Juliet Gardiner is a historian. She was editor of *History Today* for five years and has been a research fellow at the Institute of Historical Research, a publisher, and an academic. She is the author of eleven books including *'Over Here': GIs in Wartime Britain*, *D-Day: Those Who Were There* and *The Children's War*, and is the editor of *The Penguin Dictionary of British History*.

She was a historical consultant and on-screen member of the 'war cabinet' in the *The 1940s House* series for Channel Four, and wrote the accompanying book, and also that to *The Edwardian Country House*. She is a frequent lecturer and broadcaster, both on radio and television, in Britain and abroad.

Juliet Gardiner lives in east London.

'Gardiner explores every aspect of the British home front, and presents these deeply moving moments superbly. I have no doubt that *Wartime* will become the seminal work on Britain at war.' Max Arthur, *Daily Mail*

'Gardiner brings off a rare combination of social history and chronological narrative . . . Her expertise on the subject is formidable, and anyone wanting a sense of those days... will need this book: it answers more questions than a reasonable person would ask.' *Daily Telegraph*

'A minor monument of scholarship, this book is big in both size and scope, but biggest of all in terms of sheer, exhilarating readability.' *Scotsman*

' she has extensively mined archives to present the voices and experiences of ordinary Britons who lived through the war. ... In a book replete with treasures, everyone will find a special jewel.' *Times Literary Supplement*

'A magnificent achievement, which takes into account a great deal of recent research. The vivid personal testimony delivers an emotional punch that brings home the truth about the people's war as the people themselves experienced it.' Dr Paul Addison, Centre for Second World War Studies, University of Edinburgh

'Juliet Gardiner has created a literary equivalent of Radio Four's *The Archive Hour* . . . it's utterly gripping.' *Spectator*

'Juliet Gardiner's compelling *Wartime: Britain 1939–1945* lets you experience what it was really like' Andrea Levy, author of *Small Island*, *Guardian*

'a definitive and comprehensive history of the home front, a wonderfully detailed account of the people's ground-level war, using extensive archive material. Novelists and playwrights will plunder it mercilessly.' Lynne Truss, Orwell Prize judge

'Irresistibly unputdownable . . . Gardiner, a former editor of *History Today*, has a wide, scholarly perspective' Angus Calder, author of *The People's War*, *Scotland on Sunday*

'Juliet Gardiner's book is so wonderfully readable . . . This book does more than just stack up bizarre and comic details of life in a sad period, and it does so with grace and charm.' *BBC History Magazine*

'After reading this patchwork epic of courage and cowardice, crime and chronic depravation, we shouldn't be surprised that those who were there look back on it all with a sort of inverted nostalgia.' *Literary Review*

'This exhilarating book is the voice of the people. A staggering wealth of unpublished material has been discovered to provide these stories' Imperial War Museum *Despatches*

'an excellent social history about life on Britain's home front during World War II.' *Irish Examiner*

Wartime

Britain 1939–1945

Juliet Gardiner

review

First published in 2004
by HEADLINE BOOK PUBLISHING

First published in paperback in 2005 by REVIEW
an imprint of HEADLINE BOOK PUBLISHING

1

Picture Credits for Chapter Openers: 1: Hulton Archives/Getty Images;
2: By permission of the trustees of the Imperial War Museum, London;
3: © Punch Limited; 4: John Phillips; 5: Corbis; 6: Corbis; 8: © Punch
Limited; 9: © Punch Limited; 10: Courtesy of Harry Seidler and the
Mitchell Library, State Library of New South Wales; 11: Popperfoto;
12: © Punch Limited; 13: Hulton Archives/Getty Images; 14: Hulton
Archives/Getty Images; 15: © Punch Limited; 16: © Belfast Telegraph
Newspapers Limited; 17: © Punch Limited; 18: Hulton Archives/Getty
Images; 19: Courtesy of the Bodleian Library, University of Oxford;
21: © Punch Limited; 22: Courtesy of the *Orkney Blast*; 23: Reproduced
from *The Doodlebugs*, Norman Longmate (Hutchinson); 24: Imperial War
Museum, London; 25: © Punch Limited.

Cataloguing in Publication Data is available from the British Library

Typeset in Aldine401BT by Avon DataSet Ltd,
Bidford on Avon, Warwickshire

Designed by Viv Mullett

Printed and bound in Great Britain by Clays Ltd, St Ives plc

ISBN 0 7553 1028 4

HEADLINE BOOK PUBLISHING
A division of Hodder Headline
338 Euston Road
London NW1 3BH

www.headline.co.uk

CONTENTS

In memory of Charles and Dorothy Wells,
but for Pearl and Mercy Gardiner Phipps.

'Every true story has
several possible endings.'

Siri Hustvedt, *What I Loved*

FOREWORD

T HE SECOND WORLD War was a war that most British people had fervently wished to avoid, coming as it did little more than two decades after the end of 'the war to end war; the war that would settle nations once and for all; the war to which memorials clutter up the whole country – the war that was to teach the folly of war', wrote Vivienne Hall, a thirty-one-year-old shorthand typist living in London, as war threatened again. It was characterised as a 'people's war' at the time, and by historians ever since. A 'people's war' writes a contract between the leaders and the led, constituting a demand for just rewards for those who fought on the Home Front as on the battlefield: the phrase was appropriated by government to urge greater effort and suggest shared sacrifice. Yet at its simplest a 'people's war' describes the fact that in modern warfare almost the entire civilian population is mobilised for the war effort, and in the years between 1939 and 1945 would have the experience of death, destruction and deprivation on the Home Front as those in uniform would in other theatres of war.

In 1940 the writer Lionel Birch wrote an article for the magazine *Lilliput* about soldiers dreaming of how they would spend their leave. But 'when we did at last get our forty-eight[hour passes] . . . we realised the revolutionary truth: [in this war] there is no such thing as leave . . . Today war follows you around, even when you were on leave. On the platform of the London terminus it is waiting there to meet you; and as you round the bend of the village main street, you come face to face with it again. You encounter it in the eyes of your civilian friends. The burr-burr of the telephone in the empty room of the girl who has gone away convinces you. There is no such thing as leave . . .' from the demands of prosecuting the war, no relief from its imperatives, restrictions and shortages, no let-up from the fear of death or injury by enemy action.

The pervasiveness of the war is the theme of *Wartime*. But while regulations about such necessities as blackout, gas masks and rationing were uniform, and duties in the military, war production or Civil Defence compelled a large swathe of the adult population, the actual experience of war varied in ways that were multi-layered and sometimes contradictory.

War tested on the wheel many of the easy assumptions of peace: what would it mean for the Irish, the Scots, the Welsh to play an active part in the war effort of a country invariably known as England? How would those who refused to fight, or those who had come to take refuge from countries that were now Britain's enemies, or those who were native-born fascists in a war against fascism, be treated? How would women be integrated into the war effort and what would be the effect of their conscription for the first time in the history of the so-called civilised world? And what of the Communist Party with its fractured allegiances in an 'imperialist struggle' against Nazi Germany at a time when the Soviet Union was aligned with the enemy? What did going to war mean for soldiers, nearly half of whom would never leave Britain's shores? How could writers, painters, musicians and actors find a role for their art in war-torn Britain?

Britain was many places between 1939 and 1945: it was towns and cities ravaged by bombs; it was coastal regions depopulated and barricaded against invasion or cleared for military training; it was rural areas that may have escaped enemy action, yet were disrupted by large-scale evacuation.

For the British people war brought paradox: lives were transformed through unprecedented mobility, compulsion, separation, deprivation and danger. Yet war also brought new opportunities and raised expectations, boosted confidence and increased scepticism of authority. And war overwrote social, regional, political and generational divisions but without obliterating them. Many would persist throughout the six years of conflict, colouring the experience of war and shading into the peace.

During the Second World War, the writer Elizabeth Bowen found herself unable to write a novel; it was impossible to find the narrative. She turned instead to penning short stories. Sixty years after the end of the war, if the 'big picture' of a nation united in courageously facing a common enemy holds steady – as it surely does – so too do the 'short stories', the details of people's varied experiences of war that complicate and nuance that picture. *Wartime* is an attempt to keep in frame both the stories of people's lives and the dramatic circumstances in which they were played out.

INTRODUCTION

O N 30 SEPTEMBER 1938 the British Prime Minister, Neville Chamberlain, returned from a meeting with the German Chancellor, Adolf Hitler, in Munich. He was clutching a piece of paper that he waved as evidence of a peaceful resolution to the crisis that had threatened when the Führer prepared to invade Czechoslovakia. 'Peace for our time' the Prime Minister proclaimed. He was mobbed by grateful citizens cheering and singing. As far as the socialite MP Sir Henry 'Chips' Channon was concerned, 'the whole world rejoices and only a few malcontents jeer'. Chamberlain received more than 40,000 letters – 'the impression given and stated by the Premier was that these were all letters of tribute and praise' – and it was even suggested that Chamberlain's trademark furled umbrella should be broken up and its fragments sold like holy relics.

Munich would be the final desperate throw of Chamberlain's attempt to avoid war by appeasing Hitler's demands for territorial expansion in Eastern Europe. At the end of the First World War, the Treaty of Versailles had imposed punitive terms on the loser: Germany was stripped both of territory and population, it lost its overseas colonies and assets, was almost completely disarmed and was saddled with a massive war indemnity. The final humiliation had come with the Allies' insistence that Germany must formally admit to her guilt and pay reparations at a sum to be fixed by the victors – in the event, 132 billion gold marks which would have been a charge on the German economy until 1988. These harsh terms aroused intense resentment, and Germany blamed the vindictiveness of the Allies for the country's catastrophic economic and political situation: it was this resentment that Hitler would be able to exploit in the furtherance of his expansionist aims.

The crisis over Czechoslovakia was the latest in a series of events 'which seemed to bring catastrophe near'. They had started in March 1936, when German troops reoccupied the Rhineland in direct contravention of the Treaty of Versailles. Fault lines in Europe were deepening: in June that year, the Italian fascist dictator, Benito Mussolini, triumphed in his war in Abyssinia (now Ethiopia); in July the Spanish Civil War broke out when the army under the command of General Francisco Franco set out to seize power from the elected Republican government; and in November the Rome–Berlin axis was agreed, while Germany and Japan signed an anti-Comintern pact that pledged each to neutrality if the other was at war with the USSR. 'I don't know in what year I first knew for certain that the present war was coming,' George Orwell wrote. 'After 1936, of course, the thing was obvious to anyone except an idiot.'

But Britain was nowhere near ready for war – 'lamentably unprepared', said Winston Churchill. Most political leaders realised that any future conflict would be a war of attrition, demanding a level of industrial capacity and trained labour that could not be attained until at least 1940. Britain's only hope was diplomacy. Chamberlain's policy of appeasement, seeking peace by redress of Germany's grievances, was part of an ongoing attempt, which had preceded his premiership, to reconcile what would prove to be two irreconcilables: defending a very large and increasingly restless British Empire, without endangering Britain's economic prosperity and social stability by increasing spending on rearmament – and this meant avoiding European entanglements.

Isolated within Europe, unable to rely either on the League of Nations, unwilling to commit to 'collective security', diplomacy was Britain's only viable option to avoid war, and had been part of a dual strategy of appeasement and rearmament in the knowledge that it would take at least until 1940 to develop the industrial capacity and the trained labour to sustain the war of attrition that most political leaders realised would shape any future conflict.

Not that there was much popular enthusiasm for heavy spending on rearmament. The early 1930s had seen economic depression and high levels of unemployment in many parts of the country, and there were urgent social concerns that had a call on the Treasury. There was also a natural aversion to militarisation less than twenty years after the end of the First World War – indeed, in 1935 the League of Nations had secured 5 million signatures for a 'peace ballot' that rejected the proposition that military measures should be employed against an aggressor.

But in March 1938 Hitler had annexed Austria – the so-called Anschluss (or 'joining'); on 15 August the German Army was mobilised. For Virginia Cowles, a young American journalist who was working for the *Sunday Times*, it was apparent then that 'peace was dying. Everyone in their hearts knew it, but the actual fact was so appalling they clung desperately to hope.'

It was clear that neither prong of Chamberlain's policy was effective. The Anschluss hardly fitted into anyone's idea of a 'grand European strategy' and Britain's military defences were not such that this was 'the moment to accept a challenge', in his words. From then on the main plank of British strategy was to avoid a European war until the country's rearmament was complete, even if this meant trying to barter imperial possessions and redraw the frontiers of the smaller European states in a thoroughly nineteenth-century manner.

The roots of the Czechoslovakian crisis lay in Hitler's intention not just to reverse the defeat of the First World War, but to create an unassailable, self-sufficient German Empire that would last a thousand years. His exploitation of issues of nationality and self-determination that had been enshrined in the Treaty of Versailles to enable these expansionist aims, found many British politicians uneasy at the harshness of the terms of the Treaty and prepared to entertain the German case for revision.

The tinderbox was the fate of 3 million Sudentedeutsche living within the borders of Czechoslovakia, a state carved from the Hapsburg Empire after the First World War. A barrage of German propaganda in the spring of 1938 had encouraged the Sudeten Germans (who comprised about a fifth of the Czech population) to escalate their complaints against the Czech government and demands to be reunited with their homeland to the extent that to accept these demands would mean the 'smashing of

Czechoslovakia' – which was Hitler's intention.

It was in an attempt to find a solution to the flammable European situation that the frail sixty-nine-year-old Chamberlain had set out on an early version of shuttle diplomacy in September 1938. On the 15th, at Berchtesgaden, Hitler's Bavarian mountain retreat, the two men had agreed 'in principle' (and in secret) to the separation of the Sudeten Germans from Czechoslovakia. For his part, Hitler agreed to stop short of invasion.

On the 22nd, Chamberlain returned to Germany to discuss the gradual transfer of the Sudeten territories and insist that what remained of Czechoslovakia was to be guaranteed. He found that Hitler had upped his demands: the timetable for the handover of Sudeteland must be advanced, and Polish and Hungarian claims for Czech territories acceded to. Chamberlain was obliged to return to England – and the prospect of war.

Trenches were dug in parks and open spaces, gas masks were issued, bomb shelters erected, Air Raid Precaution arrangements finessed, the evacuation of children planned and, in a 'premature panic migration', thousands were reported to be leaving London. It seemed it would be a reprise of the Great War – but this time with much more horrific consequences for the Home Front. The words of Chamberlain's predecessor, Stanley Baldwin, echoed down the years. 'The bomber will always get through,' he had told the House of Commons in November 1932. 'I think it is well for the man in the street to realise that there is no power on earth that can protect him from being bombed.' And it was estimated that each single ton of bombs would result in seventy-two casualties: thousands would be killed within hours of war being declared.

On 28 September, as Chamberlain was addressing the Commons, he was once more recalled to Germany to confer with Hitler. Two days later he was back on British soil clutching that infamous piece of paper, which, he assured the nation, 'was symbolic of the desire of our two peoples never to go to war with each other again'.

The triumph was palpable. 'What a shave,' wrote Virginia Woolf, who noted 'the obvious feeling is that We don't want this war'. But within weeks relief had started to give way to unease. 'Chamberlain's private pact with Hitler . . . can't really mean a thing. Can we trust Hitler? Do we really want a pact with a Jew-baiter and a religious persecutor?'

wondered Shelagh Morrison-Bell, the daughter of a Conservative MP. 'Safe, but dirty' was a remark that resonated with Vivienne Hall, whose 'sense of shame was deepening', while a civil servant reckoned, 'We ought to have made a firmer stand . . . otherwise that fellow across the North Sea will tear off country after country like leaves off a calendar.' 'How long is "our time"?' wondered the mother of the playwright-to-be Bernard Kops as she pored over the newspaper in the Stepney tenement where the family lived within sight of Tower Bridge.

The peace indeed proved transitory. On 15 March 1939 Hitler reneged on his promises and occupied the remainder of Czechoslovakia. The policy of appeasement had run into the sand. But, at a high cost in terms of international credibility and disruption and misery in central Europe, the respite had brought Britain time to build up its capacity to rearm and to strengthen its defences against direct attack and even the invasion that was anticipated.

Chamberlain finally and publicly placed a limit on British acquiescence in German expansionism on 31 March 1939, when he announced that if Poland were to be attacked, 'His Majesty's government would feel themselves bound at once to lend the Polish government all support in their power.' It was this commitment that would lead Britain to war some five months later.

1

'BRITAIN IS AT WAR WITH GERMANY'

Today was a beautiful day
But posters flapping on the railings tell the flustered
World that Hitler speaks
And we cannot take it in and we go to our daily
Jobs to the dull refrain of the caption 'War'
And we think 'This must be wrong, it has happened before,
Just like this'.

LOUIS MacNEICE, 'AUTUMN JOURNAL'

'THE SUN IS shining, the garden never looked lovelier – everything is in bloom. Tiger [the cat] lies there in the sun; all looks happy and peaceful. But it's *not*. War has broken out between England and Germany, beastly, beastly war,' wrote a twenty-four-year-old civil servant living in Croydon on 3 September 1939. And church-goers who had gone to matins that Sunday morning had left a nation at peace:

when they emerged from church into the noonday sun, Britain was at war.

Britons had heard the momentous news over the airwaves. The wireless was regarded by the government as a vital means of communicating information to the public, and so, to ensure that essential instructions were listened to, the BBC had closed down its regional services two days earlier and reduced them to a single synchronised output. Now every programme began with the words 'This is the BBC Home Service'.

In 1939 a wireless was a central feature in most people's lives. More than 8.5 million wireless licences were issued in 1938, and 3 million copies of the *Radio Times*, priced at 2d, were sold each week. Out of a total population of 48 million, probably as many as 40 million were listening to the BBC by now. 'Literally everyone in England,' George Orwell confidently asserted, 'has access to a radio' though for some this meant listening in pubs or community halls. Most wirelesses were bulky wood or Bakelite sets – invariably positioned next to the fireplace in a living-room – since they had been built to accommodate heavy batteries, known as accumulators (the national grid had arrived in the mid 1930s but by no means all households were connected to mains electricity – by 1941 only two-thirds were). These accumulators had to be recharged about once a fortnight, usually by a local garage, though 'the accumulator man [used to] walk up four flights of stairs carrying a replacement battery' to Barbara Roose's mother's flat in Covent Garden. 'He took ours away to be charged for sixpence.'

Thus BBC programmes attracted intense concentration from their captive audience. This was particularly true of the news, especially the 9 p.m. bulletin, which was the focus of many people's evening – 52 per cent of listeners said they always listened to the news with their families, and 76 per cent preferred to.

But it was at 11.15 in the morning of 3 September that people gathered round their sets to hear Chamberlain's metallic tones (which the writer Constance Miles found 'the most delightfully *English* voice') announcing that the fretful dance of diplomacy to avoid war was over. No reply to Britain's ultimatum to Hitler that his troops must withdraw from Poland had been received by the 11 a.m. deadline, and 'consequently this country is now at war with Germany'. The tension of the past few days had been unbearable, so the announcement might almost have come as a relief – but the Prime Minister's words sounded leaden that perfect Sunday morning as the roast beef began to brown nicely in ovens throughout the country. Chamberlain spoke of 'the evil things' that the nation would be fighting, cataloguing not only brute force and bad faith, but Nazi injustice, oppression and persecution, before maintaining that right *would* prevail.

A young married woman in Leeds 'could eat no breakfast hardly and just waited with sweating palms and despair for 11 o'clock. When the announcement was made, "This country is at war with Germany," I leant against my husband and went quite dead for a minute or two.'

Mavis Carter, a teacher, had 'held her chin up high' as she sat listening to the broadcast in Chepstow with her family, but that was largely 'to hold back the tears at the thought of all the slaughter ahead', and when ' "God save the King" was played, we all stood up'. An elderly Essex woman did the same: 'I had been told by the gardener that an important announcement would be given out on the wireless. It would either be peace or war, and anxiety increased as the time drew near. Then it was the latter. I stood up for "God save the King" and my little dog got out of her basket and stood beside me. I took her on my lap for comfort.'

Angela Culme-Seymour was at home that Sunday morning. A notable beauty, she had been the wife of Winston Churchill's nephew Johnny, but was now married to Patrick Balfour (the heir to the Scottish baron Lord Kinross), a journalist who wrote 'Londoner's Diary' for the *Evening Standard*. She was living with her 'safe and temporary husband' in Maida Vale. When they heard Chamberlain's broadcast, 'Patrick and I looked at each other rather hard and I felt sick. So I said "Let's go downstairs and have a nip" with the Stowes [the butler and cook] and that's what we did. It was odd, rather like toasting the war. Then I went out for a walk by myself and stood on the bridge over the Grand Union Canal for a long time. It was entirely still and quiet and I felt very, very odd.'

'L[eonard] and I stood by,' recorded Virginia Woolf in Sussex as Chamberlain spoke to the nation. 'We as usual remain outside. If we win, – then what? . . . All the formula are now a mere formula for gangsters. So we chopped words. I suppose the bombs are falling on rooms like this in Warsaw now. A fine sunny morning here, apples shining . . . It's the unreality of force that muffles everything . . . not to attitudinise is one reflection . . . Then of course I shall have to work to make money. That's a comfort. Write articles for America. I suppose take on writing for some society. Keep the Press going.'

In Kintyre, the writer Naomi Mitchison, who had been a VAD in the First World War, was at home with her husband Dick and son Denny. As she listened to Chamberlain, she thought that he 'sound[ed] like a very old man . . . At the end Joan [a house guest] said How could he ask God to bless us? . . . As God Save the King started Denny turned it off and someone said Thank you. The maids hadn't wanted to come through: I told Annie [the housekeeper] who was wonderfully cheerful and said she remembered the Boer War, and Bella [the cook] who said Isn't that heartbreaking. After a bit she began to cry, a saucepan in her hands, and said Think of all our men going, then to me of course you've got boys too. Dick said Think of the women in Germany all saying that too, but there was no response. Then she asked When will they send our men over? But none of us had much idea.'

The writer, former diplomat and more recently National Labour MP Harold Nicolson – who would rush out a 50,000-word Penguin Special in three weeks explaining *Why Britain is at War* – reflected on the day it broke out that 'even when someone dies, one is amazed that the poplars should still be standing quite unaware of one's own disaster, so when I walked down to the lake [at Sissinghurst, Harold and his wife Vita Sackville-West's house in Kent] to bathe, I could scarcely believe that the swans were being sincere in their indifference to a Second German War'. Conservative MP Henry 'Chips' Channon still allowed himself a modicum of hope on the day that war was declared. 'Everyone is smiling, the weather is glorious but I feel that our world, or all that remains of it, is committing suicide while Stalin laughs and the Kremlin triumphs' – this last a reference to the signing of a non-aggression pact the previous month between Germany and the Soviet Union, which effectively secured Russia's neutrality for Hitler's invasion of Poland, and had come as a great shock to many British people. 'If only we can win a quick war, and dislodge the Nazi regime. That would mean a Neville victory, a November election and triumph. In London the church bells are ringing, people draw more closely together, everyone is kind and considerate, and all are quietly appreciative of what the Government has done.'

That might have been true in Channon's circle but on the south coast at Milford in Hampshire a civil servant was far from 'quietly appreciative'. 'I saw from someone else's paper that the issue of peace or war will be decided today, but I can't be bothered to hang around waiting for it. Hitler gave us the only answer he understands when he bombed Poland on Friday. I go off alone to the cliff and watch the magnificent sea. It's exhilarating down there and probably I shan't have many more opportunities to see it. I stand there a long time thinking while the wind blows me clean and wild looking . . . When I come down to dinner I'm told that we are at war and that Chamberlain has spoken. I'm glad I missed him. I don't want to hear him say "God knows I have done my best!" I don't believe it. He could have secured Russian co-operation. And I didn't want to hear the King tonight either. Sacrifice. Pull together. Justice. I'm willing to fight Fascism if necessary (and if we'd treated Russia decently it wouldn't be necessary) but I feel tricked somehow. That National Government has brought us to this by sabotaging collective security. They've not thought of justice until just recently and I and those with me who prophesied this feel no pleasure at being true prophets but only ache at the futility of it.'

The pacifist writer Vera Brittain was sitting on a camp bed in the study between her two children, Shirley (who would grow up to be the politician Shirley Williams) and John. She listened to Chamberlain whose 'voice sounded very old and trembled' and 'found that the tears were running down my cheeks – I suppose from some subconscious realisation of the failure of my efforts for peace over 20 years, for I had expected the announcement . . . Went out in the [New] forest; in the sunny quiet and gorse and heather it was impossible to take in the size of the catastrophe. To comfort myself, wrote an article for *Peace News* called "Lift Up Your Hearts".'

Some people had not been able to listen to the wireless. Muriel Green, who was eighteen, had been pumping petrol in her family's garage in Norfolk and hadn't heard the declaration of war. When a customer leaned out of his car window to tell her, she had 'a feeling of hopelessness followed by annoyance . . . Think through friends who will eventually be called up. Decide to think of them as killed off and then it will not be such a blow if they are, and it will be a great joy at the end if they are not.'

Far away from his homeland, on a yacht off the coast of California, with Vivien Leigh and Douglas Fairbanks Jr, the actor Laurence Olivier heard the news. He proceeded to get blind drunk and rowed round the other yachts, shouting, 'This is the end! You're all washed up! Finished! Enjoy your last moments. You're done for . . .'

Following Chamberlain's broadcast, a series of short official announcements instructed listeners that the blowing of whistles or blaring of horns was now forbidden since these could be mistaken for an air-raid siren. (Indeed, a survey taken a few days earlier found that one in six people did not know what the signal for an air raid was, 'despite [this] having been publicised widely by the government, also mentioned in many newspapers and on films and wireless'.) They were told that all theatres, cinemas, music halls and other places of entertainment were to be closed forthwith, and football matches and other events that attracted large crowds were forbidden – measures intended to minimise the chances of a large number of people being killed by a single bomb. The London tubes were needed for transport and would, therefore, *not* be available as air-raid shelters. Every citizen was then warned of his or her wartime responsibilities: to observe the blackout from dusk to dawn; to listen regularly to the BBC news broadcasts; to carry a gas mask everywhere; to make sure every member of the family was labelled with his or her name and address ('If I am so blown about that I can't tell my name, do you think the label will still be intact?' wondered a nurse when she was instructed never to go out without the luggage label that had been handed to her); and when the air-raid siren sounded to go immediately to a shelter and stay there until the All Clear sounded.

As the announcements drew to a close with some information 'about food' the banshee wail of the air-raid siren filled the air. The war was less than half an hour old, but it was what the nation had been led to expect: an immediate knockout blow from the air. Two days earlier a leaflet had come through doors advising 'What To Do in an Air-Raid'. It was as reassuring as it could be in the circumstances. Citizens should not be unduly alarmed by any pictures they might have seen of the bombing of Barcelona during the Spanish Civil War. British homes were more sturdily built than those in Spain, and offered considerable protection to the occupants. The direct effects of a high-explosive bomb were usually limited to within around 30 feet of the bomb. If fifty large bombs fell within a square mile there was a hundred-to-one chance of a person experiencing 'what might be called a direct hit'. People must, however, take shelter.

They should file in an orderly fashion into a public shelter – for in the previous few days 'Public Shelter' notices had been pasted on numerous buildings such as town halls, railway stations, offices and shops, and in parts of London the entrances to vaults and cellars that had been hurriedly requisitioned for the purpose. Or they could make for the nearest trench, since digging night and day – which had been abandoned after the Munich crisis the previous autumn had seemed to promise peace – had been resumed in the parks and other open spaces, and local authorities were now urged to provide stairs, seats and sanitation in these timber- or concrete-lined mud hollows, or they could go to a purpose-built brick public shelter. Far more preferably, they could take shelter in their own homes, either in the corrugated-iron Anderson shelter in the back garden if there was one, or by scurrying into their basement or cellar. But although 1.5 million free Anderson shelters had been distributed by the outbreak of war (and were optimistically estimated to be able to protect 6 million people), and 50,000 were being turned out every week, this was still a third short of target. In addition many corrugated-iron kits had been delivered but not erected, while others had been erected in such a cack-handed way (for it was a task requiring considerable strength and some dexterity) as to represent danger rather than protection. Furthermore, Anderson shelters had not yet gone on sale to those householders who were not entitled to a free one because their annual income was in excess of £250 a year.

In sum, the protection of those in key danger zones still fell far short of what was expected to be required on the day that war broke out.

Nina Masel had been playing the piano in the front room of a Romford semi when her mother, who until a quarter of an hour before 'had been convinced that a war wouldn't be needed at all, flung open the door just before 11.30 a.m. and burst in shouting "Stop that noise!" and flung open the window letting in the scream of the air raid siren, and the scuffling noise of neighbours in a hurry. Immediately my father assumed the role of administrative head of the house [as the government leaflet had told him he should] issuing commands and advice: "All get your gas masks . . . Steady no panicking! . . . Every man for himself! . . . Keep in the passage!" My small sister (11) began to sob: "Will it be alright?" she kept querying. My mother was frightened, but was trying to take hold of herself. My heart beat hard for the first few seconds, and then it calmed down. I think my brother and sister felt much the same as I did. We gathered in the passage (we have no shelter) and sat on the stairs. After a few minutes we decided that it was a false alarm or a trial, so we went to the front gate (all except my mother and small sister, who kept calling for us to come back) and remained there until the "All Clear" was given. A few babies were crying and air-raid wardens with gas masks and helmets were running up and down.'

As she was walking along Upper Street in Islington, north London, Eileen Harmer heard the siren. She and the friends she was with made a dash for the public shelter erected on Islington Green. 'As we went in an ARP warden yelled "mind those electric wires" and we realised that the shelter was still being built. I wondered how many more, up and down the country, weren't ready yet now that the war had started.'

At their London home, Morpeth Mansions in Westminster, Winston Churchill and his wife Clementine went out on to the flat roof 'to see what was going on. Around us on every side, in the clear, cool September light, rose the roofs and spires of London. Above them were already rising thirty or forty cylindrical balloons' – these were the silver-coloured barrage balloons, 66 feet long and 30 feet high, filled with 20,000 cubic feet of hydrogen and tethered to the ground by steel cables, highly effective in deterring low-flying aircraft. Churchill and his wife 'gave the government a good mark for preparation, and as the quarter of an hour's notice which we had been led to expect we should receive was now running out we made our way to the shelter assigned to us, armed with a bottle of brandy and other appropriate medical comforts. Our shelter was a hundred yards down the street, and consisted merely of an open basement, not even sand-bagged, in which the tenants of half a dozen flats were already assembled. Everyone was cheerful and jocular, as is the English manner when about to encounter the unknown. As I gazed from the doorway along the empty street and at the crowded room below my imagination drew pictures of carnage and vast explosions shaking the ground, of buildings clattering down in dust and rubble, of fire brigades and ambulances scurrying through the smoke, beneath the drone of hostile aeroplanes. For had we not all been taught how terrible air raids would be?'

In Fleet Street, newspaper editors sent their star reporters off to 'cover' the hospitals, expecting casualties to pour in. In Fulham, 'police on bicycles . . . ride up from the police station wearing "Take Cover" placards on chest and back and shout "Take cover" and "Take cover" is echoed by people in cafés and streets. People in the street begin to run frantically. People in houses and shops rush to door. Remain crowded in doorway. People in streets diving for any open door they can see. Policeman on bike waves people at café door back. "Go in". People go in and then after a few seconds return to door. Woman of about 25 with pram rushes up and is helped into café by men who push back other men in the way. Then a boy of about 15 runs up panting, looking terrified, and dives in . . .'

'Of course we were afraid. We were absolutely terrified,' recalls Shirley Annand. 'We had all read H. G. Wells so we knew what it would be like. Bombs raining down, fires everywhere, gas, hundreds of thousands dead.' George Beardmore, an asthmatic London clerk who was also a writer, thought that 'it would be impossible to convey the sense of utter panic with which we heard the first air raid warning ten minutes after the outbreak of war. We had all taken *The Shape of Things to Come* [H. G. Wells' novel] too much to heart, also the dire prophecies of scientists, journalists and even politicians of the devastation and disease that would follow the first air raid. We pictured St Paul's in ruins and a hole in the ground where the Houses of Parliament stood.'

As the warning sounded, Members of Parliament were beginning to arrive at the House of Commons to hear Chamberlain at noon. Harold Nicolson reported that the Conservative MP Leo Amery was critical when he heard it: 'They ought not to do that after what we have heard on the wireless. People will think it is an air raid warning.' 'Hardly had he said these words,' Nicolson wrote, 'when another siren takes up. "My God!" I said, "It *is* an air raid warning!" ' The MPs walked 'quickly but not without dignity into the House' where 'the police in steel helmets tell us to go down to the air-raid refuge. I do so . . . It is very hot. People chat to each other with forced geniality. After ten minutes we are released and go onto the terrace. People assert that they heard gunfire and bombs dropping. I suggest that it was merely the carpenters nailing in the asbestos linings to the windows. The terrace is flashed with sunshine, and we watch with disapproval the slow movements of the people of Lambeth trying to get a [barrage] balloon to rise. It has been dampened by last night's rain.'

Ellen Howard, a thirty-seven-year-old woman living with her husband and children in south London, had 'hardly digested the news when the sirens started wailing'. Her husband 'heard them first, or rather was the first to realise what they meant. We all flew to our tasks. I filled the bath tub, closed the upper windows, got down the tins containing our gas masks, prised them open and soaped the eye piece [to stop the glass visor from steaming up], carried my oiled coat and a box of precious things down to the shelter. K. had put earth on the boiler fire, turned off the gas, filled the kitchen sink, drawn the lower curtains and closed the windows and also put the dog's harness on him. We were all down in the shelter in four minutes. It was our first rehearsal and we were well pleased. I'd not got out the axe, K. had forgotten her gas mask and I hadn't turned on the radio [as instructed to do in case there were announcements]. Nothing happened so we took stock of ourselves, had a drink and found we'd also forgotten the oil cape to wrap the dog in [supposed to offer protection against poison gas]. H. decided to stay outside until he heard gunfire, so he went out and the All Clear went. K. and I felt a bit shaky but decided that it was excitement as much as anything else – it had all been such a scramble. Suddenly we smelt gas. It was several seconds before we remembered that no one had turned off the 'fridge before turning off the main tap. A note to remember and we also decided not to put out the boiler fire anymore – burning earth smells horrid.'

In West Hampstead, Gwladys Cox felt 'unspeakable astonishment' when the siren sounded. She turned off the gas at the mains, caught the cat and put him in his basket, and she and her husband grabbed their gas masks and 'struggled down the several flights of stairs to the street, some yards along the pavement, down the area steps, along dark winding passages' to their shelter in the basement of their block of flats, which the tobacconist, whose premises it was part of, had given them permission to use and which they had already equipped with deckchairs, rugs, candles and matches. 'My knees were knocking together with weakness while I stifled a strong desire to be sick. I was not exactly afraid, but nervous that I should be afraid; startled and bewildered, glimpsing dimly that already all my known world was toppling about my ears. And behind all these mixed feelings was one of unreality because the circumstances of this first alert had such an artificially dramatic element – as if the curtain having been rung down on peace, war planes which had been awaiting their cue in the wings suddenly swooped into view before the footlights . . . I remained in the shelter about half an hour staring at the cobwebs while Ralph reconnoitred outside. When the All Clear started, we came upstairs to make preparations for Sunday dinner.'

That morning Barbara Campbell, from Redhill in Surrey, had been on duty at the hospital where she was a masseuse. At about half past eleven she was driving to visit a patient and a policeman signalled her to stop. She thought he was going 'to advise me to have something done about my car headlights for night use. But he said "the air raid warning's on": I was astonished as I did not know that war had been declared. There were a great number of other cars on the road, and I noticed several crammed with bedding and furniture heading south. About 100 yards from my parents' house a warden in complete protective rig rushed at me and signalled me to draw into the kerb and shouted at me "Air raid. Leave the car at once". When I got home I found several residents in the road filling improvised sandbags with soil and sand from our next door neighbour's garden and stacking them in front of our garage which is built into a bank and has part of our garden on top of its concrete roof. In the kitchen mother was cooking Sunday lunch with one hand and sewing up sacking with the other. When the warning went mother suggested to my sister that she should go next door to the neighbour's for company and while there had suggested that they should make use of our garage as a shelter, putting our car out permanently in the road. This seemed a good idea so other neighbours joined in and work went on all day. When sacking ran out, I went up into the loft and found some old curtains and we ran them up too. By the evening we had a good six feet of sandbag wall and two lines in front of the doors which were protected by stair carpets and we had jointly furnished the interior. One of the neighbours had started to fix up a cable from the house to supply electric light. I think the feeling of having something definite to do was a help to us all, and certainly we spoke to neighbours we had not met before. It takes a war to get to know people it seems. It turns out that one neighbour has a five-month-old baby and an evacuated child with her, another has two children, yet another two children and their mother, and all felt the responsibility of the children. The neighbour with the baby was said to have wept hopelessly when the warning went as she had no gas mask for the baby and doubted the efficacy of her modern house to stand up to any shock making the gas proof room she had prepared rather useless. We decided to leave our garage doors unlocked so that the shelter would always be available . . .'

The alert had been a false alarm – the first of several. A sole French plane flying along the Thames had been mistaken for the vanguard party of a German attack. It lasted twenty minutes. When the All Clear sounded people emerged and got on with their Sundays, interspersing their usual late summer Sabbath activities – a walk, a rest after lunch, the Sunday papers, writing letters, tidying up the garden – with the imperatives of war concerned with blackout and shelter provision, Air Raid Precaution (ARP) duties, anxiety.

Chamberlain picked up his gas mask in its new shiny black leather case, put on his homburg hat, and walked the few hundred yards from Downing Street to the House of Commons. He told MPs of his intense feelings. 'This is a sad day for all of us, but to none is it sadder than to me. Everything I have worked for, everything that I have hoped for, everything that I have believed in during my public life has crashed in ruins.'

Winston Churchill had already 'prepared a short speech which I thought would be becoming to the solemn and awful moments in our lives and history', and when he was called to give it his distinctive voice resonated like the 'barks of a field gun' as he associated himself with his Prime Minister's sadness. His next words drew succour from the centuries that he had been mapping a few days earlier writing his history of the English-speaking peoples. There was, he said, 'the feeling of thankfulness that if these great trials were to come upon our island there is a generation of Britons here and now ready to prove itself, not unworthy of the days of yore and not unworthy of those great men, the fathers of our land who laid the foundations of our laws and shaped the greatness of our country'. 'Too much like one of his articles,' thought Harold Nicolson.

When the debate finished Churchill was told by Chamberlain that his offer to 'hold myself entirely at your disposal, with every desire to aid you in your task' had been accepted. He was to return to government as First Lord of the Admiralty with a seat in the War Cabinet of nine members. Anthony Eden, another critical anti-appeaser, was back too, as Foreign Secretary.

The day passed slowly. Monica Kerr started 'sorting out all my possessions and destroying all those letters that I've been keeping as "precious" ', and was appalled to hear some of her fellow civil servants having a sing-song after supper. 'They were singing the hit song of the First World War twenty-five years ago, "Pack up Your Troubles in Your Old Kit Bag". How *can* they?' Marion Browne, who had decided to keep a wartime diary, met an actress friend from Birmingham for lunch who was 'upset because her tour will not play in London as arranged' – since the theatres had been shut. She saw her friend off at Waterloo station on to a train that had had its light bulbs replaced with dim blue ones and sported yellow notices on every carriage instructing passengers to 'Lie down on the floor in the event of an Air Raid'. 'Station very miserable,' Miss Browne noted. 'I hate seeing mothers leaving town with their children, obviously upset at leaving their husbands. All seems so futile and I can scarcely believe that it is true. Sat in the station refreshment room for half an hour and then went to Dick Sheppard House, the headquarters of the Peace Pledge Union. But found out that the Peace Parade planned for today had been cancelled. Made some new friends and was driven home. Talked to some girls who did not intend to accept ration books. Went to bed at 11 o'clock and was knocked up at twelve to say there was a light showing through a crack in my bedroom window. Promised to put up interlined curtains the following day.'

At nine o'clock that night George VI broadcast to the nation, sadly reminding his listeners that 'for the second time in the lives of most of us, we are at war'. He called on his people to 'stand calm and firm and united in this time of trial. The task will be hard. There may be dark days ahead and war can no longer be confined to the battlefield . . .' It had been intended to print the King's message with a facsimile of his signature appended, and to distribute a copy to every household in Britain, but the exigencies of war put a stop to that. It would have taken 250 tons of paper and cost some £35,000, and the Post Office was alarmed at the prospect of delivering 15 million extra pieces of mail at a time when their staff was depleted by military call-up. The plan to have a royal message pinned up in every home was discreetly abandoned.

At the end of the day that war was declared the King went to bed alone. The Queen had decided to return to Balmoral that day to explain to her daughters as best she could what was happening. In Cricklewood, north London, Hannah Hodgson had been dozing in an armchair. She found 'this dimmed lighting is very restful' but finally roused herself to go to bed just before 11 p.m. As she stretched out like a starfish in the double bed she had shared with her husband until he had been called up two days earlier, she was thoughtful. 'So this is war, unsatisfied desire and a sense of frustration. No stimulating change of duty, no ennobling thoughts, no sense of humour.'

2

'EVACUATE FORTHWITH'

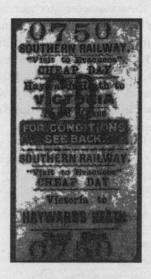

*All the time I was evacuated I used to tell myself that one day the war
would be over and I could go back home. After the war . . . I made my
way back to where I used to live. The whole area had been obliterated
during . . . the Blitz and I was quite unable to find the spot where our
house once stood. That happened more than fifty years ago . . . but
somehow I am still waiting to go home.*

JIM BARTLEY, EVACUEE

S O BEGAN WHAT Churchill called the 'Twilight War', some called the
'Bore War' and what later came to be universally known in a phrase
borrowed from America as the 'Phoney War'. Chamberlain, who had
led Britain into it, thought it 'a strange war which is more like a siege'. It
was a time of rumour and uncertainty, and it did not seem like real war
on the Home Front because war in the shape it had been sketched did

not materialise. There were no bombed cities and no charnel house of flame and death. Yet.

Despite protestations of support for 'Poland's Gallant Fight Against the Odds', the promised air attacks on Germany did not happen. When the RAF pilots set off on sorties over Germany, they did not have military targets in their sights, nor bombs in their holds. They went 'for the purpose of distributing a note to the German people': that is, to drop 10 million somewhat confused leaflets in an attempt to persuade the German people of their Führer's folly in pursuing an unnecessary war and the hopelessness of his enterprise, since his country did not 'have the means to sustain protracted warfare'. 'We are dropping *pamphlets* on Germany,' snorted Kate Phipps, a Red Cross nurse. 'Will that have any more effect than if they dropped them on *us*? We would just burn them. No doubt they will do likewise.'

In little more than a fortnight, the ostensible cause for which Britain and France had jointly gone to war was lost. 'Collapse of Poland' announced *The Times* headline on 18 September 1939. German and Russian troops had met at Brest-Litovsk in western Poland, the Polish government had fled to Romania, and the country was being partitioned – or 'raped' as *The Times* had it. Two days later the Lord Mayor of Warsaw sent a message from his city, which was under constant bombardment: 'When will the effective help of Great Britain and France come to relieve us from this terrible situation? We are waiting for it.' It never came. For the following seven months, 'the people of Britain were left with a war on their hands'. 'Both sides are waiting,' wrote the *Observer*. 'Great Britain is waiting for Germany to make a move . . . Germany is waiting until everything is ready – possibly including the weather.'

In November Chamberlain broadcast to Britain and the Empire: 'I know well that in a greater or lesser degree the war has interrupted and affected your daily life . . . Most of these hardships and inconveniences have been brought about by the necessity of providing against attacks from the air. Some of them may now seem to have been unnecessary, since the air raids have not taken place, but if they had come *as everyone expected*, and had found us unprepared, you would have rightly blamed the Government for its neglect.' There was no better example to illustrate the Prime Minister's words than the evacuation scheme starting on 1

September. In anticipation of massed air attacks, 1,473,000 people were moved, the majority in three days, from the crowded cities of Britain to safe areas in the country – or at least safer. Back in February 1939 a Local Government report had been blunt: 'In a country the size of England, there is, in the condition of modern war, no place of absolute safety.'

Plans for evacuating what were referred to in official circles as *bouches inutiles* (useless mouths) – children, the elderly and the infirm, who would not be in a position to help, and indeed would hinder, the war effort – had been discussed since the mid-1920s. But there was reluctance to activate this operation on the scale that would be necessary. As late as 1938 the government-issued *Householders' Handbook* had still laid the responsibility for evacuation on individuals, suggesting that 'if you live in a large town, children, invalids, elderly members of the household, and pets, should be sent to relatives or friends in the country if this is possible'.

But what about the poorer areas of cities where people did not have the resources to leave their homes or send their dependants away? These places were likely to be among the first targets for enemy action, since in the jumble of post-industrial urban Britain they tended to be concentrated around such targets as dockyards and factories. Like so many other early wartime initiatives, plans for evacuation were driven by the desire to avoid mass panic. But despite anxious representations from the London County Council (LCC) and other inner-city authorities, it was not until May 1938 that a 'Committee of Evacuation' was set up under the chairmanship of 'that great administrator', the former Governor of Bengal, now Home Secretary, the austere Sir John Anderson.

The evacuation would be the largest mass movement in British history: 'Exodus of the Bible dwarfed' claimed the *Dorset Daily Echo*. With 1,589 assembly points and 168 entraining stations in London alone, it would be an operation of major logistical complexity to relocate whole schools, including teachers, plus mothers with under-school-age children, pregnant women and the disabled – people regarded as a priority for evacuation. The planners saw it as comparable to a military operation, with the emphasis on the logistics of rapid transportation and much less attention given to what would happen when the evacuees arrived at their destination. This was to lead to serious mistakes both in the conception of the plan and its implementation. But had the aerial bombardment begun immediately on the outbreak of war, as had been forecast, many of these shortcomings might well have been buried under the debris of war.

Public Information Leaflet No 3 made it all sound very sensible: 'The scheme is entirely a voluntary one, but clearly the children will be much safer and happier away from the big cities where the danger will be greatest. There is room in the safe areas for these children; householders have volunteered to provide it. They have offered homes where the children will be made welcome. The children will have their schoolteachers and other helpers with them and their schooling will continue . . . Do not hesitate to register your children if you live in a crowded area. Of course it means heartache to be separated from your children, but you can be quite sure that they will be well looked after. That will relieve you of one anxiety at any rate.'

Since the Munich crisis, local newspapers had frequently imagined terrifying scenarios when the bombs began to fall in their areas. 'It does not require the exercise of much imagination to previsualise the absolute chaos, the anguish and the hopeless and helpless plight of thousands . . .' reported the *Liverpolitan* in November 1938. 'We should have screaming mothers dashing aimlessly about with crying children in their arms . . . and amidst the hysteria, the tumult and the conflict . . . Despite the best of parental intervention, the exertion of the most heroic efforts at self-sacrifice, it would be the children who would chiefly fall victims of the holocaust.' Even the more restrained *Liverpool Daily Post* spoke sombrely of 300,000 casualties a week expected when hostilities began.

In general, as had been predicted, those who took part in the official government scheme were predominantly urban working-class children evacuated with their state schools, plus other 'priority cases' who had no one in the country with sufficiently commodious accommodation to put them up for an unknown duration. The areas designated for evacuation were the most densely populated inner cities where the birth rate was higher and families larger, whereas the more affluent suburbs were more often classified as 'neutral areas', neither sending nor receiving evacuees. It was more likely to be from these areas that upwards of 2 million people would be able to make private arrangements to go to friends or relations, or rent cottages, or book hotels and boarding houses, choosing the West Country, rural Wales, the more remote parts of Scotland – anywhere that seemed away from what were thought would be prime military targets. Though there were periodically sniping references in the press to the 'funk holes' of the comfortably off, well away from danger, privately arranged evacuations could split families and cause as much heartache as an official scheme. At the end of August 1939, all families had to grapple with what was best for mothers and children in the face of what threatened to be impending attack. The difference was that some had a choice of when and where to go: others seemed to have almost none.

Public schools made their own arrangements. Dulwich College was evacuated to Tonbridge in Kent. Westminster moved in with Lancing College in Sussex; the City of London School doubled up with Marlborough, and, when a government radio-monitoring unit took over its buildings, the Oratory School moved from Reading to Henley – and never returned. St Paul's Boys' School relocated to Lord Downshire's estate at Wokingham in Surrey; Queen Margaret's School, Scarborough, was evacuated to Castle Howard in the spring of 1940 and, when part of the building, including the State Rooms, was destroyed by fire in November 1940, still stayed on. St Denis Girls' School moved from Edinburgh into one of the Duke of Buccleuch's stately homes at Drumlanrig, while Craigmount School moved from Edinburgh to Scone Palace in Perthshire. At the Duke of Devonshire's magnificent residence at Chatsworth, fine furniture and paintings were moved out, chandeliers bagged up, four-poster beds covered in dust sheets and tapestries, and panelling covered over – ready for girls from Penrhos College in North Wales whose own premises were wanted as offices by the Ministry of Food. And Malvern School, whose premises were requisitioned by the Admiralty, set up educational shop in the awesome surroundings of Blenheim Palace for a year before sharing Harrow's premises for the rest of the war. For the same reason the Royal School at Bath moved into Longleat, where most pupils felt cold for most of the time. Highgate School had informed parents at the end of the summer term that they should look out for advertisements in *The Times* and *Daily Telegraph* announcing 'Highgate School goes West', which would be the coded announcement that the evacuation of the boys' public school to Westward Ho! near Bideford was about to start.

Eton, however, stayed put, though its precautions did include warning boys not to wear their customary top hats when they went into the air-raid shelters since these took up too much space – and provided no protection against blast.

There had been evacuation rehearsals earlier in the summer, and on 28 August London children, who were still on holiday, were summoned to their schools, which would be their assembly point, for a practice. Anxious parents, many still undecided whether or not to send their children away, quizzed teachers and officials, opted for evacuation, changed their minds, and then changed them back again. Each school was allocated a number and told which was to be their station for disembarkation. Parents had all received a government leaflet instructing them that their children should bring 'a handbag or case containing the child's gas mask, a change of underclothing, night clothes, house shoes or plimsolls, spare stockings or socks, a toothbrush, a comb, towel, soap and face cloth, handkerchiefs; and, if possible, a warm coat or mackintosh' – though this relatively modest kit was to prove beyond the resources of a number of parents in deprived inner-city areas. 'The headmistress sent home a list of things which we had to take with us pinned up in a blanket,' recalled a child who lived at Elephant and Castle in south London. 'We didn't have all the things.' Liverpool schools realistically decided to substitute a pillowcase as the suggested receptacle in place of a case or rucksack. Many schools supplemented the official list: Brockley School for Boys in south-east London added 'card games, gym kit, pullover, story or reading book and school hymn book' to its requirements and detailed the food that should be packed for each boy 'to last one or two days'. A ten-year-old girl evacuated from east London to Oxfordshire didn't 'realise what war was and . . . I imagined that the carrier bag full of food that I had been given was to be my food for the duration of the war'.

Practices were arranged daily in most schools, and parents were never entirely sure when they saw their children off to school in the morning whether they would be coming home again that evening. 'Each morning my sister and I would leave home with our packed sandwiches and clothes,' recalled the cartoonist Mel Calman. 'We would say goodbye to our parents. Our labels were pinned on us and I felt sick . . . We went through this awful ritual of goodbye each morning for a week. Every morning I felt sick and kissed my parents and thought I was leaving my identity with them.'

On 31 August the Ministry of Health gave the green light: 'Evacuate forthwith . . . [though] no one should conclude that this means that war is now regarded as inevitable . . .'

In the early morning of 1 September 1939 the exercise to 'get the children away' began. Police in loudhailer vans directed the 'great trek' to and from assembly points. Helpers – teachers, local authority officials and railway staff plus members of voluntary organisations including 17,000 Women's Voluntary Service (WVS) members – wearing armbands that denoted the party they were with, and usually carrying banners so they could be identified in a crowd, set out to accomplish 'war task number one'. The children went by underground, bus or other forms of hastily assembled road transport to their designated 'entraining station', either a main terminus or a suburban station, and were marshalled on to trains clutching gas masks, luggage, food and drink for the journey – and a favourite toy if the school allowed that, though not all did.

But it was soon apparent that nothing like the expected number had turned up. A total of 3.5 million had been planned for: less than half that number – 1.5 million schoolchildren, teachers, mothers with small children, the disabled and their helpers – travelled under the scheme, though this shortfall was not admitted at the time. The rate of take-up varied widely among the various places scheduled for evacuation. The greatest proportion of schoolchildren from a single area – between 61 and 76 per cent – left from Manchester and Salford, Newcastle and Gateshead, Liverpool, Bootle and other areas on Merseyside. In London almost half the schoolchildren joined the exodus, fanning out from Land's End to the Wash. In Glasgow 42 per cent of schoolchildren were evacuated, but in other areas the total was much lower: only 24 per cent of schoolchildren left the combined Midlands conurbations of Birmingham, Coventry, Smethwick, Walsall and West Bromwich, while Edinburgh sent 28 per cent, Derby 27 per cent, Bradford 25 per cent, Nottingham 22 per cent and Sheffield only 15 per cent. Overall, less than half the schoolchildren left English towns and cities including London, and 38 per cent moved from evacuation areas in Scotland. Richard Titmuss, who wrote a humane official history of the problems of social policy in the Second World War, suggested that parents from the poorest districts, who were likely to have the least education, were more likely to accept that those in authority – teachers and the government – in some way 'knew best', and that they had little say in such matters as the evacuation of their children.

In theory, this shortfall meant that the exercise should have been easier to achieve than had been anticipated: in fact, it led to problems. When it was clear that only half the number expected needed transport, train timetables and destinations were hurriedly rescheduled to get the evacuees away as fast as possible, but that meant that the evacuees who finally 'detrained', in the official language, at towns and villages in the reception areas were often quite different from those who had been expected and prepared for.

However 'sensible' the decision to send off your children, to wave goodbye to your wife and infants, or to part from your heavily pregnant wife for an unknown length of time, it was heart-wrenching. Children had to have a luggage label attached to their coats with their name, address and school on it, but no destination. A government leaflet had explained that though the State would bear the cost of the train fare, 'it would not be possible to let all parents know in advance the place to which each child is to be sent but they would be notified as soon as the movement is over', and each child was issued with a stamped postcard to send home when they arrived at his or her destination. Richard Titmuss considered that, 'The Government was asking a great deal: it was asking parents to send their children for an indefinite period to an unknown destination, there to be committed to the care of strangers.' It was clearly admirable that so many parents were prepared to do so in the circumstances of impending war; it is hardly surprising that even more felt they could not.

There were pragmatic considerations. Children who stayed at home when their school was evacuated, would have nowhere to be educated: the LCC, for example, had made clear that 'if you do not wish your children to be evacuated you must not send them to school until further notice'; and indeed, by December 1939 thousands of children who had remained in the evacuation areas had been without education, health services, school meals or milk since 1 September. But the trust necessary for parents to agree to send away their little (and not so little) ones must also have depended on how confident they felt about the satisfactoriness or otherwise of local arrangements. Manchester was an example of efficient planning, with parents being given plenty of information in good time to take the decision: the city's reward was a 70 per cent evacuation, more than 20 per cent above the national level.

As the government leaflet had put it, 'There are still a number of people who ask "What is the need for all this business about evacuation? Surely if war comes it would be better for families to stick together and not go breaking up their homes?" ' And this was what a number of parents – and children – clearly felt despite all the brisk injunctions: 'If we die, we die together' was a wartime-long mantra for many. Again there were practical considerations. Unemployment had been high throughout the 1930s, and many mothers needed to work in wartime to supplement the family income, and that was particularly the case in 1939 if an employed husband had been called up into the Forces where a private's pay could hardly be said to be a living wage for a family. In these situations older children might be needed at home to help look after a younger brother or sister; family illness, impending confinement or a new baby could create the same dependency. It would be facile to think that those who kept their children at home were selfish or sentimental, or that those who sent them away were uncaring. The vast majority of both suffered anxiety, some felt guilt, and others a sense of loss, as did many of the children.

A young woman who had helped with the evacuation of children from Bow in the East End of London recalled 'most vividly' that while the 'children were wild with excitement . . . most mums were pale and drawn no doubt wondering when they'd see their sons and daughters again. It was certainly the first time the mothers had been parted from their schoolchildren. Very close families were the order of the day in Bow. No one had to tell you about the value of family life in the East End then because, quite frankly, we didn't know anything else.'

Bernard Kops recalled that his little sister Rose was terrified at the thought of evacuation from their Stepney tenement: 'I want to stop with you. I want to be killed with you,' she screamed to her mother as they assembled in the playground with their gas masks and labels tied to their coats. 'And then we all moved away, all the children and parents crying . . . I knew for my mother the separation from us was even worse than the thought of war.

'. . . In the train I could hardly contain myself with excitement when it moved out of the station. I jumped from window to window. But then I came back to carth with a clunk when I looked at my terrible responsibility, my crying, snotty-nosed red-eyed little sister. I had promised to look after her and not be separated from her.

' "But where will we be tonight?" she appealed to me. And I shrugged. "Your guess is as good as mine." "But will we be with strangers?" Rose had never been away from home, never been more than six inches away from my mother and now she was clinging on to me and the other children were watching.'

Many parents found it unbearably painful to part with their children even if they were convinced that it was the right thing to do. 'Come the Friday morning,' recalled Edna Kirby (later Griffiths), who was evacuated from Merseyside, 'I was up and dressed without having to be asked. My mum was on her knees black-leading the grate (it was Friday after all!) and didn't even look up when I left, and never said a word. In a child's way I thought perhaps she was glad I was going; it never occurred to me at the time that she was so upset she couldn't say anything. I ran to catch the train to school, my bundle under one arm, cardboard gas mask container bumping against my hip, tears running down my face, and thinking how sorry mum would be if she never saw me again.'

Some parents could not bring themselves to tell their children that they were being evacuated or for how long they might be away – though they had no idea themselves anyway – and the sense of apparent parental betrayal could run deep. Marjorie Lamb, who was five when she was evacuated with her school from Liverpool to Harlech in North Wales, was disturbed to notice that her father had tears in his eyes when he went off to work that morning. She had no idea why, since she assumed when she saw she was to travel on a yellow bus that she was going to visit an aunt. But when no aunt materialised to greet her at the end of her journey, 'the idea began to dawn that for some reason my mother had sent me away. Why the conspiracy of silence . . . I will never understand. Perhaps it might not have been so bad if someone had just explained to us what was going on. Why had we been sent away, we were so young?'

Other mothers, unable to face the truth, lied, telling their children they were off to the seaside for 'a bit of a holiday'. This appealed mightily to Reginald Baker, who had only had one holiday from Bethnal Green in his young life, and that had been a day in Southend when his father had spent nearly all the time in the pub, as usual, 'with the children sitting outside eating arrowroot biscuits and drinking lemonade'.

'It is now an interesting thought,' reflected Eileen Donald, many years later, 'that I, who as a child had been protected and cared for by my family, should calmly have asked them what I should do if they were killed, and written their instructions down in my diary, so as not to forget, and then gone off quite happily.'

The journalist Collie Knox observed the first day's evacuation from Paddington station in London, when a total of 9,500 children were moved out of the capital: 'All day they passed in a continuous stream over the footbridge on to the Main Line platform . . . All day through there came by way of loudspeakers calm voices giving counsel and advice . . . and these voices never tired. The station rang with admonitions such as "Hullo children! Please take your seats quickly. The train leaves in a few minutes. Don't play with the doors and windows if you don't mind. Thank you." '

It was much the same all over Britain: 40,000 were evacuated from Leeds in under seven hours; over two days nearly the same number were moved away from the Medway ports to other parts of Kent; evacuees from Southampton and Portsmouth were directed to safer areas in Hampshire, Dorset and Wiltshire; some 22,000 went from Birmingham to the Cotswolds and parts of Wales; and over five days 130,000 children, mothers and teachers left Merseyside. Most of the evacuation was completed by 3 September, with no child being lost or seriously injured in transit (if slamming fingers in train doors does not qualify), and this all took place as troops were being called up and crammed into trains bound for camps and barracks.

In order to reduce the load on the railway service where possible, evacuees were taken by sea: around 23,500 people, mostly children, were taken on boats – many of which would be deployed the next summer in evacuating British and French soldiers from the beaches of Dunkirk – from London down the Thames and then round the coast to various destinations in Suffolk and Norfolk. Betty Jones was nearly ten when she was evacuated: 'We were put on a bus to Tilbury Riverside Station when we embarked on a Thames pleasure steamer . . . I remember sitting on deck sniffing a lemon. Mum said this stopped you feeling sick. After a trip of about four to five hours, we landed at Yarmouth.'

Many trains were delayed, diverted and shunted into sidings, and two-hour journeys sometimes took six or more. A teacher evacuated from Glasgow found it 'the most depressing, deplorable and disgusting journey I have had the misfortune to take. The train took twelve and a half hours to reach Aberdeen. Half hours and hours were spent in railway sidings until the line was clear. The journey was a positive nightmare, increased by the darkness of the train (lit by blue lights) and the wretched rainstorm that greeted our arrival at the station. The evacuees were famished when they arrived having had no food for twelve hours.' It was an exhausting day for all the children, most of whom had been up since daybreak. They were hot since they were often wearing heavy coats or were togged up in all the clothes they possessed, hungry, thirsty, bored and apprehensive. For many the 'adventure' had already begun to pall and they wanted to go home again. But the worst privation was the lack of lavatories: 400 mothers and children were despatched the 120 miles from Liverpool to Pwllheli in a corridorless train; while children from West Ham in London's East End were finally decanted at Wantage in Berkshire when it was realised that it was idiocy to imagine they could travel all the way to Somerset without requiring a lavatory – and that is where they stayed. But it was not a long journey for all: Eileen Donald was sixteen when she was evacuated from Wandsworth in south-west London. 'Once on the train, we settled down to a long journey. Windsor Castle loomed up, and we waved goodbye to it because we thought that we should not see it for a long time. To our astonishment, the train stopped. Windsor was the end of the journey.' Eileen was 'whisked off on a bus' to Eton where she and two friends were billeted with two Eton masters.

The press portrayed the children's arrival at their destination (or rather *a* destination) as a triumph: it 'was carried out with the same efficiency that characterised the departure . . . For all but a few it was an enthralling but happy adventure, and homesickness and shyness quickly fled at the sight of new faces, new surroundings and new playmates . . .' The reality was rather different. When they finally arrived at their destinations, the children tumbled on to the station platforms weary, dirty, hungry and frequently tearful and uncooperative. 'It was not,' in the understated words of Richard Titmuss, 'a good start. Town and country met each other in a critical mood.'

The plan was that schoolchildren, mothers and mothers-to-be should be billeted with families in private homes. Camps did not seem the answer for young children for a protracted period; it was believed that there was not time to build them, and again, as usual, there was the question of cost when money was being spent on a host of other wartime necessities. It was also anticipated that the hosts with whom schoolchildren were billeted would act *in loco parentis* in caring for the evacuees, so that their teachers would not have twenty-four-hour responsibility for their charges.

In the months before war was declared, officials from the Ministry of Health had gone out to talk to local authorities about the evacuation scheme. They included only four women, and this, as Titmuss suggests, 'may have contributed to the failure to foresee conditions in which the mothers and children would arrive, and the kind of services they would require'. The appointment of billeting officers, whose task it was to arrange accommodation for the evacuees, was indicative of this lack of comprehension in high places about what the evacuation of hundreds of thousands of inner-city children and thousands of mothers would mean. Their duties were envisaged as being temporary, concerned with receiving evacuees, slotting them into accommodation, and then their task would be over. The officers were usually employees of district councils, librarians maybe, or sanitary inspectors; they rarely had any qualifications for what was manifestly sensitive social work, though many were kindly and well meaning. And they were volunteers, expected to be needed in the emergency and then to fade away. In fact, of course, the arrival of evacuees in the countryside was often the start of a war-long commitment dealing with a spectrum of problems: from such routine administrative tasks as handling forms, keeping a file on each evacuee in the area, auditing the money paid to householders through the Post Office, and dealing with supplies such as blankets, clothes and shoes, through to the fraught responsibility of dealing with householders who wanted to get rid of their evacuees, and those evacuees who were unhappy with their billet, or wanted to go home. Since a billeting officer usually lived in the very communities in which he or she was having to persuade their neighbours to take, or retain, evacuees, they could be very susceptible to pressure.

'No one knows exactly the rights and powers of the billeting officers,' explained Renée Humphries, a writer living in Burford in Oxfordshire. 'And no one challenges them because they seem to be exercised more rigorously on poor people than on rich, and as the poor people are often the tenants or employees of the billeting officer, they do not like to protest . . . I do not think all the ill feeling is the fault of the billeting officer entirely as they are faced with the job of getting a quart into a pint pot, and are so overworked that they have little time and chance to be tactful and find out rights and wrongs.' It was soon obvious that this amateur goodwill exercise had to be professionalised, with the chief billeting officer post converted to one of a full-time salaried employee of the local authority, supported often by a network of voluntary helpers.

The shortfall of expected evacuees, and the consequent confusion at the despatching stations, meant that numbers of reception committees were not confronted with the refugees they had been expecting. Mothers and babies bound for Tring in Hertfordshire arrived at Woodcote in Oxfordshire, to the surprise of the reception committee who had been expecting schoolchildren; at Charlbury, also in Oxfordshire, helpers awaiting 113 London schoolchildren and teachers were informed that three busloads of pregnant women were on their way and had to send loudspeaker vans around the streets appealing for additional accommodation. Anglesey had been expecting children from two secondary schools, and 625 elementary school pupils. What they got was 2,468 elementary pupils; and within a few days 4,000-odd schoolchildren, 300 teachers and helpers, and 413 mothers with 667 young children had descended on the Welsh island as well as 'an unknown number of adults outside the government scheme', while Pwllheli, which had not been scheduled to have any evacuees at all, received a message on 2 September that 890 mothers and pre-schoolchildren were on their way from Liverpool – though eventually only 492 arrived.

The allocation of billets seems to have been a mixture of haphazard allocation or householders choosing for themselves whom they wanted. Wartime 'foster parents', who had been recruited in a hurry with often the most cursory of checks on their suitability to provide a home for young children, strolled round the reception area making their selection, and within a manner of minutes the paperwork would be complete and a five-year-old child would have set off into the night clutching the hand of a total stranger. Susan Waters, a twenty-one-year-old schoolteacher who had travelled with her infants' school to Bedford, was appalled when, after a further bus journey, the party arrived at the village where they were to settle. 'The scene that ensued [on the village green] was more like a . . . slave market than anything else. The prospective foster mothers, who should not have been allowed on to the field at all, just invaded us and walked about picking out what they considered to be the most presentable specimens and then harassed the billeting officer for the registration slips which were essential if they were to get the necessary cash for food and lodging from the government.' Bill Wilkinson's experience on the Isle of Anglesey was that 'all the girls got sorted first – then it was the boys' turn but it was done in alphabetical order so of course we were at the end. It got down to the "W's" and I started to cry – there were only a few of us left – an odd "Y" or two – all the others had been collected – some by horse and cart and a few by car. There didn't seem to be anyone left to take us. My brother said "Never mind – they might send us home". But then someone came and took our cases and we only had to walk round the corner to our billet . . . a house belonging to a local headmaster.'

It seemed 'like the middle of the night and far from home' when Charles Crebbin arrived in a village in North Wales. 'We must have been tired and filthy and it felt, in that church hall where we were assembled, as though we were up for auction – and as adults came along and selected children here and there, it felt to those who were left to last (I was one of them!) that no one wanted us. We heard adults asking for "a little girl" or a "brother and sister" etc. – but no one seemed to ask for a lone little boy of six wearing glasses.' Others spoke of 'feeling like puppies in a pet shop', of 'being paraded round a ring while people made their selection', or of 'being picked out like sweets in Woolworths'. A woman who was evacuated from Merseyside remembers being 'herded like cattle round the streets of Oswestry, officials knocking on the doors of those who had put their names down as wanting evacuees. That person came out of his/her house and chose whom they liked the look of. It was total chaos . . . some children were still being walked round the streets at midnight!'

In agricultural counties, the boys were often chosen first. When a party of Glasgow evacuees arrived in a Perthshire village, a 'burly man of the soil call[ed] out that he wanted six boys! He chose the six biggest lads he could find among us. I expect he found plenty for them to do on his farm.' One boy was not chosen 'because I didn't look strong enough to help with the harvest'. Others were selected for the most capricious of reasons. 'When we had tea,' a Liverpool girl 'learnt why I had been chosen [the little girl of the household had been allowed to make the selection]. I was the only one with long hair! Very few girls had long hair in those days.'

'You are *not* to get separated' and 'You *must* stay with your sister and look after her' were many mothers' parting injunctions to their children, and this made it more difficult to get placed, particularly if there were several siblings who refused to be parted from one another. Dorothy Wharton's mother's last words to her three children had been ' "Stick together" but no one wanted me because I was too small to work on a farm. We got a few knock backs because my sister insisted that we must all stay together. Eventually a little man called Mr Edwards agreed that he'd take all three of us.'

Bernard and Rose Kops were doubly disadvantaged in the selection stakes: 'nearly thirteen years old, when I should have been studying for my Bar Mitzvah, I found myself in Buckinghamshire in a church hall at that. A picture of Christ on the wall, and my younger sister sitting beside me hiding her eyes . . . So there we were, September 1 1939, Friday night, when we should have been having lockshen soup, waiting to be billeted on a family who wanted us about as much as we wanted them. But later we really did want them because, owing to the fact that my sister and I wouldn't be separated, the billeting officer had a very hard time trying to get us off his hands. We were the last ones left in that church hall. "But you won't *be* separated – you'll be awfully near each other. Denham's [in Buckinghamshire] such a small place." Rose shook her head about twenty times and clutched me tighter. "No," she replied, "I promised my mum."

'Near to midnight the billeting officer was getting quite desperate. Then he drove us around in a car from house to house trying to sell us.

His desperation must have eventually made him a better salesman because a young woman and an old woman, standing at the door, nodded their heads up and down. We were in.' The family the Kops children stayed with was kind to them and was to give them a wonderful Christmas even though the children insisted 'it's not our festival'. When Bernard told them about his family in Amsterdam, and pronounced ' "To be Jewish is to be persecuted," Mrs Thompson sliced a tomato and put some salt on it. "Don't you worry your head about that." ' But there was a strong current of anti-Semitism in Britain that went far beyond the fascist right – and children were by no means immune from it. A survey in the 1930s had estimated that as many as three-quarters of the British population harboured unfavourable attitudes towards Jews. Many of the poorer areas of cities were populated by a high proportion of Jews, some recent immigrants, many long-established residents. In rural areas, where most families had lived for generations, any newcomer would seem strange and potentially unwelcome. Jewish evacuees seemed particularly exotic, un-English – and in some cases not to be tolerated. No one in the small coalmining village in South Wales to which the poet-to-be Ruth Fainlight was evacuated from north London 'seemed to have met or had contact with a Jewish person before. We were told we could not possibly be Jews: it was as if it were a delusion we were suffering from and of which, in natural kindness and humanity, we should be cured. When we joined in with Christmas festivities, received presents from friends and relations, and put up paper chains, that seemed to invalidate our strange claim.'

Few guidelines were given to billeting families about Jewish dietary requirements and practices of religious observation. Children arrived at their billets to be met in some cases with ham omelettes or bacon and eggs, and were required the next day, a Saturday, to run errands for their hosts in contravention of the protocols of the Jewish Sabbath. Some evacuees were even taunted as 'dirty Jews' and little was done initially to provide opportunities for worship.

Lily Mitchell, evacuated from north London to Wales where she was billeted with a staunch Baptist, Mrs Jenkins, was determined that her observant father would not find out that she was obliged to attend chapel every Sunday. 'I certainly wasn't going to tell him.' A number of other Jewish children who were kindly treated in other respects grew stoical about the bacon and sausages they were served, and the lack of opportunities for observance; they became 'assimilated', but at a cost to their religious and cultural integrity.

Catholic children could suffer similar difficulties: a majority of Merseyside evacuees were Roman Catholics and they were sent to Nonconformist Welsh villages, while many Glasgow Catholic children found themselves in strict Presbyterian homes in the west of Scotland. Both sometimes encountered lack of understanding and were refused permission to go to Mass or observe fasts, and in some cases were obliged to attend chapel or church on a Sunday since they were too young to be left behind alone. The strict observation of the Sabbath by chapel-goers was hard too: 'on Sundays we either went to church or chapel, nothing else was debated. The good book was all that we could read on the Sabbath, certainly no *Beano*s or *Dandy*s. A game of cards? Heaven forbid!' Such practices increased the children's sense of isolation and distance from their families and their former lives, and it distressed parents: their children were not only far away from home in uncertain times, but the beliefs in which they had been raised were being undermined – they were indeed living beyond a state of grace. One Liverpool priest even urged parents to bring their children home, alleging that 'the physical danger they might incur in Liverpool was trifling when compared to the spiritual danger they incurred by remaining'.

Education was the first casualty of war for many children whose schooling suffered whether they were evacuated or stayed behind. When they arrived in the evacuation areas a number of school parties were broken up and scattered over a wide area, in many cases miles from anywhere that was suitable to serve as a school. The pupils of the Mary Datchelor Girls' School, evacuated from Camberwell in south London to Kent, were taken to seven different villages. Their headmistress drove frantically around the area over the next ten days and finally managed to round up more than half of her 438 pupils, but the rest remained dispersed. Some schools, like an infants' school from Plumstead in south-east London, which was evacuated to Maidstone in Kent, was never able to function properly. The children were dispiritedly moved from village to hamlet to more remote hamlet in search of suitable school accommodation and acceptable billets throughout the autumn and winter, finally giving up and returning to London in January 1940.

When the evacuated schools did remain intact, the hastily acquired premises – such as church halls, vacant shops, above the British Legion club – were often unsuitable for educational activities, and had the added disadvantage that they kept the incomers separate from the local children, which often increased resentment and rivalries. Some evacuees were never accepted into the local community; they were isolated and, even after three years in the same village, felt like strangers, while some country children felt envious of the incomers. 'They got all the fun . . . Evacuation got nothin' to do with *bombs* . . . it's to do with parties an' new clothes an' tins of sweets an' things,' expostulates a character in Richmal Crompton's story of *William and the Evacuees*, when William and his village cronies decide to get themselves 'vacuated too' to a big house so they too can enjoy the imagined munificence bestowed on the city children.

In other instances the evacuees were moved in with the pupils of the local school regardless of the space, staff and resources available, and often with scant notice. A school in a small Berkshire village which usually had around a hundred pupils had to cram three children into desks made for two when fifty-seven children from an LCC school arrived; in West Sussex fifty evacuees were sent to a school which had space and resources for only the existing twenty pupils; and in another Sussex village ninety children arrived at a primary school where just two teachers taught everyone from five to fourteen in two small classrooms. When Upton Cross Junior School in London's West Ham first arrived at a school in Buckinghamshire, the pupils had to be educated on a shift system, with local children attending school from 9 a.m. to 1 p.m., and the evacuees from 1.30 p.m. until 4 p.m., and this early example of hot desking was by no means a unique solution to the problem of acute overcrowding.

Since nearly 1.5 million people were evacuated under the government scheme in September 1939, there could never be a single narrative of this – or subsequent – evacuations: the situations the children left behind, and those they encountered when they arrived in the country (or in some cases outer suburbs), ran the gamut of possibilities. But for all those involved – and observers and commentators too – evacuation proved a revelation. It was a chance for one half of the nation to see how the other half lived – and for those who didn't see, to draw rapid conclusions from largely anecdotal evidence. In the absence of much other war news on the Home Front in the autumn of 1939, evacuation stories dominated the newspapers.

In January 1933, at the worst of the slump, there were 2.9 million officially unemployed in the United Kingdom (including Northern Ireland), though the real number was undoubtedly much higher. Over 1 million were in receipt of poor relief. By the outbreak of war there were still just under 1.5 million officially out of work, and again this was an underestimate. Liverpool, Glasgow, Belfast and London were among the many cities where poverty was endemic among a considerable sector of the population. In such places there was simply no money to clothe children properly – boots and shoes were a particular problem – and often the housing in which poor families lived was grievously sub-standard.

Patrick Dollan, the socialist Lord Provost of Glasgow, reprimanded those who were unsympathetic to the plight of his city's evacuees – and others like them. 'Those children may not have reached aristocratic standards of hygiene, but are more deserving of sympathy than censure. They come from houses that have been denied the amenities of modern civilisation, and are victims of an environment that would have been impossible if in bygone years men had thought more of homes and families than of profits and dividends.'

Yet although the children who were evacuated under the government schemes came disproportionately from among Britain's most impoverished families, the impression of hordes of uncared-for urchins is grossly misleading. A teacher working 'in one of the poorer districts . . . was surprised at the thoroughness most of the mothers had displayed in equipping their children . . . about half of the twenty had brand-new pyjamas, new soap, new toothbrushes, new plimsolls, new shirts for the boys and new knickers for the girls. A teacher told me that one of the mothers would be paying for her children's new clothes till Christmas.' And tellingly, when Mass-Observation – an organisation that had been set up in 1937 by a poet, a film-maker and an anthropologist to 'sound the English unconscious' and was to prove invaluable in wartime in surveying public opinion and reporting on morale – asked their observers in reception areas in November to find out what were the 'main problems between evacuees and hosts', while 27 per cent complained about 'dirty, diseased or ill-mannered children', 20 per cent admitted it was the 'strain of having strangers in the house'.

A schoolteacher evacuated to Brighton found, 'The rumours of lousy, dirty, ill-behaved children bandied about Brighton were exasperating. We knew that 90 per cent of the children were well behaved and happy. But the only stories regaled to me were of the horrors of the wild London children.' Margaret Cassidy, who was evacuated from Glasgow to the village of Dunning in Perthshire, pointed out that the type of children 'who have gone on record as the typical Glasgow evacuee . . . came from . . . a slum clearance area . . . [but that she and her two sisters came from an area of mixed council and private letting houses] and all evacuees were not germ-ridden, poverty-stricken, illiterate, unused to comfort, as the picture has been painted of them.' A seventeen-year-old girl, evacuated to a unnamed town about thirty miles from London, complained that 'a great deal of publicity has been given to the hosts burdened with dirty, verminous evacuees, but none, or very little, to cases where well-brought-up, middle-class girls and boys have been billeted in poor, dirty houses where they have to do any housework that gets done'. Yet the image of the evacuee that generated most publicity was that of slum urchins, 'half-fed, half-clothed, less than half-taught, complete strangers to the most elementary discipline and the ordinary decencies of a civilised home', an example of poverty 'quite unknown to the ordinary citizen' being dumped on the doorsteps of a worthy rural population.

Welsh local authorities spoke of 'children in rags' arriving from Liverpool in a state that 'baffles description' with no change of clothes and wearing garments so filthy that they had to be burned – and indeed some small children were stitched into their winter apparel of calico or brown paper which, in normal times, would not have been scissored off until the spring. Shoes were a particular source of criticism: Liverpool became known as 'plimsoll city' for the almost universal footwear of its children, and what might have been just about acceptable for city pavements proved entirely inadequate for the mud of the countryside. Many country hosts were shocked to find their small billetees had no nightwear and, according to a Ministry of Health report, 'many Manchester and Liverpool little girls have never worn knickers, a fact that distresses and horrifies foster parents'. Reginald Baker, from Bethnal Green in London's East End, recalls that he 'never had any underwear as a child. I didn't get a pair of underpants until I was eleven or twelve at least.' In many cases foster parents found themselves having to equip the evacuees with what they considered to be the basic minimum clothing out of their own pockets. The Ministry of Health, galvanised by complaints, broadcast an appeal for second-hand clothing on 8 September, and many organisations, including the National Union of Teachers and voluntary bodies, US citizens and an Indian maharaja helped with donations of clothes and money throughout the war.

Then there were the lice. Reports flooded in of 'scenes of horror in the village street' as the heads of a number of children were seen to be 'literally crawling with nits' while others were covered in patches of ringworm or had impetigo all over their bodies – a much more serious condition than the much shuddered over but relatively easily treatable nit infestation, but all were regarded as manifestations of dirt and neglect. The most notorious example was at Bridgenorth in Shropshire, where an estimated 70 per cent of the evacuees the town received were reputed to be harbouring vermin on their persons. A Women's Institute survey reported that as many as 45 per cent of all children evacuated from metropolitan boroughs were vermin-ridden, and from Merseyside the proportion was reported to be high too, between 22 and 50 per cent. This evidence was gleefully seized on by some – most vociferously the Malton and Thirsk Conservative Association – as evidence not only of the fecklessness of the evacuees' parents, but also that funds spent on social services had obviously been a complete waste of public money. Evacuating authorities, however, refuted the figures as being grossly exaggerated. The LCC, for example, insisted that only 10 per cent of London evacuees were verminous – though later investigations showed this to be a conservative estimate. Clearly nits were no longer just a persistent itch on the unfortunate host's head but had become a site of political and social contestation, a reproach to urban living conditions and school medical services.

The Minister of Health had assured the House of Commons when the question of evacuation had been discussed in early March 1939 that all evacuees were children who were 'subject to regular examinations . . . [they] are not scrofulous and verminous children . . . they are the bud of the nation'. When this proved not to be entirely the case, the reason given for the high rate of infestation was that the children sent out to the country had not had regular medical examinations: evacuation had come at the end of the summer holidays and so pupils had not been seen been seen by 'nitty Nora' the nurse, or any other medical authorities for several weeks. Presumably such inspections could have taken place at the same time as the evacuation exercises were rehearsed in schools, or on arrival in the reception centres, but in both cases officials had more pressing concerns. But the omission led to difficulties and in some cases cruelty. In one Scottish town, the Medical Officer of Health ordered that all the evacuees should have their heads shorn without any consultation with the child or young person – and in many places children were stigmatised for their condition. But in fact the problem was not necessarily caused by the wartime conditions. In 1938 a Liverpool survey had found that more than 20 per cent of the city's schoolchildren were verminous. The ineffectiveness of the school medical system, as of many aspects of social welfare provision for the poor, became increasingly apparent when it was subjected to the scrutiny of the evacuation experience.

There was also the problem of bed-wetting, forcing an unwelcome chore on the housewife who had to wash piles of sheets every morning – invariably by hand in the 1930s and 1940s – and this lapse was frequently blamed on lax parental training, rather than the psychological trauma of evacuation and separation, which certainly must have accounted for many of the cases. Behaviour and manners were often found seriously at fault too: there were numerous reports of children who crammed food into their mouths with their hands and seemed never to have seen a fork; who refused to sit at the table to eat, so used were they to consuming food on the wing; chips, bread and jam and tea – even beer – was the only sustenance numbers of children were reported to be used to; and green vegetables and milk were regarded with great suspicion. The language issuing from many infant mouths – 'bloody' and 'bugger' peppering every sentence – was deemed offensive and corrupting of rural children. There were stories of children who defecated on the carpet, who refused to sleep in a bed since a bed was where the dead were laid out, who wilfully broke treasured possessions, who thieved money and tormented younger children and animals.

There was evidence that a number of these stories had a kernel of truth, and that there were a few deeply anti-social and disturbed children, but that many reports were greatly exaggerated, generalised or contradictory. Psychological understanding of the effects of separation on young children was heartbreakingly limited, with stories of children regularly caned or beaten with a leather strap for bed-wetting, being humiliated by having their faces rubbed by wet sheets, seven-year-olds being made to wash their soiled sheets and pyjamas themselves or do onerous chores as 'punishment', and even a report of a Liverpool child who was chained up in an outside dog kennel and left there all night when she wet the bed. But anti-social behaviour was by no means confined to the evacuees. Stories of piles of urine-soaked mattresses having been burned by harassed billeting officers came to be counterpoised with evidence that hosts sometimes invented bed-wetting cases in order to claim the 3s 6d allowance for extra laundry costs. In Llantrisant in Wales, the total of such allowances paid out rose from £43 in 1940–41 to a staggering £350 in 1941–42, until there was an official investigation, after which the reported cases declined dramatically. Special clinics were set up to deal with persistent bed-wetters, but few had trained psychologists working with them, and a Liverpool observer wrote that 'a visit to one . . . gave the feeling that we still live in the Middle Ages. In this clinic, the children were treated as little criminals, and threat and punishment were the means of teaching them clean habits. The result can easily be imagined: no progress was made at all.'

Simple practical measures could have helped: during 1940 and 1941 when children were again being evacuated, the government ensured a more effective distribution of rubber sheeting; extra payments were made to those who housed persistent bed-wetters; children with enuresis had this coded information printed on to the labels they wore, so that the reception authorities had advance warning; and gradually hostels were set up for the most disturbed and disruptive children. Systematic medical inspections were introduced and, in subsequent evacuations, local authorities were issued with such useful publications as *The Louse and How to Deal With It*.

Evacuation was a gift to the social scientist, the policy-maker and the psychologist. It offered unique, near-laboratory conditions to isolate and study the effects of poverty, separation, child development, education, class and culture in a huge cohort. Starting in 1940, there were at least 230 surveys of evacuation undertaken by university departments, voluntary organisations, Mass-Observation, 'concerned parties' and even individuals. Some of the conclusions would inform subsequent evacuation initiatives, and some would contribute towards the planning of the post-war world. Some findings confirmed what the researchers had suspected all along. Occasionally there were unexpected insights. But what most found was that evacuation offered an opportunity for redemption and social experiment. There were members of the public who felt this strongly too. The journalist F. Tennyson Jesse had been a war correspondent for the *Daily Mail* in the First World War; as a journalist and criminologist, she had 'attended many trials at the Central Criminal Court' and considered herself well placed to pronounce on such matters. 'These children, of whom country residents so reasonably complain, are bound to grow up . . . into sub human savages, unless we seize the opportunity of saving them . . . war has lifted the flat stone – these disgraces to our educational system have been forced out into the light. Do not let us . . . let them creep back beneath their stone. This is, and I repeat it with every emphasis of passion at my command, an opportunity which, if we miss it, we do not deserve to have given to us again.' A vicar's wife and WVS organiser in rural Lincolnshire would have been much happier to exclude mothers from the scheme altogether since so many were of the 'low slum type . . . Children should be removed from their mothers' care and put into nursery schools' while the errant mothers could be sent to camps where they could 'live dirtily (and happily) together and be a nuisance to no one but themselves'. Others had more 'progressive' views. Two women looking after twenty mothers and thirty children in a Devon farmhouse were shocked at how the mothers disciplined their children: 'If the mothers want their children to behave, they hit them. This was clearly unacceptable: children should be trained not beaten.'

The two-nation divide that evacuation put under the spotlight was not only between the rich and the poor, or, as it had been in Disraeli's coinage, between the industrial north and the agricultural south: rather, these were fused into an urban/rural dichotomy. The urban poor were seen as different from, inferior to, the country poor. An article in *Farmer's*

Weekly in October 1939 commented that 'there is evidently such a difference between town poverty and country poverty . . . I think of the country cottage women living near me who are managing splendidly to bring up their large families on labourer's wages . . . Poverty in the country hasn't the same ugly look as in towns.' But just as rural England was evoked during the war as the authentic England (and it was invariably named as England rather than Britain) that men were fighting to keep free, so the countryside was mobilised to redeem the 'lost' children of the industrial towns and cities. Evacuation would give such children the opportunity to flourish in the countryside as they grew berry-brown and rosy-cheeked, they would lose their wily, artificial city ways and embrace the simple, honest values of country folk. The influential report *Our Towns*, the work of representatives from numerous women's voluntary groups, published in 1943, put the case. 'Rural life has advantages of great price: clean air and sleep-giving quiet, ready access to a diet balanced by fruit and vegetables, few temptations to extravagance . . . juxtaposition of the social classes, the force of public opinion in small communities, the influence of tradition and the extraordinary interest, discipline and emotional enrichment of tending growing things which brings an element of personal responsibility and creativeness to the humblest lives.'

While many city children complained of the countryside being dull, with nothing to do and nowhere to go, and city teachers fretted about the lack of science facilities in rural schools, the shortage of books and the difficulties of preparing their pupils for examinations, the proselytisers of country values pointed out the 'true' education to be had in the fields and hedgerows, observing nature at first hand rather than mediated by mere 'book learning'. Yet while country people were confident that with all that fresh air and good country food the townies had 'grown in stature, increased in weight and there is a marked difference in their nervous condition', surveys conducted in 1940 showed no appreciable difference in the growth rate of evacuated LCC children as compared with an equivalent group of children in 1938.

Indeed, a simple picture of a deprived urban working class confronting a comfortable rural middle class is misleading. In general, it would seem that while middle-class families were more likely to have the surplus accommodation for evacuees, they were less likely to be prepared to take them. It would be reasonable to expect the upper echelons of society to find such an invasion rather less of a burden, staffed as they still were in 1939 with cooks and nannies and maids. However, Wootton Basset and Cricklade Rural District Council in Wiltshire wrote to the Ministry of Health reporting that some householders in their area would be unable to take evacuees since 'the servant problem in large houses is so acute that it would be unfair to billet children on the owners'. And well-to-do families in Surrey reported 'disgruntled butlers', maids 'that gave notice after the first week because of the extra work' and the intelligence that 'if you tell a prospective cook, when interviewing her, that you have six evacuees, most likely she will turn the place down at once'.

A WVS regional organiser found 'over and over again that it really is the poor people who are willing to take evacuees and that the sort of bridge-playing set who live in such places as Chorley Wood are terribly difficult about it all.' 'It's always the same, the poor helping the poor. There's overcrowding in every small house, and the rich still go their comfortable ways,' complained a Salisbury resident. While Mrs Miles' comfortably off neighbours in Surrey complained about the imposition, her charwoman, 'whose one sitting room is about the size of a pocket handkerchief . . . was nearly out of her mind with excitement and joy . . . "I'm having two girls, poor kiddies. Could I rest when I have a spare room and I thought of them wanting a shelter!" ' Even Lady Reading, founder and chairman of the WVS, who had at one time thought evacuees would be 'quite happy' billeted in barns and garages, came round to the view that 'Evacuation had been a terrible fiasco . . . not nearly enough use was made of the big houses of England.'

Although there were examples cited of contented pairings between evacuees and the comfortably off, the arrangement by which evacuees stayed with less well-off families seems generally to have worked rather better with fewer illusions on either side. And the money helped: in 1939 householders received 10s 6d if they had one child billeted with them and 8s 6d for each child if they had more than one. This was intended to cover 'full board and all the care that would be given to a child in their own home'. But the issue about money was not a simple matter of cost analysis: it was also about value, about the recognition women deserved for war work if it was something they were doing round the clock in their own homes, rather than in the services or munitions factories. An article in the Women's Institute's magazine,

Home and Country, argued that because housework 'brings in no money, it also brings very little understanding and respect, so little indeed that the planners of the evacuation scheme could – and did – calmly assume that the housewife need not be paid anything for the time, energy, labour and skill spent in cooking, washing, ironing, mending and "minding" and doing housework for three or four extra children. They did not ask school buses to run free services with unpaid drivers; or farmers to charge nothing for milk and vegetables, or cobblers not to send in accounts for mending evacuated children's shoes. Housewives playing their part (mostly with affection and efficiency) nevertheless asked themselves – and the billeting officer – the reason why they alone should be forced to work without pay. But answer came there none.'

For an agricultural labourer earning thirty shillings a week and with a family to keep, the money for taking in evacuees could be a significant boost to the family income. Unemployment had not only affected the manufacturing cities that the evacuees left. There was poverty in some of the reception areas too. In Wales the depression of the 1930s had hit coal- and slate-mining and other Welsh industries particularly hard and recovery, hampered by poor management–staff and falling export markets, was slow and uncertain. The rural economy had suffered too with falling demand for the staples of Welsh agriculture – wool, mutton, butter and cheese – and as a result the young men had left the mountains and valleys in search of work elsewhere. Many people who remained were elderly – and poor. In 1944 the Parliamentary Secretary to the Ministry of Health spoke of 'the appalling conditions of rural housing', and estimated that about 30 per cent of the population of rural England were not connected to mains water supplies. Evacuees from city slums were surprised to find that many of the country billets had no electricity, and two years after the end of the war nearly half of all rural households were still without a bathroom.

Aware of the problems of poverty, the government havered about reclaiming the cost of billeting, since they feared this might prove an additional inducement to bring children home, but at the end of October 1939 it was decided that the cost must be recovered 'from parents in accordance with their ability to pay'. The real cost of each child's board and lodging was reckoned to be around nine shillings, but the government proposed to reclaim six shillings per child from its parents

– though those who could afford the full nine shillings were invited to do so. Those on unemployment pay or poor relief were not expected to pay anything, while parents on low incomes were means-tested to determine what they could pay. This proved an immensely burdensome and expensive scheme to operate, and it is doubtful whether it eventually did much more than cover its costs. By the end of that year the average amount collected for each child was 2s 3d and a quarter of parents of schoolchildren were unable to make any contribution at all.

The view of society that went with a particular political inclination explained some of the tensions. In general, reception areas returned Conservative or Liberal MPs, while those sending evacuees were in the constituencies of Labour members, and each vigorously defended its particular interests. A few evacuees already had political affiliations that again were reinforced – or tested – by the experience of evacuation. Seventeen-year-old Doreen Mainwaring was a member of the Young Communist League in south London when she was evacuated with her younger sister Sheila to Deal in Kent. Her mother Dorothy wrote in despair: 'the children were evacuated last Friday . . . they were sent to the *rectory*. I don't suppose there would be a Young Communist in a million among school children, yet that one, Doreen, has to be sent to the *rectory*. However I have just had a short letter to say they are being moved as it is too much for the rector's wife . . . she has taken in four children and has four children of her own and keeps a maid who is working from morning to night. Doreen says "I am just waiting to find out what [the maid] is paid". Of course you can see why she is being moved, can't you? . . . On the first Sunday they were there the rector's wife said they had to go to church and Doreen refused to go. That did it.'

In Wales, language was an issue. In response to offers from various South American countries on the outbreak of war, the Foreign Office had decreed that the large-scale evacuation of children was to be restricted to English-speaking countries only, yet in rural parts of North Wales there were villages where almost half the population spoke only Welsh. Although the evacuees were usually taught in separate classes by teachers from home, there were difficulties when a small number of children had to be absorbed into a primary school where Welsh was the first language. And communication between Welsh and English children playing together was hard until the evacuees began to pick up at least colloquial Welsh. Elsa Chatterton, who was evacuated from Merseyside to Llanfrothen, 'went to the village school where we were taught by our own teachers . . . but once a week the local headmaster taught us Welsh. We learnt to count to ten, say the Lord's Prayer and sing "Jesus Loves Me" . . . On the way home we were taught in our innocence some different Welsh by a local teenager. When Mrs Williams-Ellis discovered what we had learnt she told us not to walk home with Owen any more!'

The protection of the Welsh language had been one of the reasons given by Welsh Nationalists for their objection to English evacuation to their country – treating Wales as an English 'reception area'. In January 1939 J. E. Jones, the Organising Secretary of the Welsh Nationalist Party (Plaid Genedlaethol Cymru), declared that 'the indiscriminate transfer of English people into Wales will place the Welsh language and even the very existence of the Welsh nation in jeopardy . . . If England cannot make its emergency plans without imperilling the life of our little nation let England renounce war and grant us self-government.' This was to prove a minority view and the majority acceptance, if not always welcome, of the evacuees held sway, but it raised uncomfortable questions that were to echo in other ways, in other arenas, throughout the war: whose war was it? In whose interest was it being fought? And what exactly were its aims?

Tensions were sharpened by the question of what the evacuees had, in the event, been evacuated *from*, since no bombs had rained down to destroy the homes they had left behind, no fires consumed the tenements they had vacated, no palls of poison gas drifted through the mean streets they had roamed. Why were rural householders put to this inconvenience when it no longer seemed a heroic act of shelter and self-sacrifice in desperate times?

Throughout September and October 1939, billeting officers all over the country were overwhelmed with requests from householders to remove their evacuees. The chief billeting officer for Windsor reported having seventy complainants calling on him each day in the first few weeks of evacuation; within the first three months of the war, his counterpart at Maidenhead in Berkshire had been obliged to arrange 750 transfers; and in London the LCC's Education Officer, E. M. Rich, had a nervous breakdown through overwork occasioned by the seemingly endless queues of people who snaked along every corridor in County Hall seeking redress for their grievances about evacuation arrangements. Billeting tribunals were established, again staffed by volunteers, and accepted arguments against having evacuees for such reasons as long-term illness (indeed, any doctor's certificate seemed to count as decisive), that the household was already housing additional relatives, or a householder was engaged in essential war work. The editor of the Cornish *St Ives Times* was barbed in his comments on those who offered excuses for not taking in evacuees in the picturesque seaside town. 'I gather that those who have the task of finding volunteers to house these children have had no light job. A number of people who a short while ago were moaning that they had no seasonal bookings this year were apparently full up immediately the question of evacuees arose. Perhaps we are to have a season after all. I hear that the numbers of people who have developed heart trouble and kindred ailments this week is staggering. I suppose we must expect to see these poor souls wheeled along the Wharf Road in bath chairs.'

Recourse to legal proceedings was invoked only in the most blatant or intransigent cases of non-cooperation. In the comparatively rare instances where those who refused to take in evacuees were taken to court, the charges were often rejected, or the fines paltry.

With parents far away and hosts sometimes hostile and uncomprehending, teachers had a pivotal role to play in the success of the evacuation scheme. Their days grew long as they attempted to mediate difficult cases of children who were unhappy with the homes where they had been placed, and hosts who had been landed with difficult children, while having to reassure parents back home that all was well. Children, particularly primary-school-age children, were dependent on their teachers as the only familiar adults in a newly configured and strange wartime world. Where there was resentment at the imposition of evacuees – and there was usually some – teachers devised out-of-school activities to try to relieve the burden on the host families and ensure that the children had as constructive and contented a time as possible. Miss Hoyles, the headmistress of Albany Road, a mixed infant and junior school in Camberwell, south London, which was evacuated to Weymouth, was one of the those who were indefatigable in trying to make evacuation a happy experience for the children – in her care arranging new billets if things did not seem to be working out, setting up a consultative committee to ensure good relations between evacuated and local schools, feverishly seeking suitable teaching space for her pupils, organising nature walks for the children to get the greatest possible benefit from their seaside surroundings, dealing with cases of infestation with vinegar and special combs, working with the police to improve the loutish behaviour of some evacuees, and even, on occasion, reimbursing shopkeepers out of her own pocket after an outbreak of juvenile kleptomania.

The hardest evacuees to place, however, were not schoolchildren but mothers who had been evacuated with their under-fives. Of the Catholic families evacuated from Clydeside, 56 per cent had four or more children, and finding a householder prepared to accept such a large-scale invasion was a daunting challenge for the billeting officer, since a mother who arrived with small children invariably insisted on having any older children who had been evacuated to the vicinity with their schools living with her. It was partly a simple question of economics and partly lack of clarity over what were not then called domestic boundaries. A householder was paid five shillings a week for each adult woman (with an additional three shillings for each pre-school child). This was for lodging only: the mother was supposed to cover the cost of her own food, presumably with money sent by her husband. There was the traditional conflict between two women sharing a kitchen, and there were inevitable tensions over what a child could or could not do in someone else's home – a situation easily regarded as 'interference' by the mother, and what the host construed as 'licence' on the part of the mother.

There were complaints that evacuated mothers were feckless, lazy, dirty and offered no help about the house. The Women's Institute reported that its members had 'found it hard to be sympathetic to women who could neither cook, sew nor conform to the ordinary standards of human decency and whose one idea of enjoyment was to visit the public-house or cinema'. For their part, many mothers felt unwelcome – as indeed they were – found the country lonely and boring, and missed their husbands and the often close-knit community they had left behind. They defended their opening-hours occupation of village pubs, pointing out that there was nothing else to do: there were no 'picture houses' nearby, a bus might only go into the nearest town twice a week, and there was a limit to how often they could push a pram round and round the village green since some mothers were shooed out of their billets after breakfast and debarred from returning before nightfall. It was mothers such as these who led the swarm back to the cities. By December 1939 nearly 90 per cent of those mothers evacuated in September had returned home.

Expectant mothers who left under the government scheme were relatively few in number – a total of 12,300 in England and 403 in Scotland – but they posed a considerable challenge. Again, plans had been made to transport pregnant women from vulnerable areas and midwives travelled in the trains with them, but few arrangements were in place to receive them. By July 1939, 75 per cent of midwives working in London hospitals had been seconded to casualty work and two-thirds of maternity beds reserved for air-raid victims, but little had been done to compensate for this in the reception areas. The first weeks of the war saw a frantic race to install beds, bathrooms, lavatories, sluices and cooking facilities in such diverse premises as boys' clubs, local authority offices, Ruskin College, Oxford, stately homes and private houses to cope with childbirth and the needs of infant care.

In medical services, as in most other emergency wartime provision, the question of cost was contentious. Who was to pay for the treatment of evacuees when they fell ill or were injured? The evacuating authority or the reception area? In the case of pregnant women, a Dorset county councillor posed the question succinctly: 'Who pays for an enjoyed conception in London resulting in an expensive confinement in Dorset?' The answer in that case, in terms of beds and accommodation, was the Ministry of Health, but new mothers, evacuated away from their extended families, also needed help to care for the new baby and probably other siblings: another unplanned responsibility for the reception area. An unforeseen problem arose when billeting officers reported finding it difficult to place unmarried expectant mothers on 'moral grounds' – though there seems no reason why the mother's circumstances needed to have been revealed. If unwed mothers could not be housed in private accommodation, they were sent to local workhouses where their 'public assistance' costs had to be borne by the reception areas. Some reception areas were so determined not to pay for this that in one instance a Somerset Public Assistance Department put two single expectant mothers straight back on the train to London.

For the children's part, despite the problems, many of them billeted with kind and tolerant foster parents adjusted reasonably well and settled down to enjoy country life, particularly if they had been evacuated with their school and were surrounded by friends and familiar adult faces. Reginald Baker found life in a village outside Bicester in Oxfordshire a pleasant change from the poverty he'd known at home in Bethnal Green, even though the village people were 'not so much unwelcoming as indifferent to us: we were "townies", they thought we were coarse and we spoke differently. I can't ever recall being invited to anyone's house the whole two years I was there.' But he was happy with his billet with the village blacksmith and his family. 'Granny Dorling' bought him Wellington boots 'which was generous of her as she only got 8/6d a week for me'. The food was good and plentiful – and they had a tablecloth on the table for every meal, unlike at home where it had been a sheet of newspaper except for the tea after the funeral for Reg's baby brother, who had died when the gas used for fumigating the rooms above to get rid of vermin seeped through the thin walls of the tenement building. 'We'd climb trees and dam streams, and paddle and collect frog spawn . . . and soon I looked different, fatter and with rosy cheeks . . . but even then we were always plotting to go home. All the kids were. They missed home even if they'd been beaten at home, and they missed their mums . . . We used to see a lorry coming through the village and it had the words "London Brick" painted on it. In fact the London Brick Company was at Luton, but we didn't know that and me and Ronnie [Norton who shared the same billet] used to plan all the time how we'd get onto that lorry one day when no one was looking and get taken back to London.'

Some children looked back on the time they were evacuated as the happiest in their lives, but many children missed their homes and families almost unbearably. This was bound to be the case if a child was ill-treated in his or her billet – there were reports of children being boarded with psychopaths, prostitutes, molesters and paedophiles. It has recently been estimated that between 10 and 15 per cent of evacuees were abused physically, sexually or emotionally, and the NSPCC did bring a number of successful prosecutions for cruelty. But others who were not so treated simply found the wrench too great, the standards too different, and either could never conform to new ways of doing things, or felt guilty that they had somehow betrayed their parents if they settled to their new foster family's ways. Many young children were anxious about those left behind and found it hard to understand why they had been sent away 'They reason, with some justification, that they can live wherever their mothers live, and that if "home" is as much in danger as all that, their mothers should not be there either.' Evacuation clearly showed the importance of family ties for the emotional stability of children.

At first there had been no official plans for ensuring that families kept in touch and it was beyond the purse of most working-class city dwellers to travel as far afield as Cornwall or Devon from London, or the Isle of Anglesey from Liverpool, for example, to visit their evacuated children. At the outbreak of war the railway companies had abolished cheap day-return tickets and it was not until November 1939 that some concessionary fares were introduced. Cheap day tickets were available on Sundays to a limited number of stations, none of which was more than 160 miles from London. This meant that some parents, none of whom had had any say in where their children had been evacuated to, had to try to find the money to traverse halfway across the country to see them, while others only had to pay the equivalent of a daily commuter's fare. A teacher, evacuated with her school to Caernarvon, noted that 'very few parents [from Merseyside] ever visited their children – in fact the children were ignored until they were fourteen when they could become wage earners'. But this was not a general rule. An Oxford survey found that of the 217 unaccompanied children, nearly 90 per cent received at least one letter a week from home and regular visits from parents, and 97 per cent wanted to go back home after the war. In some parts of Islington, for example, a social worker reported that there was 'a feeling of reproach if you did not care enough for your child to visit frequently, or even to bring him home [though these children had been evacuated to Cambridge which was not a long journey]. The week-end expeditions became social gatherings and money was often borrowed to meet the fare.'

Some parents made considerable efforts to visit their evacuated children. The father of Ronald Hodgson, who was evacuated from Neasden in north-west London to Kettering in Northamptonshire, worked for the Post Office in London, and as often as he could he would get on his bike and cycle the 70 miles each way to visit his son. Reginald Baker recalls, 'After a bit, my parents started to come down quite often because my father could work it so he had deliveries to make in the area, and he'd bring my mother. Granny Dorling would sometimes put them up in the spare room . . . I always liked to see them and I liked the 6d my Dad gave me when they came, but they never said to me "You want to come home son?" '

Despite cheerful stories in local newspapers designed to reassure parents that their children were safe and happy away from home, and that they had done the right thing in signing up to the government scheme, many were anxious not only about how their children were faring, but also had nagging concerns that in those vital years of childhood their progeny would learn alien ways and values that would make it hard for them to adapt when they came home; that over the several years they might be away, the children would form new bonds with their wartime guardians that would erode mother–child ties. A survey of children evacuated from north London found that many parents were critical of the system of billeting their children in private homes, advocating camps and boarding schools that would ensure that the children were treated more equally. This laudable aim may also have hidden anxieties about new attachments to foster parents displacing family bonds.

Many parents who had been prepared to sacrifice their children when it appeared that they were in mortal danger from enemy action decided to bring them home when it was clear that they were not. A survey of the 80 per cent of children evacuated from Islington in north London to Cambridge, who had been brought home in the first six months, found that they had returned either because their parents considered their billets to be unsuitable (dirty was the usual complaint) or because they had been moved too often. It might be for financial reasons – the cost of contributing to the child's board, lodging and extra clothes was too much of a drain on the family income and the family might have lost certain allowances because the child was away, or the child was fourteen and could leave school, get a job and contribute financially at home or help around the house. A girl of thirteen was brought back to London from Maidenhead because her stepmother 'had had a baby and I was needed to queue for food'. Or it was a simple question of 'family ties' – the child was homesick, or the parents missed the child too much.

These reasons stacked up conclusively when it was the case that the cities were no more perilous than the countryside. A number of schools, finding it impossible to operate on two sites, packed up and came back too, while most schools in the cities remained shut or had been requisitioned for use by the ARP, Auxiliary Fire Service (AFS) or Red Cross, or as decontamination stations or even temporary mortuaries, even though many of their pupils had returned, leaving the children to 'run wild' in the streets with no classes to attend. The left-wing journalist, Ritchie Calder, writing in the *Daily Herald*, named them 'the Dead End Kids' of London and the provincial cities, starved of education, numbed through lack of direction, and neglected in health'. Throughout England and Wales it was estimated that by April 1941 around 290,000 children were still not receiving full-time education – though the LCC denied that the figure was as high as this.

The government was alarmed: its policy of dispersal seemed to be in ruins. A propaganda counter-offensive was mounted: advertisements urging 'Don't Do it Mother. Leave the Children Where They Are' showing a shadowy Hitler whispering to a doubtful woman surrounded by her children in the country that she should 'take them back' to the city. The Queen was photographed visiting evacuees at a school in Sussex; there was talk of enlisting Boy Scouts, Girl Guides and the Salvation Army to give enthusiastic testimonials to the benefits of evacuation; and the BBC's gardening guru C. H. Middleton broadcast a homily among his usual offering of horticultural tips, encouraging children to stay in the country for the autumn to plant school gardens for the moral as well as the practical benefits that would accrue from this contact with the soil.

In November 1939 in a speech at the Mansion House in London, Chamberlain insisted that though the expected bombers had not arrived, the danger was by no means past and that children should not be brought back to the cities. As Christmas 1939 loomed, the government recognised that this would be a particularly vulnerable moment with parents pining to reunite their families for the festive season, so a special fund was set up to organise Christmas activities for evacuees in the country. It was no use: by January 1940 it was estimated that some 90,000 evacuees had returned home, 60 per cent of those who had left on the outbreak of war. It would take the decisive argument of the Blitz in the summer of 1940 to make many reconsider. But not all. For them it was a question of 'once evacuated, twice shy'.

3

FIGHTING THE DARKNESS

"But apart from this, life is going on just the same as usual."

It oughtn't to need a war to make a nation paint its kerbstones white, carry rear-lamps on its bicycles, and give all its slum children a holiday in the country. And it oughtn't to need a war to make us talk to each other in buses, and invent our own amusements in the evenings, and live simply, and eat sparingly, and recover the use of our legs, and get up early enough to see the sun rise. However, it has needed one: which is about the severest criticism our civilisation could have.

'MRS MINIVER', *THE TIMES*, 25 SEPTEMBER 1939

RIGHT AT THE top of almost everyone's list of things they hated most about war in the early months came the blackout. In November 1939 the *Daily Mail* had asked its readers 'What part of the war do you mind most?' and to the surprise of a Somerset farmer, 'Women in Uniform' came first and ' "Blackout" second. Some people simply put "Unity Mitford". The thing I mind most, which is shortage of animal-feeding stuffs, came sixteenth. "Evacuees" didn't come as high as I expected.'

The blackout was the most immediate transformation of daily life that war brought. Its imposition on 1 September was evidence as eloquent as the evacuation of children and the call-up of the ARP on that same day, in anticipation of immediate bombing raids on the civilian population. In 1938 lighting restrictions had been predicted as 'imposing general darkening as a permanent condition from the outbreak of war'. And that is exactly how it felt. The regulations insisted that no chink of light must be visible from flats, houses, offices, factories or shops. Illuminated signs and advertisements must be turned off for the duration of the war; street lighting would be extinguished; and cars, trains, buses, trams and trolley buses – the last dubbed 'the silent peril' since they were particularly lethal to pedestrians as they glided noiselessly and now virtually unseen along overhead cables – would be obliged to mask their headlights and to screen their interior lights; while even essential vehicles such as fire engines, ambulances and police cars would have to conform as closely as possible to restrictions. And this intense darkness settled over all the land. Earlier suggestions that the country should be divided into regions of more or less vulnerability in the way that it had been for evacuation, and lighting restrictions imposed accordingly, were rejected.

Putting up the blackout was a nightly chore for householders and it could take an exasperatingly long time in an average-sized semi-detached house to draw curtains, pull down blinds, slide brown-paper screens into place, pin up blankets or heavy bedspreads – and then nip outside to make sure that not a scintilla of light was escaping. It was much worse for some: a Cambridge clergyman's wife was appalled when she realised that their vicarage had forty-three windows; large pubs, hotels and offices had to start blacking out in late afternoon to make sure their numerous windows were covered; and a City of London textile firm calculated that to black out its fifty skylights would take 8,000 square yards of material.

Women's magazines were full of tips on how to brighten gloomy blacked-out rooms by stitching chintz on the inside of dark curtains or pinning on tinfoil stars, and Sanderson manufactured a double-sided wallpaper at two shillings a roll which could be stuck on to windows with the black side facing out and the patterned side into the room. But it was a dispiriting business. Already electricity companies had reduced the voltage, and one device to make blacking-out easier was to replace low-wattage bulbs with those of even lower wattage. Makeshift cardboard or tin lampshades were fashioned, and people groped their way along unblacked-out halls and landings and got undressed in the dark rather than turn on the light in rooms without the regulation blackout. Numerous accidents were reported in the home, as people fell down stairs and crashed into walls and furniture. Margaret Cotton, an American living in St John's Wood in north London, found the family's blackout arrangements were difficult for her maid Lily: 'with curtains drawn and improvised black paper shades about the ceilings and wall lights . . . [it was] anything but efficient for cooking. Shadows fell everywhere, into the soup and vegetables cooking on the stove, across the grill so that Lily had to strike a match to note the progress of things cooking.' It was not for several weeks that Mrs Cotton cracked the problem: 'I made some extra heavy black sateen curtains and embellished them with appliquéd cretonne roses. These curtains now permit us to have every light ablaze in the kitchen and to snap our fingers at Hitler, air raids and wardens.'

But in what was intended to be a perpetual – and comprehensive – blackout, many householders left skylights and small landing windows unmasked, claimed not to realise that the back as well as the front of a property must be blacked out, and switched on lights when they went into rooms that were not in normal use. Lord Alfred Douglas, who had in his golden youth been Oscar Wilde's beloved 'Bosie', was fined after he had gone out in the gathering gloom leaving a light on in an uncurtained room in his house in Hove on the south coast. A correspondent to *The Times* pointed out that from the roof garden of his house 'one of the highest in the West End – I can make an after dark inspection of London and most of the suburbs. I still see many top-storey lights which are difficult to detect from the streets. Some of them are showing through thin curtains; a few from apparently unprotected windows. These lights could be seen for miles from an approaching aeroplane and would thus nullify the effect of the blackout.'

Effective blackout could also be a considerable expense. Sufficient fabric for Mrs Cotton's 'kitchen window cost me a pound. I wondered how the really poor were going to manage complete blackouts, and have since noticed the many *painted* windows, black or dark blue. No doubt an economy, but how dismal those houses must be, like caves.'

The scientist J. B. S. Haldane had been concerned at the time of the Munich crisis that while he could 'afford a pot of paint and even several sets of new blinds', others could not, and he set up an example: '. . . one of my neighbours, Mr John Smith, has been out of work for eighteen months and has six children. He cannot afford to buy them the boots and butter they need. He is certainly not going to buy paints and blinds now [as the government was advising]. And even if war comes, and the shops are sold out, he will not be able to do so. As a result he will probably show a light, and my life, not to mention the King's, will be endangered . . . I think that Mr Smith ought to hide his lights as part of our collective protection. As he cannot afford to do so, I think that the government, or even the municipality, should help him do so. For this purpose paint and other necessities should be stored for issue in the event of an emergency.' But they were not, and no subsidy was forthcoming for the private householder. However, there was another notional neighbour of Haldane whose problem the government did confront: 'Miss Irene Jones . . . can afford paint and blinds but she is an absolute pacifist, who says that she will have nothing to do with war . . . She says she is going to keep her lights on, and if a bomb hits her house she will be well out of a wicked world. As I have never yet seen a bomb hit the mark at which it is aimed, I think it is much more likely that a bomb aimed at her skylight will hit me . . . if lights should be covered, as I think they should, then this should be made a matter of law, like the lighting regulations for vehicles.' Which it was.

The responsibility of ensuring that blackout regulations were observed lay with ARP wardens, who would instruct a householder to rectify his or her blackout deficiencies; but if the miscreant refused to comply, the warden's only recourse was to report them to the police. Usually a warning was given first but, in the case of flagrant or persistent transgression, a householder would certainly be prosecuted, and penalties could be harsh. In the first week of October 1939 forty prosecutions for blackout offences were brought in Oxford, a city on which no bombs were to fall, and in 1940 300,000 people nationwide were taken to court for blackout offences. In many respects this was consensual policing – at least in the early days of the war. Although individuals might feel exasperated when they were reported for emitting a gleam of light, there was plenty of evidence that the general public thought that one person who failed to cover up a source of light was imperilling the safety of all by in effect shining a beacon for the expected enemy raiders. Soon after the outbreak of war, police were called to an angry crowd outside the house of an eighty-three-year-old man in Hampstead, north London, who were shouting, 'Smash the door down.' Lights were showing from two front-room windows. Despite the man's age and his possible confusion, the court fined him £2, which was four times the amount of the weekly pension for a single man in 1939. In neighbouring Highgate, a large crowd gathered round an elderly man who had lit a bonfire in his garden, and, according to the police 'wanted to assault him'. Shopkeepers who transgressed the lighting regulations were made an example of, and fines of £50 were not unusual – when a baby Austin car could be bought for around £120.

It was not just the careless householder or shopkeeper who was culpable. Several ARP wardens from Westminster sent a stiff letter to *The Times* 'to protest most emphatically against the failure of many government Departments with regard to the lighting restrictions. Civilians in our sector . . . are making great efforts to do their part, and have always immediately remedied any defects. It is, therefore, all the more regrettable that the government offices . . . in the immediate vicinity seem to take no trouble to ensure that their windows are light proof. If we had a lead from them in this respect, civilians in general would be more willing to listen to requests from their wardens.'

But sometimes these requests seemed preposterous: when a civil servant who had moved with her department to Newcastle turned on the lights in her new flat, 'the merest glimmer appeared from the electric bulbs. The Electricity Department had switched my 210 voltages to 105. The blackout curtains were drawn and the light was insufficient to unpack my boxes of china and books. The flat was a studio one with picture windows all round, high up on the hill which overlooked the Vickers Armstrong factories. I drew one curtain and sought for a candle, placed it on top of a packing case, surrounded it with cardboard and started work. A few minutes later there was a sharp knocking on my door and a stern voice called, "Open in the name of the law" . . . A burly policeman stood outside. Without preliminaries he pushed his way in.

"We've been informed you are signalling to enemy planes and giving the location of the armament factory. Ah!" He had caught sight of the glimmer of light from my packing case and he strode forward and fell over a case of books. "But it's only a candle," I said. "It's been placed strategically to throw a beam of light for miles around," he said pompously and promptly blew the candle out. We stood in the darkness . . . "What am I going to do?" I said frantically. "I only moved in today. I'm unpacking." "You can go to bed," he said brusquely, as he stamped across the room.'

The blackout drained the vitality from people's lives and many, timorous about venturing out, found themselves enclosed in a smaller, gloomier world. But if staying in could be enervating and isolating, going out was distinctly hazardous. 'For weeks it was frightening and depressing. How dependent one is on light,' wrote Margaret Cotton. 'And how helpless one can feel without it . . . I wonder how we ever got about . . . this groping along with other shadowy figures, in a ghostly world, seemed like a fantastic game of blind man's bluff.'

Three men from the Foreign Office found the darkness 'so stygian' as they left their club in Pall Mall 'that we walked arm in arm or we should have lost each other'. For Nella Last, a Lancashire housewife, 'a tag I've heard somewhere "City of Dreadful Night" came into my mind and I wondered how on earth the bus and lorry drivers would manage. I don't think there is much need for the wireless to advise people to stay indoors – I'd need a dog to lead me.'

'My dear boy,' wrote the crime novelist Dorothy L. Sayers to 'Gerald', who was 'brought up in the country . . . of course you don't have any difficulty. There you have a blackout every night, and take your precautions accordingly. You are aware of the ditch on your right, the quickset hedge on your left, the unfenced pond in the corner, and the position of the unlit cow straying through a gap. But the town dweller is accustomed to lighted streets: there are men and women born since 1918 who never saw the dark in their lives until September . . .'

An article in the *New Statesman* railed against the sentimentality of those who found the blackout heightened their sense of adventure and beauty: 'I yield to no one . . . in my admiration of the stars, but in a town I think they look better by electric light. The common report that in ordinary times you cannot see the stars in London is a myth. Many people are now seeing the stars for the first time, not because they were not visible before, but because in the blackout there is nothing else to see . . . Moonlight, which conceals as much as it reveals, fills even the dullest street with a curious glamour. The slate roof of a Victorian public house falls under its enchantment no less than the dome of St Paul's. Moonlight is the great leveller. Mystery takes the place of bad architecture and the worst statues become masterpieces of Phidias . . .'

But Quentin Crisp – an artist's model who was to become famous as the 'Naked (and gay) Civil Servant' – who had lied about his age to get into the Army because he needed the money so badly, but was turned down on the grounds that he was 'suffering from sexual perversion', found the lighting regulations a delight, and London full of 'overtures made possible by the blackout'. Not that he ever thought that the streets of London were totally black – 'more of a cosy gloom . . . The city became like a paved double bed. Voices whispered suggestively to you as you walked along; hands reached out to you if you stood still and in dimly lit trains people carried on as they had once behaved only in taxis . . . If there is a heaven for homosexuals, which doesn't seem very likely,' he thought, 'it will be very poorly lit and full of people they can feel pretty confident they will never have to meet again.'

The headlights of cars and other vehicles were required to be shielded so that only a tiny crescent of light was emitted; some drivers used cardboard discs, or pulled an old sock over them, and stuck tissue paper over side and rear lights to reduce their intensity. A car's plastic indicators were obliged to wink only along an eighth-of-an-inch gap, and dashboard lights were forbidden – a frustrating restriction when, starting in February 1940, motorists were only permitted to drive at a maximum speed of 20 mph in built-up areas during the hours of blackout, yet could not see to check their speedometers. All car owners were obliged to paint a stripe of white along their bumpers or mudguards and running boards, and could be prosecuted if the paint got dirty and thus less effective, and they were forbidden to park facing the oncoming traffic at night. Kerbs and bollards had been painted white when war threatened at the time of the Munich crisis in September 1938; motorists tended to hug the white line painted along the centre of the road, which meant that cars going in opposite directions came into dangerously close contact with each other. A suggestion made in *The Autocar* that cars should switch sides and drive on the right rather than the left after dark so they could follow the kerb was thankfully never adopted.

Bus and tram conductors wrestled with the difficulties of identifying tickets (which were a different colour for each fare stage) and coins, while the drivers of public vehicles felt the strain of negotiating the equivalent of a pea-souper fog for several hours every winter evening. Cyclists were required to fit rear lights as well as front – as in theory were prams on the public highway – and some painted the frames of their bikes white but, whatever they did, cyclists were extremely vulnerable to vehicle drivers peering exhaustedly into the unremitting black, and casualties were high.

Pedestrians were known to walk along the white line down the centre of suburban and country roads to get their bearings – a dangerous practice. In the first days of the war it was forbidden to carry a torch, but after 13 September this was allowed if it was masked by a double layer of tissue paper with the weak beam aimed at the ground – and soon torch batteries were in short supply everywhere. Sales of fluorescent paint increased as people optimistically dabbed some on keyholes and bell pushes, and citizens were encouraged to wear – or carry – something white: a white handkerchief in a suit breast-pocket for men, or white buttonhole in a lapel, for example, or an untucked white shirt tail; a white handbag or corsage of white fabric flowers for women. Even a white Pekinese dog was mooted – portable by either sex presumably. A letter to *The Times* in November suggested that: 'walkers northwards should use the west and those walking southwards, the east pavement . . . it does not matter much at night which side of the street one walks since there are no shops or other attractions.' But such regimentation never caught on, and pedestrians continued to feel confused, disorientated and often frightened, weeping tears of frustration or near panic as they negotiated their way along city streets and country lanes in the dark, hopelessly lost, hearing their fellow citizens but unable to see them, or recognise their own front door.

Policemen controlling the traffic wore white gauntlets. A large white spot illuminated the rear of buses, though Dorothy L. Sayers' manservant pointed out that 'if the London Transport Passenger Board would place the route number *at the side* of the vehicle as well as the front and behind it might be possible to discover which omnibus had arrived at the stop without darting out before it as before an oncoming juggernaut'.

In the first four months of the war a total of 4,133 people were killed on Britain's roads, and 2,657 of these were pedestrians. Road fatalities increased by 100 per cent compared to the corresponding months in 1938. In Glasgow the number of deaths tripled; in Birmingham they rose by 81 per cent in December 1939, which saw the highest number of road deaths – 1,155 – since records had been kept, while a further 30,000 people had been injured. A Gallup poll published in January 1940 claimed that one in every five people had sustained some sort of injury in the blackout since September. In effect, for the first months of the war it was more hazardous to be on the roads than in the Armed Forces. Indeed, the first fatality on the Home Front directly attributable to the war happened on the very first day, when a conscientious policeman, noticing a light shining from an upper-storey room in London's medical heartland, Harley Street, and unable to rouse the occupants, shinned up a drainpipe with a torch clenched between his teeth, but lost his grip as he reached the third-floor level and plunged to his death.

The surgeon to the King pointed out in an article in the *British Medical Journal* that by frightening the nation into blackout regulations, the Luftwaffe was able to kill 600 citizens a month without ever taking to the air, 'at a cost to itself of exactly nothing'. And in November 1939, during a parliamentary debate on the matter, Winston Churchill argued that the blackout measures had been overdone. In Paris, he pointed out, lights still twinkled and one could drive around with relative ease, whereas in Britain the blackout was unnecessarily creating a civilian killing field and a depressed and irritable population. The Home Secretary responded that the blackout was depriving the enemy of 'the means of launching an attack unexpectedly on this country the consequences of which would be little short of disastrous' and pointed out that despite the example of French laxity, blackout regulations in Germany were even more restrictive than those in Britain. The military aim of the blackout must remain the 'dominant consideration' but, in the face of mounting public anger at the toll of deaths and injuries and the inhibition to people's everyday lives, some relaxations would be introduced. The period of the blackout was to be reduced by one hour: henceforth it would begin half an hour after sunset and end half an hour after sunrise. Just before Christmas 1939 churches, markets and street stalls were allowed partial illumination, and shop windows were permitted to be dimly lit while restaurants, cinemas and theatres, and other places of entertainment and amusement could once again display an illuminated sign. But all these concessions would be rescinded the moment the siren for an air raid sounded.

At New Year 1940 a start was made to introduce 'glimmer' or 'pin prick' lighting whereby a circle of diffused lighting of very low intensity was directed from street lights on to the ground (providing local councils were prepared to spend the money to do this). It was still painfully easy to get lost. 'A friend of mine maintains that anyone who finds it difficult to drive in the blackout is not fit to hold a driving licence,' reported a journalist. 'I do not quite agree with him. It is easy enough, I admit, to drive along the main street especially now that better lighting on cars is allowed' – in mid October 1939 headlight masks that permitted a little more light were made available to car drivers, and buses were fitted with a special headlight mask which faintly illuminated passengers waiting on the pavement. In January 1940 ARP cardboard headlight masks costing a few shillings were made compulsory for all civilian vehicles. These let light out through a narrow horizontal slit and were hooded to confine the beam to the ground in front of the vehicle. 'But choose the circuitous and unfrequented routes beloved by some taxi-drivers and you will lose your way as easily as if you had never been to London before. Take a taxi, for example . . . on a night of pouring rain during the dark of the moon and you will go through a familiar world utterly blotted out in darkness inspissated. On arriving home on such a night I asked the driver how he found his way about in the blackness. "Instinct," he said; "pure instinct." I had almost guessed that. He seemed to me on several occasions instinctively to have just missed driving into lamp posts and letter-boxes and other cars.'

In mid November 1939 Gwladys Cox had 'wanted to see the Embankment in the blackout . . . I was agreeably surprised to find how quickly the buses got along, partly because the streets are empty of cars. It was quite possible to read in the dim bus lights. The Cenotaph . . . was an eerie scene with dim figures shuffling about and bearing down on one suddenly out of the gloom . . . Big Ben, the Houses of Parliament and Westminster Abbey loomed up, huge, dark, unlit piles against the indigo sky and seemed to take on nightmare proportions. As we expected the moon to rise shortly, we walked half way across Westminster Bridge, and while waiting leaned over the parapet and watched the black hulls of barges drifting down the dark, unlit river with the ebb tide. Presently a large, orange moon rose up behind the LCC buildings making them stand out in fine silhouette and throwing a wide ribbon of gold across the black river . . . As we strolled along the Embankment, a man among the passers by put his hand stealthily on my handbag and tried to snatch it. I was holding it firmly with the leather handle wrapped round my wrist so I wrenched it away and said "No you don't!" He actually turned to look at me, blinked, the moon lighting up his face, and then disappeared among the other dim figures.'

'Summer time' came early in 1940 and that helped. In February, the clocks went forward an hour but they weren't put back again in the autumn, and summer time was retained all year round – just as it had been in the First World War. And then in May 1941 double summer time was introduced, and for the next four years it was light until late at night during the summer months. This helped somewhat to reduce traffic accidents, as did petrol rationing when it started in the third week in September, thus cutting down the number of cars on the roads, though the toll remained high. The longer daylight hours might exasperate parents of sleep-resistant children, and privacy-seeking courting couples, but they saved electricity consumption and enabled farmers, allotment holders and gardeners to labour out of doors for longer.

The general compliance with blackout regulations pays tribute to the biddable nature of the British public when convinced of the good sense of a cause, but also to a flattering over-estimation of the precision-bombing capabilities of the Luftwaffe. German planes were usually flying at between 15,000 and 25,000 feet above Britain, as mustard-keen ARP wardens knocked up householders who were showing inch-wide beams of light from not quite tightly drawn curtains, yelled, 'Put that light out!' to anyone who momentarily shone a torch on a road sign, and pounced on someone pausing to light a cigarette in a doorway. Prosecutions could be brought for all those offences, and others – including the case of a man fined for failing to obscure the glow from the heating light in his tropical fish tank.

Yet as minute attention was paid to the details of domestic blackout, lighthouses all round the coast beamed paths of light far out into the sea; batteries of light mounted surveillance over prisoner-of-war camps; electric sparks flew from rails, and railway marshalling yards were lit; the holds of ships shone forth as they were loaded; and factories in full wartime production glowed. In March 1939 a leaflet, *War Time Lighting Restrictions for Industrial and Commercial Premises*, had been sent to all employers instructing them that they must be able to obscure or extinguish lights within minutes of an emergency being declared. In effect this meant that factories would have to have their windows painted or permanently covered over and often sealed, and no one could know for sure what the effects of working all day in artificial light and stuffy air would be on wartime productivity. And that still left screening blast furnaces and eliminating the glare from slag heaps. These were expensive remedies, and it was many months before sufficiently high screens were erected to shield a famous ironworks, 'Dixon's Blazes', which burned brightly in the centre of Glasgow.

With a population of close on 48 million and with industrial enterprises scattered throughout the country, it was never going to be possible to have the entire nation blacked out: the best that could be realistically hoped for was a blanketing of areas so that it was hard for enemy planes to get their bearings from ground landmarks, estimate the limits and contours of a city, or distinguish the precise nature of industrial installations that were contributing to the war effort.

As the Phoney War on the British mainland dragged on into the winter and no air raids materialised, early vigilance and anxiety subsided, and indifference and exasperation with regulations and exhortations and officials washed over the civilian population. And when the night raiders did come, it would not be the carelessly drawn curtains, the unshaded skylight, the smouldering cigarette butt that would guide them. It would be the Luftwaffe's technological equipment, landmarks like rivers that could not be blotted out, and, the most deadly beacon of all, the fires started by the German incendiary bombs.

★

As the blackout proved the most pervasive aspect of the war in the early months, gas masks soon proved to be the most irrelevant. The useful life of a gas mask was reckoned to be two years, so the 35 million respirators, as they were officially called, issued at the time of the Munich crisis should still have been satisfactory when war broke out twelve months later. But of course many households had mislaid their masks, thrown them away, or they were damaged and useless, so these had to be replaced. But by September 1939 it was reckoned that, with the distribution of a total of about 44 million masks, 'every British adult civilian, for the first time in history, entered war with an article of personal defensive equipment'. Special heavy-duty masks were issued to ARP wardens, control centre staff and others involved in Civil Defence, and these were adapted so that wardens and switchboard operators could wear their masks when speaking on the telephone. Members of decontamination squads who would be in the front line of a gas attack carried air-purifying containers, like those used by soldiers on the battlefield, and stood ready with their supplies of chloride of lime which was considered to be the most effective neutralising agent for poison gas.

But while the great evacuation trek had been made more poignant by the sight of each schoolchild fleeing from the cities equipped with a gas mask, at the outbreak of war children under five had no satisfactory form of individual protection against gas – the best that could be advised was to 'wrap them tightly in a blanket'. In the view of J. B. S. Haldane, this was a matter of the greatest urgency which should have been handed over long ago 'to the Army Clothing Department, even if this involves a delay in the supply of full-dress uniforms for the Brigade of Guards'. But it was not until the end of October 1939 that the deficiency was made good. Infants under two were supplied with a 'baby bag' rather like a haversack, consisting of a metal-framed rubber hood with a plastic window that covered the baby's head, chest and arms, and was tied at the waist. Air had to be pumped into this distressingly military-looking apparatus with bellows, and should the person doing the pumping – invariably the mother – be overcome, then presumably the baby would be gassed too. Children aged between two and five were fitted with a 'Mickey Mouse' mask, with a harness to keep it in place, which four-and-a-half-year-old Barbara Roose thought was 'lovely'. The masks sported a strange red protuberance and a coloured rim round the eyepiece which were supposed to make the whole grisly exercise fun. In spring 1939 a BBC broadcast had queried: 'Are your little ones used to seeing you in YOUR mask? Make a game of it calling it "Mummy's funny face" or something of the kind. Then if the time comes when you *really* have to wear it, you won't be a terrifying apparition to your child.'

People were advised to wear their gas masks for fifteen minutes a day to get used to them. There were hints on how a man should put on his gas mask if he had a beard ('curl it under the chin and secure it with "bobby pins"' was recommended); how to accommodate your spectacles when you put on your gas mask; whether it was possible to wear mascara and/or a wig when wearing a gas mask; how to check the efficacy of your mask. A government leaflet advised: 'Hold a soft tissue paper to the end of the mask and breathe in. The paper should stick.' Enterprising retailers turned out fancy gas containers of fabric-covered cardboard or leather – including 'genuine crocodile' – to substitute for the utilitarian government-issue brown cardboard, and handbags and briefcases with special gas-mask compartments could be found in the shops. Lectures on gas were arranged in schools and church halls for ARP personnel up and down the country. Audiences sat horrified as they were warned that there might be 'phosgene that fills your lungs with water and produces gangrene of the extremities' or mustard gas 'that had hardly any odour but blinds you and eats your flesh away', or some nameless gas that 'smells of geraniums, one whiff and you're a goner'. ARP wardens were equipped with a larger version of the sort of wooden rattle beloved of football fans to clatter in the event of a gas attack. Post Office pillar boxes, and sometimes lamp posts, were painted a sickly yellow with a gas-detecting substance that would change colour if gas were present. Rumours were rife: the gossamer webs of spiders that blow about in early autumn and can be a mild irritant were identified as 'gas-impregnated and sent adrift by the enemy'.

It was never illegal not to carry a gas mask (though it was to damage one) but strong pressure was put on citizens to do so. Government posters urged 'Hitler will send no warning – so always carry your gas mask' and 'Take Care of Your Gas Mask, and Your Gas Mask Will Take Care of You'. Advertisements appeared in newspapers showing couples sitting up in bed in their pyjamas dutifully donning their masks when a gas attack was signalled. Responsible-minded employers were known to send staff, and teachers their pupils, back home to fetch their masks if they had forgotten them. Entry was occasionally refused to restaurants, or places of entertainment, to patrons who were without their survival kit, and John Lewis, the department store in London's Oxford Street, reminded staff that 'those who come without their [gas mask] must not be surprised if they are dismissed as unsuitable in time of war'.

But it was to little avail: a youth worker in Glasgow thought it looked like 'swank' to be seen without a gas mask in the streets in September 1939. By the end of the year, his view was that the 'swankers' were those who still carried their gas mask. Rows of familiar-looking brown boxes soon lined the shelves of lost property offices. A survey conducted on Westminster Bridge in early November 1939 revealed that only 24 per cent of men and 39 per cent of women were carrying gas masks, while in Lancashire that same day the total was 6 per cent of men and 9 per cent of women.

H. G. Wells, author of the prophetic *The Shape of Things to Come*, had already been observed not to be carrying a gas mask before the war was a month old. The 1942 film, *The Goose Steps Out*, starring the comedian Will Hay, depicted a German spy being instructed during his training that in order to pass muster as an Englishman he must *never* be seen carrying a gas mask. But as two men condemned to death turned to leave the dock, F. Tennyson Jesse was amazed to see that one of the police officers 'with a scandalised face, pointed sternly to the floor, and meekly the two rapers and murderers stooped to pick up their gas masks. I presume that, even in England with our respect for authority, they will not have to take them to the scaffold.' Others, however, found their gas masks useful even though gas attacks never materialised. Angela Culme-Seymour recalled, 'I made sure we never forgot to take our gas mask when we went into the shelter during a raid on Kensington where we were living. It made an ideal potty for the children.'

'My God, this could be my street, my family, any time . . .' realised a Cornish man as he gazed at 'a large front page newspaper picture showing a mother dishevelled and blood-spattered sitting in the street with shattered buildings just behind her head [in the aftermath of the raid on Guernica in the Spanish Civil War] holding up her tear-stained face towards the cameraman . . . across her soiled lap lies the tiny body of her young child, clothes tattered and disarrayed, some wounds evident.' The reasons why people volunteered to risk their lives to protect and aid their fellow civilians in the Second World War were numerous: practical, confused and courageous. But the perception that 'it could be my street, my family, any time' would, it was hoped, give the voluntary policy its logic, and the citizen his or her lodestar.

Among the most visible of this Civil Defence 'army of volunteers . . . old and young, men and women, rich and poor' – though in practice predominantly middle-aged or older – were the ARP wardens, and the months of the Phoney War were a testing time for them. Part of the 'fourth line of defence', as the Civil Defence services were called since they were auxiliary to the fighting services of the Army, Navy and RAF, the ARP suffered a certain crisis of identity, and the slings and arrows of their fellow citizens whom they had volunteered to protect, when there was nothing under attack on home ground. At first equipped with only an armband, a silver badge and a tin helmet stencilled with a letter of the alphabet to denote function, and maybe a logo to indicate rank, they 'found themselves confronted, not with the stimulus of action and danger but with tasks of . . . preparation and organisation' and, within a remarkably short time of the outbreak of war, attracted hostility from press and public alike. They were accused of being parasites and slackers, guilty of nepotism as they allegedly wheedled a nice little number for relatives and friends, of 'dodging' military service (though many were not eligible for conscription, while others were called up later, or in some cases enlisted), of 'standing around doing nothing', and being handsomely paid to do so. Full-time ARP workers were better paid than men in the Armed Forces, while unskilled workers earned less than a warden's £3 a week. It was convenient to overlook the fact, in this vortex of criticism, that the majority of ARP workers were part-time and unpaid.

Many members were themselves already less than happy with the organisation of the service they had joined: 'I have never seen such an illustration of incompetence in all my life' and 'There's so much red tape, it's unbelievable'; and the training: 'the lectures are absolutely hopeless . . . I've forgotten more about chemicals than these johnnies from the Town Hall seem to know'; 'I rather wish I'd joined the Fire

Service. I mean you have to go to all these lectures and sit down with a lot of old ladies. There's no guts in it for a man.'

Before the air raids started, the ARP wardens had two main tasks and both of these could make them seem officious, bullying busybodies. Apart from ensuring that householders' 'blackout was really black' in the words of a popular song, everyone living in the sector patrolled by the ARP warden had to be registered: how many people occupied a house or flat, did they have any pets and what shelter arrangements did they have? All this would be vital information when the air raids began, since knowing if people might be buried under fallen masonry could be crucial to their survival. But when no bombs threatened, it could seem like unnecessary snooping to the naturally privacy-retentive British householder.

The Home Secretary robustly defended the ARP service against charges of slackness and sponging, and upbraided the public for their lack of generosity towards this large-scale civilian effort. But he did concede that he was devising ways by which the number of volunteers could be pared down while still being in a state of poised readiness, and the service capable of rapid expansion in the event of attack. When the review was completed six months later, in spring 1940, it recommended a rationalisation of some of the functions, improvements in training and further overall reduction of full-time paid staff, but also appealed for a quarter of a million new part-time volunteers; these 'twice citizens' would now be minimally reimbursed for any loss of earnings. Grants were to be made available for 'recreational facilities' and the public was asked to donate radios, books and games to help pass the 'weary months of waiting inactivity' which still seemed, as winter turned to spring, to be the ARP wardens' unfortunate lot.

In Fulham in south-west London, ARP volunteers included clerks and typists, shopkeepers, professionals, bricklayers, carpenters, painters and decorators, housewives, a number of ex-servicemen – and 1 per cent of the wardens were 'engaged in sport or entertainment'. The reasons the burghers of Fulham gave for joining the service were 'to do my bit for my country', 'I felt I must do something to help', 'everyone else seemed to be doing it', 'I wanted to do something. I didn't want to sit at home like in the Great War', 'As a woman I felt I had the leisure and I could do something to help' – though a couple of volunteers 'didn't know' why they had joined and one confessed, 'It was the New Year. I must have been drunk. I am *strongly* anti-Chamberlain.'

The government had envisaged that the ARP service, with its neighbourhood role and focus on people, would appeal to women. But many male ARP volunteers – particularly the ex-service contingent – were less than enthusiastic about admitting women and few were recruited. In May 1938 Samuel Hoare, the then Home Secretary, decided to approach Stella, Marchioness of Reading, with an idea for a new organisation that would recruit women into Air Raid Prevention work and thus ginger up local authorities who were not taking seriously enough the need to prepare for war. Lady Reading, the forty-four-year-old widow of Lord Rufus Isaacs, a former Viceroy of India (whom she had married in 1931 five years before his death, when he was seventy and she was thirty-seven), was a woman of prodigious energy, determination and a compelling charm. She had been a VAD nurse in the First World War, and in the 1930s had been involved in the work of the Personal Service League which collected clothes for the unemployed so that they looked smart when they applied for a job. Attracted by the notion, Lady Reading jotted down what she thought was needed to 'bring home to all women, especially women in the household, what air raids mean and what they can do for their families and themselves'. Recruits to the Women's Voluntary Service for ARP, as the organisation was originally called, would be unwaged (though in some cases expenses were to be paid – though not always claimed – and eventually there was a paid administrative staff of around 200) and were to work in co-operation with local authorities which would provide premises and facilities. No one who volunteered was ever to be refused, and somehow a job was always found, and training given where necessary, for a huge range of women with very different backgrounds, skills and temperaments.

The uniform for the WVS was designed by the London couturier Digby Morton: it was bottle-green flecked with grey enlivened with beetroot-coloured touches, and a sensible felt hat gave some individuality to the wearer and would spring back into shape no matter what fell on it – or it fell into. Members were not obliged to wear the kit, but in wartime it seemed right to be in uniform, though from the ARP to the Home Guard to the Boy Scouts this was not always something those in authority fully seemed to understand – or were prepared to 'waste' money on indulging. WVS members had to pay for their uniforms – and after 1941 exchange clothing coupons for them too.

WVS gave women who wanted to do their bit for their country in the event of war the opportunity to do so, and it offered an outlet in the public sphere for the organising abilities and energies of many women that had been so often denied them since the home was seen as the focus – and container – of their lives.

Stella Reading was wont to refer to the WVS as 'Women of Various Sizes' – though one exhausted member wondered, during the Blitz, whether the initials might not stand for 'Willingness Versus Self' – and she was anxious to stress the *social* diversity of the membership as well. 'These were the wives of labourers, railwaymen, cabinet ministers, farmers, parsons, all kinds of women of every political colour,' she enthused and WVS members were told that it was their time not their money that was wanted, and that the service had 'no rank only jobs'. However, its members were bound to be women who were able to find (or make) the time, and were not obliged to take full-time paid employment. The organisers were often women with a certain status in the local community – the doctor's or vicar's wife, a member of the parish council, a school governor, a retired headmistress or civil servant, maybe a single woman of independent means – who welcomed the opportunity to exercise the philanthropic social leadership that their position in society had bestowed in a world where such attributes were being overtaken by professional social services. The claim that the WVS was democratic and unhierarchical was not entirely true – particularly in rural areas where old social patterns persisted. Although Lady Reading insisted that the service she ran with a firm grip was non-partisan and socially inclusive – and some WVS organisers were indeed active members of the Labour Party – the vast majority of the many working-class women mobilised for WVS war work remained as workers rather than leaders.

The motto was simple: 'The WVS never says no' – though it had to sometimes of course – but the service's wartime role would extend far beyond any horizon that it had been possible to imagine, and draw heavily on its members' experience, strengths, abilities – and stamina. Reviewing the WVS at the end of the war, Lady Reading was to reflect that 'we have learned that it is no good talking about things, we must do them, and . . . to do that we must take pains, dislocate our lives and our comfort . . . We have done work we never thought to approach and have carried burdens heavier than we knew existed . . . We now know that no obstacle can block, it can only impede; that tiredness is an incident, not a finality.' During the Second World War, 241 members of the WVS were killed in action on the Home Front.

Having helped with surveying the accommodation available for evacuees and then played a key role in the mass evacuations on 1 September 1939, and after helping settle the children into their new homes, WVS members went on to help where needed in almost all areas of war work on the Home Front. They collected bones, paper, tin, rags, and cotton reels (used in the construction of Army telephonic communication systems) for salvage, and gathered rosehips, horse chestnuts and other medicinal plants. They commandeered ice-cream sellers' tricycles to collect books for Army camps and those working on ack-ack (anti-aircraft) and barrage balloon sites, subverting the vendors' slogan to read 'Stop Me and *Give* One'; and they distributed gifts sent from overseas. WVS members organised volunteer car pools to take patients to hospital and run other essential errands when petrol was rationed; they took over huts on quaysides to distribute fresh vegetables to the crews of minesweepers going to sea; and ran a babysitting service so couples could have an evening out when a husband in the Forces came home on leave. In some areas members took 'jobbing classes' at technical institutes so that, with so many men away, they could take charge of unblocking drains, changing washers and fuses, replacing window-sash cords and putting up shelves.

The WVS 'adopted the feet of the Army' too, teaching soldiers how to darn their socks, and often did it for them – a Shropshire member estimated that during the course of the war, she had personally mended 3,600 socks – and they sewed stripes and flashes on to the uniforms of promoted men and returning POWs. The women also did work which, controversially, went beyond their original civilian remit – and far beyond the 'womanly work' that was the common perception of WVS tasks – when members undertook an order from the War Office to produce camouflage nets for use in disguising military installations and equipment. In addition to the warehouses requisitioned for this work

(300 by 1945 producing 3,000 nets a week), frames were set up in village halls, schoolrooms and larger homes and gardens, so that whenever a WVS member had some time to spare, she could put in a couple of hours weaving camouflage strips into nets. It was a loathsome task: 'the dust and fluff from the scrim half choked the women knotting it onto the nets and the dye left their hands and clothes deeply stained. Crawling about . . . with bruised knees and aching backs, elderly women drove themselves for that extra hour that meant so many square feet of cover for the British Army.'

No matter, however, how comprehensive and unexpected the remit, how dangerous and unrelenting the work, the WVS – which had started with five members whose names Lady Reading (she was made a Dame in January 1941) had culled from her personal address book and which had risen to a wartime peak of 1.3 million – was conscripted into the rhetoric of the 'people's war' in a reassuring way. War hadn't really changed anything fundamental. WVS members were, said the Home Secretary, Herbert Morrison, on the service's fifth anniversary in 1943, 'a million magnificent women [who] were simply applying the principles of good housekeeping to the job of helping to run their country in its hour of need'. The war had moved women's concerns up the social agenda. It would make women's everyday, timeless labour into work of national importance – digging for victory, collecting salvage, making do and mending, providing cups of tea and hot food, caring for the sick and wounded, looking after other people's children, offering solace. Their work was validated beyond the home, organised, recognised, on occasions incorporated into the national narrative of struggle and survival, and sometimes even given lustre by the praise of public men.

The interwar years had seen a proliferation of women's organisations, some auxiliaries of men's associations such as the Rotary Club, others independent. All were to take a wartime role. The Townswomen's Guilds had 54,000 members on the outbreak of war but the Women's Institute was the largest, with some 290,000 members. In peacetime the WI had largely been about organising country women's leisure with fêtes and beetle drives, competitions and folk dancing. In wartime it became 'a many faceted experience'. The numerous branches organised sewing bees and knitting circles to make and mend for the troops, organised school meals, made valuable contributions to discussions about the 'new

Jerusalem' that would be built after the war – and, of course, made jam. Thousands of pounds of jam (and there was a glut of plums in 1940) were produced in government-subsidised jamming and fruit-preservation centres in church halls and outhouses, members' kitchens and mobile units. It was estimated in 1940 that 1,170 tons of fruit that would otherwise have rotted was turned into jam and preserves by – unpaid – WI members in 2,600 village centres, and the jars were sent to hospitals, institutions and canteens or were sold in shops as part of the rations people were entitled to.

The very continuity of the work women did in voluntary organisations was seen as morale-boosting – though it wasn't always easy. 'Life in the reception areas is not all blackberrying, nor wholly knitted squares,' wrote a Women's Institute member. Most branches moved their monthly meetings to the afternoon because of the blackout, but others found their usual meeting places occupied with evacuated schoolchildren during the day, and so had little choice but to pick their way to meetings in the pitch-blackness. An editorial in the WI magazine, *Home and Country*, would claim that there 'is no doubt that in the dark days of 1940's perfect summer, when the nation was confronted by one disaster after another, the quiet customary functioning of the WIs was an important factor in the villages [where] the maintenance of morale never waived.' The English were best placed to win this ghastly war by carrying on as usual, while making monumental changes, and 'pretending that nothing untoward was happening', and this would be a responsibility particularly laid on women's shoulders in a number of guises.

This was exactly the sort of task the smug 'Mrs Miniver' relished. 'Mrs Miniver', who was to become an iconic creature in wartime Britain, was the creation of Joyce Struther (using the name Jan for her short stories, poems and journalism), who had been writing about her doings in a weekly column in *The Times* since October 1937. The detailed domestic observations of a preternaturally contented Chelsea housewife and mother – whose husband an exasperated *Times* reader rather wished would have an affair with a pretty ARP worker – soon attracted a considerable following, with mailbags of correspondence addressed to 'Mrs Miniver' as if she were a real person, rather than the good idea of a journalist.

When war broke out 'Mrs Miniver' was conscripted to the national cause (or rather she rushed to enlist). Her collected pre-war jottings were given a brief wartime coda and published as a best-selling book, and MGM made a film based extremely tenuously on the same book, starring Greer Garson in the title role. It was a huge box-office hit in America (rather less so in the UK) and played a sterling ambassadorial role on behalf of plucky, beleaguered Britain. In *The Times* Mrs Miniver continued for a while to address epistles to an imaginary sister-in-law. As her rose-tinted spectacles seemed never to leave her nose in peacetime, so they stayed firmly lodged throughout the war. Mrs Miniver managed to delight in a surprising number of things: 'the nice "damp jutey smell" of sandbags . . . the way London was beginning to look and sound like a country town with its tinkle of bicycle bells and clopping of hoofs; . . . the singing of the barrage balloon cables which made you feel you were "going to sleep, on a ship at anchor with the sound of wind in the rigging", the way Londoners were learning to carry gas masks with panache, as if they were going on a picnic with a special box of food.'

Reviewing her 'sayings and doings', the novelist Rosamond Lehmann struck a resigned note. 'Now the war is upon Mrs Miniver, as it is upon all of us. But whoever is defeated, she'll come through. Having plenty of courage and common sense, she will cope successfully with evacuees and increased taxation, even, if necessary, with bombs. The airy balloon that hovers so lightly above our heads may shrivel a little, but it won't collapse.'

Complacent – even a touch risible – though Mrs Miniver's ordered world might seem, it was just these qualities of 'courage and common sense', laced with some Miniveresque optimism and a certain stoicism, that would get the British people through the war that was unfolding all around them.

4

'HE'S IN THE ARMY, MRS JONES'

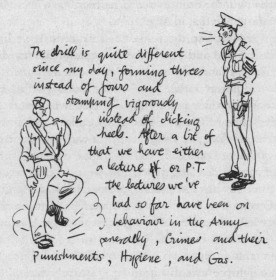

The drill is quite different since my day, forming threes instead of fours and stamping vigorously instead of clicking heels. After a bit of that we have either a lecture or P.T. the lectures we've had so far have been on behaviour in the Army generally, Crimes and their punishments, Hygiene, and Gas.

He had got known as one of the dreamy ones who get by somehow. He was most nearly bestirred when he had to regret his mother regretting the Army for him. Each time at the first glance, her eyes cried out: 'What are they doing to you now?' She saw how exposed, naïve, and comically childishly slender his neck looked rearing out of the bulky battledress collar . . . These days he held himself almost pigeon-breastedly, as though aspiring to fill out the bulky concavities of the khaki. He did not succeed . . . Had he looked more like a soldier, any kind of soldier, she might have taken it more calmly – she could have felt the authority of a real change.

ELIZABETH BOWEN, *THE HEAT OF THE DAY*

ON THE OUTBREAK of the First World War in August 1914 Lord Kitchener, the Secretary of State for War, had appealed for 100,000 volunteers. 'The crowd of applicants was so large and so persistent,'

The Times reported, that at one London recruiting office, 'mounted police were necessary to hold them in check . . .' More than 1,500 men a day flocked to the colours and, within four days of Kitchener's appeal, they were being sworn in at the rate of 100 an hour in London to fight for King and Country and a marquee had to be erected on Horse Guards Parade to cope with the numbers of eager recruits.

It was not quite like that in 1939.

Since the 1914–18 war, the role of the nation's Army had been to defend the homeland and police the outposts of the British Empire, not to engage in a land war on the Continent. Resources had been poured into air power rather than land forces. The government – convinced that everything possible must be done to ensure against the ominous prediction of Chamberlain's predecessor as Prime Minister, Stanley Baldwin, that 'the bomber will always get through' – had concentrated military spending on building a defensive air shield of fighter planes and radar against what was expected to be a knockout blow from the Luftwaffe. Millions more pounds had been channelled into strengthening Bomber Command to bomb the enemy if he would not be deterred. These priorities had resulted in years of under-funding and under-recruitment to the Regular Army, leaving it perilously short of men and equipment. The Territorial Army (TA), the part-time volunteer force established in 1907, was little better off. In September 1938, the Munich crisis – when Chamberlain's appeasement of Hitler's territorial demands in Europe narrowly averted war over Czechoslovakia – had shown that Britain was 'not prepared [indeed] had hardly begun to prepare' for war. When Hitler reneged on the Munich Agreement by occupying the whole of Czechoslovakia in March 1939, the growing threat from Germany, which had overturned the restraints of the Versailles peace settlement at the end of the First World War on the size of its army, emphasised Britain's vulnerability. By 1939 Germany had more than 4.5 million men under arms (including those in training) with 3.75 million in the Army (das Heer) which traditionally enjoyed primacy among the German Armed Forces.

Lord Halifax, the Foreign Secretary, and the Secretary of State for War, Leslie Hore-Belisha, grew concerned that Britain's modest commitment to despatch a token expeditionary force of two divisions to France to fulfil Chamberlain's commitment, given in February 1939, that 'any threat to the vital interests of France must bring about the cooperation of Great Britain', was insufficient and would leave the French to counter a German attack virtually single-handed. The French spoke bitterly of the British being ready to fight to the last French soldier, whereas what the British were doing was concentrating on making their own island an impregnable fortress. Lieutenant General Sir Henry Pownall, Director of Military Operations and Intelligence, recognised the dangers in this strategy: 'The support of France *is* home defence – if France crumbles, we fall.'

As Chamberlain had pledged not to introduce conscription in peacetime, he knew that to renege on that promise would be like a red rag to the Labour Party and the trade-union movement and could thus have a serious impact on the rearmament programme – particularly in the vital aircraft industry. An opinion poll conducted in 1937 showed opposition to be overwhelming among the public too. And of those who were recruited, over three-quarters were unskilled urban labourers. Yet he needed to demonstrate both to Germany and to France that Britain's resolution to stand up to Hitler had substance. It was not until April 1939 that Chamberlain finally conceded that voluntarism was not yielding sufficient men. Against continuing opposition in the country and from the 133 MPs who voted against the measure, the Military Training Bill was introduced in April 1939. All men would be liable for call-up in their twentieth year. They would be trained and serve full-time for six months, and then would be called on for part-time service in Territorial Units for a further three and a half years. Paradoxically, compulsion had the effect of increasing volunteers. Some men were motivated by patriotism when they realised how imminent war now seemed, while others opted to choose the service in which they would serve rather than being drafted, since this was a privilege for those who volunteered before they were enlisted.

Although a man liable for call-up was able to express a preference for which service he wished to join – the Army, Navy or Air Force – there was no guarantee that this would be respected, particularly as the RAF and the Navy proved the more popular choices, while the Army's need for manpower was by far the greatest. Call-up proceeded slowly: by

May 1940 the net had scooped up men aged up to twenty-seven, but those aged forty were not sent for until June 1941.

At the outbreak of war conscription was extended to men between eighteen and forty-one (the upper age limit was extended to fifty-one in December 1941) and the Territorial Army was in effect merged with the Regular Army into a single fighting force. 'The "Terries" . . . were whipped away,' remembered Eddie Mathieson, a fifteen-year-old apprentice joiner from Edinburgh when war broke out. 'In fact one of them was an apprentice . . . Jackie Quinn. He was cryin' when he went. He was only seventeen. And he was whipped away! He didn't want to go. He was in the Artillery and he used to go like strutting around with his spurs and bandoliers. He used to love goin' about in that. And then all of a sudden he realised it was for real. It was no a dressin' up affair. The real thing was on him. He survived the war, but he took a bayonet in the stomach in the Ardennes.' But Britain still had a fairly 'tinpot' Army of only 897,000 men by September 1939.

The majority of those drafted into the Army regarded the war as an unpleasant but necessary job that they had to despatch before they could get on with their ordinary civilian lives. Few had any ideological commitment to an anti-Nazi crusade, any particular hunger to 'kill the Hun', or even any very clear idea precisely why Britain was at war and who were her Allies. 'There is the soldier who really enjoys army life and is even prepared to stay in the army after the war . . . there are not many of these,' wrote Captain 'X' (in fact William G. C. Shebbeare, a young journalist serving in the Royal Armoured Corps) in his trenchant commentary on the British Army. 'Against these are the vast majority who dislike Army life and long for nothing so much as to get back home.'

Nella Last's son was twenty and due to be called up. She 'looked at my own lad sitting with a paper, and he did not turn a page often. It all came back with a rush – the boys who set off so gaily and lightly and did not come back – and I could have screamed aloud . . . He has never hurt a thing in his life . . . it's dreadful thinking of him having to kill other boys like himself – to hurt and be hurt. It breaks my heart to think of all the senseless, formless cruelty. . . We who remember the long drawn-out agony of the last war feel ourselves crumble somewhere inside at the thoughts of what lies ahead.'

Ethel Mattison's husband Jack, 'as a Civil Servant, though a junior one, was not called up until January 1941. I dreaded meeting any [of our friends] because naturally they would ask after Jack and I would burst into tears. He went first to a place in Shropshire to be kitted out and then to a reception camp in Yeovil. They were confined to barracks for some weeks, but at the first opportunity I went down for the weekend. I was terribly excited, but when I saw him in uniform it was like meeting a stranger. We stayed overnight in a boarding house and I was in for a greater shock when I saw the identity disk on a string round his neck. That made me realise for the first time what being a soldier meant. We were unable to make love.' In a letter to his wife Peggie, John Phillips, a graphic artist, who had been called up in the summer of 1940 and was sent to Shoeburyness in Essex to train as a driver with a Royal Artillery anti-tank regiment, confirmed, 'Uniform does something to you. I hope it isn't permanent. In that hotel room I felt quite shy with you . . . not quite myself . . .'

It was the task of the Forces to turn such civilians into fighting men who, 'for the first time in their lives . . . were in a machine which a man could not quit if he didn't like its ways'. Wartime recruits were treated like pre-war regulars. They were kitted out in battledress and were put through a basic training that, in the case of the Army, lasted about three months. In the words of Len Waller, who was in training at Chelsea Barracks in early 1940, it was designed to turn 'sloppy civilians into soldiers. It wasn't done by kindness, either. Every day we were marched and yelled at up and down the barrack square. We were cursed, humiliated, degraded and worked until we were fit to drop. At the end of each day's training we were allowed to relax by sitting aside our beds polishing and burnishing a bewildering array of equipment.'

Before the war, William Shebbeare had noticed 'soldiers used to resent it very much that they were treated as outcasts. They wore civilian clothes as much as they could because in uniform they were often made to feel unwelcome in cafés and other places of amusement. They felt cut off from the rest of the people . . .' But as soon as war was declared, this changed: '. . . every civilian has a son or brother or nephew in the army and therefore often takes a delight in doing for any soldier what he would like others to do for his or her own boy. Hot tea is brought out to troops on the line of march, soldiers are asked home and made welcome, socks are darned, baths are offered.'

A subtle change in coloration crept slowly over Britain in the months of the Phoney War. It was not only the buildings rubbed out by blackout, the seepage of camouflage over buildings, it was the preponderance of khaki in the streets and public places, and, less widespread, the slate blue of the Air Force, the eponymous blue of the Navy, the green of the WVS, gradually the dark blue of ARP wardens' overalls and a multitude of other sombre shades of war, evidence that the Home Front was also the battle front. Non Commissioned Officers (NCOs) below the rank of sergeant, and other ranks, were only permitted to wear civilian clothes off duty if their commanding officer gave them express permission, and this was usually only granted when the man's leave exceeded seven days.

But on the Home Front there were millions of men who were not in any of the Services, yet were engaged on vital national war work. The government had been determined not to repeat the mistakes of the First World War when the enthusiastic and indiscriminate recruitment of soldiers left war production seriously depleted and disabled. Chamberlain, in a broadcast appeal for volunteers for National Service in January 1939, had added a caveat: 'A schedule has been prepared of all the occupations which are so essential to the war effort that persons engaged in them should not bind themselves to undertake any other form of full time service.'

The reserved (or scheduled) occupation scheme was a complicated one covering some 5 million men in a vast range of occupations, from boiler-makers and poultry farmers to teachers and doctors, who were to be exempt from military service – sometimes after a certain age. The principles on which the schedule had been drawn up came in for widespread criticism. It was found, for example, that *chefs de cuisine* and shirtsleeve-makers were deemed 'essential to the war effort'. 'Really,' exploded the Earl of Derby, who had been Secretary of State for War in 1916–18, 'when one hears of ice-cream merchants being exempted from National Service, it does make one angry.'

The age of reserve varied: a lighthouse keeper was 'reserved' at eighteen while a trade-union official could be called up so long as he was under thirty, but not if he was over that age. After November 1939, employers could request a deferment of call-up for men in scheduled occupations but who fell outside the reserved age, and this was later extended to men in non-scheduled work.

Engineering was the industry with the highest number of exemptions. Until 1941 the designation 'skilled engineer' could cover a man working in a toy factory: if he were over a certain age, he would be as immune from call-up as a man working in an aircraft factory. But as the demand for man – and woman – power for the Armed Forces and war production grew, the basis for reservation was be reconsidered and the net of regulation and obligation inexorably pulled ever tighter across the Home Front.

Despite the oft-expressed envy of those in reserved occupations, this was far from a soft option given the hours and conditions in which such men worked. A Ministry of Information film made in late 1939 tried to counter the resentment by showing a factory worker saying stiltedly to a sailor, 'We're both doing our bit for the war effort, you in your submarine and me in my reserved occupation.'

By 1945 around a quarter of adult men under fifty were in the services. But though the Army increased exponentially – 897,000 in September 1939; 1,656,000 in June 1940; 2,221,000 the following June to a peak of 2,920,000 the month after the war in Europe ended in May 1945 – the popular image of a soldier shouldering his kitbag as he embarked for war, not to return for several years; of 'battle-hardened troops fighting through the jungle of Burma, the desert of North Africa, the *bocage* of Normandy', was not the full story. For much of the war, more than 1.5 million troops, which represented well over half the British Army, were stationed in anti-aircraft, home defence, field force, logistical training and administrative units in Britain either defending the country against attack, supporting the Army abroad or waiting to go to the battle front. After the return of troops from France via Dunkirk in June 1940, there were not enough theatres of war to absorb the numbers of men in the British Army. The emphasis was on defence, regrouping, re-equipping and retraining. It was not until four years later, after D-Day in June 1944, that the majority of soldiers were serving overseas, but even by spring 1945 around a third of the Army, some million men, were still seeing out the war at home. The experience of war for them was not one of 'daring deeds at the sharp end, but rather of a sedentary existence in camps and depots across the country polishing their brasses and wondering why they were there'.

The lives of soldiers on the Home Front were closely interleaved with those of civilians in the early years of the war since, given the rapid influx of new recruits, not all could be accommodated in Army barracks, and many were billeted in households near their camps. Mrs Trowbridge, a middle-aged, middle-class housewife living near Bradford, was one such host. 'My soldier has arrived – very thin and delicate-looking. I suspect a tendency to asthma. Wonder if a smoky room suits him – though he should be acclimatised to smoke and dirt – he comes from Burnley.' A day later she was pleased to note, 'my soldier seems quite at home now . . .' but before long Mrs Trowbridge was seriously disenchanted with the ways of the military: 'I never had a great opinion of the Army and its officers, but after the last few days I don't know how we shall win this war. At least I do know, that the Army, as now run, won't do it. Total war! And we hear still of interviewing officers who ask a prospective officer from an OCTU [Officer Cadet Training Unit] what the best white wine is to serve with oysters!!! As though he were interviewing an applicant for a chef's post! And the petty Hitlers! . . . Reactions to billeting coming in from all sides. Some boys are banished to the kitchen; others are presumptuous. Some want a private room for 18/6 per week and others offer all their lodging allowance except a 3/6 bus pass. Evidently all the soldiers in this road have agreed to pay 25/-, coming in to all meals. I think they are "getting at us" but as my soldier is very quiet and unassuming and has a ridiculously small appetite compared with my family, I couldn't in all fairness demand more.'

Many recently conscripted soldiers felt themselves to be 'cogs in [a] vast impersonal, bureaucratic machine . . . and saw little meaning in their daily activities. "Bull", petty punishments for minor infringement of regulations and endless fatigues' fuelled their discontent. 'We're here because we're here because we're here' they could have chanted, echoing the conscripts of the First World War. The narrative of a nation united, of the sacrifices and dangers of war shared by all its citizens more or less equally, was valorised by the notion that the military were primarily civilians in uniform, yet this assumption also sharpened the frustration soldiers felt in their ambivalent position to the Home Front: separate yet present, semi-detached from their families with only occasional and irregular leave, while maybe stationed only a short distance from home, concerned about their families, particularly when the Blitz started, but unable to take a regular part in the Civil Defence effort while men considered unsuitable for military service on grounds of age or health or occupation were active in this front line. The charge, particularly after Dunkirk, that they were 'under-unemployed' haunted soldiers when the air raids started, and Churchill had to intervene to insist that the Army should not be used for such Home Front duties as clearing bomb sites.

'Getting involved in this army business does seem an awful waste of time,' wrote John Phillips to his wife Peggie. 'But if I can come out of it a stronger and better person, that'll be something. It is very maddening to be the protected, trained animal with no ideas or responsibilities, just fed at regular intervals, allowed out at regular intervals, while *you* have to do everything worth doing, keep the home going on next to nothing, look after the well being of the children . . .'

By 1941 regular reports on Army morale showed that the troops in Britain were generally less than happy about their training, dissatisfied with their living and messing arrangements, critical of the lack of entertainment provided, angry about their pay, and, as the war dragged on, dispirited by military losses and reverses: in general 'bored and browned off'. 'Pay and allowances [for soldiers] amount to little short of a public scandal,' indicted Shebbeare. Until April 1944 an unmarried soldier was paid three shillings a day (or £1 1s a week). His accommodation, food and uniform were free and this, the government calculated, saved him thirty-five shillings a week. After nine months' service a soldier who qualified as, say, a wireless operator would be earning the equivalent of a civilian wage of around £3 10s. This was considerably less than the comparable pay for a skilled man in civilian life, less than a comparable rank in the RAF, and a great deal less than those working in the munitions industries.

It was worse for the women married to the military. 'It is generally accepted as *axiomatic* that a private soldier's wife with children in an urban area who had no resources other than his pay and allowances simply could not manage,' reported the War Office. In effect the government admitted this was the case by introducing 'War Service Grants'. A wife would be eligible for such a grant if, after paying rent, rates, insurance etc., she was left with less than thirty-six shillings a week – though if her husband got promotion in the Army and thus a pay rise, this extra pay was usually knocked off his wife's grant so he was no better off. The fact that hundreds of thousands of married soldiers applied for these grants for their families was irrefutable proof that the soldier's pay and allowances were entirely inadequate. Sometimes a soldier's peacetime employer might be prepared to make up the shortfall from his pre-war earnings (the Civil Service did, for example, and so did numbers of private companies), but if they didn't, his family had a penurious time. It didn't help that shopkeepers and landlords tended to regard service families as bad financial risks and were reluctant to let rooms or extend credit to them.

Wartime inflation compounded the problem. Prices had risen dramatically in the first months of the war. The official cost-of-living index – which was seriously out of date since it was based on the spending patterns of a working-class family on the outbreak of the First World War – had risen by 14 per cent from September 1939 to February 1940, and showed that the price of food – which represented about two-fifths of working-class budgets – had risen by 17 per cent, and the price of clothes was 25 per cent higher than it had been on the outbreak of war – which was undoubtedly an under-estimate. It was not until April 1944 that Army pay was marginally improved. As men disembarked to invade occupied Europe they could reflect that the allowance paid to their wives had been raised by ten shillings if they had children – but there was no increase for childless wives; and although children's allowances had gone up, grants were reviewed in light of these increases and many families were no better off under the new system. Newspaper headlines trumpeted '5 shilling Private at Last' but it wasn't quite like that. The basic pay remained at three shillings a day on entry and rose to five shillings only after three years' service and a test of special proficiency. An additional grouse was that the rates of pay and the system for calculating allowances were ridiculously complicated and hard to fathom – there were some 200 differential wage rates – and arrears and underpayment were common. Between February and April 1943 Professor John Hilton, who ran a weekly advice 'bureau' in the *News of the World*, received nearly 1,500 letters each month from soldiers and their families complaining about pay.

Death and injury added a vicious twist to the downward spiral: a private soldier totally disabled in battle was awarded only forty shillings a week (twenty shillings less than his pay had been when he was wounded), and ten shillings a week for his wife and seven shillings and sixpence for each child. Should he be killed on active service, a soldier's widow over forty, or with children, would receive thirty-two shillings a week for herself and eleven shillings for each child, and possibly some help towards the rent. If she was under forty and childless, her compensatory pension would be precisely twenty shillings a week.

About half the men in the Armed Forces during the Second World War were married despite the fact that younger men were in the majority. The rate of marriages went up from 17.2 per thousand in 1938 to 22.1 per thousand in 1940, while the age of those getting married fell: nearly three brides out of every ten getting married for the first time were under twenty-one. Couples often felt an urgency to marry before the man went into the Forces. An RAF airman pointed out that of his intake four men had married in December 1939, three of whom had not even been engaged when war broke out three months earlier. Marriage gave status to wartime romances and wartime passions, and sometimes legitimised wartime babies. It promised to bring stability to men's and women's lives, and a future to hedge against chaos, uncertainty and danger.

Relationships were sustained by letters, though these were problematic when men were posted abroad. Mail was often delayed for weeks only for several letters to arrive together before another long anxious wait for news. 'I had been more than a month without a letter,' wrote Muriel Bowmer to her husband whom she had married less than a year previously, 'and now today I have received three at once, so I can feel happy again.' Another wife who had had heard nothing for months decided her husband had ceased to care, and embarked on adventures 'to forget'. The Army recognised the problem: a military psychiatrist stationed in the Middle East advised 'delay, irregularities or non-arrival of mail were potent causes of anxiety and depression even among the most stable personalities', and the transport of mail was given priority wherever possible. When the troops landed on the Normandy beaches on D-Day, the War Office was aware of how anxious families would be for news, and claimed to have managed to get letters sent back to Britain by air from the fourth day of the invasion. By 1944 over 3 million air letters, 4.5 million items of surface mail and postcards, plus 500,000 airgraphs were passing through the Army postal services every week, sent to and from the Forces and families and friends back home.

Commanding Officers were instructed to read their men's letters, both to ensure that militarily sensitive information was not inadvertently revealed and also to gauge morale. But this seemed to most soldiers a sneaky way of fulfilling the adage 'get to know your men well' and must have inhibited many a British male who in the best of circumstances was not always gifted with a lyric pen. Servicemen were, however, allowed a certain number of 'green envelopes' each month in which to put letters that would go for censorship purposes to the base commander who would not know the sender, rather than the unit commander who would. 'I haven't used the green envelopes much,' wrote John Phillips. 'You see there's always such a lot of description in my letters that I'm always doubtful whether I may not have given something away that I shouldn't, and as you see, it says on the bottom of the green envelope "I certify on my honour that the contents of this envelope refer to nothing but private and family matters." I've never felt that I could honestly sign that. The great advantage of the green envelopes is that the contents need not be censored here and you can put more private things in. But if one *were* opened and found to contain censorable matter, the privilege of having [them] would be taken away from a large number of men for a long time. So you have to be careful.'

Letters were frequently not very informative. 'Well my darling,' wrote John Phillips to his wife Peggie, 'here I am sitting in the sunshine – it's evening of a day which I'm not allowed to tell you, and we have safely arrived at a place unknown, on board an anonymous craft of uncertain tonnage bound for heaven knows where.' With more than a hint of sarcasm, Muriel Bowmer wrote to her husband, who was (she thought) on his way to North Africa: 'Thank you very much for your interesting letter received today. Nobody could accuse you of giving away information to the enemy. It took me *ages* to work out the place we had been to for our weekend spent together . . . you are very skinny about news concerning your work. In fact you are skinny about news of every description. I bet you are the censor's monitor and give the ink out –

teacher's pet! But it makes me feel even further away from you. I shall keep on writing – a long letter at weekends and four short ones like this during the week. So you'll know *all* about me and what I'm doing without you.'

But even the most eloquent letters were a fragile thread to bind together couples who desperately missed a presence, a touch – sometimes for years. And then that snapped. Peggie Phillips had written to her husband John who was fighting in Italy about the family Christmas celebrations in December 1943. 'We went to see Father Christmas at Selfridges . . . Linda and V[anessa] are very excited about Christmas. It is the first time Linda has understood anything about it. I think it will be the last Christmas without our Daddy . . . here's hoping.' But by the time she wrote that letter, Gunner John Phillips was already dead, killed in action by a direct hit from a shell on 26 November 1943 and 'buried on a little grassy mound by the roadside . . . the chaps have made a wooden cross – the poor best we could do' wrote his Commanding Officer. And soon the last letters Peggie had written to her husband started coming back stamped 'It is regretted that this item could not be delivered because the addressee is deceased'.

One thing that did help (usually) to cement wartime relationships was leave. It became the staple of wartime novels and short stories – the snatched, intense moments, the gay little hat, the entwined fingers, feet caressing in the quiet little restaurant, the quivering lip and the welling tears as it was time for the husband or lover to go back to camp. At the start of the war, leave was haphazard and the soldier was never sure what his entitlement was. By 1940, providing that training made it possible, a soldier would get seven days' leave every three months, plus a day for travelling, and also an additional forty-eight hours which could be taken separately or tacked on to the eight days. Jack Mattison, who was in the Army Pay Corps, was stationed in Horsham in Sussex until he went overseas in 1944, and he bought a motorbike so that he could get home to London whenever he had leave. 'It was fine in summer, but nerve wracking in winter with the blackout or the fog, or both. But it did mean that we were together whenever possible.'

Soldiers about to go abroad were given embarkation leave since obviously, once overseas and in battle, regular leave was much harder to arrange, and many soldiers did not see their families between being posted and demobbed. At the start of the war, soldiers received only two travel warrants a year but this was later increased to four.

Most letters home bear testimony to hopes raised, then dashed, of leave being postponed at the last moment, or being so brief that it was not possible to get home, or the notice so short that a wife or girlfriend who had a job could not arrange to be free. Having a husband home on leave was recognised, though not always condoned, as a prime reason for absenteeism by women. In principle, a woman in the services was supposed to get leave at the same time as her husband, but again organisation often failed this ideal.

Possibilities of leave and snatched meetings infuse the letters sent between the recently married Anne and Heywood Hill, as of so many couples separated by war. He had been called up into the Army in November 1942 and was training near Maidstone in Kent, while she continued to run their Mayfair bookshop. When Heywood was transferred to Salisbury Plain, the couple managed to snatch an hour together at Waterloo station where the soldiers changed trains. In late December 1942 Heywood wrote to Anne: 'I can't get a room for you on Thursday. It's New Year's Eve and everywhere is full. We could have dinner together. You could come by a train which leaves Victoria at 5.18 and catch one back which arrives at 10.15 . . . If you stayed the night we should only have ½ an hour more together . . . It's all a bit risky because one never knows what ghastly thing will turn up. I asked the sergeant if he thought I'd get away by 6.30 on Thursday and he said he'd fix it (but he might not be about that day). If I am not on the platform go to the hotel – it's called the Royal Star – about 10 minutes' walk from the station. I've booked a table for dinner at 7. Start if I don't turn up and if I'm not there by 8.15 . . . take the train back.' There were further considerations. 'About leaves, try not to have any between 7th and 14th of Jan, or the 4th and 11th of Feb (copy this into your diary),' instructed the pregnant Anne. 'They are the days when the Curse would have been due, when one is more liable to have a miscarriage Mr Saunders [her gynaecologist] says. After 2 March I fear all dates are prohibited according to him. I shall anyhow be a mountain, I suppose.'

Some men who did manage to get home did not always receive the returning soldier's welcome they might have anticipated: the enforced absence could be a relief to both parties if the marriage was already under strain and, even if it hadn't been, the greater sense of independence and self-sufficiency that women were obliged to develop in wartime could make readjustment to a husband's presence difficult. In October 1941 Amy Briggs, a Leeds nurse with two young daughters who worked part-time at a first-aid post, recorded in her diary: 'My long weekend off. Should have a pleasant time, just the girls and I . . . Home from cinema at 6 p.m. Find hubby at home. Hell! See that I'm very, very annoyed and so we fall out. Tears and no tea for me.' Things got no better and on Sunday she recorded: 'Work at 7.10 a.m. late but glad to get out of T.'s [her husband's] way. Home at 2.40 p.m . . . Fall out immediately we meet. Wish I could hide my feelings but I just can't . . . T. leaves at 6.30 p.m. Wish he'd leave for good . . . Go to bed early ab-so-lutely fed up.'

The import of thousands of new young recruits into the Army posed a number of problems, not the least of which was welfare support for men summarily plucked from home and family. At first such provision was largely ad hoc and piecemeal but in the autumn of 1939 Lieutenant General Sir John Brown (Director General of the Territorial Army) was appointed War Office adviser on welfare, and a network of Local Army Welfare Officers (LAWOs – often retired officers), working with various voluntary agencies, provided what assistance they could to the troops in their area, and generally acted as liaison officers between the troops and the civilian population in areas of 'military occupation'. From the late summer of 1940 the Blitz added an acute strain to the lives of soldiers who were all too aware that they were often stationed in remote areas well away from the action. The situation was complicated by security regulations that made it impossible to ascertain from newspapers even the name of the localities that had been bombed, and this gave rise to wild rumours – and great anxiety. To assuage this and discourage men from going AWOL if they thought their home and family might have been affected, an air-raid enquiry scheme was instigated, by which soldiers stationed in Britain could check up with the authorities nearest to their home, and those overseas could channel their fears through the Soldiers', Sailors' and Airmen's Families' Association (SSAF). Searches were organised by the SSAF in conjunction with the LAWOs and voluntary organisations, and after a particularly heavy raid a Forces enquiry office was set up to give out information and help with such matters as evacuation and funeral arrangements.

It was within an officer's remit to grant compassionate leave to his men in addition to their ordinary entitlement. He could allow up to twenty-eight days (which could then be extended in exceptional circumstances), and in 1942 there were 38,000 formal requests for compassionate leave from soldiers based in the UK alone. It was also possible to apply for release from the Army on compassionate grounds, and by 1945 there had been some 80,000 such applications, of which around 60 per cent were successful. A Birmingham sapper in the Royal Engineers who was on embarkation leave before going to Sicily in 1943 failed to return to his regiment when his wife gave birth to a premature baby. 'It was touch-and-go with the baby so obviously I didn't go back when I should have done. The next thing I know I had the Redcaps [the military police] after me . . . they took me back to Scotland where I was stationed and I was charged with Absent Without Leave . . . my daughter was only about six weeks old, still in hospital in one of those incubators and she was less than 2lbs when she was born . . . When I was called before the Commanding Officer . . . He said "Well" he said "two lbs" he said "she'll probably be some sort of imbecile" . . . this fellow was only a Captain . . . he was only in charge when the Major was on more important business. But anyway, fortunately [the Major] came back, and he was the one who knew his men . . . and he saw what I was charged with . . . and he sent for me and when I explained . . . he straightaway said, "Oh, we'll have to do something about that . . . " he said. "I'll put you in for four days' compassionate leave." '

At some RAF stations, men were allowed to live off base during training and operations; others forbade the practice. 'This depends on the Commanding Officer,' wrote the celebrity pilot Richard Hillary, 'some believing the sudden change from night bombing attacks over Berlin to all the comforts of home to be a psychological error, others believing it to be beneficial.' A middle-class woman without children, or with children evacuated or away at school, would be more likely to be able to take advantage of this concession by renting accommodation near where her husband was stationed – be it an Army camp, RAF station or a naval port – either to live with him, or to be there for brief off-duty reunions, though throughout the course of the war this could involve a number of relocations even if the serviceman never left the country. The Second World War version of the eternal wartime figure of the camp follower could be a nightmare of packing cases and strange kitchens, loneliness and uncertainty, separation and strained relationships, and frequently little help or even sympathy from the military authorities who may have had an ideal of domestic bliss as being what the fighting man needed, but could be reluctant to engage with its realities.

Since 'war is a mass experiment in which many of the complications of ordinary life are simplified', two social psychologists decided to investigate 'assortative mating' to see why some soldiers cracked under the strain of war while others remained 'steady'. Eliot Slater and Moya Woodside found that for those who had married after the outbreak of war, when the husband was already in uniform (and a quarter of their sample had), marriage was a quite different thing 'from what it was for others, and was more a formality than an institution. It conferred a change of status, but left living habits largely unaltered. The setting up of a home was postponed or found temporarily impossible . . . the relationship was not built up in a normal way; instead, the couple would be separated for months or years, with occasional brief meetings of ten to fourteen days, which were more like honeymoons than normal life. For these . . . couples, marriage could only be described in qualified terms: "six years married, but away in the Army for five"; "happy with what we've had of it (four and a half years married, longest time together a fortnight)"; "it's been a honeymoon on the instalment system" . . . These couples realised how abnormal their situation was, how impossible it was to say how matters would work out: "we've not really been married", "we don't know what marriage is".'

For the greater part wartime brides remained at work and continued to live in their parents' home: 'it's a funny position, to be married and yet not married; you can't go out with the fellows, and so you're alone all the time'; 'war wives are like a single girl'.

It was a lonely furrow and some wives found the separation unbearable and sought comfort elsewhere. Only one woman 'mentioned the sex deprivation of separation' to Slater and Woodside, 'but probably more felt it and were too shy to say so'. A medical officer who served for several years with the Army in the Middle East had come to the conclusion 'that the fidelity of nearly all wives could stand a separation of two years but in the third and subsequent years an increasing proportion of wives lapsed', and this problem was more acute for those with husbands in the Army or Navy rather than in the RAF 'who were given as a rule a shorter overseas term'. Male infidelity seemed to have been less of a problem: 'some men admitted they had had extra-marital experiences of a transient kind while in the Army; most of them had told their wives. These women were not deeply concerned, and felt for the most part that the circumstances of war exonerated the husband. One wife said she would overlook what happened abroad but not in England.'

'Listen, darling,' said Graham Robertson to his wife Deborah as they lay in bed together the night before his embarkation overseas in Marghanita Laski's pseudonymous wartime novel *To Bed With Grand Music*. ' "I'm not going to promise you I'll be physically faithful to you because I don't want to make you any promise I may not be able to keep. God alone knows how long I may be stuck in the Mid-East, and it's no good saying I can do without a woman for three or four years, because I can't. But I'll promise you this, I'll never let myself fall in love with anyone else, and I'll never sleep with anyone who could possibly fill your place in any part of my life." He was himself a little overawed with the magnanimity of his proposal. That means I'll have to be pretty damn careful, he said to himself, but aloud he said, "Darling, will you promise me the same?" '

But 'circumstances of war' were not always seen as such an acceptable excuse when women 'drifted' – as was the terminology of the time – into affairs. Such romances 'took place under all sorts of circumstances' and Slater and Woodside reported 'two cases where workmen repaired the bomb-damaged roofs, but undermined the home foundations'. Some women started affairs with neighbours or former workmates of their husband who might have been asked 'to keep an eye on the missus' in his absence. Others met men in the wartime jobs they took, some fell in love with an overseas serviceman who was far from *his* family. 'Every married man out here is haunted in one way and another with the idea of the crack up of his marriage: some poor chaps dread the very sound of American or Canadian troops. Nothing like that has ever troubled me of course, any more than you have worried about me and the veiled beauties of the East,' John Phillips had written from Palestine to his wife. Another soldier whose wife 'kept on about Canadians' in her letters came home on leave to discover that a Canadian soldier who called at the house 'was on familiar terms with his wife, and was borrowing money from her' and that his small son called the man 'Daddy Ray'. The husband 'was in hospital and not physically fit [so] he couldn't knock this man up as he'd like. But he got in touch with the Canadian authorities and succeeded in getting him sent back to Canada.'

'Affairs in wartime were almost inevitable,' recalls Ethel Mattison, who was sharing a house in London with her brother-in-law while his wife had evacuated to Scotland with their two children, and her husband, Jack, was in the Army. 'Mac and I, two lonely people comforted each other by sleeping together and having an occasional meal out. Both Mac and I knew it had no future – which would not have been what either of us wanted anyway – but it was good while it lasted . . . Somebody, maybe Mac's cleaner who came in once a week told Jenny [her sister]. She came home for the weekend and she and Mac found a new flat. Jenny never said a word to me about it all the rest of her life. She and I had a relationship which became closer as time went on.'

Although the advice columns of women's magazines were condemnatory of women who had affairs while their men were away fighting, they were usually even sharper about the self-indulgence of confession, and piled the burden of secrecy on to that of guilt, instructing that it was *not* helpful to a man's morale to write to tell him about misdemeanours. In any case women often recognised that these wartime romances were compensatory. While her body might, for a time, be on loan to Jim or Chuck or Stanislav, her heart remained with her husband, and she still looked forward to a future with him when the seemingly endless 'duration' was over. The romantic novelist Barbara Cartland, who was a welfare officer in the WAAF (Women's Auxiliary Air Force), recalled a twenty-two-year-old woman, pregnant by another man, who 'said to me through her tears, "I love my husband – I do really. You won't believe me, no one will, but I've never stopped loving him. It wasn't me that did this to him – it was some fiend which got hold of me. Oh, I can't explain. I only want to die because I've let him down." '

Illegitimate births might have been seen as providing a concrete indication of the extent of such liaisons. Between 1940 and 1945 the number of babies born of out wedlock was twice the number in the previous six years. In 1940, 26,574 illegitimate births were recorded; in 1945, the number had risen to 64,743. But an important reason for the increase was that in pre-war Britain a woman would be most likely to have sex only with a man she intended to marry, and if she got pregnant this would simply have hastened the wedding: indeed, 70 per cent of all illegitimate conceptions were regularised by marriage before the war. In wartime things were different: patterns of courtship were disrupted and a man might find himself posted away leaving no time to marry before his baby was born. And many relationships undoubtedly were more transient and fleeting, passions heightened with the abandon of loving today since tomorrow we may die.

The figure of almost 300,000 illegitimate births during the war does not, of course, include those babies born to a married woman but not fathered by her husband, providing that the husband did not know this, or accepted the illegitimate offspring as his own and had it registered in their name, since a married woman's child is assumed be her husband's unless she states otherwise when registering the birth. In Birmingham, where a check was kept by social services, a third of all illegitimate children in the city were born to married women: half of these had husbands in the services (including five prisoners of war) while the others were divorced, widowed or living apart from their husbands. A woman could hardly hope to smuggle a new baby into the family if her husband had been away for longer than the gestation period, and she needed his permission to offer a baby for adoption. But despite the fact that most husbands made 'forgiveness' of their wife's transgression dependent on her putting the baby up for adoption, some accepted the child as their own, and indeed a Home Office survey found at least one husband sufficiently generous-hearted to bring up his wife's two illegitimate children as his own.

Abortion on non-medical grounds was illegal – though that did not mean that it did not take place either in expensive clinics or with the help of frequently medically unqualified 'back street' abortionists who could put a woman's life at risk. 'A friend of Eileen's who I know slightly, tried to get an abortion,' wrote Ethel Mattison in July 1941. 'She went to someone on Saturday afternoon, was up all night and in great pain after taking castor oil, and in pain all the next day and night. Eileen asked me to go [since Ethel was trained as nurse] so although there was absolutely nothing I could do I just had to stay there and missed two nights' sleep. On Monday morning I sent for my doctor and explained things and she managed to get the poor woman into hospital where apparently it came off fairly soon and she seems to be OK.'

In 1939 a committee looking at the issue had estimated that between 16 and 20 per cent of pregnancies ended in abortion, that is, up to 150,000 abortions a year, and a quarter of these were probably criminal. The desire not to have a baby in wartime, however, was not confined to those in illicit relationships. In June 1941, Peggie Phillips found out that she was pregnant. Her husband John wrote from his Army camp that 'much as we would like another baby [the couple already had two daughters aged three and fifteen months] these are hard times and it be wisdom [sic] to be brutal and cut off this little promise of a life until the world is a little more settled and we could find some sort of way of assuring that this new little person could be cared for in a decent way. I think this is the strongest argument for you *going* to the osteopath [sic] . . . Perhaps the most sensible way of looking at it is that we ought to get rid of "little accident" while it is early days yet and things haven't gone too far: and we can always have the baby at another time (if it *ever* gets to a more convenient time). I hate deciding the way I have . . . please write and answer this as soon as you can: then we might be able to decide finally when we've both had a say.' Peggie Phillips took her husband's advice: went to see a doctor whose eyes she 'didn't quite trust' and was sent to a discreet nursing home in Kent where for a fee of 50 guineas (which she had to raid the children's account to raise), she had an abortion. 'The woman, still in the same surroundings, feels the separation more [than the man] and has no dramatic team spirit to help her through . . .' reflected her absent husband. But as John Phillips was killed in Italy in 1943 'another time' never came.

Uncertainty about the future meant that in the early years of the war the birth rate fell dramatically: in 1941 it reached the lowest point since records had been kept – 13.9 per thousand of the population – but after that it rose steadily as couples either decided it was safe to have children or, more usually, that even if it wasn't, they were not prepared to wait any longer. 'Jack is now officially assistant editor of their journal and will get a hundred a year for the job,' wrote Ethel Mattison to her sister on New Year's Day, 1940. 'If it wasn't for this bloody war it would make all the difference between having a baby and not having one I guess, but in the circumstances it's unthinkable. Apart from the eventual outcome of the war you would never be sure that you could go on giving it proper food or anything. I always envy anybody I hear is going to have a baby almost instinctively, but my God, what an awful responsibility.' It was not for another three and half years that Ethel would announce: 'You will have heard the great and glorious news that I am pregnant . . . I decided . . . I just can't afford to wait longer.'

The Army, aware that 'one of the gravest morale problems was created by the "anxious soldier", the man who had been alarmed by reports from home about his matrimonial affairs or the wellbeing of his children', was prepared to step in and help resolve marital problems. Intelligence gleaned from reading soldiers' letters home was apt to portray women as undermining the war effort by persuading a husband to overstay his leave, trying to dissuade him from volunteering for dangerous duties and discouraging him from accepting promotion since this could lead to loss of allowances; while the wives played truant from their work when husbands were at home, and themselves could prove sexually fickle. Generally, in fact, behaving like fifth columnists when it came to undermining the men's well-being, in the view of the War Office Morale Committee. The Army Welfare Service, which enquired into applications for compassionate leave and other domestic difficulties, had a grant-in-aid of £250,000 from the Treasury for its work, so important was it considered to the well-being of the troops. In July 1942 the Army Legal Aid Scheme was set up jointly with the Army and the RAF to assist servicemen since 'the State owed an obligation to the serving soldier, whose problems had often arisen because he had been taken away from his home by the State'. Anyone under the rank of sergeant major was eligible to apply for help, and should a serviceman decide to instigate divorce proceedings he could be helped by a newly established Services Divorce Department set up by the Law Society. It was ironic that the effect of such State incursions into the private sphere was to encourage a massive increase in the divorce rate largely by making such legal action possible for those who would not previously have been able to afford it. The number of petitions filed rose from 9,970 in 1938 to 24,857 in 1945 and to a post-war peak of 47,041 in 1947 after the Forces had come home. The year before the war, 50 per cent of divorces were on the grounds of adultery; by 1945 the number had risen to 70 per cent and for the first time more husbands were petitioning for divorce than wives. Although the war witnessed an unprecedented rush to the altar – or the registrar's desk – it also pulled asunder an unprecedented number of unions, though some of those marriages must have been fragile before the impact of war, but without the resources to end them.

Faced with the problem of the infidelity of wives (or their suspected infidelity), the military authorities put in place reconciliation services, the possibility of stopping a soldier's allowance to a wife who was no longer behaving as one, and also contemplated issuing moral strictures. The idea was mooted of approaching the Archbishop of Canterbury and asking him to offer spiritual guidance on the matter, and the Army Morale Committee approached the BBC to see if a public figure, or maybe an anonymous soldier's wife, could speak on the weekly *Mostly for Women* programme on a Sunday morning. The BBC replied stuffily that the subject of infidelity was 'not one that could be discussed over the microphone' and suggested instead that the Queen, or maybe Winston Churchill, could come on instead and praise those women who had 'given their husbands to serve their country overseas'. The possibility of enclosing an appeal to the women of Britain for fidelity with every new issue of the family allowance booklet was toyed with. This was not pursued since the fact that this leaflet would drop indiscriminately on the doormat of all service wives with children was considered indelicate and insulting to the good and faithful wives.

There were other losses: in families separated by war, the men had the poignant experience of knowing their children were growing up without them, that they were becoming remote, dimly remembered figures. Mothers became effectively single parents with no one with whom to share decisions, no one to jointly shoulder the burden of discipline, and no one to rejoice in the pleasures of parenting either. When Ethel Mattison's daughter was born by caesarean section after a long and difficult labour in February 1944, a message was flashed on the screen at the cinema where her soldier husband was watching a film 'telling him to report back to barracks immediately. I came out of the anaesthetic . . .

just in time to hear Jack's army boots coming up the stone stairs. I recognised the sound . . . [he] only had 24 hours leave.' After the birth Mrs Mattison was dangerously ill and was in hospital for six weeks . . . 'Jack was only able to be with me for a week when I came home, and I didn't feel "myself" for a very long time . . . I used to breast feed the baby and sing songs like "Speed Bonnie Boat" and "My Bonnie Lies Over the Ocean" with my tears dropping on the baby's face. I didn't realise until my sister pointed it out many years later, that these were songs of separation.'

Most women tried to keep the presence of a father alive: Mary Cole's husband was called up into the Navy when their daughter Valerie 'was not quite three weeks old . . . and he didn't come back for three and a half years. Of course . . . she got to that stage where she realised that other children had daddies because most of them seemed to come home on leave. So she had photos of him and when she started talking she would jabber away to him and she said to me one day, "Daddy doesn't talk does he?" And I said, "Well Daddy does but the photo doesn't." . . . I always bought her a present on her birthday and Christmas from Daddy. I bought her a dolls' house on one occasion and I left it on the doorstep and got a neighbour to ring the bell and she went down and there was a note from Daddy, from his ship. So he was a real person to her.

'We were on the common one day and I turned around and she had her arms round the leg of a young sailor and she said "Here's Daddy." The poor boy – there were about six of them – and he was the youngest of the lot and he was covered in confusion and, of course, it was a huge joke to the others. She obviously had a picture in her mind of him.'

In contrast to those men who had joined the Army, most of whom spent the early months of the war in Britain, for those in the Navy – both Royal and Merchant – there had been no waiting for war to start, no Phoney War. As Constance Miles wrote in her diary: 'This is the period of the war in which the British mind is constantly concentrated on the sea. Every day there is some fresh sinking of some vessel great or small, and every day there are storms, rain, fog and the grim grey wild skies look down over the heaving glassy green billows. Every night we hear of some ship mined, and we are losing count of even their names.'

On 3 September 1939, a passenger liner, the Glasgow-built *Athenia*, was torpedoed by a U-boat (*unterseeboot* – undersea boat, the name commonly given to German submarines) 250 miles west of Donegal and sunk with the loss of 112 lives. On 14 October a U-boat managed to slip undetected into Scapa Flow in the Orkney Islands, the main base for the Home Fleet throughout most of the war, and torpedo the battleship *Royal Oak* lying at anchor there. More than 800 crew died. On the 16th, the Luftwaffe bombed the naval base at Rosyth on the Firth of Forth, the first time that enemy aircraft had reached Britain. The Navy blockaded German ports, neutral ships in the North Sea were subject to stop and search by the British, and it was estimated that a considerable number of the German's forty U-boats had been scuttled. But by mid November a new danger faced those on the seas: magnetic mines, which were as hazardous to fishing smacks as to ocean liners. Between the outbreak of war and the beginning of May 1940 a total of 268 ships flying the British flag – from battleships to minesweepers and trawlers – were lost as a result of enemy action: from May until December 1940 the losses were never less than fifty-seven a month.

The only good news at sea for the British came just before Christmas 1939 when the *Admiral Graf Spee*, a 12,000-ton German pocket battleship that had been harrying Allied shipping in the South Atlantic, was scuttled in the River Plate off Montevideo in Uruguay by her crew. 'The Royal Navy's Christmas present to the British public,' the journalist Mollie Panter-Downes called it.

Earlier in December, in the words of Leo Walmsley who lived in a fishing community near Whitby in Yorkshire, 'the Nazi air force unfurled its pirates' flag with a large scale attack by machine gun and bomb on vessels of all kinds . . . includ[ing] many fishing craft' such as the *Pearl of Grimsby*, which was fishing about sixty miles out to sea when she was strafed by machine-gun fire from three German planes that swooped just above mast height. This was followed by a hail of bombs that injured three crewmen, with one dying of his wounds. Similar attacks on fishing boats continued.

That autumn the Admiralty had appealed to fishermen to join the minesweeping patrols in the dangerous work of neutralising magnetic mines. 'There was no age limit, no medical examination to pass.

Minesweeping was, par excellence, a job for fishermen, a specialisation of their ordinary peacetime occupation . . . Families of fishermen, fathers, sons and even grandsons volunteered together. So did complete crews, boats included. Minesweeping after all *is* fishing . . .' The fishing boats had been adapted to perform their wartime tasks but they were unarmed, and their crews were untrained in warfare – 'their function was that of special constables, first aid and auxiliary firemen'. The majority came from the herring fleets of Scotland and East Anglia as the herring season was coming to an end, whereas boats fishing in other waters were needed to make a vital contribution to the nation's wartime food supply.

The total number of British ships lost due to enemy action throughout the war was 3,910. Though Britain managed never to cede mastery of the seas – an island nation's age-old safeguard – throughout the Second World War, those who attacked, defended, transported or harvested at sea were in the front line from the first day.

The battle cry of the Second World War was not one of sacrifice, as it had been in the First, but one of effort. The convergence of military and civilian forces, in the rhetoric of politicians as in the uniformed (and uniform) nature of British society, was unique to that war. It rewrote the nature of 'combatant' and could complicate the position of those who sought to deny this designation.

5

NON-COMBATANTS AT WAR

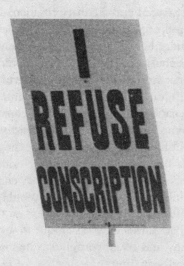

Your conscience thinks that War should cease;
But finds no fault with German peace . . .
It minds not who seduces whom
If, safe within its narrow room,
It still can hug itself and say
'We took no part in war to-day';
It will not mind who lost, who won,
So long as you have fired no gun.
  A. A. MILNE, 'A C. O. MOVEMENT'

'I ADMIT THAT IT is an extraordinarily difficult thing to judge what
   conscience is,' wrote Fenner Brockway, who had been imprisoned
for his pacifist refusal to fight in the First World War, in 1939. 'I suppose
it is a combination of intellectual and moral conviction which is held so

deeply that the individual holding it will not recognise any authority which attempts to impose on him a different course from the course which expresses those convictions . . .'

The National Services (Armed Forces) Act that had been passed on 1 September 1939, the day German troops marched into Poland, contained the proviso that if a man required to register under the Act objected to being placed on the Military Service Register and thus be eligible for call-up, he should apply for his name to be placed on the Register of Conscientious Objectors instead. He would then be called before a local tribunal to explain why he should be exempt from a service his fellow men were compelled to undertake.

In the First World War the options for Conscientious Objectors (COs) had in practice been war or prison. In the Second, the tribunals had more courses open to them. They could register the man appearing before them as a Conscientious Objector with no conditions attached; they could register him on condition that he undertook civilian work under civilian rather than military control; they could remove his name from the register of COs but stipulate that he could be called up only for non-combatant duties in the Armed Forces; or they could refuse to allow his name to be inscribed in the Conscientious Objectors' Register, in which case he would be called up into the Armed Forces. If the applicant was not satisfied with the decision of the tribunal, he could take his case to an appellate tribunal: its decision was final.

Though the procedures were clear enough, the meaning of the term 'Conscientious Objector' was not defined by the Act, as some tribunal chairmen complained. Judge Burgis, who chaired the North-Western Board, came up with a lucid interpretation of their duties. 'It is immaterial to this tribunal how many men we send [into the Armed Forces]. Conscience, and conscience alone is what we have to consider . . . All we have to consider is whether these views are sincerely and deeply felt, and we have not to determine whether they are reasonable or patriotic.'

But this did not in itself suggest the *categories* into which men should be ranked: was there a gradation of sincerity that allowed some men unconditional exemption, while others were directed to take particular work that could aid the war though not in a directly military sense? Was it possible to 'plumb the depths of men's conviction' to make sure conscience was not being 'made a cloak', as Judge Burgis had it, for cowardice or obduracy, or opportunism?

Given the choices available to them, the tribunals could grant a man Unconditional Exemption (decision 'A'), which meant he would be placed on the CO register as exempt from military service with no conditions placed on what work he must undertake. The 'B' decision meant exemption on condition that a man undertook civilian work under civilian control; while decision 'C' meant that the applicant would be registered as liable to be called up for non-combatant duties only. If the tribunal was not satisfied that an application was genuine, it would direct that the man's name be removed from the CO register and he would thus be liable for military service. This was decision 'D'.

As Frances Partridge wrote of her husband Ralph, who had been wounded fighting in the First World War and awarded the Military Cross, but had decided to register as a Conscientious Objector in the Second, 'R.'s beliefs *are* coherent and sound; the difficulty is to present them to the tribunal in such a way that they can put him into one of their preconceived categories, and convince them – not that he is a thinking man – but a believing one.'

In the First World War similar tribunals had been held under the aegis of the War Office and a military man had sat in on every hearing, but in the Second this practice was stopped. The eleven tribunals in England and Wales and the four in Scotland now came under the Ministry of Labour and National Service, which meant that they could be seen as acting in the interests of the nation's war effort as a whole, rather than as recruiting offices for the Armed Forces.

Most of those chosen for the unenviable task of trying to peer through murky windows into men's souls were local worthies and they rarely had any legal experience at all – though one Labour MP argued that this was irrelevant. What was needed, he claimed, was 'someone who has a great and deep understanding of human nature . . . who will be sympathetic and will endeavour to put himself in the place of the person who is appearing, and not someone who will calmly and dispassionately weigh up the pros and cons'. 'It is a public duty and so disagreeable that I cannot refuse to do it,' one individual was supposed to have replied to the then Minister of Labour, the Liberal MP Ernest Brown, when accepting this particular wartime poisoned chalice. Members were not young – though most of those who appeared before them were – and almost all had fought, or been involved, in the First World War, and there was frequently a notable academic on each. H. A. L. Fisher, the author of a magisterial three-volume *History of Europe*, chaired the appellate tribunal for England, and the economic historian Professor J. H. Clapham was a member of the East Anglian tribunal. Other members, mostly men, included solicitors, barristers, doctors, an ex-Mayor of Southport and an ex-Lord Mayor of Manchester, a former editor of the *Glasgow Herald* and a former governor of the Bank of Scotland who chaired the Scottish appellate tribunal.

Tribunals varied in the way they interpreted their brief. The London tribunal, which sat in Fulham, was notorious and so was the Newcastle-based Northumberland and Durham one where 'instead of the judicial atmosphere which ought to prevail in a tribunal, there is a carping, bullying, brutal attitude', complained Frederick Pethwick-Lawrence, a Labour MP who had been a Conscientious Objector himself in the First World War. The chairman, Judge Richardson, was reported to have insulted Jehovah's Witnesses, saying, 'I have the greatest contempt for your sort' and mocking 'you might pray and preach, but what good do you *do*?' and one day delivered the opinion that, 'I am certain, as sure as I sit here, that if Christ appeared today he would approve of this war'. The reaction to this statement was so hostile, with boos and whistles and stamping of feet, that he cleared the court and later apologised. But the tragedy of war permeates people's attitudes in remarkably different ways. When Judge Richardson was faced with an objector who explained that he was one of seven brothers of whom six had been killed in the First World War, told him, 'I am one of seven brothers, of whom only two are alive. I lost five brothers in the last war,' adding quietly, 'and I have a son going up next week.'

The London chairman referred to some applicants as 'these miserable creatures' and dismissed answers they gave to questions as 'What tosh!' But these excesses were not typical and some tribunals (particularly the South-Eastern) were praised for their fair-mindedness and the genuine attempts their members made to engage in a dialectic of profound theological and philosophical complexity without a rule book, at a time of grave national emergency.

During the First World War there had been 16,000 Conscientious

Objectors coming forward after the introduction of conscription in 1916. The total number of COs by the end of 1945 was 59,192, roughly 1.2 per cent of the 5 million 'called up'; this was nearly four times as many as in the First World War, but it was over a six-year rather than a two-year period and so the increase can be seen as relatively small, and registration fell throughout the war – 222 out of every thousand in 1939; sixteen in every thousand by March 1940; fewer than six by the summer of 1940.

Those who registered as Conscientious Objectors came from all over the country and from many walks of life. More came from the south of England, particularly London, than the Midlands and the North – though that might have been partly because there were more men in reserved occupations in these industrial areas. Norfolk was a traditional stronghold of pacifism, and the concentration in Wales was highest of all probably due to the strength of Welsh religious nonconformity – the Methodist Church, which dominated Welsh life, produced the largest of the Nonconformist pacifist groups with some 4,000 members. The figure also included a number of nationalists who considered the war to be England's war, and saw opposition to conscription as the ideal opportunity to force Welsh nationalist demands on to the government agenda. This is an option that the poet Dylan Thomas opportunistically considered since he did not intend 'to waste my little body (though it's little no longer, I'm like a walrus') . . . for the mysterious ends of others' – not that he was a member of Plaid Genedlaetho Cymru, the nationalist party. But this stance was not in the end taken by Thomas or hardly anyone else. The few Welsh nationalists who registered their objection did so on ethical and religious rather than solely on political grounds. The editor of Plaid Genedlaetho Cymru's journal, *Y Ddraig Goch*, A. O. H. Jarman, was one of the twelve Welsh nationalists imprisoned for their opposition to conscription.

There was no such thing as a typical Conscientious Objector. A Mass-Observation survey concluded that most 'have occupations where particular intelligence is required, or a higher standard of education . . . and even highbrow tastes in cultural matters'. Although not all were left-wing intellectuals, weedy specimens yet advocates of free love, vegetarian poets or potters, as popular prejudice had it, M-O admitted that some COs 'look odd and arty to the conventionally minded . . .

actually the chief odd things about them are a tendency to be vegetarian, love their mothers, love animals, and not all these things are unconventional'. In fact the occupations of those who registered varied from artists to Custom and Excise officials, ice-cream vendors to journalists, paint sprayers to teachers, the unemployed to window cleaners.

The majority of those who objected did so on religious grounds, and in general they were more favourably looked on than those who gave political or ethical reasons for their objections. This was particularly true if an applicant came from a family with a long history of religious pacifism like the Quakers. Of the 4,056 cases that came before the South-Western tribunal up until 7 March 1942, 71 per cent based their objections on religious grounds.

Many who had made the decision to resist conscription had to face opposition, from family, friends and workmates, long before they got anywhere near a tribunal. 'Quite frankly Jags, I think you talk a lot of tripe,' wrote a Gosport woman to a male friend in Southampton. '. . . I know it isn't the least bit of good talking to you, or even trying to change your opinion about the war, but the fact remains that you as an individual cannot do one bit of good trying to stick to what you consider to be very high ideals about fighting etc . . . Christianity does not enter into your idea of fighting, you very seldom go to church, you never read the Bible . . . and yet you have the audacity to bring God and the Church into your argument for not fighting.

'. . . You have not one good argument to put forward . . . for not fighting. You say you do not want to kill a man, well my dear, who does? No man on this earth *wants* to kill another man . . . use that dumb brain of yours and understand that men do *not* quite definitely fight to kill. They fight to defend which is an entirely different matter . . . For goodness sake, grow up. You are 24 years old, enough to go and fight like any other man who probably feels just the same as you do, but has sufficient common sense to know that he as an individual cannot possibly do anything about it . . . Go to war my lad and be a man . . . whether you live or die, you will have done your bit for your country . . . yours with love, Barbara.'

At Easter 1939 Arnold Monk-Jones, who taught classics at St Paul's School in London, had taken a walking holiday in the Lake District.

There he met Eileen Bellerby, a science teacher at Cheltenham Ladies' College. The attraction was mutual and on their return home the couple wrote to each other frequently as war drew nearer and each had to consider her or his response. Although Arnold, who was forty when war broke out, had fought in the First World War, he had come to share the views of one of his brothers, a Conscientious Objector who had worked with the Quaker Friends' Ambulance Service. Eileen, who was thirty-four in 1939, came from a family of teachers and was a Quaker. 'Our discussion about pacifism has left me rather uncertain about my own attitude,' wrote Arnold in his first letter to Eileen on returning home to Sydenham in south London. 'I am prepared to find it true that capitalism makes war inevitable, but haven't yet enough information on this point . . . But loathsome as war is, I still believe that resistance to an aggressor who prefers force to reason is probably better than non resistance . . . surely a distinction ought to be drawn between offensive and defensive power politics; just as in civil life a distinction exists between the burglar who robs with violence and the policeman who, in arresting him, knocks him over . . . Yours very sincerely, Arnold.'

'I am very interested in what you say about pacifism and I respect your point of view,' responded Eileen. 'I feel for myself that I could not take part in the beastly realities of war . . . I don't think that capitalism is entirely to be blamed for war, nor that the introduction of socialism would inevitably bring wars to an end . . . As for the distinction between offensive and defensive power politics, I can't forget that those on the defensive are the "haves" and one has a good deal of sympathy for the needy burglar who robs the house of the rich.'

'Re pacifism, you have shaken me considerably and I am very doubtful what is the best line to take,' admitted Arnold in his reply (though he did add in red crayon 'if bored omit from here to the middle of page five' at the start of his disquisition). 'I suspect that you have given more reading and thought to the question than I have; but I think that the solution is not quite so simple as a mere refusal to take part in war in any circumstances, much as I respect that attitude . . . I *think* my attitude would be to fight if required, but to try to work for peace and understanding: just as . . . I should physically resist anyone making a violent attack on anyone . . .' He added a postscript: 'I find [my pupils] very willing to listen to and consider the pacifist case – much of it of course new to them – though most of them incline to resistance to aggression . . . I do think [the First World War] has taught the youth at least of this country how loathsome war is.'

Eileen was quick to tell Arnold that 'there is no need to apologise for your "long-winded arguments". I'm glad and proud that you take the trouble to tell me what you think about it, though I feel it's a little impertinent of me for me to air my views when it means so much more to you. It's comparatively easy for a woman to be a pacifist: for a man it is a much more serious step.'

And so their epistolary debate went on throughout the last summer of peace: Arnold confessing that at one point he was 'wobbling like a jelly fish between a position I took before you shook me up (viz collective security and negotiation about grievances, and working for the ultimate abolition of war, and whole-hogging pacifism)'. He reported the views of a colleague who 'insists that once war breaks out the genuine pacifist can only kill himself, otherwise he will be living on food brought to him by the sacrifice of men's lives'. Eileen shot back, 'That is a *reductis* [sic] *ad absurdum*. A pacifist is not much use as such in wartime, except in so far as he keeps sane in all the war hysteria, but it seems to me he must help to alleviate the suffering that war brings.' Arnold read Aldous Huxley's *Ends and Means* in the hope of further enlightenment and Eileen made clever use of this to advance their romance. 'I think it is a pity for you to be spending time indoors writing down what you think about *Ends and Means* when you say how you long to be out in the country, and wouldn't it serve both purposes if you came here for a weekend? . . . If you came on a Friday evening it would leave the whole of Saturday and most of Sunday for talking over this pacifist question.' Arnold thought this an excellent suggestion, but it is clear that wrangling about whole-hog pacifism and its alternatives was not all that preoccupied the couple that weekend, for on the Monday morning Eileen dashed off a note: 'Arnold dear. I can't really believe what has happened . . . this letter is quite superfluous except to tell you that I love you very much and you have made me very happy.' Arnold replied with wonder, 'I am only beginning to realise my tremendous good fortune. You can't think how happy you have made me.' But throughout a time of great joy, the gathering clouds of war ('all this ugliness and cruelty makes our love very, very precious'), the evacuation of St Paul's School to Berkshire, the threatened requisitioning of Cheltenham Ladies' College by the Ministry of Supply (the headmistress, the redoubtable Miss Popham, put up a fight arguing, 'You won't be defending Britain if you break up the public schools!'), and, on 27 September 1939, marriage (even though Arnold recognised that 'I could hardly have chosen a more appalling year in which to ask a woman to marry me'), the couple never lost sight of the urgency of the issue that had first engaged them. In the end it proved an academic question for the Monks-Jones since Arnold was beyond the age of call-up by 1940, and the couple put their energies into running a billet for boys who had been evacuated with St Paul's School.

The first step for a Conscientious Objector – registration, which took place at a man's local employment exchange – was an ordeal. Edward Blishen, a writer and teacher, came from a military family – his father, who had been shellshocked and wounded fighting in the trenches in the First World War, wasn't sympathetic to pacifists. 'He felt that if he had fought a war, then I ought to fight one as well.' But Blishen, who had read 'the literature of disgust . . . bitter fruit of the Great War (as we called it then till this greater war came) . . . the horror of it, the rejection it expressed, had run in my veins, until I could not think of fighting without a sense of shock . . . So as I made my way to the Labour Exchange, I heard that voice within me, weeping for France [which had just been invaded by German troops], as the voice of disloyal temptation; and I registered as an objector . . . and it felt as though I were separating yourself from the rest of the world . . .'

Reginald Bottini was a shipping clerk for a family firm of wholesale importers. His father had been killed in the First World War. 'I was brought up by a widowed mother – I remember her sobbing quite often when I was a child,' and his youthful anti-miltarism had already led him into trouble when he refused to join the Officers' Training Corps at school. But he was not a pacifist 'because as far as I was concerned it has been proved that in certain circumstances violence is inevitable. But the sense in which [the Second World War] was presented in neatly labelled nationalistic packages and flags didn't go with me.' He regarded it as an imperial war and 'opposed the war on grounds of working-class solidarity. I objected to fighting the working class of another country and sacrificing the working class of this one because one knows that in the mortality statistics who comes out worst. That is not to overlook the fact that a large number of middle-class and public school officers are slaughtered as well . . .' When Bottini told his boss of his intentions to register as a CO, 'Mr Stewart used some insulting expressions and said, "Get rid of him". ' So after five years' service Bottini was given a week's notice.

It was his Christian faith that led Len Richardson, an insurance agent, to register as a CO but, despite the strength of his conviction that this was the right thing to do, he still 'hardly dared glance round for fear of seeing any of my old friends from school and the rugby field'. His work, which he continued to do while waiting to be summoned before the tribunal, meant that he called on many housewives and he found it hard to explain why he wasn't going to war 'to people whose sons and husbands had already gone . . .'

Many Conscientious Objectors belonged to one of the Christian pacifist organisations of various denominations, most of which were affiliated to the Council of Christian Pacifist Groups. There were also a number of non-religious groupings working for peace: among them the Civil Service Pacifist Fellowship, which numbered about 500; the Teachers' Anti-War Movement; a grouping of local government workers; the left-wing British Youth Peace Assembly; and the International Voluntary Service for Peace, which worked for international co-operation by arranging work parties advertised as 'pick and shovel peace-making'. It had sent men to work in the devastated areas of northern France after the First World War, and continued by helping in land-settlement schemes in distressed areas in Britain. There was the Independent Labour Party, which had always been sympathetic to objections to war; the No-Conscript organisation, which had been active in helping COs in the First World War; the Women's Co-operative Movement; and the Woodcraft Folk, a youth organisation that offered the same sorts of activities to young people as the Boy Scouts and Girl Guides, but with a very different ideology.

And there was the Peace Pledge Union (PPU), founded in 1936 by Dick Sheppard, best known for his welfare work as vicar of St Martin's-in-the-Field's, who had been an Army chaplain in the First World War, and was once described as the 'Führer of a really formidable peace army'. The largest of all the groups, it believed in an 'active pacifism, one that not simply said no to war but worked to build a better world based on international co-operation'. Among its members and sponsors, the PPU included the composer Michael Tippett; Edward Blishen; the actress Sybil Thorndike; Sir Arthur Eddington, the Professor of Astronomy at Cambridge; the sculptor and calligrapher, Eric Gill; the pacifist writer Vera Brittain; the philosophers Bertrand Russell and C. E. M. Joad; and a soldier from the First World War, Brigadier General Crozier, whose book *A Brass Hat in No Man's Land* had pointed up the idiocies of war from the inside. At its peak in April 1940 the PPU could boast a membership of 136,000, while its journal, *Peace News*, under the editorship from June 1940 of the writer (and widower of fellow writer Katherine Mansfield) John Middleton Murry, eventually achieved a circulation of 20,000 copies.

Most of these organisations were affiliated to the Central Board for Conscientious Objectors (CBCO) which was not, in the words of its chairman, the pacifist ILP MP Fenner Brockway, 'an organisation *of* Conscientious Objectors but an organisation *for* Conscientious Objectors'. Its main task was to give advice on such matters as how to register as a CO and how to appeal against a local tribunal's decision, and it closely scrutinised new legislative proposals going through Parliament that might affect COs.

Not all pacifists registered as COs (a large number were over the age eligible to be called up, while others were in reserved occupations), and not all who did register as COs were pacifists (probably about a quarter were not members of any pacifist organisation). There were those whose objection was not necessarily to all wars, but rather to this particular war, and those who resisted State compulsion of any sort and refused to register as a Conscientious Objector. Some men who were in reserved occupations registered as COs as a protest at conscription, even though it did not directly affect them.

If registering as a Conscientious Objector was an alienating ordeal, appearing at a tribunal was even more harrowing, and the Central Board for Conscientious Objectors and a number of pacifist organisations prepared their members for these occasions – and sent someone experienced along with the applicant as moral support and to testify to his character and sincerity. In the case of a religious applicant, this might be a priest or minister, while others might bring an employer – one applicant brought an Army colonel who happened to be his father – or, if not a living reference, then a letter in support, maybe outlining some social-work activities, church work or charity projects.

'Mock tribunals' were usually conducted by men who had already successfully been before a tribunal themselves, and they put the applicant through his paces with questions as similar as possible to those he was likely to encounter. Predictably they drew the ire of the popular press: 'Conchies Learn The Answers. Mock Tribunals Teach Them What To Say' blazoned the *Daily Express*. Some judges were condemnatory too, regarding the practice as negating the sincerity of objectors – though the complexity of much of the questioning could leave anyone without extreme verbal and mental agility at a severe disadvantage in expressing his convictions to the tribunal persuasively.

If an applicant objected to conscription on religious grounds, he was usually asked if he was a member of a church or other religious organisation, and then for how long he had been a member. If, as most did, he based his objections on the teachings of the Bible, he would be quizzed as to which of Christ's sayings gave him this certainty, and much convoluted discussion might follow about how comprehensive the adage 'Thou shalt not kill' should be, as biblical text countermanded biblical text like cards being dealt. Some tribunals favoured asking applicants to name all twelve apostles and, if they were unable to do so, considered this omission cast doubt on the sincerity of their beliefs. Another favourite was to ask the applicant if he thought that God would make any distinction between a soldier and a civilian lying wounded in the street, and one tribunal member remarked, 'Even God isn't a pacifist – he kills us in the end.'

If, however, the applicant's objection was not based on religious grounds but rather on ethical or political ones, the tribunal would feel it necessary to prove that this was not just an opinion but a moral conviction. He might be asked a less offensive version of the First World War probe 'What would you do if a Hun was raping your sister?' – such as 'Do you not realise that many of your old school/work friends are risking their lives to defend you?' or 'Would you not defend your wife/parents/children from the ruthless invader?' The members of the tribunal laboured to expose the fallacy of the applicant's logic and thus, presumably, the integrity of his conscience, quizzing men on whether their objection was to taking life and, if the answer was yes, riposting,

'Well, why aren't you a vegetarian then?' A man might be asked if he was prepared to accept a ration book since rationing was contributing to the war effort; and many men were asked if they would fail to go to the assistance of those injured in a train crash or traffic accident. Fred Pitkeathly, who appeared before a Scottish tribunal, was asked if he did not think that Abraham Lincoln had been justified in going to war on behalf of the slaves.

'I shall never forget the tribunal,' recalls Reginald Bottini. 'I was trembling, trembling more with indignation than anything else, but nevertheless trembling . . . I made a statement that started with . . . the fact that my father had died at the age of 25 in the trenches leaving my mother a widow as an indication, though not a justification, of where my ideas tended to come from. And the whole of the rest of my statement referred to what I believe to be the correct socialist approach to war which was that it was a struggle for raw material resources for a sub division of the world in terms of land, for domination of the imperialist-capitalist groups that I would have no part in. It was not a pacifist statement. They asked a question about what would be a just war for me. They put it along the lines of "Would you find it possible to fight in a war of socialist versus capitalist?" I couldn't lie to the tribunal on that because I'd never taken a pacifist view. On the other hand I was sufficiently pragmatic to recognise that if I said, "Oh yes I jolly well would" bang would go the possibility of registration [on the Conscientious Objectors' register]. I didn't want to play into their hands. I said I wasn't quite sure at that point in time. It would depend on the circumstances . . . And what impression that gave other than of youthful confusion, I don't know . . . I suppose they gave me the credit of thinking things out . . . I do remember though that I particularly upset the trade union representative . . . [he] questioned me very thoroughly . . . about the threat to socialist rights and trade union rights represented by Hitler. And I found his questions much more severe than that of the presiding chairman or the other member nominated by the CBI [Confederation of British Industry]. In fact I came back afterwards and complained long and hard afterwards and described him as a TU renegade . . .'

The composer Benjamin Britten was in the US when war broke out. He had written the *Pacifist March* for the Peace Pledge Union, and by the outbreak of war he and the poet W. H. Auden, another Briton in exile in the US, had agreed that their position 'forbids [us] to act as a combatant in any war', a decision Auden commemorated in his poem 'September 1 1939' with its conclusion: 'We must love one another or die.'

But by December 1941 Britten had 'made up my mind to return to England, at any rate for the duration of the war' with his musical collaborator and lover, the singer Peter Pears. Britten registered as a Conscientious Objector and was called before a tribunal in May 1942. His statement read: 'The whole of my life has been devoted to acts of creation (being by profession a composer) and I cannot take part in acts of destruction . . . I believe sincerely that I can help my fellow human beings best, by continuing . . . the creation or propagation of music.' He was asked what he would do if his country was invaded. 'I believe in letting an invader in and then setting him a good example,' he replied. A week later he heard the tribunal's decision: he was to be called up for non-combatant duties.

Britten decided to appeal. He was supported by Laurence Gillam, a BBC producer, who stated that Britten's availability to work on radio programmes was 'in the national interest', and Ethel Bridge, the widow of Frank Bridge, the man who had taught Britten composition since the age of fourteen. She recalled 'going for a walk with [Britten] through Kensington Gardens & Hyde Park and showing him the gay uniforms of the soldiers at Hyde Park (or Knightsbridge) Barracks & he would turn away & say "I hate all of it & what it stands for" . . . & this passionate hatred has remained with him all through these years that I have known him.' The composer William Walton appeared too, and it turned out that the tribunal chairman was the father of a man who had been a friend of Britten's at Gresham's public school. He proved 'a wise and sympathetic judge' and decided that Britten should be 'completely free to go on with [his] work'. Peter Pears was allowed to do the same.

Michael Tippett went before an appellate tribunal after his registration had been rejected and he too had been assigned to non-combatant military duties. But in his case the appeal only partly succeeded: 'I was given conditional registration – I had either to do full-time work with Air Raid Precautions, the Fire Service or on the land. The alternative was some kind of cultural activity. I consulted with a number of close friends [one of whom] told me to "bend with the wind" '. But 'prison . . . didn't bother me . . . Apart from the fact that I could never shoot or commit deliberate acts of violence against other individual human beings, let alone groups, there were simply two issues that mattered . . . I would brook no interference with my compositional work, which I felt was the most valuable thing that I could do; the other was a matter of principle – why should I be privileged and evade imprisonment by doing officially approved cultural or educational work, while other pacifists, particularly the younger ones, were defenceless? . . . [the composer Ralph] Vaughan Williams [was among those] who testified on my behalf even though they disagreed with my position.

'The magistrate's only option was to send me to prison for the minimum period, three months. I didn't think I was necessarily better than a colleague . . . who fought in the war with just as high a sense of morality: he thought he was defending civilisation against the evils of Nazism. But though I thought Nazism was evil, I thought war was the wrong means for defeating it . . . After all it is the innocents who suffer most on either side – the mothers and children of Dresden, of Coventry or wherever.'

Tribunal members 'could respect and sympathise with an objection to the act of killing or even an objection to being involved in the non-combatant part of a military effort, but what they considered to be a total rejection of all responsibility of the individual to the state, especially in an hour of need, stretched their tolerance to its absolute limit', and they found it hard to grant unconditional exemptions. Indeed, the chairman of the Southern Local Board announced that his tribunal was not going to grant any 'A' status at all, even though this was in flagrant disregard of the terms of the Act, and without announcing the fact many other tribunals acted in a like manner. In 1939 14 per cent of all objectors were granted unconditional exemption: as the war grew fiercer the tolerance grew less: those granted unconditional exemption fell to 5 per cent in 1940 and just 2 per cent in 1941.

In all, 18,495 men had their applications to be placed on the Conscientious Objectors' register rejected: the dictates of their conscience were not considered to be 'genuine' by whatever omnipotent criteria the tribunals worked to. The 'D' decision meant such men's names were added to the register of those liable to military service. Of those, 10,878 appealed and the remainder either accepted their fate and waited for call-up, or, unconvinced that they would fare any better at appeal than they had at local level, refused to undergo the medical examination that was the prerequisite to entry into the Armed Forces. Such a refusal was punishable by a fine or imprisonment: of the 5,852 who failed to get their 'D' registration changed at the appellate tribunal, 1,891 went to prison. In the First World War, of the 16,000 COs, approximately one in three went to prison for his beliefs. In the Second World War around one CO in ten was imprisoned.

Leonard Bird, a solicitor's clerk, had been granted exemption on condition that he did alternative work. He refused and was among the first COs to go to jail. In prison he met ex-soldiers who were there 'for committing a small theft or hitting a policeman on the nose. We knew they'd done it so they could avoid being sent abroad on active service. We had very little trouble and very little argument. We had more argument with the chaplain who didn't understand us when we asked him what "praying for our enemies" could mean.' Bird was released after a year and 'did voluntary fire watching while I was working for a firm of solicitors, but when it was a compulsory requirement . . . I refused to do [it]. I got prosecuted four times and sent to prison two more times . . . prison is a terrible experience . . . But I would do it again.'

A letter in the *Aberdeen Evening Express* pointed up the paradox of imprisoning a man for his deeply held beliefs at a time when Britain was at war with a totalitarian regime. 'Some people may be glad to see Conscientious Objectors being thrown into prison for their . . . scruples, but . . . is it not for freedom of conscience that we are fighting at this minute . . . Let the Conscientious Objectors have a chance to get on with some useful or civil work for their country . . . instead of confining them to prison at the country's expense when all hands are needed.'

Rather than deciding on rejection or complete exemption, the tribunals could choose to direct men into non-combatant work in the Forces – usually the Army: this was decision 'C'. While in recognition that 'all hands were needed' in a war that was going to put civilians in the front line, the great majority of applicants were recorded as 'B' and directed to serve in a civilian capacity on the Home Front.

Both decisions brought problems. The only certain non-combatant role in the Forces was in the Corps of Chaplains, and of course this was not a calling that a man who was not ordained could just take up as a result of a tribunal decision. The most popular alternative was the Royal Army Medical Corps (RAMC). Many found the RAMC had particular appeal: a man would be offering aid to his fellow men in time of war, but not joining them in belligerent acts. Other popular alternatives were the Royal Army Dental Corps, the Royal Army Pay Corps and the Royal Army Veterinary Corps. Although there was no guarantee that a doctor, dentist, pay clerk or vet would not be required to take up arms, the possibility was remote. Such direction by the tribunal, though, could only be a recommendation, not an instruction, and by early 1940 the RAMC was said to be full up and unable to accept more recruits. In fact there was some opposition to the deployment of COs when it was felt that people with specialist skills were being kept out of the RAMC in order to accommodate them. So, in April 1940, the Non-Combatant Corps (NCC or, as they were called at first, Non-Combatant Labour Corps – 'Nancy-Elsie to genuine warriors'), which had been established during the First World War expressly for Conscientious Objectors, was re-formed. It consisted of fourteen companies with a total of 6,000 men at its peak, and was designed to be integral to all aspects of the war effort apart from those that required the handling of weapons. NCC members would drill without arms, be trained in gas-prevention measures, passive air defence, decontamination, cooking and cleaning, and would be deployed mainly on construction work, quarrying, felling timber, filling in trenches, looking after burial grounds, laundries and baths, and 'general duties not involving the handling of military material in an aggressive manner'.

The NCC came in for criticism too, charged that COs (men the popular press were not above referring to as 'lily-livered conchies') were 'masquerading' as soldiers wearing uniforms, benefiting from a number of the perks enjoyed by the regular troops such as service canteens and half-price entry to places of entertainment, yet not facing the perils that fighting men confronted. The NCC was linked to the Pioneer Corps of the Regular Army in order to have corporals, sergeants, captains, majors. Most 'felt it was a fearful degradation, not being allowed to really go and fight but to look after a bloody bunch of conchies' and life could be made galling for the non-combatant with endless kit inspections, the absolute minimum of leave, pedantic enforcement of every pettifogging regulation and sometimes outright hostility – including from some of the officers and NCOs. Some COs reported taunts from other soldiers urging them to join a combat unit, and many were anxious about how much, and in what ways, what they were doing might be contributing to the prosecution of the war. Most suffered intense frustration at the menial and repetitive war they were condemned to by their principles. Eventually almost 2,400 of nearly 7,000 men did transfer from the NCC to other units once it was clear that they could take a non-combatant role in a combat unit while retaining their CO status. And invariably any sniping by other troops stuttered to a halt when confronted with non-combatants who suffered harrowing experiences working as paramedics at the scene of battle, laid smoke screens to hinder enemy attacks, worked with prisoners of war or undertook the sometimes deadly task of dismantling unexploded bombs (UXBs).

Eventually over 350 NCC men volunteered to work alongside the regular Royal Engineers in bomb disposal. Christopher Wren, a young pacifist 'absolutist' when war broke out, had been 'overcome by pictures [of Dunkirk] in May 1940. We felt we couldn't just stand there and let it happen . . . we were prepared to go and help – on the beaches, stretcher-bearing, first aid, and anything that was needed to save life. Germans as well – I should say that.' He heard that 'there were from time to time opportunities to volunteer for bomb disposal and . . . I thought it would be very good: to destroy armaments and at the same time protect people. Both aspects seemed to fit with why I had become a non-combatant.' Though some 'conchies' were bullied, Wren found the sappers very accepting but if 'some members of the public saw your NCC badge and someone asked what it was, I would say "Non-Combatant Corps". You knew what they were thinking so I would say I was a coward straightaway! Then sometimes they would see the bomb flash and they wouldn't know what to make of it all . . . Our way of life, through our Parliament is exceptional. Even when we are on the knife-edge of defeat we still allow Conscientious Objectors . . . by having this system we were able to get people to volunteer for jobs like bomb disposal. We were able to use the "conchies" to do it . . . so there was something to be said for our cowardice, if that's the word.'

The tribunals were required to direct men exempted from military service on the condition they undertook civilian work under civilian control into work where they could make the most useful contribution to the war effort short of fighting. But there were problems: many industries where manpower was most needed were involved in war production; a number of employers were reluctant to take on COs, fearing that the existing staff might object; agriculture, which seemed an obvious choice, was over-manned in some areas of the country at the beginning of the war, and in any case some farmers refused to employ COs. It was reported that of over 2,000 COs who had been instructed to find work in agriculture or forestry, many had been unable to – one man was reported to have applied unsuccessfully for more than forty jobs. John Middleton Murry, editor of *Peace News*, raised £100,000 to help buy a 300-acre farm in Lincolnshire through a Community Land Training Association which had been formed in the autumn of 1940 to train COs who wanted to work on the land. Similar projects were undertaken elsewhere in the country with the support of other prominent pacifists, including Eric Gill – who showed his contempt for wartime regulations by carrying a gas-mask box everywhere, but refusing to put his gas mask in it. 'Peace farms,' the *Sunday Pictorial* sneered, '. . . a nice funkhole in the country, miles away from bomb threatened cities . . . where Conscientious Objectors . . . laze about . . . and adopt an omnipotent and superior attitude to war-troubled Britain.'

The situation had eased somewhat by 1941, partly because the number of farm workers called into the services meant that many farmers were obliged to accept what workers they could get, regardless of any ideological objections they might have, and, by this time after months of the Blitz, it was clear that it could be as dangerous (if not more so) working on the Home Front as in the Armed Forces. The record of courage and fortitude of many of those COs working in Civil Defence belied the idea of a bunch of funks, though it persisted in some quarters. A Conservative MP, who was also a lieutenant colonel, demanded that it should be 'made compulsory for all Conscientious Objectors to wear a white armband with the letters CO in yellow'. But the word was spreading in rural communities, as in urban, that not all COs were limp-wristed wastrels, skivers and slackers, but hard and willing workers, and by 1944 it was estimated that there were about 8,000 COs employed on the land, most working on private farms.

An alternative to agriculture or forestry that the tribunals often recommended was working in Civil Defence, either the ARP or the AFS, but this was not the felicitous solution it might have appeared to be. Some COs refused such work as being part of the war machine – 'so you would rather [help people in an air raid] inefficiently than efficiently?' Bill Prentice was asked by a Glasgow tribunal when he raised this objection. Others were prepared to do Civil Defence work when it was voluntary, but not when compelled to do so by the State. And many local authorities refused to employ COs in these capacities. Reginald Bottini 'wrote to the 28 London boroughs telling them what I was and saying that I wanted a job in the ARP. And I had 28 letters of refusal come back. I didn't want to leave London because leaving London would mean chickening out of what was going to happen in London. And the last thing that a person like me would want is to be regarded as getting away somewhere safe while people are being bombed . . . but every borough council turned me down without saying so because I was a CO. If I'd written without mentioning my CO-ship I might have got a job, but I wasn't prepared to do that.'

Eventually Bottini was seconded to work on land-drainage for the War Agricultural Committee. And he 'never had any abuse during the war, reserved looks, people who wouldn't visit who used to visit before the war, people who avoided saying "Good morning" in the street, but no insults, or white feathers or anything like that. Just a sort of blank incomprehension as to how one could take this view, and with some men, not many, an understanding that anybody who can get out of this bloody lot is wise. But that's a masculine point of view. The feminine point of view seemed to be "my husband had to go" or "my son's had to go, why shouldn't you?" But never hysterical – it was a reluctant conviction that it had to be done and if it had to be done why didn't everyone do it?'

Although in general the attitude towards Conscientious Objectors was one of tolerance or low-level grumbling criticism about those 'who wanted to pick and choose their wars for themselves', a number did suffer abuse and material privation. 'Yellow belly, conchie. You shouldnae be here,' was shouted at Fred Pitkeathly by 'young farmhands . . . who were exempt from the Forces because of their jobs'. At moments of heightened national anxiety, such as Dunkirk, the more right-wing press was apt to resort to describing COs as less than British, certainly less than men. Rather they were effeminate cowards – 'national pansies . . . with no chins, no character and no spirit'.

A Yorkshire vicar, incensed to find that five out of the eight applicants for the post of organist at his church were COs, decided not to fill the post, but to play the organ himself as well as conducting the service and preaching the sermon. Another man was denounced from the pulpit of his local church, and members of the congregation were enjoined to pray for him, while Walter Wright's landlady reluctantly gave him notice when she found out he had registered as a Conscientious Objector: 'She didn't want to but her son was in the Army and when he came home on leave he refused to sit down at table with a "conchie" so I had to go.' In December 1940 the BBC sacked all Conscientious Objectors working for it, and stopped broadcasting the Orpheus Choir because its conductor, Sir Hugh Roberton, was a Conscientious Objector. After protests the ban was lifted in March 1941. John Middleton Murry was dropped as a reviewer from the *Times Literary Supplement* on account of his pacifist views. Derek Savage, a Cambridgeshire man who had been granted exemption, 'could find no suitable permanent job (I was not even acceptable to the sponsors of a scheme to teach beginners the rural art of straw-thatching which I really wanted to learn). I did from time to time get casual work writing out ration books in the Food Office, and sorting letters at Christmas in the Post Office . . .' Cecil Davies featured in a *Daily Express* article about Conscientious Objectors and as a result received a deluge of mail, most of it abusive, including one from someone who had 'cut out his photograph from the paper, wiped their bottom on it, and sent it to him in an envelope'.

Conscientious Objectors were sometimes sacked by their employers when their CO status became known, as Reginald Bottini had been, and the dismissal of Iorwerth Peate from the Folk Studies Department of the National Museum of Wales aroused considerable controversy. The position of local authorities was particularly pertinent since they were spending tax payers' money on employing men who refused to fight for their country. There were reports of citizens refusing to pay their rates until their local council dismissed any COs in its employ, while some women preferred to walk several miles into Northwich in Cheshire to pay their rent rather than hand it to a rent collector who was registered as a CO. On several occasions councils were faced with the threat of strikes by ARP and AFS members who refused to work alongside COs. It was unclear whether it was legal for an employer to dismiss a Conscientious Objector for this fact alone since the right to object was enshrined in law, but though the government urged councils against such action, no sanctions were enforced and in cases where COs sued their employer for wrongful dismissal, the case was invariably rejected. Discussion of what to do with COs raged through council chambers throughout the land and covered the spectrum from the brutal – 'They should be shot at dawn'; 'They are like worms and should be tramped upon'; 'Men who register as Conscientious Objectors should be treated as they are in Germany. They should be put in concentration camps' – to more measured debates about balancing the views of the councillors and members of the public with the good of the community, manpower requirements and the rights of the individual. In the end thirty-one county and city boroughs and nineteen county councils dismissed all Conscientious Objectors; eighteen boroughs and five county councils retained all objectors on full pay; while others took a middle way – giving COs unpaid leave of absence for the duration of the war, or retaining them while reducing their pay to that of a soldier, excluding them from war bonus schemes and putting a bar on promotion.

Teachers posed a particular problem: theirs was a reserved occupation after the age of thirty, and there was a shortage of teachers, but they were in the privileged position of influencing the young. 'What would be thought if a CO were to stand in front of a class of children whose relatives had gone to fight for their King and country?' wondered a member of a Yorkshire education committee as they voted to suspend a teacher without pay.

'As a serving soldier I object to my children going to school . . . at which there are Conscientious Objectors being allowed to teach,' read a letter in a Hertfordshire newspaper. 'Many parents are threatening to take their children away from school unless the teacher is withdrawn.' And Leeds Education Committee dismissed a CO who was a woodwork teacher for refusing to show boys how to make toy models of battleships. In some cases teachers were granted military exemption by the tribunals they appeared before only to be dismissed the next day by their employers. Such opposition was not deflected by the President of the Board of Education's insistence that he had 'no reason to suppose that the teachers concerned would fail to observe the principle, to which the teaching profession itself attaches great importance, that political propaganda should in no circumstances be introduced into schools'. A total of nineteen local authorities sacked their CO teachers, though the government, mindful both of the shortage of teachers and the undesirability of dismissing people for their opinions (after all, atheists and communists taught), urged local education authorities not to undertake such a purge, and the National Union of Teachers did the same – but both were powerless to halt the process if the authority was determined that young minds were at risk.

Not all who were opposed to the war sought exemption from fighting. Ernest Trory had joined the Communist Party in 1931 when he was eighteen. 'We were against the war and we wanted to bring it to an end because it wasn't in the interests of the working classes of either Britain or Germany... but we didn't register as COs. We remembered what Lenin said in the summer of 1915: "Pay no heed to the sentimental whiners who are afraid of war. Too much still remains in the world that must be destroyed with fire and sword for the emancipation of the working classes"... So when we were called up – we didn't rush to volunteer, but when we were called up – we went into the Army and learned how to use rifles and machine guns and how to drive tanks and so on because if we were eventually to stop the war, we might have to use these implements of death and destruction. [When it was my turn] to register at the Labour Exchange the manager asked if I wanted to register as a CO. So I said "Why would you think I wanted to register as a CO?" So he said "Well, I understand that you are against the war etc. and that you might not want to go into the Army." So I said "Well no. I'm not a pacifist, I'm a revolutionary."... And I said that if they wanted to teach me how to use guns, I was more than happy to learn how to use rifles and machine guns. And in any case, if workers are being called up into the Armed Forces, then that's where I want to be...

'I was in the Army approximately 10 months and I made no progress at all. All Communists who had been full time organisers [as Trory had been in Sussex] were discharged from the Army on the same day. Now that's more than coincidence. That's obviously an instruction from above... I was ordered to appear before the colonel or the adjutant. I stood to attention outside his office and was marched in. And the adjutant said "You are being discharged from the Army." And I said "May I know the reason?" He said "I'm not allowed to give it to you. But you are being discharged under sub paragraph" – I can't quote the exact number – "of King's Rules and Regulations". So I said "Well, may I know what the sub paragraph says?" And he reached for a copy and turned it up and said "I don't think you'll learn very much from it, but this is what it says: "This sub paragraph only applies to a soldier who cannot be discharged under any other sub paragraph." He apologised to me for not being able to give me any more information. And I said "When do I leave?" He said "As soon as you can get a suit of civilian clothes sent in." . . . And at the final pay parade, I paraded in civilian clothing and received my final pay packet and a travel warrant to Brighton and I was off. I was given a fortnight's leave and in May 1941 I became a civilian again.' Trory went 'to work for the Road Motor Maintenance Department of Southern Railway which had been bombed out of Battersea and moved to Brighton . . . We had to repair all the road transport connected to the railway, a good deal of which had been through the London Blitz.'

It was the drive for war production that showed that women could be Conscientious Objectors too. Many had been involved in the peace movement since the First World War, and had campaigned, written and lectured on their opposition to war. Among the well known were Vera Brittain, Rose Macaulay, Frances Partridge and Storm Jameson, and there were many less visible but equally active figures who supported and assisted COs, but were not themselves under compulsion to undertake war work and therefore had no formal vector for objection. That changed in 1941. In March all women aged between nineteen and forty were obliged to register at employment exchanges so that the Ministry of Labour could direct those considered suitable into 'essential work'. Under the provisions of the National Service (No 2) Act, which became law on 18 December 1941, unmarried women aged between twenty (reduced to nineteen the following year) and thirty-one were to be called up and given a choice between the women's auxiliary military services – the Auxiliary Territorial Service (ATS), Women's Royal Naval Service (WRNS) or Women's Auxiliary Air Force (WAAF) – Civil Defence, the Land Army or certain specified jobs in industry. The Act gave women the same right as men to register as Conscientious

Objectors and put their case to a tribunal, but no objection was allowed to industrial direction on grounds of conscience, though in practice women were usually successful in avoiding work in munitions factories, for example, if their conscience forbade it. But this did not answer the objections of those who would refuse any work that might release others to serve in the Armed Forces. The conscription of women into the military was a radical step: the first time it had happened in any modern nation, and tribunals were believed to 'wear a velvet glove' when it came to dealing with women COs. But this was not always so and many women found that they seemed to rouse the particular ire of tribunal chairmen. One young woman was told that the logic of her argument was that she should eat nothing and starve herself to death. 'That might be the most useful thing you can do,' the chairman told her. A young Bradford hairdresser who said she objected to taking life was asked by a member of the tribunal whether that included insect life. And when Alice Holmes said that yes it did, her inquisitor expostulated: 'And you a hairdresser!'

During the Second World War 257 women COs were prosecuted for refusing directions to work, and 214 were jailed. The first woman CO to be sent to prison in the Second World War was a twenty-one-year-old housemaid, Constance Bolam, who had been directed to work as a ward maid in her local eye hospital. She refused, arguing that she would not have been compelled to do the work had it not been for the war, and she was opposed both to war and to compulsion. When Miss Bolam refused to pay a 40s fine imposed by the Newcastle-upon-Tyne magistrates in January 1942, she was sent to Durham prison for a month, where she worked in the laundry but declined to knit socks for soldiers in her cell of an evening.

Another woman jailed for her objection to war was Kathleen Derbyshire (later Wigham), born in Blackburn in Lancashire. Both her parents were committed pacifists who had helped Conscientious Objectors in the First World War. 'My father wouldn't allow war toys in the house . . . We took *Peace News* at home and my mother would never let me attend the Empire Day celebrations at school.' Kathleen was 'a pacifist for moral as well as religious reasons and . . . a vegetarian because it's an avoidance of taking animal life unnecessarily'. She left school at fourteen and eventually trained to work with mentally handicapped children. After war broke out, she volunteered to help and advise Conscientious Objectors, and, as a Quaker, was involved in the movement 'to become a friend to German POWs'.

'We were told that women would be called up for industrial conscription . . . And for a long time I had been aware that I would be a Conscientious Objector when the time came for me to register . . . When my turn came I just said "I've come to register as a CO" and the young lady said "I don't know what you mean." And so I said "Well, I have an objection to war." "Oh," she said "but we don't want you to go to war, you're being directed to do hospital work." So I said "Yes, but this is only to relieve someone else to do war work and I object to that." Well she couldn't cope with that so she pressed a bell and after a while a gentleman came and took me to a little room . . , and he said "Oh you're one of those are you. We didn't expect a woman. We've had a lot of men, but we didn't expect a woman." So I said "Well I may be the first but there'll be more to follow!"

'I was called to face the industrial tribunal . . . with five people sitting round a table all of whom tried very hard to persuade me that my duty was to do hospital work. I found it very hard to get through to them that I didn't object to doing domestic work in a hospital . . . but I objected to the idea that it was releasing people to do military service. Then I was asked if I had a ration book and I said yes and they [said] "Well why do you think you've a right to a ration book if you're not prepared to do industrial service?" I replied that a ration book is essential to life and I wanted to live and that's the reason why I objected to war because I want to live and I want other people to live . . . Then they asked about gas masks and I said that I hadn't got a gas mask, I'd refused to have one. I wasn't prepared to go into a factory to make them so I didn't feel I had the right to wear one . . . They took a lot of notes . . . then they said "If you refuse to do war work do you know what the consequences are?" "Yes it would probably be imprisonment." They seemed rather surprised by that and said first it would be a fine and if I refused to pay that I would go to prison . . .

'After a few months I received a summons for £5 for having refused industrial conscription and I was given 10 days to pay. Of course I did nothing, didn't reply or anything and then after 10 days I received a second summons asking me to appear before the Court at the Session

House . . . in Blackburn . . . I gave my reasons and they actually did their best to persuade me to pay the fine. They said "We don't want to send people like you to prison. Can you not pay the fine?" And I said I *could* pay but I wasn't prepared to . . .

'On 2 July 1942 I was summoned to the Session House again . . . and the chairman scratched his head and said "Well, there's nothing more we can do but send you to prison. We are giving you the shortest possible sentence that we can possibly give anyone. We hope that this will help you change your mind. 14 days in Strangeways [Manchester]. If at any time during your sentence you do change your mind, all you have to do is let the governess know that you'll pay your fine and you'll be released immediately." They were almost begging me to pay the fine. However I managed to assure them that I knew what I was letting myself in for and I was told to stand down and a prison wardress came and took me down to the cells.

'. . . I felt very calm. I felt I was being true to my father and I knew it was the right thing to do. And I thought I knew what to expect after my work with the Blackburn Pacifist Fellowship . . . but it was far harder than I had imagined . . . I had been told that I should tell the prison authorities that I was a CO so I told [the warden] and she said "You'll be treated like all the others here. You haven't come to a convalescent home . . ."

'At night when you'd finished work – mine was sewing mail bags – you came back at 4 o'clock for tea and at 8 o'clock it was lights out so then there was nothing to do but lie down whether you could sleep or not . . . and of course everything was in darkness because of the blackout. And then the sirens would start to go and you'd hear the gunfire and the sound of bombs dropping and you'd hear women shouting "Let me out, let me out, take us to the air raid shelters." And nothing happened . . . no one even saying "shut up!" nothing at all so you got the impression that the officers and wardresses must have gone to the shelters and we prisoners were just left in our cells. I don't know if that was true, but that's how it felt. I was told the next morning that they didn't evacuate the building unless a bomb was very close, otherwise we were just left all night hearing bombs fall and knowing you were trapped, locked in your cell unable to get out and it was sheer mental torture when the raids were on . . .' In fact two male Conscientious Objectors were killed in their cells when Walton Gaol in Liverpool received a direct hit in May 1941.

'I didn't have any hostility from the other prisoners . . . The only hostility I encountered was from the warden. She'd say things like "Our men are fighting for sluts like you. Fold your blankets and carry them down to the laundry. I don't know what the country would do if there were many more like you. If I had my way you'd certainly be hanging from the end of a rope." And when she took me to the prison hospital she said "She's one of those bloody conchies." But the matron could see I'd had enough. She . . . set me to work mending nurses' uniforms and helping her push the trolley of medicines round the wards . . .'

After her release Kathleen Derbyshire was called before the tribunal again and she was again interrogated on her views: ' "Supposing you came home from work and there was a German pointing a gun at your mother's chest, what would you do?" And I just kept answering "I wouldn't have a gun" . . . We weren't getting anywhere and finally a member said "You are an ostrich with its head in the sand." ' Kathleen's witness told the tribunal about her work in the Peace Movement: ' "This young lady with several others gives a portion of her rations every week to a communal box and after a week that box is taken to an Old People's home and the food is distributed" . . . We'd done that all through the war . . . and he told them that I'd already served a prison sentence . . . The panel retired to consider their verdict and within 20 minutes they were back and it wasn't as bad as I'd expected. The chairman . . . said they felt that I was sincere in my views and was very conscientious and they'd had testimonials from various people and I had this family background of pacifism that they'd taken into consideration . . . and they had decided that it was a waste of time to give me any industrial work that would help the war effort because I was going to be obstinate and refuse to do anything . . . in the end they said "unconditional exemption from war work of any description". I was free. And that really was a triumph you might say. I was very, very pleased.'

Kathleen Derbyshire returned to Blackburn and continued working in a health-food shop, but in her free time she helped in a home where evacuees 'who were bed wetters or from large families that didn't want to be broken up were taken. They were problem children, very noisy and unruly, about 16 or 20 – a really scruffy lot. They had come from the poor parts of London, the Camden area, Euston and King's Cross . . .

'I do think that COs suffered in the Second World War. Many of them lost their jobs and found it hard to get employment. They had to find sympathetic employers. And COs did encounter hostility. There was a girl I was at school with who didn't agree with me and sometimes I would be walking past her house and if she saw me she'd go and get a bucket and swill down the pavement where I'd just walked as if the paving stones were dirty because I'd walked across them. And sometimes I felt perhaps I should walk in the gutter to save her the trouble.'

6

THE MINISTRY OF AGGRAVATION AND MYSTERIES

LIMITED ENGAGEMENT.
FULL LENGTH. NOTHING CUT BUT THE PRICE

DAVID O. SELZNICK'S
production of
MARGARET MITCHELL'S
Story of the Old South

GONE WITH THE WIND

IN TECHNICOLOR, starring
CLARK GABLE

A long face never won a war. In the present circumstances many people are asking, ought we to celebrate Christmas at all? There should be no doubt that this is the very year when we should think, not less, but more about Christmas, not only as an escape from the horrors of the war, but as a remembrance of nobler ideals . . . in being cheerful and gay we are paying our tribute to life itself, which must go on, and after all is what man is fighting for . . .

PICTURE POST, 10 DECEMBER 1939

BEING 'CHEERFUL AND GAY' had to be worked at in those first few weeks of the war. And there wasn't much on offer to help. With theatres and cinemas dark, and almost all places of sport and entertainment closed down as an immediate response to the declaration of war (with the blackout discouraging anyone to venture far after sunset anyway) and the plug pulled on television, the wireless was the main source of entertainment in the autumn of 1939 – though 'entertainment' was an optimistic description.

After 1 September, when the BBC had reduced its output to a single channel, the Home Service, almost all that could be heard by a listening public of 34 million were announcements about the war interspersed with recorded music. The most frequent sound transmitted over the air seemed to be Sandy MacPherson interminably playing the BBC Theatre Organ. A total of forty-five programmes featuring the Scotsman playing 'familiar and well-loved melodies' were broadcast in the first fortnight of the war, to the intense annoyance of many listeners left with only *Children's Hour* and the odd talk to leaven the unremitting diet of music and war bulletins, and endless government announcements and fussy instructions that were to earn the wartime BBC the unaffectionate – and persistent – sobriquet 'Auntie'. Things gradually began to improve – slightly. *For Amusement Only*, evoking a First World War concert party with jokes about the Nazis ('It's so quiet you can hear a Ribbentrop') and Liverpool-born music-hall veteran Tommy Handley singing 'Who Is This Man Who Looks Like Charlie Chaplin?' – the first song about Hitler ever broadcast by the BBC – was transmitted on 6 September. The next day schools broadcasts were resumed and drama started to reappear in the schedules, and by the third week of the war daily news bulletins were reduced to six, and public announcements were grouped together in two slots rather than being broadcast throughout the evening as had been the case at first.

Part of the problem was that though it was obvious that the BBC was going to be a vital cog in the war machine, it was not clear exactly how. *The Listener* magazine felt it knew. 'The first and most obvious function of broadcasting . . . is the dissemination of news, of pronouncements by our leaders, and of instructions to citizens on the many problems that confront them . . . But . . . the maintenance of morale is of the first importance . . . and if a dose of light entertainment helps us to forget our troubles even momentarily, there is no need to begrudge ourselves that pleasure: refreshment of this kind strengthens us to face the grimmer tasks . . .'

This breezy formula in fact posed a formidable challenge. With its dominant position in the life of the wartime nation, the BBC had the task of fostering national unity and morale, yet maintaining objectivity;

of being a trustworthy vector of information without making the public feel it was being drip-fed government propaganda; of explaining without patronising; of entertaining hugely diverse audiences in conditions that were as yet unknown. On the whole, and with reservations, the Corporation did manage to achieve remarkable success 'in maintaining national unity and national morale during a time of unparalleled difficulty'. But in the early days of the war the BBC's 'steady hand on the tiller' appeared to be a dead hand – and the government's dead hand at that.

Like the rest of the country, the BBC had been expecting a different sort of war, and when air raids didn't happen – for which essential public information and soothing music might have been the appropriate response – the Corporation was much criticised for its contribution to putting the bore into Bore War. 'The BBC monotonously repeated news which was in the morning papers and which it had itself repeated an hour earlier. While each edition of the papers repeated what had already been heard on the wireless,' the *New Statesman* complained. By the beginning of October it was worse: 35 per cent of the public were fed up with the BBC and 10 per cent had stopped listening at all, while the press used words like 'puerile', 'funereal', 'travesty', 'amateurish' and ' a paucity of ideas' to describe the wireless output.

People needed entertaining, and they also needed to know what was going on, and if the BBC was not prepared to tell them then it seemed that there were others who would. Most British households were able pick up a number of English-language propaganda stations from Germany, both official stations and the secret network of stations code-named 'Concordia'. This network first came on air in spring 1940, purporting to represent disaffected Britons hostile to their country being at war with Germany and to be broadcasting from within Britain itself. These 'black propaganda' stations included the New British Broadcasting Station (NBBS), by far the largest, which usually signed off with the British national anthem; the demotic Workers' Challenge station, appealing to a downtrodden British working class who were being sacrificed in an unwinnable war in the interests of capitalism; the anti-Semitic Radio National; the 'pacifist' Christian Peace Movement; and the 'Scottish nationalist' Radio Caledonia which used 'Auld Lang Syne' as its signature tune. But the most famous – and most listened to –

German station was Radio Hamburg, on which could be heard the voice of 'Lord Haw Haw', a name picked up from Jonah Barrington's column in the *Daily Express*: 'The gent ... speaks English of the haw-haw, dammit-get-out-of-my-way variety, and his strong suit is gentlemanly indignation.' The name was eventually attached to the broadcaster William Joyce, a naturalised US citizen who had been brought up in Ireland, had been Propaganda Director and then Deputy Leader of Oswald Mosley's British Union of Fascists and who had fled to Berlin a week before the outbreak of war.

Joyce started broadcasting on 11 September 1939 and his 'Jairmany calling' programme could be heard until his drunken signing off as Berlin fell in May 1945. His broadcasts were not mentioned in the *Radio Times*, but they were listed in *The Times*. By January 1940, 30 per cent of the population of Britain was reported to tune in regularly, and of the 16 million who listened to the main BBC news bulletin at nine o'clock, 7 million turned over to Radio Hamburg straight afterwards. Radio critics might name him 'the best entertainment in the blackout', and comedians devise ditties about 'Lord Haw Haw, the Humbug of Hamburg, the Comic of Eau de Cologne', but the Ministry of Information, responsible for the nation's morale as well as the information it received – or was prevented from receiving – was alarmed, and urgently discussed how to counteract the 'insidious appeal' of Lord Haw Haw with his talk of 'the hyenas of international capitalism' and the decadence of the English upper classes, his frequent mention of Britain's 1.5 million unemployed, his criticism of the government's social policy and how he looked forward to a time 'when the working men of England could exercise a formidable opinion'. His broadcasts often revealed startling knowledge of local conditions (such as the apocryphal story of knowing that a particular town-hall clock was so many minutes slow), and the way listeners repeated and embroidered these reports gave the impression that German spies were everywhere. 'I learn some things from Hamburg before our people tell us,' a retired Indian Army officer from Bournemouth noted.

At first the BBC chose to ignore Haw Haw's barbs and inflated claims of German successes and British reverses. Instead the popular programme *Band Waggon*, with regulars Richard 'Stinker' Murdoch and Arthur Askey, and occasional guest appearances by such stars as George

Formby, was moved to the same time as Lord Haw Haw's broadcasts were transmitted, as 'spoilers'. But in February 1940 the BBC started to acknowledge Haw Haw's existence on air, pointing out that listening was unpatriotic and played into the hands of Joseph Goebbels, Hitler's Propaganda Minister. Topical comment programmes such as *Once a Week* with the barrister Norman Birkett, and the *Postscript* series that followed the nine o'clock news every Sunday evening, were introduced to suggest that audiences might be mature people who could be trusted with serious reflection and informed criticism. *Postscript* did not catch the public imagination until the writer J. B. Priestley took over in the week of the evacuations from Dunkirk in June 1940, by which time the novelty value of Lord Haw Haw's broadcasts had begun to wear off as it was increasingly obvious that the 'news' he was giving was hardly the inside story it purported to be. With the invasion of Holland and Belgium in May 1940, Joyce's potency waned dramatically since the apathy about when the war was going to 'happen' had been definitively answered, and Lord Haw Haw's direct appeals to the British to surrender to the Nazis for their own good seemed contemptible. After the war William Joyce would be charged with treason, found guilty and hanged.

But when it came to the role of the wireless in 'keeping spirits up' in wartime rather than informing the public, there proved to be no simple formula for this either, and in the circumstances of the Phoney War too much resolute patriotic cheerfulness grated. The almost war-long success of *It's That Man Again* – introduced in September 1939, its title taken from a *Daily Express* headline referring to Hitler, and later universally known by its acronym *ITMA* – lay in its quick humour and its irreverent parody of officialdom and proliferating bureaucracy. Tommy Handley was the Minister of Aggravation and Mysteries housed in the Office of Twerps, who had 'the power to confiscate, complicate and commandeer'. New characters were regularly introduced: the German spy, Funf, played by Jack Train speaking into a glass tumbler; the office cleaner, Mrs Tickle (who would later be replaced by Mrs Mopp); Mona Lott; Sir Short Supply; Ali Oop, the saucy postcard vendor; Claude and Cecil; and the bibulous Colonel Chinstrap. The fast-paced, engagingly puerile, highly topical, excruciatingly punning programme, spiced with sexual innuendo, was soon requisite listening for most of the nation – by 1944, 16 million regularly tuned in to *ITMA*. Tom Harrisson, one of the founders of Mass-Observation, travelling by train from Streatham in south London in February 1940, noted that at two stations the porter greeted the guard with the words, 'It's that man again' – and the programme introduced a panoply of catchphrases into the lexicon of wartime, such as Mrs Mopp's 'Can I do you now, Sir?'; 'Ta-ta for now' (or 'TTFN'); 'This is Funf speaking'; Ali Oop's 'I go – I come back'; Colonel Chinstrap's 'I don't mind if I do'; and, particularly useful in the blackout, or among bomber pilots waiting to drop their loads, 'After you, Claude'. 'No, after *you* Cecil'.

'One of the surprises of wartime radio,' wrote the producer of the *Brains Trust* about his programme which went on air for the first time on 1 January 1941, 'is that five men discussing philosophy, art and science should have a regular audience of ten million listeners' – which was as many as the most popular variety shows. Originally the scientist was Julian Huxley, the philosopher was C. E. M. Joad, and the third regular panellist was Paymaster Commander A. B. Campbell, a wacky seafarer who claimed not only to be able to sleep with his eyes open, but also to have 'married a South Sea Island girl by eating some fish with her'. The *Brains Trust* had its copyable catchphrases too. Campbell tended to preface his answers with 'When I was in Patagonia . . .' (or some such far-flung place); for Joad it was 'It depends what you mean by. . .' Two different distinguished guests joined the regular panellists each week – the conductor Malcolm Sargent proved a particular success, as did the West Indian cricketer Learie Constantine – and, unusually, most weeks one of the guest panellists was a woman. Although none of the panellists had been able to name the seven wonders of the world in the first programme, week after week various 'brains' debated questions chosen from some 3,000 sent in by listeners (including, it was rumoured, members of the royal family), such as 'Is Vera Lynn harmful to morale?', 'What is democracy?', 'Why can you tickle other people and not yourself?', 'What is the point of learning algebra?' and 'Why do flies land upside-down on the ceiling? (that one ran and ran). There were inevitably complaints about the 'pinko' nature of panellists and their obsession with social questions, while the Church complained that too many agnostic views were heard, and increasingly restraints were imposed: MPs were banned from appearing, contentious political questions were weeded out, and there were complaints that BBC censorship was turning a lively and sometimes heated search for enlightenment 'into a polite parlour game'.

It was very soon clear that in wartime a single radio station was not enough for a nation with few distractions. There was also the question of how to entertain the troops in France, for whom time hung heavy that siege winter of 1939–40, as it did for British servicemen at home, particularly since the popular English-language Continental stations, Radio Luxembourg and Radio Normandie, had shut down on the outbreak of war. Overriding security objections from the Air Ministry, a second BBC service started transmitting on 7 January 1940, and within ten days the Forces Programme, regarded at first as a temporary wartime expedient, was broadcasting twelve hours a day. Its listeners were not intended to be only servicemen – and they weren't. The BBC was surprised to find that it had a large audience among working-class housewives, a group they had not paid much attention to in the pre-war years, and with its foregrounding of dance music and variety shows the Forces Programme was also particularly popular with the young. It must have seemed a staging post on the road to perdition as Reith's educative mission for the BBC – 'He who prides himself on giving what he thinks the public wants is often creating a fictitious demand for lower standards which he will then satisfy' – was traduced. The new programme was specifically designed to give servicemen and women 'what they wanted' appropriate to the conditions in which they listened, which was likely to mean that they had to dip in and out of programmes, and use the wireless as background ('tap listening' as it was disparagingly called) to their wartime activities. The Forces Programme would be '90 per cent light' since 'if we give them serious music, long plays, or peacetime programme talks, they will not listen' – though one of its most popular items turned out to be the *Brains Trust* which was then repeated on the Home Service on a Sunday afternoon.

The outbreak of war had not only narrowed the choices of wartime couch potatoes, but 'All Sport Brought to a Halt. Restart When Safe for Crowds' read a *Daily Mail* headline on 4 September 1939. Football stadiums had been closed and when they reopened at the end of September crowds were restricted to 8,000 in evacuation areas and 15,000 elsewhere, and authorisation from the police was required for every match. The Football League was reorganised to cut down on travelling, and many of the players were called up. Matt Busby, then a Liverpool player, passed out as Sergeant Major Instructor for the Army and in 1944 was put in charge of the British Army football team that was sent to raise the morale of the Allied troops in Italy. Stanley Matthews spent most of his war in Blackpool as a physical instructor with the RAF and kept playing football, while several other players including the legendary soccer inside forward Raich Carter, managed to play for local teams near the RAF camps where they were stationed.

Some clubs benefited greatly from wartime conscription. Third Division Aldershot, for example, frequently fielded six or seven international players because of the club's proximity to the Army training centre. Others did not: one Saturday, Brighton played a match against Norwich City with five of its regular players, two Norwich reserves and five soldiers recruited from the crowd. The result was Brighton and Hove Albion 0 – Norwich City 18.

Gradually the restriction on the number of spectators at matches was eased, and by 1943 attendances had picked up again, though a number of grounds had been requisitioned: the Arsenal ground became a concrete-walled ARP centre (and the 'Gunners', the leading English club in the 1930s, who lost forty-two of their forty-four players to the Forces, were obliged to move in with their London neighbour and arch rival, Spurs). One of Aston Villa's stands was taken over as an air-raid shelter; Swindon lost its ground to a POW camp; and Norwich City was obliged to relinquish its car park for a gun emplacement site for the Home Guard.

Football pools, which, it was estimated, represented a modest weekly flutter for half the adult population, escaped from its wartime ban on 7 October 1939. The refusal of the GPO to deliver the bulky postal coupons in wartime, however, led the various pools promoters to link forces to produce Unity Pools coupons. These appeared in newspapers with injunctions to the punters 'not to write in blotty ink' as they filled them in, and to increase the network of agencies in order to bypass the postal services where possible.

Greyhound racing survived by moving its meetings to the afternoon – though these were soon restricted to Saturday afternoons lest mid-week meetings proved too tempting to war workers, and the tote was discontinued. Horse racing suffered from petrol rationing which curtailed travelling to race meetings, from the requisitioning of courses – Aintree was taken over for the internment of so-called enemy aliens, Epsom was acquired by the Army and the Derby moved to Newmarket – and from a surfeit of wartime morality about gambling. The golf club that had been Edward VIII's favourite, the Wentworth near Virginia Water in Surrey, served as a billet for Conscientious Objectors who were building 'large underground offices intended for use if Whitehall were abandoned' there, and elsewhere golfers might have to negotiate newly dug allotments and trenches, and eventually bomb craters, but many courses continued to offer a round of sorts – providing players could find the petrol to drive out to them. Tennis, as a spectator sport, was severely limited – a barrage balloon centre was located at the Queens Club, and Wimbledon provided the Home Guard with somewhere flat to drill, while a donkey grazed on the tea lawn. But eight grass courts were kept going, though the balls were reconditioned, the nets mended with string and in 1941 Centre Court was pitted with bomb debris. On the whole, cricket managed just about to survive. It too lost players to the Forces and grounds to the exigencies of war – the Oval was scheduled as a POW camp – and most matches were one-day events. But even though the RAF took over the practice ground and the pavilion at Lord's, the game carried on there in attenuated form. 'I had the feeling,' said Sir Pelham 'Plum' Warner, the doyen of English cricket, 'that if Goebbels had been able to broadcast that war had stopped cricket at Lord's, it would have been valuable propaganda for the Germans.' By 1941 the turnstiles were admitting 90,000 plus an uncounted number of servicemen in uniform, who could get in for free.

Throughout the war, spectator sports were to be a battleground of old attitudes in khaki disguise. Politicians such as successive Home Secretaries Sir John Anderson and Herbert Morrison argued that sports were morale-building, an important safety valve in dark times, while Sir Stafford Cripps exemplified the opposition view. He had been particularly incensed by a boxing match at the Albert Hall in February 1942 that drew 4,500 spectators and argued that since it could not be 'business as usual' in wartime, nor should it be 'pleasure as usual', that sports such as 'dog racing and boxing displays' offended the 'solid and serious intention of this country to achieve victory'. This, however, was to disregard the extent to which many wartime charities benefited from sporting events: the Red Cross, for example, was in receipt of donations of £50,000 from greyhound racing by 1943. And when England beat Scotland 3–0 at Wembley in January 1942, the turnstile takings were sent to Mrs Churchill's Aid-to-Russia fund.

Within little more than a month after the outbreak of war, half a dozen West End theatres had reopened – though most performances were matinees, a number of evening performances started at six o'clock so that people could get home before the blackout, and 'evening dress, the mark of bourgeois respectability, disappeared completely from the stalls and dress circle'. Even so, there were problems throughout the war with audiences reluctant to travel into town during raids. Among the theatres that opened their doors was the Windmill with its 'non-stop revue' of scantily dressed girls and its boast 'We Never Close' – which it never did throughout the Blitz.

Me and My Girl, which featured 'Doing the Lambeth Walk' and had already chalked up 1,062 pre-war performances, was one of the first shows to reopen, and the Crazy Gang – an ensemble of zany comedians including Bud Flanagan and Chesney Allen with the comic juggler 'Monsewer' Eddie Grey, whose routines invariably included much custard-pie throwing – came back too. *Sandbag Follies*, a political revue written and produced within forty-eight hours of the outbreak of war packed them into the Unity Theatre, but Churchill's son-in-law Vic Oliver was out of a job when *Black and Blue* closed. He took what he could find in the provinces until he was recalled to appear in the spectacular revue *Black Velvet* at the Hippodrome which opened in 1941.

Outside the West End, Oscar Wilde's *The Importance of Being Earnest* opened at the Golders Green Hippodrome with a cast that included John Gielgud, Edith Evans, Peggy Ashcroft and Jack Hawkins. Gielgud, carrying a gas mask as did his fellow actors, said how 'delighted' they all were to be back at work, but warned, 'it won't last long for some of us. Jack Hawkins and I are waiting to be called up,' though he never was. In recognition of the morale boost that the theatre gave, actors could claim exemption from conscription providing they were not out of work for more than two weeks at a time, though not all took advantage of this concession. Laurence Olivier, back in Britain, and Ralph Richardson both joined the Royal Naval Volunteer Reserves.

Theatre audiences seemed not to want to see the war on stage. Terence Rattigan's *Flare Path*, set in a Lincolnshire hotel and featuring the wives of bomber crews waiting for their husbands' return from a raid, proved the exception, running for eighteen months after it opened in August 1942. But in general American musicals such as Cole Porter's *Something for the Boys* and *Dubarry Was a Lady*, and comedies such as Noël Coward's *Blithe Spirit* and Rattigan's *While the Sun Shines*, were what wartime audiences flocked to as the all-too-real spectacle of war played in the surrounding streets.

Entertaining the troops in theatres of war all over the world counted as 'war service'; and here the Entertainment National Service Association (ENSA) offered a lifeline to many entertainers. Set up by the theatre producer Basil Dean, ENSA also served the civilian population, who, it was apparent to Dean, would 'require morale boosters quite as much, if not more, than the troops'; and at the time of the London Blitz it would 'provid[e] entertainment of every size and description from symphony concerts . . . plays, revues, concert parties, down to one-and two-man units with "squeeze boxes" entertaining men and women on lonely gun sites.'

Dean was anxious that ENSA should not be regarded as 'a giant foxhole' for those who wanted to evade active service. But with demands on it to brighten up the lunch hours of war-production workers as well as entertain the troops at home and abroad, the available talent had to be stretched thin, and ENSA became known to some as 'Every Night Something Awful' – as what seemed like near-amateur performers, desperate for a six-week engagement that would keep them out of the Forces, strove to plug the gaps. A factory worker once leapt on to the table at the end of an ENSA concert to demand 'three cheers for the audience' for sitting through the show. Nevertheless, several top-rating popular performers like the ukulele-strumming George Formby and 'Our Gracie' Fields from Rochdale were ENSA stars, while others – Terry-Thomas and Tony Hancock included – were 'discovered' in ENSA shows.

As well as concert parties and variety shows, in October 1940 ENSA started to provide what Basil Dean called 'good music parties' which he hoped would 'meet the spiritual challenge of the hour' in factories. Unfortunately these could be rather blush-making occasions with a string quartet scraping away in a factory canteen at lunchtime as workers clattered plates and cutlery – and barracked. But they could also be the much more successful evening concerts held in halls or cathedrals for which local factory workers paid a shilling to hear such orchestras as the Hallé conducted by Sir John Barbirolli, or the London Symphony Orchestra, and listen to music by Beethoven, Rachmaninov, Debussy or Tchaikovsky – though ENSA also experimented with modern compositions by Walton, Bax and Sibelius. While many of the workers were hearing this type of music for the first time, apparently 'they listened with concentrated attention and expressed their appreciation in the most enthusiastic manner'.

'What madness is this?' the *Daily Express* demanded when a government grant of £50,000 to CEMA was announced. 'There is no such a thing as culture in wartime.' CEMA (Council for the Encouragement of Music and the Arts, which after the war would become the Arts Council) was started in December 1939 with a grant from the US-based Pilgrim Trust but by the time the Trust withdrew its subsidy in 1942, it was receiving increasing Treasury backing, to the tune of £100,000 a year and this would rise to £235,000 by 1945. CEMA's original purpose had been to rescue cultural pursuits threatened with extinction during the first winter of the war, disperse the arts – music, drama, painting and design – to the provinces, to Scottish villages and to Welsh mining districts, and encourage 'music-making and play-acting by the people themselves'. It gave money for the Old Vic to send two touring companies on the road, and helped small outfits like the Pilgrim Players, who travelled in two cars to bring religious plays to the people. 'Music Travellers' were sent off to sponsor local music-making groups and revive moribund choirs, and 'Art for the People' toured art exhibitions to enlighten citizens in 'culturally deprived industrial towns like Swindon and Barnsley' and other parts of the country.

Dismissed as 'too 'ighbrow' by Ernest Bevin, the Minister of Labour, in February 1940 CEMA began taking its repertoire of classical music into factories within a fifty-mile radius of London, starting with the

Vauxhall works at Luton where it drew audiences of 3,000 to each concert. By 1944, seventy concerts were being held in factories and thirty in churches and village halls every week under CEMA's auspices.

When the economist John Maynard Keynes – who was 'not a man for wandering minstrels and amateur theatricals' – took over as chairman in 1942, however, he professionalised the Council's enthusiastic endeavours. Insistent that CEMA should be about the arts, not the social services, he accelerated the shift away from participatory local efforts towards high culture, extending its scope to cover ballet and opera. CEMA re-formed ballet companies such as Ballet Jooss, whose founder, Kurt Jooss, had fled Germany when Hitler came to power, the Ballet Rambert and the Carl Rosa Opera Company as part of its programme of taking ballet and opera to those who had probably never seen it before. It guaranteed national symphony orchestras against loss, subsidised provincial theatres – even buying a lease on the Theatre Royal Bristol to stop it being turned into a warehouse, and reopening it in May 1943 with Sybil Thorndike in *She Stoops to Conquer*, the play that had been performed when the theatre first opened in 1776. Keynes was also determined to restore wartime London as 'a great artistic metropolis' rather than specifically concentrating on out-of-London culture, and so underwrote theatre seasons in the capital – but cut the budget of Art for the People and that of the Music Travellers too, leaving one of the Travellers to fume about having 'to refuse people we have taught to ask, break promises wholesale, with our dreams of taking music to our whole region shattered'.

The entire corps de ballet at Sadler's Wells was called up, and during the Blitz Finsbury Borough Council requisitioned their theatre to house people who had been bombed out. Nevertheless, the company rallied and toured the country with two pianos instead of an orchestra, and managed jetés and pliés on the concrete floors of factory canteens and Army barracks.

The Sadler's Wells' opera company did the same, touring with English-language productions such as *La Traviata* and *The Marriage of Figaro*, which boasted a cast of twenty-six, an 'orchestra of four and a decor consisting of two chairs and a sofa'. The Royal Opera House in Covent Garden did not rise to the challenge so well. While Sadler's Wells' productions used British singers, the outbreak of hostilities meant that operatic divas required for their Italian- and German-language productions were not able to travel. Instead the Opera House became a dance hall, popular with servicemen and women, factory and shop workers. As tangos and foxtrots replaced arias and overtures, the transformation seemed to exemplify the assertion of the *Brains Trust* panellist C. E. M. Joad that 'the distinctive cultural expression of English genius during the years 1939 to 1941 . . . is light music'.

At the end of the First World War, the first of the great *palais de danses* had opened in Hammersmith in west London. By the outbreak of war there were dance halls in most British towns and cities. Some, such as the Astoria in central London and the Locarno in Streatham to the south, were glittering palaces, part of an industry that attracted more than 10 million people a year on to the floor. During the war dance halls attracted even larger numbers – 10,000 a week might pack into one of the huge Mecca halls and several ran four separate sessions a day. When servicemen and women got forty-eight hours leave, many gravitated to dance halls to conga and rhumba, join in the hokey-cokey and 'Hands, Knees and Boomps-a-Daisy', as well as to take their partners for a tango, foxtrot, waltz and other traditional ballroom dances. Uniformed members of the Forces were usually admitted for half price – and dancing shoes were provided in the larger establishments so the soldiers did not damage the highly sprung dance floors with their hobnailed boots.

Bands led by Joe Loss, Lew Stone, Harry Roy and Geraldo (Gerald Bright) had begun to take over in the dance halls from the highly polished 1930s bands whose repertoires had largely consisted of foxtrots and 'novelty numbers' – though Victor Sylvester with his 'strict tempo' music retained his popularity well into the war. British service bands such as the RAF Dance Orchestra – better known as the Squadronnaires – the RAF's Sky Rocket, the Royal Army Ordnance Corps' Blue Rockets and the Royal Navy's Blue Marines enjoyed an enthusiastic following, as did all-girl bands such as Josephine Bradley's and Ivy Benson's. The American soldiers and airmen arriving in 1942 brought the music of Tommy Dorsey, Artie Shaw and Benny Goodman, the 'King of Swing'. The most popular of all, Glenn Miller's United States Army Airforce

Band, took as its motto 'It don't mean a thing if it ain't got that swing' from Duke Ellington, and gave some 800 performances at US Army and Air Force bases and halls throughout the country. Miller's signature tune 'Moonlight Serenade' could pack out an aircraft hangar and was guaranteed to bring tears to most GIs' eyes – his success galvanised British bands into turning to swing, too.

Throughout the war lyrics were written, or adapted, to fit the events – or the mood – of the time: 200,000 copies of the sheet music of 'There'll Always Be an England' sold in the first two months of the war; Flanagan and Allen customised Noel Gay's 1939 number 'Run, Rabbit, Run' to 'Run, Adolf, run, Adolf, run, run, run/Look what you've been gone and done, done, done'. 'We're Gonna Hang Out the Washing on the Siegfried Line', which sounded like something straight out of the First World War, was an early runaway success, as were the many songs of wartime separation such as 'Wish Me Good Luck As You Wave Me Goodbye'. As conscripts put on their unfamiliar khaki uniforms, 'Kiss Me Goodnight Sergeant Major' reminded everyone of the aching gulf between home and army life – as later did Irving Berlin's 'This is the Army, Mr Jones'. Vera Lynn may have been (some of) the 'Forces' Favourite' with 'We'll Meet Again' and 'The White Cliffs of Dover', but the soldier's song of the war was 'Lilli Marlene', a First World War German poem set to music that Rommel's Afrika Korps sang in the Western Desert. An English version was commissioned and recorded by Vera Lynn and Anne Shelton in Britain and Marlene Dietrich in the US, but the troops continued to customise their own endlessly imaginative (and mostly bawdy) versions that somehow fitted the mood and the moment even better.

'Goodnight Children, Everywhere' sung by Gracie Fields, its title taken from the sign-off of 'Uncle Mac' (Derek McCullough) on the BBC *Children's Hour* programme, sent a message to all evacuated children: 'Your mummy thinks of you tonight.' 'Blackout' songs included 'They Can't Black Out the Moon', and a verse was added to the already popular 'Lambeth Walk' – 'Down the inky avenue . . .' During the Blitz as London burned, amazingly 'I Don't Want to Set the World on Fire' ('I just want to start a flame in your heart') proved a hit, as did – more understandably – 'When They Sound the Last All Clear'. American GIs brought with them such hits as 'Chattanooga

Choo Choo', 'Ma, I Miss Your Apple Pie' and, the most famous of all, the Andrews Sisters' recording of 'Don't Sit Under the Apple Tree' ('With anyone else but me'). 'Shine on, Victory Moon' was the song of the V-1 bombs in 1944, and when it began to look as if the war really was coming to an end, the songs that caught the moment included 'I'm Going to Get Lit Up When the Lights Go on in London'; Ivor Novello's celebration of when you come home again, 'We'll Gather Lilacs'; and 'Sing Me a Song of Tomorrow Today'. For the GIs over in Britain the coming of peace meant 'Don't Fence Me In', and Glenn Miller's version of the American Civil War march 'When Johnny Comes Marching Home' – but Miller, whose music had become the soundtrack for the war, did not get to march home. His plane was lost over the English Channel in December 1944.

'A masterstroke of unimaginative stupidity,' fumed George Bernard Shaw, the octogenarian playwright, in a letter to *The Times* when he heard of the closure of cinemas on the outbreak of war. 'We have hundreds of thousands of evacuated children to be kept out of mischief and traffic dangers. Are there to be no pictures for them? ... What agent of Chancellor Hitler is it who has suggested that we should all cower in darkness and terror for the duration?' In the event, the closure of cinemas was short-lived. Those in so-called safe (or reception) areas were permitted to reopen on 11 September, and four days later cinemas in evacuation areas were allowed to open until 10 p.m. with the exception of London's West End, where cinemas had to close at 6 p.m. since they were considered to be particularly vulnerable to air attack – but that stricture was lifted on 4 November.

'Going to the pictures' had been a hugely important part of people's lives: in the 1930s, between 18 and 19 million cinema tickets were sold every week, and by 1945 the figure had reached 30 million. Probably most of those under forty went to the cinema at least once a week and many went more often. Many 'picture palaces' catered for very large audiences. The Bolton Odeon, for example, which opened its doors in 1937, could seat 2,534 with continuous showings on weekdays and three on Saturdays. The larger cinemas had bars and restaurants attached, and the most modest 'flea pit' invariably had shows for children on Saturday mornings.

The war did not portend well for the British film industry: many actors, directors, producers and technicians were liable for call-up and the government requisitioned acres of studio space for storage and war production. An entertainment tax was always attractive to a Chancellor of the Exchequer who needed to raise wartime revenue, and this was increased three times during the war, with the result that cinema seat prices rose (more than theatre seat prices). Nevertheless the war proved to be glory days for British cinema both in terms of growing audiences once most of the 4,800 cinemas throughout the country had reopened and in the quality of many of the films made. It was as if, wrote the critic Dilys Powell, 'it took a war to compel the British to look at themselves and find themselves interesting'. From a British cinema with 'no tradition' came a number of distinguished films concentrating on Britain's wartime experiences that can still be regarded today as masterpieces, including Carol Reed's *The Way Ahead*; Lauder and Gilliat's *Millions Like Us*; Anthony Asquith's *The Way to the Stars*; three of Powell and Pressburger's films, *49th Parallel, Canterbury Tales* and *The Life and Death of Colonel Blimp*; and the wartime conscription of Shakespeare's history play *Henry V* on to celluloid, starring Laurence Olivier.

Women, 'who form the bulk of the cinema-going public', tended to object to war films, certainly until 1942 when the war seemed at last to be going Britain's way. The exception was Alexander Korda's *The Lion Has Wings*, a rather obvious piece of propaganda about the superiority of the RAF intended 'to reassure the British public they weren't going to be blown to pieces in five minutes: the Royal Air Force would prevent it'. It was one of the top three box-office draws of 1939 – though there were reports that it was being shown in Berlin as a comedy. A very different sort of war film was Charlie Chaplin's first 'talkie', *The Great Dictator*, in which he played two interchangeable roles: a 'bowler-hatted jaunt[y] Jewish barber', and a 'neurotic dictator [with a Hitler moustache] . . . with childlike braggadocio dreams of ruling the world'. The film pulled in record audiences in the desperate days of 1940.

Gone with the Wind, the three-hour-forty-minute-long screen version of Margaret Mitchell's blockbuster romance of the South in the American Civil War starring Vivien Leigh as Scarlett O'Hara and Clark Gable as Rhett Butler, opened in April 1940 and ran all through the Blitz; it was not until a few weeks before D-Day in June 1944 that it was finally taken off. In 1942 –'a year of big audiences and big films' – the British offering, *In Which We Serve*, received accolades (and useful propaganda value) on both sides of the Atlantic and broke box-office records too. The film, based on the torpedoing of HMS *Kelly*, hymned a paean to England: 'This very small island, vastly overcrowded, frequently badly managed, but . . . the best and bravest country in the world.' Noël Coward wrote the script, composed the score, played the role of Mountbatten 'almost as well as Mountbatten played it', and co-directed with the then unknown David Lean. It also starred the relatively unknown John Mills, Bernard Miles, Richard Attenborough and Michael Wilding, with Celia Johnson as one of the 'wives who wait'.

Making films was something that the Ministry of Information (MoI) was charged to do among its several functions of boosting and monitoring morale, producing propaganda and acting as censor. The documentary films it produced were intended, in the words of Sir Kenneth Clark, Director of Home Publicity at the MoI (and later a household name with his 1969 BBC television series *Civilisation* about the world's greatest art), 'to help people to remember government messages by putting them in dramatic form'.

There was already an established documentary film movement in Britain associated particularly with the name of John Grierson, whose GPO Film Unit made the famous *Night Mail* in 1936 with words by W. H. Auden and music by Benjamin Britten. On the outbreak of war Grierson left to run the National Film Board of Canada, but the GPO Unit was renamed the Crown Film Unit and came under the control of the Film Division of the Ministry of Information. In the course of the war, the MoI would be involved in producing 1,887 films as well as approving 3,200 newsreels and 380 feature films. Although it was not responsible for making commercial films, the Ministry's approval was essential when it came to getting finance, distribution, and the exemption of those involved from military service.

At first the unit lacked direction and it was not until April 1940, when Jack Beddington, former publicity director at the petroleum company Shell was appointed director, that things improved and 'the MoI started using film properly as part of the war effort, or to hold a mirror up to the country, to try and articulate some of the things that were happening'.

While newsreels recorded major wartime events, 'they could not record the changing face of the whole country. Fine work was done by the newsreels: many cameramen risked their lives to cover battles on land and sea and in the air, some were killed or wounded . . . [but] the background, as opposed to the foreground, of war could not be dealt with. This was where the documentary producers came in.'

The first of the MoI documentary films was *Westward Ho!*, designed to reassure parents that it was important to evacuate their children. It was followed by eighty-six more such films, some made by the Crown Unit, others by independent production companies, all informing a captive public of what the government wanted it to know about such topics as careless talk, war savings, salvage, digging for victory, the work of the Red Cross, and how to act in the event of an invasion. The films were not universally popular either with the public or with cinema managers, who tended to show them in between programmes as audiences were moving seats, or even as the curtains were closing at the end of a performance. They were also shown by mobile cinema units to factory workers in their lunch hours and to the rural population in village halls. But although historians have found the documentary film movement very revealing of wartime attitudes, there is a 'dearth of information' about what the people who watched them at the time thought of these propaganda films, and how effective they were in raising morale and stiffening wartime resolve.

Among the finest films of the war are the semi-factual documentaries that reconstructed wartime events, using those people who would have been involved rather than professional actors, but with a fictional story line. The enduring gem among the Home Front examples was Humphrey Jennings' ten-minute film *London Can Take It* (1940). It was made to bring home to US audiences, as Ed Murrow's nightly radio broadcasts were doing, how 'the greatest civilian army ever to be assembled' was holding firm in the Blitz. The commentary was growled by the American journalist Quentin Reynolds, who concluded, 'I can assure you that there is no panic, no fear, no despair in London Town . . .' *London Can Take It* was tactfully edited to a five-minute version to show to those who actually were 'taking it', and it always brought a warm response. Jennings' other films were a study of the AFS and the Fire Brigade in the Blitz, *Fires Were Started*; his evocative *Listen to Britain*; and his rather wince-making *A Diary for Timothy* scripted by E. M. Forster. The cumulative effect was awesome: Jennings' films 'decisively shaped and defined the image of Britain at war that was to be circulated round the world and handed on to generations to come'.

Apart from imparting information, such films were one of the ways in which the MoI fulfilled another of its remits, that of sustaining – and monitoring – the morale of the British people in wartime. Morale, 'the woolliest concept of the war', was 'too complex and variable for definition' in the professional opinion of the people-watcher Tom Harrisson, and Nella Last, a Barrow-in-Furness housewife, worried too. 'What *is* "morale" – and have I got any, or how much more could I call on in need, and where does it come from, and what is it composed of?' Stephen Taylor, the Ministry's Director of Home Intelligence, had a go: morale must be 'ultimately measured not by what a person thinks or says, but what he does and how he does it'. From the official perspective low morale in wartime might include 'panic, hysteria, grumbling about those in authority, scapegoating, absenteeism', while 'high morale' was likely to encompass 'cheerfulness, co-operation, high productivity, volunteering'.

This question of morale was in the forefront of government minds throughout the so-called Phoney War, and persisted through times of military defeats and victories, rationing, shortages and the sheer grinding on-and-on-ness of wartime conditions largely because, before it was tested by war, morale had been predicted to be so frail, particularly among the inner-city poor, that the war might be lost for want of it.

Planning for propaganda in war – at home as well as abroad – had started as early as 1935 but by 1939, although Goebbels' Ministry of Propaganda was providing a formidable example of how a totalitarian state was selling the message of Nazism, there was scant interest in the matter from Chamberlain and other high-ranking politicians, and little concrete had been done to prepare for war on the propaganda – or the censorship – front. These were both initially the responsibility of the Ministry of Information, which had eventually been established on the outbreak of war, and which was very soon increasing exponentially with a growing number of academics, lawyers, civil servants and singular souls such as the poet John Betjeman, the man of letters Peter Quennell, the cartoonist and writer Osbert Lancaster, and the film producer Sidney

Bernstein. There were soon 999 of them, including a few women such as E. Arnot Robertson and P. L. Travers (the creator of Mary Poppins), in this old boys' club, while the Ministry's role, and its relation with other government departments, still awaited clarification. The MoI was housed in the neo-brutalist concrete buildings of the Senate House of the University of London, in Bloomsbury, the second tallest building in London when it was built, and said to be constructed to last 500 years. Its first (entirely unsuccessful) director was Lord Macmillan: 'this precise peer and Scottish jurist lives in another (and older) world from the world of vulgar life, the world which calls a cigarette "a fag" '. He was replaced in January 1940 by Lord Reith, formerly of the BBC (known as 'Old Wuthering Heights' to Churchill), who also proved unable to give a clear lead as to how the MoI should be encouraging morale, or to establish satisfactory relations with the press, and in May 1940 he was sacked by Churchill, who brought in Duff Cooper. Cooper found the MoI 'a monster, so large, so voluminous, so amorphous, that no single man could cope with it'. He certainly couldn't, and resigned in June 1941 with relations between the MoI and the press at their nadir. But when Churchill appointed his protégé Brendan Bracken, the Ministry 'became efficient and unobtrusive' – and respected – since Bracken enjoyed excellent relations with the press and was known to be on very close terms with the Prime Minister. Bracken was also contemptuous of efforts to exhort the British public, as his predecessors had done, with posters that talked down to the people by insisting that 'Your courage, Your cheerfulness, Your resolution will bring Us victory' or by inventing a series of irritating characters such as 'Miss Leaky Mouth', 'Miss Teacup Whisper' and 'Mr Glumpot' to warn against 'the dangers of rumour' as they had in July 1940 a year previously.

An obvious player in the morale-measuring business was Mass-Observation (M-O) which had been studying British society since 1937. The gap between the rulers and the ruled, and the failure of the press to bridge that gap, which had been revealed at the time of the abdication of Edward VIII the previous year, had led Charles Madge, a left-leaning poet and frustrated journalist on the *Daily Mirror*, the film-maker Humphrey Jennings, and Tom Harrisson, an erstwhile ornithologist turned anthropologist whose study of cannibals in the New Hebrides, *Savage Civilisation*, was a best seller, to decide that 'an anthropology of our own people', a 'mass science' to find out what 'the millions of people irretrievably involved in public events' really thought, was urgently needed. War made it imperative that the leaders understood the led. M-O (or 'Madge's lab boys') with its directive respondents, report compilers and diarists who included many professionals – barristers, doctors, journalists, vicars, teachers – plus a lot of housewives, keen schoolboys and a covey of Oxbridge (largely) undergraduates, along with other, less subjective, more statistically based, polling organisations, could offer insights into what the 'people' really thought, and thus how they might be expected to behave in what was, as everyone realised, going to be a 'people's war' dependent on the entire population for victory. The government, however, was initially wary about using M-O, in part because it was felt that the idea of an official home-intelligence-gathering organisation might alarm the British people and make them question how different their own government was from the totalitarian Nazi State; in part because in some quarters M-O was regarded as 'communist-dominated' and therefore likely to be actually subversive to morale; and in part because MPs regarded themselves as being perfectly adequate weathervanes of public opinion and did not see the need for this democratic function to be usurped. But it was too useful a resource to waste in wartime, and so M-O was commissioned to provide regular information on various aspects of public morale, and also undertake investigations into specific events such as by-elections and conditions in places that had suffered severe air raids. At first the connection was kept entirely secret and M-O was paid through Secret Service funds.

After some prevarication the government also set up its own Home Intelligence division with Mary Adams, a Cambridge science graduate who had worked as a BBC television producer, appointed in December 1939 to head the division, to supplement the work of Mass-Observation and introduce some 'quantitative' data into M-O's 'qualitative' reports on such things as shelter populations, attitudes to gas-mask carrying, shopping habits and people's reactions to government propaganda. Reports on civilian morale were also gathered from a range of regular sources such as the Ministry's own Regional Information Offices, trade unions, the Federation of British Industry, Chambers of Commerce, Rotary Clubs, schools inspectors and the Workers' Educational Association. In spring 1940 others were added, including surveys undertaken by the British Institute of Public Opinion (under the auspices of the Gallup organisation), replies to questionnaires received by the BBC's Listeners' Research Unit, reports from branch managers of W. H. Smith and of cinema chains, and from officials from the London Passenger Transport Board and those working in Citizens' Advice Bureaux. Chief Constables sent in reports from the duty rooms of police stations, while officials of political parties passed on information and members of voluntary organisations supplied numerous reports on the attitudes of the people with whom they came into contact. A comprehensive fact-finding grid was also thrown over the population by reports from Postal and Telegraph Censorship, an organisation with a staff of nearly 10,500 by 1941, whose primary function was the censorship of all mail in and out of Britain for security reasons, but who also managed to compile intelligence reports based on their scrutiny of as many as 200,000 letters a week, while telephone calls were officially eavesdropped and reported on. This jumble of information was collated into a report circulated by Mary Adams to various government departments for information, and sometimes action.

As well as generating information and encouragement, the MoI was charged with protecting national security by controlling news and information produced by others. These twin functions of exhortation and concealment were bound to be in conflict, with people often being urged to do things without being entirely sure for what purpose they were doing them – particularly in the early days of the war.

Originally, it had been the responsibility of the MoI to censor newspapers, magazines, films and radio broadcasts. The press was assured that the censor was concerned purely with military matters and would not attempt to suppress either opinion or any facts other than those that could be shown to be likely to be useful to the enemy. But who was to decide what was or was not of potential military value? The fighting services were suspicious of the new Ministry and reluctant to pass on information and allow its staff – mere laymen – to decide whether it should be published. The Chief Press Censor, Rear Admiral Thomson, recalled his arrival at the MoI in September 1939. He had been warned that 'they're a bit of a mess in there. Nobody quite knows what he's doing. It's supposed to be the place where official news is issued', and he found the present Director of Censorship sitting alone in his office on the ground floor of Senate House trying to deal with four telephones at once and barking into one of them at the *Daily Mail*, 'No, I don't know anything about the British Expeditionary Force and if I did I couldn't tell you.'

The fact that in the early days the MoI was 'a dumping ground' for people whose activities before the war were 'never remotely connected with the general public, the press and propaganda', and a safe haven for 'socially favoured amateurs and privileged ignoramuses', as the press charged, led to a number of farcical situations and capricious decisions with the Ministry of Information (or of Disinformation as it was dubbed) getting a lot of things wrong a lot of the time, and becoming the butt of jokes, satire, unease and indifference. This discredited the government, infuriated newspaper editors and led to non-news news, dull newspapers, and distrust among the general public. It was the polar opposite of what was needed, as a memo sent to the Home Office a week after the outbreak of war realised: 'The people must feel that they are being told the truth. Distrust breeds fear much more than knowledge of reverses. The all important thing for publicity to achieve is the conviction that the worst is known . . . The people should be told that this is a civilians' war, or a People's War, and therefore they are to be taken into the Government's confidence as never before . . .' (though the writer justified this policy by concluding 'it is simpler to tell the truth and if a sufficient emergency arises, to tell one big, thumping lie that will then be believed').

Under the Emergency Powers legislation, newspaper editors were in exactly the same position as ordinary citizens. Under Defence Regulation 3, they were prohibited from 'obtaining, recording, communicating to any other person or publishing any information that might be useful to an enemy', but they also had a duty to keep the public informed. Various government departments had co-operated in preparing a pamphlet entitled 'Defence Notices', which gave a long list of subjects on which it was considered information should not be published without prior advice from the censor. This list was circulated to censors and newspaper editors on the outbreak of war.

The press censorship system was a voluntary one and depended on the goodwill of editors accepting that the censor's decisions were reasonable. When they were not, or when it was clear that the armed service departments were unnecessarily withholding important but not militarily sensitive news, editors ignored rulings and risked prosecution by publishing what they deemed acceptable. It was some time into the war before a 'case load' of ad hoc decisions was built up on such thorny questions as could it be mentioned that the employees of Battersea Power Station were to play in a football match since that identified the power station and made it a target for German bombers – though they must have known of its existence anyway? Or why could a photograph of a school where children were having gas masks fitted not be identified since this was happening in every school in the country?

Journalists were often young men liable for call-up, and by the end of 1943 well over a third of the nation's 9,000 journalists were in the Forces, or doing non-journalistic work. Newspapers had to obtain War Office permission to send correspondents to report from overseas theatres of war. By the end of 1943 there were a hundred of them wearing uniforms with special insignia that allowed them to carry out their work without too much hindrance. Fifty war correspondents from Britain and Europe were killed in the line of duty. The press photographer corps was severely depleted – most papers lost some three-quarters of their photographers to the war effort, so there had to be much pooling of photographs and frequently the same image appeared in a number of papers.

Not that there was much space any more for pictures, or copy. The government control of paper had reduced the typical national daily to some six pages; later it fell to four, and in June 1940 the circulation was pegged at existing levels. The 'quality' press – *The Times*, the *Daily Telegraph* and the *Manchester Guardian* (as it then was) – managed to keep eight or ten pages throughout the war, but they did so at the cost of severely limiting their circulation.

Regular features had to be dropped, including reviews, puzzles and 'kiddie's corners', while sports coverage went down from twenty-five columns to four or five in the *Daily Herald*, for example. Astrology, however, flourished, with four or five out of every ten people professing to have some belief in it (though this fell off towards the end of the war as the fates seemed easier to read) and the 'stars foretell' section of the popular newspapers and magazines was sacrosanct, no matter how short space became.

Newspapers printed the time of the rising and setting sun – vital information since it dictated the hours of blackout. But another peacetime newspaper staple – and indeed perennial topic of British conversation: the weather – was never mentioned. It was considered that weather forecasts could be of help to the enemy, and it was forbidden to print or broadcast them – or make any reference to the weather for the previous ten days.

In 1940, when the Germans occupied the whole French coast and could actually see the cliffs of Dover on a fine day, it seemed ludicrous to continue to ban reports of weather conditions in the Straits of Dover, so 'an arbitrary rule' was drawn up whereby the English Channel up to and including the foreshore was excluded from the ban. Henceforth it was remarkable how interested the BBC considered the population of Britain were in weather conditions off Dover.

The uncertainty of the first Christmas of the Phoney War meant that many were determined to take the advice offered by *Picture Post* to make it a festive season to remember. 'Midnight Mass at the Oratory. Lovely prezzies – got my ants' nest and Madame Bovary and Freud,' rejoiced Joan Wyndham, who was seventeen and living with her strict, religious mother and her eccentric female companion in Chelsea. Joan had also requested 'an indecent pink gauze nightdress, the kind you can see through', having just fallen in love with a much older 'dissolute German sculptor' who called her Pussy (or sometimes the nicer Pussy Willow), lent her Ezra Pound's *Cantos* and got her to mend his clothes. 'Everyone over-ate. Alfred ate so much he got indigestion and couldn't go to the carol service.'

'Christmas Day. Everything was perfect and the war scarcely worried us at all,' recorded Veronica Goddard, a London schoolgirl, on 25 December 1939. On the same night eighteen-year-old Muriel Green went to bed 'feeling quite sick through eating continuously all day' (including turkey for supper). Her family's Norfolk village shop and garage was closed for the holiday, and on Boxing Day she went with her mother and her sister 'to whist drive and dance . . . There were only 4 soldiers in uniform and 1 RAF man at the dance out of 200 people. More girls than men. They had "Lambeth Walk" (still very popular) and "Boomps-a-Daisy".'

That first Christmas of the war, Gwladys Cox had managed to buy 'a fine holly bough for 1/3d – the finest I ever saw . . . Also a very nice Christmas tree for 2/6d . . . Christmas cards are beginning to come in . . .' She found a number of them 'rather dingy as if in an effort to damp down Christmas high spirits. One plain card without the relief of a robin or any holly wished me "A Merry Xmas" in plain black letters!'

The toy display at Harrods department store in Knightsbridge was also 'a dismal sight . . . The toys are there all right, but the children are missing. Only occasional groups wander up to shake hands with Father Christmas, chivvied along by anxious parents who have sneaked them up for a day from the country and who are sandwiching the fair between a haircut and a visit to the dentist.'

The availability of toys was going to be a serious matter because supplies of raw materials to make them were being diverted to war production, and toy buyers were already anxious about how much stock they would be able to get for next Christmas. But that year at least the 'Father Christmas tradition has been maintained generally, [but] outstanding among the toys which are clearly an outcome of the war are the model trench scenes and troops in action and models of the Maginot Line . . . Lead soldiers, even the enemy, have gone well, although of course they in particular are old fashioned. Uniformed dolls and model ARP units and equipment reflect more war time influences and conversations overheard in the shops indicate the desire of adults to move with the times when gift buying. A woman member of the AFS, for example, wished to buy a boy of six a model fire engine.'

All over the country churches cancelled traditional midnight Mass services because of the difficulty of blacking out stained-glass windows, while carol singers were reminded that the light their lanterns threw all around must be directed at the ground, and hand bells must not be rung in case they were mistaken for the warning of an air raid or gas attack. The annual carol service at Westminster Abbey was not held that year because the choir boys had been evacuated to the country.

'This Christmas saw as many presents as last year after all good resolutions about no presents owing to war were entirely in vain,' noted Constance Miles from her home in the village of Shere near Guildford in Surrey. On Boxing Day 'the evacuees' parents . . . are being entertained by the village . . . there are 45. They eat, they smile, they make speeches of thanks. They leap in the fields with their children and return to eat again. Madge [who did the cooking] returns exhausted and has a hot bath as the parents travel back Fulhamwards and many of their sons and daughters go to bed in the cottages weeping.'

At her home near Coventry, Clara Milburn's Christmas was tinged with anxiety by the knowledge that her son would soon be posted abroad. Alan, an only child, worked as a draughtsman for a nearby Coventry motor manufacturer and was a member of the Territorial Army. On 1 September 1939 Second Lieutenant A. J. Milburn had been called up. He was home on leave 'shortly before Christmas' and Mrs Milburn 'drove to Warwick and Leamington where I had the pleasure of being a proud mamma, with my soldier son walking through the stores and going to different counters with me. Christmas shopping was in full swing and we meant to have a good one this year, so I bought the last little luxuries.' Three days after Christmas Alan had to return to his unit and his mother 'watched the red tail light [of his car] out of sight . . . I came in thoughtfully, closed the gates, and wondered as I walked up the snow-covered path how long it would be before he came home again . . .'

By Christmas 1939 there were over 1.5 million men and 43,000 women in the Armed Forces, the majority of whom were in the Army. Most of them – with the exception of those serving in the Navy – spent the first Christmas of the war in Britain (and most did not manage to get leave) as they would for several more years.

Five Regular Army divisions had been shipped to France as Britain's contribution to the Anglo–French Alliance, starting on the day after war was declared. This British Expeditionary Force (BEF) was a defensive army with no armoured division, few tanks and insufficient air power to mount an offensive action. Throughout the winter of 1939–40 the BEF waited 'for the balloon to go up' in bitterly cold weather, and inadequate and sometimes filthy billets and barns in a particularly dreary industrial region of France. They spent their time 'digging and wiring in' since the priority was to establish and fortify the defensive line along the British sector of the Franco-German border. Otherwise it was route marches, weapons training and battlefield tours – mobile exercises would largely grind to a halt in the exceptionally severe weather in the first months of 1940, for fear that track marks in the snow would be visible to German spotter planes in the skies overhead. The life of a private involved little training but a lot of time spent whiling away the days in local bars and cafés, though some managed to strike up acquaintances with the local population, and a soldier with the 4th East Surrey who spoke the language passably was invited to Christmas lunch with a French family.

The New Year is traditionally pantomime time and 1940 was no exception, with wartime references alongside the usual Widow Twankey and the Baron routine, with songs like 'Please Leave My Butter Alone' and 'Kiss Me Goodnight Sergeant Major'. Performers could even now slip in jokes about the Führer if they so chose – which had not been the case the previous year when Herbert Farjeon's ditty 'Even Hitler Had a Mother' had been banned by the BBC.

On New Year's Eve Joan Wyndham 'got rather tiddly' and 'just hope[d] that 1940 turns out to be more exciting than 1939'.

7

THE KITCHEN FRONT

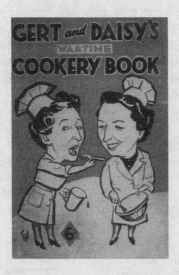

*Julia . . . noticed drops of thick blood running from the shopping bag.
The* Daily Worker *(for Eleanor now veered towards class-consciousness
under the influence of the visiting carpentry master) is an admirable
newspaper in many ways, but for wrapping up any meat other than
imported pork it is entirely inadequate. When she had unstuck the liver
from the racing news she sped upstairs . . . 'I don't like to have our meat
wrapped up in other people's newspapers,' said Roddy, meaning 'in
newspapers that have probably been read by the working class'.*

ELIZABETH TAYLOR, *AT MRS LIPPINCOTE'S*

THE WINTER OF 1939–40 was the coldest for forty-five years. Water pipes froze, coal supplies ran out, roads and pavements were like sheets of glass. The Thames froze over, as did the River Ribble in Lancashire, and for three weeks ice in the Humber held ships prisoner.

Cars stuck in snowdrifts, villages were cut off and 1,500 miles of railway were blocked by snow. Ice more than a foot thick covered the water tanks the AFS would need if an air raid came to London. Milk froze solid on the doorsteps, and on larder shelves. The shops were bare of vegetables, which could not be dug from the iron-hard frozen earth, and in the New Year another privation hit British households that was nothing to do with the weather and everything to do with the war.

Food rationing began on 8 January 1940, though the necessary ration books had started to be issued after National Registration Day on 29 September 1939. On that day each householder had been obliged to fill in a form giving details of everyone living in the house and, when these were collected, an identity card was issued, and the information was used by food offices to fill in names and addresses on ration books and post the books out.

In the First World War food supplies had not been a particular problem until 1916, when the effects of submarine warfare led to shortages, price rises, queues and industrial unrest. Rationing of sugar, fats and meat was introduced in 1918 and continued until 1920. It was 'an immediate and almost unqualified success', wrote Sir William Beveridge, who had been Permanent Secretary to the Minister of Food at the time and was appointed to chair a sub-committee in 1936 to plan 'food supplies in time of war'. The intention was that 'every member of the public would be able to obtain a fair share of the national food supply at a reasonable price'. But it was not only a matter of making sure that everyone had an equal entitlement to food: it was also a pressing matter of ensuring that there was going to be enough to eat in wartime.

Britain, as primarily an industrial and urban country, was a net importer of food: some 70 per cent of cheese and sugar, nearly 80 per cent of fruit, 90 per cent of cereals and fats and around 50 per cent of all meat was imported. After twenty years of peace and cheap food imports, many British farms were almost entirely given over to pasture and, to make matters worse, livestock was almost entirely dependent on imported foodstuffs. As a matter of extreme urgency, land had to be turned over to growing crops such as corn, potatoes and cattle fodder. The Emergency Powers Act had given the Minister of Agriculture authority to direct and control food production, including the right to take possession of any farm, or terminate any agricultural tenancy where the land was neglected or poorly cultivated. The government took full powers to fix the prices of farm produce, encouraged the raising of sheep over cows since they did not require imported foodstuffs, and in December 1939 decreed that livestock for slaughter had to be sold to the State at an agreed price. A War Agricultural Committee was appointed for each county and these bodies (known as War Ags), immediately set about increasing home food-production. The so-called 'Ploughing-Up' campaign aimed to turn grassland to growing wheat, oats, barley and potatoes for human consumption rather than animal feed, meaning a decrease in the amount of meat produced – but the government decided that this would have to be a wartime sacrifice. In spring 1939 farmers were offered an incentive of £2 an acre if they ploughed up fields that had been grass for at least seven years or brought other fallow land into cultivation. The hope was to have 1.7 million more acres producing food by the harvest of 1940. Farmers worked round the clock with tractors and horses and, given blackout conditions, there were many wavy furrows to be seen, but by April the target had been reached.

The rose grower, Harry Wheatcroft, recalled how he had to get rid of his 'luxury crops'. 'We put the plough through a field of some hundred thousand trees – a heart-breaking job. We tore from the greenhouses the bushes that were to give us blooms for the spring flower shows, and so made room for the more urgent bodily needs of the nation.

'Pigs now wander about where our Polyantha roses bloomed. There's wheat and barley where acres of Hybrid Teas coloured the land – even the humble cabbage stands where our standard roses once held majestic sway. The odour of our greenhouses has changed too. Here half a million onion plants have taken the place of the roses. They in turn will be succeeded by tomato plants and fruit; then lettuce, while the light still holds, and afterwards the humble mustard and cress.'

The War Ags could be draconian on those they felt were not doing all they could to make their land productive, and there were disturbing stories of farmers who had held tenancies for half a century being evicted or dispossessed at days' notice because their yield was deemed too low, or they ignored some Ministry directive – though there was rarely any financial assistance to implement such instructions. The Minister refused to review procedures, so in December 1944 a Dispossessed Farmers Supporters Association was set up to try to seek redress for its members

– many of whom had been forced to find jobs in factories after a lifetime working on the land – but though it attracted 5,000 members, the association's successes were negligible.

Bringing unproductive land into cultivation could involve elaborate drainage schemes for marshland, clearing acres of scrub and trees, cutting a canal in the Somerset wetlands, ploughing up thousands of acres of rabbit-infested South Downs in Sussex, and clearing a Welsh mountainside of bracken and gorse in order to plant potatoes – though that particular scheme in Montgomeryshire was a failure. Despite the persistent problems of labour shortages and low rates of agricultural pay, pre-war forethought, cash incentives to farmers, increased mechanisation – as tractors and threshing machines increasingly replaced horse-drawn equipment – and the growing use of fertilisers, meant that by 1944 the amount of land under cultivation had increased from 12.9 million acres in 1939 to 19.8 million, food production had risen 91 per cent, and in effect Britain was able to feed itself for approximately 160 days a year instead of only 120 days as had been the case when war broke out.

It wasn't just farmers who were encouraged to increase the food yield. In September 1939 householders received *Growmore Bulletin No 1*, produced as a collaboration between the Ministry of Agriculture and the Royal Horticultural Society to give amateur gardeners simple instructions on how to grow vegetables in their back gardens or allotments. Unfortunately it had been published in a hurry and was riddled with misprints – including the recommendation of 3 inches instead of 3 feet spacing when planting marrows – and in most people's opinion advocated giving far too much space to leafy green vegetables when it was potatoes that were needed for wartime fuel food. (The winter of 1939–40 was so severe that most green vegetables turned black and were inedible anyway.)

By 1940 the much more catchy 'Dig for Victory', first coined by a newspaper, became the slogan, and early in 1941 a second bulletin was published, bearing a photograph of the sturdy, booted foot of Mr W. H. McKie of Acton in west London, doing just that. By the end of the war twenty-four more leaflets had been distributed, giving advice on all sorts of suggestions for wartime horticulture such as digging up your lawn for a vegetable patch, and tearing asters and sweet peas out of your herbaceous border to substitute such good croppers as runner beans and turnips. If that wasn't practical, a gardener could grow marrows, carrots, dwarf beans or tomatoes on the requisite 15 inches of soil on top of the Anderson shelter, and flat dwellers could cultivate (small) vegetables in a window box. In Barrow-in-Furness, Nella Last planned 'to keep hens on half the lawn. The other half of the lawn will grow potatoes, and cabbage will grow under the apple trees and among the currant bushes.'

Local councils set up horticultural committees to advise gardeners, and often the local park superintendent was the key mover, organising practical demonstrations and discussions that were well attended since 'people soon found out that if they didn't grow it themselves they didn't get it'. The Ministry of Agriculture also helped out with lantern-slide shows; the Royal Horticultural Society sent out experts to talk to groups up and down the country; and 'brains trusts' were arranged in village halls – all to interest and encourage optimum food production. But with men called up into the Forces, women needed wartime horticultural expertise too, and so in the summer of 1939 Elizabeth Hess was appointed agricultural adviser to the National Federation of Women's Institutes. She travelled the country speaking to large groups of WI members and advising them on digging, planting and pruning for victory.

In the First World War the King, George V, had 'directed that potatoes, cabbages and other vegetables should replace the normal geraniums in the flower beds surrounding the Queen Victoria Memorial opposite Buckingham Palace and in the royal parks. The Prime Minister let it be known that he was growing King Edward potatoes in his garden at Walton Heath, and the Archbishop of Canterbury issued a pastoral letter sanctioning Sunday work.' The results of these patriotic examples proved astonishing: by 1918 it was claimed that 'for every five occupied houses throughout the two kingdoms [England and Wales] there is one allotment! Truly we have a nation of gardeners to be able to record such a startling result . . . which culminated in the production of 2 million tons of vegetables.' In 1939 would this 'new short-sleeved army' of some 1.3 million men and women allotment-holders be able to hold 'the pass with the spade while the country [is] in danger of semi starvation?' They didn't exactly have a head start. Many First World War allotments had been returned to their previous recreational use, and by 1929 the number in England and Wales had fallen to below a million. The movement did revive somewhat in the mid 1930s with the encouragement of such bodies as the Society of Friends and the Land Settlement Association, who encouraged the unemployed to become small stockholders and tried to revive long-derided notions of self-sufficiency with pigs and chickens (and thus manure) on the plots, as well as vegetables.

On the outbreak of war there was plenty of official encouragement for these evening and Sunday morning horticulturists. In a broadcast on 4 October 1939 the Minister of Agriculture said he was confident that 'half a million more allotments properly worked will provide potatoes and vegetables that will feed another million adults and one and a half million children for eight months of the year', while a Cultivation of Lands (Allotment) Order in 1939 empowered councils to take over unoccupied lands for allotments, and in 1940 appealed for 'half a million more allotments'. The call was given a spiritual dimension when a special allotment service was broadcast from St Martin-in-the-Fields in Trafalgar Square. It included a blessing to increase production, and the lesson was read by Mr Middleton, the BBC's stalwart gardening expert.

Allotments were dug in public parks, private, gated squares, recreation grounds and football pitches (33 acres of oats were grown on ground in Hackney in east London that had previously been occupied by seventeen football pitches), railway banks, seaside promenades and municipal flower beds – in short, wherever there was room to wield a spade and manoeuvre a hoe. By the end of May 1941 Bristol had more than 15,000 allotments, Nottingham 6,500 occupying 570 acres, Norwich had 4,000 over 400 acres and the number of Swansea's allotments had doubled its total since the outbreak of war, while in Tottenham in north London there were almost 3,000 allotments covering an area of 150 acres. There were allotments on school playing-fields, and some factory owners encouraged employees to dig allotments on their land. The LMS railway had 22,000 which, it was estimated, would stretch from London to beyond Dumfries if put end to end, and the wife of the Keeper of Coins and Medals at the British Museum planted rows of beans, peas, onions and lettuces in the forecourt. After the Blitz, allotments were cultivated in the ruins of bombed-out buildings, fighting with the ubiquitous rose-bay willow herb for sustenance from the thin soil. In Bethnal Green in east London local people founded a Bombed Site Producers' Association and by August 1942 there were 300 members working on thirty sites, sieving soil with punctured dustbin lids to clear the ground of bomb debris.

In February 1940 George Britton 'went to a lecture . . . under the auspices of [Walthamstow] Borough Council on "How to Cultivate an Allotment" . . . allotment holders have suddenly become very important people although I hear some of the ground which has lately been turned into allotments is absolutely hopeless. I put my first row of peas in yesterday.' His wife complained that 'vegetables are very dear, Savoy and cabbage 4d a pound, sprouts 5d [and by the time she had finished the letter she was writing to her daughter in California about this, they had gone up to 6d] and not much good at that. Potatoes [though] are very good, 5lbs for sixpence'. Mr Britton spent a lot of his limited free time cultivating his allotment.

By the middle of the war it was estimated that over half the nation's manual workers had an allotment or a garden, and by the end there were probably 1.5 million allotment holders producing some 10 per cent of all food produced in Britain. For it was not only vegetables that the gardens and allotments of Britain yielded: domestic hen-keepers were supplying roughly a quarter of the country's officially known supply of fresh eggs, and there were 6,900 pig clubs throughout the country with the animals kept in straw on allotments and back gardens – and much more unlikely places including the (drained) swimming pool of the Ladies' Carlton Club in Pall Mall. Twenty policemen stationed at Hyde Park station built a sty out of timber from bombed-out houses and subscribed £1 each to buy eight pigs, which they fattened on scraps from local hotels and killed every six months; they then bought another litter to begin the cycle again. Most urban pigs were fed on scraps collected from strategically placed pig bins in the streets, and fattened up to be killed for pork, bacon and ham for the small neighbourhood or workplace consortia that usually owned them.

Since priority had to be given to shipping men and matériel for war, food imports to Britain halved from 22 million tons before the war to between 10 and 11 million tons by 1944. Canned food was virtually eliminated, while meat was imported boneless and as much food as possible dehydrated to save space since it was estimated that pre-war 'we brought in with our food imports 3,000,000 tons of water a year'. But increased home production to make up the shortfall was only half the answer: as Beveridge's committee had recognised, there would also have to be a system that made sure that scarce food resources were fairly allocated.

On the outbreak of war there had been stories of panic buying and hoarding, when chauffeur-driven cars pulled up outside grocers' shops and stripped their shelves bare. A grocer in London's East End told of how 'the shortages are bringing in the rich people from the West End to take the poor people's food. They come in their cars . . . and buy . . . nightlights and candles, tinned goods, corned beef and that sort of thing . . . they go mad on sugar. I've been rationing sugar for the last three or four days. A good shopkeeper keeps some back for his regular customers.' Many shopkeepers had been operating an informal rationing policy so, when it became official, rationing not only helped the consumer, it also helped the retailer who had been coming under pressure from customers who could afford to buy in bulk.

Food rationing had not been introduced at the same time as the blackout and evacuation, since politicians were concerned about the public's opposition to the regulation of their eating habits. Churchill (then First Lord of the Admiralty) argued that there were 'signs in the Press that public opinion was becoming increasingly critical of government control and interference with the liberty of the individual'. No doubt he was particularly thinking of the campaign against rationing run by the *Daily Express*, which was owned by his good friend Lord Beaverbrook. An editorial in November 1939 read: 'the public should revolt against the food rationing system . . . There is no necessity for the trouble and expense of rationing, merely because there may be a shortage of this or that inessential commodity. Why should old women be forced to wait here and there before the shops for their supplies? This form of folly is difficult and almost impossible to understand.' It was an attack that the *New Statesman* saw as part of 'a general campaign against . . . every piece of state activity which threatens to co-ordinate business activities in the interest of the whole community' and it regretted that because the *Express* 'has two and a half million readers [and] . . . is representing itself as public opinion . . . rationing has been repeatedly postponed from November 13 until December. In December it was postponed again until January 8.'

Every household received a ration book for each member and was obliged to register with a retailer. A person could register with a different retailer for each rationed food – though in practice not many did – but they could exchange their coupons only with the shopkeeper with whom they had registered. This was in order to guarantee supplies, since the shopkeeper received stock replacements based on the number of registered customers he (or sometimes she) had. In theory this prevented consumers playing the system and getting more rations than they were entitled to, since shopkeepers had sufficient supplies only for their registered customers. Everyone over six (later reduced to five) had a buff-coloured ration book, while those under that age were issued with a green one. There were special ration books for travellers, gypsies and seamen who could not be tied to one specific retailer, and for servicemen and women when they went on leave. If a person went away for more than a few days, it was necessary to exchange his or her ration book for a temporary ration card since the host's rations would not stretch to cover a visitor's needs for more than a self-denying day or so.

At first shopkeepers were required to cut coupons out of customers' ration books and return them to the local food office. Not only was this an administrative nightmare for the shopkeeper at the end of each day, but it was soon obvious that it was a monstrous waste of time to check off every coupon in food offices – had it even been physically possible – and the system was open to abuse by dishonest retailers. So after January 1941 shopkeepers were required to stamp their customers' ration books as proof of purchase – and that saved paper as well as time.

Institutions, such as hospitals, boarding schools and prisons, had the aggregate of their 'inmates' calculated and rations allocated accordingly; hotels required guests to hand over their ration books for the duration of their stay, while restaurants and cafés had their rations calculated on the basis of 'past performance' – the number of meals they had been serving before rationing was introduced.

The first foods to be rationed were butter (4oz), sugar (12oz), bacon and ham (4oz) per person per week. Meat was rationed from 11 March 1940 to the value of 1s 10d per person per week, the theory being that this gave a choice between purchasing a small amount of expensive meat like a roast, steak or chops, or a larger amount of cheaper meat for stewing and braising. Cheese was first rationed on 5 May 1941. Preserves (jam and marmalade) and syrup and treacle were rationed at 8oz per month from March 1941, but from June 1943 the ration could be taken as sugar, which had been a summer concession since 1942. In the following July rationing was extended to tea (2oz), margarine (6oz in conjunction with butter: the ratio initially the customer's choice) and cooking fats (2oz – though at first this could be taken as margarine if preferred).

Allowances varied throughout the war: the meat ration fell to 1s 2d and then to 1s in 1941; sugar fell to 8oz in 1940 and again in 1942; from 1oz in May 1941, cheese rose to a bountiful 8oz in July 1942, but fell back to 3oz in May 1943. The rationing of meat led to more complaints than any other (except perhaps cheese) since meat and masculinity were inextricably linked and manual workers were vociferous in their complaints that they couldn't be expected to do a full day's heavy work on the 'pansy' rations they were allowed. By February 1943, it was reported that 72 per cent of men in heavy industry were convinced that their diet was inadequate for the work they had to do, and for most it was lack of meat that was the biggest deprivation; and the Minister of Labour, Ernest Bevin, voiced his concern that morale could be in 'serious danger' unless the meat ration was increased.

These were the only foodstuffs that were rationed: since the supply of eggs and milk was seasonally affected and could not be guaranteed, these were 'quasi-rationed' or 'allocated' rather than 'on the rations', with the expectation (a forlorn one sometimes) of rather less than one egg a week per person, and more for children and expectant and nursing mothers. Those who kept chickens – or bantams, ducks or geese – were at first 'invited' to forgo their egg rations, but by the end of 1942 supplies of poultry food were dependent on being able to prove that family and friends had registered with them as their egg provider. Dried eggs in tins were introduced in June 1942 and people were allowed one tin (the equivalent of twelve eggs) every eight weeks. 'During most of the year, the dried egg was to swamp completely the shell egg in the housewife's larder. Not unnaturally the British public was a trifle diffident at first,' reported the official history of rationing with masterly understatement. 'We were expecting this and laid on the fullest possible measure of persuasion and cajolery, and before long the dried egg came into its own as a thoroughly acceptable food' – an assessment many would have disputed.

The milk allowance was progressively cut until the end of March 1942, when it stood at 3 pints a week. There were lots of suggestions for other foods to be rationed including canned and processed foods, dried fruits, rice, breakfast cereals and biscuits, but this was not practical since demand for such food varied at different times and in different regions. In any case their supply could not be guaranteed – a cardinal tenet of the rationing system, though one that the government came perilously near to being unable to fulfil on occasions.

There were frequent calls for tobacco to be rationed to the consumer but these were rejected (though the supply to manufacturers was rationed) partly because it was thought it would be bad for morale and partly because the Exchequer valued the tax-raising properties of tobacco. There was always a far greater demand from the public for cigarettes and tobacco than suppliers could fulfil, though after 1941 this eased somewhat when tobacco leaf was included in the terms of the US Lend Lease programme. By this scheme, President Roosevelt agreed to supply Britain (and other countries at war with Germany, Italy and eventually Japan) with whatever goods were needed for their defence, including food – and tobacco leaf. When Virginia leaf was in short supply, manufacturers would mix in a small percentage of 'oriental leaf', but beyond this British smokers were unwilling to smoke Turkish cigarettes and frequently notices would appear in shops announcing 'No Cigarettes Only Turkish'. It was discovered that some Sheffield steelworkers were leaving their jobs on production lines, essential to the manufacture of war weapons, to queue for tobacco and cigarettes when a delivery was expected locally. Hearing this, Beaverbrook managed to persuade the government to permit canteens in factories with more than 200 employees (as well as Forces NAAFIs) to sell 'smokes' to their workers – on the basis of forty cigarettes per worker per week.

Beer too was a source of tax revenue, and continued to be produced in large quantities throughout the war – albeit a watered-down version – and its consumption rose by a quarter, due to both rising wages and the shortage of spirits. Bread was never rationed during the war (though it was afterwards), since it was believed that, along with potatoes, it would make up the bulk in the diets of manual workers who were not receiving much higher rations than anyone else despite the calories they were expending. But in order to save on wheat (most of which was imported in the early years of the war) the extraction rate of flour was raised, to produce the much more nutritious but widely disliked wholemeal 'National Loaf'. Fruit and vegetables were coupon-free as was poultry, fish (except after 1943 to catering establishments), game, sausages and offal, though such meat was by no means always available.

Just because something was not rationed, it did not mean it was in plentiful supply – quite the reverse. It was unrationed foods that led to the symbol of wartime drudgery: endless queuing, in the hope of getting tomatoes (particularly scarce after 1940 with the occupation of the Low Countries and the Channel Islands from where most of Britain's supplies came) or onions (80 per cent of which had come from France or Spain before the war) or other scarce foods. Until 1944, when oranges became somewhat more plentiful, shopkeepers who managed to get hold of any of the scarce fruits were supposed to keep them for children for seven (later reduced to five) days, but after that could sell them to anyone.

Theodora Fitzgibbon recalled how she managed her wartime housekeeping in Chelsea, where she lived with her lover in a mansion flat and worked as an artist's model. 'Fish was . . . unrationed, but with mines and U-boats at large it wasn't plentiful and sometimes it didn't seem all that fresh. Chicken was expensive and kept "under the counter" . . . for good customers. Technically offal was ration free, but as the war progressed it was remarkably difficult to find. When I remarked to the butcher that all animals seemed to be born without tongues, tails, hearts, kidneys, liver or balls, he winked at me, a great arm went under the counter, and he flung up half a dozen half-frozen oxtails. I had never cooked one before, but even today I can taste the thick gravy and see our grease-spattered lips as we chewed on the bones. Unrationed rabbit was the salvation for many people in a low-income group. I made jellied pies with scraps of bacon and onion; braised rabbit in dark beer with prunes, which made it taste vaguely like pheasant, or with cider and tomatoes; or with curry spices and paprika; or stuffed and baked rabbit, when we would pretend it was chicken; and, if it was very young, Peter would joint it and we would fry it in a crisp batter. Frying was quite difficult, as lard was rationed and olive oil only obtainable at a chemist on a doctor's prescription, so sometimes we were reduced to liquid paraffin. At least we didn't suffer from constipation! Another "filler" was pasta which could be bought freshly made in Soho; rice disappeared as the war went on, and even in Chinese restaurants spaghetti cut up to look like rice or pearl barley was served . . . I spread the ration books over different shops, for each one would give a mite over, which added up on three books . . . We didn't complain, because it was the life we wanted to live, and we hardly knew about housekeeping in any other circumstances. For those who took the challenge, it produced good, imaginative cooks who, once the war was over, felt they were in clover.'

At the beginning of December 1941 the 'points' system was introduced, initially restricted to tinned fish, tinned meat and tinned beans, and its popularity meant it soon spread to many other foodstuffs. Its introduction was helped by the influx of US tinned meats – such delicacies as spam – that were coming into the country under the newly agreed Lend Lease. Everyone received a number of points (or coupons) – for most of the war, around twenty per four weeks – which could be spent anywhere on any item of choice, though there was never any guarantee of a fixed quantity of a specific commodity: the only guarantee was that all points could be spent on *something*. The points needed for items could be varied according to their availability, and customers could choose whether to blow the entire week's allocation on a luxury item like a tin of red salmon (thirty-two points by March 1941 as compared to two points for pilchards or a tin of baked beans), or spread it across several lower 'points cost' items.

A further refinement was the 'personal points' system, which covered sweets and chocolates since 'little Willie would wish to make his own selection at the shop, yet little Willie could not be trusted with the vital main ration book'. At first everyone (over six months of age) was allowed 8oz of chocolate and confectionery a fortnight, then 16oz and finally 12oz for the remainder of the war – and well beyond. Chocolate was darker, rougher and more powdery than the pre-war variety and, with tin foil needed for other purposes, was wrapped in wax paper. The most prized treat – certainly for adults – was 'blended chocolate', a mixture of plain and milk. Mars Bars were a rare treat and, due to transport zoning restrictions, much more likely to be available near Slough where they were manufactured, while aniseed balls, pear drops, gobstoppers, humbugs and occasionally toffees tended to be what children wanted as they piled into sweetshops at the start of ration week one.

While of course there were grumbles and complaints about various aspects of rationing, particularly when amounts were cut, it was generally welcomed as a fair system and a shared sacrifice. A Gallup poll taken in November 1939 had showed that 60 per cent thought food rationing was necessary – though that figure fluctuated during the war and as early as March 1940 only 36 per cent of the population welcomed more foods being rationed, while 54 per cent thought the system should be voluntary. However, complaints were more often about how hard – and how expensive – it was to obtain unrationed food, which, logically should have inclined people to press for *more* controls, and for this reason both the 'points system' and 'personal points' proved popular when they were introduced.

Rationing was never going to be an entirely fair system: prices had risen dramatically since the start of the war: '. . . fresh butter has gone up from 1/3d to 1/7d, salt from 1/- to 1/6d [and] syrup has soared from 9d for two pounds to 1/', Ethel Mattison reported to her sister in America in October 1939. 'I would send you a cutting but no printed matter of any sort is allowed out of the country. It seems to me that there is a higher percentage increase on all things essential to poorer people . . . can you wonder that there is so much feeling against the rise in the cost of living and the inability of the government to control it?' At the end of January 1940 the bacon ration had been raised from 4oz to 8oz: 'the 4 ounces was fixed on the assumption that everyone would take up their full ration, but as very large numbers of people cannot afford to eat bacon at 2/- a pound stocks have been accumulating and deteriorating in a dangerous manner,' commented Helena Britton. 'That is how we all "share and share alike".'

A survey from the Cambridge area in 1941 pointed out that the diets of the 'poorer section of the community' had been less changed than those of the well off. For the poor, 'the acquisition of food has always been a major problem' – and there were indications that 'the poorer people themselves do not regard their food position as materially altered. It seems that so long as bread and potatoes are available the position will be tenable,' whereas among the higher income groups not only was food now 'one of the chief topics of conversation', but they have 'suffered a considerable reduction in their standard of living, though a greater proportion of their income is now spent on food than in peace time'.

By the end of 1939 the cost-of-living index had risen by 12 per cent since September – and would rise by 33.5 per cent by the end of the war. This was partly due to scarcities, and would be exacerbated later in the war by growing full employment (unemployment fell from 1,710,000 in 1938 to a low of 54,000 in 1944) and wage rises in some sectors of the workforce (average weekly wage rates in all industries rose by over 50 per cent during the war, and those in manufacturing industries by 80 per cent). In response to this, Sir John Simon, the Chancellor of the Exchequer, announced in January 1940 that food prices were to be pegged by the introduction of subsidies, and by 1943 £35 million a year was being used to keep down the price of bread, and some £25 million to subsidise the cost of both meat and potatoes. By 1945 subsidies were costing the government around £225 million, and a number of unsubsidised foods were price-controlled as well.

Subsidies could also be used to encourage eating habits. In April 1941, the effects of shipping losses in the Atlantic meant a reduction in the import of wheat, so the price of bread was raised and that of potatoes reduced. An outpouring of Ministry of Information recipes worked with the price change to encourage housewives to fill their families up with more potatoes and less bread. But customers complained that such manipulation did not always work to their advantage: if the price of tomatoes, for example, was capped, they would disappear until it was made worth the greengrocer's while to start selling them again.

Wartime conditions fitted over people's ordinary lives: inevitably the British came to the war with the attitudes and material circumstances that they had enjoyed or endured in peacetime. While there is much informed debate about the standard of living in the interwar years, for a sizeable proportion of the population these were indeed the 'hungry 30s'. Writing in 1938, John Boyd Orr estimated that the diet of half the population of Britain was deficient in some nutrients, while a third had a seriously inadequate diet, and this was confirmed by subsequent surveys: the better-off consumed more of everything – except margarine and condensed milk. During the war, to a considerable extent, this dietary imbalance was redressed. Ethel Mattison, an ex-nurse, started to work at 'the Food Office dealing with the issue of new ration books' in May 1940. It turned out to be 'a very boring job, just writing names and

On 24 September 1938, during the Munich crisis, local authorities in all densely populated areas were asked to provide trenches to shelter 10 per cent of their population within three days. In Arundel Square in Barnsbury, north London residents take their own action against the expected air raids.

Men prepare for the Second World War in the shadow of a memorial to the dead of the First. Sandbags being filled in front of the 1925 statute to the Royal Artillery by the sculptor C. Sargeant Jagger at Hyde Park Corner.

London evacuees with their gas masks and suitcases waiting at an unknown reception area to be taken to their new homes. In September 1939 393,700 school children left London in school parties without their mothers.

Mothers and children evacuated from Glasgow arriving in Perth. Unlike England where they went with their schools, Scottish school children were evacuated with their mothers. In September 1939 some 175,000 had left Glasgow, but most had returned by the time the raids came in May 1941.

Civil Servants from the Ministry of Health who had been evacuated to Blackpool working in the solarium sun room of the requisitioned Norbeck Hydro Hotel. The ballroom was converted into offices for the pensions department, and mail was sorted in the front reception area.

Hulton Archives/Getty Images

Hulton Archives/Getty Images

White lines and arrows painted on the road in Piccadilly in London as a guide to drivers in the blackout. In the first four months of 1939 4,133 people were killed in road accidents, almost twice the number killed in the same period in 1938.

Courtesy of Liverpool Daily Post & Echo

Practising for war. At a nursery in Wavertree, Liverpool, toddlers are acclimatised to wearing gas masks in the playground. The crime writer, Marjorie Allingham's description of 'elephant foetuses' seems particularly apt.

'O my darling, O my pe* / Whatever else you may forget / In yonder isle beyond the sea / Do not forget you've married me.' A wife visits her soldier husband in his barracks as the troops prepare to go overseas.

Women and children line a railway station platform on 31 May 1940 to welcome the soldiers of the British Expeditionary Force back from Dunkirk. 'The rejoicing which sprung from relief at a miraculous escape was misconstrued as an expression of congratulations upon victory,' wrote one of the returning men.

Osterley Park School, Middlesex where members of the Home Guard were trained to be 'first class irregulars'. The Director of Training, Tom Wintringham, an ex-Communist, Spanish Civil War veteran, lectures the guardsmen on anti-tank weapons.

A soldier guarding the perimeter fence at Huyton Alien Internment Camp on 21 May 1940. A Liverpool Corporation housing estate that had been left unfinished on the outbreak of war, Huyton served as a transit camp where prisoners stayed pending their transfer to the Isle of Man, or deportation overseas.

Sir Oswald Mosley the British fascist leader, under house arrest at his temporary home, a half-deserted pub in Oxfordshire, following his release on the grounds of ill health in November 1943 after three and a half years in prison.

Mr Guillioti, an Italian ice-cream vendor, reads the news that Italy had declared war on the Allies on 10 June 1940. Like many Italians – 4,000 of whom would be interned – Mr Guillioti was a long-time British resident with two sons serving with the BEF in France.

Heinkels into Spitfires. A German bomber brought down 'somewhere in south-east England' is put on show and a collection made for Lord Beaverbrook's fund to build more fighter planes for the Battle of Britain in 1940.

People leaving caves in Dover where they had taken shelter from cross-Channel shelling on the Kent harbour. The cave in the chalk cliffs ran under part of the town and were sufficiently commodious for 800 people to shelter there.

Carry on London. The juxtaposition of two potent symbols of the Blitz: St Paul's Cathedral stands intact above the ruins of the city, and a postman attempts 'business as usual' by delivering letters to bombed-out premises

A bus that had fallen into a crater in Mornington Crescent near Euston station in London after the raids on the night of 8/9 September 1940. By October so many London buses had been damaged as a result of enemy action that London Transport appealed to provincial bus companies for vehicles on loan.

Hulton Archives/Getty Images

Queen Elizabeth talking to demolition workers on a bombsite. While Churchill considered the royal couple to be invaluable to the nation's wartime morale and 'most beloved' of the people, others found such visits 'a distraction when clearing up has to be done'.

The ruins of Coventry Cathedral the day after the city was blitzed on 14/15 November 1940. By the early hours of the morning 'the whole interior was a seething mass of flames... all night long the city burned and the Cathedral burned with her'.

addresses on ration books all day . . . I think as more nurses are needed they will have to allow married ones to be non resident and then I shall be able to get a job', and she explained to her sister more about what she was doing. 'Milk has gone up ½d a pint owing to the increased cost of distribution, but in order to prevent undue suffering amongst people who need it most, a new scheme has been introduced. It enables expectant and nursing mothers and children under five to have a pint per day at half price (i.e. 2d per pint) irrespective of income, and for those who have less than a certain income to have it free. I have the job of interviewing the applicants and showing them how to fill the form in . . . I am enjoying that part . . .'

Although the intention was fair shares for all, there were some necessary variations. Vegetarians who forwent their meat ration were entitled to extra cheese in lieu, as were Jews and Muslims who could exchange their bacon rations. The Ministry of Food rose to the challenge of providing 'so far as the supply position permits it, kosher meat for those Jews who want it' since this could be supplied through Jewish butchers. But this did not happen when it came to kosher cheese for the 10,000 or so Orthodox Jews. The government feared that, since this would be handled by regular grocers, it might look like 'favoured treatment being meted out to the Jews' and fuel ever-nascent anti-Semitism.

Margaret Cotton, a well-off American living in St John's Wood in north London, was concerned towards the end of the war as she surveyed 'the pinched, or the puffy (varying with individual metabolism) look upon people's shadowed faces produced by a diet unhealthily heavy in starch, frighteningly short on fats, sugar and meat, almost completely lacking in vital fruit juices and with only ½ pint of milk every other day! . . . Although the English people have enough to eat in *quantity* throughout this war, the nutritional value of food has been so reduced that the average diet has undermined people's vitality.'

In fact some attention had been paid to the most obvious cases of inadequate diet. Certain groups of invalids were entitled to extra food – and people over seventy were allowed the comfort of an extra allowance of tea after 1944. Pregnant women and nursing mothers were entitled to extra priority foods such as oranges and bananas when available, extra eggs (both shell and dried), milk (an extra 7 pints week in addition to their normal entitlement from 1940) – free for those who needed it – and vitamin supplements. Vitamins were added to flour, and to margarine to bring it up to the nutritional level of the best quality 'summer butter'. After 1942 expectant or nursing mothers received subsidised orange juice and cod liver oil for the first time, and these were free of charge for those on low incomes. There was, of course, no guarantee that women made use of these benefits, or that they were not simply absorbed into the provision of household meals, and the take-up of vitamin supplements was low, but, prior to the advent of the National Health Service, such women were now integrated into a welfare system should they choose to use it. Their supplementary ration book came with advice: 'All the extras provided . . . are essential for you in addition to the full share of your ordinary rations. You should also visit a doctor or local clinic regularly. If you do and follow the advice given and also take all the extra food and vitamin supplements provided by this book, you are doing all you can to ensure your health and that of your child.'

Children were a special category too – at least until they left school. Babies, children and adolescents received virtually the same rations as adults, though with no tea for the under-fives and half the meat ration for children under six, and they were also entitled to extra foods like milk and eggs that were necessary for healthy growth. Babies between six and eighteen months were allocated three eggs a week, when older children and adults were lucky to get one. Children under five were entitled to 7 pints of subsidised or free milk a week, and from 1942 such children were entitled to subsidised or free orange juice and cod liver oil. With the exigencies of evacuation and rationing, school meals lost the stigma of poverty that they had had before the war, and every child received a third of a pint of milk a day at school at a subsidised cost or free, plus an extra 3½ pints at home. During the war working-class children from industrial towns and cities were drinking as much milk as children from higher-income groups had in the 1930s. After the war, the Labour Party was able to point to the contrast between the 1940s and the 1930s and claimed 'in spite of shortages, the children are rosy cheeked, well clothed . . . They are taller, heavier and healthier than before the war' and, though again this was part of a longer-term trend, infant mortality rates for England and Wales fell from 51 per thousand in 1939 to 46 in 1945 – but environmental factors for the poorest continued to militate against the gains of 'fair share' rations.

Despite the rhetoric of 'fair shares' and the general satisfaction with rationing as the way to shoulder equal sacrifices, there would never be total equality in a society with such differentials of wealth as there were in Britain. All rationing could do – and this was by no means negligible – was to ensure a fair distribution of basic essential items, be they food or clothing. Coupons regulated supply; cash was needed to pay for goods, and those who had more money obviously had an easier war when it came to food and material goods, just as they had an easier peace. Since game, poultry, offal, fish (including shellfish) and fruit were never rationed, if you could afford them you could have them – though many who did have the money baulked at paying 7s 6d for a single peach (when a private in the Army was earning £3 a week) or £1 5s for a bunch of grapes. The diaries of wealthy bon viveurs such as Chips Channon and Harold Nicolson are larded with such references as drinking 'four magnums of champagne' with friends at the Dorchester in November 1940. 'London lives well: I've never seen more lavishness, more money spent or more food consumed than tonight.'

Several surveys recorded the public's resentment at such obvious examples of the advantages the rich enjoyed over the poor, and many could not see why meals in restaurants should not have to be paid for with coupons as food in shops was. In February 1941 Gallup found that 29 per cent of those polled were convinced that the 'wealthy can always supplement their rations' and 23 per cent 'complained that those who ate in restaurants were able to eat more than the rationing scheme would allow'. Concerned about the effect this inequality of sacrifice could have on morale, the Ministry of Food considered various schemes, and in 1942 a maximum price of five shillings was introduced for all restaurant meals. This restriction was easily circumvented by charging fabulous amounts for wine or cover charges or tips 'expected', and there was no limit on the *number* of five-shilling lunches or dinners that could be eaten in different restaurants. Throughout the war luxury gourmandising continued – and resentment continued to simmer.

An initiative that proved rather more popular was the setting up of what were first called Communal Feeding Centres, until, at Churchill's suggestion, they were renamed more appealingly 'British Restaurants', usually run by local authorities. The first of these had opened in autumn 1940 during the Blitz to provide hot food for those who had been bombed out of their homes or had lost their cooking facilities. The restaurants were open to anyone; the Ministry of Food supplied the sort of necessary equipment like saucepans and crockery that was all but unobtainable in wartime; and the enterprise was virtually non-profit-making since prices were kept low with an average cost of 2d for soup, 8d for a main course of meat and two vegetables, 3d for a pudding and 1½d for a cup of tea or coffee. So for less than a shilling a hungry customer could have roast beef (or braised tongue perhaps) with two vegetables, treacle tart and custard, bread and butter and a cup of tea. The London County Council provided around 250 restaurants in London in schools, halls, municipal buildings and such unlikely venues as the Victoria and Albert Museum, the Royal Veterinary College and the banqueting hall of the Fishmongers' Company, and soon there was one every half mile or so in London's East End. Others were run by voluntary organisations such as the WVS.

Though the number of British Restaurants never approached the government's target of 10,000, any town with a population of over 50,000 had at least one, and by 1944 the country was latticed with such eating establishments serving on average 600,000 meals a day. They may have sounded grand and patriotic, but such places were in fact unpretentious and cosy self-service cafeterias – a novel idea then, and one that was soon copied by commercial caterers anxious to save on labour. Customers were known to complain at the size of the portions – 'one potato, one piece of carrot and a 2" by 3" rectangle of boiled beef' – while a Conservative MP opined 'one needs to be British to "take it" in a British Restaurant'. Nevertheless, they were useful for those working in shops, offices and factories without canteens. However, they did little to ameliorate the problem of feeding a family, and a survey in 1942 and 1943 showed that only 20 per cent of the population had eaten in a British Restaurant, and that only 1.3 per cent of housewives had done so.

Country dwellers might be able to get to a British Restaurant in a nearby town, but petrol rationing, which had been introduced in September 1939, was one of the limits to that possibility. Private motorists who were non-essential users were limited to a basic ration of approximately 1,800 miles per annum, and this was gradually whittled away until July 1942 when the basic ration was abolished altogether. Various local authorities and voluntary organisations experimented with mobile canteens, though again petrol restrictions and the problem of keeping food hot was a disincentive. The most successful scheme was the WVS meat-pie scheme, whereby village bakers cooked pies containing a pennyworth of meat and these (or sometimes sandwiches when times were particularly hard) were taken by various modes of transport – foot, bicycle, pony and trap – to workers in the fields. At the height of the scheme's popularity in 1943 something like 1.5 million pies a week were being sold.

But if the rural population envied the urban its canteens and restaurants, town and city dwellers coveted the supply of eggs, milk, ham, bacon and rabbits that was supposed to be the country person's natural bounty – or booty. Farmers were allowed to kill a calf every three months and two pigs a year, and could slaughter a certain number of sheep for household consumption or to feed extra workers at lambing time or harvest season. Without doubt more meat went into the cooking pot than was recorded on official forms. The *Farmer and Stockbreeder* helped farmers' wives make use of every possible part of the animal by printing recipes for sheep's heart in pastry, fried bullock brains, fried bacon with dock leaf pudding, stuffed pig's trotters and lamb's tail brawn. A Buckinghamshire child, living with her grandmother as her father had been called up and her mother was working in a factory making parts for aircraft, recalled: 'We grew up on a diet of vegetables and pancakes that were made of flour and water and fried. Sheep's head made a stew most days because sheep's heads and pig's heads were off ration . . . we ate dandelion leaves for salads, stinging nettles for cabbage, hawthorns, raw turnips and carrots. Wild raspberries, strawberries and blackberries were collected by us children.'

It was also, of course, much easier to 'dig for victory' in the country than town, with rather more space to grow cabbages, potatoes, Brussels sprouts, root vegetables and other staples than was afforded by the small back gardens or allotments that served as the city dweller's vegetable plots. The principled pacifist Partridges, Ralph and Frances, managed particularly well as they entertained their Bloomsbury and other friends at Ham Spray in Wiltshire. 'Home to a dream of a lunch,' wrote Frances

in May 1941. 'Lampreys in a marvellous sauce, foie gras and champagne.'
A month later 'a policeman arrived and told us that by order of the
Government all domestic pigeons were to be executed. He didn't know
why but it was something to do with invasion. So ours were killed and
eaten in a pie, but a snow-white one managed to escape and now wheels
about against a green landscape.'

Secrecy surrounded the announcement of any commodity that was to
be rationed for the first time to try to prevent a rush to purchase and
hoard. On February 9 1942, the rationing of soap was announced. As in
the case of clothes (which were rationed from June 1941), this had to
happen overnight with no warning. Soap came under the control of the
Ministry of Food rather than the Board of Trade since it was – rather off-
puttingly – made from the same substance as margarine: whale oil.
Everybody received four coupons per four-week period and these could
be 'spent' on toilet soap, hard soap, washing powder or soap flakes. This
was regarded as inadequate by most people (except small boys of the *Just
William* persuasion) and soon the amount was doubled for those with
babies up to a year since they generated a lot of nappies that needed
washing.

The whole notion of rationing – controlling what had previously been
freely available – would suggest an area ripe for behaviour that was
illicit, though not always seen as criminal, in the community. The
black market was the inevitable consequence of regulation since 'what
were once perfectly innocent private transactions can be transformed
into criminal activities and the increase of official surveillance and
interference increases the temptation for individuals to conceal what
they have previously done openly, or to switch into illegal activities,
which are less visible'. Such offences could range from large-scale
activities of theft and fraud that would be crimes by any definition, to
petty 'fiddling' that essentially constituted non-compliance with control
orders, and many otherwise upright citizens 'trafficked' in the black
market in minor ways at some time during the war.

In November 1942 there was an outcry in the press about people
giving food that they had obtained using their ration books to friends
and neighbours, which was illegal. Rations were not supposed 'to be
transferable whether by sale, barter or gift except . . . within the
household'. If you didn't need your rations for your own household,

you should not draw them, and if everyone who could be was so self-denying that would save even more shipping space. But of course everyone swapped rations with friends, gave away anything they had an excess of, or contributed what they could on a special occasion such as the making of a neighbour's daughter's wedding cake. The nonsense of this regulation meant that you could give a friend a cake but it was illegal to give them the ingredients to make a cake.

Churchill sent a note to the Minister of Food, Lord Woolton, saying that he hoped 'we are not enforcing vexatious regulations of this kind. It is absolutely contrary to logic and good sense that a person may not give away or exchange his rations with someone who at the moment feels he has a greater need. It strikes at neighbourliness and friendliness.' Woolton entirely agreed: 'The public would never agree that adult people should not give away their sweet ration if they were so disposed: neither would they agree that they should not make presents of surplus tea and sugar if through taste or abstinence they had some slight surplus . . . Self respecting people following the harmless practice of generous instinct ought not to be made into law breakers and they ought not to be at the mercy of any malicious informer or overzealous official who could cause them, as the law stands, to suffer the indignity of trial in a police court.' After this interchange, the order was amended to allow gifts of rationed goods, 'though barter or trade in any rationed foods will still be an offence' and new regulations were issued to control gifts of food from producers.

During the Second World War the analogy of the 'battle front' was brought into the home. Women were in the front line, their kitchen front represented as being critical to victory as they fought to feed their families against the odds of shortages, absences and uncertainties. Rationing was essentially something that women organised and mediated. As a Ministry of Information leaflet recognised: 'Many vital decisions for the home front have been taken by Ministers of the Crown for the whole nation, but the housewives have had the task of translating national economy into domestic practice.' It was invariably women who shopped, juggled with coupons, queued, learned that when you shopped it wasn't a question of what you wanted but what you could get, and adapted recipes accordingly – and often went without. Rationing regulated what came into a household, not how it was distributed once it got there, and there are numerous stories of women who gave their meat rations to their menfolk, went without cheese and/or butter, preserves and fresh fruit, and never ate a shell egg throughout the war years to ensure that their children could eat properly.

Good Housekeeping saw the housewife's contribution to the war effort as being rather scarily pivotal: 'Yours is a full-time job, but not a spectacular one. You wear no uniform, much of your work is taken for granted and goes unheralded and unsung, yet on you depends so much. Not only must you bring up your children to be healthy and strong, look after your husband or other war-workers so they may be fit and alert, but you must contrive to do so with less help, less money, and less ingredients than ever before. In the way you tend your family, especially, your skill – and your good citizenship – are tested. Thoughtlessness, waste, a minor extravagance on your part may mean lives lost at sea, or a cargo of vitally-needed bombers sacrificed for one of food that should have been unnecessary . . . We leave it to you, the Good Housekeepers of Britain, with complete confidence.'

By 1943 there were approximately 8.75 million women in Britain who were full-time housewives, the majority of whom were mothers of children under fourteen (the school-leaving age). In addition there were some 7.25 million who were in the Forces, Civil Defence or working in industry (an increase of just under 2.5 million in female employment since 1939). Although this figure included 90 per cent of the single women and 80 per cent of married women or widows without young children, it meant that many women were holding down two jobs in wartime: that of housewife and paid worker. In addition thousands of women were undertaking voluntary work or (sometimes and) had evacuees, troops or war workers billeted with them. Women were increasingly seen as essential 'manpower' in the war effort, and yet a woman's presence in the home, whether or not she had children, was regarded as vital. If women were compelled to go out to work 'home life will vanish and it will be hard to revive after the war. Men coming home on leave will find they can only see their wives for an hour or two a day. Men in reserved occupations will come back to cold and untidy homes with no meal ready. Friction in the home will be greatly increased and with children evacuated there will be nothing to hold the family together.'

If a woman was looking after a man, such as a widowed father, she could obtain exemption from conscription or direction, but if she were looking after a female relative, that did not qualify. A woman made a home, but she made it *for* a man (and maybe children).

Housekeeping in wartime was hard: two-thirds of households had mains electricity, and around three-quarters had a gas cooker, but the only gadgets that were at all usual were a carpet sweeper, perhaps an electric iron, and maybe a pressure cooker. Water was heated by fuel-burning boilers and rooms heated with coal fires; convenience food was rare and expectations of three or four meals a day – a cooked breakfast and midday meal followed by tea and supper or dinner – normal. Wash day (invariably a Monday) was highly labour-intensive: water had to be heated, and clothes were scrubbed by hand before being put through the mangle and pegged out to dry. Moreover, the responsibility for household chores was the woman's whether she had a job outside the home or not. Some husbands may have helped, but as a wartime husband said, 'I don't queue; my wife does that' – an assertion that many wartime photographs bear out.

Queuing could also be frustrating for housewives who had more time, as Gwladys Cox found. 'No errand boys now!' she sighed as she queued at the fishmonger's in West Hampstead in September 1941 with '13 people in front and 14 behind'. The next month she noted that 'there are always long queues now . . . there is an acute shortage of matches, only one box a week allowed at the grocers. I managed to get half a pound of prunes recently, the first for a year.' A few weeks later, 'there being nothing whatever in the larder', she telephoned the fishmonger to hear that 'Gow's expected no fish at all today. Rang MacFisheries who were quite vague as to any possibilities, and could promise nothing at any time. Found Jones the fishmonger in West End Lane closed. I took a bus to Oxford Circus to met Ralph for lunch as arranged, pouring out my tale of "fishlessness". So we investigated a fish shop behind Jays which had a notice "No fish until after 1 p.m." After lunch we decided to split forces and I went off to Selfridges where I managed to pick up some conger eel, all they had. Ralph got nothing in town, but in West Hampstead he managed to pick up a small tail of cod.'

On average a woman could expect to queue for between fifteen and thirty minutes each at the fishmonger's, butcher's and grocer's, and towards the end of the war buying cakes, biscuits and sweets also often necessitated queuing. The Ministry of Food wasn't over-keen on queues either. One official saw them as 'hot beds of discontent' with women standing wearily in line gossiping and spreading rumours like wildfire, and it was suggested that as scarcities couldn't be controlled maybe queues should be, with a ban on the number of people queuing. But fortunately this authoritarian suggestion never gained acceptance.

When they finally got their food home, there was no shortage of advice for housewives on how to cook it. The Ministry of Food issued regular bulletins, *Food Facts*, which appeared in national and regional newspapers, and in the *Radio Times*. These instructed people to 'grow fit not fat on your war diet! . . . Cut out "extras"; cut out waste; don't eat more than you need. You'll save yourself money; you'll save valuable cargo space which is needed for munitions and you'll feel fitter than you ever felt before', and detailed categories of 'body-building foods', 'energy' foods', and 'protective foods' giving seasonal information, recipes and news about the introduction of such delights as spam and other tinned meats. The Ministry also produced cookery leaflets that could be picked up at any food office and were handed out at food office cookery demonstrations: No 1 promoting the use of oatmeal appeared in 1940, and the last, No 24, with advice on 'drying and salting', came out in June 1945. The Ministry also published booklets with such titles as *How to Eat Wisely in Wartime* and *The ABC of Cookery*. The Good Housekeeping Institute published Ministry of Food recipe books, and most newspapers came out with cookery books of their own. The *Daily Express* was the first with its *Wartime Cookery* in 1939.

Ministry of Food publications, the rhetoric of which combined patriotism with practicality, advised shredding vegetables and cooking them as quickly as possible with as little water as possible since this conserved vitamins – or 'health value' in wartime parlance – though this was hardly in the British tradition. They also suggested steaming food by placing a colander or a sandwich tin or saucepan lid with holes punched in it on top of a saucepan so that only one gas ring need be used (conserving fuel was, of course, another wartime priority). Housewives were cautioned never to use the oven for only one dish but to cram it full with casseroles (or 'one-pot meals' as they were known), pies and cakes (eggless). They were advised how to make a hay box using scrunched-up newspaper if they had no supply of hay for 'stews, soups, haricot beans, porridge or root vegetables to cook by themselves . . . all day or all night'. When there was a glut of a particular vegetable, as there frequently was of carrots or potatoes, the Ministry introduced cutesy anthropomorphised vegetables – 'Potato Pete' and 'Dr Carrot' – who shamelessly self-promoted. 'Dr Carrot' promised, 'Call on me often enough and I'll keep you well.'

The style was homely: one 'Food Fact' intoned, 'Those who have the will to win/Cook potatoes in their skin/Knowing that the sight of peelings/Deeply hurts Lord Woolton's feelings'; and friendly chats along the lines of 'the grocer/the butcher/the greengrocer say' explained such things as why there weren't any onions, or why corned beef was plentiful, or why some people seemed to be getting more than their fair share of what was going. Then there was a cast of imaginary characters, first appearing in 1942, who always needed putting straight since they seemed to 'have got their facts wrong'. 'Cows aren't fifth columnist', Mrs Doubtful was told sternly when she worried about lack of milk for 'Dad's duodenal'. Poor Mrs Simple was reprimanded when she asked if she should take 'that bit extra the butcher had offered her'. There was also Miss Lightfoot, who 'works in a factory all day . . . doing her bit . . . but even in wartime conditions is seldom tired, never ill, never nervy on account of eating potatoes and carrots every single day'.

There was even a 'Food Facts Quiz' published at Christmas, and families were encouraged to sit round the fire at the festive season quizzing each other with such teasers as: 'Which is the correct way of mixing milk powder?' 'How much is fresh-salted cod per pound?' 'Which vitamins does cod liver oil contain?' and 'What is (or are) Rose Hips? A Russian folk dance? The name of a famous woman spy? An eastern dance? Pods of wild roses rich in vitamin C?'

It was all very patronising, particularly for women who had been cooking on tight budgets for generations. Home Intelligence reported in 1943 that while 'working-class housewives are . . . more receptive to the Government's appeals than are women of other classes . . . some of the economies that have been suggested are regarded as "piffling" by working-class women, on whom such forms of thrift have long been imposed by necessity . . . Neither posters nor leaflets are thought to "cut much ice", and are considered by some housewives to be a waste of paper . . . except for leaflets giving food recipes or gardening hints.'

New recipes were necessary, though, since pre-war cookery books with their suggestions for dishes involving half a dozen eggs and half a pint of cream, and recipes for veal cutlets and cheese soufflés, were redundant for the wartime housewife. With shortages of her staple ingredients, and untried and sometimes unknown substitute and ersatz food all that was available, most housewives needed new maps for this culinary wasteland. The war made reluctant near-vegetarians out of those who had previously regarded such people as free-love cranks, and the most famous vegetarian dish was the Minister of Food's eponymous 'Woolton pie' (though it was in fact the invention of an under-chef at the Savoy hotel). It consisted of a mixture of whatever vegetables were plentiful mixed with oatmeal and topped with potato pastry – and a grating of cheese should you be so lucky as to have any left. Apart from the stream of 'without' recipes – stock without bones, roly-poly without jam, cakes without eggs, bottled rhubarb without sugar – one of the most optimistic of initiatives on the wartime kitchen front was the recipes for 'mock' dishes. There was mock duck (sausage meat, cooking apples, an onion – if you could get one – and sage), mock goose (potatoes, apples, cheese – and sage again), mock cream (margarine, sugar, milk powder or milk, cornflour or arrowroot), mock apricot flan (which substituted carrots for apricots), mock marzipan (essentially adding a little vanilla essence to haricot beans and ground rice), mock hare soup (in which the hare was represented by a meat stock cube in a broth of vegetables and oatmeal) and even mock oyster soup (fish trimmings with herbs, a little milk, some artichokes and an onion or leek).

'Are you collecting these useful advertisements?' housewives were asked by 'Food Facts'. 'Start now and pin them up in your kitchen.' Some did, most didn't, but a very large number took the advice on the bottom of each leaflet: 'Listen to *The Kitchen Front* at 8.15 every morning.' Allocated a five-minute slot after the eight o'clock news, it was timed 'before the housewife sets out to do her shopping'. The cookery writer Ambrose Heath presented the programme, and so did Freddie Grisewood (known as 'ricepud'). Marguerite Patten was a contributor, and Lord Woolton made regular appearances. Elsie and Doris Waters (real-life sisters of the actor Jack Warner) had taken the part of two cockney 'chars', Gert and Daisy, in a series of 'Feed the Brute' routines, which had followed the Ministry of Food's Economy Campaign broadcasts earlier in the year. In their sketches, 'Gert and Daisy' recommended alternatives to meat, suggested ways of cooking new foods and using up leftovers, propagandised for green vegetables and advised how to save fuel – all the things that 'Food Facts' were doing, but delivered with warmth and down-to-earth humour. Within a fortnight of the first programme, 30,000 people had written in for their recipes.

At the end of 1940 'Gert and Daisy' were enlisted in *The Kitchen Front*, and sometimes did a double act with Lord Woolton. At Christmas 1941 the sisters gave a recipe for 'murkey,' stuffed mutton in place of almost unobtainable turkey. 'How do you do that?' Gert asked. 'Use your imagination,' Daisy replied. 'Do you get that at the butcher's too?' shot back Gert. It seemed a fair question.

Grandma Buggins, played by the actress Mabel Constandurous, was a stock character, meeting the culinary efforts of her long-suffering 'daughter' with a sniff and the comment 'Another disguise for parsnips, I suppose'. Recipes were tested in the Ministry of Food's kitchens in Portman Square (where Eileen Blair, George Orwell's first wife, was one of those responsible as well as writing some of the programme's scripts) and listeners sent in questions and recipes – and sometimes even turned up with dishes cooked from the previous day's recipes. The programme managed to fit in a great deal of information, promoted British Restaurants, and included the odd stricture: 'It's not funny to get more than your fair share.' It attracted an impressive audience of 5 million listeners, 15 per cent of the available audience, and four times the audience of any other daytime talk programme.

A very popular feature of *The Kitchen Front* was the talks given by the genial Radio Doctor, 'the doctor with the greatest number of patients in the world', Dr Charles Hill, Secretary to the British Medical Association who, after the war, as Lord Hill of Luton, was appointed Chairman of the Independent Television Authority, and then of the BBC. Hill pulled in up to 7 million listeners with his frank talk of 'bowels and bellies', his advocacy of prunes – 'that humble black worker to keep you regular' – and his robust common sense about health and food: 'Don't "assassinate" vegetables by over-boiling' (though they would hardly have turned out *al dente* after the recommended half an hour) and 'Don't give Father extra butter, Mother, that's *your* ration.'

Although *The Kitchen Front*'s presenters were avowedly middle class (Freddie Grisewood kept a cook at home), it nevertheless managed to attract listeners across a wide age range, and working-class housewives listened in dispro-portionately high numbers – though there were continual complaints that the recipes broadcast were too expensive.

But however popular and useful *The Kitchen Front* was in wartime, the programme failed in its long-term ambition of changing the nation's eating habits. The foods most people thought were essential to their well-being were the foods they missed most – tea, bread and meat. Only 38 per cent of mothers gave their children cod liver oil in 1942, and only 54 per cent orange juice, and this had not increased significantly by 1945. Although the majority of housewives claimed to eat green vegetables 'regularly', that turned out to mean at least once a fortnight in season. No data exists on how many cabbages, cauliflowers and Brussels sprouts continued to be 'assassinated' in British kitchens, and almost without exception the British looked forward to the return of white bread.

Easter Sunday in 1940, which fell on 24 March, wore an air of peacetime normality for many people. In London Veronica Goddard was delighted to be given 'a really nice collection of Easter eggs – no scarcity there!' A friend of Constance Miles came to tea and reported that the youngest of her three evacuees from Fulham in west London 'had never seen a lamb before – there arc so many in the fields now – and he came home in great excitement to tell [her] "It was a little animal, no bigger than the *Daily Sketch*".' And one of Mrs Miles' son's friends arrived to stay for the holiday weekend at her Surrey home. Mickey was in the Coldstream Guards training at Pirbright where 'hardly any of the soldiers buys a paper . . . they joined up for patriotic reasons but none of them follow the news in the press or on the wireless. Nothing like being in the Army for forgetting the war . . .' Mickey would be killed fighting the Japanese in 1944.

A week after Easter, two of Vivienne Hall's colleagues in her City insurance office announced their spring engagement. 'Much screaming and laughing and "ooh isn't it lovely" from younger members of staff,' she wrote. 'Truly Cupid is working overtime because of this war!' But as she walked home up the hill from Putney station, Miss Hall recalled that the previous evening she had heard on the radio that 'Goering has made an impassioned speech, vowing that Germany is just waiting for Hitler's word to loose all Germany's strength upon us and to end the war . . . it seems that there is a campaign to almost taunt Germany into starting the war – our newspapers and statesmen are all trying, by diplomatic and "wrapped-up phrases", to be saying "garn, come out and fight, you big bully" – what a strange war!'

8

'FROM THE HORIZON
TO THE MAP'

When no allies are left, no help
To count upon from alien hands
No waverers remain to woo,
No more advice to listen to,
And only England stands . . .
DOROTHY L. SAYERS, 'THE ENGLISH WAR'

WAR HAD COME to the lonely Orkney Islands off the coast of Scotland over a week before Easter. On 16 March 1940 James Isbister, a twenty-seven-year-old labourer who worked for Orkney County Council roads department, had been standing in the doorway of his croft in the hamlet of Bridge of Waithe watching 'the flashes of bomb explosions and the strafing of the enemy raiders by anti-aircraft fire when planes roared over the district and bombs began falling'. Bomb fragments splintered his body and Isbister had the unwanted distinction of being the first civilian to be killed by a bomb dropped on the United Kingdom in the Second World War. It was a mystery why the hamlet had been bombed: there were no military targets anywhere near at the time. The most likely explanation is that in the failing light the Luftwaffe pilot mistook the Bridge of Waithe for a nearby airfield.

'Poor James perished leaving a wife and baby up in the remotest of islands,' noted Constance Miles who, living within thirty miles of London, had been expecting the war to come to *her* doorstep for the last six months.

Four days earlier the Allies had suffered a setback when Finland was lost to the Soviet Union. Finland had secured its independence following the Bolshevik Revolution in 1917 but, under the terms of the Nazi–Soviet non-aggression pact of 1939, a secret protocol had promised the USSR a sphere of influence in Finland. When the Finns refused a request to cede to Soviet demands for a strip of territory required to safeguard Leningrad, Russian troops advanced across the frontier on 30 November 1939. Support for the resistance of the 'gallant Finns' had grown in the British press, and 300 volunteers and a number of British planes were sent to the front. But public opinion remained unconvinced by what the Labour politician Hugh Dalton called the 'midwinter madness' of intervening in contravention of Scandinavian neutrality, and ranging another powerful enemy against the Allies. So no effective help was offered to the Finns just as it had not been to the Poles, and on 12 March 1940 Finland finally capitulated.

Chamberlain's policy in October 1939 had been to 'Hold on tight. Keep up the economic pressure, push on with munitions production and military preparedness with the utmost energy, take no offensive until Hitler begins it.' If this was the course pursued, he 'reckoned we shall have won the war by the spring'. The spring arrived. On 4 April, reviewing the progress of the war, the Prime Minister delivered what was, in Churchill's view, 'a speech of unusual optimism' reassuring MPs that things were going well for the country: seven months had enabled Britain to redress the weaknesses she had in September 1939 compared to Germany, and added enormously to her fighting strength, whereas Germany now had few reserves left to call on. It was clear, Chamberlain concluded, that 'Hitler has missed the bus' in seizing the offensive.

Three days later German troops invaded Denmark and Norway. 'This,' announced Churchill, 'is the first crunch of the war.' When George Beardmore's wife Jean heard the news 'she phoned me at the office to be sure to bring my gas mask home'.

As German forces advanced, the Norwegian government called for help, and British troops, who lacked 'aircraft, anti-aircraft guns, anti-tank guns, tanks, transport and training', embarked on 'a ramshackle campaign' to retake Narvik and Trondheim in a country that was 'covered with snow to depths which none of our soldiers had ever seen, felt or imagined' without either 'snow-shoes, nor skis – still less skiers'. The result was that 'a mixed and improvised German force' some 6,000 strong – many of them sailors fighting as infantrymen – held some 20,000 Allied troops at bay for six weeks 'and lived to see them depart'.

'It was,' wrote Churchill, who was to be the political beneficiary of this crisis (and also as First Lord of the Admiralty in large part its architect), 'the stroke of catastrophe and the spur of peril [that] were needed to call forth the dormant British nation.' The 'tocsin sounded' on 8 May 1940. The day before, the House had assembled for a debate on the Norwegian fiasco. When Chamberlain came in, he was taunted with cries of 'missed the bus' and, in the partisan eyes of Harold Nicolson, 'made a very feeble speech and is only applauded by Yes-men'. A poem in the *New Statesman* recalled the disaster in the Crimea entitled 'Stand of the Old Brigade':

> Members in front of him,
> Members each side of him,
> Members *behind* him
> Volley'd and thunder'd.
> Why had the Nazis won?
> Why were we on the run?
> What had been left undone?
> What would be left of him
> If he had blunder'd?

The debate rolled on. None of the speeches in Chamberlain's defence was more than mediocre. One of his own party, Leo Amery, an ex-Cabinet Minister, flung at his Prime Minister the words that Oliver

Cromwell had used to the Long Parliament: 'You have sat too long for any good you have been doing. Depart, I say, and let us have done with you. In the name of God, go!' Churchill wound up for the government with 'a slashing, vigorous speech, a magnificent piece of oratory'. Hugh Dalton was moved to see the lobby 'full of young Conservatives in uniform – khaki, Navy blue and Air Force blue all intermingled', and many of them must have joined their elders in condemning the conduct of the war. The Conservative majority fell from 213 to 81. It was clear that Chamberlain could hardly carry on in the circumstances but, given the wartime situation, going to the country was not an option, and Labour leader Clement Attlee indicated that his party would probably be prepared to join a coalition government. But they would probably not be prepared to join one that was led by Chamberlain, and Labour participation was essential to guarantee trade-union support for wartime industrial policies.

Who should Chamberlain advise the King to call on to form a new government? Lord Halifax was the obvious choice. The Foreign Secretary was an aristocrat of gravitas and experience, and his effortless rise to political power had fingered him as Chamberlain's natural successor, while Churchill was not credited as having the essential qualities needed for a Prime Minister. But Halifax recognised that in the extraordinary conditions of war, it was precisely Churchill's qualities that were needed. And Churchill recognised it too. He listened to Halifax's self-abnegating reasoning: 'I thought Winston was a better choice. Winston did *not* demur.' 'Winston licked his lips,' reported twenty-five-year-old John (Jock) Colville, one of Chamberlain's private secretaries, who was not present.

On Friday 10 May Joan Wyndham was sitting in the studio of her artist lover, Leonard, hearing why he thoroughly approved of masturbation. 'Just as it was getting interesting and I was going to ask him how it was done, another artist conchie rushed in waving a newspaper. "They've invaded Holland and Belgium!" he panted. So there it is. We looked at one another. The war had really started . . . Leonard and the conchie looked pale and horrified. They will probably be forced to fight now, for every man will be needed.' Later the couple went for a walk through 'hot and dusty' London. 'There wasn't any noise. Only a man with a piano on wheels playing "It's a lovely day tomorrow". Leonard looked at the green trees at the end of the road and said, "Isn't it unbelievable, seeing the sky and the leaves and smelling the air and thinking how good it is to walk on the earth, that anyone should ever want to make war?" '

The *blitzkrieg* in the west had begun. Airfields and rail junctions in the Low Countries were bombed and paratroops and glider-borne engineers landed on bridges and key installations and blew them up, as German anti-aircraft guns were moved in place to deal with any Allied counter-attack. Maybe, thought Chamberlain, this meant he should soldier on as Prime Minister. Was a time of military crisis an appropriate one for the Prime Minster to go? 'It's like trying to get a limpet off a corpse!' exclaimed the infuriated Brendan Bracken, loyal henchman of Churchill. Wiser colleagues persuaded Chamberlain that he shouldn't stay, and the decision of the Labour Party at its conference in Bournemouth made it plain that he couldn't. The Prime Minster told his War Cabinet that he would resign and went to see the King. George VI was disappointed to hear that 'H[alifax] was not enthusiastic . . . as I thought H. was the obvious man . . . Then I knew that there was only one person I could send for . . . who had the confidence of the country . . . I sent for Winston and asked him to form a Government. This he accepted . . . He was full of fire and determination to carry out the duties of the Prime Minister.' If the King had misgivings about his new Prime Minister, 'prompted by the kaleidoscopic nature of his past career', these were certainly shared 'by the staff at 10 Downing Street, the Cabinet Office, the Treasury and throughout Whitehall', and by the City, *The Times*, the Opposition and the majority of Conservative MPs who, according to the éminence gris of the party, Lord Davidson, simply 'don't trust Winston', regarding him as a self-seeking renegade and an adventurer. The 1930s had been Churchill's 'wilderness years' when, out of office, he issued what seemed Cassandra-like warnings about German aggression and the need to rearm. When Germany invaded Poland Churchill had been vindicated and brought into the Cabinet as First Lord of the Admiralty, the post he had held in the First World War.

So, on the worst day of the war to date, with newspaper placards reading 'Paris raided' – 'Brussels bombed' – 'Lille bombed' – 'Many killed at Lyons' and, finally, 'Bombs in Kent' (a false alarm), the country was in new hands. Cecil King, director of the *Daily Mirror*, was exultant. 'So at last my campaign to get rid of the old menace has paid off. I consider this is the best bit of news since war was declared.' George Beardmore was pleased too but not sure quite why. 'I have always been a Churchillian because he writes well, which in the circumstances doesn't seem an adequate reason.' Hearing the news, Nella Last reported that the men in the shipyard at Barrow-in-Furness had been very impressed with Churchill when he had paid a visit. 'One man had said "To stand by him was to feel as if he had more pulses than ordinary men".' Whereas Mrs Last felt that if she 'had to spend my whole life with a man, I'd choose Mr Chamberlain, but I think I would sooner have Mr Churchill if . . . I was shipwrecked. He has a funny face, like a bulldog living on our street who has done more to drive out unwanted dogs and cats that seemed to come round than all the complaints of householders.' But a trainee nurse wondered, 'Isn't he a bit long in the tooth for such a position at this critical stage! They say he's an old bulldog, but shouldn't we be better served by a younger one of the same breed? Perhaps there aren't any.'

Churchill's first act was to prune the War Cabinet from nine members to five, but he resisted the right he felt was uniquely his 'to pass a sponge across the past'. Chamberlain was retained as a member of the War Cabinet. It was a magnanimous gesture and a necessary one, but it was short-lived. Within six months Chamberlain was dead from cancer. Halifax stayed as Foreign Secretary. The Labour Party chose to cease acting 'as patriotic gadflies' on the government, and take a full part in the direction of the war. Attlee and Arthur Greenwood, the deputy leader of the Labour Party, agreed to serve. Although there were no Liberals in the War Cabinet, the coalition spirit saw a Labour MP (A. J. Alexander) at the Admiralty, a Liberal (Archibald Sinclair) at the Air Ministry and a Conservative (Anthony Eden) at the War Office.

In addition to the role of Prime Minister, Churchill appointed himself Minister of Defence – a duality without precedence. The 'Ministry' consisted of a single office headed by a Chief of Staff, Major General Hastings 'Pug' Ismay, helped by a small staff, and it meant that Churchill was overlord of the military chiefs of staff since the Army, the Navy and the Air Force were not directly represented in the War Cabinet. As Churchill concluded 'with a profound sense of relief' as he prepared for a dreamless sleep that night, 'at last I had the authority to give direction over the whole scene. I felt I was walking with destiny . . .' But inevitably this gathering together of functions did not only mean that the Prime Minister considered himself to be without constraint when it came to pronouncing on military matters, but also that he had less time to focus on civilian issues in a time of total war. 'His interests,' observed Jock Colville, 'were predominantly defence, foreign affairs and party politics. He cared less for domestic problems or the home front except when he was roused for sentimental reasons.'

'Winston has slipped into the Prime Ministership in a very quiet atmosphere,' noted Constance Miles. 'Public attention is completely arrested by the progress of events in Belgium and Holland and there is only the most meagre amount of space in the newspapers devoted to the new regime.' The weather in England in early May was perfect, with 'blue sky, everything green bursting out', as across the Channel the German troops smashed relentlessly through the Low Countries. It would be like that throughout the summer of 1940: the contrast between perfect days of tranquil blue skies and sun-bathed landscapes and the jagged horrors of war, adding a sense of disbelief and unreality as news, invariably guarded and inconclusive but always disturbing, washed over a nation 'glued to their wireless sets' and anxiously scanning their depleted newspapers. The song of the blackbirds 'who seem to think that they are still in the Garden of Eden' unsettled J. B. Priestley, the bluff Yorkshire playwright and novelist. 'There's almost a kind of mockery in their fluting. I think most of us have often felt that we simply couldn't believe our eyes and ears: either the War wasn't real, or this spring wasn't real.'

Churchill addressed the House for the first time as Prime Minister on 13 May 1940. 'I have nothing to offer but blood, toil, tears and sweat,' he told the assembled MPs as 'strong German forces advanced in a number of directions' along the Western Front. 'We have before us many, many long months of struggle and of suffering. You ask, what is our policy? I will say: It is to wage war, by sea, land and air, with all our might and all the strength that God can give us; to wage war against a monstrous tyranny, never surpassed in the dark, lamentable catalogue of human crime. That is our policy.

'You ask, what is our aim? I can answer in one word: It is victory, victory at all costs, victory in spite of all terror, victory however long and hard the road may be; for without victory there is no survival . . .'

'Everyone is asking where the Maginot line ends,' noted George Beardmore as the highly mobile German panzer (armoured tanks) divisions, the pride of Hitler's Army, pushed through Luxembourg outflanking the highly sophisticated fortifications built between the wars along the Franco–German border, on which the French had pinned their hopes for the defence of their country against a German offensive. 'And all are utterly stupefied to discover that it doesn't extend as far as the coast. Another three days and those armies will be staring at us across the Channel.' By 12 May the panzers were on the banks of the Meuse in eastern France. The next morning came news that Rotterdam had been bombed. Rumour had it that 30,000 had been killed. In fact it was around a thousand, but it began to look as if the Armageddon that everyone had expected since the previous September was nigh. That same day Queen Wilhelmina of the Netherlands was brought across the North Sea by a British destroyer. George VI went to Liverpool Street station to greet a fellow European sovereign whom he had never met. The Dutch government followed her into exile after the surrender of Holland on 15 May.

Now the domino effect moved to Belgium. It was assumed that the reasonably well-equipped Belgian Army would be able to hold the Germans along the network of rivers and canals for a couple of weeks, to let the Franco–British forces get into position. But this was a *blitzkrieg* war and German troops swarmed through the country as the roads became clogged with terrified, fleeing refugees, hindering any possible Allied counter-attack. Finally, on 27 May, King Leopold surrendered and the Belgian troops ceased firing at dawn the next morning.

Before then, at 7 a.m. on 15 May, the French Prime Minister, Paul Reynaud, had telephoned Winston Churchill to tell him that the Germans had broken through the French defences, and tanks and armoured vehicles were pouring into France. 'We are beaten,' he said sombrely. 'We have lost the battle. The road to Paris is open.' On the afternoon of 16 May Churchill set off for Paris where he found 'utter dejection was written on every face'.

'I don't know if the government have prepared any plan for evacuation,' Harold Nicolson wrote to Vita Sackville-West who was at their home in Sissinghurst not many miles from the Kent coast, 'but you should think it out and begin to prepare something. You will have to get the Buick in a fit state to start with a full petrol-tank. You should put inside it some food for 24 hours, and pack in the back your jewels and my diaries . . . I should imagine that the best thing you can do is to make for Devonshire. This all sounds very alarming, but it would be foolish to pretend that the danger is inconceivable.' As Nicolson was anxious that his diaries should be packed into the getaway vehicle, Chips Channon was burying his in the churchyard at his country seat, Kelvedon, in Essex – or rather his head gardener was. 'Mortimer has promised to dig a hole tomorrow evening after the other gardeners have gone home,' he recorded. 'Perhaps some future generation will dig them up.'

By 20 May the Germans were at the coast of France looking across the English Channel. On 22 May the entire British fighter force of some 300 planes was withdrawn from France and in future operated from British bases near the coast at the limit of their range. The refusal to commit the RAF fully to the battle for France led to recriminations that this was a significant factor in the country's defeat. The French had assumed that the BEF, 'more a symbol of Allied solidarity than an effective fighting force', equipped with inadequate tanks and heavy guns, would be supplemented by the full force of Fighter Command. But Air Marshal Sir Hugh Dowding, its commander-in-chief, insisted on placing a strict limit on the number of RAF fighters in the battle for France. 'I saw my resources slipping away like sand in an hourglass,' wrote Dowding, who was determined to conserve his aircraft for the protection of Britain. His intransigence was to be vindicated a month or so later when Britain needed every plane the country possessed in the defence of her own skies.

Another cause of French bitterness was the decision taken by General Lord Gort VC, commander-in-chief of the BEF, to evacuate his forces, a decision he took without informing them. On 22 May, Gort realised his troops were in danger of being encircled so he began to pull units out of the firing line towards the coast at Dunkirk. With their flank exposed by British withdrawal, the French were compelled to retreat towards Dunkirk too, but what was in their mind was consolidation and counter-attack, not exit.

On 24 May Hitler inexplicably ordered the German panzers to halt. The Führer was confident that there was no way in which the British troops could get away, and he wanted to conserve his troops for the march on Paris rather than dissipate them in what he considered an already-won cause. In this, Hitler overruled his generals – and in so doing asserted that *his* was the ultimate wartime command. He might have won an internal power battle that day, but it was a pyrrhic victory. The forty-eight-hour delay in the German advance towards Dunkirk was decisive for the Allies – and it has been argued that it cost Hitler the war.

On 26 May the order went out for Operation Dynamo, the total evacuation of the BEF from France, to commence. It was a desperate operation: three days earlier, General Sir Alan Brooke, who was in command of one of the two British corps in France, believed that 'nothing but a miracle can save the BEF now, and the end cannot be very far off!' The Germans had already reached Calais, and bombers swooping over the town could be seen from Dover. The plan had been to evacuate British troops from Boulogne, Calais and Dunkirk, but this was now no longer possible. Dunkirk would be the only exit point and already the port was ablaze as a result of intermittent air raids. There were known to be over 200,000 British troops to be got out of France, and many were scattered as far as 60 miles from Dunkirk. Thousands of non-essential British personnel had already been evacuated. Now the Admiralty reckoned it had two days to get the rest of the men out before 'it is probable that evacuation will be terminated by enemy action'.

The British public were unaware of the desperate situation across the Channel until the 6 p.m. news on 31 May, when they were told that 'All night and all day men of the undefeated British Expeditionary Force have been coming home . . . From the many reports of their arrival and of interviews with the men, it is clear that if they have not come back in triumph they have come back in glory; that their morale is as high as ever; that they *know* they did not meet their masters; and they are anxious only to be back again soon – as they put it – "To have a real crack at Jerry".' Although the public had not been told, the evacuation had begun five days earlier, and tens of thousands of exhausted soldiers were already arriving at south coast ports and being decanted on to special trains. The only people to be officially informed were the military and a few civilians such as railway organisers, and volunteers like the WVS who provided practical help and comfort to the traumatised soldiers.

The Cotton family had their first intimation that something was terribly wrong five days earlier when, near Winchester, they 'were halted by a long column of lorries and buses filled with soldiers. Used as we were to such military sights, the first lot did not impress us. But after 30 or more lorries had rumbled past, we began to wonder . . . These soldiers were not the usual – they neither smiled nor sang. The men looked half dead. Some were asleep. All were dirty with sun-baked, swollen-eyed faces . . . Dick exclaimed, "Those boys are coming back from France! The English must be retreating – clear into England. What in God's name can be happening?" '

As the news of the evacuation became known, the BBC broadcast an appeal for the owners of small fishing craft, private yachts and cruisers to place themselves immediately at the disposal of the government. In Whitby, Leo Walmsley's flustered mother told him: 'All our boats have been ordered to stand-by for orders to go to France. They've got to take enough food with them to last three days' – but she had little more than two jam tarts in the larder, so though she 'wasn't going to do my week's baking till tonight, I've been at it ever since and I'm only hoping the orders won't come until I've got two meat pies done'. Walmsley hurried down to the harbour where he found a group of fishermen frantically trying to refloat two keelers that had been beached for painting and repair – in normal times it would not have been possible to get them off the shingle until the next spring high tide. But this was an emergency. And 'half the town wanted to go', including a man who was 'getting on for eighty' and had two sons fighting in France. Most seemed excited . . . but Walmsley experienced 'a sudden horrible sensation in the pit of my stomach. What about the Nazi dive bombers? If the British Army had been driven to the coast and were being evacuated, it wasn't likely the Nazis were going to allow this to take place peacefully.' But soon he too had 'caught the excitement of the crowd . . . To hell with the Nazis and their bombers! We'd show 'em whether they could smash up the British Army. If only we had a few rifles and machine guns to take with us.'

Finally, the boats were floated and the would-be heroes waited all day for the order to go, but at five o'clock that night came the news 'no more boats wanted for France . . . they've got all the boats they want . . . By the time we'd got there, there'd be nowt for us to do.' There was much disappointment at not having the opportunity to take a swipe at the Nazis with a boat hook but, as Walmsley's mother reminded the men, 'most of our lads being safe [is] summat to thank God for, and not rave because you haven't had an 'and in it'.

The armada that was volunteered for France was a heterogeneous array of (usually) seaworthy craft, large and small – trawlers, drifters, shrimpers, crabbers, small open fishing boats and summer pleasure boats as well as lifeboats, while amateur sailors who usually did it at the weekend turned out with their yachts, cabin cruisers, rowing boats and even canoes. The removal firm, Pickfords, sent its lighters – flat-bottomed barges built for transporting goods between the Solent ports and the Isle of Wight. The London Fire Brigade sent its tender, *Massey Shaw* (which almost ended up as a tragedy when its huge water cannon, which looked like a gun, led to the ship being mistaken for a German warship by a British destroyer). The German destroyer *Dracula*, which had been sunk at Scapa Flow in the First World War but subsequently raised, joined in. There were eleven boats all called *Skylark*; Port of London tugs – *Sun One* through to *Sun Fifteen*; small rowing boats with names like *Girl Gladys*, *Yorkshire Lass*, *Gay Crusader*, *Desirée*, *Lazy Days* and *Bluebird*. The aviator, Tommy Sopwith, contributed his racing yacht, *Endeavour*, and a number of motor launches went – 'resembling nothing so much as elongated motor buses with their rows of slatted seats' – which in peacetime cruised elegantly up and down the Thames. One of those launches that came back was the *Marchioness*, which was still working as a pleasure boat when it collided with a dredger on the Thames in 1989 and was sunk, with the loss of many party-going passengers.

If anything half suitable was spotted, it was requisitioned. The idea had been that the boats should be taken to the Small Vessels Pool at Sheerness on the north Kent coast and handed over to the Royal Navy.

But by 30 May the Navy was fully occupied, so a number of civilians simply set off themselves in their boats. A Hertfordshire chicken farmer who took his power cruiser, *Sundowner*, across had been second officer on the *Titanic* when it sank in the Atlantic in 1912, but others had never even been across the Channel before. Some had no compass, while others weren't entirely sure how to use one. But it didn't matter – once the boats reached the other side 'it was like Piccadilly Circus' and you just followed the crowd.

The boats were needed to take over some of the burden from the civilian-manned larger vessels and Navy transports that had been plying the Channel for days, many of whose crews were beyond tiredness and chastened by heavy losses. The captain of the Southern Rail steamer *Canterbury* refused to sail again to Dunkirk on 28 May, saying that his crew was exhausted after two trips across the Channel. There were rebellions on three of the ferries, and the captain of the *Malines* simply disobeyed orders and sailed off towards Southampton rather than cross the Channel again, saying that his crew were too debilitated 'to be depended upon in an emergency'.

June 1 was a grim day: the Luftwaffe sank thirty-one ships and seriously damaged eleven others, and sailors at sea and soldiers on the beaches began to ask, 'Where is the RAF?' as Dowding fought to conserve his planes for the next battle he knew was coming. As Lieutenant Peter Hadley recalled, 'To lie helpless in a trench or ditch while enemy aircraft do what they like overhead is one of the most demoralising ordeals that a soldier can face' – though in fact planes flying from their bases in southern England were drawn into the battle in the last desperate days, and occasionally achieved air superiority over the Germans above the beaches. But it didn't help when the BBC inflated this prowess, claiming for example that thirty-seven enemy planes had been shot down without loss when in fact the figure was less than half that. The realisation that such lies were counterproductive, destroying the government's (and the BBC's) credibility in the eyes of the public, was one of the important lessons of Dunkirk.

As the Little Ships (and they have been capitalised ever since) made their uncertain way across the Channel, weather was good – a 'beautiful calm sea'. Even so, the attrition rate was high with boats breaking down, and their gunwales being pulled off by the ropes towing bunches of them across the sea. The 'bawley boats', small old wooden fishing boats fitted with ancient engines, which in peacetime puttered around the Essex coast catching cockles and winkles for cockney treats, could not be used effectively on the beaches since they were so heavy that they ran into the sand as soon as a few soldiers climbed in; they had to be put to use ferrying men within the harbour. Some boat owners had refused to go at all: the men of the local fishing fleet at Rye in Sussex all declined, and none of the fishing-boat crews from the Devon fishing ports of Brixham and Dartmouth volunteered. Consequently the Navy had to man their boats, but since they were diesel-powered and their sailors had no experience of such engines, they kept breaking down and could not be repaired. Apart from the Ramsgate and Margate Royal National Lifeboat crews, and the coxswain and engineer of the Dover lifeboat, no lifeboat crews were prepared to go across, though 'they were probably right. The lifeboats were built with deep and heavy keels, for stability in rough seas, and they were wholly unsuitable for work off the beaches of Dunkirk.'

The record of some craft was outstanding. Lieutenant C. W. Read of the Royal Naval Reserve, in charge of the 35-foot motor launch *Bonny Heather*, managed to bring some 450 soldiers back from Dunkirk to Ramsgate, ferried a further 650 from the Dunkirk mole (jetty) to waiting transport ships, and in addition rescued forty French soldiers from SS *Scotia*, an Irish mail boat that was holed and sunk on 1 June.

For anyone with a man fighting in France and Belgium, the anxiety of the nine days of Dunkirk was unbearable. News was vague and often inaccurate, and people at home in England had no idea where their men were fighting. In total 68,111 men of the BEF were killed, wounded or missing in France.

Virginia Woolf, walking in the sun by Kingfisher pool near her home in Sussex on 30 May, 'saw my first hospital train – laden, not funereal, but weighty, as if not to shake bones. Something what is the word I want: grieving & tender & heavy laden & private – bringing our wounded back carefully through the green fields at which I suppose some looked.'

For Clara Milburn, Friday 31 May was 'the longest day ever! Every time the telephone rang one expected news' of her son Alan who was with the 7th Battalion, Royal Warwickshire Regiment in France. On 1 June she heard that 'one of ours' had been killed and there was unofficial news that there had been another death. There was still no news when the evacuation was called off, though 'the telephone rings all day with rumours and snippets of news from one or another, but nothing definite about our boys'. A week later a friend called with news that she and her husband 'had definite confirmation now' that their son, who was in the same regiment, had been killed. 'Cooper from the garage reports that a man named Smith in Alan's platoon saw him near Dunkirk, but one wants to see the man and hear his story . . . and so the days go by with hopes rising and falling, the telephone ringing and still no definite or genuine news.' It was not until 16 July that, coming back from walking the dog, Mrs Milburn was met by her husband who called that a telegram had come from the War Office: 'Alan is a prisoner of war,' he said. It was not to be until midnight on 10 May 1945 that Alan Milburn finally arrived home.

'There is no need for me to tell you how serious things are, nor that you will be called upon to undertake many and difficult tasks during the coming weeks and months,' wrote Lady Reading to her WVS county organisers on 31 May 1940. But it seemed at first that the full implications of the evacuation were not realised. WVS members were initially asked to provide darning needles but soon, as the mayor of a coastal town reported to Lady Reading, 'as the troops returned from Dunkirk in every kind of boat, we shoved them into cinemas, churches and halls. As they came through the door, many of them fell down fast asleep. You should have seen your women rolling them into lines, removing their equipment, their boots and socks, washing their feet as they lay there; and taking off their socks to wash them and then returning them.' As the WVS worked in Folkestone to prepare food and first aid, they could see the pall of smoke that hung across the French coast. Soon 'a never-ending stream of exhausted men was passing through the canteen . . . They could only answer greetings with a nod or a dazed smile, but they drank mugs of tea that were thrust into their hands and then reached the waiting trains and fell asleep . . . Owing to the need for absolute secrecy only the original six or seven volunteers were allowed into the harbour, and neither reliefs nor extra helpers could join them . . .'

Along the south-east coast similar arrangements were made, including in some places provision for the wounded. Canteens were opened at the stations through which troop trains passed – sometimes a train carrying as many as 900 soldiers would arrive every twenty minutes.

'The amazing welcome [that] we received' struck Peter Hadley as 'more suited to a victory parade than the return of a vanquished army which had made an ignominious withdrawal, saving its own skin but abandoning almost the whole of its equipment.' 'Typical of the reception is the provision that is being made for them, voluntarily, by civilians in Ashford,' reported Tom Harrisson, who was recording the scene for Mass-Observation. 'Some men, but for the most part women and children, stand by the track outside the station, it is on a small embankment there, ready with food and drinks and postcards for the troops.' The Mayor of Basingstoke and 'an energetic lady' raised £500 to buy refreshments and treats for the soldiers, while local bakers and confectioners worked through the night. At the first stop along the lines from Dover and Folkestone, at Headcorn, the staff at the small station somehow managed to provide food for 145,000 soldiers prepared in a large barn and carried 'across some fields to the Up platform'. The 'stupendous bill of fare' included 'jellied eels, sardines, cheese, oranges and apples and that culminating romance of every railway lunch, the hard boiled egg . . . [these] were reckoned in thousands; so were meat pies, rolls and sausages . . . washed down by oceans of tea and coffee, in the making of which nineteen stoves were unresting day or night. The whole of Kent could hardly have produced cups enough and the drinks were handed into the trains in tin cans. When the time was up the RASC [Royal Army Service Corps] on the platform shouted to the BEF in the train "Sling them out"; a shower of tin clattered on to the platform, the train passed away and the staff . . . fell to washing the tins and preparing for the next train.' At Tonbridge station a collection was taken from civilian passengers in trains or waiting on the platform, and soon £1,000 had been raised, while milk churns filled with water from a garden hose through the window of the platform refreshment room were on hand for parched soldiers. At a Penge station the Salvation Army band played stirring music for each train as it came in, and then held a fund-raising concert in the evening. Along the line 'a Union Jack is seen flying from a small house . . . "Someone come 'ome I expect," a woman says.' Outside Dover Harrisson saw 'Welcome' chalked on a platelayer's hut, and nearer London 'Vive La France' on a similar building. As Peter Hadley's train 'passed through London the little back gardens of dingy houses were gay with Union Jacks, and the words "Well Done the B.E.F." were chalked on innumerable walls and railway wagons . . . The rejoicing which sprang from relief at a miraculous escape was misconstrued as an expression of congratulations upon victory; and many who only a few hours before had succumbed to panic, or felt the chill of fear now wrote the letters "B.E.F." on their tin hats and shoulder straps, and stepped forth straightaway in the guise of heroes, accepting unquestioningly the homage paid to them by an adoring public, whether it took the form of admiring glances or manifested itself more practically in the shape of free drinks.'

Irene Phillips, a WVS worker, had her instructions. 'The men were to be got out of Kent and to be sent as far away from the coast as possible. It was thought that there might be the danger of air raids now that the Germans were in possession of the French ports . . . Only those who had to be operated upon immediately or really were too bad to move were to be left behind. The hospital train which was to convey them to hospitals in the west of England was to be run from our station and the men were to be brought in Green Line buses converted for the purpose, and put into the train on stretchers.' It was Mrs Phillips' 'first experience of badly wounded men, and I shall not forget the courage and endurance I saw during that time. The last day that week, a Saturday (1 June), was the worst, as the heat was even more intense, and the men were put out on the platform in rows and fed there before attempting to load them. The cases that day were bad, and I felt when I returned home at the end of it that I would never smile again . . . But throughout the whole three days I never heard a word of complaint pass the lips of anyone . . .'

Kate Phipps, who had worked for the Red Cross, was training to be a nurse at University College Hospital in London when in May 1940 she was evacuated to the Emergency Medical Service Hospital in Ashridge in Hertfordshire. At the end of the month the nurses 'were told to stand by for a convoy from France . . . and then suddenly it came . . . All our off duty leave had been cancelled, and around lunch time a whole lot of ARP men with stretchers arrived and helpers from the village . . . There was a buzz of excitement . . . for we had been practising for so long, and really did want to put on a good show . . . Our staff nurse was a bit jittery, her fiancé was with the BEF, and some nasty rumours had been floating around to the effect that they were being evacuated under fire. But nobody knew anything definite and half the tales we heard might be untrue. Sister McCabe . . . said "You must not be upset if the casualties smell a bit . . . I remember the stench of dried blood, just go ahead and clean them up, as if it were an everyday business, and make a bit of a joke, men like that." Then a car drew up . . . Two officers got out, limping and were helped into Ward 10 . . . Then it dawned on us that indeed things were wrong . . . the officers were dirty, and untidy, one lacked a uniform coat, the other had a bloody sling on his arm . . . They looked as if they had come straight from the battlefield . . . but we were not a first field dressing post, we were a base hospital . . . the terminal point in fact. What could have gone wrong?

'. . . the men dragged themselves in helped by the ARP and then collapsed! . . . One arrived in a pair of black striped trousers, another sported a tweed suit. Another had a nice business coat over his uniform trousers. And in the next ward my roommate told me that someone came in a woman's blouse and the Belgian flag . . . but he came on a stretcher. It appears that these were men from Dunkirk who had swum out to the rescue boats, or whose boats had been sunk at sea. They had discarded soaked uniforms (or had taken them off to swim) and then been hit in the water. Others (wounded) had stood packed like sardines all the way across the Channel, bombed by stukas from time to time but luckily not hit. At one moment I thought we had a prisoner because the man wore a Nazi helmet, but he was French and not at all sure where he was, and figured he'd stick to his find because he'd lost his own helmet.'

In the first ward Nurse Phipps worked on, with one exception the men 'are all French . . . Being the only one in the ward who spoke French, I have to try and translate for Sister, and a job it was to be sure for I have little knowledge of French medical terms . . . for the most part we have to guess at what the labels meant, but it was some consolation to have labels at all . . .

'We now hear that many of the men should never have walked at all, they ought to have been stretcher cases . . . but at the time they got on the boats, no stretcher cases were being taken, there just wasn't room. As the French put it *"Les brancards . . . les grands blessés, il fallait les laisser. Les vaisseaux qui auraient pu les prendre sont coulées."* [We had to leave the stretcher cases and the badly wounded behind. The ships that might have been able to take them had been sunk]. I did not pass on this sad piece of information at the time because "staff" was still worried about her fiancé (alas she has since heard that he was killed).

'The French seem to have a very fatalistic outlook and when asked for addresses of next of kin, shrug and say "It is *inutile* [no use] they are all dead." . . . When one asks for details one discovers all this is surmise. They have no evidence of death, they just presume it because things are in such a mess over there . . .

'Then the Green Line buses arrived and started to unload, they were mostly stretcher cases so the ARP men were kept busy. They wore beards, and . . . splints stuck out at all angles and blood stained head bandages. They looked dirty, and did they smell! I was glad Sister had warned us about the stench of dried blood. We wanted to smile a welcome, but felt more like crying . . .

'Pathetic little bits of equipment came in with the men, the odd gas mask, a few tin hats. Out of forty men we have only been able to collect three rifles, eight gas masks and twenty tin hats, and men under fire as these have been will stick to their tin helmets whatever else goes! What can have happened we asked each other and the men. But they didn't know: said the Frenchies had let them down and the bloody panzers were everywhere. But an army making a planned withdrawal doesn't send its wounded home in that condition, neither do men abandon their equipment!

'What little uniform they had was in a bad state, we had to cut it off in most cases. "Down the seams, nurse, it may have to be used again!" We found some of the wounds had field dressings still on that had stuck, and had to be soaked off. Their feet were in a bad state from marching and socks too had to be cut off. My scissors got so blunt in cutting through the heavy khaki, that in the end it was like sawing, but somehow we got them undressed . . . The men seemed dead tired, and we had to wash many asleep.

'. . . We stayed on duty until nearly midnight . . . It took me a long time to go to sleep, in spite of being so tired. I could not help thinking of those wounded who had not been collected, lying out there in ditches or fields with no help at hand . . .'

Barbara Roose's Uncle Harry was a sergeant in the Royal Fusiliers serving in France. 'Auntie Olive, his wife, and the rest of the family listened to every news broadcast on the wireless to hear if the men were safe. He just appeared one day on our doorstep [in Covent Garden]. He had come straight from Dunkirk, given a cup of tea by the WVS and put on a train with a week's leave before reporting back. He looked like a tramp with his uniform creased and dirty from being soaked and dried on him countless times. One of his trouser legs had been torn off to the knee. He had lost his boots and the only shoes that could be found on his return to Dover was a pair of woman's. They were so tight he refused to take them off in case he couldn't put them on again. His face was gaunt and there were several days' stubble on his chin. He looked utterly exhausted. He came in and said [to his sister] "Hello, Lou, I've just popped in on my way home for a cuppa."

'Mum rushed round making him tea and sandwiches while he recounted some of his experiences. They were stark and simple. "We queued up for days for a boat and I lost my boots when I started to swim out to a boat. I didn't get that one. My feet were cut to ribbons running over the beaches without boots. My men and myself finally swam a mile out to sea to a naval ship, but some of my mates never made it and were drowned." We were so glad that he was alive. He wouldn't stay after tea. "I must get back to my Olive, she doesn't know I'm safe." He hobbled down to Charing Cross station and mum went to see him off. He looked like a scarecrow. When he finally got home to Auntie Olive, she gently took off the shoes. The bottoms of his feet were raw flesh and congealed blood. He was one of the lucky ones.'

A number of the men who came back from Dunkirk had been severely traumatised by the endless sleepless nightmare they had escaped. As they had trudged along the roads clogged with fleeing French refugees, the soldiers had witnessed civilians mown down from the air, and they had been forced to abandon badly wounded comrades to their fate. On the beaches most were in a state of zombie-like exhaustion, some almost paralysed with fear, as the Stukas dive-bombed the soldiers waiting in lines to be taken off the beaches, and panic threatened to break out every time a boat appeared, with men rushing forward and grasping its side.

Several officers and men cracked, running screaming through the dunes, or burying themselves in the sand. When the Dunkirk veterans arrived back in Britain, some had not slept for more than five days and nights. A doctor in a London hospital was shocked at the number of men in states of 'total and abject neurotic collapse'. 'Men swarmed into the hospital, some raging mutinously at officers for having deserted them in a panic, and others swearing that they would never fight again. So complete a loss of morale in some was scaring to behold.' Kate Phipps had 'a case of shell shock' on her ward. 'A lot of the men still "hear" the guns, but this one jumps at every noise, moans and groans when he thinks anyone is paying attention, and refuses to talk.'

Sometimes it seemed as if the lessons of the trauma of battle in the First World War had been ill learned. At the Fazakerly hospital in Liverpool, the director, William Johnson, was a neurologist who had run the Army's treatment centre at Passchendaele in 1917. His younger psychiatric colleagues, John Bowlby and Kenneth Soddy, were convinced that the men in their care were mentally ill, suffering from acute 'anxiety and depression brought about by the loss of close friends, or the horror of the treatment of refugees', and needed psychotherapy. Johnson refused to condone this. All that was needed for those traumatised at Dunkirk, he insisted, was a short rest and then the 'scrimshanks' (as he was wont to refer to them) should be given forceful 'encouragement' to rejoin their units as soon as possible.

Between 27 May and 3 June, when the evacuation was officially halted, 338,226 soldiers arrived in British ports from Dunkirk, and to this number can be added 28,000 non-essential British personnel who had already been evacuated before the start of Operation Dynamo. Six destroyers, one gunboat, seventeen minesweepers, five anti-submarine trawlers, seventeen miscellaneous craft including personnel and hospital ships, and sixty-three small craft with names like *Albatross*, *Black Arrow*, *Clara Belle*, *Dumplin*, *Eastbourne Queen*, *Lark*, *Little Ann*, *Miranda*, *Skylark* (three by that name of the eleven that went), *Southern Queen*, *Sunshine* and *Willy & Alice* were at the bottom of the sea, along with an estimated 2,000 men.

It is the armada of Little Ships that has become the prevailing image of Dunkirk, but as the historian Nicholas Harman points out, the majority of the troops evacuated from Dunkirk came home on Royal Navy ships or boats crewed by members of the Royal Naval Reserve who were 'as much part of His Majesty's armed forces as any peace time civilian recruited for the duration. They had put on uniform, picked up their guns and gone to war.' Figures can be inaccurate: checking off a tally was not the priority in those terrible nine days, but Harman suggests that before 'the secret was lifted' on the six o'clock news on 31 May, '72,000 soldiers left the beaches mostly in craft manned by the Royal Navy or by the soldiers themselves. After the secret was revealed, when civilian volunteers began to come forward, 26,500 were rescued from the beaches' while thousands more left from the port.

There had been concern about how the manifest weakness of British fighting forces might affect civilian morale. 'I'm afraid there is going to be a considerable shock for the British public. It is your duty to act as shock-absorbers, so I have prepared with my counterpart at the War Office, a statement which can be published subject to censorship,' Major General Mason-Macfarlane, the BEF's Director of Military Intelligence, told a gathering of British correspondents on their return from France on 28 May. But in the event, that didn't seem much of a problem. As Frances Partridge wrote, 'no retreat can ever have taken place with a greater blaring of trumpets and headlines'. The *Daily Mirror* proclaimed it was 'Bloody Marvellous'; *War Illustrated* told 'The Immortal Story of Dunkirk'; broadcasting his popular *Postscript*, J. B. Priestley constructed the whole episode as 'typically English [and when he said English he hastily admitted that he meant 'typically British'] in the way in which when apparently all was lost, so much was gloriously retrieved. Bright honour was almost "plucked from the moon". What began as a miserable blunder, a catalogue of misfortunes and miscalculations, ended as an epic of gallantry. We have a queer habit – and you can see it running through our history – of conjuring up such transformations . . . here at Dunkirk is another English epic. And to my mind what was most characteristically English about it – so typical of us, so absurd and yet so grand and gallant that you hardly know whether to laugh or cry when you read about them – was the part played in the difficult and dangerous embarkation – not by the warships, magnificent though they were – but by the little pleasure-steamers. We've known them and laughed at them, all our lives . . . And our great grand-children when they learn how we began this War by snatching glory out of defeat, and then swept onto victory, may also learn how the little holiday steamers made an excursion to hell and came back glorious.'

'Cato', the collective pseudonym of three Beaverbrook newspaper journalists, one of whom was the future Labour leader Michael Foot, picked up the refrain. 'A miracle is born. This land of Britain is rich in heroes. She had brave, daring men in her Navy and Air Force as well in her Army. She had heroes in jerseys and sweaters and old rubber boots in all the fishing ports of Britain . . . In all the south-east ports of Britain there was not a man or a boy, who knew how to handle a boat, who was not prepared to give his own life to save some unknown, valorous son of his country who had faced without flinching the red hell of Flanders in the cause which he knew to be his own . . .' But the main thrust of this adulation, written just as the evacuation ended, was a powerful indictment of the policies of appeasement. *Guilty Men* was published in early July 1940 and, despite being banned by major distributors, sold 200,000 copies. Speaking in the language of Priestley, its authors emphasised the point by contrasting the deluded, despicable 'men of Munich' with the 'ordinary people' who had turned Dunkirk into victory.

At home in Barrow, Nella Last got caught up in the nobility of it all as she read 'the accounts of the Dunkirk evacuation [in the newspaper] . . . I forgot I was a middle-aged woman who often got tired and who had backache. The story made me feel part of something that was undying and never old – like a flame to light or warm, but strong enough to burn and destroy trash and rubbish . . . I felt everything was worthwhile, and I felt glad that I was of the same race as the rescuers and rescued.'

Basil Dean decided that ENSA, which he had set up to entertain the troops, should put on cinema shows for the returning humanity: 'they could no longer be called troops, for they were without arms or unit formations of any kind; Frenchmen, Belgians and the British in seemingly inextricable confusion, as they jostled one in long lines in the dining-halls and canteens'. In Bridport in Dorset 'the town was crammed to suffocation. In a small pub . . . we listen[ed] to the seething soldiery (that is the only adjective to use) expressing blasphemous resentment at what had happened to them. There was a typical "Sergeant Troy" in the bar whose loud-mouthed criticism of the junior officers of his Ack-Ack unit in seizing the only available transport and making for the French coast, leaving their N.C.O.s and men to fend for themselves was gaining angry corroboration among his listeners. These dismayed men, savagely wounded in their pride, were seeking relief in bitter criticism of those set over them. We promised each other that whilst the war lasted we would never speak of what we had heard that night, and we never did.'

The Woolfs heard a similar account from Harry West, the brother of the Woolfs' servant Louie who lived in a cottage in Rodmell. 'Harry came back on Monday,' Virginia wrote on 21 June. 'It pours out – how he hadn't boots off for 3 days; the beach at Dunkirk – the bombers as low as trees – the bullets like moth holes in his coat – how no English aeroplanes fought; how the officer told them to take their shoes off & go past a pill box on all fours. Then went himself with a grenade and blasted it. At Dunkirk many men shot themselves as the planes swooped. Harry swam off, a boat neared. Say Chum Can you row. Yes, he said, hauled in and rowed for 5 hours, saw England, landed – didn't know if it were night or day or what town – didn't ask – couldn't write to his mother so was despatched to his regiment. He looted a Belgian shop & stuffed his pockets with rings, which fell out in the sea; but watches pinned to his coat survived . . . He saw his cousin dead on the beach; & another man on the street. He was talking to a chap, who showed him a silk handkerchief bought for his joy lady. That moment a bomb killed him. Harry took the handkerchief. Harry has had eno' war, & is certain of our defeat – got no arms & no aeroplanes – how can we do anything?'

Towards the end of 1940, Cecil King of the *Daily Mirror* lunched with the Director of Statistics at the War Office who confided that 'the Dunkirk episode was far worse than was ever realised even in Fleet Street. The men on getting back to England were so demoralised they threw their rifles out of the railway-carriage windows. Some sent for their wives with their civilian clothes, changed into these, and walked home!'

After nine months of non-activity, the only campaign in which British soldiers had been directly involved had been a failure. The BEF had retreated and tanks, lorries, guns, fuel – all the equipment of war – had been destroyed to prevent it from falling into enemy hands, or abandoned on the beaches of France. But had the soldiers stayed on to fight, it is likely that this always small force would have suffered more dead, more wounded, more prisoners of war taken. Nevertheless, it was a defeat. As Churchill said sagaciously in the House of Commons, 'We must be very careful not to assign to this deliverance the attributes of a victory. Wars are not won by evacuation . . .'

But Margot, Cecil King's first wife, had seen 'a motorised column of troops going through Henley yesterday. So far in this war, very unlike the last, the people have shown no interest in, let alone enthusiasm for, our soldiers. But this time, the streets were lined with people watching, many of whom darted into shops, bought cigarettes and fruit and threw them into the soldiers' lorries as they passed. This is the first account of the kind I have heard, and it is perhaps due to Dunkirk and all that.' In welcoming the troops back from their ordeal – and their 'betrayal' by gutless foreigners as many British believed – it was possible to begin to divine a higher purpose in all the niggling irritations of wartime privations and regulations, to luxuriate in the 'quite extraordinary capacity [of their new Prime Minister] for expressing in Elizabethan English the sentiments of the public' (even though he forswore mention of the Little Ships) as he memorably assured the House of Commons that, 'We shall not flag or fail. We shall go on to the end. We shall fight in France, we shall fight on the seas and the oceans, we shall fight with growing strength and growing confidence in the air, we shall defend our island whatever the cost may be. We shall fight on the beaches, we shall fight on the landing grounds, we shall fight in the fields and in the streets, we shall fight in the hills, we shall never surrender . . .'

But it wasn't just columns of defeated soldiers that were coming across the Channel. It was the war. Twenty-one miles of water was all that now separated Britain from the German forces. Dunkirk might have been a military retreat but it had to be a fresh start. The axis had swung from the 'old guard', with their indictable political misapprehensions and military unpreparedness, to the 'people' – soldiers, sailors and airmen – and civilians who had somehow got caught up in the resilience and initiative and fortitude too, and were going to be called upon 'to defend our island'. For after Dunkirk, the war Britain was going to fight was the one the country had been schooled to expect all along. Under the pugilistic leadership of Winston Churchill, Britain was going to fight Chamberlain's defensive war.

In the next five years the unity of the people would be of paramount importance. There would be times, as in the trenches of the First World War, when those on the Home Front would feel that they were 'lions led by donkeys', let down by those who had a duty of leadership, and of care, in a morass of bungling and ineptitude. The 'people' were going to have to be prepared to resist invasion, and to survive the bombs of the Luftwaffe. They were going to have to be the heroes. And so it was just as well that they had managed to construct for themselves an enduring heroic narrative. Dunkirk kept Britain in the war: with the British, against all rational odds, still believing that they could win it.

9

WAITING FOR HITLER

"I've laid your uniform out, my Lord."

Last night a Stand-To was ordered. Thirty men of us here
Came out to guard the starlit-village – my men who wear
Unwitting the season's beauty, the received truth of the spade –
Roadmen, farm labourers, masons, turned to another trade.
CECIL DAY-LEWIS, *WORLD ALL OVER*

'HOW BLACK CAN you take it?' a friend had asked the Coopers –
Duff, the recently appointed Minister of Information, and his
wife Lady Diana – as they arrived for dinner, 'having groped our way
[through the blackout] into Max Beaverbrook's house to learn what
seemed the worst of all news . . . The Channel ports had gone. Now we
were truly naked to our enemies. Italy was against us too, bitter but
expected news.' The Coopers had just moved from their house in Chapel
Street, Mayfair, into a top-floor suite in the Dorchester Hotel (known as

'the Dorch', its reinforced concrete structure making it reputedly the safest hotel in London). 'From its high windows [in Park Lane] one could scan nearly all London beyond the green sea of Hyde Park, sprawled out for slaughter, dense with monuments, landmarks, tell-tale railway lines and bridges. How red would the flames be I wondered, when our hour struck?'

On 11 June 1940, Count Ciano, Mussolini's Foreign Minister and son-in-law, had announced that Italy was entering the war in support of Germany. On the 14th Paris surrendered. On the 16th Reynaud resigned as Prime Minister; Marshal Pétain took over and sued for peace. On 17 June, the rearguard of the BEF was rounded up and loaded on to the great Cunard ocean liner, *Lancastria*, at Saint-Nazaire. The ship was bombed and sank within half an hour. It was announced that of the 6,000 passengers aboard, 3,000 perished. The true figure was probably nearer 5,000. 'When the news came to me,' wrote Churchill, 'I forbade its publication saying "The newspapers have got quite enough disaster for today at least." ' On 18 June the French Under-Secretary for War, the relatively unknown, imperious Brigadier General Charles de Gaulle, broadcast on the BBC. Often referred to in the British press as 'an expert on mechanised warfare', he had escaped to London and would settle in Petts Wood in Kent. He asserted, 'The flame of the French resistance must not go and will not go out', and he urged his fellow countrymen to fight on. He invited those in Britain to join him so the Free French could continue the struggle.

On that day, the 125th anniversary of the Battle of Waterloo when Britain had defeated the forces of Napoleon, Churchill spoke to the House of Commons and reiterated that 'whatever happened in France would make no difference to the resolve of Britain and the British Empire to fight on "if necessary for years, if necessary alone" '. He ended with the prediction that now the Battle of France was over, 'I expect that the Battle of Britain is about to begin. Upon this battle depends the survival of Christian civilisation. Upon it depends our own British life, and the long continuity of our institutions and our Empire. The whole fury and might of the enemy must very soon be turned on us. Hitler knows that he will have to break us in this island or lose the war. If we can stand up to him, all Europe may be free and the life of the world may move forward into broad, sunlit uplands. But if we fail, then the whole world including the United States [he added pointedly] . . . will sink into the abyss of a new Dark Age . . . Let us therefore brace ourselves to our duties and so bear ourselves that if the British Empire and its Commonwealth lasts for a thousand years, men will still say, "this was their finest hour".'

For the millions who heard the speech repeated on their wirelesses at home, this proved to be the most memorable of the Prime Minister's wartime broadcasts. Virginia Woolf found it 'reassuring about defence of England; not all claptrap. Now we're fighting alone with our backs to the wall. Bombs first then invasion.' Yet, despite the impact his speeches had, Churchill broadcast only five times during the entire course of the war – and on one of those occasions he spoke for only two minutes. He was aware that 'it was only words' and that rhetoric doesn't win wars any more than evacuations do, that Britain's position was perilous – perhaps hopeless. But the retired Bishop of Durham, who had thought the speech 'another magnificent achievement', recognised that 'there are moments when *words* are the most potent *facts* and this is one'.

Despite reassuring words, the Army was desperately short of equipment; the depleted forces were recovering from their ordeal in France, and regrouping and training to re-enter the battle. The Air Force was counting its losses and trying to calculate its strength to counteract the Luftwaffe. Churchill was told by his scientific adviser Lord Lindemann that the RAF had lost an estimated 1,393 planes between 10 May and 28 June, and that the UK air strength totalled 4,732 aircraft – including reserves: hardly a match for the 11,600 aircraft the Germans were believed to still have despite heavy losses.

On 3 July, in order to ensure that it did not fall into German hands, a large part of the French fleet was sunk by the British at Mers-el Kebir near Oran in Algeria, with the loss of over a thousand French sailors and a further embittering of Anglo–French relations.

A decision had to be made about the Channel Islands. The military chiefs of staff argued that the islands could not be defended, but to Churchill it was 'repugnant . . . to abandon British territory which has been in the possession of the Crown since the Norman Conquest', and he argued that British sea power could stop a German invasion. But the Channel Islands, until then regarded by most Britons as sunny holiday resorts, tax havens and the source of tomatoes, were now to be treated as part of the abandoned Continent as Churchill acquiesced to his military advisers. The islands were 'demilitarised' after one air raid on Jersey; a number of Channel Islanders plus some livestock were evacuated; and when the German troops arrived on Jersey, Guernsey, Alderney and Sark on 1 July 1940 practically every house flew a white flag in a gesture of surrender to their invaders. At first the Germans controlled the Channel Islands with a much lighter hand than they exercised in occupied France a few miles away; fraternisation was not discouraged, and a blind eye was usually turned when islanders tuned into BBC broadcasts – but the occupation grew much crueller as the war progressed.

Despite the worst possible military news when 'in most people's minds the Channel has shrunk to something no bigger than the Thames', morale seemed to be remarkable. 'For the first time I understood what the maxim meant: "England never knows when she is beaten",' marvelled the American journalist, Virginia Cowles. '. . . I not only understood the maxim; I understood why Britain never *had* been beaten.' The King wrote to his mother, 'personally I feel happier now that we have no allies to be polite to and pamper'. Air Marshal Dowding wrote to Churchill from Fighter Command HQ: 'Well! Now it is England against Germany, and I don't envy them the job!' Diana Cooper was sure that 'without reason the English felt better after the fall of France. I know I did. It was a challenge, which is always invigorating. Insane that it should have been so, but we had Winston to stiffen our sinews and teach us how to war.' Leonard Woolf 'had that strange sense of relief – almost exhilaration – at being left alone, "shut of" all encumbrances, including our allies – "now we can go it alone" in our muddled, makeshift, empirical, English way.'

Others were more resigned than robust – and some were afraid. On 17 June 1940, Joan Wyndham had got home to find her mother 'white as a sheet and telephoning wildly. She said "France has surrendered – you'd better leave London tonight! . . . your Aunt Lalla says she'll have you. I'll take you down tomorrow." I fought tooth and nail but it wasn't any good – a lot of balls about being young and having your life before you. If London is going to be destroyed I'd rather I'd stay with it as long as possible and go on working and being with my friends until we're all blown up . . . I think it's the bloodiest thing I ever heard of, being shuffled out of the way like this.' Vivienne Hall, who worked for an insurance firm in the City of London, noted that most people were still hopeful and 'only one or two announced gloomily that we might as well put our heads in a gas oven as the Germans would be here any minute'. There was reported to be 'defeatist talk' in Fulham, and news from Greenwich and Deptford suggested that the 'possibility of our not being victorious is now being considered by some people'. The writer Rebecca West recalled strolling in the rose gardens in Regent's Park in those early June days: 'people . . . walked among the rose beds, with special earnestness looking down on the bright flowers and inhaling the scent, as if to say, "That is what roses are like, that is how they smell. We must remember that, down in the darkness." Most of these people believed, and rightly, that they were presently to be subjected to a form of attack more horrible than had ever before been directed against common man. Let nobody belittle them by pretending they were fearless.'

But newspaper magnate Cecil King didn't think 'the country is seriously worried. They are depressed by the continued lack of good news, but life continues much as usual.' In east London, which was to suffer more than anywhere in the coming months, the 'Stop the War' candidate in the Bromley-by-Bow by-election held on 12 June 1940 polled only 509 votes, and only 6 per cent of those asked favoured peace at any price. A Gallup poll taken in mid June showed that only 3 per cent of the population believed that Britain might lose the war. 'It would be difficult for an impartial observer to decide today,' wrote Mollie Panter-Downes for the *New Yorker* magazine, 'whether the British are the bravest or merely the most stupid people in the world. The way they are acting in the present situation could be used to support either claim . . .'

Air raids had already started. As the German Army made its final assault on Paris, the Luftwaffe flew intermittent bombing raids over Britain. Their targets were aerodromes but most bombs missed and fell harmlessly in open countryside. During 18 and 19 June, 120 German bombers attacked eastern England; nine people were killed in a raid on Cambridge when a row of houses was destroyed; an oil fire was started on Canvey Island; and the first bomb to fall in the London area fell at Addington near Croydon. Small-scale raids continued on the capital for the rest of the month.

Between 2 and 10 July bombs fell on every seaside town south of the Tyne, at least on one night and sometimes more. On 4 July, 'They bombed the train at Newhaven: the driver died this morning. Passengers lay under seats. Rails wrecked. Today a plane – ours – crashed at Southsea. So the Germans are nibbling at my afternoon walks [on the Sussex Downs],' wrote Virginia Woolf. On 9 July Norwich had its first raid: at Colman's mustard factory a plane appeared in the sky. 'The older men remembering the sound of falling bombs from the First World War threw themselves to the ground at the same time shouting to the women "Down!" The women and girls did not immediately abandon their bicycles – bicycles were precious possessions in those days of low wages and represented the only alternative to long walks to work – and they did not throw themselves to the ground.' Several workers were killed, many seriously injured, and flying debris and glass scarred the surrounding buildings. Daylight raids penetrated further inland to the Thames Valley, and to Norfolk and even parts of Wales, and bombs fell on ports including Falmouth, Plymouth, Portsmouth, Weymouth and Dover; shipping in the Channel and the North Sea was attacked. On 12 July there was an air attack in Aberdeen: no sirens had sounded and more than fifty people were killed or seriously wounded.

It seemed to most people that now that the Germans had overrun Holland, Belgium and France, their next logical step must be an airborne assault on Britain. On his arrival in London from the Netherlands, Prince Bernhard, Queen Wilhelmina's son-in-law had spoken nervously about the Germans sending 12,000 troops by parachute to land in his country, and added equally implausibly that the Dutch had managed to kill 10,000 of them. In Britain the fables ballooned. *The Times* reported that a Dutch government minister had claimed that Germans had landed in Holland 'disguised as nuns, Red Cross nurses, monks and tram conductors'. The rest of the press took up the story with gusto, writing of men dropping out of the sky 'like a vast flock of vultures'. Some were wearing Allied or Dutch uniforms, others were dressed as policemen and as soon as their feet touched the ground they began to direct (or misdirect) traffic and confuse the Army. Stories spread of parachutists dropping wearing women's skirts and blouses and clutching machine guns – though it was not clear whether these were warlike women or men in drag. There were reported sightings of men wearing sky-blue uniforms dangling from transparent parachutes that made them almost invisible as they floated down. *The Times* warned that 'enemy parachutists [dropped in Britain] might speak English quite well. Some might be sent over in civilian dress to act as spies. The general public must be alert.'

'We talked endlessly of parachutists,' remembered Lady Diana Cooper, 'of how they would come and deceive us by being dressed as nurses, monks or nuns with collapsible bicycles concealed beneath their habits. An English uniform would have been a better disguise.' The matron at the Emergency Hospital in Hertfordshire where Kate Phipps was nursing had assembled the staff 'and announced that we are to sign a book if we go out of the grounds in our off duty times. There is some talk that parachutists might drop on us as they have in France, and "Nurses, it is said that they are drugged and very dangerous, so please be very careful!" ' A couple of days later Matron stepped up the precautions: 'there will be classes in ju jitsu for any nurses who wish, so that they can equip themselves for coping.'

In the country Frances Partridge noted that 'everyone makes jokes about the likelihood of German parachutists landing in our Wiltshire fields dressed as nuns or clergymen – a good farcical subject on which to let off steam. This afternoon I was alone in the kitchen when the doorbell rang, and there on the step stood three tall bearded men who addressed me in strong German accents, and wore something between clergymen's and military dress! Aha! I thought, the parachutists already. But [then] I realised that it was some of the Brüderhof, a community of Christian Pacifists of all nations who live the simple life near Swindon.' The next day, walking on the downs with Julia Strachey, Partridge was 'almost brained by a wounded pheasant. "Perhaps it's a disguised parachutist," said Julia. On the wireless we hear dreadful stories of a German advance, calling up pictures of giant machines, a sky black with aeroplanes, and the unceasing crash of bombs and explosives. "Well. It's fucking awful, that's all I can say," said Julia. Yet I think a strange calm possesses us all.'

As the Dunkirk evacuation was in its final stages Churchill had proclaimed that Britons would 'defend our island, whatever the cost may be'. Some had taken action already. Lady Helena Gleichen, a Herefordshire landowner and cousin of Queen Mary, the Queen Mother, was concerned about landings along the thinly populated Welsh borders and had seized the initiative in March 1940. She organised seventy of her estate workers and tenants as the 'Much Marcle Watchers', giving them stencilled armbands proclaiming their affiliation. When her request to the King's Shropshire Light Infantry for the loan of eighty rifles, and some ammunition 'with a couple of machine guns if you have any', was turned down, she armed her troop with pikes, halberds and flintlocks that were hanging on the walls of her ancestral home.

A friend of Kate Phipps was 'running an anti-invasion post at Bledlow, up on the hill, and local women go there on two hourly shifts at night . . . to watch out for parachutists! . . . However, none have yet been sighted to date,' she wrote on 16 June. 'There have been objections by husbands to wives being out at all hours. Recently one of our planes came down (or maybe was shot down) and the pilot bailed out . . . to be met by fierce farmers armed with pitchforks. He was escorted to the police station, just in case . . .' A group of cyclists had been regularly patrolling the Dumfriesshire coast since April, and in Essex the Bishop of Romford reported that a company 'about 100 strong' had been guarding vital spots and keeping a lookout for parachutists and was petitioning for recognition – and to be armed. Reports came in of farmers all along the east coast 'oiling up their fowling pieces ready to receive what they called "those umbrella men" '.

In the debate over the Norwegian fiasco that had brought Churchill to power in May 1940, the Labour MP Josiah Wedgwood had suggested that civilians should be trained in the use of rifles: 'We should use them like *franc-tireurs* [armed fighters who, if captured, would not be accorded prisoner-of-war status]. They would no doubt be shot if they were taken. But they would be able to harass any small invading forces and not wait until some regular troops came to help.' Harold Nicolson winced, thinking the excitable MP 'gave the impression of being a little bit off his head'.

But such suggestions began to seem less and less like the fantasies of the unhinged as stories filtered in from across the Channel, and it was clear that the Regular Army was currently indisposed due to exhaustion, shortage of manpower, post-Dunkirk disorganisation and an acute lack of arms and equipment. At the start of June there were precisely fifteen infantry divisions and one armoured division to defend southern England, and on average the infantry divisions were only half-strength and possessed only about a sixth of the artillery they needed – and most of that was obsolete. The lack of transport would mean that 'the bulk of troops, if ordered to move faster than they could march, would do so in hired motor-coaches driven by civilians unprepared for the conditions which might await them in the event of a German landing . . .' And this could mean 'that in some instances a whole day and night, would elapse before the troops would start'. Ammunition for the army was in such short supply that hardly any could be spared for training purposes, and the total number of tanks in the entire country was 463. An attack could be expected anywhere along 400 miles of coastline facing the Continent, and airborne troops might land well to the rear of the forces guarding the most vulnerable coastline. The chiefs of staff were forced to concede that 'should the Germans succeed in establishing a force with its vehicles in this country, our army forces have not got the offensive power to drive it out'. It did rather seem that Churchill's question to the Lord Privy Seal the previous October could no longer be ignored. 'Why do we not form a Home Guard [as Churchill would always call the force] of half a million men over forty (if they like to volunteer) and put all our elderly stars at the head and in the structure of these new formations?' he had asked.

At last on 14 May 1940, immediately after the nine o'clock news, Anthony Eden, the Secretary of State for War, broadcast to the 'countless ordinary citizens, especially those not eligible to enrol in the armed forces, who had asked to be allowed to serve in the defence of their country in its hour of peril . . . Well, now is your opportunity.' The nation wanted 'large numbers of men who are British citizens between the ages of 17 and 65 to come forward now and offer their services . . . This appeal is directed chiefly to those who live in country parishes, in small towns and in less densely populated suburban areas . . . The name of the new force will be the Local Defence Volunteers (LDV). This name describes its duties in three words. You will not be paid but you will receive uniforms and you will be armed. In order to volunteer, what you have to do is to give your name and address to your local police station, and when we want you we will let you know . . .'

Constance Miles' husband, a retired major in the Royal Artillery, had been reduced to 'starting a war scrapbook and sticking in articles from the *Daily Telegraph*' and lecturing his local ARP HQ 'about the importance of arming men in villages' in his frustration at having his military experience go to waste, as he saw it. But Robin Miles instantly forgot the irritation he felt at his wife's frivolity in planting blue lobelias on the 'very dark day' that Holland fell when 'he heard on the wireless that the Local Defence Volunteers were to be formed which would actually – poor eager Robin! – include men of his age'.

Like hundreds of thousands of others, Miles set off for his local police station first thing in the morning to put his name down, and the next day declined to leave the house to accompany his wife on a shopping trip to Guildford 'because I might be called up to join'. He was disappointed to find that by lunchtime the same day 'nothing had happened'.

Many police stations had not been alerted to this new initiative and were flummoxed when long queues started forming at their doors. The morning after Eden's broadcast, the novelist Ernest Raymond 'was at our police station after breakfast. I confess I expected some praise for this promptitude . . . It was not forthcoming. The uniformed policeman behind the desk sighed as he said "We can take your name and address. That's all." A detective-inspector in mufti . . . explained the absence of any fervour. "You're about the hundred-and-fiftieth who's come in so far, Mr Raymond, and it's not yet half past nine. Ten per cent of them may be some use to Mr Eden, but 'lor' luv-a-duck we've had 'em stumping in more or less on crutches. One old codger who we knew for a cert is seventy-odd came in and swore he was sixty-one . . . And the kids! . . . we've had 'em coming in and swearing they were seventeen last March. We've taken their names, but Gawd's truth, this is going to be Alexander's ragtime army." '

Within twenty-four hours of the broadcast, some quarter of a million men had put their names down. By the end of June there were nearly one and a half million volunteers and Eden admitted that his expectations 'have been far exceeded'. The eager recruits spanned the social spectrum. In Burford in Oxfordshire the platoon included the local MP, lorry drivers and farm workers; in a nearby village 'carpenters, masons, farm labourers, carters, shepherds, gardeners, bakers, game-keepers, woodmen, farmworkers, storemen, farmers, quarrymen, grocers. A good country collection' signed up. Cricket clubs, local hunts, and Eton College formed units, and an LDV waterborne section patrolled the Thames. The staff at Buckingham Palace volunteered a platoon, and a number of Americans working in London formed a detachment with red eagles on their arms. The Ambassador, Joseph Kennedy, who was sceptical of Britain's ability to defeat Hitler, was said to disapprove.

Moreover, although what is remembered as the Home Guard is usually associated with the countryside – and indeed many Cornish volunteers were reputed 'to have poaching in their blood, which is the secret of good field craft' – enthusiasm was not confined to rural areas. In towns and cities volunteers signed on in even greater numbers, and Civil Defence organisers grew alarmed at the number of ARP wardens and administrative staff who were defecting to this new militia. Ernest Raymond was one, though 'all that happened was a white brassard on my arm with the letters L.D.V. instead of one with the letters A.R.P.'

Factory owners sponsored LDV defence groups, while the railways had their own unit, as did a number of collieries. Lord Beaverbrook took the opportunity to boost morale in the aircraft production factories over which he presided. He accepted weapons from an organisation called the Committee of American Aid to British Homes, which, finding that the wheels of official bureaucracy ground exceeding slow, was quite prepared to ship the large number of rifles and revolvers it had collected direct to Beaverbrook. He also managed to acquire a large quantity of armour plate and produced several hundred special armoured cars known as 'Beaverettes' for the use of his Ministry of Aircraft Production Home Guard. Neither these nor the US-acquired weapons was 'the Beaver' prepared to make available to the home forces. 'The whole thing was fantastic,' General Sir Alan Brooke, who took over from Ironside as commander-in-chief Home Forces on 20 July 1940, wrote, 'at a time when I was shouting for every armoured vehicle I could lay my hands on with which to equip regular forces . . . How could individual armies have held out, and what part could they have played once the main battle for this country was lost?'

Subsequently – and to a large extent at the time – what was to become the Home Guard has been seen affectionately as a loyal 'Dad's Army'. The average age of its recruits was indeed that of a dad, though there were boys who were too young for conscription, patriotically playing at being soldiers with broomsticks and obsolete guns. There were some grandads too ('Long Dentured Veterans'), including an ex-company sergeant major who had served in the Sudan campaign in 1885 (and subsequently in the Boer War and the First World War) and was still serving on his eightieth birthday.

Half the LDV had seen service in the Great War, and in some units it was estimated that 75 per cent of the volunteers were ex-servicemen, and almost a quarter of those enrolled in the Northamptonshire LDV within two days of the broadcast appeal were officers or NCOs. By Saturday Major Miles was getting tetchy 'at the usual sight of a cricket match on the village green, everybody in white flannels. "Oh," says Robin, all on edge and bitter about the delay . . . "why don't they invite some parachuters to come and play next Saturday? They could lay down their hand grenades and give us a game before killing us." '

It seemed clear that the LDV had been formed primarily as a response to the public's call for action, and resentment grew that it was an example of the government involving the people in a patriotic gesture without giving the matter any substance. A retired major general, who was also a Conservative MP and a member of the Westminster LDV, Sir Alfred Knox, reprimanded Eden, telling him that the public was waiting for something concrete to be done about the force beyond simply the taking down of names.

Tom Wintringham, who had been the military correspondent for *Picture Post* since the start of the war, came up with the idea of circumventing this inertia and getting in on the ground floor in building up a citizen army. Wintringham was a complex character who saw himself as part of the tradition of radical, bloody-minded Lincolnshire dissenters. A founder member of the Communist Party of Great Britain (CPGB) in 1920, he had built a reputation as the Left's most formidable military theorist as the question of war became ever more salient in the 1930s. In 1936 Wintringham was sent to Spain to cover the Civil War for the CPGB newspaper the *Daily Worker* and he was drawn into fighting on the Republican side and soon commanded the English-speaking battalion of the International Brigade. Wintringham saw many possible parallels between the Home Guard and the Spanish socialist POUM, a people's militia. 'Superficially alike in mixture of uniforms and half uniforms, in shortage of weapons and ammunition, in hasty and incomplete organisation and lack of modern training, they seemed to me more fundamentally alike in their serious eagerness to learn, their resolve to meet and defeat all the difficulties in their way, their certainty that despite shortages of time and gear they could fight and fight effectively.'

In collaboration with Edward Hulton, the owner of *Picture Post*, and its editor Tom Hopkinson, Wintringham set up a private training school. *Picture Post* provided the publicity and the Earl of Jersey the premises: the extensive grounds of his mansion Osterley Park just outside London – though 'he hoped we wouldn't blow up the house as it was one of the country's showplaces and had been in the family for some time'. 'Could we dig weapon pits? Loose off mines? Throw hand grenades? Set fire to old lorries in the grounds?' Wintringham asked. 'Of course! Anything you think useful,' the obliging Earl told him. The staff consisted largely of other Spanish Civil War veterans including the surrealist painter Roland Penrose, whose strength lay in camouflage, and Stanley White, a chief instructor to the Boy Scouts, employed to teach stalking techniques. Wilfred Vernon (who would be elected a Labour MP in 1945), a former senior technical officer at the Royal Aircraft Establishment, was brought in to improvise mines, grenades and other forms of destruction, and three Spanish anarchist miners, veterans of the Civil War, showed how to lob high explosives at approaching tanks.

The school was an instant success – its classes could have been filled three times over – and eager recruits queued up to join the two-day programmes and learn how to ambush tanks, engage in hand-to-hand combat and hit-and-run raids, heat dynamite in a saucepan – it doesn't go off when heated, it goes off when compressed, Vernon reassured Hopkinson – and other techniques of guerrilla warfare. As short of equipment as Home Guard units, they had a single shotgun with one cartridge intended for deer shooting 'to destroy these formidable invaders', so Hopkinson set out to equip the men. With the purchase of another shotgun and a .22 rifle, 'we became the most heavily armed unit in the neighbourhood' and when they heard that all the government intended to provide the Home Guard with were notorious pikes, they too turned to individuals in the US. Soon a formidable haul of privately owned weapons awaited collection at Liverpool docks – including long rifles used in the Louisiana Civil War of 1873, a number of ancient buffalo guns, modern pistols, revolvers and even gangsters' tommy-guns.

While some correspondents to *Picture Post* saw the whole Osterley Park enterprise as evidence of 'a Buffalo Bill mentality' and wondered what the organisers intended 'to do with your little jam pot bombs and Boy Scout poles', others sounded off about 'Marxist hooligans' – which was rather nearer to official thinking. Known communists and fascists were debarred from joining the Home Guard by a government order of 27 May 1940, and the police were given the task of weeding out from the lists of eager applicants those it was considered unwise to arm and involve in the defence of the country. M15 was told to vet Wintringham (who had resigned from the Communist Party for personal reasons in August 1938) and his colleagues as potential security risks, and Brigadier (retd) James Whitehead ordered his command, the London Home Guard, not to attend courses at Osterley Park – which of course greatly increased their attraction: the number of attendees rose from 1,000 in July to double that in August 1940.

The writer George Orwell had fought against fascism in Spain too and volunteered for the Army in the Second World War, but he was rejected on medical grounds. When Eden broadcast his appeal, Orwell saw a new opportunity for an anti-fascist force at home. He enrolled in the 5th (London) LDV battalion, which had its headquarters in St John's Wood, within a few days of its inception, wearing 'a crumpled uniform that had been cut to fit him by a good tailor ... and an expression that was Cromwellian in its intensity'.

Orwell was made a sergeant and his platoon – where he was known by his real name of Eric Blair – included Fredric Warburg, the publisher of his book about Spain, *Homage to Catalonia*, a piano manufacturer and his nephew, a van driver, a factory worker, a plumber and an unemployed ex-soldier, who were taught 'as much as [Orwell] could remember of the guerrilla tactics learned in Spain'. Orwell had been given the rank and command because of his experience of modern warfare, 'despite the forebodings of the authorities who were inclined to regard him as a dangerous red'. He proved a popular leader among his men, knowing a lot about weapons (even if he made occasional errors) and street-fighting techniques, but having scant regard for military bull and spit and polish.

The LDV 'uniform', the War Office announced, was to consist of a stencilled brassard or armband. 'Parashots', as the press dubbed the LDVs, could not have been less apposite. Weapons (or rather lack of them) were the burning issue. Ernest Raymond's local area had produced 300 volunteers but the only weapons available were a dozen old Lee Enfield rifles. 'In the absence of sufficient rifles we were given flat wooden slabs, cut more or less into a rifle's shape; and with these our old N.C.O. (in a trilby hat) taught us how to slope arms, ground arms . . . and even present arms to him, as he walked past us with the port and the hauteur (as he conceived them) of a Commander in Chief.' Other volunteers set off straightaway in defence of their country without instructions, mounting guard at what they considered to be vulnerable targets and going out on night patrols, armed with weapons that ranged from shotguns to pikes to cannons borrowed from local museums, from sharpened butcher's boning knives to paper bags filled with pepper.

Since re-equipping the Army had to take priority, emergency orders were sent off for 75,000 First World War rifles from Canada and 100,000 from the US. Until these could arrive the call went out for anyone possessing a rifle or shotgun to hand them into the local police station. Meanwhile, LDV members were taught how to make Molotov cocktails. In Lancashire the men filled beer bottles with 'petrol or paraffin, with Bengal matches or strips of photographic negative tied to the neck'. A Cornish unit favoured filling screw-topped glass bottles with a mixture of 'two thirds petrol and one third creosote. We discovered a large dump of bottles near Truro, and there [we] created our arsenal . . . we made thousands of them. Boxes of them were buried near every cross-road for miles around' – where some may still remain today. By the third week of June, even though the first batch of guns had arrived from Canada, it was estimated that there was still only one rifle per six men.

The issue of arms highlighted the confusion about the precise role of the LDV. Was it to 'harass and attack the enemy' with the intention of 'maiming or killing him'? Or was theirs to be more the role of a special constable, observing, reporting and checking (or 'Look, Duck and Vanish' or even 'Last Desperate Venture' to match their initials as some sceptical wits had it)? On 18 June the parliamentary goad, Josiah Wedgwood, sought reassurance from the Minister for War that 'the Local Defence Force is . . . genuinely intended to act in the service of this country, not as an extra policeman to guard the German soldiers when they march through London, but as an active defence force'.

Eddie Mathieson, an apprentice joiner, was only fifteen when he joined the Edinburgh battalion. 'It was young boys and old men, that was what the [LDV] was comprised of – the very last line of defence. My Dad was in [it] too. The . . . trainin' really was invaluable to me. We saw no action of course. We spent our time plowtering around on golf courses. We could throw hand grenades, dismantle a hand grenade, take a Lewis gun apart with a blindfold on, things like that. I learnt about . . . the old Lee Enfield rifle which was a 1914–18 weapon. All these old soldiers in the Home Guard knew everything about them.'

The father of Irene Thomas (who was to become a BBC quiz celebrity in the 1970s), had fought in the First World War, and when the formation of the LDV was announced he was one of the first to join up. 'He was very quickly issued with a rifle, a great heavy thing with a khaki webbing sling which he kept propped up just inside the front door, all ready for the moment when we would hear the church bells ringing – the signal for invasion – and began fighting street by street, for our lives . . . My father was never the veterans' association type, never went to regimental reunions, never talked much of army life . . . For such a reserved, peaceable man, the prospect of another war must have been acutely depressing, but he had a quietly stoical sense of duty, hence the rifle by the front door.'

Ernest Raymond and his fellow defenders spent 'the long summer evenings – and what a summer it was in 1940, radiant and calm and ever-unfading over the fields of England – we gambolled about the countryside in extended order and sometimes flung ourselves onto our bellies (though "flung" is too flattering a word for many of us) so as to practise firing at a deep and wide tank-trap dug across our meadows. We made Molotov cocktails . . . with these amateur bombs we manned road-blocks newly made at the entrance to our town and practised hurling this death at approaching tanks. Once we were allowed to use real Molotovs, tossing them at a derelict car till it was well aflame. We enjoyed that.'

Not everyone had such an enjoyable time. Arthur Wootten, who was a member of his local Home Guard in Kent, had been practising throwing bottles filled with 'a sticky mixture of benzine, rubber solution and phosphorus, which ignited as soon as the phosphorus was exposed to the air' at an old car lying at the bottom of a chalk pit when the contents splashed over Wootten who immediately ignited. His fellow guards' attempts to beat out the fire were completely ineffective so with great good sense Wootten flung himself into a nearby slimy-green sheep-dip trough which did extinguish the flames, but, when a local doctor removed his clothing, his skin reignited and he was plunged back into the tank to try to relieve his agony. Wootten was taken to hospital in Canterbury where he was given a massive injection of morphia so that the phosphorus could be scrubbed from his burnt flesh.

The fact that so many members of the LDV were ex-Army officers added to the government's discomfiture: such men were confident they knew what was needed, and moreover they had influence and friends in high places (a number of them were themselves MPs) and proved effective lobbyists. Soon tin helmets, greatcoats, leather gaiters and belts were being promised to replace the armbands. On 19 July Field Marshal Lord Gort, who had been commander-in-chief of the BEF (defunct) in France, was appointed Inspector of Training, and Eden had accepted the idea that 'attack' should be part of the LDV's lexicon.

In the middle of June, his attention now wrenched from the fallen Continent to the defence of the home shores, Churchill began taking an interest in the 'men of valour' and pressed his chosen nomenclature of Home Guard rather than LDV. Herbert Morrison, the Home Secretary, was inclined to agree that 'local' was a bit of a turn-off and suggested something along the lines of 'Town Guard' or 'Civic Guard', but to Churchill such phrases conjured up the Committee of Public Safety and other names adopted by 'the wild men of the French Revolution'.

Eden was rather put out by the idea – and the implication that the warrior-premier was going to move into his spotlight – and huffily pointed out that LDV had 'passed into the public jargon', and what about the profligacy of destroying a million-odd LDV-stencilled armbands and replacing them with HG ones? (The estimated cost of the name change was £40,000.) But Churchill was not to be deflected, and so from the end of July that 'sadly costive trio of abstractions "Local Defence Volunteers" . . . became in three simple, stirring words "The Home Guard" '.

'Static defence in every village by [road] blocks [or anything that might just conceivably halt an advancing column of troops, lorries and tanks] . . . thousands of Molotov cocktails thrown down from the windows of houses . . . we just want the courage of men . . . No defence is any good if the men behind it run away,' General Ironside, commander-in-chief Home Forces throughout June, noted in his diary. The Home Guard might be the authorised defenders of the island fortress (alongside any regular troops that could be mustered), but everyone had a part to play. No one could afford not to be vigilant for the arrival of the enemy. 'Orders and suggestions overwhelmed us,' reported Lady Diana Cooper. '. . . We must not spread alarm or dismay . . . We were advised to feed the enemy's cars with sugar to neutralise their petrol . . . [and] a difficult suggestion that had a foolish appeal for me was to equip one's car with an all-covering armour of small pebbles between sheets of tin . . . Place-names were obliterated on roads and stations. Barricades of wagons and tree trunks were successfully obstructing our own movements. We must "Be Like Dad and Keep Mum" (very funny we thought), and our children must not have kites or fireworks. We had killed our black-widow spiders when war came, and now the Zoo's Home Guard were trained riflemen. To have been hugged to death by a bombed-out bear would have been an anti-climax . . . We had given all our weapons, binoculars and dainty opera glasses to the Home Guard. In June the ringing of church bells was stopped, so that they might ring again for the invasion.'

Motorists were instructed to immobilise their cars by locking them in their garages and removing not only the ignition key but also the distributor arm, and anyone who parked their car in the street with the ignition key still in would face arrest. Drawings from various angles of a

Junkers JU52 – 'the one normally used for parachute dropping' – appeared in *The Field* and other magazines. 'The Government has asked us to publish these pictures of German Troop Carriers to help you distinguish the enemy,' ran the caption. 'Take a piece of cardboard and stick this page on it, and hang it in a prominent place.'

Someone was given the task of preparing a booklet *If the Invader Comes* (Harold Nicolson and Sir Kenneth Clark both claimed authorship) but, from whoever's pen it sprung, the pamphlet was approved and issued to every householder in Britain on 13 June 1940 – over a month after German tanks had first invaded the Low Countries. It laid down seven rules:

1   If the Germans come, by parachute, aeroplane or ship, you must remain where you are. The order is 'Stay Put' . . .
2   Do not believe rumours and do not spread them. When you receive an order, make sure you know it's a true order and not a faked order. Most of you know your policeman and your ARP warden by sight, you can trust them . . .
3   Keep watch. If you see anything suspicious, note it carefully and go at once to the nearest police station, or officer, or to the nearest military officer . . .
4   Do not give the Germans anything. Do not tell him anything. Hide your food and your bicycles. Hide your maps. See that the enemy gets no petrol . . . Remember that transport and petrol will be the invader's main difficulty . . .
5   Be ready to help the military in any way. But do not block the road until ordered to do so by the military or LDV authorities.
6   In factories and shops, all managers and workmen should organise some system by which a sudden attack can be resisted.
7   Think before you act. But always think of your country before you think of yourself.

They were tricky instructions to follow. Although 70 per cent of the population expressed itself in favour of all citizens being armed, and the Queen was being instructed every morning in how to fire a revolver, arming everyone seemed a long way off. Yet it would be hard to feel that you were 'putting your country first' if all you were doing was 'staying put' (or 'staying firm', which the instruction was more felicitously changed to later). As Harold Nicolson recognised, 'it is absurd to expect people to stay in their homes without telling them what to do.' He had made up his mind what to do, though: 'I shall kill myself and Vita will kill herself if the worst comes. Thus there will come a point where Hitler would cease to trouble either of us.' And on 15 June he was 'lucidly aware . . . that the probability is that we shall be bombed and invaded . . . [and] in three weeks from now Sissinghurst may be a waste and Vita and I both dead.' He was, however, remarkably sanguine about this grisly prospect: indeed, he wrote to Vita that 'being in so central a position' – at the Ministry of Information – made him feel 'I can do some good, and I am *embattled*. I did not know that I possessed such combative instincts . . . I feel such contempt for cowards.' Others were less sure exactly how to channel 'their combative instincts'.

The Minister of Information, Duff Cooper, whose job it was to inform, was scant practical help. 'We are continually hearing the demand that people should be told what they have to do, that they are ready enough to do it, but that they are awaiting for instructions. Now it is the policy of the Government to give people as full instruction as possible; but at the same time people should be encouraged to think for themselves . . . We do not want now to become like Germans or inhabitants of other totalitarian states, who cannot move or think without being told what to do.' The confusion of course bespoke a genuine conundrum: the entire population could not be armed (even if it had been wise to do so) and the collapse of the Low Countries and France had shown how disastrous it was if the population didn't 'stay put' but fled in the face of the invader, clogging roads, disorganising troop movements and supplies, thus making any effective defence or counter-attack difficult if not impossible.

The British government could only conjecture about the strength of the German forces: the fear, expressed by 'Tiny' (so named since he was massive) Ironside, was that 'the Bosches[sic] have sufficient aircraft to transport 9,750 lightly equipped men in one flight. The number of flights will vary from 1½ per day for East Anglia to 3 for Kent. Taking into account air opposition and ground opposition, it is thought that the numbers can be calculated upon the basis of 10,000 for East Anglia and

20,000 for Kent . . . Sea planes and gliders may add to these numbers. Such air-borne expeditions will be followed by sea-borne expeditions pushed forward with the utmost brutality.' It would need only 5,000 parachutists to seize the seven vital RAF sector stations and effectively ground Fighter Command, the Air Staff in London estimated, and, if there were also heavy bombing raids, these would provide a sufficient diversion for transport planes to bring in reinforcements. If the Germans tried to bring 20,000 men and tanks across the Channel, the Royal Navy would be powerless to stop them – providing their Navy had special landing craft.

In fact this was an over-estimate: it is doubtful whether the Germans could have mustered 2,000 parachutists – and there would not have been sufficient parachutes for even that number. The German Kreigsmarine did not have any 'special landing craft' at this time and, given the size and nature of his forces and the difficulties of landing men across a wide front, its commander Admiral Raedar did not regard a seaborne invasion as feasible. On 30 June General Jodl, head of operations at Oberkommande der Wehrmacht (OKW), the supreme command of the German forces, submitted a memorandum to the Führer advising that the best way to bring Britain to surrender was a blockade by sea and air 'allied to propaganda and periodic terror attacks, announced as reprisals'. An invasion should be regarded as a last resort, and then only when the country was paralysed and 'practically incapable of fighting in the air'. But Hitler was still of the view that the British could be persuaded to surrender since their position must seem so hopeless. The ruthless sabotage of the French fleet at Mers-el Kébir gave the lie to that expectation. Clearly the British intended to carry on the fight. So on 20 July 1940 Hitler issued Directive no 16, *Preparations for the Invasion of Britain*, Operation Sealion, though he still hoped that Britain would be prepared to negotiate either before the offensive was launched, or as soon as German troops landed on British soil. Ironically the expected parachutists against which the British were honing their every means of defence were not part of the plan. Rather, Hitler invited 'suggestions as to the use of airborne troops, and in particular whether it would be advisable to keep them in reserve for use only in the case of emergency'.

Though it was possible, using a strong pair of binoculars on a clear day, to tell the time by the clock tower in Calais from the battlements of Dover Castle, and though Hitler was later to speak of the Channel as nothing more than 'a ditch 37 kilometres [23 miles] wide', as the British and German forces in effect faced each other across this narrow divide the British had no answer to their urgent questions: would the Germans invade? How would the Germans invade? Where would the Germans invade? When would the Germans invade? Ironside had to rely on intelligence passed on from the analysis of photographic reconnaissance and attempts to intercept radio messages, monitor broadcasts and the press, listen to reports from neutral countries and speculate and hazard what was hoped were intelligent guesses in those June days. He had to deploy his meagre twenty-eight under-strength divisions accordingly – but always with some in reserve in case the predictions were wrong. With or without a parachute invasion, the Germans would have to get the bulk of their Army, tanks and guns across the Channel by sea. Would an invasion come along the south coast – from Weymouth in Dorset along the Sussex and Hampshire beaches? Or would the enemy attempt to land on the east coast south of the Wash? Or was the danger from the north with landings in the Shetland Isles and the coast of Scotland by troops coming from Norway?

Such precautions as could be were taken. Vulnerable parts of the coastline and estuaries were designated 'Defence Areas'; children were evacuated; anyone who could leave did so; and special permits were required for those who had reason to enter the areas. Mines were laid, and at high tide waves lapped at the huge coils of barbed wire festooning the beaches, while concrete pillboxes and tank traps were hastily erected to prevent vehicles from getting off the beaches and along possible invasion routes. Piers jutting out to sea that might have helped the enemy to unload heavy equipment or troops to invade, as the east mole at Dunkirk had helped the BEF to evacuate, were partially dismantled. At Brighton the west pier had a gap made in its structure halfway along, and under the aquarium stood a huge tank of petrol ready to be used to 'set alight the sea' in case of invasion. Farmers immobilised tractors and heaved obstacles into their fields to deter planes or gliders from landing, and rusty vehicles, broken carts and old bedsteads soon littered fields, recreation grounds and sports fields.

A salvage appeal for iron to be turned into weapons resulted in railings being torn up from municipal parks – meaning they could no longer be locked at night, which, along with the blackout, was seen as a yet another encouragement to wartime immorality. The gardens of London squares, previously the preserve only of the key-holding residents, now gave access to any hoi polloi who wished to sun him or herself on their immaculate lawns, or to children to kick a football around. Country-house owners looked on ruefully as their ornamental gates were unhinged, and some pondered on the fact that their railings would have made a fine spear for when the parachutists landed *without* being melted down. Suburban houses surrendered the chains that looped between their fence posts, a small village near Maidstone in Kent managed to produce 11 tons of railings in a single weekend, and the William Hickey column in the *Daily Express*, called for the railings around the British Museum to be torn up for the same patriotic purpose. In Cheltenham two imposing cannons that had been captured from the Russians during the siege of Sebastapol, in the Crimean War, were reluctantly removed from their plinths and handed in to be turned into modern weaponry.

Rumour and conjecture flew around: the King and Queen had fled to Canada with the little princesses and the entire government was poised to follow if an invasion were mounted; the Duke of Windsor was to be installed as the puppet ruler of a Nazi state; heavy bombing raids had already started, and such and such a town had been razed to the ground. Concerned about public morale and possible defeatism, the government resolved to crack down on scaremongering and spreading rumours. A 'Rout the Rumour' rally was organised at Hendon in north London in July 1940 to steady any defeatist feelings, and between 10,000 and 20,000 people turned up to be told to 'remember it's guts as well as guns that's going to bring us victory'. The crowds joined in singing such stirring numbers as 'Rule Britannia', 'God Our Help in Ages Past' and 'Pack Up Your Troubles' ('In your old kit bag'), and cheered when a Ministry of Information official told them that 'the secret weapon of Great Britain is the gallant, cheerful spirit of its ordinary people'. Mass-Observation concluded, 'People enjoyed it, but the event ended on a note of bafflement and mystery.'

It began to seem to members of the public that, while they were inextricably and inevitably involved in the war, any discussion of it was liable to be suppressed as unpatriotic and dangerous. Proceedings were instituted against individuals for spreading 'alarm and despondency' – a Mrs Watson of 145 Empire Court, Wembley, who had been reported as saying that officers at Dunkirk had fought to be evacuated before their men, found an officer from Scotland Yard on her doorstep. At the insistence of Churchill, the Ministry of Information promulgated a heavy-handed 'Silent Column' campaign in the press and on the radio which had none of the light irony of the cartoonist Fougasse's earlier 'Careless Talk Costs Lives' series. 'Do you know one of these?' asked the posters and showed a series of photographs of such 'characters' as Mr Secrecy Hush-Hush, Mr Pride in Prophecy; 'Mr Know All – He knows what the Germans are going to do and when they are going to do it. He knows where our ships are and what Bomber Command is going to do. With his large talk he is playing the enemy's game. He is so worried by the enemy's strength that he never thinks of ours'; and ended by exhorting in capital letters 'Tell These People to Join Britain's Silent Column'.

'There is no doubt that our anti-rumour campaign has been a ghastly failure,' wrote Harold Nicolson. 'Partly because our silence campaign and the prosecutions which have taken place in the country have caused justifiable irritation. And partly because the country is in a bad state of nerves during this lull before the storm.'

If indeed the country was 'in a bad state of nerves' this might also have been manifest in anxieties about those who would be ready to lend a hand with the invasion, the so-called 'fifth columnists', the 'enemy in our midst' who were ready and waiting to collaborate with the Germans. It was after all fifth columnists who were supposed to have facilitated the defeat of Holland and Norway, though post-war investigation showed this to be largely mythical, and the successful invasions were almost entirely explicable in purely military terms.

A Cardiff householder reported he could hear his neighbour tapping out Morse code signals to the enemy. The regular beat turned out to be a leaky cistern. Wall chalkings and graffiti on telephone kiosks and lamp posts were scrutinised to see if a code could be divined. A Cambridge don suggested that the number of empty Craven A and Player's Weights cigarette packets and discarded bus tickets strewn around his area should not be attributed to the fact that 'the British are one of the filthiest races on earth where litter is concerned'. Rather, the trails were being laid to guide the expected invaders, and were 'meant to attract attention (from the right people) and to indicate either nearby messages or routes to be followed'.

However, although they were expected to be on their guard for them, according to a Mass-Observation survey most of the public 'hardly realised what the phrase ['fifth columnists'] meant ... [and that] the level of ordinary people's feelings was much less intense that that expressed in some newspapers'. The term had come, it seems, from the Spanish Civil War, when General Mola, an associate of Franco, had threatened the Republican defenders of Madrid that as well as the four columns of troops ready to march on them, there was a fifth column within the city prepared to rise up and fight for Franco. Identifying and apprehending this British 'Trojan Horse' – described by the *Sunday Dispatch*, a newspaper owned by the pre-war fascist sympathiser, Lord Rothermere, as being packed with 'Fascists, Communists, peace fanatics and alien refugees in league with Berlin and Moscow' – was a role taken by government when it came to interning fascists and so-called 'enemy aliens', and mounting surveillance of communists and 'peace fanatics'.

In the first week of June General Ironside had assured members of the LDV (as it was still called then) at York, 'we do not want a spy complex', but his tone was belligerent. He urged his audience that when the enemy came they must 'shoot them ... without taking any kind of care of their future', but also that in the meantime they must be ever vigilant and suspicious of their fellow citizens. 'We cannot be too sure of anybody,' he proclaimed, and a local organiser came away from the meeting convinced that 'we have the *right to arrest, search etc.* suspected persons and *then* take them to the police ... remember that a person making his or her way to a rural area, is *ipso facto* suspect. If resistance is offered, slosh him. Warn him that if he tries to escape, you shoot to kill. Remember that the greatest and best-behaved members of the public will often turn out to be the most effective Fifth Columnists.'

Many members of the Home Guard had had no experience of military discipline at all, while others had had what they considered to be quite enough to be able to override orders in the higher national interest – as they saw it – and all were giving their time (often a lot of it) voluntarily, so it is hardly surprising that things could be volatile. Home Guard zeal could be hard to control. The volunteers manned checkpoints demanding proof of identification, and on one occasion in August the *Daily Express* reported that a man had been stopped twenty times on a journey of eight miles; a citizen taking a stroll could be required to produce his or her identity card by a Home Guard who had known them for years; policemen were sometimes stopped and challenged at gunpoint to produce their warrant cards; ARP wardens reported being halted on their way to their command posts and watching valuable minutes slip by as their papers were scrutinised by an assiduous Home Guard; and on one occasion fire engines and rescue vehicles were unable to get to a blaze in Chiswick at the start of the Blitz because the local Home Guard had erected a roadblock on Western Avenue and was refusing to let anyone pass.

Trigger-happy volunteers led to a spate of what might now be referred to by the misnomer 'friendly fire' tragedies, when on the night of 2/3 June 1940 LDVs shot and killed four motorists at separate locations; on 22 June it was reported that two motorcyclists and their passengers had been killed and wounded in the north of England and Scotland; on 26 June an ARP warden was shot dead when he ignored (or maybe didn't hear) an LDV challenge; and in Romford in Essex a car exhaust backfiring prevented the driver hearing the command to stop: four passengers were shot dead and a fifth seriously wounded. This patriotic lawlessness was evident in August when the pilot of an RAF Hurricane on fire after a dogfight with some German fighter planes near Southampton bailed out, only to be shot at by Home Guards under the mistaken impression that he was an enemy parachutist. The pilot officer was killed and the badly burned flight lieutenant sustained further serious injuries from rifle fire.

Nevertheless the Home Guard was regarded by politicians as a potentially important adjunct to the Army as, in desperate times, the Armed Forces were rebuilt, and also as a vital ingredient in maintaining the morale of the people and their will to win. Despite all the scoffing in the early days, it could have had formidable responsibilities that called for very brave men. Each village, or other central point, was designated as a nodal point. The whole country was covered by the Home Guard,

'as with a net, and the villages were the knots . . . at these points we were
to fight, and so deny the use of the roads to the enemy'. The Home
Guard was instructed to 'hold their allotted positions to the last man and
the last round to enable the Field Army to destroy the enemy. Mobile
units . . . will, within their prescribed area of activity, harass and delay
the enemy with the same purpose.'

Yet the force was still without what its members wanted most: a full
complement of weapons, and no amount of proficiency badges (which
were introduced in April 1941 as the invasion scare was waning) could
compensate for the fact that one year on the men were far from fully
armed.

In some desperation the War Office had started issuing truncheons
in June 1941, and the next month ordered the production of 250,000
long metal tubes with a blade welded on to the end. Beaverbrook,
who was concentrating on increasing aircraft production, was
dumbfounded: 'Why not bow and arrows?' he queried, and made a
note to lay in plenty of supplies of string since 'string is very short,
too'. Alternatively he could supply flint from the garden of his home
in Surrey that could be turned into flintlocks – 'Would these be of any
use?' he enquired disingenuously. The *Daily Mail* was scathing too,
suggesting that 'Crossbow men of the thirteenth-century might be
useful behind hedges. Archers with poisoned arrows might take
tips from Harold at Hastings. The War Office may be studying
reproductions of the Bayeux tapestry and using medieval manuscripts
as military manuals.'

It got worse. In December 1941, Churchill again intervened in Home
Guard affairs, this time to suggest that 'every man must have a weapon
of some kind, be it only a mace or pike'. Even if pikes were an
improvement on 'bare fists or stones' most Home Guard commanding
officers were well aware of the contempt with which their men would
regard the issue of such weapons, which might have been just about
acceptable at the beginning of June 1940 but were wholly insulting well
over a year later, and declined to issue them.

The answer seemed to be the mass production of somewhat basic
weapons specifically for the Home Guard. In addition to the ubiquitous
Molotov cocktail, there was the 'Woolworth bomb', basically 'a lump

of gelignite in a biscuit tin'; and the 'sticky bomb', which consisted of a glass container filled with nitroglycerine and covered with a sock coated in adhesive. 'Sticky bomb. Make one million,' ordered the Prime Minister despite the fact the thrower had to be careful or the bomb would adhere to his clothing and blow him up. Then there was the Northover Projector, named after its inventor, which consisted of a hollow metal tube, mounted on an iron tripod. It cost only £10 to manufacture and fired grenades using toy-pistol caps. By August 1941 8,000 of these were in service despite their Heath Robinson-like appearance, and tendency to fail to work and to obscure the target with a cloud of smoke when they were fired. One advantage was that the Northover required three men to operate it, making them 'forget for the moment that they haven't got a rifle' each, according to Brigadier Whitehead, the London organiser of the Home Guard. Then there was the Blacker Bombard (again named after its inventor), which Churchill was very keen on ('one of his pets', sniffed Brooke) even though (because?) it had nearly killed de Gaulle when it was first demonstrated. It looked like a medieval siege gun and had a heavily sprung steel rod inside a short barrel which shot out a projectile towards the target. Soon renamed the Spigot Mortar, which sounded a bit less medieval, it was incredibly heavy to move and its performance fell far short of its promise, though when it did work it could deliver a 14lb anti-personnel and 20lb anti-tank mortar bomb. This hardware proved very absorbing for the Home Guard, making them feel they were being taken seriously, but such weapons did not necessarily improve their fighting capacity – which fortunately never had to be put to the test.

As more weapons – and possibly more effective weapons – became available it began to matter even more in whose hands these weapons were. The secret War Office memo of 27 May that had barred communists and fascists from joining the Home Guard was followed by a purge of possible subversives. Any identified 'communist' who had inadvertently slipped through the security net and signed up to defend his country was summarily 'discharged under the heading "services no longer required" without amplification' and the police were informed. The Osterley school was simply 'incorporated'. In September 1941 Hulton agreed to the military authorities being involved in running the school, on condition that the existing staff were kept on. The oxygen of publicity was cut off and it was increasingly marginalised as a smaller school under the command of a Regular Army officer was set up near Dorking with Wintringham as a consultant but emasculated of any real authority. Instead he, Hugh Slater, John Langdon-Davis and another left-wing journalist, John Brophy, wrote instruction booklets for the Home Guard to be distributed by the War Office. They also continued to suggest radical ideas about the role and organisation of the Home Guard that were largely ignored. Frustrated, Wintringham resigned as a consultant in May 1941.

It was all part of a process to rein in the Home Guard, check tendencies to 'loose cannon' behaviour and bring it more closely in line with War Office control and the practices and procedures of the Regular Army. Battalions were affiliated to county regiments, into which factory and workplace units were integrated, and a ranking structure was introduced. Henceforth a man would be required to salute his superior officers, rather than casually addressing his platoon commander or section commander. The package was sold in terms of greater efficiency now that more weapons and equipment were soon to become available – as the Under-Secretary of State for War assured the Commons when he introduced the measures in November 1941. But Tom Basford wistfully recalled the early days of the North Cotswold LDV when it was all 'Tom fall in; Bill go over a bit' but as we got more professional we had to address each other by rank, no matter if it was your brother or your uncle'. While this militarisation 'might have been welcomed by the retired military men . . . with only a house full of domestic servants to command . . . it came hard to those who had no such background and saw themselves as a band of neighbours who had banded together for the common weal'.

It did rather look as if the Blimps were back in control and, as one London Home Guard commander pointed out, those officers who set store by a sense of rank 'are those least suited to hold it'. There were uncomfortable examples of chaps who weren't quite out of the top drawer seeing newcomers with the 'right' credentials promoted over their heads, even though they had been serving since the days of Dunkirk with a garden hoe for a weapon. In Oxford the new ranks led to something of a realignment of former hierarchies when Maurice Bowra, the Warden of Wadham College, became a lieutenant, as did the Keeper of the Ashmolean Museum, while the Head of the Geological Department was promoted to the rank of colonel and commanding officer of the battalion, whereas the university's former Vice-Chancellor and President of Magdalen remained a private.

Although large numbers of young women had voluntarily enlisted in the Auxiliary Territorial Service (ATS), the Women's Royal Naval Service (WRNS) and the Women's Auxiliary Air Force (WAAF), the Home Guard resisted them.

Churchill always accepted that 'even women, must, if they wish, be enrolled as combatants' in the Home Guard. Indeed in his speeches the Prime Minister frequently elided 'home' as in 'Home Front' to connote both country and the place where a person lives, and these two uses might have been expected to position women in the front line of defending both since home (dwelling) was seen as primarily the woman's sphere. By November 1940 some MPs were beginning to ask where women were in the total mobilisation of the people in the defence of the homeland. Some, of course, were used in an informal auxiliary capacity – wives asked to type letters, provide tea and buns, deliver notices and so on – but without formal recognition of their contribution. Indeed in June 1940 the War Office had announced 'women cannot be enrolled in the LDV' – though some local Home Guard commanders made women welcome in their units in contravention of the edict. The most vociferous proponent of women being allowed to be full members of the Home Guard – and that meant bearing arms – was the Labour MP Edith Summerskill, with the support of Mavis Tate, a Conservative MP, and the social reformer Eleanor Rathbone, who sat as an Independent. But their lobbying got nowhere. They were fobbed off with the excuse that there weren't enough uniforms and equipment for the men, and when during a debate in November 1940 the Minister for War recited a list of male military heroes, Summerskill's interjection 'What about Boadicea?' was ignored.

In July a War Office memo had reiterated 'Under no circumstances should women be enrolled in the Home Guard . . . it is undesirable for women to bear arms in the Home Guard, and I do not think that anyone should be enrolled in the Home Guard who is not under an obligation to bear arms when called upon to do so.' The War Office was not alone. The US correspondent Ed Murrow reported the reaction of an English friend of his to the idea in May 1940: 'a few million women with rifles was the most frightening prospect a man could face'.

As the age-range of conscription was widened, the Home Guard became short of manpower. This led to regulations compelling men aged from eighteen to fifty-four who were not in the Armed Forces, or other Civil Defence work, to serve part-time in the Home Guard. But there was still no place for women despite the fact that some male MPs had come round to the view that since both sexes were in danger should there be an invasion, it made no sense to deny women the means of defence. 'Why should women not be taught the use of hand grenades and revolvers?' demanded one.

There were organisations dedicated to precisely this. One of these was Women's Home Defence, the first unit of which (calling itself the Amazon Defence Corps) was formed in June 1940 and included among its 'fifty indignant female patriots' Marjorie Foster, who had won the prestigious King's Prize on the rifle range at Bisley in 1930. Its intention was to prepare 'every woman in the country to be of maximum use in the event of an invasion' and it offered training in musketry, bombing, how to use a tommy gun, and the rudiments of unarmed combat. Technically it was an illegal organisation – a private army – since it was a uniformed force providing training in the use of rifles, but the War Office declined to prosecute, recognising the outcry this would cause among women if they did. By December 1942 there were alleged to be 250 units. But no prosecution did not mean no criticism: one MP railed against it: 'a woman's duty is to give life not to take it, and the training which your movement gives in unarmed combat, signalling, fieldcraft and musketry, is abhorrent . . .'

Increasingly pragmatic considerations meant that more and more Home Guard units were admitting women to their ranks to make up the numbers, and Summerskill used evidence of this to chip away at the War Office intransigence. Finally, in April 1943, a grudging concession was wrung. From that date Women's Home Guard Auxiliaries could be nominated by such recognised organisations as the WVS. The women must be between eighteen and sixty-five (and preferably over forty-five). Their only uniform was a plastic badge and they would not receive weapons training since their task was solely 'to perform non-combatant duties such as clerical work, cooking, and driving'. They were not to be full members of the Home Guard and, if the Germans did eventually invade Britain's shores, women would not be there to meet them with a rifle, or ready to pull the pin out of a hand grenade. Women were clearly intended to obey Churchill's injunction to 'defend our island' in their traditional roles: building a field kitchen out of bricks, tin sheets and a stove pipe in the back garden, and making slit trenches and shelters comfortable as the Women's Institute advised, laying in supplies of food and bandages, nourishing, nurturing, typing, driving, making notes, taking telephone messages, brewing up – and keeping mum.

In a country with a long-standing suspicion of a professional army, the Home Guard was in the tradition of a 'people's militia', raised at a time of threat from within or without. It was 'the nation in arms', or, put another way, a means of arming the people, or rather the male people. And if the people were to be armed, that made pertinent the question of what the British people were fighting this war for in addition to the defence against Hitler. Harold Nicolson pondered this after a long talk with the Labour leader (and Deputy Prime Minister) Clement Attlee. 'The Germans are fighting a revolutionary war for very definite objectives. We are fighting a conservative war and our objectives are purely negative. We must put forward a positive and revolutionary aim admitting that the old order has collapsed and asking people to fight for a new order.'

One of J. B. Priestley's popular *Postscript* broadcasts raised the same issue. 'It so happens that this war, whether those at present in authority like it or not, has to be fought as a citizens' war. There is no way out of that because in order to defend and protect this island . . . it has been found necessary to bring into existence a new network of voluntary associations such as the Home Guard, the Observer Corps [volunteers watching for planes crossing the coast where they could no longer be tracked by radar] and the ARP and fighter services and the like . . . They are a new type, what might be called the organised militant citizen.

And the whole circumstances of the war favour a sharply democratic outlook.'

George Orwell had fought in Spain too and blamed the defeat of the Spanish Republican forces largely on the suppression of POUM, the Spanish people's militia, by the communists who were also fighting against Franco. He might have been expected to argue, as he had done in 1937, that 'Fascism is . . . only a development of capitalism, and the mildest democracy, so called, is liable to turn Fascist' and refuse to support an internecine capitalist–imperialist war as many of his friends in the Independent Labour Party (ILP) did. But he had decided '. . . that I was patriotic at heart, would not sabotage, or act against my own side, would support the war, would fight in it if possible.' His loyalties lay with England. 'It is all very well to be "advanced" and "enlightened", to snigger at Colonel Blimp, but a time comes when the sand of the desert is sodden red and what have I done for thee, England, my England?" ' he asked.

From the moment war was declared Orwell had been writing articles urging 'Arm the People' and suggesting that gunsmiths should be stripped of their weapons, which should be distributed among LDV members. A volunteer army needs to be fired with political idealism – the reason why its members will take up arms – and in the summer of 1940 Orwell saw the potential of that fervour to be a socialist patriotism, men prepared to fight for their country for a new world order, not on behalf of the 'guilty men' of appeasement but against unemployment and class privilege. He was quick to point out that he was 'not suggesting that it is the duty of Socialists to enter the Home Guard with the idea of making trouble or spreading subversion. That would be both treacherous and ineffective. Any Socialist who obtains influence in the Home Guard will do it by being as good a soldier as possible, by being conspicuously obedient, efficient and self-sacrificing.'

There was, however, something of an obstacle to seeing the Home Guard as a 'quasi-revolutionary people's army' since its backbone consisted of the old military establishment – high-ranking officers and members of the peerage peppered every platoon, particularly in the south of England. Colonel Blimps were prominently in evidence: as far as the *Daily Worker* was concerned, the Home Guard was controlled by 'the hunting-shooting-fishing oligarchy'. As Orwell's biographer,

Bernard Crick, says, 'Orwell helped the Left to respect patriotism, but he could not guide the patriots towards socialism.' Though as well as 'nostalgic veterans clustered round the local squire' on the downs of Sussex and Hampshire, a third of the Home Guard's members came from the industrial working class, and in many cases belonged to units organised by factories and workshops.

The Home Guard has come down to us today as a laudable if ramshackle form of straightforward patriotism – a 'Dad's Army'. It was that, but it also provided a mirror for many of the complexities and contradictions of wartime Britain.

10

'COLLAR THE LOT'

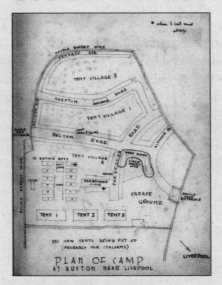

What is the barbed wire doing
Set up everywhere I see?
Is it meant to keep the world out
Or protect the world from me?
LIVIA LAURENT, *A Tale of Internment*

ON 25 JUNE 1940, Heinz Bing, a twenty-five-year-old German who had been studying chemistry at Imperial College in London and who was very near to completing his PhD, resolved to keep a diary in order 'to keep contact with all that is most important to me. To keep my spirit and as a remembrance for Lore [Meyerheim, his fiancée] . . . I know that my greatest wish is to read it to her in the near future before time has broken both of us . . .' Bing, who had come to Britain when he was nineteen, was that day on his way to Kempton Park racecourse where a camp had been hastily set up for numbers of those people who had technically become 'enemy aliens' the day that war broke out. He was to be interned there as part of the 'Urgent measures to meet an attack' recommended by the military chiefs of staff as Britain prepared for a German invasion.

In 1933, when Hitler came to power as German Chancellor, the ostracisation and persecution of Jews began. In April that year an Aliens Restriction Committee was set up in London to consider what the government should do about the flood of refugees to Britain that the persecutions would be likely to trigger. Meanwhile the Anglo–Jewish community also set up a committee to organise the reception and care of Jewish refugees, and urge the government to grant permission for all such refugees to be allowed to come to Britain, at least until they could be found a permanent home elsewhere. The committee pledged that the Jewish community would support the refugees financially so that they would be no charge on the state, and members of various scientific and artistic organisations worked to help fellow scientists and artists who had fled from Germany. Despite these financial guarantees (which would prove impossible to sustain by 1939), the government was reluctant to breach its existing policy of restricting immigration to those with capital – financial, intellectual or industrial – or women prepared to work in domestic service, and insisted that Britain was predominantly a country of transit, that most refugees were accepted only on a temporary basis until they could be re-emigrated to the US and other destinations. The government gave as a primary reason fear of an anti-Semitic reaction to workers 'flooding the labour market' in times of high unemployment.

As the climate in Germany grew more menacing, so the flood of refugees increased from the 2,274 allowed in for temporary residence in 1933, to a total of 20,000 refugees registering with the Central Refugee Committee between January and December 1938 – including a mass exodus in the wake of *Kristallnacht* in November, when Nazi gangs rampaged through Jewish neighbourhoods, smashing shop windows, looting and killing. A further 27,000 registered up to July 1939, plus 7,752 children, of whom 5,673 were Jewish, brought over by the Movement for the Care of Children from Germany. These figures may be an underestimate as some refugees came over under their own steam and did not register with the authorities.

At the time of the Munich crisis in September 1938, it was apparent that if war came Britain would thus have a large number of aliens within its shores from the country with which it would be at war. That month the War Office started to draw up arrangements for internment, and appointed a sub-committee which first met in January 1939 to consider the control of aliens. While it was intended that only certain categories of aliens, those who were potentially inimical to British security, would be interned, all aliens would be restricted in ways that the native-born population was not. MI5, the military intelligence secret service responsible for counter-espionage and the surveillance of groups deemed to be subversive, estimated that, within the definition of 'suspect enemy agents', provision should be made for the internment of 5,500 civilians within forty-eight hours of the outbreak of war.

On 1 September 1939, 415 suspected Nazi sympathisers and possible agents, all of whom figured on MI5's special list, were rounded up and taken to Olympia, the exhibition halls in Hammersmith, west London (which had been used for the same purpose in the First World War), with only as much luggage as they could carry in one hand. Others had been warned that if they did not leave the country, they would be arrested. Although the Nazi sympathies of those who were arrested were supposed to be a threat to national security, several men hardly seemed to fit the profile. One was Eugen Spier, an Orthodox Jew, who had come to Britain in 1923. He was one of the key organisers of a movement called the Focus for the Defence of Freedom and Peace, of which the politicians Sir Austen Chamberlain, Sir Archibald Sinclair, Lady Violet Bonham-Carter and Duncan Sandys and the diplomat Sir Robert Vansittart were also members. They met regularly and were behind a huge anti-Nazi rally held at the Albert Hall on 3 December 1936 that Churchill addressed. On the eve of war Spier went to the Home Office to offer his services to Britain; later that same day he was arrested and thrown into prison, where he remained for two years.

Others arrested on 1 September were a disparate group whose only shared characteristic was that they were German or Austrian. They included the flamboyant Bavarian 'Putzi' Hanfstaengel, an intimate of Hitler who had quarrelled with his boss, Goebbels, and fled to Britain to sit out the war until he could return to Germany to head up the Fourth Reich; the aristocratic Count Albrecht Montgelas, a former correspondent of a leading Weimar Germany newspaper who made his living in Britain selling German beer; the journalist and playwright Karl Wehner, who had been interned on the Isle of Man in the First World War; and Dr Alex Natan, a journalist and champion athlete who had written for trade-union papers before he fled from Germany in 1933, and also became a PT coach to the Middlesex Regiment of the British Army. From Olympia these internees, along with others rounded up throughout the country, were taken to Clacton-on-Sea in Essex where they were housed in a former Butlin's holiday camp, now surrounded by coils of barbed wire.

As the days went on and the round-up continued, the refugees and anti-Nazis were outnumbered by fascist supporters, including a Pastor Wehrhahn, padre of the German Embassy, a virulent pro-Nazi whose services included prayers for German success; and thirty-seven merchant seamen from a banana boat, the *Pomona*, stranded in the London docks on 3 September, who marched into the hall at Olympia barking 'Heil Hitler'. Jews, Catholic priests, Lutheran pastors and other opponents of the Nazi regime were increasingly vilified, humiliated, abused and denied accommodation separate from their anti-Semitic fellow countrymen, while the bayonet-carrying British guards largely ignored their plight and declined to differentiate between those who had fled from the persecution of the Nazi regime, and those who were its enthusiastic supporters.

As well as the enemy aliens who were interned at the start of the war, the government decided to scrutinise every single one of the 73,355 Germans and Austrians over the age of sixteen who had registered with the British police, as they were required to do. Tribunals were to be set up to ascertain the possible risk that such people posed to Britain's security. They were to be graded in three categories: class 'A' was for those it was considered could be expected, given the opportunity, 'to help their own countrymen, or hinder the war efforts of this country', and thus might constitute a security risk. Such people were to be immediately interned. Class 'B' were aliens whose loyalty was for some reason in doubt, and who therefore were to be supervised and subject to various restrictions: they could not move more than 5 miles from where they lived without police permission, and were forbidden to possess such items as maps, charts, cameras, binoculars and firearms. Class 'C' aliens were considered sound, their loyalty not in question, and they were to be left at liberty. 'C' aliens were further subdivided into those who were 'refugees from Nazi oppression' ('friendly enemy aliens') who would be 'hostile to the Nazi regime and ready to assist this country rather than to assist the enemy', and those who had lived in Britain for some time and who had 'definitely thrown in their lot with this country rather than . . . assist the enemy'.

The 120 such tribunals, chaired by a legally qualified person, usually a county court judge or barrister, started the process of alphabetically calling aliens to account at the beginning of October 1939. They were held in secret. Those who appeared before them were not allowed the services of a lawyer and, although a representative of one of the voluntary aid associations with whom the refugee had registered was usually present, there was no obligation for an interpreter to be provided, and frequently there was no one at the hearing who could translate for the confused appellant. The common-law presumption that a person was innocent until proved guilty was turned on its head since the alien had the responsibility of proving that he or she should not be interned – that is, was 'innocent' of any potential disloyalty. Furthermore, the Home Secretary was not bound to accept the findings of a tribunal. He could order the immediate internment of an alien if MI5 or police reports recommended it.

The tribunals would examine some 73,000 German and Austrian nationals in total: only 569 people were graded category 'A' – high security risks; 6,782 were graded 'B' – 'doubtful cases'; and 64,000 were placed in category 'C' – 'no security risk'. Of those graded 'C', 55,457 were termed 'refugees from Nazi oppression', and this represented around 85 per cent of all those examined; of that number probably between 80 and 90 per cent were of Jewish or part-Jewish origin.

The tribunals varied wildly in their classificatory decisions: an alien appearing before a Manchester or Croydon tribunal was most likely to be categorised as 'C'; whereas those in Reigate in Surrey and in Leeds favoured 'B'; and some tribunals classified all unemployed aliens as 'B' but told them they could be reclassified as 'C' if they got a job. But there was no real precedent for such bodies and, as their work expanded, they essentially defined their rules as they went along. Decisions sometimes showed uncertainties about the regulations, and on many occasions revealed prejudice and ignorance, such as when a couple who had been supporters of the Weimar Republic were informed by the judge that this was evidence that they were communists; since the Nazi–Soviet pact was still in operation, they were immediately interned, even though the Communist Party was not a proscribed organisation in Britain. The *New Statesman* reported the Kafkaesque case of R. R. Kuczynski, a distinguished population statistician, who was questioned about his association with 'that espionage system at Bloomsbury House' (in fact the headquarters of an interdenominational agency concerned with welfare relief), and put into category 'B'. When he protested that he was a lecturer at the London School of Economics, that sealed his fate. 'I know all about the LSE,' replied the chairman, who obviously saw its Fabian proclivities as signalling a hotbed of revolution, and put Mrs Kuczynski in category 'B' too since she was living under the subversive influence of her husband. Their son Juergen, later to become a leading theoretical economist in East Germany, was classified as 'A' because he had been a member of the Stepney Peace Council and had penned some socialist pamphlets. The fact that he also gave lectures inveighing against the dangers of Nazi Germany seemed to be no counter recommendation.

Writing in the *Spectator*, the journalist Cynthia Saunders gave a vignette of a tribunal when at about 4.15 p.m. the last case for the day came in. The woman applicant 'spoke very little English, and answered every question in monosyllables. She was not a refugee. She had two sisters over here in domestic service like herself, who had gone back to Germany shortly before the war. Why had she stayed? No answer . . . Would she like to go back now? No. Was she a member of the Arbeitsfront [Germany's Nazi-established labour organisation]? . . . It was getting late and the Tribunal was getting no further . . . Suddenly Miss Simmons [the interpreter] had an idea. Had the young woman any special friend in England? Yes. Who? "My employer." "Are you engaged?" "He's the father of my child." That, too, may be the price of refuge.'

Questions were asked in Parliament about the anomalies and injustices of the tribunals, particularly by Eleanor Rathbone who worked tirelessly on behalf of the refugees, and by Josiah Wedgwood, MP, intrepid promoter of many causes. As a result class 'A' aliens were given the right to appeal to the Central Advisory Committee chaired by Norman Birkett KC (who was knighted in 1941) and, under further pressure, the government agreed to set up twelve regional committees to deal with cases referred by the Home Secretary, and also to review 'B' cases – though this latter initiative was so poorly publicised that many who had been assigned to this category did not realise that they had the right to appeal.

In a reply to a suggestion in the Commons on 1 March 1940 that German and Austrian domestic servants in the Aldershot area (where a large number of military establishments were located) posed a particular threat to national security, the Home Secretary Sir John Anderson was judicious: 'I think it is a mistake to assume that every German domestic servant is a menace to the security of this country; and, in my view, there would be no justification for a policy under which all aliens of German and Austrian nationality were treated alike, without regard to the fact that most of them are refugees from Nazi oppression and are bitterly opposed to the present regime in Germany.' As Chairman of the Advisory Committee, Norman Birkett felt much the same. 'I cannot bring myself to send some simple German girl for years of detention, when I am quite satisfied that she has been in the country in some household for years and is not the slightest danger to anybody. So we keep some small element of Justice alive in a world in which we are supposed to be fighting for it . . .'

But throughout the spring of 1940 an anti-alien, pro-internment xenophobia was growing in the popular press. Innuendoes of sabotage and espionage were rife, but never confirmed: reports appeared of enemy aliens breaking such wartime regulations as the blackout with the implication that they were not really behind the British war effort. The *Hackney Gazette*, an east London newspaper, talked of allowing '60,000 enemies to be at large'; the *Daily Mail* argued that every German was a German first and an ideologist afterwards. A letter to the newspaper suggested that 'all Germans and unfriendly aliens [should] be put in a camp and have Poles as guards. I guess none would escape with their lives.' And on 23 March the *Mail* printed a suggestion from a brigadier urging that enemy aliens should be compelled to wear armbands stating their country of origin – much as Jews in Hitler's Germany were compelled to identify themselves with yellow stars.

The invasion of Norway in April 1940 and the rumours that this had been made possible by 'fifth columnist' activity intensified the media frenzy. 'Intern the Lot' and 'Round up Every Enemy Alien' read headlines in the *Daily Mail* and the *News Chronicle*. A number of German refugees who had fled to Norway from Nazi oppression escaped to Britain – and were interned – and Citizens' Advice Bureaux reported some growing anti-alien feeling, which in Liverpool and Manchester was linked to anti-Semitism. But on the whole public opinion remained unstirred, with little concern about 'the alien enemy in our midst'.

This changed fundamentally from 10 May 1940 with the German invasion of the Low Countries and rumours again rampant about 'fifth columnists' who aided the invaders. Churchill urged his Cabinet colleagues that 'there should be a very large round-up of enemy aliens and of suspected persons in this country. It would be much better that all these persons should be put behind barbed wire, and internment would be much safer for the Germans', but the Home Secretary, Sir John Anderson, continued to resist wholesale internment. Nevertheless, despite Anderson's assurance that the intelligence services had no evidence whatsoever that Germans and Austrians resident in Britain had any plans to aid the invading forces – if they came – he issued a new set of regulations. Starting on Whit Sunday, 12 May 1940, all male Germans and Austrians between the ages of sixteen and sixty who lived in areas of possible military operations would be immediately interned, regardless of their categorisation by the tribunals. Initially the east and south coast was targeted, but by 16 June the territory would be extended to cover areas around London where there were military installations. On 17 May it was agreed that category 'B' male aliens between sixteen and sixty were to be interned as what the Home Secretary called 'a precautionary measure', regardless of where they lived, and individual internment orders would be issued for anybody else who gave grounds for suspicion.

The vice tightened when on 27 May 1940 the Home Office issued directives to police forces throughout the country to intern all category 'B' males aged sixty to seventy and all German and Austrian women aged sixteen to sixty in category 'B', other than those who were infirm, in an advanced state of pregnancy, or had dangerously ill children. Special consideration was also to be given to male Germans and Austrians who were categorised as 'C' but had specialist knowledge that would be useful to the war effort. The WVS agreed to provide women 'of sound character and integrity' to help with the arrests and most of the female internees were taken to Holloway Prison or to provincial jails, and spent as long as six weeks in prison alongside convicted criminals before being shipped out to one of the two women's camps on the Isle of Man. Some had young children whom they had to take with them to prison, since many had no family or close friends in the country to whom they could entrust their offspring. And, in reply to a parliamentary question, the Home Secretary admitted that 300 of the internees were pregnant.

The *Evening News* urged 'there will only be security when all of them are safely under guard'. The Rothermere group, whose newspapers included the *Daily Mail* and the *Sunday Pictorial*, continued its campaign, making allegations of 'pretty German women' offering their favours to male munitions workers, while John Gordon's column in the *Sunday Express* suggested that many British were delighted to see the back of what he called refugees but meant Jews. But when a Labour MP queried how many refugees from Nazi Germany were known to have committed hostile acts, the answer was that not a single case had been proved by a court of law.

As the German troops advanced across France at the end of May, refugees started arriving across the Channel, including Poles and Czechs as well as Germans and Austrians who had taken refuge in these now-occupied countries. When a number of German Jews, including sixty-five children – mainly orphans – who had managed to escape from Holland on the last boat out arrived at Dover, the Jews were separated from the rest of the passengers, shut up in the hold of the ship without sufficient water and food, and then sent straight to an internment camp at Huyton near Liverpool.

The entire Jewish refugee population in Britain, most of whom had already suffered persecution and were desperately concerned about the fate of their families and friends back home, felt increasingly under threat. The Jewish Board of Deputies, anxious to protect the refugees for whom they had assumed responsibility, tried to make them as invisible as possible. The board appointed a public relations officer, who toured areas of high refugee settlement warning people in the street not to speak German loudly, cautioning café owners not to display German-language newspapers, and generally encouraging the refugees to monitor their community and control what had tragically become 'anti-social' behaviour in a tense and paranoid situation of fear and prejudice.

The situation became significantly more fraught by early June, following a recommendation from the War Cabinet on 27 May, as British troops prepared to evacuate Dunkirk, that 'the most ruthless action should be taken to eliminate any chance of fifth column activities, including the internment of all enemy aliens and of members of subversive organisations. Alien refugees are a most dangerous source of subversive activity. The number of new refugees admitted to Britain must be cut to a minimum and those admitted must be kept under the closest surveillance.' And for the first time it was recommended that the 'most dangerous characters of all' among the refugees should be deported.

On 10 June 1940 Mussolini appeared on the balcony of the Palazzo Venezia in Rome to announce that Italy was at war with Britain and France. 'Like everyone else', Joseph Pia, the son of an ice-cream-shop owner from Lazio, who owned a chain of sweetshops in Edinburgh, 'was flabbergasted. "What the hell is Mussolini coming in for? He's on a klondyke making money" – you know, supplying both sides. "Stupid ass, coming into the war!"'

That night mobs ransacked Italian property, mainly businesses, all over Britain. George Orwell strolled through Soho 'to see whether the damage to Italian shops etc. was as reported' and concluded that 'it did seem to have been exaggerated in the newspapers, but we did see, I think, three shops which had their windows smashed'. No violent demonstrations were reported in either Birmingham or Manchester despite the presence there of a substantial Italian community. However, in Liverpool Italian shops were attacked, and in Cardiff, Newport and Swansea the violence was considerable and police charged the crowds with batons. The worst violence took place in Glasgow, Clydebank and particularly in Edinburgh. The *Scotsman* reported smashing and looting in Leith Street with arson attacks, the crowds singing patriotic songs, people taken to hospital with head injuries, many arrests and rumours of a shopkeeper being killed. 'Restaurants, ice-cream shops, fish and chip shops, hairdressers' establishments and the premises of a firm of wine-importers had their windows smashed . . . The wrecking activities seemed to be led by a comparatively small number of irresponsible young men . . . many expressions of sympathy for the occupants of the shops were heard, as it was known that some of the shopkeepers were British subjects, and indeed the proprietor of a well known restaurant, whose premises were among the most severely damaged in the city, fought throughout the last war in the ranks of a Scottish regiment. Another man, whose premises were subjected to considerable damage, has two sons at present on active service with the Black Watch it is believed . . . Nearly 100 arrests were made, but only about 20 of them were detained . . .' reported the *Edinburgh Evening Dispatch*.

Mobs stormed through the streets of Glasgow, throwing bricks and stones at all Italian premises as the owners and their families barricaded themselves in back rooms, and along the Clyde coast the police had difficulty in containing the rioters. The writer Naomi Mitchison heard about anti-Italian riots in Campbeltown: 'three Italian shops had been broken up. The old man had been rather rash, saying that England needed a totalitarian govt and so on, but the younger ones were all decent good citizens who gave money to charity and paid their taxes . . . one of the youngest generation was in a mine sweeper . . . if the tide had been in they would have put the old man in the harbour . . . half of them [the assailants] were no good, on public assistance and so on.' The entry of Italy into the war seems to have been the excuse for some, mainly young, men to vent their xenophobia, frustration at unemployment (the incidents were most serious in areas of high youth unemployment) and, in Scotland in particular, anti-Catholicism. In Joseph Pia's opinion, 'these fellows who smashed Italian shops after Italy entered the war, it wasn't patriotism, it was pinching. I would say half the Italian shops in Edinburgh got it.'

The next day, Churchill ordered that all male Italians between seventeen and seventy years of age who had been resident in Britain for less than twenty years and all Italians, male or female, on the MI5 suspect list should be interned – 'collar the lot', was the phrase he used. Some 4,000 people – of whom 600 were British-born – were 'combed out' of densely populated Italian areas such as Soho and Clerkenwell in London (there were some 10,000 Italians in London according to the 1931 census); others were arrested in Scotland. In towns throughout the country where there might be only a handful of Italians, all of whom were likely to have been known individually to the police, there was also an indiscriminate collaring.

In Edinburgh, Joseph Pia was woken at four in the morning after Italy declared war. He was taken to the local police station and the police told him that they were looking for two more Italians, Mario Campanile and Vincent Macogni. 'I said ". . . you'll not get them. They're in the Forces . . . I know Mario Campanile's in the Royal Air Force and Macogni's in the British army." I mean they were Britishers like me. They mentioned another couple of names. "They're in the army too," I said. "Is that where they are?" they said, "because we were wondering why we couldn't find them." '

Those left behind tried to hide their origins. George Orwell noticed that in Soho 'the majority [of Italian shops] had hastily labelled themselves "British". Gennari's, the Italian grocer's, was plastered all over with printed placards saying "This establishment is entirely British". The Spaghetti House . . . had renamed itself "British Food Shop". Another proclaimed itself Swiss, and even a French restaurant had labelled itself British. The interesting thing is that placards must evidently have been printed beforehand and kept in readiness.' Bertorelli's in Charlotte Street in London put up a notice proclaiming 'The proprietors of this restaurant are British subjects, and have sons serving with the British Army', while in Swansea an advertisement in a local paper read 'Virgie Cresci – 51a High Street – wishes to inform the public that he and his Family are British subjects. His brother Nesto is at present serving in the Royal Welsh Fusiliers and his brother Orlando is serving in the British Mercantile Marines. His wife and her family are native-born British subjects – Cresci's cafe is Carrying On as Usual.' A Manchester Italian ice-cream vendor tied a Union Jack to his cart, and in Leeds one was decorated with a large photograph of the British royal family on one side and the exiled Italian royals on the other. The *Yorkshire Evening News* reported that a Leeds organ-grinder had chalked 'I Am Brittish [sic] And the Monkey Is From India' on the side of his instrument.

Those who were called upon to decide the fate of such Italians seemed to have little understanding of the 18,000-strong community in Britain, many of whom had been living in the country for decades. To be a member of the Italian Fascist Party was not the clear indicator that it was in the case of Germans who were members of the Nazi Party. Prior to 1938 it did not necessarily impute ideological pro-fascism – the acronym

PNF (Partito Nazionale Fascita) could equally stand for Per Necessità Familiare (for the family's sake), since a membership card for such an organisation was as essential 'as, say, a birth certificate in a democratic country', explained Professor Bruno Foa, a lawyer and himself an Italian Jewish refugee who had worked for the British Consulate in Naples and the BBC in London, in a memorandum arguing for the release of Italian internees.

Joseph Pia reckoned that '90 per cent of the Italian community of 5,000 in Edinburgh would be in membership of the Italian Fascist Club . . . We used to have boxing . . . billiards and snooker. And then on a different night . . . we used to have table tennis . . . If Mussolini had been a Communist we would have had a Communist Club. If he had been a Liberal, we would have had a Liberal Club. We were a Fascist Club – not that there was any Fascist activity . . . They had a hall – they called it the Fascisto Hall – in Picardy Place in Edinburgh where they used to have a thing above the wall. "Respect the country which has given you hospitality" . . . There was certainly no political activity in the Edinburgh area. I was never active politically. None of the Italian boys were, absolutely nobody that I knew was. The leader of the Fascist group in Edinburgh, my Uncle Alfonso Crolla, he used to run dances . . . getting the lads and lassies to meet each other, maybe with the intention of getting them married. So the Fascist Club was a social club . . . The Italian Fascist Club had no connection with the British Fascist movement, none whatsoever . . .'

Italy had fought on the same side as Britain in the First World War and, until 1935, the government had applauded the order that Mussolini brought to what they saw as his feckless and disordered country. The Roman Catholic Church – a strong cohesive force in the British–Italian community – was a strong supporter of Mussolini, and some traditional feast days had become days for political and social celebration. The Feast of the Day of the Assumption (15 August) was the day that members of the Italian *fascio* in Britain chose for their annual reunion.

Most Italians in Britain were 'simple patriots' and nostalgic for home, while a few were active anti-fascists; but there were also a number of committed Mussolini-supporters. But MI5 was not prepared to recognise these gradations, though the Foreign Office was more inclined to accept that membership of a fascist organisation was not necessarily an adequate test of disloyalty to Britain. It was decided that 1,500 Italians who represented a real danger to the country, according to the government, should be repatriated to Italy (or deported) along with other males between sixteen and seventy who had less than twenty years' residency in Britain. Italian internees were taken to local police stations, transferred to collecting points throughout the country and then most were sent to Warth Mills, a disused cotton mill outside Bury in Lancashire. This had minimal sanitation (the 'lavatories' were sixty buckets in the yard, while eighteen cold-water taps for washing served 2,000 internees), straw palliasses on the floor to sleep on – if men were lucky, many had just bare boards – no electricity, and oil and grease everywhere, rain coming in through the roof and a rat infestation. Furthermore, the internees were served inadequate and irregular meals. From here, most were transported to the Isle of Man where the 'aristocrats' of the Italian community – restaurant proprietors and wholesalers from Soho – were held in one camp, and ice-cream vendors and fish-and-chip-shop owners in another.

On 30 May the Canadian government was asked to come to the assistance of Britain by taking aliens considered to be high risk, and a similar request was made to Australia, Newfoundland and South Africa. Britain would provide the transport and the military guards: it would be the Dominions' responsibility to provide secure accommodation when the internees arrived. The matter had not been discussed in Cabinet, which was presented with a fait accompli on 11 June, and the public was not told what was happening. South Africa declined the request; Newfoundland agreed to take a maximum of 1,000 while Canada set an upper limit of 7,000, but Australia did not insist on a quota. It was understood that the Dominions would receive only those internees whose 'continued presence . . . in [Britain] would constitute a most serious danger in the case of a German invasion'. Between 30 June and 10 July 1940, 7,715 people were despatched to Canada on four ships. The 'dangerous types' who were to be deported included 'A' class internees; German seamen who had been removed from non-German ships and who had been stigmatised as Nazis – but many of whom were members of the socialist International Seamen's Union; 1,596 Italians; and a total of 950 German POWs, most of whom were Luftwaffe pilots who had been shot down. But there were also a number of 'B' and 'C' class aliens. Two hundred Italians, and 2,732 Germans of all categories, were despatched to Australia on the *Dunera*.

The internees were under the impression that they were to be taken to camps on the Isle of Man. It was only when they saw the size of the ships awaiting them in Liverpool docks that they realised their destination was across the Atlantic in some cases, and halfway across the world in others. PhD student Heinz Bing, who was classified as 'C' (no security risk) – had been moved from Kempton Park to Huyton Camp near Liverpool. He had had his chemistry thesis – the result of three years' study – confiscated, and on 2 July was writing to his fiancée Lore Meyerheim when he was told 'to pack for an unknown destination. Lost hope of ever seeing Lore again.' He and Lore, who was nineteen, had made an application to marry since her father, living in Berlin, had refused his permission. The magistrate dismissed the application; 'he thought it was most undesirable that a woman who was German should marry a man who was German, the girl's father being resident in Germany'. Had they been married, Lore imagined that she and Heinz would be interned together but, despite assurances to the contrary, wives and children never accompanied, or followed, those internees who were deported. Bing was taken 'to Liverpool docks and went on board ship [the *Ettrick*]. Conditions are terrible. No air and no room. Can't stop crying. Am frightened that Lore will end her life. Very bad night, slept on table.' But after a few days at sea Bing had 'recovered from the first shock. I will try to start a new life in Canada if I have a chance. Time is no longer a factor in our lives. Hours are like years . . . Our fate is unknown to us.'

Dominic Crolla, an Italian from Edinburgh, had been sent to Canada on the *Ettrick* too. 'Of course the Canadians, far away from Europe, had a terrible opinion of the enemy and they had prepared a great reception for us. Barbers were there the night we arrived to cut our hair, starting from the front . . . the cropped style. We had to strip off our clothing and were given a blue uniform with a large red patch on the back. We were all given a number.

'. . . During the interviews . . . we were asked what we did . . . About 180 of us answered . . . that we worked in chip shops and spaghetti shops and ice cream shops, and that we had been taken from our homes and shops and shipped to Canada. This was a big shock for the

Canadians: "We were expecting dangerous prisoners-of-war and they've sent us a bunch of harmless shopkeepers." Believe me, the phones between Toronto and London must have been very busy the next day.'

As the *Ettrick* sailed up the St Lawrence River, Bing learned that 'a transport with P.O.W.s and "A" aliens has been sunk in the Irish Sea'. The *Arandora Star* had left Liverpool in the early hours of 1 July 1940, crammed with German merchant seamen, German and Austrian class 'A' internees and 734 Italians, a probable total of 1,564 men. It did not have an escort. Early the next morning the ship was hit by a German torpedo. It took just twenty minutes to sink, and 446 Italian civilians – including some notable anti-fascists, one of whom, Decio Anzani, had lived in Britain for thirty years and was secretary of the League for the Rights of Man – and 175 Germans were drowned. The survivors were landed at Greenock in Scotland. The confusion was heartbreaking: there were no proper records of who had been on the ship, and a number of families were either erroneously informed of a bereavement, or reassured when in fact their loved one was dead. The survivors were eventually issued with postcards bearing the legend 'I'm safe' to send to their families, but within a week all were back on the high seas again, bound for Australia or Canada. Questions were asked in Parliament about why the ship hadn't been travelling in convoy, and whether there were enough lifeboats. One MP questioned the War Office's assertion that all aboard were Nazi sympathisers, since it was clear that several known Italian socialists, trade-union activists and refugees from Mussolini's regime were on the *Arandora Star* – not that all category 'A' internees *were* Nazi sympathisers in any case.

The *Dunera,* which sailed from Liverpool on 10 July and reached Australia on 7 September, was a converted troopship built to carry a maximum of 2,000. No fewer than 2,873 were packed aboard, of whom 2,732 were internees, mostly category 'B' and 'C' refugees, some of whom had been interned for only a couple of weeks; there were also 444 survivors from the *Arandora Star*. The ship was grossly overcrowded and insanitary, the food was inadequate and the internees were kept in intolerable conditions for hours on end in a dark, fetid and airless hold, many sleeping on rough straw palliasses on the floor. The number of lavatories was derisory, water was pumped in from the sea and there was rarely soap. But it was not just the material conditions that were insupportable: with a very few honourable exceptions, the British military guards were brutal and frequently sadistic in their treatment of their charges. Internees had their belongings pointlessly confiscated – including letters, family mementoes and their precious identity documents – and these were tossed overboard. They were taunted, beaten up and robbed, but although one internee committed suicide and others became ill or seriously depressed, somehow with tremendous courage the majority survived the two-month journey, by arranging educational classes and lectures without books or even paper and pencil, improvising chess sets using stale bread for chessmen, putting on theatrical and musical performances, and keeping their different religious faiths alive with services and ceremonies.

Largely as the result of the persistence of the indefatigable champion of human rights, Josiah Wedgwood MP, a court martial of three of the escort troops, including the commanding officer, was held in May 1941. Two men received a severe reprimand, and one was dismissed from the service and sentenced to a year's imprisonment. Wedgwood was outraged, considering the proceedings a cover-up. The government decided to compensate the *Dunera* passengers prior to an official enquiry: those who claimed for the loss of their possessions received approximately £12.

As well as wishing to 'collar' the Italians, Churchill suggested a wholesale round-up of all Germans and Austrians, with any sorting out of the 'well-disposed' later. Again, Anderson stood his ground, arguing that 'once large numbers have been collected in concentration camps, a serious danger arises that aliens previously well-disposed to this country will be disaffected by contact with more dangerous characters'. Churchill wavered, recognising that 'many of our enemy aliens have a great hatred of the Nazi regime; it will be unjust to treat our friends as though they were our foes', and he rehearsed the idea of a sort of 'aliens' brigade' which could 'for instance be used in Iceland' – even though there were insufficient arms and equipment for the Regular Army, let alone the Home Guard, at the time.

Notwithstanding these doubts, all chief officers of police were informed on 21 June 1940 that the government had taken the decision to intern all male Germans and Austrians except those under sixteen or over seventy; with a few exempt categories, that left some 25,000 eligible for incarceration. Internment would proceed in stages with non-refugees and unemployed refugees being taken first.

Some voices continued to speak up against this sledgehammer approach. The *Manchester Guardian* kept the issue alive in reports and editorials, and only two letters to the paper were in favour of mass internship. In the Lords, the Bishop of Chichester, Dr George Bell, asked wearily, 'What sense is there in putting men and women who were rescued from Hitlerism and who were full of gratitude to this country behind barbed wire?' and decried the waste in imprisoning expert and able men and women who could manifestly contribute to the war effort if only they were allowed to.

Some 30,000 men and women were interned between the outbreak of war and mid-July 1940. The most virulent pro-Nazis had been very gradually separated from the refugees and sent to Swanwick Camp in Derbyshire. Lingfield racecourse in Surrey was pressed into service, and category 'A' internees made themselves as comfortable as possible in horse boxes, enjoying such privileges as a daily newspaper and visits from their families. But by the middle of June 1940 Lingfield, like another racecourse, Kempton Park, had become one of the twenty-odd transit camps around the country for the influx of category 'C' inmates rounded up in the 'intern the lot' excesses. This was because the majority of 'A' internees – and a large number of others chosen for reasons that were never made clear – were being deported.

During the last week of June and the first two weeks of July 1940, 23,000 enemy aliens were interned in Britain. Many who had already suffered persecution in their homeland tried to avoid the early morning knock on the door, the policeman's request 'I wonder if you would care to . . .', being bundled into a Black Maria and driven off to who knew where. They would stay out all day, sitting in parks, cafés or public libraries, wandering the streets, hoping that the due process of this ill-conceived law would eventually run into the sand. Some were never apprehended; most were, and they often left home without any possessions. They were essentially imprisoned without trial and without respect for their human rights.

To Dominic Crolla, who had returned to Britain to work as an interpreter in an Italian POW camp after three years' internment in Canada, 'Prisoners-of-War are proud people. But internees are very sad ones. The military go to war with bands playing, people cheering, to defend their homes and country. Internees are picked up by the police from their homes and businesses and taken to camps with barbed wire and soldiers with machine guns . . . there is a Geneva Convention about the protection of prisoners-of-war; there is no law about how the treatment of civilian internees goes.'

Friedel Liebmann, a lawyer from Wiesbaden in Germany, had married Fritz Hallgarten, also a lawyer, who managed to work importing wine from the family firm into Britain, and had come with their baby to London in 1934. 'It was very hard [in Britain]: as a Jew you could not take employment, you had to be self-employed and you had to have £1,500 capital which was a lot of money in those days. Women could only take employment in domestic service. My family was very well off, I had had to do nothing for myself, so I wasn't really qualified to take a job like that and it would have been hard too because I had a small child. And in any case there weren't many positions because at the time unemployment in Britain meant that there were more people looking for jobs than there were posts . . . Most people did not understand why we were refugees. They could not understand in these civilised times before the Second World War how there could be a country that would turn against its own citizens, who had led blameless lives and who, in many cases, had contributed to the fame and welfare of the country. This was incomprehensible to English people and of course it made our lives very difficult. Only later on, when more atrocities were known about, did they begin to understand.'

When war broke out Friedel Hallgarten's father advised her to take the children to the country 'because in the First World War he had been a gas instruction officer and he knew exactly what gas would do . . . So we went to Chipperfield [in Hertfordshire] . . . our husbands [she had gone with a friend and her child who stayed a short time] had to get permission from the police to visit us because we were more than 5 miles from the part of London where they were living. One came one week, and one the other. We went before a tribunal in Watford and we were called category "C" which meant the friendliest of all. The Tribunal chairman made a joke saying that he didn't need to interrogate my younger son, who was two at the time, "because he's too young to be a spy".

'We then took a house in King's Langley [nearby] and lived there until the end of the war. It was a very pretty place. But the inhabitants did not take to us. It was not that we were Germans, it was not that we were Jewish. It was that we came from London . . . A few days after the fall of France I got a telephone call from some very good friends, Ronald and Gaby Stent . . . who said "We have to leave our house within 48 hours because we live in a prohibited zone . . . Can you take us in?" I said "Of course". And they came with their little girl who was a year younger than my younger son.

'The next day there was a knock on the door at six in the morning. The large village policeman who we knew by sight and another one said "I'm sorry we have to come so early, but we have to look round to see if there are any subversive books in the house, especially maps." . . . They started turning out the bookcases and they found a Green Line [bus] map that I needed to go to London, which they duly confiscated . . . And they said "I'm sorry Mr Hallgarten and Mr Stent but we really came here to intern you . . . the car will be here in a few minutes . . . We don't want the neighbours to think that you are spies, the car will be waiting round the corner . . ." which I thought was most tactful . . . My husband was very cheerful. He said, "I'll be back in a few days. Don't worry." I took it more seriously and said to him that should the Nazis come, I would know what to do. They wouldn't find me alive . . .'

'No proper arrangements had been planned by the Home or War Office to care immediately for a large number of internees' read a Home Office memo, and camps had to be set up in various not very satisfactory places, including the winter quarters of Bertram Mills' circus, camps in remote Scottish glens, Lingfield racecourse in Surrey and Huyton, just outside Liverpool, which accommodated a considerable number of male internees in a bleak, unfinished council housing estate. But it was the Isle of Man that was ultimate host for the majority who remained in Britain. Some internees felt a grim foreboding about the location: had they been moved to an offshore island facing Ireland so that, should an invasion arrive, they would be cut adrift, abandoned to their fate as the Channel Islanders had been?

There were six camps for Germans and Austrians, two for Italians, two for women, and one for British citizens interned under Regulation 18B, under which a person could be detained on the grounds that their actions could be prejudicial to national security. The 'camps' were in fact rows of terraced boarding houses and small hotels lining the shore in Douglas, Ramsay and smaller seaside towns on the island, which had been requisitioned and cleared of their usual summer visitors, surrounded by double coils of barbed wire and armed sentries, and given over to internees. Most of the camps were named after the largest hotel around which they were grouped – Hutchinson, Palace, Metropole, Central. The internees catered for themselves: a house supervisor (or father) was elected; above him was a street supervisor and above him was a camp supervisor, or commandant. A 'mini civil service evolved' with men chosen to be in charge of welfare, the canteen, educational activities and artistic ventures. Accommodation was acceptable, though most had to share a bed with a stranger – some decided to pull the mattress on to the floor, while others demarcated their territory with a rolled-up blanket down the centre of the bed. A few didn't mind, or welcomed a new intimacy.

Just as on the deportation ships, most of the camps organised ambitious educational and artistic projects for themselves. Inmates lectured on philosophy, religion, history, art history, literature, geography, technical drawing, science, economics and politics. Artists scratched designs – mythical scenes, nubile nymphs, a copy of part of the ceiling of the Sistine Chapel, exotic animals – on the blacked-out windows, printed with lino cuts, painted and sculpted. The Dadaist Kurt Schwitters fashioned collages from cigarette packets, string, nails, torn linoleum, sweet-wrapping papers, seashells, postage stamps – whatever he could find – and constructed magnificent edifices from stale porridge. Other artists made paint from minerals and dyes extracted from food rations mixed with oil from sardine tins, and fashioned paintbrushes from hairs plucked from inmates' bushy beards. Others composed music, wrote and performed poetry and arranged concerts – the pianist Maryan Rawicz of the Viennese piano duo Rawicz and Landauer was interned in Hutchinson camp – or organised debates and printed ambitious camp newspapers on duplicators. Sea bathing was sometimes possible in the summer, as were country walks within the precincts of the camp (when enterprising prisoners grubbed up wild leaves and herbs to supplement their diet), and even the occasional cinema visit under escort was allowed. But, however ingenious the distractions, the greatest enemy was boredom. It was sometimes almost insupportable for active men and women confined with no real work other than menial chores – though from August 1940 voluntary and paid work was permitted outside the camps, and a circular alerted local farmers and market gardeners to the availability of internee labour. Bishop Bell, a tireless champion of the refugees' cause (or, as the *Isle of Man Examiner* put it, 'that self-appointed champion of captive Nazis and Fascists'), visited Onchan camp on the island and despaired at the 'unforgettable depressing picture, seeing men of high quality [150 of whom he estimated had already been interned in concentration camps in Germany] wandering aimlessly about behind high palisades of barbed wire'.

On the Isle of Man the nearly 3,000 women internees were housed in one of the two camps, Port Erin or Port St Mary – again in small hotels and boarding houses, though in their case the landladies were retained to house and feed the inmates – and the women were not as segregated from the islanders as the men were. The women's concerns again were how to keep themselves occupied, but in their case it was also how to keep the children entertained. Two Froebel-trained internees started a kindergarten, and the head of a German progressive school who had fled from Germany to North Wales was put in charge of the camp school.

The women knitted, spun, sewed; they arranged lectures on history, English language and literature, art classes, and vocational classes on such subjects as carpentry and manicure, and from early September developed a co-operative with a barter economy that issued tokens for 'service exchange' – so that a woman with hairdressing skills could do the hair of someone who could sew well, or repair shoes, or do carpentry in return.

At first married women were not allowed to see their husbands, many of whom were in nearby camps, but by August 1940 visits were permitted and the couples and their supporters lobbied for a mixed camp where families could live together – albeit behind barbed wire. This was not granted until late in 1941.

In Parliament and the broadsheet press, criticism was persistent. The economist John Maynard Keynes claimed that he had 'not met a single soul, inside or outside government departments, who is not furious at what is going on'. Civil servants actively assisted François Lafitte, a young Oxford graduate and social policy researcher, to write his condemnatory Penguin Special *The Internment of Aliens*, which was rushed out in November 1940. The Labour MP Michael Foot wrote an article in the *Evening Standard* asking 'Why Not Lock Up General de Gaulle?' and insisting that 'there are German de Gaulles and Italian de Gaulles; Germans who have been fighting Nazism for years; Italians who have been fighting Fascism for years. What have we done with them? . . . sent them off to internment camps . . . We need a totally new policy to deal with foreigners who come to our shores . . . a quick realisation that they offer the opportunity to change the whole character of this war. We need a policy which will banish the words "refugee" and "alien" from the English language. Instead we must learn what Hitler learned years ago, that this war does not recognise national frontiers. It is a war of ideas on a scale Europe has not seen since the Reformation.'

On 10 July 1940 the House of Commons debated the issue, with members such as Victor Cazalet, Eleanor Rathbone, George Strauss, Sidney Silverman and Josiah Wedgwood arguing that the system was wasteful of human resources and was bringing the name of Britain as a nation fighting for the values of a liberal civilisation into disrepute abroad.

No official announcement was ever made, but the internment of enemy aliens stopped on 15 July, and after that date only a few special cases were interned. A report was prepared by Clement Attlee, on conditions in what he referred to as 'concentration camps', and five different committees were set up to consider the problems that arose from interning aliens. At the end of July the first White Paper detailing 'Categories of Persons Eligible for Release from Internment' and the procedures for applying was published. It was a utilitarian document that concentrated on the usefulness the internees could be to the British war effort rather than on rectifying the injustice of their incarceration. There were eighteen possible criteria for release, with a nineteenth added in August 1940: this offered freedom to a man of whom 'enough is known of his history to show that by his writings or speeches or political or official activities, he has consistently, over a period of years, taken a prominent or public part in opposition to the Nazi system and is actively friendly towards the Allied cause'. Failing that, the best way out was for a man to enlist in one of the unarmed 'alien companies' of the Auxiliary Military Pioneer Corps. In such outfits men would help build roads and airfields, shovel coal, load and unload railway trucks and generally act as odd-job men for the Armed Forces. There were some reservations, particularly among the Italians, about effectively joining the Army of a country fighting against their native land, and anxiety about what punishment might be meted out to them or their families at the end of a war. But scouts for the corps visited the camps on the Isle of Man and elsewhere, and some 5,000 men signed up; they were soon dressed in the same khaki uniforms that their guards wore, and were subject to military discipline. It was to be some time, though, before the authorities decided that those ex-internees who wanted to join combat units were sufficiently trustworthy. Most of those who did became sappers, troopers, riflemen or gunners; a few flew aircraft; some joined the commandos or the Parachute Brigade, while others were commissioned and employed to interrogate POWs from their native countries, and even on top-secret Intelligence work. These ex-internees thus contributed to the Allied cause in almost all theatres of war.

Friedel Hallgarten 'wasn't anxious about [my husband]. I knew he was safe on the Isle of Man. But he worried about us . . . They had no news either. So they didn't know where was being bombed and if their families were at risk . . . I don't think my sons reacted too badly to their father's internment because I told them he was safe and other children's fathers were soldiers. The Hertfordshire Regiment, where King's Langley is, had been fighting in the Far East and many people had been taken prisoner in Japan, Singapore, Burma, that sort of thing. So their fathers were away too – and in greater danger.'

Heinz Bing was in despair: no letters from Lore had arrived at the camp in Monteith, some 600 miles from Quebec, since he had been taken into custody at the end of June. 'Has something happened to you? One of my most horrible thoughts is of you being interned,' he wrote. As air raids devastated London in September 1940 Bing waited anxiously for news. 'Our letters don't seem to arrive at all. The Liverpool office must be a frightful muddle.' It was: when Bishop Bell visited the camps on the Isle of Man in August 1940 he heard again and again how the internees felt like forgotten people. The lack of letters was their principal complaint. The bishop went straight to the Central Postal Censorship Office where he saw hundreds and hundreds of unsorted mailbags. He protested vehemently, and within three days shoals of letters had started to arrive at the camps.

'There is nothing but red tape,' Bing complained as September passed into October and there was still no news of his release. 'One feels lost and deserted by the whole world.' Alexander Patterson, a Home Office commissioner who had been sent out by the British government to investigate conditions in the Canadian camps, arrived on 25 November. 'Interview of all "C" cases who want to return. I hope I may be one of the lucky ones . . . but somehow I can't believe it any longer.' But permission was granted and on 27 December, in a fourteen-ship convoy, Heinz Bing left Canada on his way back to Britain – and to Lore.

For her part, Lore Meyerheim had suffered agonies of uncertainty and loneliness, a Jewish refugee from Berlin in a strange country at war. 'I could not yet believe it [when Heinz was interned]. I could not realise what it all meant . . . the days were dreadful without you . . . To be a German now seems to be an outlaw, something similar to being a Jew in Germany . . . Oh Heinz . . . I am thinking of you all the time . . . I long for you to love and kiss me. Why did we never sleep together? It is absurd to say that it would be nice to have a baby from you . . . But still, I sometimes think it would be a sort of comfort to have something that is part of you . . . Where are you darling? Did they send you to Canada or Australia or where on earth to? We shall perhaps never see each other again. I shall love you as long as I live . . . If only I could get a letter from you . . . I do not allow myself to think that you may no longer be alive.'

On 8 August 1940 Lore Meyerheim was finally given an address in Canada where she could write to Heinz. 'I shall do anything I can to get you out . . . I shall go to every lawyer, every solicitor. Whoever may be able to help . . . I shall see that you are not forgotten.' Although unwell – a fact she did not convey to Heinz – her life in Finsbury Park, north London, carried on: she worked as a part-time secretary to one of the refugee aid agencies in Bloomsbury House; she met the sister of George Bell, the Bishop of Chichester, who was 'very kind yet full of class prejudice . . . she argued that the British government had more important things to worry about than the plight of refugees'. She continued to lobby the Home Office, the International Students' Association and the Society for the Protection of Science and Learning for her fiancé's release, though she had still received no letters from him after 'thirteen weeks tomorrow – a quarter of a year', and she put the delay down to the fact that 'the U boats have been particularly active and sunk several ships'. She wrote, 'There are nights when I cannot stand it any longer . . . But human beings can stand far more than one thinks. You can die a hundred times and the next morning get up just as usual and carry on.'

On 1 October the first letter from Heinz arrived – 'I was so excited to see your beloved scribble after three months' – and a week later Lore received a communication from the Home Office Aliens' Department that arrangements for Heinz's release were being made. 'I still cannot grasp the importance of that letter for us both. I expect we will frame it and hang it up somewhere when you are back. I shall only believe it, though, when I have you in my arms.'

Heinz Bing finally arrived at Liverpool on Sunday 12 January 1941 and 'only had thoughts of [Lore] . . . 9 a.m. off boat; 11 customs; 11.50 police wait; 2.15 train to London.' That same day Lore Meyerheim died, probably of tuberculosis, before the lovers were reunited. She is buried in the United Jewish Cemetery, West Ham, in east London.

Throughout that year and the next, men and women emerged from their barbed-wire confinement and regimented days and returned to a semblance of normal life in wartime, some scarred and anguished by their experience, others remarkably stoical and forgiving. A small number remained in internment camps until the end of the war. These were either people who the government considered to constitute a serious security risk, or a few intransigents who argued that since they had never asked to be interned, why should they apply to be released?

Friedel and Fritz Hallgarten 'wanted to put this time behind us. We . . . felt it might have been necessary to intern people. Practically everyone who was interned was innocent. I would say 99 per cent. But how could the government know at the time? There were quislings and fifth columnists everywhere. We found as everything ended well for us, the episode should be forgotten. Our greatest feeling was that England had given us a new home and we could forgive some minor mistakes like this.'

On his return from the Isle of Man, Fritz Hallgarten worked as 'an ARP warden for a time and then in the Home Guard and he enjoyed that'. Nevertheless when his wife applied to the King's Langley WVS to help in their war effort, 'after some consideration they finally took me on. But not as a full member. They ran a canteen for bombed-out Londoners, women and children who were living in the village. And once a week I went there cleaning vegetables, washing up, and in the end I was made a cashier because I never lost any money. But I never had a badge.'

In that paranoid summer of 1940, though, Churchill's 'collar the lot' injunction would also extend to include those native-born citizens who might be found crouching in a Nazi Trojan Horse, and put Oswald Mosley, the man popularly seen as Britain's most plausible candidate for quisling status, behind bars.

11

THE ENEMY WITHIN

*Love your enemies is one of those precepts whose motive force, like a
foreign currency, is instantly frozen in time of war. The State demands
of us, an additional income tax as it were, a ready and sustained
flow of hatred . . . [yet the enemy] is . . . closer to us, more intimately
a part of our own being during time of war than at any other period.
It is when we are, officially at war . . . that we are, unofficially, most
susceptible to each other's influence.*

BETTY MILLER, 'NOTES FOR AN UNWRITTEN AUTOBIOGRAPHY'

IN 1931, THE poet John Betjeman had hymned 'The Mitford girls, the
Mitford girls,/I love them for their sins . . .'

On 29 June 1940 Diana, the third oldest of the six Mitford sisters, was
arrested and taken to Holloway Prison in London where she was given
a small cell in F block.

Eight years earlier Diana had met the man she called Kit – Sir Oswald Mosley – at a twenty-first-birthday dinner party in London. 'He was completely sure of himself and his ideas, he knew what to do to solve the economic disaster we were living through, he was certain he could cure unemployment. Lucid, logical, forceful and persuasive, he soon convinced me as he did thousands of others.' From a 'long line of landed gentry on whose land Manchester was built', Mosley, whose grandfather had been known as 'John Bull', had fought in the First World War, was invalided out of the trenches before he was twenty, and in the 'khaki election' of 1918 became a Conservative MP. He subsequently crossed the floor of the House and joined the Labour Party, and in 1929 was appointed Chancellor of the Duchy of Lancaster in Ramsay MacDonald's government. With the almost equally clever John Strachey, Mosley 'devised an economic solution . . . to the intractable problem [of unemployment]' which the Labour MP (and later Minister and diarist) Richard Crossman was to describe thirty years later as 'brilliant . . . a whole generation ahead of Labour thinking'. It was rejected: Mosley resigned.

Convinced that 'none of the old parties . . . would be adequate . . . to translate his ideas in action', Mosley formed his New Party in reaction to the 'old muttons'. But since the New Party won no seats in the 1931 General Election – indeed, twenty-two of its twenty-four candidates lost their deposits – public meetings became the only way of propagating Mosley's ideas. When Diana Mitford met him, Mosley was 'about to launch' the British Union of Fascists (BUF) which to her 'seemed at the time the only dynamic movement in England' though he 'did not underestimate the difficulty of his attempt to change the course of history', and she was smitten. 'He had every gift . . . Of course I fell in love with him, and decided to throw in my lot with him.' She finally married her fascist on 6 October 1936 in a secret ceremony in the drawing room of the Berlin house of Goebbels, the German Minister of Propaganda, and his wife Magda. Hitler, who was a guest, gave them a large photograph of himself in a heavy silver frame topped by a double-headed eagle as a wedding present.

The peak of BUF activity had been in 1934. Groups were set up in a number of British public schools and universities, and newspaper baron Lord Rothermere was persuaded by Mussolini to give the BUF favourable publicity in the *Daily Mail*; in January the paper described the BUF as 'a well organised party of the Right ready to take over responsibility for national affairs with the same energy and purpose that Hitler and Mussolini have displayed'. Such recommendations brought a sharp increase in membership but, as a political party of influence, the BUF was marginalised even at this propitious moment, with only a handful of Conservative MPs expressing mild interest, and increasing hostility from the Communist Party, Labour supporters and trade-union activists. The crisis in British society that Mosley had predicted in 1932, and recognised was essential to the success of his movement – as it had been in Hitler's Germany – failed to ignite, and the BUF had notably little success in most areas of high unemployment in the North and the Midlands where traditional Labour loyalties remained strong. What drew members was Mosley's charismatic oratory, his revolutionary ideas, and for many the aura of excitement and potential for violence the BUF cultivated with paramilitary blackshirt 'troops', the use of armour-plated vehicles, the insistence that no heckling was permitted at meetings, and the use of such weapons as knuckledusters and lead-filled hosepipes (though these were to be banned by Mosley).

Members of the BUF included the forceful orator William Joyce, whose fanatical commitment to fascism had deepened after his face had been slashed with a razor while stewarding a Conservative Party meeting at Lambeth Baths in 1924. Joyce resigned in a factional battle in 1937, and started a new virulently anti-Semitic organisation, the National Socialist League, before fleeing to Germany on the eve of war where he was to become the voice of Nazism in British homes in the guise of Lord Haw Haw. The brilliant military strategist and advocate of tank warfare, Major General J. F. C. 'Boney' Fuller, and the strongly anti-Semitic A. K. Chesterton (second cousin of the more famous G. K.) were also members of the BUF.

On 7 June 1934 the BUF held a rally at London's Olympia – the largest indoor venue in London. There were at least 12,000 people present, including 2,000 blackshirts acting as stewards. It was a highly orchestrated affair with echoes of Hitler's Nuremberg rallies, but in fact its apogee was the start of the BUF's nemesis. The violence at the meeting marked it out as a thugs' party and frightened away many who had been attracted by Mosley's radical ideas, his oratory and powerful presence.

Anti-Semitism had been incipient in the BUF since its foundation, but from 1934 Mosley adopted it as a political strategy, inveighing against both what he called the 'big Jews' of international finance and the 'little Jews' who threatened to 'swamp' the cultural identity of the neighbourhoods in which they had long settled. Jews were 'a nation within a nation' who owed no allegiance to the British State and thus 'offended' British patriotism.

After 1935 Rothermere decided to stop the *Daily Mail*'s support and the BUF became increasingly alienated from all 'respectable' opinion. It lost any potential as a national movement aiming to revolutionise the structure of British politics, and degenerated into a series of localised organisations playing on anti-immigrant fears in some areas in the East End of London – Bethnal Green, Stepney, Shoreditch – and drawing a motley membership from those who could not adjust to the post-1918 world, people who W. E. D. Allen, a Mosley sympathiser, characterised as being involved in a 'mutiny against destiny'.

But in 1939 the BU (the organisation had dropped the F for Fascist in 1936) enjoyed a brief revival in its guise as a peace party ('Britons Fight for Britain Only'). The revival was a chimera. With fascist Germany and fascist Italy threatening Britain, it was hard for a British fascist party – even if it had dropped the designation – to play the peace card as a patriotic card.

However, although a number of enemy aliens considered to be inimical to British security were rounded up and interned when war was declared, the authorities considered the BU, with its estimated 22,500 members, to be a nuisance, whose wilder shores of paramilitarism and incitement had been controlled by the passing of the Public Order Act in 1936, rather than a danger. The organisation was not proscribed, nor were its leaders interned.

Most other fascist and pro-Nazi parties in Britain, such as the Nordic League, the Right Club and the Greater Britain Movement, had closed down immediately as a defensive act on the outbreak of war, since Defence Regulations 18B promulgated on 1 September allowed the authorities to detain those who they had reason to believe were capable of prejudicial acts against the State, without charge, trial or the length of their sentence specified. Since it was never suggested that anyone detained under Regulation 18B was guilty of any crime, the process of arrest, interrogation, appeal and judgement was bound to be extremely subjective and arbitrary. Lady Redesdale, Diana Mosley's mother, found the procedure baffling: 'Why don't the government give them a fair trial and shoot them if they are guilty of treason? Or let them out if they are innocent?' The Home Office had an explanation: 'As a matter of fact, it is precisely because the potential for mischief of certain persons could not be brought within the scope of the criminal law that parliament was persuaded that it was in the interests of national security to confer these exceptional powers of detention without trial.' Though if there was sufficient evidence 'on which to base criminal proceedings' a detainee could be brought to trial subsequent to his or her detention. It smacked of Alice's Red Queen – or a totalitarian state.

The BU continued its activities, organising well-attended but hardly influential meetings in London and Manchester during the autumn and winter of the Phoney War. The measure of its support was indicated in the three by-elections held at this time: even in Silvertown, near the heart of the BU's supposed stronghold in east London, the candidate polled less than a sixth of the votes that went to the Communist Party's Harry Pollitt.

By the end of April 1940, only thirty-six British citizens had been detained under the powers granted by Regulation 18B. The collapse of Norway changed everything for the fascists as for refugees and foreign residents. Once fighting started in earnest, propaganda for a negotiated peace could look like surrender to the Nazis, and a great deal of activity could fall under the encompassing umbrella of 'hindering the war effort'.

At first, the Home Secretary, Sir John Anderson, was reluctant to embark on wholesale internment of fascists, as he had been of 'aliens', since there was no evidence of fifth-column activity among either fascists or communists, and such wholesale internment would seriously over-extend police resources. But there were a number of factors that overrode this consideration. One was the affair that involved the organising secretary of the Right Club; a fanatically anti-Semitic White Russian, Anna Wolkoff; and another member of the club, Tyler Kent, a cipher clerk at the US Embassy, who had been intercepting coded communications sent between a 'Naval Person' (Churchill, who was still at the Admiralty) and President Roosevelt. This was potentially a grave matter, since Roosevelt was privately negotiating to increase aid to a beleaguered Britain. The presidential elections were due to be held in November 1940 and, if news of any intended compromise of US isolationism leaked out, Roosevelt's hopes of re-election would be jeopardised, and along with them would go Britain's hope of US help in defeating Hitler. The Secret Service also believed that Mosley, along with fellow fascist Captain Archibald Maule 'Jock' Ramsay, the Conservative MP for Peebles, were having highly secret talks about uniting the various British fascist, anti-Semitic and pro-peace groups. These organisations might welcome a Nazi invasion, either assisting them directly, or staging a government coup d'état and negotiating surrender terms with the invaders – though it is doubtful that the government actually believed either possibility to be very likely. But the internment of fascists in general and of Mosley in particular had become a matter of public morale. In the confused and anxious weeks of late May and early June 1940, not much decisive action could be taken: seizing those who had long expressed admiration and affinity for Nazi Germany, and emulated some of its viler practices, was one thing that could.

Although there was little direct evidence of subversive fascist activity, and Mosley's pronouncements, though they were anti-war, were couched in strongly patriotic language, the decision was taken to intern some twenty to thirty leading members of the BU, since MI5 estimated that some 20 to 30 per cent of the organisation posed a serious security risk. On 22 May 1940 Defence Regulation 18B was amended to authorise the Home Secretary to detain any members of an organisation which in his view was either subject to foreign influence or control, or whose leaders 'have or have had associations with' leaders of enemy governments or 'sympathise with . . . the system of government' of enemy powers. The law was deliberately framed to catch any member of a fascist or proto-fascist organisation the government wanted put away, since, by definition, they would 'sympathise' with fascist regimes. By the end of June some 750 individuals who were associated with the BU had been interned; and on 10 July 1940 it was declared a proscribed organisation and closed down.

On 23 May 1940 Mosley had been arrested and taken to Brixton

Prison, where 'he found a large number of our people were detained', while others were taken to 'a concentration camp at Ascot . . . [and] some Northerners were thrown into jail in Liverpool where conditions were the worst of all'. A number of fascists were eventually moved to camps on the Isle of Man where they were housed in segregated camps separate from those interned as 'enemy aliens', but Mosley remained in Brixton, the authorities concerned that his oratory might whip up disaffection in the more autonomous and communal situation on the Isle of Man.

Mosley's defence, which he put to the Advisory Committee in July 1940, was essentially that his wish for peace was a legitimate expression of political opinion – had not Chatham, Fox, Cobden, Bright and then, in the twentieth century, Lloyd George all opposed war? Did that make them traitors? In neither his speeches nor his writings, he maintained, had he ever expressed a wish to see Germany defeat Britain. Indeed, in the interwar years he had pressed for rearmament. He did not see the Tyler Kent affair as decisive in the decision to intern British fascists – and he had only heard about it in prison.

Other prominent fascists incarcerated in Brixton included Maule Ramsay, who had been convinced by *The Protocols of the Elders of Zion*, actually a pernicious forgery describing a worldwide Jewish conspiracy, published after the First World War. Maule Ramsay's epiphany had been the Spanish Civil War, which he saw as evidence of communist domination – and then he started to see it everywhere. By 1938 he had decided that Bolshevism was Jewish and that the hand of Jewry was behind most historical crises, and Germany, and only Germany, had grasped the full significance of these happenings and 'perceived behind the mobs of native hooligans the organisation of World Jewry'. *Mein Kampf* joined *The Protocols of the Elders of Zion* as his bible. It was unlikely that the Crown would have secured a prosecution of Maule Ramsay under the Official Secrets Act so, again, internment was the solution.

Another internee was Arnold Spencer Leese, the son of a baronet from Lincolnshire. An ex-veterinary surgeon, who had sent a textbook he had written on the diseases of camels to George V, he was also the Director General of the Imperial Fascist League (IFL), which he had turned from a patriotic anti-socialist organisation into a fanatical anti-Semitic one. With his hatred of the Jews and his views on racial purity, he was the nearest thing on offer to an 'English Hitler', though without any of the Führer's charisma. The IFL published a magazine, *The Fascist*; its members wore a uniform consisting of a black shirt, khaki breeches, puttees and an armband with a swastika superimposed on a Union Jack. Meetings ended with a 'Heil Hitler' salute, and one of their members advocated sending half the Jewish population to gas chambers and the other half to zoos. The ILF may have been of marginal political importance, but it was a deeply disturbing organisation for Britain's Jewish population, particularly as news of the Nazi treatment of the Jews in Germany began to become known. Leese was ordered to be interned in June 1940: he went into hiding for four months and, when the police came to arrest him, the powerfully built, 6-foot, blond fascist put up a violent struggle, booting a police constable in the backside, and smashing his police cell when he was finally taken into custody, protesting against his loss of liberty without due process of law. Leese started his internment with a three-month prison sentence for assault and wilful damage.

It is important to contemplate the gradation of views even among those that are repugnant. Not all fascists were pro-Nazi: the First World War veteran A. K. Chesterton was every bit as virulently anti-Semitic as William Joyce, yet he fought against Hitler with the British Army in East Africa. And for most British fascists there was a genuine conflict when war broke out between their admiration for German and Italian fascism and their strong sense of British nationalism; many members left the BU because their patriotism seemed at variance with Mosley's regard for European fascism and calls for a negotiated peace, while some who desired peace at any price flocked to join. But the invidious venom of irrational anti-Semitism ran through almost every fascist organisation, certainly after 1935.

Admiral Sir Barry Domvile, ex-Chief of Naval Intelligence and ex-Chief of the Royal Naval College at Greenwich, was also interned in Brixton Prison in a cell 'a little larger than a telephone call-box, and roofed in wire netting'. He had run an association to promote Anglo–German friendship called the Link, which provided a vector for Josef Goebbels, the Minister of Propaganda, and Joachim von Ribbentrop, the Foreign Minister, to influence British opinion, and was openly pro-Nazi. He was also something of a libertarian who was irritated by pub closing hours and customs restrictions among other things, and found much to admire in Germany, particularly the fact that 'you can drive your car at any speed that your reason considers safe . . . there are no speed limits in Germany' and the efficiency of the SS – 'men of splendid physique . . . brought up with patriotic ideals'. He was confused about what he thought of Jews until he was interned, and then he became quite clear about the 'Judmas' ('my copyright title'), the Judaeo-Masonic conspiracy that he blamed for his predicament.

Also interned in a cell on F wing in Brixton Prison twenty-two hours out of twenty-four was Captain H. W. Luttman-Johnson, a Scottish landowner and former cavalry officer in the Indian Army. In 1933 he had become the secretary and organiser of the January Club, a dining club and discussion group in which all who were interested in various forms of fascism could participate. Though the BU gradually took over the club, it had started as a more ecumenical group (Luttman-Johnson had been advised 'clubs should not have too clearly defined names. The Fabian Society was not called the Slow-Progress-Towards-Socialism Club'). Its members included such establishment figures as Sir Philip Magnus, the historian and biographer; the writer Sacheverell Sitwell; and Major Edward 'Fruity' Metcalfe, who was a close friend of Edward VIII – and was married to Alexandra 'Baba' Curzon (known as Ba-ba Blackshirt on account of her enthusiasm for fascism), who was Mosley's one-time sister-in-law (and sometimes lover). Mosley himself, his first wife Cimmie, and his mother were also members, as was William Joyce. Luttman-Johnson had been a member of the BU for only a month when he was interned, while other January Club leading lights had never joined Mosley's party.

Charles Watts, of the BU Westminster branch, was interned on the evidence of a fellow BU member, Olga Bonora. Bonora was an ARP warden and when she visited the Westminster BU offices she saw a number of steel helmets and ARP badges there. She 'had asked Watts how they had come to be there. He told her . . . it was intended to take them to various branches in the East End and that during the air raids Fascists would wear them. They would pose as air raid wardens, and in the general confusion proceed to "beat up" all the Jews they could find.' Bonora reported this plot to the authorities.

When Diana Mosley was arrested at the end of June, she was offered the opportunity to take her eleven-week-old baby, Max, with her to Holloway Prison. She decided, however, that given 'the bombing of London which . . . was expected hourly', he would be safer in the country with his nanny and brother, Alexander, who was not yet two. But, trusting in the assurance that she would be away only for the weekend, Diana Mosley asked the police to stop outside a chemist where she purchased a breast pump so she could go on nursing her baby on her return. It was to be nearly three and a half years before Diana Mosley was back home with her children again.

Of the 747 BU members imprisoned under Defence Regulation 18B, ninety-six were women. One was Lady Domvile, wife of Admiral Sir Barry; another was Miss Elsie Steele, who had already been imprisoned in April 1940 for telling a large crowd in Bethnal Green in east London, 'you don't see any of the rotten Government leaders in khaki. Remember it was Chamberlain, dictated by his Jewish masters, who declared war, not Hitler.' Like Diana Mosley herself, the women BU internees remained intensely loyal to Sir Oswald, and on his forty-fourth birthday held a tea dance in Holloway to celebrate.

Mosley's appeal against his conviction was turned down. In his submission he had asked the Advisory Committee 'what shred of evidence can they [the police] produce to support the allegation that I would play the traitor to my country?' The Committee chairman Norman Birkett KC reported to the Home Office that the evidence that the BU was under foreign control was 'somewhat scanty', and concluded that 'although there is abundant evidence of fierce criticism of British policy, there is nowhere any evidence that the leaders of the BU desire a full German victory, or have any other concerns than to take the fullest advantage of the present situation in order to bring BU to power with Mosley as its leader.' Mosley admitted to an anti-Semitic policy. He disputed the fact that the BU's emblem and the use of banners at rallies were copied from Germany, arguing that the Durham Miners' Gala was more the model than the Nazis, and denied receiving funding from Italy (although he had). He agreed that the BU attracted extremists but argued that a lunatic fringe was the cross many political parties had to bear. The most damning evidence against him seemed to be attempts to set up a radio station in Germany; these had been intended to be commercial stations on the lines of the successful Radio Luxembourg and Radio

Normandie. The idea was to make money to enable the BU to fund its political activities at a time when its finances were penurious – somewhere around 1935 Mussolini's funding had dried up.

Birkett concluded that the radio station 'does not assume the importance which at first sight it appeared to have', but nevertheless endorsed Mosley's internment on the grounds that he was a member of a now-proscribed organisation, and that, in view of his deviousness and evasiveness over foreign funding and respect for the law, and because of his 'inordinate ambition . . . to undisputed even autocratic power . . . it was necessary to exert control over him' even though there was no evidence of planned fifth-column activity, or indeed any misconduct or planned misconduct – any more than there was in the case of almost all of the enemy aliens similarly detained.

Lady Mosley's appeal was not successful either. She had never been a member of the BU but she was a dedicated fascist. In 1933 she had gone with her younger sister Unity to Germany and attended the first Parteitag (Party Congress) held in Nuremberg after the Nazis' seizure of power. Diana was enthralled: 'when Hitler appeared an almost electric shock passed through the multitude . . . it was a thanksgiving by revolutionaries for the success of their revolution. They felt the black years since their defeat in the war were now over and they looked forward to a better life.' Unity returned to Munich the next year to study German and set about her self-appointed task of engineering a meeting with Hitler, which she finally achieved after many months of positioning herself at a table near to the one he habitually occupied in the Osteria Bavaria. Excitedly, Unity urged Diana to come to Germany to meet the fascist leader too, and over the next few years Diana 'saw . . . this extraordinary individual . . . fairly often, though nothing like as much as Unity . . . who adopted the whole creed of the Nationalist Socialists including their anti-Semitism, with uncritical enthusiasm'.

The last time that Diana met Hitler was in August 1939 when she and Unity were his guests at the Bayreuth Festival, dining together every evening. On 2 August, he told Diana that war was inevitable. That evening the party attended a performance of Wagner's *Götterdämmerung*. Diana returned to England. Unity, despite Hitler's warnings, stayed on in Munich. On 3 September she heard the news of war from the British consul and that same day went to the Englische Garten, sat on a park bench and pulled out the small automatic revolver she had taken to carrying in her handbag, and shot herself. But though the bullet lodged in her brain, Unity did not die but was seriously brain-damaged. At Christmas her mother ('Muv') and sister 'Debo' (Deborah Mitford, later the Duchess of Devonshire) set out to bring her home from Switzerland, to where Hitler had helped her to escape. Unity lingered on in a pathetic state until she died in Scotland in the spring of 1948.

The ostensible reason for Diana's internment was that she had acted as an intermediary between her husband and the German government and Hitler (this related to the radio station proposal), had transmitted instructions from her husband after his arrest about carrying on the BU (paying staff etc.), had supported her husband, and held fascist views. An MI5 officer described her as an 'extremely dangerous and sinister young woman'. Even her sister Nancy, the novelist, had been 'thankful Sir Oswald Quisling has been jugged . . . but think it quite useless if Lady Q is still at large' and went to see a government official 'to tell what I know (very little actually) of Diana's visits to Germany. I advised him to examine her passport to see how often she went . . . Not very sisterly behaviour but in such times I think it one's duty.'

When Diana Mosley finally came before the Advisory Committee in October 1940 the decision was almost a foregone conclusion. She felt intense hostility towards Birkett: he nursed identical feelings towards her. She answered irritably his 'silly questions' about the fact that she had visited Hitler frequently – 'this friend of yours is now bombing London', he pointed out. Did she agree with Nazi policies towards the Jews? 'I am not fond of Jews,' Lady Mosley stated baldly. She subsequently claimed that the transcripts of the investigation of her and her husband, which were kept secret for several decades, were tampered with, but what is clear is that there was never the slightest intention of releasing either of the Mosleys: it was far too sensitive a political issue and would have been likely to inflame public opinion. In effect, however repellent her views, Diana Mosley was being interned for being Mosley's wife, as Churchill recognised: 'Sir Oswald Mosley's wife,' he wrote in November 1941, 'has now been 18 months in prison without the slightest vestige of any charge against her . . .'

By spring 1941 nearly all the other fascist internees with young children had been released: the Mosleys remained in prison, he in Brixton, she in Holloway. What would make internment bearable for Diana would be to be reunited with her husband, who was allowed only a half-hour visit every fortnight. It was out of the question, she was told, and Sir Oswald's petitions were turned down too. Finally Diana's only brother, Tom, while dining at 10 Downing Street with Churchill, whom he called 'cousin Winston' (though it was Clementine Churchill who was actually the cousin – she had been a bridesmaid at the Redesdales' wedding), pressed their case. Churchill, 'a great cutter of red tape', did so for Diana, and after eighteen months the Mosleys were reunited to live in a house in the grounds of Holloway Prison, allowed to cook their own food, with prisoners convicted of sex offences ('so clean and honest') to clean for them, and a patch of earth where they could dig for their own private victory, growing vegetables and strawberries. Thus the Mosleys 'saw the seasons come and go', for unlike prisoners who had been sentenced, they had no idea how long they might remain incarcerated.

Reluctantly, Herbert Morrison, who had succeeded Sir John Anderson as Home Secretary in October 1940, agreed to Mosley's release on medical grounds and to Diana's on humanitarian grounds. The Home Secretary assured Parliament that there was 'no undue risk to national security' any longer, and he had no wish to 'make martyrs of persons undeserving of honour'. But the Minister of Labour, Ernest Bevin, dissented, arguing that the decision would 'weaken morale and have an unfortunate effect on negotiations and discussions in the industrial field'. The Mosleys were finally released early in the morning of 20 November 1943 and placed under house arrest.

Mosley was reputed to remain remarkably 'unembittered' by his experiences – though he did name one of his cows after a prison wardress.

Admiral Domvile was released in July 1944, as was E. Quentin Joyce (the brother of William Joyce, Lord Haw Haw), who had been imprisoned on the outbreak of war, and other prominent BU members; but it was not until 26 September 1944 that Maule Ramsay was set free. Morrison had thought it impossible to release a Member of Parliament, presumably because he could not be required to abstain from all political activity, and indeed Maule Ramsay resumed his seat in the Commons

the next day to the fury of the Communist MP Willie Gallacher, whose
son had recently been killed in action.

MI5 reckoned that in 1939–40 there were around 9,000 paid-up
members of the BU – and probably at least as many again who
supported or sympathised with the movement. The Communist Party
of Great Britain (CPGB) had a membership of some 20,000 in March
1940. At weekends when volunteers were out on the streets selling it,
the party's newspaper the *Daily Worker* sold around 100,000 copies
compared to the BU's weekly *Action* which shifted around 14,000 each
issue. Along with the Peace Pledge Union (not a political party though
generally associated with the Left and with a membership exceeding
130,000 and a circulation of over 40,000 for its newspaper *Peace News*),
the CPGB and the BU were the most vociferous in opposing the war
and calling for peace. If the charge of being 'under international
influence or control' could be levelled at the fascists, how much more
true was this in the case of the Communist Party of Great Britain
through its membership of the Comintern (the Russian-controlled
Third International committed to establishing communist parties
throughout the world to aid a proletarian revolution)?

The CPGB was put in a difficult position when Germany signed
the non-aggression pact with the Soviet Union on 23 August 1939.
Nevertheless on 2 September the party's Central Committee
announced qualified support for a war 'that need never have taken
place. One that could have been avoided . . . had we had a People's
Government in Britain.' A pamphlet written by the General Secretary,
Harry Pollitt, *How to Win the War*, published on 12 September,
emphasised the party's support for the war since it believed it to be a
'just war'. The penny pamphlet sold 50,000 copies, and when, at a
meeting of the Political Bureau on 12 September, the CP's theoretician
R. Palme Dutt argued that his comrades should reconsider whether it
was in fact a 'just war', he received scant support.

When the Central Committee met on 24 September, however, it was
already clear that Comintern HQ held a different view and had decided
that the party policy should be one of 'revolutionary defeatism' ('the
main enemy is in your own country' in Karl Liebknecht's First World
War formulation), with workers in every bourgeois nation working

towards their own country's defeat in this 'imperialist war', and seizing the opportunity to ferment a revolutionary situation. Later that evening Dave Springhall ('one of those Communists who talk like a concrete mixer') arrived back from Moscow where he had been acting as British representative to the Comintern, and informed the assembled members that his instructions were that the war was indeed an imperial one to which no working-class movement should give support.

The Committee argued bitterly for two days but when the vote came to fall in line with Moscow's edict, only three members – Pollitt, John Campbell, the editor of the *Daily Worker*, and the West Fife MP Willie Gallacher – voted against it. On 7 October the CPGB renounced its cautious support for the war and produced a manifesto announcing that 'This is not a war for democracy against Fascism . . . [it] is not in the interest of the people of Britain, France and Germany', and argued that British reactionaries had supported Hitler as a bulwark against Bolshevism. 'Thereby it forged the weapon which has been turned against itself. That is the basic cause of the war,' glossed Palme Dutt in an article published a few days later. The manifesto called for the election of a new government to carry on peace negotiations. Harry Pollitt relinquished the post of general secretary and went to work in the Manchester district, while Campbell moved out of the editor's seat at the *Daily Worker*.

'It was a terrible time,' recalled Ethel Mattison, a CP member. 'We argued and argued but we just couldn't argue our way out of the feeling that it was a complete *volte face* but we still stuck by the party. There was no question of doing anything else.' Although a few left the party, most stayed and others joined: by March 1940 the party's membership was higher than it had been at the outbreak of the war; and the *Daily Worker*, and *Labour Monthly* edited by Palme Dutt, who had taken over the responsibilities but not the title of General Secretary, almost trebled their circulation between January 1939 and December 1940. The reasons why members stayed were various: partly solidarity with the Soviet Union, which was seen to be a country – the only country – to be struggling to build a socialist state on the ashes of capitalism; partly the belief that Chamberlain's bellicosity towards fascism was a recent and not very convincing stance. And it was hard to argue that Britain was fighting for democracy when four-fifths of its empire had no democratic rights of any sort and India had joined the war without consulting the representatives of its people at all. There were also those who remembered the First World War and believed that millions of working men had lost their lives in a war fought ultimately for imperial gain; and there were those who believed, or half believed, all these things, but above all felt intense loyalty to a working-class party that put unity above everything. There were too many enemies on the outside, waiting to pounce, for divisions to be made public.

Throughout the Phoney War, MI5 continued to have fears about Russia using the British communists as a fifth column in the event of war between the Soviet Union and Britain, and suspected that German, Austrian and Czech communists who had come to Britain as refugees in 1938 and 1939 were actively propagating communist propaganda under the cover of refugee organisations, and that some were 'trained revolutionaries'. However, despite the Security Service's call to intern some and restrict the movement and activities of all, the Home Office decided that it was not justified in interning refugees solely on the grounds that they were communists.

As enemy aliens were rounded up wholesale, leading fascists were interned and the BU proscribed in June 1940, there were continuous discussions about whether the CP should not be similarly treated. In early July 1940, the Cabinet deliberated long and hard before deciding to suppress a CP pamphlet, *The People Must Act*, although the Scottish Office refused to instruct the police in Scotland to seize copies of it, arguing that it knew no grounds in law on which such an action could be justified and that a challenge in the courts would be likely to succeed. A challenge was never mounted in England or Wales but, had it been, the Home Office would have argued that thrusting leaflets into the hands of people who have not asked for them could lead to a breach of the peace.

Throughout May and June 1940 CP members complained of increasing police harassment, with a reported forty-five arrests for using 'insulting words and behaviour' when speaking at open-air meetings, selling the *Daily Worker* and distributing leaflets. Members' homes were searched and police broke up meetings, demanding to see the identity cards of those present; and the National Council of Civil Liberties reported that employers were being informed if their workers were seen at CP meetings, and such information frequently led to dismissal. The

Home Office also suggested that all newsagents should be required to furnish a list of those of their customers who placed a regular order for the *Daily Worker*.

In October the party published a pamphlet, *How to Defend Yourself: a Practical Guide for Workers*. It advised that while apparently legal charges such as 'obstruction' and 'breach of the peace' and 'insulting words' were in fact political charges, members should never give the authorities any unnecessary opportunity like 'shouting provocative slogans'; they should be careful to choose 'a spot where it seems unlikely that you could cause any obstruction' when selling a CP paper. Members were cautioned *never* to consent to having their homes searched, and that they should be careful not to carry anything that might give information about themselves or anyone else on their person since, if stopped, they were bound to be searched. 'The emptying of pockets is better than the wringing of hands,' it counselled sagely.

The 'problem' the authorities had with communists during the Second World War exemplified the delicate balancing act of a liberal democracy fighting a 'people's war' against a totalitarian regime in the name of freedom. The Ministry of Information, concerned about the possible effect on public morale and on the authority of both central and local government of communist propaganda against the war, called for a defence regulation that made it an offence 'to attempt to subvert duly constituted authority'. However, wiser counsel prevailed, since such a move could provide 'subversive forces' with such potent ammunition that they would be strengthened rather than weakened. Moreover, it 'would be inconsistent with the historic notions of English liberty. Our tradition is such that while orders issued by the duly constituted authority must be obeyed, every citizen is at liberty to show, if he can, that such orders are silly or mischievous and that the duly constituted authorities are composed of fools or rogues . . .' Such activities were 'only subversive if they were calculated to incite people to break the law or topple the government'. 'A most admirable statement of principle', declared the Home Secretary, Sir John Anderson, and no action was taken against the CPGB.

So if communists were unlikely to assist a fascist invader, Britain was not at war with Russia, and there was no evidence that a communist 'fifth column' had operated in Scandinavia, the Low Countries or France, nor was there any indication that they were inciting revolution, what was the danger the party posed? There were several possible answers.

The most convincing was the influence of communists in the trade-union movement, serving as shop stewards in particular. In 1941 the party leadership reaffirmed that 'the Communist Party can never be victorious until the main strength of the party is organised in factories. The factory is the basic unit of our party; members of the party are primarily organised in the place where they work, not in the place where they sleep.' During the war the party's grievance was essentially that employers were using the need for greater productivity to exploit the workers, imposing longer working hours, suspending Factory Act legislation about health and safety, and permitting 'dilution' – the working man's First World War complaint – with women and youths substituting for skilled men at lower rates of pay. The right to strike was removed on 19 July 1940: individuals could be prosecuted for taking strike action, the penalties being imprisonment or a heavy fine.

The issue was particularly salient in the aircraft industry – an industry that was increasingly vital to the prosecution of the war – where the party had built up a strong base among shop stewards. By November 1939 there had already been go-slow movements, bans on overtime and sit-ins protesting at working conditions; and the circulation of the industry's union journal *New Propeller* had risen to 31,000. In April 1940 a conference was convened to link workers in the aircraft industry with those in other engineering industries, since it was argued that in wartime the boundaries between them were increasingly permeable. This resulted in setting up the Engineering and Allied Trades Shop Stewards' National Council, the aim of which was 100 per cent union membership – a closed shop – and the co-ordination of the activities of shop stewards from all sectors of the industry: the union's general secretary was a communist. Despite the opposition of the largest union in the engineering industry, the Amalgamated Engineering Union (AEU), it was clear that the new union represented a powerful force in a vital wartime industry and care would have to be taken to ensure that it was not provoked unnecessarily.

While the historian of the Communist Party claims that 'a handful' of communists were arrested under the terms of Regulation 18B (including the Welsh poet – and dentist – T. E. Nicholas, though this was clearly a blunder by the police and he was soon released), the score of the official historians of the intelligence service is only one: John Mason, a Yorkshire steelworker, trade-union member and shop steward who had joined the Communist Party on the outbreak of war. He was arrested in July 1940 and interned for eleven months and, though his offence was not made public and he was never brought to trial, Morrison defended Mason's internment, saying that he was involved in attempts to slow down production. It seemed that the government was indeed wary about using Regulation 18B against communists for the hostile reactions it might provoke in factories.

Coalmining and shipbuilding, two other industries that were vital to the war effort, also had a long history of industrial militancy. The President of the 135,000-strong Miners' Federation in Wales, Arthur Horner, was a communist, and so were a number of members of the executive. And Welsh miners emphatically did not share the rest of the nation's fervent admiration for Winston Churchill: memories – albeit false – of his use of troops to fire on striking miners at Tonypandy in the Rhondda in 1910 were part of their bitter history, as was their recall of Churchill's role in breaking the General Strike in 1926.

In Scotland, the Communist MP Willie Gallacher was a veteran 'Red Clydesider', a representative of the workers in the Glasgow engineering and shipbuilding industries, which had been hit hard in the Depression years. They would be revived by the exigencies of war, and having their workforce on side would be vital to its prosecution.

Writing in the Labour Party paper *Tribune* the week after war broke out, Stafford Cripps (the post-war Labour Chancellor of the Exchequer) and Aneurin Bevan (the post-war Labour Minister for Health and Housing) argued that it was the 'duty' of socialists to assist 'the anti-Fascist forces' while demanding a change of government, and to work to stop the war degenerating into 'a simple struggle between rival imperialisms' – which did not sound very different from the communists' call for a 'war on two fronts'. Cripps defended Russia's invasion of Poland and then the invasion of Finland in November 1939 as a defensive move – though the board of *Tribune* demurred and in March 1940 the editor, who was considered to be too pro-communist, was removed. In fact there was very little in the expressed views of the CP that a number of Labour MPs had not said at some point. Part of the reason for the government's caution in moving against the CPGB was that what communists were saying was what a number of people were clearly thinking.

While opposition to war was painted as unpatriotic – or worse – the usual channels of dissent seemed blocked. Although they were not members of the coalition government until May 1940, Labour leaders supported a war prosecuted by a government still run by Conservative appeasers, those they castigated as the 'Men of Munich', and the electoral truce agreed between the parties meant that Labour and the Conservatives agreed not to contest seats in by-elections previously held by the other party. Although all stressed that this was not a political truce, many Labour Party members worried that it was, and local Labour parties and trade-union branches continued to pass anti-war resolutions throughout the months of the Phoney War. Moreover, the ban sapped the life out of local parties by giving them nothing to do in the way of political activity. The truce was not, of course, binding on the Communist Party or any other party or individual who chose to enter a by-election fray. But among the population as a whole the anti-war platform was not one many wished to clamber on to: when Harry Pollitt stood as a candidate in the Silvertown by-election in east London in February 1940, although he polled six times the votes of the BU candidate, he only received a derisory 966 votes – just over 6 per cent of the poll.

Since many of the members of the CP were young men in their twenties and early thirties, and since most were not pacifists though they were opposed to the war, there was, by the end of 1940, a considerable communist phalanx in military uniform. Conscripted men were advised to 'go under cover' and leave their membership cards at home but, as a historian of the CPGB says, many continued to act as communists in the Forces as they had in Civvy Street. A London communist, Harry Berger, appeared at the Trades Union Congress (TUC) conference in October and addressed the delegates as any other worker might, complaining about Army pay and conditions; and by November 1940 the *Daily Worker* had a regular 'soldiers' page' which soon became a weekly 'Our Page for Soldiers, Sailors, Airmen', publishing letters – usually signed with initials only – telling about life in the Armed Forces with gripes about low pay, the embedded nature of the class system, the authoritarian structure, bureaucratic incompetence etc.; and 'Gabriel' (Jimmy Friel, who worked on the paper until he quit over the Hungarian uprising in 1956) drew cartoons to illustrate the squaddies' plight. The page became a hugely popular read among the ranks regardless of their political persuasion.

After the fall of France the party made an attempt to broaden its appeal. The Central Committee issued a manifesto on 22 June 1940 calling for a 'People's Government', claiming that 'the same kind of leaders who brought France to defeat are in high places in Britain'. There should be a scourge of all 'the guilty men of Munich', for if British workers ousted their own ruling class that would encourage German workers to bring down Hitler. 'People's Vigilance Committees' were set up to fight instances of the abuse of civil liberties, and by the end of June 1940 these had begun to coalesce into a movement to rally support for a People's Government, including support from groups outside the confines of the CP such as local Labour parties, some of which had been disaffiliated at the Labour Party conference in May, who continued to oppose the war.

The Chairman of the national People's Vigilance Committee (which soon changed its name to the 'People's Convention') was D. N. Pritt, a lawyer and MP for Hammersmith, who had been expelled from the Labour Party over his support for the Russian invasion of Finland. The manifesto, issued in September, was signed by 500 people 'from all walks of life. Largely from trade unions, but from many other sections of society too including MPs, parliamentary candidates, borough councillors, distinguished writers, scientists, actors, artists and clergymen. Over a quarter of a million copies were distributed calling for the appointment of delegates to a "People's Convention" in support of six aims: defence of living standards; defence of democratic and trade union rights; adequate ARP; friendship with the Soviet Union; a People's Government; and "a people's peace that gets rid of war".'

But how could these aims be achieved in wartime without endangering the fight against Hitler and fascism? Popular agitation would give a lead to popular discontent, and it would bring new men to power. This new People's Government would set an example by giving independence to India, introducing socialism at home and proposing reasonable peace terms. The German working class would rise up and overthrow the Nazis. Proletarians in other countries would do likewise, and peace-loving socialist regimes would produce a stable peace throughout the world.

The convention was held in London on 12 January 1941. The organisers claimed there were present '2,234 Delegates directly representing 1,200,000 of which 1,136 delegates represented 1,004,950 in Trade Unions and factories and on jobs' (which was a gross exaggeration), plus various other political organisations, youth organisations, shelter committees and tenants' associations. 'Left-wing psychopaths,' a Home Intelligence report dubbed them irritably. Nehru's daughter Indira (who, as Indira Gandhi, would become Prime Minister of India) attended, as did Krishna Menon (who would be High Commissioner of India in London after independence and then Minister of Defence). Menon addressed the delegates, telling them that Nehru would have sent support had the British not just put him in prison, and denied that there was any such thing as 'democratic imperialism', just as it was impossible to find a 'vegetarian tiger'. Messages of support were received from the singer Paul Robeson, and the US novelist Theodore Dreiser, chronicler of the Depression, and 'fraternal militant party greetings' came from Mao Tse-tung to the 'representatives of the British working class and toiling masses and all progressive elements' who were gathered together in the Royal Hotel in Woburn Place; the overspill was in the nearby Conway Hall.

Celia Fremlin, a Mass-Observer who had been a member of the Communist Party but had resigned over the Nazi–Soviet Pact, went along and noted that those present were 'very predominantly' middle class, a small number of 'student and intellectual types' and about 25 per cent were working class. The ratio of men to women was three to one and 'the great majority' were aged between twenty-five and thirty-five. While there was 'of course, a liberal sprinkling of CP and extreme left-wingers – particularly among helpers, bookstall assistants etc. the vast majority of the rank and file were, however, ordinary trade unionists etc. of various shades of left-ish opinion'. She noticed 'perhaps about 20 soldiers and airmen in uniform present . . . most were in battledress . . . a curious mixture of soldiers and clergymen received big applause simply on appearance. There seemed to be a similar feeling about both – that they represented deeply-rooted traditions in our society, whose support is of intrinsic value.'

What struck Celia Fremlin at the convention was the 'overwhelming feeling' . . . of hope – a hope that somehow a way would be found out of the present mess – *into* exactly what was very vague in most minds . . . A feeling that struck one rather curiously with the realisation that for months past this feeling has been almost absent from public gatherings.'

The press was generally hostile, charging that the CP was exploiting the grievances of the people for its own sinister purposes. The *Daily Mirror* was more sympathetic, noting that while 90 per cent of the delegates were 'honest-to-God British citizens . . . [with] no wish to see Hitler victorious . . . They have too many grievances the government leaves unanswered. They expected Labour ministers in the government to be their champions. They are disappointed in them. Labour ministers behave like pale imitations of Tory ministers. So the people feel themselves leaderless. They are beginning to turn to the Communist Party.' Nevertheless Malcolm MacEwen, who wrote for the *Daily Worker*, thought that faith in the proposition 'that a "people's government" would conclude a "people's peace that gets rid of the causes of war" was another of our fantasies . . . we were deluded by the idea that the German workers would respond to the establishment of an anti-Imperialist British government by overthrowing Hitler'.

The writing had been on the wall for the *Daily Worker* ever since Herbert Morrison, who was viscerally anti-communist, took over from Sir John Anderson as Home Secretary in October 1940. The day after the People's Convention the Cabinet finally agreed to Morrison's order to suppress the *Daily Worker* and the communist journalist Claud Cockburn's roneoed sheet *The Week*, which, in Morrison's mind, advocated the same views as the *Daily Worker* 'in a style which has a less popular and more "intellectual" appeal' striving 'to create in the reader a state of mind in which he will be unlikely to be keen to assist the war effort'. But despite his claims on occasions, Morrison had been unable to establish that the *Daily Worker* was funded from Moscow. 'What is the *Daily Worker*'s real crime?' asked Professor J. S. B. Haldane, the scientist, who had recently been appointed to chair the newspaper's editorial board. 'A very serious crime indeed. It is the only daily newspaper that opposes the government.' The papers ceased publication on 21 January

1941 and, when the matter was debated in the Commons, only fifteen MPs voted against the ban.

It seemed clear, however, that support for the CP was not crumbling away. In the Dumbarton by-election at the end of February 1941, Malcolm MacEwen, challenging Labour, polled 15 per cent of the votes, a much larger proportion than in the two previous wartime by-elections the party had fought. A few days after the People's Convention, the BBC decided it would not employ any of its supporters, who included the actors Michael Redgrave and Beatrix Lehmann and the band leader Lew Stone. There was an outcry: the writer E. M. Forster withdrew his services, and the novelist and critic Rose Macaulay cancelled a broadcast. The composer of the classical music of deepest England, Ralph Vaughan Williams, refused permission to broadcast a choral work the BBC had commissioned, in protest against its ban on the work of the communist composer, Alan Bush; while J. B. Priestley and the cartoonist David Low were among those who wrote to complain. The ban did not last long: forty MPs tabled a motion protesting against 'political discrimination' and Churchill himself led the retreat. 'Anything in the nature of persecution, victimisation or man-hunting is odious to the British people,' he stated, and on 20 March 1941 the BBC relented.

At 4 a.m. on Sunday 22 June 1941 everything changed for the Communist Party and for the fiercely anti-Bolshevik Churchill when, without any declaration of war, German tanks invaded Russia along a 1,800-mile front. Harry Pollitt quit the London shipyard where he had been working and, his views vindicated, resumed the post of General Secretary. He sent a letter to members: 'It is an axiom of Marxists that the Communist Party formulates all its policies in accordance with the concrete situation that exists . . .' From that day forward the CPGB line was clear: it was now a war fought against fascism, not in the interest of imperialism. Membership rose to a record peak of 56,000. Everyone could unite and pull together and, except for calling vociferously and prematurely for a 'Second Front Now' in the west to relieve the pressure on Russia fighting along the Eastern front, that's what the CPGB did. But Morrison refused to lift the ban on the *Daily Worker* until August 1942.

The Prime Minister broadcast to the nation that Sunday evening: 'No one has been a more persistent opponent of Communism than I have for the last twenty-five years,' he acknowledged. 'I will unsay no word that I have spoken, but all this fades away before the spectacle which is now unfolding . . . We have but one aim and one irrevocable purpose. We are resolved to destroy Hitler and every vestige of the Nazi regime . . . Any man or state who fights against Nazism will have our aid . . . It follows, therefore, that we shall give whatever help we can to Russia and the Russian people.' To John Platts Mills, a far-Left barrister, Churchill gave the task of running a pro-Soviet campaign saying: 'I've been teaching the British people since 1918 that the Russians eat their young. Take as much money as you need and change the public perception of them.'

12

SPITFIRE SUMMER

"... 'Borough of Grimstone' calling 'Metal-Workers' Guild' and 'Ethels of Empire.'"

It must be here, I thought, the line we shall hold for ever: the line that must never be passed if we were to survive and make the world whole . . . here is the Ebro, the Yangtze, the Volga, here is the Channel: let us stand and fight, retreat no more . . . we can lose no more territory. Such a point comes in every war. So far as Hitler's advance westward is concerned, I think it was reached at our village [the cliffs above Dover] in 1940 – there and in the sky above it.

VINCENT SHEEAN, BETWEEN THE THUNDER AND THE SUN

THEY WERE SNAGGED on hedges, dangling from tree branches, lying sodden in ditches, their green and yellow pages glinting in the early morning light. On 2 August 1940, people living along the south coast looked out of their windows to find that the previous night had brought a shower of leaflets – *The Last Appeal to Reason by Adolf Hitler*. Delightedly, householders collected all the leaflets they could find. Some threaded them on loops of string and hung them over the privy door for use as lavatory paper, while a number were auctioned in aid of the Red Cross.

There had been other 'messages' from Hitler since early July, with bombs dropped on shipping convoys in the Channel and, moving inland, probing British defences to find any weaknesses that could be exploited when the major assault began. But this time the message was an appeal to 'reason and commonsense'. The Führer could, he said, 'see no reason why this war need go on' and was 'grieved to think of the sacrifices it must claim . . . A great Empire will be destroyed', he warned, '. . . an Empire which it was never my intention to destroy or even to harm . . .'

In Britain the appeal met with a dusty answer. Halifax was due to give a routine broadcast on 22 July on the BBC (which until a month previously had persisted in the courtesy of referring to 'Herr' Hitler and 'Signor' Mussolini), and he used the opportunity to rebuff Hitler's overtures. Invoking God seventeen times in his short speech, the Foreign Secretary ended with a peroration that Churchill had suggested: 'Hitler may plant the swastika where he will, but unless he can sap the strength of Britain, the foundations of his Empire are based on sand.' When the War Cabinet met, the peace offer was not even raised.

The appeal for peace came three days after Hitler had issued his directive for the invasion of Britain (or England as he always referred to it), should all other political and military initiatives fail. Alerted to the almost insurmountable difficulties of a seaborne invasion at present, the Führer had decided to 'sap the strength of Britain' with an all-out attack on her Air Force. On the same night that German planes set off to leaflet Britain, the order went out to 'overpower the English Air Force . . . in the shortest possible time' by attacking planes, airfields and supply lines, and also aircraft production factories. If Hitler couldn't get peace – the complicity with Britain he sought for his war in the east – then it would have to be all-out war, though always with the hope that, brought to its knees, Britain would see sense and agree terms.

Thus began what has become encoded as the 'Battle of Britain' when the RAF and the Luftwaffe battled for mastery of the skies above southern England, etching swirling, twisting vapour trails in the blue yonder as they fought screaming dogfights that coalesced into the battle for Britain's survival.

Fighter Command's strength had been depleted in the battle for France: it had only 768 planes in operational squadrons, and of these only 520 were fit for operations. Replacement planes ordered from North America were only trickling in, while the Soviet Union parried requests to buy aircraft from them. Britain would have to fight the battle with only what its factories could produce.

Deeply concerned with what he considered to be 'the muddle and scandal of the aircraft production branch', one of Churchill's first acts on coming to power in May had been to appoint Lord Beaverbrook to the post of Minister of Aircraft Production (MAP), charging him with 'the solemn duty to ensure that our air crews were adequately and properly supplied with whatever type and quantity of equipment they required'. Beaverbrook was a Canadian newspaper magnate who had come to Britain in 1909. He owned both the *Daily Express* and a Sunday version, and acquired the London *Evening Standard* in 1923. His prodigious energy – or bullying – during the crisis over the abdication of Edward VIII in 1936 had earned him the sobriquet 'Tornado', and it was this tornado that Churchill sought to harness in May 1940. The 'Beaver' never drew a salary (he was, after all, a multimillionaire), largely appointed his own staff rather than using civil servants, declined most of the time to write memos or reports, and had scant regard for committees, boards or what he saw as excuses. 'I am a cat that walks alone,' he boasted, and ran MAP much as his own fiefdom, in a blaze of publicity: 'as a drama', in the words of his biographer and largely uncritical admirer, A. J. P. Taylor, or with 'ballyhoo' as less smitten contemporaries described it. Beaverbrook justified all his excesses by saying, 'I asked very much to get very little.' He took the whip hand in deciding what aircraft should be produced and in what numbers, since he declared that he knew the factories' capacity, and jealously guarded aircraft for the defence of Britain, determined that the country should stay in the fight until the US came into the war (as he was convinced it would), and was loath to release planes for training or service overseas.

Beaverbrook boasted of working seven days a week and expected others to do likewise. He might have been inspired by his own slogan,

'Work Without Stopping', but it was a foolish one since the productivity of exhausted workers declined – men were reported to be working for thirty-six-hour stretches on rush jobs. Factories were in production twenty-four hours a day, bank holidays were cancelled, and though this 'Dunkirk spirit' increased production by a quarter in the week after the evacuation, it had fallen back to almost normal levels a month later. Kathleen Church-Bliss and Elsie Whiteman, who worked at an aircraft component factory in Croydon, were told by a workmate that 'after Dunkirk they all worked 13½ hours a day, Saturdays and Sundays included, for two months. She doesn't know how they did it. Her eyes fill with tears at the recollection.' At the end of June 1940, the Minister of Labour, Ernest Bevin, stepped in to demand a restriction on the hours worked by women and young people to a maximum of sixty a week, and he urged that the same limit should apply to men.

'Working without stopping' included, in Beaverbrook's view, when the air-raid siren sounded: he 'wanted the factories to go on working unless they were actually being bombed, or maybe even then'. This was in direct contravention of government instructions telling everyone to seek shelter as soon as the alert sounded. This tension between worker productivity and worker safety was to exercise politicians, employers, trade unionists and workers throughout the war.

Jennie Lee, a former and future Labour MP (and the wife of Aneurin Bevan), was appointed by Beaverbrook to troubleshoot. If delays were reported in an aircraft factory, she was to get down there and sort out the problem. She was sent to Reading where work was being disrupted as soon as the sirens sounded because, although there were adequate concrete shelters at the factory, the men would be off home across the fields to be with their loved ones. In return for an assurance that they would cease sprinting off at the first ululating note, Lee promised she would provide adequate shelters for the men's families. Even though there was an acute shortage of cement at the time, Beaverbrook managed to procure some. 'This was just one of the many times when he nipped in quickly and had supplies intended for the Navy and Army diverted in his direction before the rightful recipients were fully awake. The great point was that he never let you down. You chanced your arm, made a promise and he was prepared to move Heaven and Hell to help you keep it.' But despite her admiration for 'the Beaver's' ability to rip through red tape, Lee was bound to concede that 'there was a time limit to this hectic, chaotic way of waging war'.

Beaverbrook took – and was given by Churchill – the credit for the remarkable increase in aircraft production. Between January and April 1940 2,729 planes had been produced. By August the total had risen to 3,576. Between 1 June and 1 November 1940, an average of sixty-two Hurricanes and thirty-three Spitfires were leaving the factories each week. In total 4,283 fighter planes rolled off the assembly lines in 1940. The Germans were producing fewer than half that number. In addition, the RAF and the Civilian Repair Unit (which was part of MAP) were performing 'miracles' in managing to get 160 damaged planes a week back into service, a total of 4,196 between July and December 1940. Whenever possible, damaged aircraft were cannibalised to make one serviceable plane out of two or three damaged ones: a third of the planes issued to fighter squadrons during the Battle of Britain were salvaged rather than new.

But miraculous as such an achievement was, it could hardly be accounted for by the energy and drive of one man who only took up the gauntlet on 11 May: Beaverbrook's contribution was to the public's morale as much as to aircraft production. At a time when Britain was fighting for survival, he gave the impression of action, and involved the people of Britain in the fight, reinforcing the message of the need for an all-out effort from everyone.

Spitfires were his opportunity. They were the planes that captured the public imagination: they became iconic of the Battle of Britain; its alternative name was 'Spitfire Summer' – though in fact Hurricanes outnumbered Spitfires in a ratio of 3:2. Those who flew them regarded 'Spits' with their top speed of 350 mph as more than a match for the Messerschmitt and they had the edge over a Hurricane. A Spitfire was better at altitude, it was faster, it was more agile. And with its slim fuselage and graceful elliptical wing, it was beautiful. 'What looks right is right' was the engineer's old saw, but the pilots who flew Spitfires were more lyrical. 'A greyhound', 'a thoroughbred', 'like driving a racing car', 'a musician's plane'. Whereas flying a Hurricane was more like driving a truck – its (or rather her) virtues those of stability, strength, ruggedness, 'steady as a shithouse', a wonderful platform for guns, strong, a 'brutal machine' when it was brutality that was needed in those desperate summer days. For those on the ground it was always the far away, instantly recognisable Spitfire with its delicate lines, its swoops and flips and wheeling turns engaging ME 109s through the clouds, that thrilled. It seemed a symbol of defiance and of hope. As an American journalist wrote, 'the flash of the Spitfire's wing . . . through the misty glare of the summer sky, was the first flash of a sharpened sword'. And it was the Spitfire that the people of Britain would give their hard-earned money to buy, their prized household goods to help make.

Housewives could participate in the battle. At lunchtime on 10 July 1940, the head of the WVS, Lady Reading, broadcast an appeal: '. . . The Minister of Aircraft Production is asking the women of Great Britain for everything made of aluminium, everything that they can possibly give to be made into aeroplanes – Spitfires, Hurricanes, Blenheims and Wellingtons. Now you are going to be able to have a chance of doing something positive that will be of direct and vital help to our airmen, and of doing it at once . . . I am asking for the things that you are using everyday, anything and everything new and old, sound and broken, everything that's made of aluminium . . . Very few of us can be heroines on the battle-front, but we can all have the tiny thrill of thinking as we hear the news of an epic battle in the air. "Perhaps it was my saucepan that made part of that Hurricane".'

Just as when Eden had broadcast for LDV volunteers, the response to Lady Reading was instant and overwhelming. Almost before she had finished speaking, saucepans, kettles, dishes, colanders, zinc baths, metal hot-water bottles, clothes hangers, preserving pans, jelly moulds, fish slices, toys, tennis-racquet presses, a clapped-out racing car and even the occasional aluminium artificial leg were being handed in to WVS centres (the limbs were politely refused). The little princesses gave a set of miniature metal teapots and kettles they had been given by the people of Wales, and it was rumoured some well-off patriots had been buying brand-new sets of saucepans to donate. Art students in Falmouth paraded the streets wearing home-made sandwich boards appealing for aluminium, and a baby Austin car was driven around the town of Bodmin with a placard tied to the back pleading for 'pots and pans to crown Adolf'. A housewife in Cardiff handed in a set of saucepans bought in Germany fifteen years earlier, announcing that she was pleased to be able to return them in the form of an aeroplane. In Portsmouth the response was so overwhelming that forty-five depots were opened in different parts of the city and the first collection filled four railway trucks; by the end of August the city had amassed over 8½ tons. In total the WVS reckoned that their collection added up to nearly a thousand tons of aluminium by the time the appeal finished in mid September.

Beaverbrook's 'Saucepans for Spitfires' campaign exemplified the patriotic gesture – and the needless sacrifice. Families generously handed over essential household items they would bitterly regret losing when it became impossible to replace them; there was still plenty of new aluminiumware in the shops that could have been requisitioned, and most scrap dealers had piles of it lying around.

Under another of Beaverbrook's schemes anyone could help pay for a Spitfire. The idea originated in Jamaica where a letter appeared in the *Daily Gleaner* in May 1940 referring to Churchill's call for more planes to fight the Luftwaffe. An account was set up at Barclay's Bank in Kingston and money began to pour in for the 'Jamaica Plane Fund'. The idea was taken up in other parts of the empire and by the beginning of August the *Straits Times* of Singapore had cabled £250,000; the Gold Coast sent £100,000, Ceylon had raised £395,000, Natal £201,000, the Falkland Islands £50,000 and Bengal £40,000. Beaverbrook recognised this as a perfect opportunity, settling on the conveniently round figure of £5,000 as being what it cost to build a Spitfire (though the true cost was nearer £12,000) as the basis of his appeal. He then went on to itemise a Spitfire's constituent parts so that every component was 'priced': £2,000 would buy a wing, £5 a compass, a guinea (£1/1) a thermometer, 15s the blast tube of a machine gun, and for mere pocket money (6d), a rivet could be contributed. It was a brilliant stroke in the 'people's war': 'as you put your daily shilling in the collection box, there was a feeling that it connected you – intimately if indirectly – with tremendous and heroic events and in a way that a cheque to the Income Tax inspector rather failed to do'.

The Spitfire Fund proved a public relations coup: almost every town and city in the British Isles set one up. In Cardiff 'collections were made in the clubs, pubs and places of work' to contribute to the Lord Mayor's Spitfire Fund. 'Two boys spent their August holidays collecting golf balls which they sold to raise ten shillings for the fund, while school children sent in their pocket money. Such was the spirit of 1940.' The city raised

£20,000 – enough to buy four Spitfires according to Beaverbrook's maths. The Durham miners sent a cheque for £10,000; the isles of Lewis and Harris in the Outer Hebrides, with a scattered population of 30,000, raised £6,400. Guildford in Surrey launched its Spitfire Fund on 20 August 1940 and within a week £2,500 had been received.

And the Austrian parents of the first baby born in Guildford to refugees who had fled to Britain from Nazi persecution raised 14s 8d in 'Spitgift' money by charging 2d to see their new baby.

In Hackney, a poor inner-London borough, donations poured in: 10s from the children of a local school, £4 raised by the tenants of a block of council flats, and many more. Penzance in Cornwall decided to go the extra mile to raise £5,500 so that the Spitfire they 'bought' could 'go into the air as a fully equipped fighting unit', and an enterprising group of evacuees decided to go blackberrying and sell the fruit to the locals at 2d a pound as their contribution. Soon Truro, Falmouth, St Austell and smaller towns all over Cornwall were joining in the drive, vying to see who could raise the most money.

It was the same all over the country that summer: the citizens of Wolverhampton subscribed £6,000, and those of Worcester raised enough to buy two Spitfires, while Southampton felt they had a particular responsibility since 'the designer of the Spitfire, the late Mr R[eginald]. J. Mitchell CBE, was himself a citizen of this borough until his untimely death three years ago [aged only 42] . . . Nothing could be more appropriate, therefore, than that Southampton should present one or more Spitfires to the country in memory of this great man whose genius may yet prove to be the means of enabling us to emerge triumphant from the greatest trial to which we have ever been subjected in our history.' The Mayor's appeal raised £15,527.

The *Belfast Telegraph* launched a Spitfire Fund on 12 August 1940, setting a target of '£5,000 for one plane', but by the end of the year donations had flooded in from all over the provinces at such a rate that £51,000 had been raised – apparently more than enough for ten times that number.

Those who bought a Spitfire could have it named after their town, company, a person, or any other legend they chose, in 4-inch-high letters painted on to the fuselage. Thus Dudley in the Midlands designated its plane 'The Dauntless'; the City of Hull chose 'Argonaut'; Lewis's, the

Liverpool department store, loyally named the plane they donated 'Woolton' after their ex-chairman and now Minister of Food; and Ely chose 'Pride of the Isle'. Four Spitfires flew bearing the name City of Birmingham, and two cities that were to suffer so grievously in the Blitz – Coventry and Liverpool – each had three planes. Dozens of towns had a single Spitfire bearing their name take to the air. The money raised by the *Belfast Telegraph* was used to pay for Spitfires named after places in the Six Counties. The LNER replicated the names of two of its trains, 'The Flying Scotsman' and 'Cock of the North', on Spitfire fuselages. Bristol Civil Defence, Bow Street Home Guard and HRH the Nawab of Bahawalpur used their own names, while Newmarket Racing Stables chose 'Blue Peter' and the Hulton Press opted for the title of its popular wartime magazine, *Picture Post*. The British community in Buenos Aires funded four planes named 'Pampero I–IV'. The Corn Exchange and the Stock Exchange both donated eponymously labelled planes while the Bank of England selected its nickname 'The Old Lady' (presumably 'of Threadneedle Street' would have just been too long). Lady Davidson, the wife of the Conservative Party Chairman, christened 'her' Spitfire 'La Rosalinda'; while the Hon. Mrs Ronald Greville's was 'Margaret Helen' and a Mrs Crawford chose 'Mabel'.

The names of some organisations or companies, or the products associated with them, offered particularly apt choices: Hoover came up with 'Sky Sweeper'; the Anti-Aircraft Command with 'On the Target'; the battery company Ever Ready with its brand name. The Co-operative Wholesale Society went for 'Defiant' and the building firm, Wimpey, chose 'Popeye's Pal'. H. J. Heinz – which did not manage to provide 57 planes – nevertheless did some subtle product endorsement with 'Foremost', 'Trustworthy' and 'Perfect'. ABC Cinemas christened four Spitfires Miss ABC I, II, III and IV, while the catering company J. Lyons chose the name of its popular waitresses: 'Nippy'. Smith's were straightforward with 'Crisp', Bryant and May elegant in using their trademark 'The Swan'; and Marks and Spencer hopeful with 'Marksman', while the Kennel Club was justified in laying claim to 'The Dog Fighter'. Some names were less well chosen, perhaps: it is hard to imagine a young pilot's heart soaring as he took off on yet another dangerous mission in a plane labelled 'Metal Box' (after the sponsoring company) or 'Concrete' (chosen by Portland Cement).

One of the organisations that Beaverbrook had singled out for praise in the pages of the *Daily Express* was the 'Dublin Spitfire Circle', members of which made collections – or arm-twisted donations – for the fund from employees of such companies as the Great Northern Railway, Guinness and the unfortunately named Swastika Laundry Company. But in October 1940 the Irish Department of External Affairs objected, claiming Eire's neutral status was endangered, and the Minister of Justice drew a distinction between collecting money for funds 'for the purchase of armament, equipment or comforts for the armed forces of any other state', which the *Gardai* (police) should stop, and 'any collection . . . which may be organised to raise funds for the relief of civilian victims of air-raids in Great Britain', which was allowable.

But imaginative and invigorating though these initiatives were, they made only a marginal difference to producing a sufficient number of Spitfires to win the Battle of Britain. It wasn't so much the money to build planes that was lacking in 1940: £13 million was finally raised, but it was productive capacity that was in short supply and 'the fund was an irrelevancy' to that.

A crucial factor for Britain's aircraft production had been the decision taken in 1938 to set up the Shadow Factory Scheme, with the Air Ministry taking over valuable industrial space to create reserve productive capacity. Aircraft production was the key priority, and a number of factories – many of which had been turning out cars or car parts in peacetime – were adapted and equipped to do this. The Merlin engines that powered all Spitfires were produced by a shadow factory built by Rolls-Royce at Crewe when it was clear that their Derby works would not have sufficient capacity; and additional shadow factories were constructed at Trafford Park, Manchester and near Glasgow for engine production, but these were not ready until the Battle of Britain was effectively over. A number of Beaverbrook's own schemes to convert underground quarry works for aircraft production, such as moving the Bristol Aircraft Corporation engine production from Filton to a disused stone mine at Corsham in Wiltshire, proved costly failures. However, the system of back-up aircraft production was triumphantly vindicated when on 26 September 1940 the Luftwaffe effectively destroyed the large-scale Spitfire production factory near Southampton and production was halved for the next six months. Had Castle Bromwich, near

Birmingham, not already been equipped as a shadow factory to produce Spitfires, the situation of fighter-aircraft production in the summer of 1940 would have been grim indeed.

It was not only those working in the huge factories who were involved in aircraft production: the manufacture of components was farmed out to hundreds of small firms, workshops and garages all over the country – Rolls-Royce, for example, put work on its engine components in the way of over ninety small companies in the Derby area. Such outworking could lead to serious bottlenecks, as in one case when hundreds of Spitfire wings subcontracted off-site were found not to fit the fuselages. When the need became acute, aircraft production turned into a home industry with women holding so-called 'filing parties' in their kitchens to smooth the rough edges of mysterious metal components 'for an hour or two after tea', and after lessons many school workshops were filled with boys hammering aircraft parts under the supervision of a technically inclined teacher.

'We knew it was a battle, but we did not know it was *the* battle of Britain,' wrote an American journalist. To the young men of Fighter Command, and to the population of southern Britain who watched from the ground, trying to make sense of the screaming air fights going on above their heads, reading newspaper billboards that made it all sound more like a cricket match than war, and frantically thumbing through plane-spotter manuals to see which far distant flash of silver was 'one of ours', that summer and early autumn of 1940 had a narrative all its own. 'The fate of civilisation was being decided fifteen thousand feet above your head,' wrote the journalist Virginia Cowles, 'in a world of sun, wind and sky . . . [aircraft could be seen] falling earthwards, a mass of flames, leaving as their last testament a smudge of black against the sky.'

Because of the limited range of the German fighter planes, the battleground arced over southern England. Although the fall of France gave the Luftwaffe bases in northern France, the Messerschmitt ME 109 fighter could still carry only sufficient fuel to reach as far as London. Since heavy combat used more fuel, the contest for superiority in the air was confined to the skies over Kent, Hampshire, Sussex and Surrey – with the fighter planes accompanying the bombers having to head back to France before their fuel ran out.

By the beginning of August, just before the full German offensive got under way, many of the aircraft losses of the Battle of France had been made good. Fighter Command now had 1,032 aircraft ready to take off from airbases, and a further 452 in storage units ready for use, and despite terrifying rumours of the strength of the Luftwaffe, the number of British fighters was roughly comparable to those of Germany at that time.

But planes in the air were only part of the equation of battle. It had to be possible to spot approaching enemy aircraft as early as possible, estimate the intended target, plot the height and route, convey this information to the airbases, get the planes into the air to apprehend the attackers, and feed them information as they flew. 'The war will be won by science thoughtfully applied to operational requirements,' wrote Air Marshal Dowding in November 1940, and nowhere was this more axiomatic than in the complex communication system of 'command and control' that lay at the heart of Fighter Command's success. Constant observation and early warning were vital, and this came from a number of sources that interconnected and interlocked.

The first came from Radio Direction Finding (RDF) apparatus, better known as radar. In 1935 it had been discovered that aeroplanes reflected back to ground short-wave radio pulses, which could be captured on cathode-ray tubes. It was certainly an improvement on Britain's previous aircraft detection resources, a massive mirror housed in a 200-foot-long, 25-foot-high concrete block facing expectantly out across the Channel from Romney Marsh in Kent with microphones dotted along the top. So impressed was Dowding with radar's potential – its 'magic sight' – that the Treasury were persuaded to sink an initial £10,000 in its development. By the start of the war there were twenty-one radar stations dotted round Britain's coastline, stretching from the Shetlands to the Isle of Wight, isolated units consisting of 350-foot-high steel towers for transmission and 240-foot-high wooden towers for reception – both of which were impossible to camouflage. At the base was a 'receiver hut' where personnel – often members of the WAAF – sat intently studying the blips on a cathode-ray tube. It was essential to be able to distinguish Allied aircraft and avoid 'blue on blue' incidents, so RAF planes were fitted with an IFF (Identification Friend or Foe) device that blipped in a stronger, V-shaped signal, but still on the same frequency, on to the RDF screen.

The radar chain was theoretically able to detect the height and range of aircraft as far away as 200 miles. In fact the average was more like 80 miles, but that was adequate for detecting German aircraft across the Channel. The system was by no means perfect. Height readings could be dangerously inaccurate – it was impossible to detect aircraft flying at below 1,000 feet. So after the outbreak of war a second ring was established to pick up low-flying aircraft and coastal shipping. The existence of radar was kept a tightly guarded secret from the public, and all sorts of fabulous stories circulated of carrot-eating pilots (the most famous of whom was 'Cat's-Eyes' Cunningham) whose eyesight could penetrate the dark, to account for the success of Fighter Command in locating and engaging enemy planes.

Radar only worked scanning out to sea. Inland, aeroplane detection was the responsibility of the Observer Corps, which was staffed by some 30,000 volunteers manning 1,000 observation posts. Once alerted by the radar stations, they plotted enemy aircraft that had crossed the coast, with the help of binoculars, grid maps, aircraft-spotter manuals, telephones, map markers – and tea-making equipment. Largely self-taught in plane detection, often observing in remote vulnerable locations in the middle of fields and moors or perched on rocky outcrops, observers spent many lonely, cold hours of boredom during their essential vigils, for posts had to be manned round the clock. Such observation was effective in fine weather, but rain or low cloud made the task almost impossible since all the observers could report was the noise of an aircraft overhead, and even in good weather it is very hard to judge by eye the height of aircraft. The reports were fed into the Observer Corps HQ at Horsham in Sussex and from there out to Operation (Ops) rooms at all levels – Command, Group and Sector – so the sightings could be co-ordinated with the information received by radar.

Information of 'enemy blips' on the cathode-ray tubes in the radar stations was relayed by telephone to Fighter Command Headquarters housed 42 feet below ground in Bentley Priory at Stanmore in Middlesex, a few miles from central London. The HQ acted as a communications hub: information was first received in the filter room and, once verified, was simultaneously transmitted to the HQ Ops room next door and to the Ops room of the four Fighter Command Group

HQs that covered the country, and to any sector with raiders heading their way. This system enabled Fighter Command to deploy its forces where they were needed as quickly as possible, rather than rely on aircraft patrols which could mean that planes were using up fuel unnecessarily – and could be in the wrong place when required.

The Sector Controller would know the state of readiness of the various squadrons in his sector – those who were already 'scrambled' (airborne), those who were on 'thirty-minute readiness' and so on. He would decide which additional units to 'scramble', and guide them towards the enemy planes once the Luftwaffe was in their area and the order had been received from Group HQ.

A 'Pip Squeak' device fitted in each aircraft allowed Sector Control to plot the path of its squadron in the air, and work out the point at which the paths would intersect and the air battle take place. The Sector Controller would issue vectors (directions) to the squadron leader in the air, expressed in compass bearings, but if he was already occupied with two squadrons – the maximum one person could control – NCOs or WAAFs sitting on either side of him would speak directly to the pilots, while the pilots' voices were relayed through a large speaker on the wall. Once the planes had seen the enemy, control passed from the Sector Controller to the fighter leader in the air, who directed his squadron into battle by issuing instructions over his radio transmitter. The whole process from first blip on the radar screen to planes in the air was intended to take a matter of minutes – as it needed to, since it took only six minutes for aircraft to cross the Channel.

Sector Controllers had the awesome task of assessing information, deciding how many squadrons to hold in reserve, when to break off combat, when to recall a squadron to refuel and pick up more ammunition – and how much their men could take of an intense battle. Plotting was stressful work too: it demanded intense concentration, since a misread signal could direct a squadron into danger, or leave it unaware of approaching planes. Aircraft plotters were frequently members of the WAAF. Known as 'clerks (special duty)', they were sworn to secrecy about what they did under the terms of the Official Secrets Act. But though Joan Wyndham felt confident after the 'long, harrowing weeks' of her WAAF training that 'we are now fully fledged Filter Room Plotters, ready to keep track of anything that flies up from a wild goose to a Heinkel', the women in the Ops rooms were not always welcomed in this role by their male counterparts, who could be scornful about how they anticipated women would react under stress – and WAAFs were paid about a third less than the men for the same or equivalent jobs.

Monitoring radio transmissions could be harrowing work. A WAAF sergeant working at Hawkinge airfield in Kent recalled a German reconnaissance pilot who would banter cheerfully with her in English: 'Would you like me to drop a bomb on you? Whee . . .' One day his plane was intercepted by Spitfires who shot him down in flames. 'He was unable to bail out and we listened to him as he screamed and screamed for his mother and cursed the Füehrer. I found myself praying "Get out, bail out, oh please dear God get him out." But it was no use. We heard him the whole way down until he fell below our reception range. I went out and was sick . . . I realise[d] that I was in part his executioner.' A WAAF might hear a German squadron leader order an attack on an unsuspecting RAF pilot below. 'I would often hear one of the WAAF operators murmuring, "Oh God, oh God, please . . . *please* look up," and I knew how helpless she felt,' recalled Aileen Morris.

The main constraint on Fighter Command in 1940 was people rather than planes. There simply weren't enough ground staff at the airfields – fitters, instrument mechanics, maintenance and construction workers – nor were there sufficient personnel working in the communications side of the operation. There was a shortage of pilots to fly the planes too: Churchill's 'the Few' to whom so much would be owed by so many in the Battle of Britain. In the spring of 1940 it was vastly over-estimated that the Germans had around 16,000 pilots and at least 7,300 in operational units, and there was 'a flurry of activity to raise pilot training to match these numbers'. Training was overhauled and speeded up so that soon after the fall of France 115 new pilots passed out every two weeks rather than the previous thirty-nine. Airmen from overseas who had fled the advancing Germans, or had volunteered or been posted to Britain, were recruited too.

August 10 1940 had been designated 'Adlertag' (Eagle Day): the start of the operation in which Reichsmarschall Hermann Goering – Hitler's 'man of steel' and himself a First World War fighter ace, now commander-in-chief of the German Air Force – ordered the Luftwaffe to 'wipe the British Air Force from the skies'. But bad weather forced its postponement, and in the event the attack went off at half strength on 13 August with attempts made to recall planes as cloud cover was so heavy, and resulted in a series of poorly co-ordinated raids on airfields in southern England. Southampton docks were badly hit; Eastchurch, a temporary home for 266 Squadron, was hit; several airmen were killed, the hangars torched and ammunition blown up; at Detling near Maidstone the commanding officer was killed as were sixty-seven other personnel when Stukas dive-bombed the airfield. Hangars were torched, the runway wrecked and twenty aircraft on the ground destroyed, plus the Ops room, cookhouse and mess were all put out of action – but somehow essential services were working again by the next afternoon.

Other airfields were badly hit too, including Debden, Kenley, Tangmere, Croydon, Luton, Hornchurch and North Weald. In an attack on Eastchurch, a Coastal Command station, again the Ops room was destroyed and planes on the ground put out of action. And as it was so often to be during the Battle of Britain, Manston was another casualty.

At home at Ham Spray that day, the pacifist, Frances Partridge, 'suddenly heard terrific air activity, and planes seemed to be dashing about in all directions, though many were invisible behind the clouds. Then a great grey mushroom of smoke rose from the direction of Newbury . . . four large bombers swooped over the Downs making a deafening noise . . . The extraordinary thing is that even when I stared up and saw an unfamiliar mark like a cross on their wings, I *still* didn't realise they were German bombers. But I did think how easily they could have machine gunned our two little figures, I so conspicuous in my red shirt . . . the mushroom cloud had been from bombs dropped near Newbury. There had been something like an air battle over Inkpen. I felt unreasoning excitement for ten minutes or so.'

It was not until 18 August 1940 that it was apparent to the British that the German air offensive had dramatically intensified, moving inland to attack the entire structure of the fighting force. Ominous columns of Heinkels, Dorniers and Junkers escorted by ME 109 fighters droned over the coast, aiming primarily for airfields and mounting smaller raids on industrial installations, RAF supplies, communications and radar stations, hoping to stretch Britain's fighters as thinly as possible. Between 12 August and 6 September there were fifty-three major attacks on airfields. Those nearest the coast suffered most – Manston, Lympne and Hawkinge – and all were briefly shut down following a series of attacks. The Luftwaffe started bombing by night as well as day, making it difficult for damage to be repaired and airfields got back into commission. Desperate efforts were made to keep the airfields operational and, after a series of continual heavy raids, the Air Ministry agreed that at least one bulldozer and one excavator would be provided at each airfield, and a team of 150 government supply workers was set up that could be drafted to wherever the men were needed most.

On 30 August came the heaviest raid on an airfield when Biggin Hill – known as 'Biggin the Bump' as it was sited on a plateau on the Kentish Weald – was hit by a devastatingly accurate low-level attack. Felicity Peake (who was to become Director of the Women's Royal Air Force in 1946 aged only thirty-two), an ex-deb who was already a war widow at twenty-six as her husband Jock had been killed in a night-flying accident, was Section Commander of the 250-strong WAAF contingent at Biggin Hill. She had dived into a trench for cover when the station siren went. As the Ju 88s began their descent Peake (or Hanbury as she was then) radioed for help: 'Bandits approaching . . . they're approaching Biggin Hill, they're bombing Biggin Hill, they're bombing me! . . . Bombs fell pretty continuously, the noise was indescribable, yet through the intervals I could hear the put, put, put of machine-guns as plane after plane dived on its target.' When she was finally able to emerge, Peake found that another trench sheltering airwomen had received a direct hit, catapulting all twelve occupants violently to one end where they were buried in falling earth. 'Airmen were digging to rescue the trapped women [but] the dry summer had made the ground unusually hard and their task was no light one . . . one by one, the airwomen were brought out.' Although several were badly injured, miraculously only one had been killed. In all there were thirty-nine dead and twenty-five injured, though few aircraft on the ground were destroyed.

The raids continued – including one that disturbed the funeral service for those killed on 30 August. The padre was so terrified of the dogfights raging overhead that he jumped into a freshly dug grave for shelter. 'If any aerodrome is in the forefront of the battle and right in the front line, it's Biggin,' observed a young pilot whose squadron had just been posted there. 'The whole place had a desperate air of total war and mortal combat. Broken Spitfires and Hurricanes, hangars in ruins, filled-in bomb craters everywhere and so much general bomb damage that one is left in no doubt whatever that this is total war. In spite of all this, the fighters still fly and the station is still fully operational.'

Again and again the bombers came back to demoralised and depleted Manston in Kent, the nearest airport to France, where some of the airmen had taken to the catacombs in the cliffs in their terror and were refusing to emerge, culminating in a raid on 24 August 1940 when twenty Ju 88s razed buildings to the ground and destroyed the communication circuit before wheeling off to drop 500 bombs on the nearby seaside town of Ramsgate – leaving unexploded bombs littering the airfield. A local fireman who arrived on the scene was 'appalled at the damage done. The hangars were ablaze, planes on the field were blazing, and in pieces . . . there was . . . not a soul to be seen except an RAF officer who stood gazing at the scene . . . pipe in mouth and hands in pockets with tears streaming down his face.' That day almost all the station staff were moved out as civilians moved in to loot tools, equipment and live ammunition. Manston was never operational again.

With a few exceptions – Ventnor on the Isle of Wight being one – remarkably little damage was done to radar stations since the Germans did not fully appreciate how valuable they were in warning of attack, and did not give them a high priority. The communication network was also relatively unscathed and, far from German reports that eight airfields had been completely destroyed and the rest of the system severely depleted, Fighter Command proved resilient and adaptable. Planes were moved to airfields further inland, and a squadron would be sent up to hover over its airfield to protect it from attack. New fighting tactics were deployed, with RAF fighters encouraged to avoid combat over the sea, and at the first alert Spitfires were detailed to attack Luftwaffe fighter planes while Hurricanes went after the bombers.

Both sides exaggerated the losses of the other: the Germans claimed that the RAF had lost nearly 900 planes during August: the British tally was about half that. This was partly the natural triumphalism of battle, but mainly because in the terrible noise, smoke and confusion it was often very hard to see which side had shot the other down, and double accounting was almost inevitable.

The loss of pilots was salutary: in August the casualty rate rose to 22 per cent, which meant that men were dying at a faster rate than they could be replaced by those graduating from Operational Training Units, even though these were turning out 320 pilots a month. Training was cut from six months to four weeks with 'the final polish' supposed to be given in the squadrons – in battle – and in mid August it was slashed again to a bare two weeks. Commanding Officers were obliged to take men with far less training and experience than they would have liked. When Geoffrey Wellum, then aged eighteen years and nine months, received his first posting to the prestigious 92 Squadron at Northolt in May 1940, his CO told him at his first interview, 'You are not much use to this squadron . . . half-trained youngsters who think they know all the answers are a pain in the neck in an operational squadron in time of war. You've never even seen a Spitfire I gather, let alone flown one . . . apart from the time involved which we haven't got, I just can't be bothered with taking untrained people if I'm unsure whether they are going to measure up. It's not fair to them or to the rest of the pilots and if anybody doesn't attain the standards that I set myself and the rest of the squadron then they are out so bloody quickly that they don't even know what's hit them . . .' Despite this less than encouraging welcome, within a matter of weeks Wellum was to be a distinguished Battle of Britain pilot, awarded the Distinguished Flying Cross for his skill and bravery.

The pilots were heroes: they all seemed young – as indeed they were. Flying in combat was not reckoned to be a job for anyone over thirty. The RAF did seem to choose a preponderance of young men from minor public schools – the 'Brylcreem Boys' was what these smart young RAF types were called. There were also career RAF pilots who'd been at the job through the 1930s, there were men of the Auxiliary Air Force, and members of the Volunteer Reserves whose numbers had swelled the RAF by thousands, when war threatened such men whose style has become iconic of the battle – though that was by no means the full story. The image of the 'weekend fliers', many of them young varsity fellows with sports cars, wearing blazers and silk cravats, with a fondness for 'popsies' and for drinking and playing poker, is of men seemingly possessed of courage to the point of recklessness, who appeared insouciant at the thought of death. They were exemplified by Richard Hillary, whose book *The Last Enemy* was a best-seller when it was published in 1942, but whose face and hands were so badly burned when he was shot down that even the skill of the pioneering New Zealand maximofacial surgeon at East Grinstead hospital, Archibald MacIndoe, could not do other than partially release Hillary's clawed hands and stretch his face back to what resembled a taut and inflexible carapace. For Hillary, the Battle was 'war as it ought to be, war which is individual combat between two people . . . I shan't get maimed: either I shall get killed or I shall get a few pleasant putty medals and enjoy being stared at in a night club.' Determined to return to flying, Hillary was killed on 8 January 1943 when his Spitfire spiralled out of control and crashed to the ground: the impact was heard for miles around and the plane burst into flames. It was said that the fire was so fierce that Hillary's coffin had to be filled with sand in semblance of a body inside.

If an airman was on alert he would wait 'in readiness' for when enemy planes were sighted. The order would go out to 'scramble' and the pilots would run to their aircraft to be helped into the cockpit by their ground crew. Throttle released, 'chocks away', the Spitfire or Hurricane would taxi along the runway and then become airborne in search of the enemy. Then in the lonely sky, every man for himself: 'ten bandits many of the snappers [ME 109s] below at one o'clock. Estimate about three to four thousand feet below. Going in.' Remembering the adages 'Never stay still, dart in the sky'; 'A pilot flying the same course for longer than thirty seconds is a dead man.' Climbing high to take aim on the bombers, coming in fast from behind with a rat-tat-tat of ammo fire on the fighter planes, watching as smoke poured from the undercarriage, the plane losing height rapidly and spiralling down to land or sea. But as the novelist Derek Robinson wrote, the odds were stacked against you in that small, plexiglass cockpit: 'a speck of dirt on your windscreen could turn into an enemy fighter in the time it took to turn round and back. A little smear on your goggles might hide the plane that was coming to kill you.'

At last the pilots would be recalled, the mission completed or abandoned – no point in giving chase across the Channel, the cloud cover too heavy to locate enemy planes. They headed back to base – at least if the plane hadn't taken a hit. Perhaps the radio transmitter was on the blink and there was no calm, clear voice to guide a pilot home; maybe the oxygen supply had been disconnected, and flying at heights greater than Mount Everest in an unpressurised aircraft could lead to the pilot blacking out in mid-air. The squadron pancaked on to the runway at irregular intervals, each plane making for its own anxiously waiting ground crew. Sometimes a pilot would judge that his fuel level was too low to get him back to his own field or his plane was limping from a hit, and he'd come in at a nearby airfield and phone in. Not all the planes would return. Then it was the efficient ritual of death in war – closing over the abyss to get on with the job: a thin black line drawn under a name in the mess ledger, the bunks reallocated, personal possessions, shaving kit, leisure clothes packed up, a bedside book put into the box along with the photographs and the man's souvenirs of war – and the pin-up calendar tacked up above his bunk rolled up and thrown away. The letter the CO had to write as a follow-up to the official Air Ministry telegram – 'We regret to inform you . . .' to try to soften the terrible loss with words of admiration and gratitude: 'the bravest of men in defence of his country', 'very popular with the other chaps – a born leader'.

For the survivors, it was off down to the pub. Piling into someone's old Humber for a pint – or several – at the Dog and Duck, the White Hart, the New Inn, the Old Jail, a game of darts maybe and an attempt to forget. 'If I wasn't flying, I was plastered,' one pilot remembered. The airmen didn't talk much about the loss of a colleague – 'gone for a Burton' (a beer) was the usual epitaph. As the Battle wore on they were careful not to get too friendly with men they knew they might never see again, but they still felt the loss keenly, sorrow in the midst of thankfulness that it hadn't been them today. That it might be them tomorrow. Between July and October 1940 a total of 481 Fighter Command pilots were killed, posted missing in action or taken prisoner over enemy territory, and 422 were wounded or injured.

By August, Air Marshal Dowding was acutely conscious of the exhausting strain on the airmen. During July one fighter squadron had flown 503 sorties in three weeks and spent more than 800 hours in the air. Not every flight led to a battle, but all demanded the same level of concentration. Six German planes had been downed, but the price had been the death of six British pilots. The men, like so many others, were almost at the end of their tether. 'Stuffy', as Dowding was called – though this wasn't how most of the men who served under him saw it – had thereafter decreed that each pilot – his 'chicks' as Churchill called them – must have eight hours in every twenty-four off, and take a twenty-four-hour rest period every week. Pilots were sent far away from their airfields for some uninterrupted sleep, while more games and physical exercise were introduced on the stations, dances were arranged, string bands toured the bases.

The aerial circus that was the Battle of Britain as seen from the ground of southern England drew in its civilian spectators in multiple ways: they saw young pilots drinking in village pubs, and, watching a plane weaving and diving far overhead, fancied that one of the boys they had watched down a pint the previous night was in the cockpit – maybe it was one of the 'aces' who was up there. For months the people of southern England never seemed able to get away from the relentless noise of screaming aircraft and the crash of shrapnel and bullets. A woman who, as a child, lived near Biggin Hill, remembers that during raids on the airfield she ran from her house to the garden shelter using a dustbin lid for protection, but even 4 feet below ground with three thick overcoats wrapped round her head, the noise was still deafening.

The writer Elizabeth Jane Howard spent the summer of 1940 in Sussex where 'the Battle of Britain was fought over our heads – literally. It became common practice for the family to rush to crashed German planes to prevent the local farmers attacking the aircrew who'd survived. Feeling was running very high. I remember a bomber belching black smoke, scraping the trees on each side of our lawn; Colin and Bill . . . both six years old eyed it dispassionately. One of them said "Junkers eighty-eight." "Eighty-nine," the other responded. They didn't mention its state or the enormous explosion when it crashed in a neighbouring field. The weather was cloudless; sometimes one could count up to sixteen parachutes descending after the zooming noise of engines banking steeply or diving upon their adversary.'

During the Battle, the journalist John Gale was a teenager living in Surrey. One night 'a Heinkel III was shot down at Caterham, not far away'. The next morning he and his nine-year-old brother cycled over to have a look. 'We found the Heinkel, which had come down . . . it was not completely destroyed. "This belongs to *them*," we thought . . . While we were examining the wreckage, the air raid sirens sounded . . . while most people, including the sentries that had been guarding the aircraft, were in the air raid shelters, we crept out and returned to the Heinkel, pulling from the wreckage a large piece of metal, which I took to be aluminium. It was a good souvenir. I tied it on my bike and we rode home . . . That evening we showed the piece of Heinkel to our father. "Hullo," I said, turning the metal over. "What's this? There's some writing." We read the words clearly printed on the piece of Heinkel, MADE IN BIRMINGHAM. My father laughed: "That's what war's all about," he said.'

Dover had been in the front line of the war since the start with naval patrols setting off from the harbour. 'We're Cinque Port people,' a Dover man told the US journalist Ben Robertson. 'We've always had to fight.' Looking out from Dover was 'a narrow dark film on the water which was the coast of France, where the enemy was looking across at us' and from early June the town had been subjected to intermittent pounding from heavy guns mounted at Calais. Housewives continued to queue as shrapnel and machine-gun bullets shattered nearby shop windows, and a journalist was offered a table in a hotel restaurant with the recommendation that it was 'away from the broken glass' of the blown-in windows. Over half the population had fled into the hinterland for safety, while other townspeople took shelter in the caves, carved out of the chalk cliffs in medieval times and now used as their wartime habitat.

Throughout the summer and early autumn of 1940, the shell-pocked town was a ringside seat at the air battle for Britain, its so-named Shakespeare Cliff between Dover and Folkestone providing a press box for commentators, 'a superb place from which to watch battles'. The battle-scarred Grand Hotel near Dover Castle provided them with accommodation (since the only other hotel that hadn't been requisitioned by the government, the Shalimar, was a temperance hotel), while the King Lear pub at the foot of the cliff was their watering hole.

It was from Dover that the BBC commentator Charles Gardener had broadcast his excited cricket-score style commentary on a dogfight, which had attracted some admiration and much opprobrium; it was from Shakespeare Cliff that the diminutive, red-haired Hilde Marchant of the *Daily Express* – 'a sort of a Spitfire herself attached to the ground', admired an American pressman – had written of the RAF planes overhead making 'an aluminium shield' in the sky. And it was on Shakespeare Cliff that the US press corps staked its claim, among them the newsreel cameraman, Art Menken, Vincent (Jimmy) Sheean of CBS, the beautiful Helen Kirkpatrick of the *Chicago Daily News* who was also reckoned 'to have a fine mind', and Virginia Cowles of the *New York Herald Tribune* who was now filing reports for the London *Sunday Times*, moved in the best circles and numbered government ministers among her friends. Occasionally Whitelaw Reid, whose family owned the *Tribune*, was there, all of them sitting in the sun, in the long grass, waiting, watching, listening and trying to make sense of what they saw and heard.

'The daily spectacle was out of all ordinary experience or easy credibility,' wrote Sheean. 'In colour alone it defied description. Sometimes the Messerschmitts would attack our barrage balloons with green or yellow tracer bullets; the silver balloons would explode in flames and sink gracefully to earth [other watchers found them less graceful, more 'like a tortured slug']; our Bofors guns around the port would attack the Messerschmitts with balls of fire. The intrepidity, indeed foolhardiness, of the Messerschmitt pilots was fabulous. I saw one Messerschmitt dive over the port to get a [barrage] balloon . . . at sundown one evening; he had to come down to not much more than a thousand feet; he missed the balloon and the Bofors guns got him, so he plummeted into the water; from any point of view his was a useless death.'

And it was here on the white cliffs of Dover that some of the Americans had an epiphany – or less an epiphany, rather a slow-burning realisation – that this time it wasn't necessarily going to be about watching the right side lose as it had been in Spain or France (for several of them had covered those campaigns). That maybe even if Britain was an old-fashioned, ill-resourced power with imperial pretensions, its people had the dogged determination to repel the invaders – somehow. 'It was at Dover I think,' wrote Sheean, 'that the side of England became "our side" in my eyes.' And if that was the case, what was the US government going to do about helping? After all, Churchill had clearly implicated

America in Britain's fight, calling on the New World to help liberate the old in his 'we will fight them on the beaches' speech of 4 June, and on 18 June he had done the same again: '. . . If we can stand up to [Hitler], all Europe may be free, and the life of the world may move forward into broad, sunlit uplands; but if we fail, then the whole world, including the United States, and all that we have known and cared for, will sink into the abyss of a Dark Age . . .'

For Churchill, there were two arguments that would bring the US to Britain's aid – aid he knew was essential to win the war. The first was US dependence on the Royal Navy, the second the heroism of the British stand which suggested that, despite what seemed like ridiculously long odds, Britain would hold out, could grasp victory. Like many other Americans, Roosevelt had been deeply shaken by France's collapse, and was sceptical about Britain's chance of survival. His personal estimate put it as low as one-in-three in June 1940. If Britain was doomed, as he feared, any American aid would be used against the United States by the Nazis within a year.

The heroism of 'the Few' in the Battle of Britain was the country's greatest propaganda asset. Churchill believed that the facts would speak for themselves, arguing that, 'Propaganda is all very well, but it is events that move the world. If we smash the Huns, we shall need no propaganda in the United States.' But the British Ambassador in Washington, Lord Lothian, thought differently: the American people needed to be told the story of Britain's brave fight in graphic terms as seen through the eyes of their own countrymen and women. So, despite obstacles put in the way by a nervous Ministry of Home Security, visits were arranged for US journalists to army barracks and airbases so they could see for themselves 'British planes getting back, but only just getting back because they have been so battered and riddled by the enemy [which] would provide a dramatic picture of the drain on our resources . . . provide invaluable evidence of our spirit and our needs.'

What was needed to help engage the sympathy of the American public was to actually see the human face of war. Lord Lothian came up with the notion of sending 'one or two ace fighters' to the US. He found an ideal candidate. William Fiske III, the twenty-nine-year-old pilot officer son of a wealthy New York banker, had married an Englishwoman and moved to Britain, and in March 1940 he signed up for the RAF Volunteer

Reserve. The idea was that Fiske should be sent back home to tell US senators, editors and other opinion formers how it was in battle. The Air Ministry agreed, but was reluctant to participate in anything that smacked of a public relations stunt: Pilot Officer Fiske must experience combat first. He was assigned to the 601 City of London Squadron and soon proved 'a natural as a fighter pilot', his exploits unquestionably the ideal way to 'give the hero-worshipping public of the United States a feeling of identity with the conflict'. On 17 August 1940 Billy Fiske was wounded in a fierce battle with some Ju 87s: he was badly burned but made it back to base, and this blooding seemed the crowning publicity achievement as the 'Yank in the RAF' began his convalescence prior to taking up his ambassadorial role in Washington. Tragically, that was never to happen, for Fiske unexpectedly collapsed and died. There were to be more no more token Yanks: the 'lone eagle' was replaced by the all-American 71 (Eagle) Squadron of the RAF that became operational in January 1941.

Fiske had not been the only American who fought in the Battle of Britain, and Americans were not the only men from overseas who had risked their lives in the sky for Britain – and would continue to do so, and on land and at sea, for the duration of the war. Of the 2,917 Fighter Command aircrew who are recognised to have taken part in the Battle of Britain, the vast majority – 2,334 – were British by birth and they came from all over the United Kingdom. But many of those who fought alongside the British were from the empire.

These men had often paid their own fares to join the peacetime RAF and later fight for Britain; during the Battle they provided half of the eight 'ace' fliers – pilots who had shot down at least five planes – and a disproportionate number of the dead. Over 40 per cent of Australians and South Africans who fought in the Battle of Britain were killed, compared to an average of 20 per cent of other Fighter Command pilots.

Few had more reason to fight the Germans than the Poles and the Czechs – and few airmen proved more adept at doing so than these 'homeless men. Motivated often by a hatred bordering on despair, they fought with a terrible and merciless destruction.' One hundred and forty-five Poles joined the Battle, many flying with the 302 (Polish) and 303 (Polish) squadrons, and alongside them flew 88 Czechs, 20 Belgians and a Frenchman.

*

On 4 September 1940 Hitler changed the tactics of the German air assault. The Luftwaffe switched the main force of its attack to cities: London would be the main target and from 7 September the capital was relentlessly bombed by day and by night. At the time this was believed to be a retaliation raid, a violent response to the RAF bombing raid on Berlin on the night of 25/26 August. But the first attack, and those that followed, fit the context of Hitler's attempt to defeat Britain by whatever means necessary. It was obvious by mid August that their air attack would not allow the Germans to attempt an invasion. The 'collapse of England in the year 1940 is under present circumstances no longer to be reckoned on', the Führer told his HQ staff. But Operation Sealion was not cancelled. Instead the air assault moved into the next stage. German Intelligence reports led Goering to assume that Fighter Command was all but decimated: the rest of the country was now to be attacked to complete the task and clear the way for invasion. Industrial installations, transport and communication links around the main urban centres were to be targeted – Bristol, Liverpool, Birmingham, and other Midland cities were heavily bombed – and bombs had been falling on the suburbs for nearly three weeks before the main attack on London started.

Whatever the reason, and however terrible the new assault was for the civilian population, the switch from bombing airfields gave Fighter Command an essential respite to regroup and revive. But the Battle of Britain was not over: the most crucial week was still to come as Fighter Command adjusted its tactics in line with the new threat. The bombers that attacked London flew at a high altitude with the German fighter planes darting in and out of the stream of bombers. This made defence more difficult, since it was harder for radar to estimate the altitude of the incoming bombers, and more difficult for fighter planes to climb above them for the most effective form of attack.

The crucial week in the Battle of Britain was 7–15 September 1940. On the 15th, more than 200 German bombers flew with a heavy fighter escort towards London. The attack was met by over 300 Spitfires and Hurricanes. Although 158 bombers managed to get through, visibility was poor and bombs missed their targets and were widely dispersed. The RAF pursued the retreating Germans to the coast, and in the course of the raids thirty-four German bombers were destroyed and twenty were extensively damaged – a loss rate of 25 per cent, which was unsustainable. Three nights later the Luftwaffe again sustained heavy losses when they attacked the capital with seventy bombers. After that they switched to night-time raids which exacted a less heavy toll on their aircraft.

September 15 has ever since been celebrated as Battle of Britain Day. The day when it was clear that however long the struggle might be, Britain had retained mastery of its skies, and there would be no quick or easy German victory – though no quick or easy British victory either. Five days later Hitler postponed Operation Sealion indefinitely. The threat of military invasion was replaced by an entirely unprecedented test of civilian endurance. 'I think we have avoided losing the war,' wrote Harold Nicolson to his wife Vita as the Blitz raged around him and the Ministry of Information where he was working was 'struck on the boko by the Luftwaffe . . . But when I think how on earth we are going to win it, my imagination quails.'

13

BLITZ, 1940

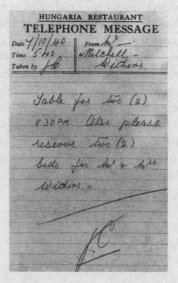

HUNGARIA RESTAURANT
TELEPHONE MESSAGE

Date 7/10/40   From Mr
Time 5.40   Mitchell —
Taken by JC   Withers.

Table for two (2)
8.30PM Also please
reserve two (2)
beds for Mr & Mrs
Withers.

Autumn seems a funny time to be bombed. By nature it is a hopeful start of the home year. The colours burning in the trees and the weed fires burning in the garden ought to be enough. Autumn used to be a slow sentimental fête, with an edge of melancholy – the children going back to school, the evenings drawing in. Windows lit earlier. Lanes in the country, squares in the city crisp with leaves. (This year, leaves are swept up with glass in them.) In autumn where you live touches the heart – it is the worst time not to be living anywhere. This is the season in which to honour safety.

ELIZABETH BOWEN, 'LONDON 1940'

THE PEOPLE OF the East End of London, of Poplar and Canning Town, Limehouse and Shadwell, Beckton and North Woolwich, Rotherhithe and Bow, knew the sickle side of the Thames that carved up their neighbourhoods. Boats sank, children fell in, lives were lost, the flotsam and jetsam of the metropolis lapped its muddy banks. But this same river had brought prosperity to the capital for almost two millennia: it had always been a river of commerce transporting the produce of the world. 'London's broadest street', J. B. Priestley called it, and one-quarter of all British imports came through the London docks. In return, the Thames sent down to the sea Britain's exports, many manufactured from the raw material it had imported. Commerce and industry fetched up on its shores and for the East Enders the Thames meant a livelihood on the boats, in the docks and on the wharves and quays that were cut behind the shoreline throughout the nineteenth century. It was often hard, poorly paid and unreliable work, and yet it was the reason why so many lived close by this deep, fast-flowing, tidal, often malodorous river.

In wartime the Thames again revealed its dark side: it was a fifth columnist, waiting in a besieged city to show the enemy the way. Like a seductive, sinuous thread that couldn't be pulled out, it mapped the targets for German bombers; it looped round the Isle of Dogs as if to draw attention to its significance, marked out docks, warehouses, gasometers, electricity substations, the ordnance factory at Woolwich. When all around was darkened by the blackout, the Thames – the name derived from the pre-Celtic *tamasa*, 'dark river' – still glistened, a perfidious silver reflection of the moon, seeming insouciantly to mock the efforts of those who struggled nightly to cover cracks between drawn curtains, stick brown paper over tea-tray-sized skylights, or bawl warnings to anyone who lit a cigarette in a blacked-out street. In peacetime a full moon on a clear night had been called a hunter's or a poacher's moon: in wartime it was renamed a 'bomber's moon' since on such a night aircraft crews could see 'every detail on the ground from an altitude of 3,500 feet' wrote a German pilot in his diary. It was propitious weather for death and destruction.

Although in the First World War the docks had been the Germans' main target for aircraft and Zeppelin attack, they had been relatively unscathed. Just one bomb damaged the Port of London, and the Authority put in a bill for only £3,000 for war damage to the hub of the activity on the Thames. But in the Second World War the port became 'the most consistently and heavily bombed civilian target in the British Isles' with nearly 1,000 high-explosive bombs and thousands of incendiaries falling on it. A third of its warehouses and transit sheds were destroyed, and the Thames itself threatened to silt up since it couldn't be dredged for the six years of war.

The first bombs of 'Black Saturday', 7 September 1940, fell on the docks. Three days earlier Hitler had promised a rally in Berlin revenge for an RAF raid on the city on 25/26 August in which ten civilians had been killed and twenty-nine wounded. 'When the British Air Force drops two or three or four thousand kilograms of bombs, then we will in one night drop 150, 230, 300 or 400 thousand kilograms,' he thundered. There was near-hysterical applause from the audience as he continued: 'When they declare that they will increase their attacks on our cities, then we will *raze* their cities to the ground . . . so help us God!'

London had been experiencing intermittent raids for several weeks. 'Nuisance raids', George Orwell called them, and most people would have agreed: sleep was the main casualty and the population grew used to 'going to ground' every time the siren sounded, but they were tired, irritable and apprehensive of what was to come. 'Most people believe that when the Germans decide to bomb, it'll be a real blitz,' noted the American journalist Ed Murrow at the end of August.

There had been air attacks on the rest of mainland Britain too. It was clear that the raids were becoming less random: a pattern was being established that gave the Luftwaffe valuable training and information-gathering opportunities, while doing considerable damage to Britain's docks, industry and infrastructure as well as killing and wounding its citizens. Just over 1,000 people were killed in August 1940. By the first anniversary of the outbreak of war, almost 4,000 civilians were dead or seriously injured, and thousands more had sustained less serious injuries, all as a result of enemy action.

But 'Black Saturday' was of a different order. This was the start of the Blitz, and for Londoners there would be no respite for fifty-seven consecutive nights – and the bombers often came during the daytime too.

That year had seen a memorably good summer, a compensation for the bitter winter, and Saturday 7 September was particularly perfect, a hot sun in a blue, almost cloudless sky. But soon after four in the afternoon the sky darkened as what seemed like a thousand planes streamed overhead, the steady, determined drone of the bombers menacing the hazy peace. At No 11 Group airfields, the sector that covered south-east England from Southampton through to Suffolk, where the camouflage paint was drying in the sun on recently repaired Spitfires and Hurricanes, Sector Controllers looked up anxiously, reluctant to commit their planes to battle until the raiders split up to make for their allocated airfield targets. As the men of the Observer Corps phoned in their reports of the number of planes passing overhead 'and still counting', Fighter Command realised that this was not the sort of raid they had become used to: the raiders were not going to split up to attack airfields. They were coalescing in two waves: the whole lot aiming straight for London.

The siren wailed in London at 4.43 p.m., and though most East Enders dutifully trooped down to the public shelter or took cover in whatever makeshift arrangement they had, no one was unduly worried: it had happened like this before. The All Clear would go soon and with any luck they might catch the last of the sunshine. But an off-duty fire officer gazing contentedly at the azure sky in his garden in Dulwich saw something that made him jump up and hurriedly struggle into his uniform. The sky was filled with an ever-darkening rash of black dots that he realised were planes in numbers he had never seen before – and they were all making for the East End. A little later Barbara Nixon, an actress who was a volunteer ARP warden in Finsbury, realised that it wasn't like anything anyone had ever seen before. From some 4 miles away she could see that 'the East End were getting it . . . we could see the miniature silver planes circling round and round the target area in such perfect formation that they looked like a children's toy model of flying boats or chair-o-planes at a fair. It was almost impossible to imagine that they were doing damage . . . As one plane flew off, another V-formation would fly in, stretch out into a "follow-my-leader" line and circle round as its predecessor had done. Presently we saw a white cloud rising; it looked like a huge evening cumulus, but it grew steadily, billowing outwards and always upwards. A fire-engine went by up the main road. The cloud grew to such a size that we gasped incredulously; there could not ever in history have been so gigantic a fire. Another fire-engine raced by, then a third, then a fourth, clanging their bells frenziedly as they shot across the traffic lights; our local sub station turned out, nearly every fire appliance in London was heading east.'

Jim Goldsmith, a regular fireman stationed in the City who set off towards the inferno, recalled that the men 'didn't need any lights or maps to find the way, you just headed for the glow in the sky'. George Woodhouse had joined the Auxiliary Fire Service (AFS) a voluntary organisation run by local authorities under government instruction. Before the war there had been some 1,600 locally organised Fire Brigades in Britain; few had more than twenty full-time firemen, almost all were ill equipped. The AFS, with over 200,000 members by September 1939 and trailer pumps pulled by saloon cars or London taxis painted grey, supplemented this force. But its members were frequently resented by the regulars and when the Blitz came it was indeed a baptism of fire for these often fairly raw recruits. Woodhouse, who was stationed at Holloway in north London, was 'ordered out, our destination the London Docks . . . People were frantically waving their arms at us begging us to stop but of course we were not allowed to. Arriving at the docks I drove through a large pair of gates to find the whole dockside area was jammed solid with fire appliances, literally nose to tail . . . The whole scene was one of utter devastation, not one of the pumps was being used. People just stood and stared . . .'

The Royal Victoria Docks and the Surrey Docks, which edged the U-bend, the 'bight' the Thames makes before it straightens out to flow west, were in the eye of the firestorm. Woolwich Arsenal was a prime target, and so were the Beckton gasworks, the largest in Europe, which supplied central London – when that was hit, very soon after the first arrival of the bombers, rumours spread round Silvertown, the area of narrow streets around the Royal Victoria Docks, that the enveloping sulphurous smell meant that the Germans had dropped mustard-gas canisters. Within minutes flames leapt into the sky along the banks of the Thames from burning warehouses and factories hit by the 300 or so bombers that savaged the area. Acrid black smoke from the bombed warehouse of the Silvertown rubber factory rolled through the nearby streets. Molten tar from another factory flowed across the North Woolwich Road, bogging down fire engines, ambulances and Civil Defence vehicles. The ghastly fumes of rubber, tar and paint mixed with a sweet odour of caramel as Tate & Lyle's sugar barges blazed. At the

Surrey Commercial Docks, 250 acres of pitch pine, which had come in
from Scandinavia and lay piled 25 feet high on the wharfside, was ablaze,
the flames soaring hundreds of feet into the sky, and soon even the
wood-block paved roads were on fire. An army of rats swarmed from a
soap factory in Silvertown. A grain warehouse was on fire too – and
when a large quantity of wheat burns, as the firemen found, it leaves a
sticky residue that was in danger of pulling off their boots. The mooring
ropes of barges burnt away, setting the smouldering craft adrift down
the Thames – later they would come back on the incoming tide still
alight – bumping into the fire barges manoeuvring to pump water ashore
to feed the land pumps, while boats as far as 300 yards from the docks
making their way down the river had their paint blistered by the intense
heat. The warehouse frontage downstream from Tower Bridge was
ablaze continuously for 1,000 yards – one unbroken wall of flame.

Soon after 6 p.m. the All Clear went, and stunned East Enders emerged
from public shelters, from flattening themselves in alleyways and under
bridges, or crouching in understairs cupboards or beneath tables in their
houses – since there were few Anderson shelters in these cramped,
gardenless streets where a small backyard might have just enough room
for a piece of string strung across as a washing line. The sight before
them was devastating: fire hoses snaked across the streets, while the
docks burned out of control as firemen tried hopelessly to contain the
great conflagrations and prevent smaller fires linking up to form new
ones. Falling slabs of masonry and coping stones crashed to the ground
from burning buildings, making the firemen's task even more perilous,
and the water mains proved entirely inadequate to provide the vast
amounts of water needed to deal with the fires.

The East Enders' respite was momentary: the conflagration meant
terror to those on the ground but to the raiders it was a marker. If the
light was so bright that Barbara Nixon standing in Shaftesbury Avenue
could see to read a newspaper, if people standing on the Brighton Downs
60 miles away could see the glowing crimson penumbra over London,
the same furious red glow enabled the Luftwaffe to home straight in on
their target. Just after 8 p.m. the bombers came back – squadron after
squadron of Heinkels and Dorniers – some 250 of them droned over
the coast to attack the capital, dropping 330 tons of high-explosives and
440 incendiary canisters 'with the object of destroying the city's harbour

installations, supplies and power sources'. But given the nature of the tidal basin of Silvertown, this meant civilian death, injury and destruction too, for industry and domesticity were jumbled together with hundreds of small houses hard by the Royal Victoria Docks which had been built for those working on the docks in the 1850s, and where those working there in 1940 still lived. These small, cheaply built houses crumpled under the impact of bombs and blast, their inhabitants thrown into the street where they lay sprawled and motionless, or buried under piles of masonry, rubble and dust.

Water pipes and gas mains were shattered by explosions and telephone cables were severed. Communication between the fire services and Civil Defence was kept going only by the courage of motor-bike despatch riders or teenage messenger boys – on bikes painted yellow and with a tin hat and an armband to identify them – skidding through tunnels of fire, skating round unexploded bombs and pushing through rubble and masonry-strewn streets to carry messages from fire crews to control rooms and back again, and from the ARP control rooms to the posts.

It went on all that night: the noise of planes overhead, the whine of falling bombs and the deafening crash as they hit buildings and exploded; the acrid smoke, blotting out the light and pressing into lungs, the dust from masonry that powdered hair and clothes so people staggered out from damaged buildings looking like figures on a sarcophagus. There were acres of warehouses on fire, molten tar flowed into the bomb craters making lakes of liquid fire. A rum warehouse at East India Docks was 'a raging inferno against which were silhouetted groups of pigmy firemen directing their jets at the wall of flame', while the pepper from a burning warehouse stung the lungs of the firemen so they felt they were breathing in the fire itself. At Woolwich Arsenal firemen fought the flames surrounded by boxes of live ammunition and crates of nitro-glycerine. For many, it was their first actual experience of large-scale fire-fighting: they had joined as auxiliaries and had been taught that a thirty-five-pump fire was a large one. Now they were facing blazes that needed upwards of a hundred pumps, and notices pinned at several places on the large map of London that hung in the Regional Fire Headquarters in Lambeth read 'Fire Out of Hand', while the pegs that represented the availability and location of London's hundreds of fire-fighting units had all gone. By the early hours of the morning forty-two engulfing fires were raging: 300 pumps were fighting one blaze and 130 were needed at another. 'Send all the bloody pumps you've got,' pleaded the fire officer at the Surrey Commercial Docks. 'The whole bloody world's on fire.' Calls went out for additional fire engines – 1,000 were in use in the docks area alone; West Ham needed another 500, and Barking and East Ham were also running short of vehicles. They came from all over London, and from as far away as Birmingham and Bristol.

It wasn't until 4.30 a.m. that the last bomber turned back and the All Clear sounded. Although more than 430 were dead and some 1,600 seriously injured, it seemed incredible that more had not been consumed in the inferno. The docks of Bermondsey and West Ham were pulverised, with many buildings still burning, and the destruction had fanned out to Stepney, Whitechapel, Poplar, Bow and Shoreditch. There was no gas, electricity or water, the trolley lines were down, phone cables were cut, paving stones broken and in many places roads were impassable because of craters, masonry or unexploded bombs.

That was how life would be for many months. There were piles of rubble where houses had stood, while some still standing were a grim cross-section of their former lives, the protection of their outer walls peeled away as if a giant tin-opener had ripped them open exposing fireplaces, shreds of curtains, torn strips of wallpaper, broken furniture, sometimes even a mirror still intact above a mantelpiece – the intimacy of domesticity defiled in the grey morning light. Jagged ziggurats of glass lay everywhere, and a heavy pall of greasy smoke hung over the East End.

Firemen had been working all night to contain fires that fed on themselves, the heat drawing in draughts of cold air that increased the reach of the flames, which tossed out burning timbers that in turn started other fires; and wood that had been drenched by their hoses steamed dry and reignited in the intense heat. As the fires continued to burn and smoulder, many of the firemen were to work forty hours or more since there was little relief: the fire service was at full stretch. For the next three weeks, the London fire brigades and their reinforcements would fight 10,000 fires and learn how best to deploy their inadequate resources, how to strategise their response to fire calls, identify those fires that had the greatest potential to spread, be deliberately neglectful about those blazes destined to burn themselves out, estimate how many pumps each fire would require, and be vigilant for the signs of the impending collapse of a building.

The next morning Winston Churchill paid a visit to the East End, where he and his chief of staff Pug Ismay found 'the destruction was much more devastating' than they had imagined. 'Fires were still raging all over the place, some of the larger buildings were mere skeletons, and many of the smaller houses had been reduced to heaps of rubble. The sight of tiny paper Union Jacks, which had already been planted on two or three of these pathetic heaps brought a lump to one's throat.

'Our first stop was at an air-raid shelter in which about forty persons had been killed and many more wounded by a direct hit [when a bomb fell down a ventilation shaft in Columbia Road, home of the Flower Market in Shoreditch] and we found a big crowd, male and female, young and old, but all seemingly very poor. One might have expected them to be resentful against the authorities responsible for their protection; but as Churchill got out of his car, they literally mobbed him. "Good old Winnie," they cried. "We thought you'd come and see us. We can take it. Give it 'em back." Churchill broke down, and as I was struggling to get to him through the crowd, I heard an old woman say, "You see he really cares; he's crying". Having pulled himself together, he proceeded to march through dockland at breakneck speed, and, anxious to see and be seen, Churchill spent much of the day in the East End inspecting the damage and meeting the East Enders.'

Though the raid had been heaviest over the East End, other parts of London had suffered on Black Saturday too. In west London, it seemed to Vera Brittain that 'between 2.0 & 3.0 [in the morning] bombs seemed to drop every 5 minutes. Lay in shelter most of night face downwards with pillow over my head. In afternoon . . . went round and saw damage done last night. Warwick Gdns was a devastated area – no glass anywhere. House at corner of Pembroke Gdns and Earl's Court demolished – windows all round broken; clock & windows smashed on St Philip & St James's Church.' The following day Brittain decided to leave London 'for a few days' rest . . . taxied to Waterloo; found it closed (Vauxhall Bridge [had] been bombed). Took taxi on to Clapham Junction; part of area round station sealed off for delayed-action bomb; air-raid alarm sounded on station, but we went on; ran into raid, train bombed and machine-gunned, people running for their lives; got onto floor. Changed at Surbiton – reached Woking half-dead, and SLEPT.'

As the second wave of bombers were loosing their deadly cargo over London on Black Saturday, there was panic in other areas of the country too. An urgent signal was sent out to Eastern and Southern Commands and all troops in the London area. Operation Cromwell meant that an invasion was considered imminent. In some areas, Home Guard commanders assumed that this meant that German parachutists were already landing in the fields, and that German boats were slithering up the beaches. As instructed to do in such an emergency, they forced an entry into church towers to ring out the bells to summon their men. The alert was found to be without foundation, and procedures were tightened up. In future only if a member of the Home Guard had seen a *minimum* of twenty-five German parachutists descending with his own eyes, were church bells to be rung and the local population alerted.

The bombers came back on the Sunday night: this time, for nine and a half hours 200 bombers targeted the City of London as well as the docks, and soon twelve huge conflagrations were burning: 412 Londoners were killed and 747 seriously injured; quays, factories, offices and homes were laid waste and every railway out of London to the south was put out of action.

As the bombs fell, some 600 East Enders who had been bombed out of their homes were taken to a temporary rest centre housed in South Hallsville primary school in Canning Town. The extended families and lifelong neighbours were still waiting for transport to get them out of the area, tired, hungry – and fearful 'in this shelterless school' – on Monday 9 September when the alert sounded again at 8 p.m. It was 4.50 the next morning before the All Clear went. That night 370 were killed and 1,400 wounded. Included in that number were seventy-three (or so the Council said later) who had been killed in South Hallsville school by a bomb that fell just over an hour before the All Clear. It had been a direct hit and the roof had caved in, crushing people under slabs of concrete, burying them under layers of bricks, pushing them down into the crater the bomb had made as it sliced the school in two. As the rescue workers dug frantically in the grey light of early dawn, no one could answer the questions: Why were they still there? Where were the buses? Had they been 'misdirected' – gone to

Camden Town instead of Canning Town? No one even knew for sure who had been sheltering there, or how the various body parts that were pulled from the wreckage – and carefully carried to the local swimming pool that had been turned into a temporary morgue – could be pieced together for identification, to give families the bodies to decently rest in peace. ARP workers and local volunteers went on digging for twelve days before conceding that of course they'd never bring out anyone alive, or even whole, now. Entire families had been wiped out. The seventy-odd known dead were buried in a mass grave. But the locals reckoned nearer 200 had died, and believed that more than a hundred still lay incarcerated in the site the authorities concreted over.

'Where are the bloody guns?' was a question that echoed round the shelters on those first dreadful nights of the Blitz. It seemed as if the Luftwaffe was having it all its own way and Britain was 'taking it' a bit too docilely. There were two squadrons of night fighters detailed for the defence of London, but on 7 September the smoke from the fires was so heavy that the Blenheims stationed at Hornchurch were unable to get off the ground, and the single-seater fighters that were available were notoriously ineffective for night flying except when visibility was very good. It would be up to those on the ground employing barrage balloons, searchlights and anti-aircraft guns to try to parry the assault. But barrage balloons hovered too low for the high-flying night raiders, which flew too high for searchlights to be effective either. There were seven anti-aircraft (or ack-ack after the noise the guns made) divisions, but there was a grave shortage of weapons. Only half the heavy and a third of the light guns that had been considered essential before the war were in place. Ack-ack guns had been deployed to guard factories and airfields during the Battle of Britain, so when the Luftwaffe switched to London the capital was perilously vulnerable, its defence resting on an entirely inadequate total of 264 anti-aircraft guns.

'We had depended on anti-aircraft guns . . . and apart from a solitary salvo loosed at the beginning of the raids, no gun had been shot in our defence – and morale was by now pretty low . . . we felt like sitting ducks and no mistake,' wrote Violet Regan, sheltering in a school in Poplar. General Sir Frederick Pile, commander-in-chief of the Anti-Aircraft Command, realised that 'something must be done immediately.

'Within twenty-four hours . . . reinforcements from all over the country were on their way to London and within forty-eight hours the number of guns had been doubled.' Pile instructed 'that every gun was to fire every possible round . . . every unseen target must be engaged without waiting to identify the aircraft as hostile. The result was as astonishing to [Pile] as it appears to have been to the citizens of London and apparently to the enemy as well.' On 10 September, the fourth night of the Blitz, men – many of whom had only just finished training and who were having to work round the clock to repel daylight raiders as well – let off deafening volleys of shells. They were firing blind and 'few bursts can have got anywhere near the target' since the tactic was to throw a enormous barrage of time-fused shells in front of a bomber formation and just hope that some of the planes would fly into it. Anything better than one hit per 2,000 shells was considered spot-on aiming, and that assumed approaching aircraft could be seen in advance so the guns could be pointed in roughly the right direction. Nevertheless the tirade, coming as it did after three nights of the Luftwaffe having an almost uninterrupted passage to their targets, seems to have forced the bombers to fly higher and even some to turn back. But most importantly 'it bucked people up tremendously' and those Londoners sheltering from the raid could feel some confidence that there was, at last, some semblance of a battle – even if most soon suspected that for some time it would be more sound than effect.

Every night that September – the month of the 'knockout blow' in German expectations – the bombers came back, occasionally as few as fifty, sometimes as many as 300. The death toll mounted: by the end of the month 5,730 people had been killed and nearly 10,000 seriously injured. Industries, public buildings, shops were destroyed; a number of the hospitals to which the dying and injured were taken were repeatedly hit as they treated Blitz casualties; railway lines were smashed, stations bombed, roads cratered and made impassable by debris; trolley lines were down; gas, water, electricity, gas and telephone supplies fractured; and thousands of houses demolished or damaged.

Four-fifths of all bombs dropped during the Blitz were high explosives (HE) – SC-Sprengbombe-Cylindrisch, or General Purpose as they were known in Britain – the sort designed to cause maximum impact. They were made of thin steel to maximise the effect of the blast, and varied greatly in size. Some had a cardboard tube like an organ pipe or an adapted bayonet scabbard, attached. These, known as the 'Trumpets of Jericho', emitted an eerie whistling sound as the bomb plunged to earth and were expressly designed to terrify the civilian population. The smallest and most common were the 110lb bombs, while towards the other end of the scale was the 2,200lb bomb, nicknamed Hermann after the portly Goering, Commander-in-Chief of the Luftwaffe. The 'Satan' bomb weighed nearly 4,000lb, and could produce a crater that 'could comfortably accommodate several double-decker buses'. The 'Max', the largest bomb ever to fall in Britain, weighed a massive 5,500lb.

Incorrectly named 'land mines' would fall from the air during the Blitz, too. These were similar to the magnetic mines used at sea to blow up shipping, and their usefulness as land missiles was probably discovered only when some accidentally fell on coastal towns. Since they floated down and did not penetrate the ground, the damage they caused was widespread. Designed to smash through modern prestressed-concrete industrial buildings in residential areas, the parachute mode of delivery meant that the mines were impossible to target accurately, and made a mockery of any claim to be aiming at military and industrial targets as they reduced Victorian domestic terraces to rubble.

While most HE bombs exploded on impact, some 10 per cent failed to do so. This might be due to a mechanical or electrical fault, but sometimes it was because the bomb had been set with a delayed-action mechanism. Unexploded bombs (UXBs) caused enormous disruption: invariably a considerable area had to be closed, streets blocked off and premises evacuated – London and Birmingham suffered particularly badly from this inconvenience and potential danger. Bomb disposal was now a job for the Royal Engineers – the sappers (called after the 'saps', the trenches they had built in earlier wars). The bomb-disposal unit had the skilled and dangerous task of removing the device or making it safe. And of course bombs did not just lie conveniently on the surface where they fell, but often penetrated through earth and tarmac to lie deep underground, making it extremely difficult and perilous to defuse them.

Throughout the war, bomb disposal was a perpetual deadly game of being one step ahead. As soon as the sappers worked out how one fuse could be neutralised, it seemed the Germans would adapt it or invent another that would test the ingenuity – and courage – of the soldiers (and those 350 or so commanding officers who had volunteered to help) to the very limit. By the end of 1940 there were over 3,000 bombs still waiting to be defused.

Incendiary bombs could be lethal too unless they were put out as soon as they fell. The most widely used bombs were packed into a canister that burst open above the ground, scattering its contents over a wide area. The 9-inch-long bombs, 2 inches in diameter, were made of a magnesium alloy. When ignited by a small impact fuse, they burned for ten minutes at a temperature sufficient to melt steel, and could throw particles of burning metal up to 50 feet. Though incendiaries could be extinguished with a stirrup pump, smothered with earth or sandbags, or even doused in a bucket of water, they presented a deadly hazard in unoccupied properties where fire could seize hold in minutes. Later in the Blitz, a small additional charge was fitted into the tail of the bomb, which exploded a minute and a half after the incendiary had ignited. By 1942 this delayed action had increased to six minutes, and the incendiaries had become much heavier and could penetrate through the roof of a building and the storey below before starting to burn.

People became expert at judging what bombs were falling in their area during a raid: 'That was, I think, an incendiary that came down a moment ago,' wrote Mea Allan, a thirty-one-year-old journalist, during a raid on London in late September. 'It was if the *Evening Standard Guide to Air Raid Sounds* is anything to go by . . . On the other hand it might be noise Number 3 which is a Molotov breadbasket . . .'

Each bombing raid brought an aggregate of death and destruction but each comprised numerous individual tragic incidents: on 15 September a bomb fell on an Anderson shelter that had been dug into the garden of a small terraced house in Barking, east London. A family of six had been sheltering there and the strength of the blast blew their bodies apart. A torso landed on the roof of what had been the family home, and a woman's arm was found with an engagement ring on one of the fingers. It transpired that it belonged to a twenty-year-old girl who was to have been married the following Saturday. The rescue van was equipped with only one shroud, so an ARP warden sent a colleague to the local greengrocer for some potato sacks and the men filled a number of these with the human remains. When the mortuary van arrived to collect this grisly cargo, the local residents were shocked to see that what was being used for the purpose was a council dustcart – thoroughly cleaned and painted black.

By the middle of September the Luftwaffe was sustaining such heavy losses in the battles fought over southern Britain that its strategy began to change. Daylight raids decreased after the 15th when fifty-six German aircraft were destroyed, and that month the German Air Force flew 6,135 night sorties over London, and all over Britain towns and cities were bombed – Hull, St Helens, Warrington, Cardiff, Plymouth, Merseyside, Filton near Bristol, and Liverpool were all attacked in September, though London remained the main target. 'Every night, one's only prayer is for morning!' wrote Vere Hodgson, who did welfare work for a charity in Notting Hill in west London.

Harold Nicolson at the Ministry of Information was concerned about the effect on public morale if it appeared that the East End was suffering while the 'toffs up west' got off lightly. 'There is much bitterness. It is said that even the King and Queen were booed the other day when they visited the destroyed areas . . . If the Germans had had the sense not to bomb west of London Bridge there might have been a revolution in this country.' But by mid September 'the Germans [had] smashed about Bond Street and Park Lane and readjusted the balance' (somewhat) and on 9 September, while the King and Queen were at Windsor Castle, which they repaired to each evening in an armoured car to avoid the night raids, a random bomb hit the north side of Buckingham Palace, shattering windows on all floors, including those of the King's study where he had been working the previous day. The royal couple moved into apartments in the inner courtyard, but on 13 September, 'All of a sudden we heard an aircraft making a zooming noise above us and saw 2 bombs falling past the opposite side of the Palace. And then heard 2 resounding crashes as the bombs fell in the quadrangle about 30 yards away . . . The whole thing happened in a matter of seconds. We all wondered why we weren't dead. Two great craters had appeared in the courtyard . . . The aircraft was seen coming down the Mall below having dived through the clouds & had dropped two bombs in the forecourt, 2 in the quadrangle, 1 in the Chapel & the other in the garden. There is no doubt that it was a direct attack on the Palace.'

The bombing of Buckingham Palace had great propaganda potential for the royal family. Forty journalists were sent to cover the story and the incident famously enabled the Queen 'to look the East End in the face', usually ensuring a welcome for her and the King when they went walkabout, not only in the East End but in other parts of the country to see the suffering of their subjects and the damage caused to their nation. On such occasions, travelling by royal train (in which the royal couple could eat and sleep to avoid putting too much strain on the resources of war-torn towns and cities) or in 'an ordinary-looking saloon with military number plates and splinter-proof windows', George VI chose the most appropriate uniform, 'wearing in turn the dress of each of the high ranks he bore, as Admiral of the Fleet, a Field-Marshal, and Marshal of the Royal Air Force [for by making] no further public appearances in mufti [after the outbreak of war] he gave visible notice that he considered himself as continually on duty as any fighting man in the services', in the words of an admiring booklet published at the end of the war. Since his military role was purely emblematic (even his one major tour of the war to French North Africa in 1943 was spoilt by 'desert tummy') and the nation already had a siren-suited warrior prime minister at its helm, the job opportunity was for a 'people's king', a comforter and morale booster.

It was Oxford Street's turn on the 17th. That night 350 tons of bombs dropped on London – more than the total number that had landed on the whole of Britain during the First World War – and the department stores D. H. Evans and Bourne & Hollingsworth were badly damaged. The John Lewis store was completely burned out, looking 'like a charred skeleton with its blackened walls and gaping windows and rust orange girders and its wax models lying like corpses in the street', and a smell of soot pervaded the air. But soon an enterprising manager had set up a trestle table on the pavement and was doing a brisk trade in underwear salvaged from the debris.

But for every large department store damaged, there were dozens of small shops put out of business every week by the raids, their owners' sole means of livelihood lost, and these incidents went largely unreported, judged to be of interest only to those in the immediate locality. There might just be a 'terse notice saying "Bombs were dropped in — district; there were a few casualties".'

Bad weather at the start of October brought lighter raids, but the respite was short-lived, and the toll of damage and destruction was mounting: in the six weeks since the start of the night attacks on London, more than 76,000 buildings had been damaged, 16,000 of which were totally destroyed or damaged beyond repair.

On the night of 1/2 October in West Hampstead, 'the bottom of [Gwladys Cox's] world dropped out! Last night, most of our home together with the whole top floor of Lymington Mansions was destroyed by incendiary bombs . . . There was a terrible crash quite close . . . making the building stagger . . . almost immediately the plunk, plunk, plunk of incendiary bombs above on *our own roof*!' When the All Clear came, 'to our surprise at 11.15 p.m., we . . . peered about us. Above us flames from our living room roof reddened the sky, while searchlights swept the heavens, and then the firemen told us bluntly that no one would be allowed to return to the flats, we at last realised that we were literally homeless. We had always counted on being able to shelter in the cellar in the event of being bombed, but we had reckoned without A.F.S. flooding – the area was already inches deep in water. As Mrs Sepp had so often asked us to go to her in an emergency . . . we determined to take her at her word. So tired, wet and bedraggled, clinging to each other and to coats and wraps and Bob's [the cat's] basket, we floundered along to Lymington Road – literally floundered for the pavement was rough with loose stones and rubble, the result of the raid.' The next morning the Coxes returned to their flat to find that their neat and orderly home was a scene of indescribable desolation. 'The dining room was completely burnt out, neither roof nor windows remained. Ralph's beautiful antique desk, which, besides our marriage certificate, Fire Insurance Policy, contained all the letters I had written to him . . . covering many years, not even the ashes remained; his hundreds of books, his chief hobby, collected during a life-time, were congealed black masses of cinders; hundreds of gramophone records had vanished into thin air. In the drawing room, the roof had fallen in and what remained of the sodden furniture was covered with a shining layer of molten lead from the burning roof; the carpet was inches deep in a wet mixture of ceiling-plaster and burnt rafters.'

At first Luftwaffe bomber units were allocated specific targets such as the West India Docks, or Battersea Power Station (known to German crews as the 'Packet of Woodbines' because of its large towers). But it was soon obvious that such precision was just not possible, and from 8 October 1940 bombers were directed to a target such as the area inside the U-loop of the Thames, or the area around the Elephant and Castle to Blackfriars Bridge and taking in part of the East End, in which would lie a number of specific targets. But even these were hard to target with any real degree of accuracy using only visual aids on a moonlit night, and on cloudy nights there was a near zero chance. So crews, who had no wish to return to base with bombs on board since this could be lethal to them in the event of attack, and made landing hazardous, aimed their bombs roughly in the direction of where they thought the target was, aided by whatever fires were burning.

When the sirens sounded on the evening of Sunday 13 October 1940, most of the residents of Coronation Mansions in Stoke Newington, north London, one of several nineteenth-century blocks of flats erected by the Four Per Cent Industrial Dwellings Society in the area, went down to the shelter in the basement of the block. They were joined by several passers-by and local residents since the basement had been designated as a public shelter. A heavy bomb fell halfway along the block: the floors above caved into the basement, crushing and trapping those below and filling the air with dust, smoke and brick particles. Fallen masonry, heavy furniture, girders and general debris made it impossible for any survivors to crawl out of any of the exits, and the explosion was so powerful that it ruptured the water mains, sewage pipes and gas mains. Water and effluent started to pour in and, as the rescue parties arrived, those entombed in the basement were gasping for air while their lungs filled with liquid. There was nothing the rescuers could do. The entire family of a member of the Finsbury Rescue Service was buried under Coronation Mansions. 'For days on end he watched the digging, although there was no hope at all. They tried to persuade him to go away, but he only shook his head. His wife had wanted to stay at home that night, and he had himself insisted that she and the children should go to the shelter.' The Stoke Newington bomb was 'the greatest bombing tragedy of the whole of London', thought the journalist Hilde Marchant of the *Daily Express*. It took ten days to dig out the victims: many could be identified only as 'female blown to pieces'. Of the 154 people who died that night, some twenty-six were never identified.

The following day a bomb falling on Balham High Street in south

London made a crater so large that a double-decker bus fell into it and only the roof could be seen sticking out. The bomb also penetrated the underground station, where around 600 people were sheltering. The platform was plunged into darkness and within minutes the panic-stricken shelterers were engulfed by water pouring into the station 'like a waterfall'. 'All you could hear was the sound of screaming and rushing water. We managed to get to the platform by wading along through the sludge on the track, and it was terrible,' recorded Bert Woolridge, an ARP warden. 'People were lying there, all dead and there was a great pile of sludge on top of them. Lots were curled up in sleeping positions on the platform. One of them – he was a porter – had had his clothes ripped off by the bombs; he lay there naked. We put people on stretchers and carried them away through the water. I don't think we found any survivors that night.' London Transport staff managed to wrest open the floodgates but sixty-eight people still died.

On 28 October a bomb exploded at the east end of the crypt of St Peter's Church, Walworth, which was used as a public shelter. For its rector, who was also a chief ARP warden, 'Those early hours of the morning were so hectic that my memory of it is confused . . . Early on the [ARP] Post was invaded by walking casualties, brought out of the crypt or found staggering around the churchyards, dazed and covered from head to foot in white dust . . . I found an old lady, who lived just round the corner, sitting on [a] chair . . . where one of the wardens had put her. She was grey with dust from head to foot, and where her skin was exposed it was beginning to peel off. Otherwise she did not seem to be injured, and was fully conscious. In fact, she died later from the effects of the blast . . . later we reckoned on 250 seriously hurt, and over 70 killed, with several hundreds of lesser casualties, caused mainly from the splinters from wooden partitions, dividing the various parts of the crypt, which ripped into people and their belongings . . . The blast in the confined space of the crypt was greater than it might have been because both bombs exploded on the floor of the crypt, having in one case gone through the roof and ceiling of the church, then the organ, on through the stone floor . . . they literally bored their way through successive layers . . . the combined blast produced some bizarre results, some of which were studied by Air Ministry experts later on . . . A strange case was that of a young woman, who was sitting in a chair by the brick pier supporting one of the arches in the crypt. One of the bombs exploded just the other side of this brick pier, blowing to bits a whole family, six members of which I commended to Almighty God a few days later at a funeral service in a neighbouring church. The young woman, just a few feet from them, was uninjured, except for a burst eardrum . . .

'One of the problems, with which I had to deal, as we got most of the casualties to hospital in two hours, was the disposal of the dead. I decided that the considerable risk of panic among the wardens and local population would be heightened if they had to see rows of dead laid out waiting for mortuary vans. I had the bodies taken straight into the undamaged west end of the church, where they were laid out in rows in one of the aisles. In the morning there were 35 stretchers of the remains waiting for the vans. Their blood stained the flag stones; I was glad I was able within a week to establish our altar on that very spot . . . where we offered prayers for them and for ourselves, and all the world, during the following years.'

The toll for October was 6,334 civilians killed and 8,695 seriously injured. There seemed no reason why it should ever end. Though raids were lighter when the weather was bad, the night bombers still managed to get through, and seemed to be meeting remarkably little resistance.

On the night of 3/4 November bad weather meant that there were no raids at all, the first time since the night Blitz had started. Throughout the rest of the month London was again subjected to heavy attacks – 142 people were killed and over 430 injured on 15/16 November when all but one of the metropolitan boroughs were bombed, as were 76 out of the 95 districts in the London area. But raids on the capital were less heavy than in the previous two months, though there was still extensive damage to life and property.

'It's an awfully anxious life,' wrote Helena Britton from Walthamstow to her daughter in America. 'It's about nine weeks now since dad and I undressed to go to bed . . . Last Monday we spent eleven and a half hours in the [Anderson] shelter from 7.30 p.m. to 7 a.m., and last night it was from 7.25 to 6.45. We have made it as comfortable as possible, but we all get so stiff owing to restricted movement . . . Lots of people are leaving town . . . but I don't want to leave our little home if it's possible to stay . . . you mustn't worry about us, dear. We shall pull through.'

'We are speechless with fatigue,' wrote Vere Hodgson. 'I shall sleep if bombs fall all round my bed!'

London did not suffer the Blitz alone. All around the country Luftwaffe attacks had been increasing, particularly on such natural targets as ports and industrial centres. By 31 December 1940 the bombing raids on the rest of Britain read like a gazetteer to the whole country: London had been attacked 126 times, and Liverpool 60; in the Midlands Birmingham had suffered 36 raids and Coventry 21. Attacks ranged from Aberdeen (3) and Edinburgh (4) in Scotland to Cardiff and Swansea in Wales (11 each). The raiders swooped down to Cornwall and round the coast blitzing Plymouth (13), Portsmouth (13), Hastings (4) and Hull (4) among other ports and seaside towns; they continued to bomb airfields across the country, and more than 100 other towns and cities felt the fury of the Luftwaffe attack on one or more occasions.

The severity of the raid on Coventry, on 14/15 November, would add a new word to the lexicon of war in both Germany and Britain: *Koventrieren* or to Coventrate – to lay waste by aerial bombardment.

Coventry was a thriving industrial city, whose population had grown fourfold to nearly a quarter of a million in the past twenty-five years as people flocked there in search of work in local factories: when war came, these and a mass of small workshops making car and aircraft parts had been turned over to war production. In addition, Coventry was the location of a number of 'shadow factories' understudying war production. The city was thus a prime target in Hitler's mission to knock out Britain's war economy, and had already suffered seventeen attacks between mid August and the end of October, resulting in 180 dead and 750 injured. But the mid-November attack was beyond parallel.

Coventry's Civil Defence received no advance warning of Moonlight Sonata, the German code name for the raid, though Intelligence sources had signalled a very heavy raid that night. Its location was unknown, and early that afternoon the RAF Counter Measures Unit had worked out that the X-Gerät beams, the device by which the Germans directed their planes to their target, intersected over Coventry, indicating that the city was that night's Luftwaffe target.

The first wave of Heinkels was over the city by about 7.20 p.m. and dropped more than 10,000 incendiaries which started eight major fires and a mass of smaller blazes. Soon the red glow in the sky could be seen by the incoming German planes even before they had crossed the coast in endless waves of bombers that kept coming all through the night.

Every night the Coventry and Warwickshire hospital, near the ordnance factory, displayed a lighted red cross on its roof to show its status. But at the yellow (stand-by) alert, staff covered every patient with a mattress as some form of protection. When the bombs began to fall that night, nurses were wheeling beds down from the top floors and lining them along the ground floor away from the flying glass. A woman who was recovering from an operation woke 'as the sirens sounded to see the wall opposite my bed disappear. A doctor and nurse were lying on top of me to protect me from flying glass and debris . . . I was carried down a large curving staircase in my bed by soldiers to the basement . . . As they left me, a bomb screamed down and I screamed with it. One soldier ran back, folded me in his arms and rocked me. Other patients then joined me and all night the noise of screaming bombs was terrible. I saw an incendiary stuck in the wall just like a torch. Twenty high explosive bombs fell on the hospital, five were direct hits and all but around a hundred of the 1,600 windows were blown out. At dawn came the All Clear and it became eerily silent except for the crying of a baby, some said, newly born . . .

'My father turned up looking haggard and afraid. Where my bed had stood in the ward was a large hole, so he thought the worst. My family had watched from the village, fearing for me, their eldest, helpless in the hell that was Coventry. My father helped to carry me out to a waiting ambulance, pulling the blanket over my face because he said it was cold, but really so that I should not see the rows of bodies lying there.'

The All Clear did not sound until six the next morning. Since so many electric cables had been severed, the sirens in the city centre didn't sound and only a faint eerie echo of the 'white signal' carried through the dawn mist from the outskirts of Coventry. The police toured shelters, calling, 'It's safe to come out now' and the citizens of Coventry emerged into a ravaged city. The BBC reported the scene as one in which through the drizzle and mist 'it was impossible to see where the central streets . . . had been . . . It seemed hopeless . . .' 'Coventry is a city of the dead, utterly devastated,' wrote a Coventry woman to her daughter in London.

'We have no gas, electric light and, in most cases, no water. We have no milk or bread at the moment. Mobile vans are going round the town with bread and water. Loud speakers are going round telling the homeless where to meet to be taken out of the city.'

The centre of the city had been devastated by over 500 tons of high-explosive bombs and 30,000 incendiaries. A 'major raid' was classified both by the Luftwaffe and by the British authorities as one in which more than 100 tons of high explosive bombs were dropped – and Coventry received more than five times that. A hundred acres of the city centre were laid waste. The 600-year-old cathedral of St Michael's was gutted by fire from incendiary bombs – by morning all that was left was a shell with the 300-foot spire still pointing to the sky from which its destruction had come. Bombs blocked every railway line out of the city, and the stations, many of which were also damaged, had to be closed. In a 'very rough estimate' the Ministry of Home Security calculated that one-third of the city's factories had been completely demolished, or so badly damaged as to be out of commission for many months. In a city that had already had a housing shortage before the war, one in twelve of the houses and flats was either destroyed or rendered uninhabitable, and two-thirds of the remainder were damaged that night.

Nearly everybody knew somebody who had been killed or injured, or was missing. In a city of 238,000 inhabitants, 568 people were estimated to be dead, and over 1,200 injured, most of them badly. The toll – 'a civilian had a 60 per cent greater chance of being killed or seriously wounded during that one night in Coventry than during the whole six years of the war elsewhere' – would have been worse had not thousands, alarmed by the earlier raids, trekked out of the city at dusk each day to find shelter in nearby towns and villages or in the countryside. The city had seventy-nine public shelters that could accommodate 33,000 people, and these had sustained relatively little damage, while those huddling in Anderson shelters and reinforced basements had been protected too.

Nevertheless the survivors were totally stunned by their fearsome ordeal as they gazed around their ruined city. 'The centre of the town is roped off,' reported a local woman, 'and no one is allowed within half a mile of it. There are so many unexploded bombs about, they are talking of blasting the town because none of the buildings are safe . . . one can't

get near the Council House for people waiting for death certificates . . .
we are indeed a stricken city.'

The great fear was that the bombers would come back again to finish
their work the next night. They didn't, but the horror was not over yet.
Bodies lay stacked in the mortuary with luggage labels tied to them
marked in indelible pencil indicating their identity. But during the raid a
bomb had hit a nearby gasometer that exploded and took the roof off the
mortuary. Two nights later it poured with rain, the bodies were soaked
and the labels rendered illegible. 'We had as many as three or four
persons identifying the same body as a different person, particularly the
bodies which had suffered the full effect of bomb blast. It was quickly
recognised that some other method should be adopted and, finally, each
body was stripped and all belongings, clothing etc., were put into a
sandbag; each body was put into a coffin supplied by Regional Control,
and both given the same number and entered into a register. It was
gruesome work that was done by stretcher party personnel. A bottle of
brandy was very useful at the outset . . . subsequent bodies were
identified by their clothes, jewellery etc . . . and there were very few
who were not finally identified.'

In every blitzed city so far, most of the victims had had a private
burial, but the scale of the deaths in Coventry led the city's Emergency
Committee to decide that a mass funeral would be less painful than a
long-drawn-out series of individual interments. They thus 'tried to
persuade people who were clamouring to go to the mortuary and take
the bodies away that . . . they ought to remember their friends and
relatives as they had known them in life.' People were 'persuaded to
accept a civic funeral and that the bodies should be interred in a
communal grave'. It was not a popular initiative but it did overcome the
problem of identification without necessarily admitting that there was
one. The first mass funeral took place on 20 November 1940, a grey and
dismal day, while elsewhere in the city bodies were still being recovered
from the debris. One of the officiating clergy recorded looking 'back
over the long line of mourners still approaching. It was a pathetic sight;
women carrying wreaths; here and there a bunch of flowers, the black
suits and dresses relieved by a slash of colour of the uniform of a husband,
a son, or a brother on compassionate leave. It seemed as if there were no
end to this long dark line, which moved slowly across the grass. At last

the great crowd was gathered around the graves . . . In the distance against a grey scudding sky, a Spitfire wheeled and twisted; the sound of its engine came fitfully to us down the wind.'

That day, 172 were buried, and a similar ceremony was held the following Saturday at which 250 were interred. The devastated city then began its slow haul back to something that approximated to 'normal life' in wartime, and to full industrial capacity.

Nearby Birmingham was to show a similar resilience. Like Coventry, it had turned many of its factories over to war production, making among other things components for radar equipment, rifles and aeroplanes, and it too was dotted with 'shadow factories'. It had been bombed intermittently since early August – the university, the art gallery and town hall were all hit and fire had damaged the cathedral and the council House; 400 citizens had already lost their lives. But the heaviest raid started on 19 November: for four consecutive nights a number of factories were hit, including the BSA factory at Small Heath with the loss of fifty workers; the GEC and Lucas plants were also damaged, along with the usual sad litany of shops, churches and thousands of houses. The heaviest night of the Birmingham Blitz was the eleven-hour raid on the night of 22/23 November that started 600 fires. Fire brigades came from as far away as Cardiff, Bristol and Manchester to help. Many of the water mains were hit and firemen drew water from the canals that intersected the city; the fires were all under control by the time the All Clear sounded. Over seventy factories had been hit in the nights of intensive bombing, though only four had been destroyed or severely damaged. But almost 800 people had been killed, more than 2,000 injured, and 20,000 civilians made homeless. The Luftwaffe was to come back to Birmingham for three nights in December, but the object of the raids was not achieved. As in Coventry, production was not seriously affected, and what damage had been done to industry was soon repaired.

Just as much a target as industrial centres were Britain's ports – in fact, going by the number and intensity of attacks, Merseyside, which included Liverpool, Bootle, Birkenhead and Wallasey, was 'Hitler's number one target outside London'. The Mersey was lined with granaries, power stations, dry docks and gasworks. Ocean liners brought supplies from across the Atlantic to Liverpool's docks, and already by the end of

September over 300 people had been killed and nearly 600 injured by bombing raids on this vital area. The toll mounted in October with a further 300-odd casualties, but it was on 28/29 November that Liverpool had its night of hell, when more than 350 tons of high-explosive bombs, thirty huge land mines (eight of which failed to explode) and 30,000 incendiaries blanketed the area, killing almost 300 people.

The worst single incident of that terrible night happened at the Ernest Brown Instructional Centre in Durning Road, Edge Hill. About 300 people were sheltering in the basement, some of whom had got off a tram and crammed in at the height of the raid. At 1.55 a.m. the school was hit by a parachute mine. The three-storey building collapsed into the shelter below, crushing many of the occupants and burying others. Boiling water from the central-heating system and gas from a fractured main poured in, and the fires raging all around made the rescue work hazardous and difficult. Mrs Taft, an ARP warden who was in the shelter with her three-year-old grandchild, 'was magnificent in her courage and her common sense. Even as we heard groans from the dying, some of them children, she never cracked up. None of us thought we would ever get out alive, but Mrs Taft kept cheering everyone up. When people said, "We'll never get through," she just replied, "They'll get us out all right." . . . The mass of people made it almost impossible to move about. The roof came through under the enormous weight of the debris and the best we could say was that we believed the victim's end was instantaneous. The horror of it all did not rob people of their courage. None of the women screamed. Nobody fainted . . . We tried to scramble for the exits. Mrs Taft said, "Keep calm and try the emergency exits." They were jammed too. We all thought we were lost. Then to add to our troubles, a fire started somewhere in the main section. I could see it over the brickwork . . . smoke poured into our part and people nearly choked with fumes. Water from the burst boiler and the broken water main slowly flooded the floor of the shelter. It rose to our knees. We didn't know where it was coming from or when it would stop . . . Then Mrs Taft shouted, "I can see a light." She had found a small window leading out of the shelter that had not been blocked by the terrific amount of debris and she shouted for volunteers to dig a way through. Four men came forward. They flashed a torch and someone outside saw it. Rescue work began.'

Joe Lucas was one of a family of six children who lived in Chantry Street near the school. He had been suffering from whooping cough and other shelterers complained that his cough kept them awake, so on the night of 28 November Joe's mother decided that she would keep him and his baby sister Brenda at home with her, but she sent the other four children to shelter in Durning Street in the charge of the oldest, Florence, aged seventeen. All four children were killed that night: Florence, George aged eleven, Francis aged nine, and Winifred, aged seven. 'The trauma of that night was so terrible that for six months my mother couldn't speak. She never spoke a word. Brenda was only a babe in arms, but for a long time Mam wouldn't let us more than an arm's length away from her.'

A total of 164 men, women and children were killed and many more were seriously injured. 'Almost everyone in the neighbourhood knew someone who'd lost someone that night,' Marion Browne remembered. 'When I went to school the teacher kept saying "So and so won't be coming to school anymore".'

Portsmouth, Southampton and Bristol were among the ports that suffered repeated attacks in the final months of 1940. Bristol suffered its heaviest attack to date in November. With a large docks complex at Avonmouth, and its engineering works including a number of aircraft-manufacturing centres, notably the Bristol Aeroplane Company at Filton on the outskirts of the city, it was another natural target. Bristol had been considered sufficiently far west to be a safe city, a reception area for thousands of evacuees and a suitable wartime home for the BBC's main studio centre. This optimism had already been shaken when Filton suffered considerable damage and casualties in raids in late August and September. On 24 November the siren went at 6.22 p.m., but as it was the 338th alert that the city had suffered, no one seemed particularly anxious on that cold, foggy November Sunday.

The first of five major raids on the city lasted for six hours, and though the damage to the docks and factories was relatively limited, the shopping centre was very badly damaged and fires were in danger of conflating in the area: there were more than seventy large fires each needing a minimum of five pumps to fight it, so that meant at least 350 pumps. But Bristol only had 224 appliances available, and the Fire Brigade was nearly eighty men short. So the city burned and 200 people died, including eight firemen, twenty-two ARP wardens, two ARP messenger boys and two ambulance drivers. St Peter's Hospital, among the finest remaining Tudor mansions in the country, was damaged beyond repair, and the shopping centre round Wine Street and Castle Street and Broadmead was badly damaged. The Dutch House, one of Bristol's seventeenth-century architectural treasures, was hit, and was demolished by the Army two days after the raid. Only the top floors had been badly damaged and the building could probably have been restored had people had time and energy to think about organising a conservation protest in the midst of the bombing.

With Luftwaffe attention mainly directed elsewhere, it was not until 8 December that London suffered its worst raid for two months, when over 400 aircraft delivered a total of 380 tons of high explosives and 115,000 fire bombs. The extensive damage was a reprise of the attacks on the Surrey Commercial Docks on the first night of the Blitz. Offices of the Port of London Authority were hit, as were many factories involved in war production, shops, houses and blocks of flats. The capital was seared that night in an arc that stretched from Shoreditch to Wanstead in the east, and to Marylebone in the West End, and bombs also encircled London from Croydon in Surrey, via Slough to the west and Dagenham and Woodford to the east. The raid caused more than 1,700 fires and killed some 250 people, with more than 600 seriously wounded. A bomb fell in front of the BBC's Broadcasting House in Portland Place but, though the noise of the blast could be heard by listeners at home, transmissions were not interrupted.

After this raid, Londoners had some respite – not so the north of England. Sheffield, one of the world's great arsenals ever since Henry Bessemer had invented the process that revolutionised steel-making in the 1850s, had been expecting a raid since the attacks on industrial centres started. Appropriately, Operation Crucible was the code name assigned to the Luftwaffe attack. It came on 12 December, when for nine hours high-explosive bombs and incendiaries cascaded down, causing a great deal of damage to the city centre where many shops burned unchecked since there were not enough fire-watchers at the time to keep them safe. That night Marples Hotel, which stood on the corner of the High Street and Fitzalan Square, 'got a direct hit' – its seven floors of offices, concert halls, orchestra dais and heavy furniture came crashing down on the cellars where seventy people were buried in the ruins. Although the search for survivors went on for twelve days, only seven people were got out alive and only fourteen bodies could be properly identified. Three nights later the bombers came back: thousands of incendiaries caused widespread fires, and bombs hit factories and railway lines, blocking the line to York; there were nearly 400 UXBs scattered over the city, and that night 6,000 Sheffield residents were made homeless. Many bombs probably intended for Sheffield were wide of their target, falling instead on Leeds, Barnsley and Batley. Although many of Sheffield's factories were hit in the raids, most of the machinery remained undamaged and production was not affected for long, but over 1,200 business premises were damaged with the result that jobs were lost and thousands suffered the additional hardship of unemployment. The casualties were also tragically high in Sheffield: in the two nights of aerial bombardment more than 750 civilians were listed as dead or missing and around 500 were seriously injured. Geoffrey Hill, a fifteen-year-old Sheffield boy, recalled that it was not until the morning after the raid that 'we realised how bad it was. On street corners there were stretchers with bodies on them covered in tarpaulin waiting to be moved . . . For weeks water wagons had to supply people [and there were] no toilets or electricity.'

Merseyside was hit again, three weeks after the attacks in late November. On 20 December the docks were set ablaze by another heavy raid, and warehouses and timber yards ignited – the Dock Board, the Cunard Building, the Central Police Station and the town hall all burned, and the Adelphi Hotel was badly damaged. As the lights went out in the restaurant, the hotel orchestra struck up with 'There'll Always Be an England' and the diners joined in. A bomb struck a railway viaduct in Bentinck Street where people were sheltering under the arches below, killing forty-two. The concrete blocks were too heavy to move at first, and it was several days before those trapped in the debris could be brought to safety and the dead bodies removed. The next night, the raid was even heavier and several of the docks blazed; St John's Fish Market, packed with Christmas poultry, burned; St George's Hall was threatened by incendiaries and the great organ only narrowly escaped the flames; the Law Library burned down. The Liverpool to Leeds canal was breached, the railway goods station at Canada Dock was flooded and Liverpool's parish church, St Nicholas, Pier Head, was completely gutted. Seventy-four civilians were killed when a public shelter in Anfield received a direct hit, and the death toll for the two nights was over 700.

Manchester, one of Britain's largest cities and another important industrial centre now in the front line of war matériel production, suffered what had become the pattern: a double raid on successive nights – 22 and 23 December 1940. Flares and incendiaries were dropped to mark the target zone and the German pilots were further helped by the illumination from the fires still burning in Liverpool after the previous night's raid. There were widespread attacks on factories and commercial premises, and soon thousands of incendiary bombs had started upwards of 400 fires in the city centre and at Stretford. The main roads in the city – Deansgate, Oxford Road and others – were blocked by bombs and debris. The lack of fire-watchers in commercial and business areas affected Manchester badly, and a large number of the city's 3,500 full- and part-time firemen had been called to Liverpool to help fight the fires there. By morning one side of Piccadilly 'stood like the ruins of Ypres', the evocative image of First World War devastation.

All those provincial cities and towns that suffered such ruination did so in a way that was different from London's experience. They did not have the long-drawn-out continuity of attack that the capital had endured for three months, nor was the sum of the total damage comparable to that of London; but the concentration of attack on much smaller areas brought a particular intensity of destruction and misery. 'There was no question of the attack moving from one part of the target to another, some distance away as the night wore on. Every moment the onslaught bore down on the centre of the city and its environs . . . such a concentration of missiles means that most of the inhabitants heard, or felt, the fall of every bomb . . . there is something fearfully exposed, naked and unbefriended about a city of limited size under heavy attack . . .' 'It was possible to stand at certain points in or near their centre, and hardly know where one was. Not only did the raw wounds gape and the smoke curl weirdly among endless arcades of twisted steel, but the very contours of the city had been battered out of recognition.'

*

There were no raids anywhere over Christmas – 'on the Führer's orders', wrote Field Marshall Erhard Milch, who was in charge of the day-to-day operations of the Luftwaffe. But for London, the lull was brief: following a short, sharp attack on the capital on 27 December, which left 600 dead and wounded, over fifty of them in a public shelter in Southwark that received a direct hit, the City of London was the target of a massive raid on 29 December. Within half an hour Luftwaffe pilots claimed they could already count fifty-four major fires from the air. In just three hours 120 tons of high explosives and 22,000 incendiaries were dropped on the City.

The Thames was abnormally low that night, down to the bed of the river, and firemen found it impossible to get their suction pipes through the mud and into the water. Within a short time, bombs had fractured water mains, and soon the hydrants that drew on the river to feed the firemen's pumps ran dry. As buildings crashed to the ground and rubble blocked access for the Civil Defence services, the City seemed doomed, its heritage destroyed as it had been in the Great Fire of 1666. Eight Wren churches were destroyed including the 'wedding cake' church of St Bride's in Fleet Street (no Wren church was to escape damage during the Blitz), of which all that was left were the four walls and the steeple of the 'madrigal in stone'. The fifteenth-century Guildhall was set on fire by the burning embers from the church of St Lawrence Jewry next door and seriously damaged. A bomb landed near the Monument, designed by Wren to commemorate the Great Fire.

It was in those old brick-and-timber buildings that fires could take hold with such ease; the newer city office blocks with their steel and concrete structures might despoil the cityscape in the eyes of many, but they did not burn easily and they survived the blast of high explosives better.

Fires burned around St Paul's Cathedral, and to those who watched from other parts of London it seemed impossible that the capital's most famous landmark would not be consumed by the flames. St Paul's had become a symbol to Londoners of their capital's defiant resistance to the Nazi attackers – even though, as the Dean recognised, many were not quite sure what the building was and were apt to point it out as the Old Bailey. In April 1939 the Chapter of St Paul's (the Dean and his canons) had formed a watch, to protect their cathedral from the bombs they felt certain would fall. They were right: on 12 September a 2,200lb bomb had fallen close by and had to be removed in a perilous operation by the bomb-disposal squad, and taken through the streets of London – which had been cleared of traffic and people – to Hackney Marshes, the 'bomb cemetery' in east London where the 8-foot-long missile was exploded in controlled conditions. If a fire got hold in the timbers between the cathedral's inner and outer dome it would spread undetected until the brick cone collapsed, and burning timbers and molten lead would cascade down on to the nave and choir far below.

The Dean, Walter Matthews, and the Cathedral Surveyor, Godfrey Allen, had arranged for the installation of water tanks and rising mains, and some of the cathedral staff were trained in fire-fighting. The Dean had also decided that he needed men who understood the structure of the cathedral, and he approached the Royal Institute of British Architects for volunteers. He collected an illustrious crew who donned blue uniforms and steel helmets and learned how to haul hoses, tie knots and operate hydrants, and familiarised themselves with the labyrinthine layout of St Paul's.

The watch's greatest test came this night of 29 December. After a fire in the library aisle had been put out the water mains dried up. All that was left were sandbags, buckets and stirrup pumps. Soon after 6.30 p.m. came what everyone had feared: an incendiary pierced the lead and lodged in the timbers of the dome. Burning lead was already dripping on to the crossing below: any minute the Grinling Gibbon carved choir stalls and organ screen might catch fire. The red glow could be seen from Fleet Street, and the US commentator Ed Murrow broadcast the cathedral's obituary: 'The church that means most to London is gone. St Paul's Cathedral, built by Sir Christopher Wren, her great dome towering above the capital of the Empire, is burning to the ground as I talk to you now.' But it was a premature death knell. 'I build for eternity,' Wren had said, and inside the cathedral two teams from the watch crawled gingerly along the wooden beams high above the nave with stirrup pumps to try to extinguish the incendiary. Those who took 'the dome patrol' were 'selected from amongst those with a head for heights and with a leaning towards acrobatics', according to the Dean, 'for they were expected, if necessary, to walk along the slender beams of the Dome to reach their bombs, or to thrust the nozzles of their stirrup pumps into the heart of an incipient fire. The dome was not a healthy place in the height of a Blitz and the patrol was changed at half-hourly intervals.' Suddenly, having burnt its way through the wood, the bomb crashed on to the floor below and 'was easily put out!'.

Few other City buildings were as vigilantly guarded as St Paul's. So many were empty and unattended that Sunday night that fires could swiftly get a hold on the ancient bricks and timber in the close-packed streets and alleyways. The GPO's Central Telegraph Exchange in St Martin's-le-Grand received a direct hit and burned 'without a bucket of water to put it out'; three City telephone exchanges housed nearby were burnt out, inflicting the worst blow of the war on the telecommunications network throughout the capital. Across the Thames from Bankside the city looked like a seamless sheet of flame: a warehouse storing Brasso polish was 'like a blast furnace'; a paint warehouse was ablaze; and fires burned out of control in the wharves that ran between Queen Victoria Street and Upper Thames Street. By now the mains were dry and every fire station in central London was 'down to bare poles' – emptied of everything except the pole the firemen slid down to get to their vehicle.

It was clear that fire brigades could not cope with the carpet of incendiary bombs that fell nightly without more help from the community. As was so often the case as the war progressed, the voluntary nature of service was replaced by compulsion, since 'Some of you lately, in more cities than one, have failed your country,' Herbert Morrison chided on New Year's Eve 1940. 'This must never happen again . . . every group of houses and business premises must have its fire party. Fall in Fire Bomb Fighters!' This 'watcher on the roof of every building' would be a volunteer where possible, but if these did not come forward in sufficient numbers, the local authority could enrol street fire-watching parties and compel participation, and fire-watching patrols were made mandatory for all business premises. Men between sixteen and sixty were required to train for fire-watching duties and put in forty-eight hours each month on the roof tops. But as the population of London was now around 75 per cent of what it had been before the war – the same was true of most other inner cities – and many of those left were already volunteer members of the ARP and other Civil Defence services, this left a small pool from which to draw. Those who had been working all day might well be prepared to do a stint of fire-watching, but understandably preferred to do it nearer home rather than travel to protect their workplace.

Though the press acclaimed this fire-watching initiative, it was strongly criticised by the trade unions, who had not been consulted and who objected to workers having to protect their employers' premises at considerable risk and without remuneration – in effect unpaid, compulsory overtime – and large numbers of workers all over the country refused to comply. It was estimated that nationwide around 60 per cent of those required to do fire-watching claimed exemption; in Norwich, out of 25,000 men required to register, 24,750 claimed exemption, 80 per cent on the grounds that they were already doing fire-watching.

Conscientious Objectors were not automatically exempt from fire-watching duties and numerous prosecutions were brought – including one of a CO employer who refused to make fire-watching arrangements for his own Newcastle-upon-Tyne premises. Ironically, a number of COs who had been acting as voluntary fire-watchers now, in the face of compulsion, refused to carry on doing so. On 19 September 1942, the compulsory principle was extended to cover women for the first time. Those who were pregnant or had children under fourteen living with them were exempt, but all other women aged between twenty and forty-five were required to take turns at fire-watching at work, and local authorities were instructed to register women within the eligible category who were not fire-watching at work, so they could be called on for local duties.

Fires were still burning fiercely as dawn broke on the morning after the 29 December raid on the city of London, and the smoke hung in palls, visible for miles, for several days. As commuters started to arrive for work it was to a scene of utter desolation: Guy's Hospital, next to London Bridge station, had had to be evacuated, and commuters had to negotiate bomb craters, broken glass and rubble strewn all over the pavement, and pass smoke-grimed and exhausted firemen still at work trying to put out the fires – to find that their place of work was now nothing but a pile of rubble.

As she came out of the station, Dorothy Barton 'looked at Wren's masterpiece. I felt a lump in my throat because, like so many people, I felt that while St Paul's survived, so would we.' The whole of Cannon Street east of Bread Street had burned to the ground. But when the smoke cleared, Londoners had a better view of St Paul's than even Wren himself had had. Fire and bombs had laid waste so many buildings that night that a person standing in Cannon Street could see the whole east end and south transept, the dome and the south baroque tower of the cathedral – only the tower of St Augustine's Old Change, left standing, interrupted the vista.

As she crossed London Bridge, Dorothy Barton saw 'a group of exhausted firemen, with smoke-blackened faces and clothes [who] were rolling up their hoses after battling with fires all night. Quite spontaneously, the office workers burst into a cheer and several shook hands with the firemen as they passed. I was in tears as I walked along, it was such an emotional moment. I don't think that anyone should ever forget that firemen were heroes during the entire war, especially during the Blitz.'

When she reached her office building, Barton 'found it was the only one still standing, comparatively undamaged in a street blocked with rubble . . . Suddenly a policeman rushed in and said "Everybody out, there's an unexploded bomb in the backyard". Pausing only to grab my handbag and the ledgers I was responsible for, I made my way to the end of the street again, where all the staff had gathered with various bits of office equipment in their arms. After a while, someone in another firm nearby offered us space in their building, so we made our way there.

'It was a bitterly cold day, with a smattering of snow on the ground, and there was no gas, water or electricity in the City, which meant no heating and no cups of tea. We worked in our temporary office with all our outdoor clothes on, and it was obvious that unless we found hot food and drink fairly soon, we should all have to return home, so Jean (our other typist) and I took an early lunch break and went to see what we could find. We had both worked in the area for some time and thought we knew our way about, but after a few minutes of detouring around blocked off streets we were completely lost without familiar buildings to guide us.

'Suddenly we fancied we could smell something cooking, so walking along sniffing like a couple of Bisto kids, we followed the tantalising smell until it led us to a small restaurant, minus all doors and windows, where the enterprising owner was cooking sausages and mash over bottled gas stoves. We joined the all male queue and . . . were handed a plate of two sausages, a pile of mashed potatoes, and huge mug of hot strong tea for very little money.

'We were looking round for seats when a voice said from behind the counter, "Upstairs please, ladies, it's quite safe, we've checked it", and then I noticed a sign on the wall in gold letters which read "Ladies' dining-room" . . . pointing up the stairs. Jean and I took our food upstairs and ate it in solitary splendour, looking out of non-existent windows over an almost non-existent City, and giggled at the absurdity of not being allowed to eat with the men.'

In the biting cold wind John Pope-Hennessy, the art critic, who was writing a book *History Under Fire* for which Cecil Beaton was taking the photographs, 'ran about the glowing, smouldering mounds of rubble where once were the printer's shops and chop houses of Paternoster Row. We have trundled under perilous walls, over uncertain ground which, at any moment might give way to the red-hot vaults below . . . We could not deny a certain ghoulish excitement stimulated us, and our anger and sorrow were mixed with a strange thrill at seeing such lively destruction – for this desolation is full of vitality. The heavy walls crumble and fall in the most romantic Piranesi forms. It is only when the rubble is cleared up, and the mess is put in order, that the effect becomes dead.' The aesthetes 'went to St Paul's to offer our prayers for its miraculous preservation'.

Over 160 people had died in the raid, and 500 were injured. A bulging wall crashed down on some firemen fighting the blaze near Fleet Street – 'all we could see was a heap of debris with a hose leading to it', wrote an observer at the scene at which eight of the sixteen firemen who perished that night were killed: a further 250 were badly injured, most of them with severe burns.

The Luftwaffe had failed to gain mastery of the skies above Britain, and though its losses since September had been relatively light, and most of these had occurred at take-off or landing or over occupied France rather than because aircraft were shot down by British defences, it was by no means clear that the British war economy was on its knees nor was there any evidence that the morale of its people had been broken. Indeed, the Führer admitted that 'the least effect of all [operations against England to date] has been made on the morale and will to resist of the English people' and 'no decisive action can be expected from terror attacks on residential areas'. But that did not mean that the Blitz was over.

Battle Camp: Crawling in Wales by Miles Chace, a Lieutenant in the Royal Artillery, depicts the ludicrous side of military training as soldiers wriggle past a farmer's wife feeding her chickens.

A moment frozen in the busy responsibilities of Sir Ernest Gowers and other senior officers in the London Regional Civil Defence Control Room, painted in ultra realist style by Meredith Frampton in 1943.

Capturing the civilian's war. Evelyn Dunbar's painting *A Canning Demonstration* is a wry comment on the contribution women were expected to make to the war effort. Under the auspices of the War Artists Advisory Committee (WAAC), Dunbar depicted a range of their activities including making camouflage nets and queuing.

Coupons Required 1941 by Leonora Green. This was the year when Britons were in greatest danger of going hungry and having an inadequate diet. So what looks here like a day's feast is in fact a week's allowance.

Dinner/Vitamins Enlisted to Win the War, by Hugo Dachinger, a Jew who had fled from Vienna and was interned in Huyton camp. Newspapers were forbidden at first but Dachinger persuaded the guards to give him discarded pages, and it was these he used as his 'canvas'.

A Crashed Aeroplane, Devon by C. J. Pearce. Such scenes were replicated all over southern England during the Battle of Britain in 1940, and as firemen rushed to extinguish the flames and rescue any survivors, so did souvenir hunters and those anxious to mete out rough justice to any Luftwaffe survivors.

A Balloon Site, Coventry by Dame Laura Knight. A painter of the circus and ballet in peacetime, Knight considered this and her other painting of women involved with barrage balloons, *In for Repairs*, among her best wartime work.

The Bells Go Down by John Piper, 1942. A neo-romantic painter, Piper continued his fascination with ruined buildings by chronicling the 'instant ruins' of the Blitz as an official war artist.

'...and, on the approach of the unauthorised persons, to call them to 'alt with the words...' Punch's view of the continuing responsibility of the stalwart Home Guard still on guard to repel an invasion in the summer of 1942.

Medical Inspection by Rodrigo Moynihan. A private soldier who was invalided out of the Army after a nervous breakdown, Moynihan revisited his military experiences in this painting for the WAAC in 1943.

Land Army Girls Going to Bed by Evelyn Dunbar. At first Land Girls tended to live on the farms on which they worked, but complaints about primitive conditions and loneliness meant that increasingly premises were requisitioned as hostels for them: by January 1944 there were 696, housing over 22,000 Land Girls.

Utility fashion, June 1943. Three women model Utility dresses designed for the manufacturer Berketex by Norman Hartnell. Hats were not utility standard, nor were coupons required for them.

'Purely from a publicity point of view, the necessity for camouflage suits us very well.'
Every cloud has a silver lining, or profiting from regulations. *Punch*'s take on wartime opportunism, October 1943.

VE Street Party, 1945 by Edwin La Dell. Bunting was 'off ration' and every household would contribute something from hoarded rations – or even pre-war delicacies – to ensure a splendid spread to celebrate the coming of peace at last.

14

'WE WERE
UNDERGROUND PEOPLE'

"In any case you're well over the white line."

*The bodies had become part of the debris; they had become one constituent
of the many constituents of the mound. They had been crushed and pressed
into the decomposed raw material of the five houses. Like the clay of the
London sub soil, their clay, now quiet, had lost its individual existence and
become indissolubly a part of its environment.*
JOHN STRACHEY, *NEW STATESMAN AND NATION*, 9 NOVEMBER 1940

THE BLITZ HAD brought death and destruction to Britain. It had also
brought exhaustion. 'Good Yawning everybody' ran the headline
on Hannen Swaffer's column in the *Daily Herald*. In London, and other
towns and cities where raids were frequent, lives fell into a dreary routine
of disrupted utility services and transport, shortages of all kinds – and
disturbed sleep.

'Am sitting in pyjamas, dressing gown and coat, sipping cup of tea,

one ear waiting for the 8 o'clock sirens that blow nightly without fail,'
wrote the journalist Mea Allan, who also worked for the left-of-centre
Daily Herald and was living with friends in north London after she had
been bombed out of her flat off the Strand. 'One does one's day's
work, with no time for lunch, one gets to one's abode, gulps down
something solid, has a bath and changes into night attire, has handy gas
mask, quilts, cushions, chewing-gum and other shelter comforts – and
then when the hell's symphony breaks loose legs it for safety.'

Gwendolen Watts (later Stewart) had left Birmingham for London
with her mother and sister, and they returned not long after the Blitz
started: 'But by this time we'd got used to the bombing, it was just a way
of life. I'd leave the office, catch the tram home – all . . . the windows
were blacked out. Straight into the house. My mother would have tea
ready, we'd eat our tea, we'd get partly undressed and go down into the
shelter. My father had dug a huge crater in the garden and put the
Anderson shelter in right down deep and covered it with earth so it was
right underground . . . He had put steps there that went round and
round so that if there was a bomb blast it would stop it coming straight
into the entrance. He'd painted the inside of the shelter white and he'd
got butterflies painted on the walls. He had a little stove down there, it
was a real little home from home. He'd built bunk beds on each side for
us because he was always out fire-watching. As soon as we'd had our
meal we'd go down there with our books and knitting, whatever we
were doing.

'So that became my life: home from work, have a meal, down the
shelter, sleep all the way through, of course you'd be wakened if there
were bombs falling. But on nights when there weren't any bombs we
would still sleep in the shelter to have unbroken sleep instead of getting
up and coming down.

'When Dad was out fire-watching he'd come home every half hour or
so to see that we were all right . . . The next morning you'd come out of
your shelter and there would be incendiaries everywhere. The factory at
the end of the street was still burning. And you'd have to pick your way
through the hosepipes and the rubble. The trams weren't running but
you had to get to work in the morning no matter what had happened in
the night. My job was right across town and I had to walk through
Birmingham city centre as best I could – me and everyone else – going

round craters, stepping over hosepipes. Chaos everywhere, the smell of burning, broken glass, picking my way through. And even if you arrived at the office at 11 o'clock they were still pleased to see you because everyone was making the same effort.'

Where to go in an air raid had dominated everyone's thoughts. Those who had basements or cellars in their houses or blocks of flats were often able to make these reasonably comfortable with improvised bunks, or deckchairs draped with cushions and rugs, and could often arrange some form of rudimentary lighting, heating and at least the facility to boil a kettle so they could make tea during a raid – which invariably lasted into the early hours of the morning. For those with Anderson shelters, the persistent problem was damp. The shelters often flooded after a rainstorm, and it was unwise to leave bedding there. They were usually sited at the end of the garden so when the alert went families had a trek through a dark and often muddy garden carrying supplies for the night. 'There'll be more deaths from pleurisy than bombs,' predicted a middle-aged woman.

The first shelters issued had skimped on space to save money. They were too small to accommodate bunks and the night was spent crouching on the floor or on an upturned box. Most had no light other than a flickering candle in an upturned flower pot (which was what was recommended) or a torch, by which to read, sew or knit. Heating was a problem too: oil and paraffin heaters were not recommended since if knocked over – which was fairly likely – they could start a fire, and in a confined space such appliances used up oxygen; while electricity could short-circuit in the damp. And far from shutting out the terrifying din of explosives and falling masonry, the metal Anderson shelters magnified the noise so that incendiaries falling sounded like the rattle of coal scuttles being emptied. In a survey of what people wanted from their shelters, soundproofing came first, followed by sociability (Anderson shelters didn't usually offer that – more cooped-up family tensions), and only a third came 'bomb proof'. In Poplar, east London, Charles Key, the local Labour MP, who so impressed Herbert Morrison that he made him Special Commissioner for Shelters in 1941, recognised the problem and his borough issued 140,000 pairs of earplugs free to its citizens.

Exhaustion, stress, a certain fatalism and the inconvenience of this subterranean life meant that more and more householders decided not go to their shelters when the siren wailed but waited until the unmistakable sounds of a raid could be heard overhead, and increasingly not always then. In the first air-raid-shelter survey published in November 1940, after nearly three months of bombing, it was estimated that only 27 per cent of the 3.25 million people who lived in the district covered by the London County Council (LCC) were using their domestic shelters.

If a family had no Anderson or cellar, all they could do in a raid was crouch in an understairs cupboard if they had one, or under a table pushed against the wall, both of which might offer some slight protection from falling masonry and wood, broken glass and shrapnel. Or they could go to a public shelter. These might be in the town hall, railway station, or a requisitioned building – offices, shops, cellars or vaults – and since the Air Raid Precautions Act of 1938 the strengthening of such premises attracted a government grant. Reinforced trenches in parks and public open spaces, and brick-built public surface shelters, had been intended for people caught out in a raid and unable to get home, and it had been envisaged that they would need to be used for only short periods. Department stores often made their basements available to customers in the case of a raid – Dickins and Jones was generally considered the best. 'What a lot of time is wasted nowadays – an hour here, or an hour there, sitting in some blooming shelter,' complained the American Margaret Cotton, living with her family in St John's Wood in north London, who had had a foretaste of shelter life during a daytime alert just before the Blitz proper started. She had been buying some furnishing fabric in John Lewis in Oxford Street when 'the Banshee Howl drove me, along with everyone else into the basement. Such an extensive layout of rooms and corridors, a regular maze of them – like the catacombs! . . . There, in the shelter below Oxford Street, were hundreds of people, mostly women shoppers, crowded on wooden benches set back to back in close rows filling the basement rooms. I found a place among them and settled down to read. Almost everyone carries a book nowadays as well as a gas mask. Certain of the store staff, men and women, wearing arm bands reading "Head of Personnel", "Shelter Warden" or "First Aid". Salesgirls circulated through the rooms selling sweets, biscuits, soft drinks, small sixpenny books, embroidery patterns and silks, and even offering free wool in navy, khaki and Air

Force blue complete with needles and directions. "Won't you please knit for the Forces at John Lewis' expense?" Music was furnished by a gramophone and every so often, an attendant sprayed the air with disinfectant. An hour and a half spent thus is not too bad. But still it is an aggravation and a waste of time.'

'Communal domestic shelters' had been erected as protection for those who had none for their personal use. These usually stood in the centre of a street, and were designed to serve groups of houses or blocks of flats nearby. Again in the anticipation of short, sharp raids – three or four hours maximum had been predicted before the war – and in line with the general government policy of dispersing people to reduce the risk of large numbers being killed as they sheltered in the same place, these communal shelters proved entirely inadequate for the ten- or twelve-hour assault that could be the reality of the Blitz. They invariably had poor ventilation, no lighting and minimal seating – if any: 'rheumaticky old ladies had to sit upright on their benches for six to twelve hours on end, with their feet propped up on a couple of bricks', recalled Finsbury ARP warden Barbara Nixon. There was no sanitation other than maybe a bucket, and no facilities for making cups of tea or providing food. Most shelters soon became damp, fetid, litter-strewn, vermin-infested health hazards, avoided by many. But others found some comfort in the public shelters: the press of bodies, the illusion of safety in numbers.

The desire not to be alone, to be somewhere with familiar faces particularly during night raids, drew people to places they knew, yet which were in fact no safer than their own homes. 'The public showed a strong tendency to be irrational in their choice of shelters,' a government report concluded sadly. The vicar of Haggerston in east London frequently pointed out that his reinforced-concrete church hall had been refused designation as an official air-raid shelter when war broke out, since no part of the building was below ground. But when the parishioners of his church, St Augustine's, in Shoreditch, a borough in which 'the supply of shelters is not superabundant', asked 'if they might be allowed to sleep in it by night, and take cover in it by day' he 'did not feel able to say nay' but stuck up notices 'both within and without the building' warning 'THIS IS NOT AN AIR-RAID SHELTER. They who use it as such do so at their own risk.'

No shelter could promise safety in the event of a direct hit (as the tragedies at underground stations and basement shelters demonstrated) but the fragility of some surface shelters made them little more than talismanic. The ongoing disputes between government and local authorities about which would pay for Civil Defence provision meant that several authorities seized any opportunity to fulfil the obligations placed on them as cheaply as possible. Thus several were reputed to have 'misread' a government circular and built brick shelters in their boroughs using no cement in the mortar; others employed cowboy builders who used mainly sand, but, whatever the facts, such shelters – well over 5,000 in London alone – were in danger of collapse. Surface shelters 'soon became known to us as "Morrison sandwiches" [so named after Herbert Morrison, the Home Secretary]. They were topped with a slab of reinforced concrete about 9 inches thick, which was . . . unkeyed by any reinforcing to the walls . . . in the actual Blitz, too often the blast of a bomb would suck the walls outwards and the concrete top would sandwich the occupants to the ground.' 'They are no damn use at all,' one man told a Mass-Observer, 'a breath of wind would knock them over,' while another admitted, 'I don't trust them. They wouldn't stand up to an air gun.' And there were those who declined to use surface shelters because they thought that from thousands of feet up the bombers could recognise the distinctive squat brick structures for what they were, and make them a target.

The most notorious shelter in London was in Stepney. The Tilbury shelter was a vast 300-foot-long warehouse 'half full of margarine and other merchandise' on Commercial Road. The journalist Ritchie Calder regarded it as 'definitely unsafe' and on those 'dreadful nights that hell was let loose on East London', the Tilbury shelter was home to as many as 16,000 people – the Commissioner for Civil Defence for London reckoned it was more like 8,000 when he visited, but it must have been very hard to tell, and Calder had an agenda to shame the government into action.

A Mass-Observer was equally appalled. 'Over everything is sprawled a vast mass of human beings and their bedding. The dirt and stench is indescribable. The place is used by horses in the day time, and it is apparently nobody's job to clear away the horse dung before nightfall. The bedding is just spread over it. To the odour of horses is added that of thousands of unwashed humans. (It is to be hoped that margarine is not retentive of odours of this kind.) . . . The place was crowded with all creeds, colours and races of people. Hardly any floor space was not covered by bedding or deck chairs, and people were already beginning to overflow on to the margarine and the carts and trucks. In the dim light men were reading newspapers and Penguins, rabbis were reading their sacred books, dog-collared clergymen sat cheek by jowl with unkempt Jews, mothers were pouring tea, some were already trying to sleep, others were heatedly arguing about the possession of a few feet of dung-strewn floor.' A sixteen-year-old girl observed that 'everyone there was working class. The shelter is near the dock area . . . mostly cockneys, but also many Jews and Indians. On the whole, the Jews lay on the right-hand side, the cockneys in the middle and the Indians on the left. Race feeling very marked . . . in fact presence of considerable coloured element responsible for drawing cockney and Jew together, in unity against Indian . . .'

'People should not have had to put up with those conditions in addition to the hell of bombing,' reported Nina Hibbin for Mass-Observation. It was not even safe. Should the Tilbury shelter receive a direct hit, the M-O report concluded, 'the resulting stampede would kill ten times as many people as the bomb'.

In Bristol an old railway tunnel that ran from the port was used by 'men, women and children huddled together sleeping on mattresses, planks or straw. Some had corrugated iron sheets or pieces of sacking and canvas placed overhead to catch the water that dripped from the rocky roof of the tunnel. The air was thick with fumes of oil stoves, oil lamps and various odours of cooking food . . . When the corporation employees opened the doors in the mornings the stench and fumes came from within like a fog. It was a picture of Dante's Inferno. Many of the people were nervous wrecks. People stayed in the tunnel by day, afraid to lose their places. There was hardly any room between the rough beds. Some performed their natural functions alongside the beds. It was unbelievable that people could be driven by fear to endure such conditions.'

People felt safer underground in vaults, cellars or crypts. The crypt of the Rev. John Markham's church, St Peter's in south London, was officially allowed to shelter 230 but usually housed more than double that number. The rector went down there as little as possible during raids and when he did, 'I had to tread delicately between the bodies of the shelterers, lying like sardines on a variety of beds, mattresses, blankets or old carpets which they brought down with them. Some sat on deck chairs, some lay on the narrow wooden benches provided by the borough. The stench from the overflowing Elsan closets and unwashed humanity was so great that we had to buy gallons of Pine Fluid . . . The shelter wardens had a whip round among their flock to buy electric fans, which did stir the foetid air a trifle, giving an illusion of freshness. I suppose you can get used to those sorts of conditions if you stay in them for 12 hours night after night. At least one family stayed there almost 24 hours, rather than go home and risk losing their place. Places were as precious, to the regulars, as seats in some theatres, so that queues formed outside hours before the sirens wailed, and I had to provide wardens to regulate the flow of would-be shelterers, some of whom came from some distance, even by taxi.'

Where they were available, natural shelters were appropriated, for example the privately leased caves at Chislehurst. These had served as an ammunition store in the First World War – an adjunct of Woolwich Arsenal – and more recently had been used for cultivating mushrooms. The dry, sandy floors and natural, airy hollows that could be turned into private 'rooms' made them attractive places to shelter – though some were dangerously near the surface – and during the autumn of 1940 some 12,000 to 15,000 Londoners, many from the East End or south London, took specially laid-on trains out to Kent nightly and set up home in the caves.

At first conditions were primitive, with bare earth floors, candles or torches for light and a single cold-water tap and an oil drum containing creosote for sanitation. But soon electric lighting was installed; donkeys carted away ash bins that were used as lavatories; the local council provided beds; the Red Cross opened a medical centre that included an operating theatre and a canteen; and the children's ward of a local hospital was evacuated to the caves. There were regular film shows; a dance hall was constructed and a piano brought in – people would gather round for a sing-song. Shelterers had originally been charged a halfpenny to enter, but now forked out sixpence to help pay for the amenities, and 'captains' were appointed to oversee the shelterers and keep order. In November 1940 the caves were taken over by the local authority and designated as an official public shelter, though strenuous efforts were made to continue the 'self-help' initiatives of the early days.

Caves hollowed out of Dover cliffs were used for shelter too, with rows of bunks installed along the walls, and 'as there was no current of air, you can imagine what it was like when slept in night after night by those with no homes, and little facilities for washing. Rather like a rabbit hutch.'

Yet government air-raid provision policy generally ran counter to the instinct to burrow in the face of danger. This was partly for reasons of cost – an Anderson shelter for six people cost around £7 10s to manufacture, while the cost of producing bomb-proof deep communal shelters was reckoned to be around £12 to £15 per head. It was partly the fear of mass slaughter if a large number of people were concentrated in one place when a bomb fell. But it was also the apprehension of what was referred to as 'deep shelter mentality' whereby a mass of 'timorous troglodytes' would go underground and refuse to surface, thus bringing the economy of the capital to a grinding halt. A scheme proposed by the London borough of Finsbury to provide sufficient shelter for its entire population (though admittedly it was one of the smaller London boroughs) was the work of the avant-garde architect Berthold Lubetkin, and used the services of Ove Arup (who was famous for the concrete, spiral penguin pool at the London Zoo) as consulting engineer. The borough claimed that such a scheme would be cost-effective, since no other Civil Defence measures would be needed: the 59,000 people of Finsbury would be all together, way under the ground, when the bombs started to fall. But government experts were concerned about the concentration of so many people in one place, and particularly that thousands of people would converge on the shelter entrances within minutes of the alarm sounding, jostling to get down the spiral ramps, and the proposal was turned down.

A half-mile stretch of disused tunnel that ran below Borough High Street in south-east London was converted into an underground shelter for 8,000 people, but this was a tiny section of a huge complex of potential underground shelters in the city: the underground railway network – the tube. During the First World War, the London Electric Railway

Company had allowed over eighty of its stations to be used as air-raid shelters outside normal opening hours, and as many as 12,000 people would go underground at Finsbury Park and 9,000 at King's Cross. Special constables were employed to maintain order, and questions were asked in Parliament about insanitary conditions and the risk of disease, but in 1917 the Metropolitan Police concluded that in the main shelterers had been 'orderly and obedient'.

But despite this favourable precedent, in 1924 Sir John Anderson, in his capacity as Chairman of the Air-Raid Precautions sub-committee, effectively ruled out the use of underground stations and tunnels as air-raid shelters in any future conflict, giving as his reason the need for trains to run freely to get Londoners to work and disperse them away from the capital in the evening before raids started, and to evacuate casualties. This policy was maintained despite the fact that reports appeared in the press of an underground tunnel being prepared under Windsor Castle to shelter the royal family, and a catacomb of tunnels being dug out and strengthened under Whitehall for the safety of the government. The Communist Party led the campaign for better air-raid provision, including the opening up of the tubes. Its newspaper, the *Daily Worker*, claimed that 'the shelter policy of the government is not just a history of incompetence and neglect, it is a calculated class policy . . . [a] determination not to provide protection because profit is placed before human lives . . . the bankruptcy of the government's shelter policy is plain for all to see . . . safe in their own luxury shelters the ruling class must be forced to give way'.

Smart London hotels and restaurants also provided secure underground accommodation for their customers. At the Hungaria, illustrious diners bedded down on camp beds in the cellars during night raids, and, if they were not able to get home until morning, were served breakfast. The Dorchester, which was considered to be pretty bomb-inviolate anyway with its reinforced-concrete structure, turned its basement gymnasium into an air-raid dormitory. Lady Diana Cooper felt 'quite secure' . . . as she lay 'hugger mugger with all that was most distinguished in London society', watching 'monstrous profiles projected caricaturishly on the ceiling, magic-lantern style. Lord Halifax is unmistakable.' Writing to her son who had been evacuated to America, she wistfully admitted that, 'It's certainly more pally in the Underground where families go in about five p.m. with bedding, babies, buns, bottles and settle down to community singing, gossip, making new friends, exchanging bomb stories etc. I should rather like it, but can you imagine Papa's reaction if he had to join the party?'

The 'party' had not been easy to arrange. As bombs fell intermittently on London in the summer of 1940 notices were displayed at tube stations directing travellers to go to the nearest surface shelter in case of a raid, and staff refused entry to those they did not consider to be bona fide travellers. But on 'Black Saturday', 7 September 1940, some East Enders defied the ban. Bernard Kops, who had been evacuated but returned to London just before the Blitz started, was among those 'thousands upon thousands . . . that pushed their way into Liverpool Street Station, demanded to be let down to shelter. At first the authorities wouldn't agree to it and they called out the soldiers to bar the way. I stood there in the thick of the crowd with my mother and father and brothers and sisters thinking that there would be a panic and we would all be crushed to death . . . The people would not give up and would not disperse, would not take no for an answer. A great yell went up and the gates were opened . . . "It's a great victory for the working class," a man said. "One of our big victories." '

Within days the occupation had spread like wildfire: people either vaulted over the ticket barriers and swarmed down the escalators to seek shelter on the platforms below, or bought a penny ticket for a short journey and then refused to come up again. Although at the height of the Blitz only some 4 per cent of those living in central London were using the tubes for shelter, that still meant 177,000 people. At the beginning of October 1940, Herbert Morrison – an ex-Mayor of Hackney who, it was hoped, would be rather more in tune with Londoners in their darkest hours than the somewhat austere Sir John Anderson whom he had replaced as Home Secretary – bowed to the fact and acquiesced in allowing the use of the tubes for shelter 'insofar as it does not interfere with the transport of London's workers'. The government continued to insist, however, that the shelterers' presence was a concession, not a right. A government campaign suggested that it was unmanly to seek shelter underground and that such places should be left for women, children, the aged and the infirm. There were reports of police turning away young unattached men who sought shelter, though their need for safety and a good night's sleep was great too. 'I am just as much in the frontline as any soldier,' complained a twenty-nine-year-old single working man. '. . . it is really unreasonable to abuse chaps who are waiting to be called up.'

An account in the *South London Press* described the scene at the Elephant and Castle tube station on 1 October 1940: 'From the platforms to the entrance the whole station was one incumbent mass of humanity . . . it took me [the reporter] a quarter of an hour to get from the station entrance to the platform. Even in the darkened booking hall I stumbled over huddled bodies, bodies that were no safer from bombs than if they had lain in the gutters of the silent streets outside. Going down the stairs I saw mothers feeding infants at the breast. Little girls and boys lay across their parents' bodies because there was no room on the winding stairs. Hundreds of men and women were partially undressed, while small boys and girls slumbered in the foetid atmosphere absolutely naked. Electric lights blazed, but most of this mass of suffering humanity slept as though they were on silken sheets. On the platform, when a train came in, it had to be stopped in a tunnel while police and porters went along pushing in the feet and arms which overhung the line. The sleepers hardly stirred as the train rumbled slowly in. On the train I sat opposite a pilot on leave. He looked dumbly at the amazing platform. "It's the same all the way along," was all he said.'

'We were underground people,' recalled Bernard Kops. '. . . What sort of victory had we achieved? Every family for itself now . . . The soldiers forced us to get into trains, to go further up the line. Liverpool Street was the closest geographically and umbilically, was the most popular. So we were forced to move on and we tried the next station along the Central Line, and then the next and the next . . . I would scoot out of the train ahead of the family and under the legs of people . . . and I bagged any space I could along the platform. The family followed and we pitched our "tent", then we unravelled and unwound and relaxed. And out came the sandwiches and the forced good humour. Here we were back on the trot wandering again, involved in a new exodus – the Jews of the East End, who had left their homes and gone into the exile of the underground. Our spirits would rise for a while, we were alive for another night, we would see another dawn.'

With many shelters becoming night-time homes during the Blitz, something had to be done urgently to improve them. A committee was set up under Lord Horder, doctor to George VI, to examine shelter conditions both above and below ground. The members toured the East End shelters nightly and reported that what was needed to counteract the effects of 'gross overcrowding' was regular cleaning and inspection, and improved sanitary arrangements. First aid posts were needed, and shelter marshals should be appointed in the larger shelters. Local councils were authorised to spend money installing lighting, seating and wire-netting bunks in their surface shelters. But improvements were slow, and even by April 1941 many people were still having to stand or sit on the floor all night in public shelters. But by March 1941 bunks had been installed in most of the seventy-six tube stations that were used as air-raid shelters for nearly 23,000 shelterers.

By mid October 1940 chemical toilets had been installed in almost all London shelters, but these were easily knocked over – excrement overflowed and generally added to the stench. In spring 1941 local councils were authorised to provide waterborne sanitation in large shelters. No washing facilities were installed in either the underground or public shelters, and people – many of whom had to go to their jobs first thing in the morning – had to find public baths which took to opening early specially to offer such facilities, or trek home for a quick wash, shave and change of clothes.

At Churchill's suggestion, a short, superfluous branch line at Aldwych on the Piccadilly Line had been closed at the end of September and adapted as a shelter, and this was to provide a prototype for the adaptation of a further seventy-nine tube stations that autumn. The walls were whitewashed, the lighting improved, the track was boarded over and 200 three-tier bunks were installed, improved lavatory facilities replaced the original buckets, and a system of tickets was introduced to provide a bunk or reserved floor space for regular shelterers – many of whom trekked up from the East End. In recognition that this was likely to be a way of life for the long term in its borough, Westminster Library donated 2,000 books; educational lectures were arranged and ENSA gave a series of concerts throughout the winter; there were film shows and, ambitiously, Shakespearean plays were put on. A canteen serving hot food and drink was supplied by a local restaurateur; nurses from Charing

Cross hospital ran a rota of medical services; and every Sunday a padre who was a regular shelterer himself conducted a service of worship. The same thing happened in other larger shelters: the LCC ran classes on such disparate subjects as dressmaking and current affairs. Then there were the self-generated entertainments – knitting, card games, quizzes, sing-songs – 'Roll Out the Barrel' and 'Maybe It's Because I'm a Londoner', were particularly raucous favourites – drinking, fornicating, fighting. One memorable night, the shelterers at Marble Arch tube station were treated to an impromptu concert by Glenn Miller and his band, who had been practising in a nearby theatre when the alert was sounded, and hurried into the tube station still clutching their instruments.

But ever ambivalent about large numbers of people congregating together during an air raid – particularly underground – the government was reluctant to admit the long-term need for shelters, or to make them attractive places. The Ministry of Health was concerned that 'too much publicity on improvements and amenities now provided in shelters in London had had a harmful effect . . . in encouraging considerable numbers of people to return from reception areas where facilities for entertainment were limited'. A report to Herbert Morrison warned that it was 'undesirable to give excessive publicity regarding Christmas festivities and general amenities provided in shelters. The general impression should be that shelters were clean, but not gay.'

Although Morrison had been forced to concede that the tube could be used as an air-raid shelter, the government was still determined that trains should be as little interfered with as possible. Stations were policed to ensure that people did not go underground for the purpose of sheltering before 4 p.m., and when they got to the platforms they found two white lines painted along the edge. Before 7.30 p.m. the shelterers had to remain in the space between the wall and the first line to allow passengers to get on and off the trains on their way home from work. After 7.30 p.m. they could commandeer the space up to the second line and occupy the passageways and stairways.

Veronica Goddard, a sixteen-year-old Kensington schoolgirl, was critical nevertheless, reporting that a friend 'had a frightful time getting home from work . . . because so many people have taken to sheltering in the underground that it is practically an impossibility to get anywhere near a train. Regardless of all the poor workers trying to get home, they settle themselves down on the platforms . . . a terrible hindrance altogether to those trying to get home quickly.'

Queues started to form outside tube stations as early as ten in the morning – only a few hours after the shelterers had come up from the previous night's incarceration – and various sharp practices developed. There was a thriving black market trade in pitches selling for as much as 2s 6d – which, since the average wage of an underground worker in 1940 was £3 a week, was a considerable sum. Known in London as 'droppers', these racketeers would persuade a sympathetic guard that their health would not allow them to stand hours in line, so they would be let in early and, when the rest of the shelterers were allowed in, they would find that all the best pitches had been bagged by having clothes or strips of bedding piled on them.

The only solution was some form of ticketing, as was in operation in the Aldwych. Printed reservation tickets were issued by shelter marshals and wardens appointed by the various local authorities in whose borough the tube stations were located, though roughly 10 per cent of the accommodation was unallocated so people who found themselves in the area in the event of a raid could use it. Late arrivals had no option but to cram in the passages or somehow make themselves comfortable on the staircases and (switched off) escalators. In Holland Park station, where people started arriving at 2 p.m., every space had been taken by 7 p.m. and those who arrived after that bedded down at the top of the emergency stairs 'underneath a glass roof with no deep shelter protection at all'.

The routine of the tube shelterers' lives, with its regular hours, allocated sleeping spaces and shared dangers, forged a community of sorts – though it could be a disputatious one. Shelter Users Committees were set up. They organised collections for first-aid equipment (when none was forthcoming from the local authority), and for Christmas parties for the children, and distributed toys sent by America's Air Raid Relief Fund. And several committees produced Gestetnered newsletters – *The Subway Companion*, *The Belsize Park Tube Magazine*, *The Holborn Shelter News* and *The Swiss Cottager* were among the most regular. These emphasised the rules about not overstepping the white line and not bringing in camp beds since 'three camp beds occupy the space of four blankets', about not expecting 'home comforts or elbow room', and about keeping the platforms free from litter. They offered hints about 'guarding against colds and infections . . . a face mask can be made of a few square inches of surgical gauze, or even butter muslin . . . sprinkle with a little oil of eucalyptus and tie over the face with a strip of tape at bedtime'. The underground press could be a campaigning organ too, trying to quash outbreaks of xenophobia and anti-Semitism.

At the height of the 1940 Blitz an additional 340 basements in central London were requisitioned and strengthened for air-raid protection for a further 65,000 shelterers. On 29 October Herbert Morrison made another volte-face over deep shelters, announcing his intention to extend the existing tube-shelter network by constructing a series of linked tunnels. Eight new shelters to accommodate 64,000 people were planned for north and south London, all fitted with purpose-built lavatories sited off the main shelter, bunks, canteens and medical facilities. The intention was to transfer tube station shelterers to these new underground caverns.

The tube was not a guaranteed safe haven: bombs falling on Tottenham Court Road station, Trafalgar Square, Bounds Green, Camden Town and Balham, when sixty-four shelterers were killed, and Bank, when fifty-three died, proved that. But for an average of 120,000 people nightly, many of them East Enders, the inconveniences, privations and possible dangers of the underground were balanced by a greater feeling of security, camaraderie, and oblivion to the noise of the raids.

An unbreakable rule at tube stations and public shelters was no animals, for reasons of hygiene and also because it was hard to predict how they might behave in the event of a heavy raid. At least 400,000 pets – mainly cats – were destroyed in the week war broke out, and the RSPCA reported that their ovens 'could not burn the bodies fast enough as they had to damp down furnaces owing to the blackout'. Some vets were rumoured to be so distressed by this slaughter that they moved their practices to reception areas and accepted pets there. The Animal Defence League started a scheme for evacuating pets, and other pet owners responded to advertisements in the press and found that the going rate was roughly ten shillings a week for an average-sized dog, but only a penny a day for a budgerigar.

The RSPCA had issued a booklet in 1936, *Air Raid Precautions for Animals*, with various suggestions, for example advising against attempting to put a canine gas mask on a dog – instead the animal should be sedated and wrapped in a wet blanket. The National Air Raid Precaution Animals Committee provided rest centres for animals, and an appeal was broadcast to the public for stables or garages for working horses that were caught in the street when an air raid started. The King was among those who responded, with an offer of the Royal Mews. There were some 4,000 horses in the London area at the start of the war, and they grew increasingly useful for transport and deliveries as petrol rationing bit. Horses presented a particular problem in an air raid: they were so terrified that they would refuse to leave a burning stable and could rear dangerously and injure their would-be rescuer. Various solutions were tried, including covering their heads with a feed bag, or stabling a goat with them so it could be led to safety with the horses (reputedly) following meekly.

Canaries, as a species used to work in coalmines, were credited with being natural Blitz survivors, whereas budgerigars ingested dust and died, and fish had no chance if their tank or bowl was shattered in a raid. But despite these hazards, many owners were reluctant to part with their pets, who gave them comfort and companionship. Dogs, and occasionally cats, were often credited with animal intuition – and superior hearing – so they could act as a personalised alert system, hearing enemy raiders before the siren wailed and either diving for cover or, more heroically, agitating for the family to take shelter. But inevitably animals were killed in the raids, injured, trapped or abandoned, or they ran off, and by early autumn a feral colony of homeless and dispossessed cats was to be found roaming bomb sites scavenging for food.

When the alert sounded – 'Wailing Willie or Wailing Winnie', as most called the ululating sound – everyone in the area made their shelter dispositions for the night, or decided out of a sense of fatalism or exhaustion to stay in their beds. For the ARP wardens, however, this was the start of the night's real work.

The ratio of ARP wardens varied from city to city, borough to borough, but for most the standard was ten wardens' posts to the square mile. Each post – which might be a shop, hall or basement, or even the front room of one of the wardens – would have a post warden and usually a deputy, and would be divided into sectors with perhaps three to six wardens controlled by a senior warden in each sector, and there might be sub-posts in the sector too. In rural areas the sectors would be much larger than those in towns; wardens would be posted to cover a number of villages and be expected to have more all-round competencies, since there were fewer of them and the support services had further to come.

An ARP officer was invariably local: it was essential that a warden knew his or her patch, and a conscientious warden would know the habits of the people who lived in the streets for which he or she was responsible, who had been evacuated, who was away for the night, who had visitors or billetees, who slept where, so that when a bomb fell or a fire raged ('an incident' as these were referred to in an attempt to defuse the drama) the emergency services could be directed at once to where survivors might be buried. About nine-tenths of ARP wardens were part-timers who came on duty after they had finished their day's work, and one in six was a woman. There had been an alarming haemorrhage of Civil Defence workers during the Phoney War, and the government had not helped by putting a halt on recruitment. Once the air raids started, it was obvious that there was an acute shortage of Civil Defence personnel. In June 1940 it was announced that men aged between thirty and fifty liable for conscription could opt for the police or fire service in preference to the Armed Forces, and those already in post were 'frozen' in their jobs – not permitted to resign. This stricture had been extended to rescue and stretcher parties in July, and in October, a month after the start of the Blitz, full-time ARP wardens in London were also 'frozen' in their jobs and the age of reservation was lowered so fewer were drained off into the Forces.

Barbara Nixon had become a voluntary part-time warden in Finsbury in May 1940. When she became a full-time warden (for which she was paid 'the magnificent sum of £2 5s a week') she was transferred to Post 13, where there 'were the toughest set of wardens in the borough' and it was 'unwise' to ask what people had done before the war because, 'owing to the fact that race tracks, boxing rings, and similarly chancy means of livelihood closed down at the outbreak of war, there was a large percentage of bookie's touts and even more parasitic professions, in the CD services, together with a collection of workers in light industry, "intellectuals", opera singers, street traders, dog fanciers etc. In the early days the Control Rooms were crowded with chorus girls.' There was also an ex-burglar, a trade unionist, and two men who hoped that joining the ARP would defer their call-up papers; the post warden had been an electrician. Importantly, all the wardens except Nixon 'had been to the same local school, though at different times, and they knew the family history of nearly everyone in the neighbourhood'.

When she joined the ARP Barbara Nixon had been 'given a tin hat, a whistle and a respirator' – and a badge. It was not until May 1941 that full-time and regular part-time wardens were finally issued with blue serge uniforms with an overcoat, beret and boots. Training was rudimentary and often largely irrelevant. It was on the job at the height of the Blitz that Nixon, like so many wardens, became aware of the 'multitudinous things a warden needed to know, from the names of the residents in each house, and which shelter they used, hydrants, cul-de-sacs, danger points in the area, to the whereabouts of the old and infirm who would need help in getting to shelter, telephone numbers and the addresses of rest centres etc.'

Wardens would report to their post when they came on or went off duty, and part-time wardens were supposed to put in about three nights a week, though this increased greatly when the Blitz was at its height. They would sit around drinking cups of tea, smoking, reading the paper, playing cards or darts, gossiping or snoozing until the yellow 'stand-by' warning alert sounded and then they would leave the post to patrol the streets of their sector on foot.

When the red alert – 'raiders overhead' – sounded, the siren would wail, and the Chelsea wardens would hurry 'to the shelters, ticking off the names of the residents in their areas as they arrived, then back they went to hurry and chivvy the laggards and see that those who chose to stay in their houses were all right . . . They carried children, old people, bundles of blankets, and the odd personal possessions which some eccentrics insisted on taking with them to the shelters.' It was a similar story throughout Britain, and, until the All Clear sounded, those wardens who were not fully engaged at an incident would tour their sector, usually in pairs, at considerable personal risk from bombs, shrapnel and falling masonry, making sure that throughout the night they regularly put their head in at all the public shelters on their beat, partly to see if anything was needed, but mainly to maintain morale. The sight of a tin hat and the knowledge that someone was 'out there', and in control, was reassuring as the raids raged overhead.

If a bomb fell, the wardens who were nearest to the spot would hurry over to assess what help was needed, and rush back to their post to ring through to the control centre with a report before returning to the incident. 'I go into a house, decide who's alive and who's dead, tot up the number of victims and what is necessary in the way of fire services, ambulances, demolition etc . . .' wrote a Kent ARP warden who thought 'that women warders are better than men in most cases, not all. They can see in a moment who is in the house because they know what to look for. If the kettle is on the stove they know the occupants are probably downstairs and have not gone to bed; if there is a cot they know there is a baby about somewhere.'

If an incendiary had started a small fire the wardens would try to put it out themselves with any passing help available, without summoning the fire services; they would administer first aid if there were minor casualties, and direct anyone who no longer had a habitable home to a rest centre.

If an incident was clearly a major one, the ARP wardens would do what they could until the arrival of the other Civil Defence services that had been alerted by the control post. By law, the police were in charge of all such incidents but, if a policeman tried to assert his statutory right, he might get short shrift from the warden in charge, who would argue that he knew the procedures – and the people. The warden would want to know if there were any premises nearby that had a phone that could be used, and if there was anything potentially lethal in the area like a store of petrol, oil or chemicals. The fire service would drive up with pumps appropriate to the size of the blaze (if they were not all engaged elsewhere), the Heavy Rescue Squad would arrive and the men would start trying to lift masonry and debris to get at anyone trapped in the ruins. As soon as they arrived they would cut off the supply of gas, water and electricity since, ironically, gas masks offered no protection against domestic coal gas, and all too often people trapped under masonry were killed by being gassed – or drowned – after they had survived the collapse of their building. The rescue party would use jacks, blocks and tackles and sometimes oxyacetylene cutting equipment to try to get out the injured. They worked frantically, throwing debris into baskets or in piles on the ground, scrabbling with tools and sometimes their bare hands as their lungs filled with brick dust that made talking difficult. Their eyes watered from the acrid smoke that swirled around, and they were in constant danger from falling masonry. Other than the illumination of the flames, the scene would invariably be pitch-black while the Alert was in progress, and the rescuers would be required to shield their torches and point them downwards in the confused belief that such a tiny glimmer of light could be seen by the bombers overhead. Periodically the leader would call for absolute silence in the hope that faint cries might be heard coming from the twisted mass of wood, metal and plaster. And all the time enemy planes would be circling overhead, the threatening crump and whine of bombs fell all around and the ack-ack guns would volley deafeningly in response.

It was the awesome responsibility of the leader of the rescue team to decide when the hope of finding anyone alive was such a faint possibility that he had to move his team on to another incident, despite the entreaties of watching relatives who could not bear to give up hope.

A first-aid party (called a stretcher party in London) would arrive to treat minor injuries on the spot and gently lift the more seriously injured on to stretchers – or a door or plank if there were no stretchers available – and into vehicles. All casualties had to be labelled at the incident with any information that would help in their treatment – X for internal injury, T for tourniquet applied – written in indelible pencil on a luggage label or, when these ran out, in pencil or lipstick on the casualty's forehead. Non-critical casualties would be taken to one of the first-aid posts, which were staffed round the clock on a rota system throughout the war by a doctor, at least one trained nurse, and a team of first-aid workers who would be on hand to treat the victims – clean and bandage their wounds, pick splinters of glass and metal out of their skin and strap up broken bones. The purpose of the posts was to prevent casualty wards from becoming overwhelmed with relatively minor injuries that needed a doctor to treat them, but did not require hospitalisation. There was also a fleet of mobile first-aid posts which could be sent out from ambulance stations to serious incidents, or to places where there was no first-aid post nearby.

At a major incident, or where serious injuries had been reported, ambulances would arrive to convey the wounded to first-aid posts, or hospitals. These might be regular peacetime ambulances camouflaged with dark-grey paint, but were just as likely to be a commercial van that the owner loaned to the ambulance service every night after work, or taxis or private cars adapted to take stretchers on the roof, though again, as the war dragged on, more custom-built ambulances came into service. An ambulance driver in Exeter trained on an old laundry van 'wearing a gas mask and all the equipment' and then drove an Austin Seven, one of the old cars that had 'been picked up for about £25 each . . . they just put on a canvas top and stencilled on the letters ARP'. In Liverpool, Tim Clarke, whose only uniform was a tin hat and an armband proclaiming 'AMBULANCE', noted that it was mainly bread vans that served as ambulances, since their owners couldn't get the petrol to keep them in service.

The WVS would arrive too, in their bottle-green uniforms and sensible felt hats, ready to be an 'auxiliary' to anyone who needed their help and plug any gap in the services that they could. The women would drive a mobile canteen to serve cups of tea and buns to the parched and dusty rescue workers at a major incident, and they learned how to improvise when gas, electricity and water supplies had been put out of action. They would help with casualties, take traumatised bombees (as those who had lost their homes in a bombing raid were called) to rest centres, direct those who were shocked and bewildered, but not badly injured, to the homes of those who ran their Housewives' Service – women who wanted to help but were tied to their homes with heavy domestic responsibilities – for a cup of tea, a bath and somewhere warm to sit. They would go over lists with ARP wardens to make sure that everyone was accounted for in the sector, and soon moved in to run rest centres, organise mobile laundries for those who had been bombed out, and provide shelter marshals who went on duty every time an Alert sounded. Later in the war, the WVS took responsibility for setting up Incident Inquiry Points (IIP) at major incidents where they often had the grim task of breaking devastating news to those whose homes or workplaces had been hit, and sometimes of accompanying the bereaved to the mortuary to identify the dead they had loved. Like all members of the Civil Defence services, it was during the Blitz that WVS members came to realise, in the words of their founder, that 'tiredness is an incident, not a finality'.

Later would come the mortuary vans to take away any bodies, which would have been neatly laid on the ground covered with a torn curtain, a blood-soaked sheet or bit of sacking to preserve some propriety in death. Into these requisitioned vans that sometimes offended onlookers if their peacetime function of house removals or butcher's van had not been obliterated, would also be loaded parts of bodies that had been collected in a basket to be taken to the mortuary. Here they would be reassembled, a macabre human jigsaw that gave relatives and friends a collection of parts they could imagine was a body to bury, the semblance of an unseen loved one to mourn. 'It became a grim and ghastly satisfaction when a body was fairly constructed,' recalled Frances Faviell, an artist who had studied anatomy at the Slade and so was particularly useful for this terrible task where 'the stench was the worst thing about it, that and having to realise that these frightful pieces of flesh had once been living, breathing people . . . if one was too lavish in making one body almost whole, then another one would have sad gaps. There were always odd members which did not seem to fit, and there were always too many legs . . . I think this task dispelled for me the idea that human life is valuable – it could be blown to pieces by blast, just as dust was blown by wind.'

But post-raid clearing-up operations, no matter how efficient, did not always effect closure. Sometimes the dead lingered where they fell. Just after Christmas 1940 Bernard Regan, a builder who worked for the Poplar Heavy Rescue Squad on the Isle of Dogs in east London, received a panic call. Some more victims had been found at a school that had been bombed three months previously. 'After all this time, there is no big stuff to be moved, just one big heap of small rubble and concrete, which has settled into a tight mass and requires hand work.' Since there couldn't possibly 'be any survivors after all this time', Regan and a workmate, George Jillings, worked systematically to clear the site. 'After an hour or so, George called me to help with a doormat he had found but could not pull clear. It was black, and of a thick curly texture, so I fished around for a while loosening the packed rubble, then George came back with a length of iron to prise it out. I told him then that it was a bloke, and I knew who he was, Warden Herbie Martin . . . Meanwhile everyone had gathered at one spot, so we went over to find out why. They had found two more bodies and sent for the Light Rescue to come and take them away, and while I watched two more bodies were uncovered. I know none of us are very happy having to handle corpses, and it shows. They had uncovered two young girls, about eighteen years of age, quite unmarked, they looked as if they were asleep. I looked round at the other men. Most of them were shocked and a bit sick: we usually found bodies mutilated, and we just lifted them out by their hands and feet and quickly got away. Major Brown sees one man being sick, so he fishes out a bottle of rum to be handed round.

'By now I am feeling a bit angry at the prospect of these girls being lugged by their arms and legs, so I got down beside them. They both have only their knickers and short petticoats on, and the dry weather we'd been having, and the rubble packed tight round them had preserved them. Their limbs were not even rigid. They were lifelike: I could not let them be handled like the usual corpses. I know I would have belted the first one that handled them with disrespect, but nobody makes a move to shift them, and they just stand there, gawping.

'I looked at George, and I just said: "stretcher – blanket." Then I put my right arm under [one of the girl's] shoulders with her head resting against me, and my left arm under her knees, and carried her up. I laid her on the stretcher, "You'll be comfortable now my dear." I did exactly the same with the other one. I stood up and waited for some smart Alec to make a snide remark, but nobody did. I cooled down a bit after I had smoked a cigarette. I wonder, why had I been so angry?'

The air raids that assaulted London and then many other towns and cities throughout the country did not, fortunately, result in anything like the number of deaths and serious injuries that had been the predicate of pre-war planning. What they did was to destroy or leave uninhabitable far more houses and blocks of flats, and leave far more people with nowhere to live and with only the clothes they stood up in, than had been planned for. While tens of thousands of papier-mâché coffins were left uncalled for, and numbers of emergency beds remained unfilled, the tide of the homeless and dispossessed threatened to overwhelm the boroughs that were worst hit in the early weeks of the Blitz. The nature of the war had been miscalculated, and so 'when the storm broke [on 7 September]', judged Richard Titmuss, 'the relief services of London were overborne'.

In October 1940 Mea Allan had 'been doing aftermath of raids stories every day. It's harrowing and I feel a furrow perpetually on my brow. There seems no light or laughter anymore and one knows the test is still to come. But no one is depressed at heart. Those who are homeless are *angry*. And of course bus talk etc. is all about What Happened Last Night . . . Ritchie Calder brings sad tales back from the Isle of Dogs where people are just wandering around like unclaimed mongrels, too stunned to even ask where they can get food and a new home and dragging their bits of bedding and children about with them. [Ritchie Calder] is furious and keeps ringing up all the Ministries in turn and taking half the cabinet out East to show them their job.'

A person who had been bombed out needed shelter, food, clothes and money straight away. In the longer term they needed somewhere to live, furniture – and compensation. Though there was never a total breakdown in services, it came pretty close in at least two London boroughs, Stepney and West Ham, where the government, having lost faith in inefficient local administrators, wrested control from them, and in Plymouth and Coventry – and almost everywhere there was confusion and great hardship endured particularly by those who had few resources.

Local authorities had been allowed only £20 to convert premises into a rest centre; in consequence these places, often in schools or church halls, were bleak and unwelcoming, equipped with little furniture, none of it comfortable, and with a lamentable shortage of blankets; often the only food on offer was a hunk of bread and margarine, and a cup of tea, 'Blitz broth' as it became known. The centres had been envisaged as places where people would stay for a few hours – indeed they would not be allowed to stay for longer – after which they would be able to make their own arrangements for accommodation or return home.

A social worker wrote of the 'unforgettable' picture of the rest centres in those early days. 'Dim figures in dejected heaps on unwashed floors in total darkness: harassed, bustling but determinedly cheerful helpers distributing eternal corned beef sandwiches and tea – the London County Council panacea for hunger, shock, loss, misery and illness . . . Dishevelled, half-dressed people wandering between the bombed house and the rest centre salvaging bits and pieces or trying to keep in touch with the scattered family . . . A clergyman appeared and wandered about aimlessly, and someone played the piano.'

Nineteen days after the first attack on London there were 25,000 people still in rest centres. It was the voluntary organisations that stepped in first: the Canadian Red Cross provided 50,000 blankets, 100,000 assorted items of clothing and 50,000 tins of food, and Canadian soldiers helped load this bounty on to lorries and distribute it to the rest centres. Social workers and community-minded priests moved in to staff the centres and cut away the red tape that tied up much-needed supplies of food, clothes, blankets and coal. The local MP for Whitechapel, Jimmy Hall, was one, and Father John Groser, 'he of the flying cassock', the inspirational priest of Christ Church off Commercial Road, who slept every night with his flock in the railway arch shelter in Watney Street, not only helped the rescue squads during the first mass raids and broke open official food stores on his own authority to feed the homeless, but with Hall 'battered away at Whitehall, endeavouring to get things done . . . about evacuation and better shelters'.

Finally the 'machinery of government was unclogged of its peacetime entanglements, and geared to a wartime tempo'. It abandoned former parsimonies and parochial niceties, which had dictated that local authorities should consider those who had been bombed out and had come from neighbouring boroughs as 'refugees', obliging the authorities to enter into complicated negotiations to recoup the cost of such items as blackout and latrines. Instead it allowed councils to deal with the problem as they thought best, appointing staff, extending the number of rest-centre places and, most important of all, it recognised that this was a national not a local crisis – and responsibility. Camp beds and blankets were ordered in immense numbers and officials were sent out all over the country to scour for supplies of teapots, mugs, kettles and chairs. Feeding centres were set up at rest centres, and those who no longer had any cooking facilities could also use these to buy a hot meal. But though rest-centre facilities generally improved considerably after the first desperate weeks, there were boroughs that simply failed to cope.

Around 2.25 million people were made homeless between September 1940 and May 1941: almost two-thirds of these lived in London, so in effect one person in every six in the London area was without a home. A family standing on the pavement in front of their badly damaged house, or perhaps just a pile of bricks where their house had been, may well have had no idea where the nearest rest centre was, or even that such places existed, and often the shelter marshals and police didn't know either. Few acted as fast as the Hackney ARP controller who, within days of the first raid, was plastering the area round an incident with directions to the nearest rest centre. In Stepney 'the local Information Centre has not functioned at all' during the worst of the raids. When notices did go up, they were often in obscure places, written in an officialese that was unintelligible to the average East Ender, using words like 'incapacitated' and 'household effects', and, unlike ARP notices, were never translated into Yiddish, the only language of many who needed to read them. When a rest centre was finally located, most turned out to be woefully deficient in providing any information about the multiplicity of things such a family needed to know. Were they officially homeless and therefore eligible for official billeting? Or were they categorised as 'temporarily homeless' since their home had been damaged but might be considered repairable – providing a surveyor could be located to pronounce on this? What if they had been driven out by a UXB in the vicinity – and therefore were not eligible to be rehoused, or even, strictly speaking, to use the rest centres? Where should they apply for emergency cash grants if they had no money, for war damage compensation, where could they replace their identity cards, ration and pension books and gas masks, where could they they get clothes, who would help them salvage any furniture, how might they set about getting their house repaired if that was feasible – and how were they to find somewhere to live in the meantime?

All this was in essence one problem: the rehabilitation of homeless citizens, but it involved the overlapping efforts of half a dozen different government departments, and people would find themselves trailing miserably from pillar to post, when in no fit psychological state to surmount so many obstacles to getting their life back on track.

In an attempt to simplify this labyrinth, the Ministry of Information printed some 50,000 leaflets for distribution to a number of blitzed towns in January 1941, giving such information as:

You can get drinking water at . . .
Drink only boiled water and milk
Rest centres are at . . .
Transport for . . . will leave at . . .
For help and information go to . . .

Staff were sent into rest centres to give advice, and Public Assistance Board officers turned up too to make hardship payments on the spot and set up mobile offices that could be sent to any bombed area. Most radically, what would now be called 'one-stop shops' started to be set up in mid October 1940 to bring the various services together in areas that had experienced heavy bombing; and in areas with less acute problems the WVS (whose idea it had been) established information centres, often run in collaboration with Citizens' Advice Bureaux, to tell people what they were entitled to and how they should go about getting it. By the end of May 1941, where none had existed eight months earlier, such centres could be found in almost all London boroughs, run by a variety of voluntary and welfare agencies and subsidised by the government.

If rest centres were going to be the battleground clearing centres they had been intended to be, all these matters were of the greatest urgency. The throughput had to be fast, and yet by mid October out of every ten of the 19,000 Londoners in rest centres, four had been there for at least ten days. Furthermore this number did not account for all the homeless, since some had taken up permanent residence in shelters or down the tube, while others effectively squatted in their bombed-out homes in order to guard their few surviving possessions and not feel entirely deracinated in a world in which they had lost almost all of what was familiar to them.

A special commissioner for the London homeless was appointed at the end of September 1940. Rehousing became an active service, with officers going into rest centres with the express intention of emptying them as fast as possible: 'halfway' houses were set up for those families with problems that made it difficult to billet or rehouse them straight away, and the terrible confusion and feeling of helplessness that air-raid victims felt began to be addressed.

At the start of the Blitz only a few boroughs had lists of empty houses that could be requisitioned, or where the homeless could be billeted, and it was not until April 1941 that local authorities were permitted to requisition unoccupied furnished houses; in May they were empowered to take these over in advance of the need for them so that a stock of immediately habitable houses could be built up; and in July that year the most draconian of the measures, the right to requisition occupied houses in exceptional circumstances, was granted. But there was almost no provision for providing furniture or bedding for those who had lost everything. Little thought had been given to salvaging furniture from bombed-out houses, and in any case there was often nowhere available to store it. Most local authorities found their obligation to repair bombed houses totally daunting since the damage was so much greater than had been anticipated.

Insurance companies had declined to insure the population against war damage a couple of years before war broke out, so in 1940 the War Damages Commission was set up to make payments to those whose land or buildings had been damaged by enemy action. The intention was that this money would be recouped from tax payers via a complicated inland revenue scheme. A helpful booklet written by a solicitor, *When the Raid is Over*, explained the position to owner-occupiers, who, by the end of the war, made up only 26 per cent of households; to the 13 per cent who occupied local authority (council) houses; and the remainder who rented from private landlords.

The situation was unequivocal: 'the Government's intention is to give war damage for property at the end of the war and not before.' And how much that would be would depend on 'the amount of the damage and the financial position of the country at the end of the war'. The payment would only be for actual physical damage incurred and not for consequential losses such as loss of trade for a shop, or having to provide alternative accommodation. The amount awarded – and in many cases it was several years after the war that the money was paid out – was calculated as the cost of 'reasonably reinstating the property to its former condition in line with building costs in March 1939'.

In the meantime, the house owner or landlord should carry out necessary repairs, or the council would do so 'if there was a housing shortage or the owner or landlord was unwilling or unable to do so' – and presumably if the local authority had the necessary manpower which many didn't. The owner or landlord would have to foot the bill though there were grants available and the cost should be able to be reclaimed after the war.

A tenant whose home had been seriously damaged could either give up his lease and not pay rent, or if he elected to hold on to the lease he must repair the property (or have it repaired) as soon as possible, but would not have to pay rent until his home was habitable again. However, if the landlord was not prepared to release the tenant from his or her lease, he had to make the premises fit to live in as soon as possible, and no rent was to be paid until they were. If part of the house was habitable, then part of the rent would be due – the niceties to be decided by the courts if necessary. For those buying a house on a mortgage, usually no one was bound to make good war damage, but it was hoped that the lender would act like a landlord and repair the property if this was possible, though the mortgagee would still be liable to pay interest or instalments and to repay the capital: 'damage to or destruction of the premises does not affect this liability.' If, however, the property was unrepairable and the air-raid victim needed somewhere to live or carry on their business, they could claim an immediate grant of up to £800 which they were supposed to use to pay off any outstanding mortgage if they had one, on the assumption that their building society would be prepared to renew the mortgage on any replacement property they found.

The destruction of or damage to furniture, appliances, cars, clothes and jewellery could also be claimed for after the war at market or repair value 'at the date of damage', but taking into account 'the condition of the article before damage'. In the meantime, advance payments could be made and the amount depended on the income of the claimant – but when the household income exceeded £400 per annum it was presumed that money put by would mean such State help was not required. Grants were also available if furniture needed to be put into storage, but not to replace it if it had deteriorated as the result of being left in a bombed-out house.

When it came to persons killed or grieviously injured by enemy action, only physical injuries counted: 'mental injuries, e.g., the shock of seeing someone killed do not come with this definition.' A person could claim an injury allowance for up to six months (longer in exceptional circumstances) if they were off work for that time. A married man would receive 25s 6d a week when he was in hospital and 33s when he came out; a bachelor or widower would receive 11s and 20s respectively; but 'women and girls' were valued at less: they would get 9s 6d if they were in hospital and 18s if they were not. War pensions for women permanently injured or disabled were also less. Pensions started at 34s 2d a week for men over twenty-one and were 10s less for women of the same age. If a housewife were injured she would not be entitled to a pension. Rather, if someone else had to be engaged to do her housewifely duties, her husband (for 'whom the household duties were performed') might, depending on his income, be entitled to a pension, though 'he must continue to maintain the injured woman'. There were frequent protests from women's organisations that 'bombs don't discriminate' and finally, in 1943, the injustices were rectified.

Although the government had feared a mass exodus from the cities once the Blitz started, many people instinctively wanted to stay in their home territory, even if they hadn't actually got a home any more. When tens of thousands had to leave Silvertown temporarily in the first days of the Blitz – because their homes had been destroyed or damaged, or were threatened by UXBs, and water supplies were contaminated – the Ministry of Health offered them a one-off opportunity to evacuate their blighted neighbourhood, whether they were homeless or not: fewer than 3,000 took up the offer.

Mea Allan wrote an article on 'East London comes to Belgravia' in the *Daily Herald* on 20 September 1940. 'I found half a dozen of them in Lord Linlithgow's home in Chesham Place knitting wool squares for a baby's quilt. They looked rather lost like commercial travellers who have missed a train, doing crosswords in the hotel lounge. They said they were very happy. One old lady in a grey shawl kept nodding by the fire "Most kind, most kind" like Florence Nightingale. Another woman said "Well I wouldn't like to go back there – not after *this*. Hot water and all conveniences." '

But that does not seem to have been the general reaction. Local authorities were reluctant to accept the responsibility for rehousing or billeting people from outside their boundaries, and invariably the people didn't want it either. At a time of great disruption, they clung to the familiar: relatives and neighbours, local churches, pubs they frequented, cut-price shops and street markets. And when in October the raids were no longer mainly concentrated on the East End but spread across London, what was the point of leaving your own home in order to be bombed in someone else's? Although fourteen London boroughs – including Westminster, Paddington and Hampstead – had been asked to requisition and prepare as many houses as they could for homeless East Enders, by November 1940 it was recognised that this transference was not working, and after that the policy was only used as a last resort. The aim instead was to find accommodation – or make habitable their own houses – for people where they wanted to live: in their own scarred and battered neighbourhoods.

Even if a house was not badly damaged, the violation of one's home could be a distressing experience. The shipbuilding town of Barrow-in-Furness, up the Lancashire coast from Liverpool, had 'a night of terror' on 3 May 1941. Ten people were killed and 2,000 made homeless. Nella Last and her husband had been at home. The following morning she took stock: there were 'few windows left in our district or roof tiles! Land mines, incendiaries and explosives were dropped and we cowered thankfully under our indoor shelter . . . I've a sick shadow over me as I look at my loved little house that will never be the same again. The windows are nearly all out, the metal frames strained, the ceilings down, the walls cracked and the garage roof showing four inches of daylight where it joins the wall. Doors are splintered and off – and there is the dirt from the blast that swept down the chimney. The house rocked and then the kitchenette door careered down the hall and plaster showered onto the shelter. I'll never forget my odd sensations, one a calm acceptance of "the end", the other a feeling of regret that I'd not opened a tin of fruit salad for tea – and now it was too late! . . . I've worked and worked, clearing glass and plaster and broken china – all my loved old china plates from the oak panelling in the hall. With no sleep at all last night, and little on Friday night, I've no tiredness at all, no dread of the night, no regrets, just a feeling of numbness. All the day, the tinkle of glass being swept up and dumped in ash-bins has sounded like wind-bells in a temple, together with the knock-knock as anything handy was tacked in place over gaping windows. We have brought the good spring-bed into the dining room both for comfort and safety . . .'

After the raid on Coventry in November 1940 it had become clear that house repairs could no longer be relegated to second place after repairs to railways, public utilities and war industries. Since the main problem was shortage of manpower, the War Office finally agreed that men could be released from the Army for the purpose, and by July 1941 5,000 soldiers were working in mobile gangs that would be sent to wherever the need was greatest. Since nearly 5 million private houses were damaged during the war, repair work had to be perfunctory, usually a matter of patching up houses to make them wind- and rain-proof using whatever material was available. It was essential to clear bombed sites as soon as possible, both for reasons of morale and so that traffic could flow. Millions of bricks were salvaged from demolished houses, and while most were used to strengthen air-raid shelters in the early days, some later became available for house repairs. Much of the rubble of the London Blitz was initially dumped in the parks – the level of the northern end of Regent's Park was (and remains) raised by several feet. Later in the war debris was put to use as hard core in the building of airfields for the US Army Air Force in East Anglia.

At the start of the Blitz there were over half a million children of school age in the London evacuation area, the mass exodus of 1939 having been followed by an almost equally mass return. When the air raids started, about 20,500 unaccompanied children left; by October the number had dropped to 15,000; by November it was down to 4,000 and in December only 760 children were evacuated. Singed by the experience of the first evacuation in September 1939, local authorities were loath to sponsor the evacuation of mothers and children, and it was soon apparent that even homeless mothers from the East End who were offered this opportunity felt the same. The scheme was extended to all LCC boroughs and several outside, but still the response was relatively lukewarm despite a vigorous campaign to persuade mothers that they were not acting in their children's best interests by keeping them in the blitzed city.

In London voluntary evacuation was so limited, and the problems of the homeless so pressing, that the government came nearer than it did at any other time during the war to make the evacuation of children compulsory. In the end it wisely didn't, because it was clear that the reaction to such an edict would be uniformly hostile.

In any case, evacuating children to 'safe' areas was no longer the confident calculation it had been in 1939. By the early summer of 1940 the threat of invasion had turned coastal towns into no-go areas, and children who had been evacuated to such places as Eastbourne, Folkestone, Margate, Clacton and Southend were hastily moved out again, along with large numbers of the usual peacetime population. And as the raids spread out from London across the country from September 1940, there seemed few guaranteed havens from the matrix of destruction.

Those driven from the cities fanned out more widely across the country: some areas that had been designated as neutral were now reclassified as reception areas for evacuees; local authorities in England and Wales were prepared to send evacuees to Scotland; and towards the end of 1940 to Northern Ireland and Eire too.

In 1940, after the experience of the previous year, strenuous efforts were made to ensure that this time the evacuees stayed evacuated. In reception areas, government or local authorities organised 'Mother's clubs' and occupational centres – usually run by voluntary groups – that provided such activities as 'make and mend' groups, boot-repairing and toy-making classes, places where mothers could meet each other, do their washing and ironing, have a canteen meal and where their children could be minded while they went shopping or did a part-time job.

In order to avoid some of the difficulties of the 1939 evacuation, when householders had protested at having what they considered to be dirty, verminous or badly behaved children billeted on them, the government decided to abandon its earlier opposition to providing hostel accommodation. Unfortunately, however, instead of these being temporary arrangements where problems were sorted out and suitable accommodation was found for each individual child, the hostels in effect became dumping grounds – 'Hostels for problem children' as some of the children themselves headed the notepaper on which they wrote to thank American families who had sent over toys – without appropriately trained staff or proper assessment of the children's needs. Within a year things had begun to improve with more attention given to the individual welfare of the children, staff being better trained, and psychiatric advice and treatment provided.

Nurseries were provided for the collateral casualties of war: orphans, and children whose mothers were no longer able to care for them. Sigmund Freud's daughter Anna, herself a distinguished child psychologist, who had arrived in Britain with her father from Vienna in 1939, made a particular study of children in nurseries who had been bereaved or in other ways traumatised by the Blitz. Some local authorities established 'rest and recuperation' and convalescent hostels in the country for mothers and children who had suffered in the air raids. The Oxford House Settlement in Bethnal Green set up two residential schools in Wales for children whose anti-social behaviour made them hard to billet, and a voluntary country-holiday scheme meant that over 2,000 nursery-age children were given some rural respite from the horrors of the Blitz.

In London the 'shelter derelicts', the aged or chronically sick who had no one to look after them and had taken up almost permanent residence in shelters and rest centres, presented a problem. It was decided to treat these people as 'air-raid casualties' by evacuating them to hospital beds in reception areas, thus raising morale in the shelters and freeing up space in rest centres. But while many undoubtedly needed to be hospitalised, others, though they were unable to cope with air raids, were resistant to being bundled away from their familiar surroundings, perhaps parted from a spouse and forcibly bedridden. The spectre of the workhouse reared its head, and yet it was clearly impracticable to expect householders to offer a billet to the elderly and infirm. What was required for such people were hostels. An informal committee set to work searching for premises, and by June 1941 1,500 aged but able-bodied Londoners were settled in these rural retreats, which were usually staffed by voluntary helpers.

Vera Brittain, the pacifist writer, agonised over what to do with her own children, John and Shirley, who were then aged ten and eight. As the German Army overran Europe in May 1940 and the threat of invasion seemed very real, numbers of British parents had decided that their children would be safer overseas in 'new territories unhampered by the evil nationalistic traditions of the quarrelsome Old World' as Brittain saw it. Private arrangements had been made since before the war by those who had the contacts and the money to send their children overseas – the sea crossing to America cost around £15, the equivalent of a month's salary for three-quarters of British working men in 1939. When the news from France became increasingly grave at the end of May 1940, offers of hospitality started arriving in Britain first from Canada, then Australia, New Zealand, South Africa and the United States. Such offers had been broached before, but the government had rejected them as 'good hearted but impracticable', and likely to suggest panic and defeatism since whenever morale was strained rumours grew that the royal family – and sometimes the Cabinet – had decamped to Canada, or were about to. However, on 17 June, the day that France fell, the War Cabinet agreed that these offers should be accepted with alacrity, and children of the less privileged given similar opportunities for a safe passage out of war-torn Britain. The Children's Overseas Reception Board (CORB) was set up to organise the exodus. It was learned that Americans had applied to give a wartime home to a total of 5 million refugees. Though this seems an inflated figure, there was clearly a groundswell of sympathy evidenced by the United States Committee for the Care of European Children, chaired by the President's wife, Eleanor Roosevelt, which received thousands of offers from all over America to take British children. The *New York Daily Mirror* urged, 'America must say to England "Our bars are down to your children. Send them by the thousands, it is our duty and privilege to give them a home."'

The response was overwhelming. 'A queue of parents began to stretch from the office door [of Thomas Cook, the travel agents in Berkeley Street, where CORB was housed] into Piccadilly. The opportunity of safe-guarding the children's future appeals equally to the small households of Mayfair and the large dockyard families from Bermondsey and Chatham,' noted Vera Brittain. Mindful of accusations of privilege, it was announced that the scheme would favour children from areas considered the most dangerous, and preference would be given those from the least affluent families. The children's passage would be free, though most parents would have to contribute to their children's maintenance as they would if they been evacuated within Britain. Parents with children at fee-paying schools would be required to pay £1 a week maintenance and contribute £15 towards the cost of travel.

In just two weeks 211,448 applications for children aged five to sixteen to be sent overseas had been received. In gratitude for her own children's (privately arranged) evacuation to the US, Vera Brittain volunteered her services to CORB, where she worked several hours a day interviewing applicants in order to appoint 'five hundred dependable men and women' to act as escorts (for a payment of £5 if they went to Canada, or £20 if it was Australia or New Zealand) for the 200,000 'seavacuees' already registered under the scheme.

Unlike the evacuation of children within Britain, there was no government pressure to send them overseas, no guarantee of safety and no commitment to bring the children back at any specified time. Churchill was not in favour of the scheme, which, he told the War Cabinet, 'encouraged a defeatist spirit . . . and should be sternly discouraged', and indeed the Cabinet was taken aback by the great public enthusiasm with which the possibility of overseas evacuation had been greeted. Duff Cooper, the Minister of Information (who sent his own son to school in Canada), was instructed to dampen expectations by pointing out the considerable risks in crossing the Atlantic, the transport difficulties, and the fact that only a small number of children could ever be expected to get away under the CORB scheme.

Announced on 20 June 1940, the CORB scheme closed its application list a fortnight later on 4 July for want of a ship – or several. It had been agreed that no child sent overseas under the scheme should travel in a convoy without a battleship escort, but because of the continuing threat from U-boats, the withdrawal of US shipping from belligerent waters, and the fact that the few passenger ships available were being used to convey enemy aliens to Canada, there was not sufficient shipping to transport large numbers of children or to provide a naval escort. Had the scheme all been an elaborate camouflage, angry Labour MPs demanded, designed to allow the rich to get their children out of danger without undue charges of privilege and of leaving a country in danger? A feeble gesture to the working-class families that the government had never really intended to see through?

It could seem like that. The American Secretary of the Rhodes

Scholarship, Frank Aydelotte, had appealed to Rhodes scholars throughout the US to take in 'one or more children of Oxford and Cambridge dons, or those children of dons from other universities'. Douglas Fairbanks Jr suggested setting up a colony of British actors' children in Hollywood, and the elite Cambridge Tutoring School in New York offered to take British boys for a fee of £100, specifying 'Boys from a cultural background only can be accepted. Sons of army and navy officers and professionals would be welcome.' The list of those who sent their children abroad by private arrangement in the summer of 1940 did read rather like a pocket version of *Who's Who* with a particular emphasis on politicians, present and future. There were Hambros and Rothschilds (though, being from prominent Jewish families, they had particular reason to fear Hitler's notorious 'black list' should there be a Nazi invasion of Britain, and to wish to get their children away from danger) and Guinnesses. Lord Mountbatten despatched his wife Edwina and his sons, and the juvenile Jeremy Thorpe, much later to be leader of the Liberal Party for a time, was sent. Duff Cooper and his wife Lady Diana despatched their son John Julius, who would grow up to be a diplomat and a writer, with instructions that he was 'not to get spoiled by riches; buses not taxis, drug stores not restaurants, and not too many cinemas . . . Nanny will buy him clothes cheaply – from Bloomingdale's please, not at Saks . . . Tutor him hard in American history and current events (war and peace). I'd like him to be braver than most and not taught "Safety first".' The boy's picture appeared in the *Daily Mirror* 'sitting on your pathetic bottom on your pathetic trunk. You looked like all the refugees in the world rolled into one wistful little victim of the Nazi-follow-my-leader.' Chips and Honor Channon sent Paul, 'my dauphin', his father called him, who would one day be a Conservative minister. And 'the real Mrs Miniver', Jan Struther, not only sent her two children to America, but went herself as well.

While the official scheme was suspended 'but not abandoned' and ships continued to sail, parents who wished to make private arrangements could do so, providing CORB granted an exit visa and parents agreed to accept the risks involved. Some 4,200 children (accompanied by 1,100 adults) went to individual sponsors in the US by private arrangement, and probably about 13,000 went to Canada the same way. The number of children finally evacuated under the CORB scheme was just over 2,500.

Towards the end of September 1940 dozens of parents who thought that their children were on their way to a safer life overseas received a heartbreaking official letter from CORB headquarters. 'I am very distressed to inform you,' it read, 'that, in spite of all precautions taken, the ship carrying your child to Canada was torpedoed on Tuesday night, 17 September. I am afraid your child is not among those reported as having been rescued, and I am informed that there is no chance of there being any further lists of survivors.' The SS *City of Benares*, the 11,081-ton flagship of the Ellerman City Line, which in peacetime plied between London and India but was now camouflaged in dark-brown paint for her wartime duties, had set off from Liverpool on Friday 13 September with a contingent of evacuees whose cheerful rendition of 'Wish Me Luck As You Wave Me Goodbye' carried on the breeze as the ship sailed out to sea. After five days the naval escort accompanying the convoy was called away for duties elsewhere and the convoy sailed on unaccompanied. Nearly twenty-four hours later, and with the convoy slowed down by a force eight gale, a 500lb torpedo shot right through the *City of Benares* just below the cabins where the CORB children were sleeping, and water started to pour in. The force of the explosion killed two of the children instantly. The order was given to abandon ship just before it disappeared below the waves. The sea was rough, wind and hail lashed the bitterly cold mid Atlantic, and many of the lifeboats took in water as they smashed into the sea. Passengers were thrown out and one boat, containing the captain, sank like a stone.

As the dreadful night dragged on, those who had managed to clamber into a lifeboat that had somehow stayed upright prayed and watched helplessly as 'the little ones faded out, quite unable to stand up to the awful conditions . . . All we could do was to hold them above water until they were gone . . . We gave them what comfort we could.'

On 20 September HMS *Hurricane*, the destroyer that had managed to pick up some of the *Benares* survivors, edged into Gladstone Dock in Liverpool and a padre went aboard to hear the tragic tale of 'a cold grey sea and a cold grey mist . . . kissing little children that their mothers kissed . . .' in the words of a poem written by the *Hurricane's* bitter and angry commanding officer. But miraculously more than fifty more survivors were rescued over a week after the *Benares* had gone down.

Of the ninety CORB evacuees, seventy-seven perished, along with six of the adult escorts and fifty-one other passengers; 121 members of the crew also died. There were twenty parents who lost more than one child in the disaster, and the Grimond family of south London lost five of their ten children: Augusta, Violet, Constance, Edward and Leonard. One of the passengers who drowned was Ruby Grierson. She had made a series of short films for the Ministry of Information and was sailing on the *City of Benares* to make a film about the children for the National Film Board of Canada, which her brother, the legendary British documentary-maker John Grierson, now ran.

On 24 September, Churchill announced to the War Cabinet that he was anxious for the overseas evacuation scheme to be discontinued. Not everyone agreed. The ferocity of the Blitz was a compelling argument for thousands of parents, rich and poor, while politicians were anxious not to offend the Dominions who had offered hospitality (though South Africa had stipulated 'no Jews'); and there were those in high places who saw CORB as a form of dialogue that it was vital to keep going with America to ensure the continuing supply of war matériel, and one day an on-side combatant in the war against Hitler. Indeed, when Geoffrey Shakespeare, the Parliamentary Under Secretary at the Dominions Office who was in charge of the scheme, went to Liverpool to see off contingents of embarking CORB evacuees, he would lay on the children the awesome responsibility of being ambassadors for Britain on top of all their other stresses. If they behaved well, he insinuated, 'People will say "What splendid children these are: we must do everything we can to help their parents win the war".' But finally the muddle-headed official overseas evacuation scheme was halted on 3 October 1940, and four groups awaiting evacuation were sent home, though exit permits continued to be granted to parents who wished to send their children overseas and could make their own arrangements.

The Blitz had shown that what people in such extraordinary conditions needed was not strictures and exhortations but information, and that was what was often so sadly lacking – not just from local authorities and government, but from the press and radio too, as Mary Adams, the director of the Intelligence Division of the Ministry of Information, realised. She grew intensely irritated by the insistence on a caricature

'Cockney (or Liverpool or Portsmouth) sparrer' clambering out from beneath the debris of a bombed-out house with a cheery smile on his or her grimy face, calling for a cup of tea and whistling 'There'll Always Be an England'. By March 1941 she felt able to make suggestions to the BBC about the nature of broadcasts after a raid. 'Generalisations on the state of morale should never be given. It is inevitable that many people listening will find themselves an exception to any generalisation . . . Morale should never be over-played. The raid will have made many people frightened and far from "heroic". They will resent a standard being set which they know to be impossible . . . Damage should never be minimised . . . Examples of local efficiency should be praised, but deficiencies should not be deliberately concealed. Concealment is likely to be recognised and lead to mistrust of official news . . . Opportunity should be taken of pointing out that this particular raid . . . is an incident on the whole war front. The raided town courageously endures its experiences in common with others: all make their contribution to the general war effort.'

This was particularly important away from London, where people often felt that the entire focus of the war was on the capital, and that the extent of the damage to their cities and towns, and their suffering, difficulties – and heroism – were going largely unnoticed.

At the start of the war the Deputy Director of the Ministry of Information's News Division, and an ex-editor of the *News Chronicle*, Tom Clarke, recognised that the frankest possible disclosure was vital to sustaining morale. 'Detail kills the public mistrust of vague announcements . . . and no news of actual air raids or of civil casualties ought to be suppressed or delayed except in so far as this is vitally necessary on grounds of national security.' Regional Information Officers would be authorised to put up lists of casualties in their regions, while at a national level the approximate number of dead and injured would be released as soon as possible, and the names of large towns raided normally given. Exceptions were to be made in the case of damage to armament factories, main railway stations and similar installations. But in fact, apart from large cities like London and Liverpool, the names of towns were not usually mentioned in case this helped the enemy to correct his navigational techniques. Censors were told to use their common sense – and they invariably erred on the side of caution. The damage to the house of an eighty-five-year-old woman could be reported, it was decided, since this seemed to underline the inhumane nature of air attacks, but the city where the house was located was not to be named, nor a description given. Photographs destined for newspapers and magazines that were considered harmful to morale were suppressed by the censor, and anything that might identify the specific location of a bomb incident had to be cropped. On 3 July 1940 the War Cabinet decreed that the right to know would be further restricted: in future casualties were to be described only as 'slight', 'considerable' or 'heavy' and no figures were to be given.

Despite such official fears, public morale did not crack under the stresses of the Blitz, mass panic did not ensue, nor were psychiatric hospitals filled to overflowing (suicide rates fell during the war, and psychotic incidents did not notably increase). There were sometimes acute local – but usually short-term – crises, such as in Coventry, Plymouth, Portsmouth and Southampton after particularly heavy and/ or sustained raids. There was much (often justified) criticism of officials, local authorities and of the government for the ways in which they had bungled and 'let the people down', but there was no widespread defeatism, and the rumours of East Enders petitioning Churchill to end the war were apocryphal. As 1940 drew to a close, though, there would be nearly five more months of intensive bombing still to come to test the resources and resolve of the British people.

15

BLITZ, 1941

The street was as flat as this 'ere wharfside – there was just my 'ouse like – well part of my 'ouse. My missus was just making me a cup of tea for when I come 'ome. She were in the passage between the kitchen and the wash 'ouse where it blowed 'er. She were burnt right up to her waist. 'Er legs were just two cinders. And 'er face – the only thing I could recognise 'er by was one of 'er boots – I'd 'ave lost fifteen 'omes if I could 'ave kept my missus. We used to read together. I can't read mesen. She used to read to me like. We'd 'ave our armchairs on either side o' the fire, and she read me bits out o' the paper. We'd a paper every evening. Every evening.

ARP WARDEN, HULL

NIGHT AFTER NIGHT in early January 1941 temperatures fell below freezing. The task of the fire-fighters in the Blitz became close to unbearable. The turntables on fire engines were immobilised by ice, and had to be set in motion by using blow lamps. Hosepipes turned solid if the water pressure fell – which it often did – while icicles hanging from buildings and ladders made conditions even more hazardous for firemen, whose wet clothes froze on their bodies. The vehicles of the ARP, rescue parties, repair squads and other services responding to calls for help were slowed down since the streets often resembled sheets of ice.

The official notion of 'fit for human habitation' was pushed to its very limit in those bitter January days, as families whose homes had been damaged by the air raids lived with icy winds whistling through hastily boarded-up windows, and flurries of snow crept in under the flapping tarpaulin that substituted for a roof. It was always a hardship when water mains were fractured and gas and electric supplies cut in a raid: in these winter months it could precipitate tragedy for the very young and the elderly.

The German strategy for 1941 was to attack 'the most important English harbours for imports, particularly port installations, and ships lying in them, or building [and] to attack shipping especially when homeward bound'. Such targets, 'whose destruction supplements our naval war', would bring a New Year's raid to Cardiff in South Wales, which figured along with Leith, Sunderland, Hull, Grimsby, London, Manchester (Ship Canal), Liverpool, Swansea and Bristol-Avonmouth as places where 'vital harbour installations' were to be destroyed on the orders of the Führer. On the night of 2 January over 100 bombers released high-explosive bombs and 14,000 incendiaries on Cardiff's docks and steelworks. A rubberworks, paint factory and transport offices were hit, railways were put out of action, and large swathes of commercial and residential property, particularly in the west end of the city, were damaged. Within the first half-hour of the raid, more than sixty civilians had been killed in the Riverside suburb, including a funeral party who had decided not to seek shelter: seven of them were killed when a land mine hit the house, and a car parked outside was blasted 100 yards. A few streets away a rescue party dug for six hours to rescue a six-year-old boy trapped under the staircase where he had been sheltering. Throughout the rescue the child was reported to have sung 'God Save the King'. His father, a coalminer, had told him that when men were buried underground 'they kept singing and singing' to guide their rescuers, and the national anthem was, the child claimed, the only tune to which he knew the words.

At around eight o'clock a parachute mine exploded outside the south porch of Llandaff Cathedral, taking the roof completely off the nave and the south side and leaving the interior 'a scene of desolation . . . stout oaken doors were split like matchwood and torn from their hinges . . . the floor was cluttered with fallen timber and broken slates, heavy pews had been thrown about and severely damaged'. The top of the spire was dislodged, making a huge crater in the churchyard and hurling tombstones as far as half a mile away. Fortunately twelve valuable stained-glass windows had been removed to a place of safety on the outbreak of war, and the famous Rossetti triptych, *The Seed of David*, had been put in a packing case and covered with sandbags, and that too was undamaged. A land mine exploded in Cardiff Arms Park and the white Portland stone Civic Centre looked 'like a wedding cake' as everything around it burned, but little damage was done to it as fire-watchers and firemen raked the incendiaries off the roof as fast as they fell and smothered them or tipped them into the Glamorgan canal.

That night 165 people died. Many were given a mass civic burial in Cathays cemetery a week later, and those who could not be identified shared a communal grave. Roughly the same number were seriously injured. Almost a hundred homes were totally destroyed and around 650 damaged to a greater or lesser degree, but the economic dislocation to the port and city was limited.

It was bitterly cold the next night too, on 3 January, when Bristol, which had already suffered heavy raids in November and December 1940, was again the target for the Luftwaffe. And again the city centre was badly damaged: the Guildhall was gutted and so was St Augustine's Church, one of the oldest in the city. The Royal Exchange and Temple Meads station burned, shops and offices in the High Street were demolished, and more houses destroyed or damaged. As firemen fought the blaze, 'two houses might be seen side by side, one in flames with the firemen at work on it, the other hung with long icicles where the streams of water had splashed and frozen'. Eight firemen and two fire-watchers were among the 149 killed that night. The raid lasted intermittently for twelve hours, and a 'Satan' bomb measuring nearly 9 feet (without its tail) and weighing nearly 4,000lb was dropped on the city, but fortunately failed to explode. The next night it was the turn of the Avonmouth Docks, but hundreds of volunteer fire-watchers managed to deal with the fires before they took a hold, and the same was true when the bombers came back during a snowstorm twelve days later.

On 10 January it was ports on the south coast that were in the bombers' sights: Portsmouth was devastated, and Southsea and Gosport were badly damaged too. Portsmouth's Guildhall was gutted by fire, warehouses and timber yards burned out of control, and much damage was done by incendiary and high-explosive bombs. Southsea shops were destroyed and the harbour Central station was badly damaged, as was a ship in the harbour, HMS *Vernon*. The toll for that single night's raid was some 250 dead and injured.

On 9 January 1941 Hitler had given orders for preparations for Operation Sealion, the invasion of Britain, to cease as his focus widened to take in the threat in Italy and the Balkans, and the battle for North Africa. These altered objectives, coupled with the bad weather, gave Britain some respite from air raids, though Southampton, which had had its own 'great blitz' on the two nights of 30 November and 1 December, was again attacked on 19 January, and the bombers returned to London – which had luxuriated in a relative calm since the devastation of 29 December – in January too, mounting four major raids on the capital between the 11th and 29th. The raid on the 11th was short but intense: Liverpool Street station was hit, killing forty-three people including eighteen who were on a passing bus. Bank underground station was hit at a minute to eight in the evening by a high-explosive bomb that made the booking hall and circular gallery cave in. A huge crater opened in the road, disrupting traffic until May, and 111 people including fifty-three shelterers and four staff died in the attack. 'It is said that the blast blew many people on to the live rails and they were electrocuted immediately,' reported Vere Hodgson. The next night it was the turn of the docks, and incendiaries started fires at the Victoria and Albert Docks and at Woolwich Arsenal. Lambeth hospital was hit, with loss of life, and overall around a hundred people were killed in the capital that night. A week later Beckton gasworks, which had been a target on the first night of the Blitz, was hit again, and it was the turn of south London on 29 January, but fortunately the casualties and destruction of property were limited.

In January the countrywide total was 922 killed and 1,927 seriously injured, and in February the diminishing number of raids meant it fell to 789 and 1,068. The Luftwaffe moved across the Bristol Channel to the port of Swansea, which had been heavily attacked on 17 January, and for three successive nights they bombarded the city. On 21 February – the final and worst night – the angry red glow from the mile-square fire raging out of control in the city centre could be seen from the north Devon coast. By morning over 40 acres had been razed to the ground including 575 business premises and the large David Evans department store. During the January raid and the three nights in February, 230 people were killed and 6,500 made homeless. In total Swansea suffered more deaths and material damage from enemy action than anywhere else in Wales during the Second World War.

As the weather improved the bombers came back with renewed ferocity. From March until May many of the same cities that had been so cruelly attacked in the autumn were again subject to heavy raids, with the Luftwaffe intensifying its attacks on western seaports in an attempt to destroy Britain's sea trade, and on industrial cities to do the same to Britain's wartime production.

Merseyside, which had already had a baptism of fire in November and a follow-up just before Christmas, was again heavily bombed on 12 and 13 March – a full moon – with the docks and Cammel Laird shipworks the main target. On such a clear night the harbour and the river proved as perfidious to Merseyside as the Thames had proved to be to London. The docks were badly damaged, with cold stores and granaries destroyed, two ships sunk and terrible damage inflicted on the small houses in the area. Several Liverpool landmarks burned that night, including the Cotton Exchange, the General Post Office and the White Star Building, but it was Birkenhead that suffered the most casualties when three hospitals were hit and thousands made homeless – 264 died there. Among the many tragic stories was one of a Roman Catholic priest, Canon J. J. Tallon, who had just returned from administering the last rites to parishioners who had been mortally wounded in the raids, when the presbytery of Our Lady's Church in Price Street received a direct hit and he was killed. Nearly 200 people died in Wallasey, and nearly fifty in Liverpool. On 16 March, rescue workers in Wallasey heard what they took to be a kitten mewing in a bombed house in Lancaster Avenue, but as they listened it grew stronger and they clawed away debris to find a baby girl, just a few months old, who had been buried for three and half days. They were able to gently extract her from the ruins, covered in dust and rubble, but tenaciously alive. Her parents had both been killed. The total casualties in Merseyside for the two nights were 1,300 killed or injured.

The toll went on: there were smaller raids on 7 and 26 April 1941, and for the first eight nights of May Merseyside experienced almost unremitting night-time bombing with the night of 3/4 May being 'without the slightest doubt the worst in the city's history' as almost 300 bombers converged on the city and 'the tally of famous buildings damaged and destroyed reads like a guide book to Liverpool'. The seven storeys of Lewis's department store blazed after being hit by a stick of incendiaries, as did Blackler's a few yards away, and the shop's entire stock was destroyed, including a newly arrived £10,000 consignment of silk stockings. The museum was hit, and an aquarium in the basement – housing a seal among other species of water life – was destroyed; the Central Lending Library lost its entire sheet music collection and most of its Picton Reference Library to the flames. Generally regarded as a lesser tragedy was an incident at the Inland Revenue Building. After it had gone up in flames, a staff officer opened the fireproof doors and the draught ignited the previously untouched tax records and reduced them to ashes.

The SS *Malakand*, a steamer packed with 1,000 tons of shells and bombs in her hold, bound for the Middle East, was moored in Liverpool's docks when she was hit. It proved impossible either to bring the blaze under control, or to scuttle the ship, and a few hours after the All Clear had sounded she blew up, with flames shooting 1,600 feet into the air. The ship's anchor was thrown 100 yards and some steel plates ended up over 2 miles away. It took seventy-four hours for all the *Malakand*'s cargo of ammunition to explode. That night half the dock's 144 shipping berths were rendered unusable, and for some time only a quarter of the usual quantity of cargo could be handled. Fifty-seven vessels had been sunk or destroyed, and the mouth to the harbour was blocked so shipping could get neither in nor out. The overhead railway and roads in were also severely damaged. 'I shudder to think what would have happened if the Blitz had gone on for three more days,' said Admiral Sir Percy Noble, commander-in-chief Western Approaches, since another such period of intensive damage would have put Liverpool's port out of action for several months to come – with disastrous consequences for the prosecution of the war.

Away from the docks, Bootle had experienced very heavy bombing: some 200 homes were demolished and a further 3,000 damaged on 3 May. The town hall, a dye works, a cold storage plant, Bryant and May's match factory and the offices of Vernon's football pools were damaged. Mill Road Infirmary was hit by an exceptionally heavy bomb that destroyed three hospital buildings and many nearby houses, and caused heavy casualties. Twelve WVS workers were killed when a rest centre, in which they were caring for victims of the raid, received a direct hit.

The next morning the centre of the city of Liverpool was a scene of utter devastation, with fires still burning as more than 6,000 demolition and clearance workers – including over 2,500 troops drafted in for the purpose – started on the daunting and depressing task of clearing up the city and getting it to function again. But it still wasn't over for Merseyside. At a minute to midnight on Sunday 4 May the bombers came back in waves, attacking Bootle, and laying waste the Belgian Seamen's hostel and a ship, the SS *Sandal* in Liverpool. St Silvester's School was gutted, as was a famous landmark, the Rotunda Theatre in Scotland Road, where Dan Leno and other music-hall luminaries had entertained generations of Scousers.

The raids were a body blow to Merseyside. In the 'May week', 1,900 people were killed and 1,450 seriously wounded; 66,000 houses were destroyed and some 70,000 people were made homeless. That terrible week was, recorded the official historian, 'the longest, unbroken series of serious attacks on any provincial area of the whole war'. A local MP called it 'simple murder'.

In the early spring of 1941 Clydesiders had begun to dare to believe that their city might be spared the assault on the seaports. They were optimistic that Scotland was too far north, out of range of the fighters that flew to protect the German bombers. It was a vain hope. Glasgow, Britain's second largest city, with a population of more than a million, had a concentration of heavy industry – iron, steel and chemical works –

and the world-renowned shipbuilding yards: Harland and Wolff, John Brown, Beardmores, A&J Inglis, which between them had built ships totalling over 750,000 tons in the 1930s – more than a third of Britain's total output. That and the acres of dockland, where ships were serviced and fitted and vessels from overseas berthed, made Clydeside an inevitable target for an enemy determined to cripple Britain's economy and to destroy its capacity to wage war.

For the two consecutive moonlit nights of 13/14 and 14/15 March 1941, the Luftwaffe came to bomb the docks: 200 planes dropped 272 tons of high explosives and almost 60,000 incendiaries, setting alight a timber yard and starting a massive fire at Rothesay Docks. In Glasgow the university was hit and so was a hospital and a school. Eighty workers were killed when a bomb hit a shelter at Yarrow's shipyard, and the communications centre at Clydebank was put out of action, which made the work of the Civil Defence services almost impossible.

The fires were still burning – visible in the sky from up to a hundred miles away – when the bombers came back the next night. The Rolls-Royce aero-engine factory at Hillington was hit, as were oil storage tanks at Dalnottar and a power station at Yoker. A conflagration took hold at Princes Dock, Govan, but despite the extensive damage the docks and shipyards were not disabled and continued to function. The Lord Provost of Glasgow remained confident that 'Glasgow houses are more solidly built than those that collapsed from concussion in London', but his optimism was sadly misplaced. The homes and workplaces of Clydeside suffered grievously, and the Civil Defence services were overwhelmed at the scale of the attack. Only eight of Clydebank's 12,000 houses escaped damage and thousands of people had to be evacuated to rest centres. It was clear that there was nothing like sufficient shelter accommodation for such a concentrated onslaught.

It was the turn of the people of Glasgow itself, when bombs fell in great numbers on residential areas of Drumchapel, Maryhill, Partick and Govan. In a particularly horrifying incident a parachute mine landed on a tenement building, killing eighty-three people. In the raids 55,000 Clydesiders lost their homes, over a thousand were killed and around 1,600 seriously injured – though it was not at first admitted that these figures were so high. As there had been a shortage of shelters for Clydesiders in life, so there was of coffins in death. Their violent death in the Blitz was robbed of any dignity as bodies were trussed in sheets tied with string at neck and waist for mass burial, a practice the District Commissioner, Sir Stephen Bilsland, complained bitterly was 'indecorous'.

While poor weather limited the activities of the Luftwaffe in late March and early April, 172 aircraft returned to Clydeside on 7 April, causing more loss of homes and lives and severe damage to transport and utility services, but little additional damage to the already stricken dock areas. The entire country had been on alert that night and almost all areas reported raids. The Germans were no longer concentrating on one place each night: the bombing had become simultaneously nationwide with previously untouched places such as Crewe, Ipswich and Great Yarmouth (where twenty civilians were killed) suffering air raids. Clydebank was attacked again on 5 and 6 May: high-density tenement blocks were demolished, with considerable loss of life; John Brown's Clydebank shipyard was hit, as were Yoker's at Rothesay Docks and Singer's factory and timber yard; the gasworks at Greenock exploded and commercial property all over the area was damaged. J. P. McHutchison, the former Education Officer for Clydeside, considered that the area had suffered 'a bad knock, probably severer than Coventry or any English town since the whole town "got it" and no single area or district escaped. It is difficult to discover another place of similar size in Britain that was virtually obliterated.'

Almost 90 per cent of the children who had been evacuated in 1939 from Clydeside had returned home long before the March Blitz came. However, a second evacuation was organised and over 100,000 mothers, children and others who were eligible left Glasgow, Clydebank, Dumbarton and Greenock. By July 1941 around 142,000 evacuees were living in Scottish reception areas.

Raids on Britain's ports and industrial centres continued throughout March and April, and into May. Cardiff and Southampton were bombed several times, and Portsmouth suffered its thirty-seventh raid on 11 March: another attack on the docks, shipyards and factories sent 193 high-explosive bombs – many of them as heavy as 5,500lb – and 46,000 incendiaries raining down on the town. Fires were started in fuel storage depots and at the Royal Naval Barracks, and bombs fell nearby at

Hamble, Selsey, Littlehampton and on the Isle of Wight. On 17 April Portsmouth was attacked again, and again the docks burned, electricity supplies were cut, houses destroyed. Great Yarmouth was raided again and an attack was made on Bawdsey Manor radar station further along the Suffolk coast near Aldeburgh. On 26 April a bomb hit the Ferry Inn at Horning on the Norfolk Broads and twenty people drinking in the bar were killed. On 27 April the Luftwaffe came back to Portsmouth and started major fires in the dockyards; parachute mines struck several buildings, severely damaging the casualty ward at the Royal Portsmouth Hospital (which had already been hit twice before in previous raids). The patients had been evacuated but several staff were killed. The central railway station was hit and so was Madden's Hotel where twenty-eight people were killed, and Portsea Island suffered considerable damage to its residential and commercial properties. Over the two nights 102 people were killed and 140 seriously injured.

Bristol was again a German target in March and April. On 16 March incendiaries caused over 150 fires in the city, and the electricity supply was cut. Eastville, Fishponds and Whitehall districts were particularly badly damaged that night, and a public shelter in the city was hit, killing twenty-five people. The crypt of St Barnabas Church received a direct hit and fifteen people died. Several fine Regency terraces in Clifton were irreparably damaged and scarcely a parish church throughout the city escaped; warehouses and factories were destroyed, and 6,000 homes were added to the list of those already demolished or severely damaged. On 3 and 4 April it was again the turn of Avonmouth Docks, which were showered with 80 tons of high explosives and 2,000 incendiaries – but again managed to continue to operate.

Decoy fires lit in the surrounding countryside succeeded in deflecting a number of bombs away from their intended target. Known as a 'Starfish' site, these decoys were built within the vicinity of an important industrial town or city to lure enemy aircraft off target to drop their bombs in the countryside. The system imitated the construction of dummy airfields (complete with dummy aircraft) and dummy factories that had proved moderately effective in deceiving the Luftwaffe earlier in the war. The bonfires were ignited electrically as soon as bombs had begun to fall, in the hope of luring subsequent bombers away from their target, while fire-fighters worked frantically to extinguish the fires that had been started by incendiaries hitting the 'real' target. By March 1941 there were 108 Starfish sites, and 164 by the end of the year. London initially had a Starfish site in Richmond Park, though it was moved to Hampstead Heath in May 1942. Because of its proximity to residential areas it was, however, used only in exceptional circumstances with the express permission of the chief of air staff.

Good Friday fell on 11 April in 1941, and that night 150 people were killed and nearly as many badly injured when Bristol and Avonmouth were deluged with 200 tons of high explosives and 35,000 incendiaries that yet again damaged the docks, the centre of the city, Clifton, Horfield, industrial and commercial premises, Colston girls' school and a public library. Taylors, a department store, and St Paul's Church in Bedminster were destroyed, communications were put out of action, and St Philip's Bridge was destroyed. Known locally as the 'Half Penny Bridge' – it had replaced a ferry in 1841 and charged a toll until 1875 – it was next to the power station serving the tram system, which was not badly damaged – but the supply cable in the bridge was and Bristol was never to have a tram service again. By the morning of Easter Saturday more than 140 Bristolians had been killed and many more were homeless, bereaved, injured and traumatised. It was, however, to be the last major raid that the city would suffer.

That night Winston Churchill was on his way by train to Bristol from Wales. He had been told of the 'uneasiness' existing in the country on account of 'the gravity of the war situation', and had been on a tour to see for himself what it amounted to. The Prime Minister had gone 'to some of our great cities, seaports which had been most heavily bombed . . . To leave the offices in Whitehall with their ceaseless hum of activity and stress, and to go out to the front, by which I mean the streets and wharves of London or Liverpool, Manchester, Cardiff, Swansea or Bristol, is like going out of a hothouse on to the bridge of a fighting ship.' The Prime Minister had spent that morning among Swansea's 'battered ruins' accompanied by the Australian Prime Minister Robert Menzies and the US Ambassador John Winant, to whom Churchill, as Chancellor of Bristol University, was to present honorary degrees the next day. Their train was held in the sidings overnight, and the distinguished guests were woken by the sound of the sirens and the bombs falling, and could see and hear the distant raid. The next morning

Churchill toured the streets of Bristol where fires still smouldered, 'sitting on the hood of an open car and waving his hat'. 'There was devastation such as I had never thought possible,' reported his secretary Jock Colville who was with the party. Later that day the degree ceremony went ahead. Many of the audience 'kept on arriving late with grime on their faces half washed off. They had their ceremonial robes over their fire-fighting clothes which were still wet.' As Churchill's train pulled out of Temple Meads station his eyes filled with tears. 'They have such confidence,' he choked, hiding his face in a newspaper. 'It is a grave responsibility.'

Terrible devastation came to Plymouth in March and April 1941, a city that had had intermittent small raids since the previous July. Earlier in the day of Thursday 20 March, the West Country town had had a visit from the King and Queen, who had taken tea with the local MP, Lady Nancy Astor, the first woman to take her seat in the House of Commons, and her husband, and local people had 'enjoyed a gala day with bands and dancing on the Hoe' – the 'high place', a large promenade commanding an excellent view of the sea from where Sir Francis Drake is reputed to have espied the Spanish Armada in 1588 as he played bowls. Hardly had the royal couple departed when 125 bombers droned over the city, aiming for the port and the docks. Numerous fires started: in the city centre Messrs Spooners, a department store, was gutted by fire, as was the Royal Hotel nearby; the new post office and the county court were destroyed, and all public utilities were severely disrupted. A particularly large fire in the Great Western Docks could be seen from miles away. The next night 175 bombers came, and by the morning after the second raid little remained of the centre of the city. It was 'a brick-pitted desert' with just the skeleton of the Guildhall left standing, while the City Hospital, St Andrew's Church and the Law Courts were in ruins, like dozens of other buildings – department stores, schools, churches of all denominations, a synagogue and two Salvation Army halls. Shops, cinemas, cafés, pubs, hotels, libraries, hospitals, offices and the Promenade pier were destroyed, while Derry's Clock Tower, a notable local landmark, was still erect but with its mechanism smashed.

On the Hoe a bomb-disposal team were preparing to lift a UXB on to a lorry when it exploded, killing all five men. In the two raids more than

18,000 houses were destroyed or damaged, 5,000 people made homeless, 336 killed and 283 seriously injured. A seventeen-year-old ambulance driver was sent to 'a park where a land mine had dropped on a maze of underground shelters, full of people'. Her job was to take the injured to hospital. 'When I arrived soldiers with lights [were] digging people out at the sides of the crater. Some were just parts of bodies and, where it was possible, we had to attach a label to the body or parts, with my name and the name of the first aid post and whether it was male or female. We then went into the shelter, and there were all these people just sitting, some with children still on their laps, people with glasses on, and the glass still intact, and they were all dead, killed by the blast . . . their hair looked like wigs, sort of lifeless and dusty.'

The water supply ran out, fires had to be left to burn themselves out and the Civil Defence services proved 'quite inadequate' to feed, house and clothe the population. But before Plymouth and Devonport had time to begin the process of recovery, the bombers were back, this time for five nights – 21 to 23 April and then again on the 28th and 29th. Their tactics were now familiar: a vanguard of planes would drop flares and incendiaries that set the area alight and acted as a beacon for the subsequent waves of bombers. As the result of these raids, the city was 'eradicated'. Whole streets were rubbed out with 'nothing but twisted girders and rubble' to be seen, a shocked WVS worker driving a mobile canteen noted. A Mass-Observation team and the US journalist Quentin Reynolds, both used to seeing the devastation of blitzed cities, were appalled by what they saw. 'Nothing I had seen had prepared me for the sight of Plymouth,' wrote Reynolds. M-O reported, 'The civic and domestic devastation exceeds anything we have seen.' Neighbouring Devonport was also 'practically wiped out'. It was reminiscent of Silvertown on the night of 7 September 1940, with whole streets of houses clustering round the docks destroyed. A shopkeeper wrote that he could 'stand in the central shopping area of Plymouth and Devonport without being able to see an inhabited building and practically without seeing any walls standing.' 'Scarcely a house seems to be habitable,' wrote Jock Colville, who had accompanied Churchill to the blitzed city on 2 May. '. . . I saw a bus which had been carried bodily by the force of an explosion, on to the roof of a building some 150 yards from where it had been standing . . . the whole city is wrecked except, characteristically, the important part of the naval establishment' which had been the real target.

Earlier in the day the Prime Minister and his party had visited the Royal Naval Barracks 'where bombs had killed a number of sailors. There was a gruesome sight in the gymnasium: beds in which some forty slightly injured men lay, separated only by a low curtain from some coffins which were being nailed down. The hammering must have been horrible to the injured men, but such was the damage that there was nowhere else it could be done.' The Admiralty refused on security grounds to give details of damage to the docks but it was extensive, with such landmarks as the Royal Marine Barracks, the Army Gun Wharf, the Royal Naval Hospital and the Royal William Victualling Yard all hit.

Seventy-two civilians were killed when a bomb hit an underground shelter in Portland Square. Though the casualties were heavy, they would probably have been heavier had the centre of the city been more crowded: an 8.30 p.m. curfew imposed after the March raids ensured that it was relatively sparsely populated. In March and April 932 died. Of those some fifty policemen, members of the fire services, ARP wardens and a Heavy Rescue worker had been killed in the line of duty. The social dislocation was immense: 40,000 people had been made homeless and were in need of shelter, food and clothing at a time when the many of the communication and distribution systems were out of commission. On the night of the 23rd, at around midnight, the staff of the *Western Morning News* realised that it was no longer possible to produce their paper in the blitzed city, yet for the sake of morale they considered it essential that there was a newspaper the morning after. This was particularly the case as the first BBC broadcasts had spoken of the 22 April raid as being 'short and sharp', which had incensed the locals and led Lady Astor to demand an apology both from the BBC and the Ministry of Information – which she dubbed the 'Ministry of Inflammation'. The newspaper's editorial and printing staff crammed into cars and, leaving the burning city, sped to Exeter where they managed to get out an edition.

In its agony Plymouth – like Coventry and Liverpool and Glasgow – became the focus for all the concerns about how a community could cope with the effects of mass bombardment, how its people could be cared for, its morale sustained.

One way that people in devastated cities tried to escape from the bombs conformed to the timeless image of refugees fleeing war, trudging along roads out of the cities into the countryside. Families with their possessions heaped in a handcart, in a pram, on the back of a bicycle, or just carried in a bundle, cramming into cars, lorries, taxis. People who had little idea where they were going, just knowing they had to get away. It was a spectre that had haunted the British government since the summer of 1940 for such a movement suggested morale had cracked, the will to 'stay put' and fight had seeped away: it was resonant of the *exode* in France in May and June when thousands of French citizens fleeing the advancing German troops had clogged the roads, making it almost impossible for the Allied soldiers to mount a counter-attack, hindering the tanks, making surrender all but certain. After the raids on Coventry in November 1940, a *Daily Herald* journalist had encountered the first large body of refugees as he approached from Rugby: 'children were being carried in their father's arms and pushed along in perambulators, luggage was piled high . . . rugs, blankets, anything they could carry from their ruined homes . . . There were also many motor cars parked by the roadside in which people would pass the night despite the intense cold, rather than stay in the city.' Likewise from Barrow, Bootle, Liverpool, Hull, Clydebank, Belfast and particularly Plymouth, people began to stream out of the cities before nightfall.

Some of those leaving had not lost their homes but were so traumatised by the ferocity of the raids that they were determined not sleep another night in the city. As Londoners took to the tubes, those in provincial cities and towns trekked into the surrounding countryside. With its belief that such behaviour was inimical to morale, the government tried to discourage it, but it was almost impossible to identify the trekkers from the homeless, and they could hardly be refused food or shelter.

After the Clydeside Blitz on two successive nights in March 1941 some 35,000 people out of a population of 47,000 were homeless. By April there were reckoned to be only about 2,000 people sleeping the night in the town. Some had moved to Glasgow or other nearby towns, several thousand were evacuated to Port Leven and thousands more trekked away from the city each night. But after a few days most were back at work despite the fact that many were billeted as far as 30 miles away and the largest employer, John Brown's shipyard, was reluctant to provide a hot meal for its workers.

On April 24 1941 as many as 50,000 people wearily walked away from Plymouth. This stream invariably included the mayor and several city councillors who did not seem to consider they might have a responsibility to provide leadership, having failed to provide adequate facilities. The trekkers found that many of the rural rest centres were already crowded with homeless people. A YMCA canteen organiser reported that when they stopped at Yelverton Moors in April and she called out in the darkness for customers, a queue had formed in no time of people who had scrambled out of the ditches and heather.

When Merseyside was raided for seven successive nights in May 1941 the city was reported to 'have a depressed and sordid atmosphere. This is partly due to the blackness and the number of very poor seen in the streets, and is enhanced by the Blitz debris.' The local authorities in the area were reported to be 'too easily satisfied with the provisions made and are inclined to ignore public opinion . . . [and] to be on the defensive and unwilling to discuss difficulties'. There was a notable lack of co-operation between the ARP and voluntary organisations, food supplies were limited and dispersal, particularly of the elderly, bordered on the chaotic. Liverpool had its own version of Stepney's notorious Tilbury shelter, and in many other public shelters conditions were 'indescribable'. In such a situation there was criticism of the authorities, scapegoating of Jews – as there was in the East End of London – and a mass desire to get out of the area. On 10 May 1941 as many as 50,000 trekkers clambered on to the extra buses and trains that had been laid on to get them out of their blitzed cities and into the countryside of Cheshire and North Wales. The small town of Maghull was one that absorbed the exodus: its normal population of 8,000 had made preparations to receive 1,750 should this be needed. In the event 6,000 people arrived, and they had to be crammed into every school and church hall in the area, and a large hospital was opened to accommodate the overflow.

In Bootle a total of 262 people were killed in the May week raids, but only about one house in ten escaped damage, and one person in every four was homeless; a third of all shops were destroyed, all main roads were blocked and of twelve rest centres in the town, eleven were put out of action. On 8 May, the last night of the raid, nearly half the population had fled into the surrounding countryside, and ten days later nearly a fifth were still trekking up to 20 miles every night to get away from Bootle – though after a few days many came back into the town each day to work.

The 'Funk Express' was the name given to the train that ferried hundreds of businessmen away from Liverpool during the Blitz weeks, and some Bristolians referred to trekkers as the 'yellow convoy', complaining that their departure left the city's fire-watching forces depleted and imperilled those who stayed put as the government urged. The nightly exodus suggested fear, certainly – but it was largely in response to the unwillingness of many provincial towns and cities to learn the lessons of London and prepare for the homeless and the disorientated, as well as the dead and injured. 'It seems that each city and town had to experience a major attack before making adequate plans for the relief of the community.' In this context trekking can be seen neither as a tendency to scuttle nor as mindless flight, but as a largely rational response to a desperate situation.

The east coast of Britain also had raids in the spring of 1941, but until May these were generally less severe than those on London, the western ports and the industrial Midlands. Hull experienced a major raid on 18 March, and in the fog many of the 300 tons of high-explosive bombs and 77,000 incendiaries missed their target – the port – and fell on commercial and residential properties, killing sixty-two civilians. The city suffered more raids on 31 March when bad weather over Merseyside diverted bombers from Liverpool. This time the ARP HQ was hit by a parachute mine, and the Deputy Medical Officer of Health, Dr David Diamond, who could have congratulated himself on the success of his recent blood donation scheme in the town, was killed instantly as he talked to the newly appointed Civil Defence Medical Officer in the basement. Fire-watchers on the roof were also killed and all that was ever found of PC Robert Garton, the policeman who had been standing guard at the door, were fragments of his uniform.

Sheffield had originally been the Luftwaffe's target on the nights of 7 and 8 May, but again the weather was not propitious so Hull made the unenviable move up the ladder of destruction from secondary to primary target. As 800 fires raged – visible from the coast of Denmark – the docks were badly damaged, Riverside Quay was gutted, timber stacks flared up and burning embers from the wood started other fires. Rank's flour warehouse was destroyed and a nearby stable was hit – the terrified horses had to be led to safety with sacks over their heads so they could not see the flames; some of the huge grain warehouses were bombed and their contents smouldered for days. The railway network was damaged, and the main bus garage was set alight with buses burning until nothing was left but charred iron skeletons. Hull was left without gas after the raid since mains were either fractured or flooded. A total of 279 civilians were killed and 550 injured – many seriously; 30,000 houses were demolished or rendered uninhabitable, and the task of feeding and providing accommodation for thousands stretched to the limit the resources of the Hull Civil Defence services and the 1,200 members of the WVS.

Hull suffered its fiftieth raid on 2 June 1941. Many previous raids had been relatively small-scale, as was this one, but this time there were serious consequences since 'All Clear raiders passed' was signalled prematurely, and as people were making their way back home from the shelters a number of bombs dropped, killing twenty-seven. The Deputy Chief Constable was also killed as he drove to a bomb site believing the raid over.

In February the South Shields coast between St Abbs and Flamborough Head had been raided: seven people were killed and twenty-four injured, and a number of houses destroyed or badly damaged. Newcastle had been the target for a five-hour, 120-bomber attack on 9 April 1941, and 150 tons of high explosives and 50,000 incendiaries carpeted the city and towns as far away as Jarrow, Gateshead, North and South Shields, Hebburn, Wallsend and Tynemouth. The Tyne docks burned, timber sheds went up along with warehouses, and many houses and commercial premises were destroyed or badly damaged. The Queen's Theatre in South Shields was set on fire and so was Sunderland's town hall; gas mains and sewers were hit and telephone and electric cables severed, while bombs fell on railway lines 'where passenger coaches were flying about like toys'. Though the damage was widespread over Tyne and Wear, the scattered nature of the raids meant that casualties were fewer than might have been feared, with some forty people killed and 100 seriously injured.

★

The Midlands did not escape in what was to be this final phase of the Blitz: Birmingham was again attacked on 11 March, and again on 9 and 10 April when 40,000 incendiaries and 280 tons of high explosives set the Bull Ring, the High Street, New Street and Dale End alight as well as houses on the city's outskirts. The next night 245 bombers came back and this time the greatest damage was sustained by the residential areas such as Small Heath, King's Heath, Aston and Nechells. In the two raids, 350 died and hundreds more were injured. On 16 May, as hundreds of German bombers were moving their bases from France to attack eastwards, Birmingham was again attacked. This time many of the bombs missed the city and fell on nearby Nuneaton, where more than eighty people were killed. Those bombs that did hit home on Birmingham caught the Wolsey car plant and the ICI chemical works, with the usual devastation of shops, offices and houses, and over thirty people were killed.

Nottingham had escaped heavy air raids until 8 May 1941, when a navigational error deflected the major attack planned for the Rolls-Royce factory and other industries in Derby. In his memoirs Churchill claimed that the raid was an example of the British successfully interfering with the German navigational beams, and the official historian repeated the claim, but it has not been substantiated from German sources. The Intelligence 'success' left Nottingham with 156 dead. Nearly 90 per cent of the bombs that fell on the city during the entire war fell that night. Almost a hundred fires were started in the city centre, half of which could be classified as major; 350 houses were made uninhabitable, and more than 430 civilians were killed in Nottingham and the surrounding area – forty-nine when bombs struck night-shift workers taking cover in two air-raid shelters beneath the Co-op bakery. The shelters received a direct hit: the bomb entered at an angle and skidded across the floor 'looking like a dustbin coming straight at me', recalled a member of the works' fire-watching party. The vicar of a nearby church, St Christopher's, also destroyed in the raid, was dissuaded from entering the devastated shelters. 'There was nothing I could do . . . the wreckage was all mixed up with marmalade and jam and flour and bodies. It was terrible.' The historic Moot Hall and Lace Market were damaged, as was University College. The cricket ground at Trent Bridge was hit by a bomb and so was Notts County football pitch.

The Starfish decoy, which had worked well in Bristol, worked spectacularly in March 1941 when an attack on Cardiff, Penarth and Barry was 'diverted' and 102 HE bombs fell on the decoy site, helping to save the vital ammunition depot at Barry; and again on the night of 17/18 April, when 90 per cent of the bombs intended for Portsmouth fell instead on the Starfish on Hayling Island.

Between March and May 1941 there were six major and a number of lesser raids on London, the first coming on 8 March after a break of two months. Across London, 30,000 incendiaries fell, causing a number of fires and damaging three railway terminus stations and some rolling stock. The North Lodge of Buckingham Palace received a direct hit and St Bartholomew's Hospital was damaged. That night two bombs fell on the Rialto cinema near Leicester Square and crashed through to the basement Café de Paris, advertised as 'the safest and gayest restaurant in town, 20 feet below ground'. It was reputed to have been constructed on the site of a bear-baiting pit, and was similar in design to the ballroom of the ill-fated *Titanic* which had been built around the same time. That March night it was packed with officers on leave and elegantly dressed women, sitting at tables round the dance floor sipping cocktails and listening to the jazz played by the legendary Ken 'Snakehips' Johnson and his band. Snakehips had just started on the second chorus of 'Oh Johnny' when two 110lb bombs crashed down. One failed to go off, but split open spilling its contents on the floor; the other exploded in front of the stage killing Johnson, a member of his band and the head waiter Charles. Thirty of the diners were also killed, and Betty, the daughter of the former Prime Minister Stanley Baldwin, was among the injured. A dustman who happened to be passing stood with tears running down his cheeks as he watched 'young men in uniform carrying out their dead girlfriends'. It was a hideous sight inside too, with the dead and injured lying among the rubble, twisted metal, glass and broken furniture. A misdirected call meant that some of those who were seriously injured had to wait over an hour for an ambulance, and meanwhile looters stepped over bodies, emptying handbags, searching jacket pockets for wallets and wrenching rings from the fingers of the dead and dying.

'It was a gory incident,' conceded Finsbury ARP warden Barbara Nixon, '. . . the melodramatic nature of the incident caught the fancy of reporters and for three days the papers were full of the gallantries of expensive girls who had torn their expensive dance frocks into strips to make bandages . . . but the same week another dancehall a mile to the east of us was hit and there were nearly two hundred casualties. This time there were only 10s 6d frocks, and a few lines in the paper followed by "It was feared there were several casualties." Local feeling was rather bitter.'

The next four raids were increasingly ferocious. 'The Big Blitz Back Again' the newspaper headlines read. On 15 March the south and east of London suffered when over 100 tons of explosives and 16,000 incendiaries falling across thirty boroughs damaged the docks, and three hospitals along with shops, offices and houses. The worst incident, though, was in north London when a bomb fell on Southgate, killing forty-two civilians. On 19 March 500 planes dropped 122,000 incendiaries and 470 tons of high-explosive bombs over a period of six hours, aiming at the docks – but sending down hundreds of parachute bombs. It was impossible to target these accurately and they fell on Stepney, Poplar and West Ham, razing rows of houses. The devastation was enormous since several of the bombs were SC 2500s – known as the 'Max', weighing 5,500lb. At least eight hospitals were hit, as were public buildings as far apart as Bromley on the borders of London in Kent and Leyton in east London, and some public shelters were demolished including one in Poplar where forty-four civilians were killed. As many as 2,000 fires were started. Public services were seriously disrupted and railway lines broken and buckled. Churchill was dining at Downing Street that night with Averell Harriman, the US Special Envoy, and Anthony Biddle, the recently appointed US Ambassador to the Governments in Exile in Britain. When the raid started, the Prime Minister took his guests on to the roof of the Air Ministry, in the words of Jock Colville, 'to watch the fun'.

Nearly a month later, on 16/17 April, came the heaviest raid of the Blitz so far. For eight and a half hours the planes came – some making as many as three flights shuttling bombs from France in a total of 685 sorties. The total tonnage of bombs dropped on London was 890, and this included 150,000 incendiaries. The targets were, as usual, the docks, warehouses and factories around the Thames, but this time 'up West' was again a victim too. More than sixty public buildings were hit during 'The Wednesday', as the raid came to be known, including the Houses of Parliament, the Admiralty, the Law Courts and St Paul's Cathedral, the ultimate symbol of London's survival. New vistas were opened up as parts of buildings were sheered off. Cordite and particles of burning wood hung in the air as shops in Leicester Square and Oxford Street were blown apart, nineteen churches were destroyed or badly damaged and eighteen hospitals suffered some damage, railway termini were closed and the underground brought to a halt in several places. Most of London was affected: there was damage recorded in sixty-six boroughs, and over 2,000 fires burned, of which fifty were 'major' or 'serious'. Bromley was hit by eighteen bombs, and seventy-four people were killed.

In Walworth two fire-watchers in the Rev. John Markham's patrol were killed when a large bomb hit one three-storey block of flats near the Elephant and Castle and badly damaged another. The next morning most of the rescue parties had left the site of devastation, convinced that everyone had been accounted for, but Markham's lists showed there might be two casualties trapped somewhere. 'We called and listened by a heap of bricks and mortar. Then we heard what sounded like the faint mewing of a cat. I told the [one remaining] Rescue Squad to dig, and very soon we found two girls, one dead under the remains of a kitchen table, where she had sheltered, the other still alive, sitting in the remains of an armchair nearby. She was the source of the faint sound, which was all she could make when she regained consciousness six hours later. Her throat and lungs were choked with white mortar dust . . . She was rushed to hospital, where she recovered quite quickly from a broken arm and severe bruising. I do not think she ever knew how close we had been to leaving the site that April morning before we heard that faint mewing sound.'

The night's casualties reached an unprecedented high: 1,180 killed – including many ARP workers who died in the line of duty – and 2,230 seriously injured.

But three nights later that figure was exceeded when 1,200 Londoners were killed and over 1,000 badly injured on 19 April, which was for ever after referred to as 'The Saturday'. The Royal Naval College at

Greenwich was hit and so was St Peter's Hospital, Stepney; houses and flats were left in ruins, many with their inhabitants dead or maimed. In Chelsea the Royal Hospital was hit and nine Pensioners were killed – one of whom was 101 years old. The remaining veterans declined to be evacuated.

A four-roomed mansion flat off Cheyne Walk near the Thames Embankment in Chelsea, for which Theodora Fitzgibbon and her lover paid £2 a week since 'rents had dropped considerably owing to the evacuation of many people to the country', was badly damaged by a bomb explosion that night. 'The window blew in and a dense cloud of greenish dust moved slowly through the gaping hole, forming into the shape of a weird monster . . . I could move only my head, for the bed was covered with lumps of plaster, broken glass, wood and what looked like small stones . . . From the first floor someone shouted up: "Come down slowly by the wall, the stairs may not be there." . . . We sat down, slithering on our bottoms like children. In the street were the occupants from the lower floors, wardens, ambulances, nurses, firemen and police, all lit by torchlight, the wardens with their log-sheets hanging round their necks. Someone tried to herd me into an ambulance but I pulled away, and Peter and I went into the Crossed Keys, which was wide open, the door and one wall was blown into the bar. The elderly couple who ran it . . . were sitting down sipping brandy, covered in white plaster looking very tired and very old . . . We soon left, and went to see if we could help. The nurses' home of the Cheyne Hospital for Children had a top floor blown off: a neat nurse's bedroom, the ceiling light still shining, looked like a stage set. A warden perilously climbed up the bombed staircase and switched it off, although there was a flaming gas main burning around the corner which floodlit the whole area. The church was nothing but an immense heap of timber and stone, flames licking through it . . . The New Café Lombard and all the large and small houses at the end of Old Church Street had been flung together into a giant mountain of shale-like destruction, all lit by the fires of the gas main. Under that fantastic mountain were people, some still alive. Heavy stones were flung aside like pebbles: the local grocer of the street, Mr Cremonesi, put his hand down through a space and felt warm flesh. A naked unhurt woman was pulled up . . . A curious rattling sound like a time bomb made us cautious: a battered tin was moving on a piece of stick. Below, the young woman had forced it through the bricks to attract attention. She was rescued by a war reserve policeman. A sixteen-year-old girl, pinned, only her head showing, talked to a rescue worker: she was freed but died several hours later.

'Young and old brought buckets of water to supply stirrup pumps to douse the fires. The dust was like a great fog. Charred paper and smouldering wood choked the helpers. Still the raid continued with whining bombs, cracking, thudding guns, droning aeroplanes, both German and our own night fighters. Huge chandeliers of flares hanging in the sky like Roman candles illuminating the bombers' targets. Our hands were cut and bleeding . . . I felt suddenly sick.'

The next day, 'dressed in borrowed clothes', Theodora Fitzgibbon struggled into work half an hour late. 'No one was interested in my bomb story, they had become like fisherman's tales, I was "the one who got away".' That night she went home to the block of flats where she and Peter Rose Pulham lived. He greeted her, 'Not a flat any longer, Pussy, a bed-sitting room . . . There's nobody else in the whole block but ourselves.'

The figures stacked up: a total of 6,065 civilians killed nationwide during April 1941.

On 10 May 1941, eight months almost to the day since the Blitz had started, London was again the target of a devastating raid. It was the worst attack of the Blitz and the last major one – but no one could know that at the time. A few days earlier, as Jock Colville walked round the streets, he had looked 'at London's landmarks more carefully now, with a feeling that it may be the last time that I shall see them'. On that cloudless night, with a full moon and the Thames at low ebb, the Royal Naval College at Greenwich was struck again; the War Office was hit, along with Westminster School and the British Museum where 250,000 books were destroyed. A bomb fell on the Houses of Parliament, destroying the Commons debating chamber and setting Westminster Hall ablaze. The litany of landmarks destroyed or damaged also included the Law Courts in the Strand, the Public Record Office in Chancery Lane and the Palace of St James; in the City the Mansion House was hit, as were the halls of a number of companies including Butchers', Cordwainers', Mercers' and Salters'. City churches included St Mary-le-Bow and St Stephen's Walbrook; Westminster Abbey was bombed as was the fashionable church for weddings, St Margaret's Westminster. Fourteen hospitals were hit, including St Thomas's, which stood across the Thames from the Houses of Parliament.

Throughout London more than 2,000 fires burned that night, from Shadwell and Whitechapel in the east along the river to Southwark and Westminster. As well as the Thames running low, a number of vital water mains were fractured – making the water pressure so low that the firemen faced the fires with hoses that often ran dry or dribbled out water that made little or no impact on the ferocity of the flames. At the Elephant and Castle, a medium-sized fire was fanned 'into a great conflagration because every water main was dry'.

Cecil King, chairman of the *Daily Mirror,* had seen out the raid on the roof of the paper's offices in Fetter Lane. 'Towards morning the smoke was such that you could not see that it was a full moon with no clouds; the air was full of flying sparks; every now and then there was the roar of a collapsing house . . . The lines from Paddington and Euston were blocked, King's Cross had a direct hit, and most Southern railway termini were closed . . . The Temple Church, one of the great monuments of English history, was on fire . . . St Clement Danes had been gutted, and only the spire was alight half way up the top and sending out showers and sparks – an odd and rather beautiful spectacle.' As he drove home later, King realised just how extensive the damage had been: there was an unexploded bomb in Regent Street, and the road was blocked by a land mine on the corner of Bond Street; there was 'a large fire' on the opposite side of Oxford Street and another in Cavendish Square. 'At Marble Arch a small bomb had hit the façade of the Regal Cinema. Down the Bayswater Road there was a fire burning', which he thought 'might be the Roman Catholic convent at Tyburn. I was directed into Connaught Street, where there was a huge crater in the road. So back to the Bayswater Road and a diversion for another blazing house, then to Notting Hill Gate where the road was covered in broken glass. From that point there was no sign of the raid,' though King 'picked up a man on his way to Bristol. He had spent the night in the Rotherhithe Tunnel. He could not get through Commercial Road or Aldgate, and had to go back down the tunnel and go to New Cross, which was mostly on fire.' And when he finally reached home at Culham in Oxfordshire, 'you could see the great cloud of smoke from burning London in the morning sunshine'.

That night in May, 5,000 houses were destroyed, meaning that some 12,000 people lost their homes, while nearly 1,500 lost their lives and nearly 2,000 were seriously injured. Once again many of the dead and injured were those in the front line – firemen, ARP wardens and other Civil Defence workers. On the 13th of that month, Herbert Morrison announced that the 1,666 organised Fire Brigades that had existed before the war, few of which had more than twenty firemen, were to be reorganised into some fifty 'fire forces', which would include the AFS too, all under a unified central control. It was not a universally popular move particularly when AFS men moved into some of the top jobs.

Chips Channon had been at his country house and returned to London the day after the raid where he found 'bits of paper fluttering about the streets, and broken glass everywhere. The rubble and debris are heaped high in the streets.' He tried to 'get to the House of Commons but the crowd was so large I could not fight my way through; but I could see the hole in Westminster Hall roof. I met Jim Thomas who tells me that the chamber is gutted: no more shall we hear fiery and futile speeches there . . . gone is that place, as I always foresaw. Itself the protector of democracy in the end it went a long way to kill what it created . . .'

In those nine seemingly endless months of the Blitz, over 43,500 civilians nationwide were killed by enemy action, and it is not possible to be sure exactly how many were injured. The official estimate was some 71,000 seriously injured and 88,136 slightly injured, while 98,500 were treated at first-aid posts, a fifth of whom might then be sent to hospital. This is almost certainly too low, since those reporting 'serious' and 'slight' injuries might use different criteria; many injured people never went to hospital or to a first-aid post, so did not show up in the official statistics; records were sometimes destroyed in an 'incident', and during the days and nights of ceaseless bombing it must often have seemed more of a priority to attend to its victims than to keep on top of the paperwork. But what can be said is that in 1940 and 1941 the Home Front was the front line, and it was 'not until over three years [of war] had passed . . . that the enemy had killed more soldiers than women and children'.

A formal recognition of the great bravery shown during the Blitz had been announced on 23 September 1940 when the King, in a broadcast from Buckingham Palace 'with its honourable scars', instigated the George Cross and the George Medal, both named for England's patron saint. They were to be 'a new mark of honour' for men and women who showed outstanding valour on the Home Front. The George Cross was intended to be the civilian equivalent of the Victoria Cross that was given for extreme bravery in the field of battle, in Churchill's view for a 'few outstanding deeds of éclat', while the George Medal should 'be given by the thousands over the whole area of non military good conduct and valour'.

The first recipient of the George Cross was Thomas Alderton, an ARP leader from Bridlington in Yorkshire. During the course of the war around a hundred people would receive the George Cross 'for gallantry', but the distinction between civilian and military proved harder to make than had been anticipated. As the Blitz faced civilians with battle conditions, it also involved soldiers in such heroic tasks as defusing UXBs that were not 'under the direct orders of commanders in the battlefield', with the result that more of these 'civilian' awards – seventy-six out of the first 100 – were given to soldiers rather than to civilians.

Churchill frequently complained that George Medals were not being handed out to Civil Defence workers in the thousands he had envisaged: by the end of 1940, seventy-one had been awarded, but by the end of 1941 the total had risen to 535, and this included members of the Home Guard. But at almost any incident during the Blitz, the selfless bravery of rescue workers – civilian or military – made them a candidate for honours in most victims' eyes.

16

THE ISLAND FACING
THE ATLANTIC

CITY AND COUNTY BOROUGH OF BELFAST

URGENT NOTICE

Any Builder free to undertake First Aid
Repairs and make Dwelling Houses
reasonably habitable to communicate at
once with Mr. Wilshere, Education
Architect, Old Town Hall.

R. B. DONALD, *City Surveyor*.

On the Shankill, on the Falls,
You forget oul' Derry walls.
You'se run as the bombs begin to fall,
Says good oul' Rule Britannia.
A POPULAR SONG OF THE BELFAST BLITZ

ON 3 SEPTEMBER 1939, as Neville Chamberlain was informing the people of Britain that the country was at war with Germany, Eamon de Valera, the Irish Taoiseach (Prime Minister), reaffirmed that the aim of *his* country's policy 'would be to keep our people out of a war . . . with our history and experience of the last war, and with part of our country unjustly severed from us, we felt that no other decision and no other policy was possible'. Éire would be neutral.

De Valera would honour his guarantee that he would never allow Ireland to be used as 'a base for attacking Britain' and would maintain his commitment to defend Ireland against all invaders (though quite how that was to be done given the country's declining defence budget was not entirely clear). While the Taoiseach did not compromise Éire's neutral status by interning enemy aliens or breaking off diplomatic relations, he managed to maintain a generally friendly pro-British neutrality (or rather non-belligerence, which grew more benevolent after the US entered the war in 1942 and it was clear that Britain would be victorious). A close watch was kept on German agents and their possible sympathisers, and secret liaisons and strategic links between Britain and the US were fostered; and, after 1942, UK or US pilots who crashed in Éire were sent straight to Northern Ireland, while Germans were interned for the duration of the war. Not that Churchill always saw it like that. He recalled not only the danger that Dublin might have posed in the First World War when it appeared that the 1916 Easter Rising would be supported by German guns, but also earlier centuries when French and Spanish ships had tied up at Irish ports to revictual before sailing on to attack England. The ambiguity of the situation disturbed him and he wrote to Halifax that Éire 'is not a Dominion . . . It is certainly under the Crown . . . Legally I believe they are "at war but skulking".'

In 1938 Britain had returned to Ireland the ports ceded to them by the 1921 Anglo-Irish Treaty, with the vague, but never formalised, understanding that in time of war these would be handed back again. By 1939, with the U-boat war intensifying, the use of harbours such as those at Berehaven, Cobb and Lough Swilly, and fuel-storage facilities for ships and aircraft at Haulbowline and Rathmulen, would have aided the war effort. 'It is,' said Churchill 'a heavy and invidious burden which Britain should not have to shoulder,' since the ban reduced the British range of action by approximately 400 miles. De Valera remained intransigent. Contingency plans were drawn up to reoccupy the ports by force if necessary, and diplomatic exchanges flirted with the idea of British support for Irish unification in return for the south abandoning its position of neutrality and declaring for Britain. This came to nothing: Ulster would never have accepted the proposition, while de Valera regarded such an idea as fatally compromising Éire's sovereignty – and he did not believe the British government would be able to deliver anyway.

If de Valera was to ensure his country's neutral stance, he had to neutralise the Irish Republican Army (IRA), who would naturally see in England's difficulty, Ireland's opportunity. In fact the IRA had been at war with Britain since January 1939, when posters had appeared in the streets of Dublin and in every town and city in Northern Ireland, proclaiming, 'The hour has come for the supreme effort . . .' and demanding that Britain withdraw her institutions and representatives of all kinds from Ireland. It was signed by six members of the IRA constituting themselves as the 'Government of the Irish Republic'. The ultimatum was rejected by the British government and immediately a war came to mainland Britain that would last for fourteen months: the IRA mounted a bombing campaign with explosions at gas and electricity stations in London, Liverpool and Manchester. A fish porter was killed in Manchester and two other men were injured when incendiary devices that had been placed in manholes exploded; electricity pylons were found to have time bombs attached to them – though most turned out to be faulty and the charges didn't detonate. Suspect Irishmen were rounded up, and on 2 February 1939 twenty-one people were charged in London and Manchester with causing explosions in the name of the IRA. The violence escalated: in February there were explosions on the London underground – bombs had been placed in attaché cases in left-luggage offices. Eight people were injured, two of them seriously.

Throughout the summer the campaign continued with tear gas emptying cinemas, bombs posted through shop letter boxes, windows smashed, a wave of letter and parcel bombs, and balloon acid bombs posted into pillar boxes. A bomb placed in Madame Tussaud's waxworks destroyed the model of Henry VIII, and only quick action saved the tableau of Red Riding Hood and the Wolf on the floor above. A Prevention of Violence Bill was rushed through the Commons at the end of July 1939, giving the police the power to fingerprint and register – and if necessary deport – Irish people they had a reason to suspect. Since the beginning of January there had been 127 attacks in England; one man had been killed and fifty-five injured, and large quantities of gelignite, potassium chlorate, sulphuric acid, aluminium powder and detonators for making bombs had been seized. Sixty-six Irishmen had been arrested, including a sixteen-year-old Dubliner

Brendan Behan (later to memorialise the experience in his memoir *Borstal Boy*), who was charged with attempting to blow up Hammersmith Bridge. As the Bill was being debated in the Commons, there was an explosion at King's Cross railway station in London, which killed a young Scotsman who was waiting in the left-luggage office and severely injured his wife and fourteen other people; and another bomb went off at Victoria station.

On 25 August, as the whole country anxiously anticipated war with Germany, Broadgate in the centre of Coventry was crowded with shoppers when, at 2.30 in the afternoon, there was a tremendous explosion: the smoke cleared on a scene of devastation – broken glass, rubble, debris and twisted metal, with bodies lying on the pavement. Since a plane had been spotted flying overhead a few minutes earlier, it was presumed that, without a declaration of war, the Luftwaffe had attacked. Five people had been killed, including an old man of eighty-one and a schoolboy of fifteen, and some forty injured. But it was not an air raid: it was the work of the IRA on the ground. A bomb had been placed in the basket of an errand boy's bicycle. Although there were further explosions a couple of days later in Blackpool and Liverpool, the Coventry bombing was the most serious of the campaign and a small foretaste of the devastation the city would suffer the following year; on 14 December 1939 two Irishmen, Peter Barnes and Frank Richards (alias James McCormick), were condemned to death for the killings.

The IRA campaign in England was effectively over by the time war broke out, though sporadic incidents continued throughout the Phoney War. But before the British government had legislated to control Irish terrorism, de Valera had moved to declare the IRA (of which he and many of his Cabinet had been members in former times) an unlawful organisation on 15 June 1939. A year later, at the height of the invasion threat, the Dáil brought in emergency legislation to intern Irish-born citizens and set up military courts to try specified offences punishable by death. The main target was the IRA, and IRA headquarters were frequently raided and leading members interned.

Germany had drawn up detailed plans for an attack on Ireland (including Hitler's notion of a destabilising invasion of Northern Ireland on the twenty-fifth anniversary of the 1916 Easter Rising): these were soon abandoned. But throughout 1940 and 1941, British unease about Irish succour to the Germans in any attempt to invade Britain by the back door, and about German espionage in Éire, persisted. The anxieties proved of little substance, partly because of a fortuitous admix of lack of knowledge about Ireland and the IRA (other than that they too were prepared to bomb Britain) on the German side, and the general incompetence and disorganisation of the IRA. The most important German spy to be parachuted into Ireland, Captain Herman Goetz, failed dismally to succeed in any effective subversive activities. He committed suicide after nineteen months in the Republic, and wrote a valedictory epitaph on the IRA, an organisation he considered 'worthless' in which 'nobody knew how the game was played . . . There was no code, they had not a single wireless operator, they made no attempt to learn messages discipline; their military training was nil. I once said to one of them whom I admired for his personal qualities: "You know how to die for Ireland, but how to fight for it, you have not the slightest idea." '

On 31 May 1941, after the main Blitz on Britain was over, Dublin was bombed. Thirty-four people were killed – over half of them women or children – and 145 injured; while more than 350 houses were destroyed or badly damaged. It was an immense shock and outrage to the people of Dublin – and their leaders.

The German Minister to Éire, Edouard Hempel, 'was staggered . . . my very first immediate reaction was one of suspicion and I wondered if the bombing had been done by the British with captured German planes. It could have been easy for them to have done something like that to upset Irish neutrality and to get Ireland into the war.' When analysed, the bombs were found to be of German origin, and the Germans admitted responsibility.

Later, Hempel decided that the raid had been an accident, an unforeseen result of British interference with the radio beams the Germans used to locate their targets, and this was the explanation Winston Churchill favoured too. The historian Brian Barton suggests two other possible explanations: one that this was a deliberate German attack, a retaliation, or a warning to Éire that its neutrality was not so watertight as was required. When Belfast was blitzed the previous month, de Valera had sent fire crews to help and southern Ireland's borders were open to refugees fleeing from the raids. There was a marked discrepancy in the treatment of downed German and Allied airmen. Furthermore, RAF planes had recently been known to engage German fighters in battle over Dublin.

The benign explanation is that the bombs were dropped by planes that intended them for Liverpool, but were either blown off course by strong winds or were lost in low cloud and, reluctant to fly back with a full load of bombs, unleashed them on a likely target without realising it was the neutral city of Dublin. Several years after the war the German Federal Government agreed to pay £327,000 in final settlement.

Despite their government's neutrality, individual citizens of Éire did fight for Britain during the Second World War. Churchill was to praise them in a victory broadcast in May 1945 when he contrasted the 'temper and instinct of thousands of southern Irish men who hastened to the battle front to prove their ancient valour' with 'the action of the Dublin government'. Indeed, in November 1939, as Churchill thundered against the refusal of Éire to surrender the Treaty Ports, Commander Edward Fogarty Fegen from Tipperary was earning himself a posthumous VC when he attacked the German battleship *Admiral Scheer*, in mid Atlantic. Though his ship, the HMS *Jervis Bay*, was no match for the German vessel, Fegen's valiant action saved thirty-eight Allied merchant ships in the convoy he had been escorting.

The numbers are difficult to obtain, but a historian, Richard Doherty, working with figures of those killed, estimates that 98,296 Irishmen served in the British Army during the Second World War and that does not include those in the Royal Navy (estimated by the Admiralty in early 1945 as 715 men and women) and the RAF (on the Air Ministry's calculations 11,050). Southern Irishmen serving with the British Army won a total of 780 decorations, including eight Victoria Crosses.

Nothing was done by the government of Éire either to encourage or discourage volunteers. Men (and some women) joined for a variety of reasons: some came from families with a tradition of fighting with the British Army and, in the words of James Hickie from Dublin, would 'have been given the white feather' by their families if they had not enlisted. Others joined up because they 'believed that that bloody little monster from Germany had to be stopped'; some of the minority Protestants in Éire had a residual loyalty to Britain; while other Irishmen, driven by high rates of unemployment and the fact that the

pay in the British Army was higher than that in the Irish Defence
Forces, crossed the water. When a serviceman came home on leave to
southern Ireland, he was not permitted to wear his uniform, and piles
of civilian clothes lay at Holyhead to enable a quick change before
getting on the ferry.

Censorship rules meant that decorations for valour could not be
published in Irish newspapers during the war, nor could obituaries for
those killed in battle. And though the British Prime Minister might
praise the Irish volunteers, and, when it was permitted to do so after the
war, the *Irish Times* trumpeted 'the Irish heroes . . . with their outstanding
fighting quality', Éire's most famous playwright, Sean O'Casey, referred
to them bitterly as 'blossoms of blood on our sprig of Green', and most
returned home unsung to an uncertain future.

For Northern Ireland, the Second World War might have been expected
to give the Six Counties an opportunity to demonstrate their intense
loyalty to the mainland in its hour of danger, a golden opportunity for
Unionists to contrast their patriotic allegiance with southern Ireland's
declaration of neutrality. The day after war was declared the Prime
Minister, Lord Craigavon, assured Stormont (the Northern Irish
parliament) that there would be 'no slacking in [Ulster's] loyalty. There
is no falling off in our determination to place the whole of our resources
at the command of the [Imperial] government . . . anything we can do
to facilitate them . . . they have only just got to let us know.'

A 'khaki invasion' of Allied Forces arrived, ostensibly to help protect
the country against a possible threat of German invasion. By November
1940 there were 70,000 British troops living in Northern Ireland, under
canvas at first but gradually moving into specially built Nissen huts. By
April 1941 the number had grown to 100,000. Belfast was 'jammed with
officers' and the population of Londonderry was boosted by an influx of
40,000 military personnel by 1943, while it was reckoned that a quarter
of Fermanagh's wartime population consisted of servicemen. In Belfast
'hundreds of men in uniform could be seen wandering the streets . . .
with nothing to do and nowhere to go' – though the Lord's Day
Observance Society suggested that 'brighter worship' might make up
for the fact that the cinemas and pubs were closed on Sundays. But the
influx provided interest for the women of Northern Ireland – or some

of them. 'Life here, for women at any rate, has been revolutionised by the presence of all these men, and is one round of canteens, sherry parties, regimental entertainments, dances etc. Sole topic of conversation is the "soldiers" and their doings . . . Canteen work everywhere is astonishingly popular,' reported Moya Woodside, a Belfast welfare worker married to a surgeon. 'Well-off women from fashionable parts of town neglect their homes and husbands to spend hours and hours every week doing work as cooks and waitresses and dishwashers – jobs which at home they would have left to maid or charwoman . . . I . . . came to the cynical conclusion that it was our old friend SEX which was so largely responsible for the enthusiasm displayed . . . The acid test is: can one visualise all these women working and slaving in a similar manner in a canteen which catered for other women?'

A number of British government departments had also relocated to Northern Ireland, and in the autumn of 1940 the first refugees began arriving from the bombed cities of the Midlands and the North East, all of which put a strain on the country's resources. However, the 'occupation' brought some welcome jobs to the economically disadvantaged North, which had the highest rate of unemployment anywhere in Britain in 1939, and the highest death rate and infant mortality rate, and among the worst housing conditions. But in many areas unemployment persisted: the shipyards benefited from government contracts for battleships and submarines, but when Harold Wilson, then a young civil servant, Secretary to the Imperial Manpower Committee of the War Cabinet, visited Belfast in December 1940, he was shocked to find that Northern Ireland's munitions industry was running well below capacity and that unemployment, which had halved in the rest of Britain, was actually rising, with 25,000 'fit young men and women standing in the dole queue'. The problem wasn't easy to solve; the linen industry had all but collapsed, and Northern Ireland's factories were not winning munitions contracts because they just did not have the skilled labour or manufacturing capacity to fulfil them – a legacy from the pre-war years.

The anomalous position of Northern Ireland – its physical separation and yet avowed political loyalty to Britain, the religious and political divisions within the Six Counties, their 170-mile border with independent, neutral Éire and the undercurrent of suspicion with which the British government regarded Ireland (North as well as South) – was made transparent by the war. 'If trouble comes to this country,' opined the commander of the British Army in Northern Ireland on 2 September 1939, 'it will come from within the borders.' While the BBC all but ignored Northern Ireland in its morale-boosting attempts for the British war effort, censorship – 'spying and snooping' – introduced in May 1940 was particularly irksome to those who regarded themselves as 'ultra loyal to Britain'. Moya Woodside reported that a university student friend who was 'returning to Belfast with full credentials, permit etc. had her entire trunk turned out on Stranraer platform, her scientific notebooks perused, her private diary read, her handbag searched and a number of letters from her fiancé read – at length – before she was allowed to board the steamer'. Then Mrs Woodside heard tell of 'letters addressed to people here [Belfast] from England or Scotland, and which were returned to sender by the censor as they contained (a) packets of special 'invisible' hairpins, unobtainable locally (b) photographs cut from a Yorkshire newspaper of my maid's brother's wedding (he is a sergeant in the Army and was married in uniform) (c) a printed instruction leaflet on how to knit a pullover for the Forces. And people are being paid £3.5.0. a week for this sort of thing.' The final straw came with 'more censorship ineptitudes! No hand knit woollies are allowed to be sent to Ireland by private individuals. Two English friends . . . living here are very fed up about this, as formerly the presents knitted by adoring grandmothers and aunts in England kept their children in clothes . . . It is hard to see how this sort of thing will help to win the war.'

Northern Ireland seemed to be having a rather different war in other ways too. Although wartime regulations about blackout and food rationing were extended there, food was invariably more plentiful than it was in the rest of Britain, with increased agricultural productivity and, in the early years of the war, rather less official scrutiny about what was produced and how it was disposed of. Troops stationed in Fermanagh were able to send generous food parcels home to their families in mainland Britain. Milk was always available as were vegetables and pork – and eggs until mid 1943. Moreover, Ulstermen and women could always slip over the border to stock up on supplies of butter, meat, eggs, cheese, bacon, jam, chocolate and cigarettes. Smuggling was endemic, with supplies coming from Éire by train with the complicity of border guards, or being rowed across the loughs – until the British government made it illegal to use a rowing boat on British tidal waters without naval authority. Gradually the trade petered out, mainly through the Royal Ulster Constabulary offering hefty rewards to anyone who brought a smuggler to justice. But northerners who could afford it still crossed the border for holidays in Donegal and Galway and, until it was bombed in May 1941, Dublin sparkled as brightly as ever with its shops, pubs and restaurants, theatres and music halls all pulling in people eager for a good time.

The impression that Northern Ireland's war was not quite like that of the rest of Britain persisted when it came to the defence of the civilian population, too. The Westminster government had 'absolutely turned down' Stormont's request that the province should be included in Parliament's legislation for Civil Defence – the provision of shelters in particular. This was largely on grounds of cost, but also because many, including Major General Pug Ismay, Secretary of the Committee of Imperial Defence, considered that Northern Ireland was an unlikely military target – a complacency largely shared by Stormont on the eve of war. In March 1939 Ismay drew the analogy between the province and a Woolworths store, to which the only entrance was through Carringtons, the biggest jeweller in London. And as late as June 1939 the Parliamentary Secretary to Northern Ireland's Minister for Home Security argued that there was no need to implement Civil Defence regulations that placed an obligation on large factories and commercial firms to build air-raid shelters for their employees, since Belfast '. . . is the most distant city of the United Kingdom from any possible enemy base. It is 535 miles from the nearest point in Germany. An attack on Northern Ireland would involve a flight of over 1,000 miles. For aeroplanes of the bombing type, loaded, this is a very big undertaking. To reach Northern Ireland the attacking plane would pass over targets which would appear to be more attractive than anything the North of Ireland has to offer.' In the months between these assessments and the outbreak of war, Northern Ireland's vulnerability to attack and the paucity of its provision for civilian defence were increasingly recognised, but only limited preparations were made to protect the most likely targets, such as Belfast harbour – though there were lengthy deliberations about how exactly the statue of the Unionist political hero, Lord Carson, should be protected at a time when Belfast had no air-raid shelters for its citizens. 'The inadequacy of Ulster's political leadership was never more vividly demonstrated,' concludes a historian of Ireland.

On the outbreak of war there was an acute shortage of ARP workers and their equipment, and local authorities in Northern Ireland were under no legal compulsion to prepare air-raid defence schemes. Blackout observance tended to be somewhat cavalier – and it was hard to insist it was essential when two-thirds of Ireland burned brightly in the night sky.

'If you really want to help us,' Neville Chamberlain was reported to have said to Lord Craigavon in May 1939, 'don't press for conscription. It will only be an embarrassment . . . He was frightened of the issue being complicated by Mr de Valera kicking up the dust, though Ulster affairs have nothing to do with him,' wrote Craigavon's wife. Indeed, there was widespread opposition to the idea not only from de Valera, who thought that the imposition of conscription would be equal to 'an act of war against our nation'; the Roman Catholic Church was opposed, the trade unions were opposed and, on the other side of the water, the British press were opposed. The Unionist MPs at Westminster, however, were affronted. They felt snubbed and emasculated – the 'loyal and the brave' had been prevented from 'doing their duty'. There was nothing to prevent men from volunteering for the British Army, but not very many did. In the opening month of the war there were around 2,500 volunteers, and by the spring of 1940 the number had fallen to 1,000 a month. A recruitment drive in the countryside yielded disappointing results, and legislation was considered to withhold benefit payments from the unemployed of military age who refused to enlist. This was rejected, though some informal withholding probably went on. By December 1940 the level of volunteers had fallen still further, to around six hundred a month, and continued to decline thereafter. The notion of conscription would be revived after the Belfast blitz in May 1941, but it was again rejected, in no small measure because the Roman Catholic hierarchy remained adamantly opposed (organising a No Conscription campaign that attracted 10,000 to a rally at the end of the month). Since a large number of Northern Irish Protestants were in reserved occupations, the brunt of any call-up would fall on the Catholic population, and that was likely to lead to sectarian unrest in Northern Ireland and inflame the South.

When Anthony Eden broadcast 'the opportunity to countless ordinary citizens . . . who were unable to enrol in the armed forces yet who wanted to serve their country' to join the Local Defence Volunteers in May 1940, the all-embracing spirit of his appeal was lost in Northern Ireland and, from the start, the Home Guard was a sectarian body. Craigavon decreed that a policy of recruiting anyone who wanted to join in the defence of their country would allow Republicans to infiltrate the militia – and arms to find their way into the hands of the IRA. He thus made the Northern Irish Home Guard a branch of the special constabulary, the Unionist 'B specials', whose commanders 'selected' members from their own localities, and the force was placed under the control of the Royal Ulster Constabulary (RUC) Inspector-General rather than the military as it was in the rest of the United Kingdom. By the end of August 1940, 26,000 volunteers had come forward, which was as many as the authorities felt they could cope with. There were accounts given to Stormont of Catholics being turned away at recruiting offices, and those few who did manage to join soon left when they realised the extent of the control of the hated 'B Specials'.

In London, prominent Home Guard officers petitioned Westminster for an end to sectarianism, at the same time as the Craigavon Cabinet decided to divert the pressure on it by referring the matter to the British Parliament, since one of the functions of the Home Guard was external defence and that was the remit of Westminster rather than Stormont. It was a sensitive issue, and the government was divided: the Home Secretary, Herbert Morrison, considered it politically expedient to recognise that 'there are good Catholics in Northern Ireland' who should be allowed the opportunity to join an imperial rather than a sectarian defence force; while the Minister of War, David Margesson, was convinced of the 'absolute necessity of not involving the Army in the religious animosities of Ireland'. After much deliberation Sir John Anderson, who had been asked to look at the problem, concluded in March 1941 that, as Catholics were unlikely to join a predominantly Protestant force no matter who controlled it, the status quo should pertain – though the minimum publicity was to be given to the pronouncement.

Despite events in Europe and the threat of invasion and air attack, wranglings about Westminster's contribution to the cost of protecting the citizens of Northern Ireland continued and, to the growing unease of several politicians, including Craigavon and the Minister of Labour, John Gordon, by June 1940, there were only 200 public shelters for the entire population of Belfast.

Moreover, the people themselves still seemed largely unconvinced of the dangers. When John MacDermott, a lawyer and Unionist MP for Queen's University, who had been appointed to the post of Minister of Public Security on 25 June 1940, ordered the evacuation of some 17,000 children from Belfast on 7 July, only 7,000 turned up, and a second evacuation arranged in August was no more successful. Although the alert had sounded twenty times since October 1940, Moya Woodside persisted in her belief that 'we are another 240 miles and back from Liverpool and why should the Germans come all that distance when they have plenty of important targets to hand?' She thus declined to emulate some of her air-raid-conscious neighbours 'in this professional and middle-class suburb [who] are excelling themselves in the varied treatment of their windows, and soon [ours] will be the only house to remain normal. I prefer to run the risk of bombs falling nearby rather than live for the duration in rooms which remind one of a dungeon or a meat safe! Besides, it has never been proved, or if it has, I haven't seen it stated, that all this sticky paper and muslin etc. are of the slightest use. If the propaganda authorities want something sensible to do, why don't they survey results of different methods of window protection in already bombed areas; and publish their finds for the benefit of those in remoter parts? As all but the vaguest references to raids and their effects is chopped out of letters from England, people over here are completely in the dark as to what is effective and what isn't. The shops are making a grand profit anyway.'

But not all Belfast's citizens shared Moya Woodside's scepticism. When the bombing started across the water in mainland Britain, Emma Duffin, who had nursed on the Western Front in the First World War, 'wondered if Belfast's turn would come next. We knew its ARP measures were far from ready. There were rumours that the Germans had said on the wireless that they would like to reduce [the city] to a ploughed field for not having stayed neutral like Éire.'

Given the German strategy of attacking docks and shipbuilding on the western side of Britain from October 1940, it began to seem unwise to assume that Belfast would be spared, particularly as it was home to the huge Harland and Wolff shipyards and the aircraft factories of Short and Harland. And since MacDermott was forced to concede that Belfast was 'less well-defended than any comparable city or port in the United Kingdom', he started to send delegations of civil servants over to see the effects of the Blitz on British towns and cities, and a fast-track Civil Defence programme began. Moya Woodside noticed 'in one of the poorest districts of the city . . . the air raid shelters have mostly been built at the edge of narrow pavements (in some streets barely three feet wide) thus blocking out light and air from the houses opposite. The effect in an already narrow street is oppressive; and to judge from the smell, they are being used as a public convenience!' But by the spring of 1941 still fewer than 15 per cent of Belfast householders had air-raid protection in their homes, and there were roughly 750 public shelters capable of holding 37,500 people ready for use; this meant that at least three-quarters of the population of Belfast had no shelter provision of any kind.

Northern Ireland's military defence provision was equally scant: in the entire province there were only twenty-four heavy anti-aircraft guns, fourteen light anti-aircraft guns, one RAF Hurricane squadron, six radar stations, no efficient Observer Corps, a single bomb-disposal unit and two barrage balloons. In Belfast itself there were no searchlights, no night fighters and no provision to throw up a smokescreen to confuse the enemy.

But in April 1941 Belfast proved to be neither beyond the reach of the Luftwaffe, nor remote from its intentions to bomb ports and centres of industry.

The first raid on the night of 7/8 April was brief, with seven relatively minor attacks by aircraft, most of which were on their way to, or returning from, attacking targets in Britain in raids that were among the most extensive and widespread of the war so far. Before the sirens sounded, the people of Belfast heard the planes and an ARP worker on his way to his post was injured by shrapnel. The Luftwaffe attacked the docks and shipyards, igniting a timber yard and setting grain and tar ablaze. Water mains were fractured, flimsy working-class housing round the docks was destroyed, and two AFS men were killed when a parachute bomb – which the firemen at first assumed to be a German parachutist – exploded. Incendiaries rained down 'like hailstones' and the most serious of the night's fifteen fires gutted St Patrick's Church of Ireland Church, leaving just the east window and altar standing. Half an hour before the All Clear at 4 a.m. the Rank Flour Mill by the Pollock Basin was hit by a parachute mine that ripped open the structure, trapping men in the twisted steel and asbestos: twenty died. At about the same time a parachute bomb was blown on to the roof of Harland and Wolff's aeroplane-fuselage factory. Workers who had emerged from the shelters believing the raid was over rushed towards what they too were fooled into thinking was a German parachutist, and several were killed in the explosion. A total of thirteen people died that night, and more than eighty were injured.

The government, seeming either unshaken or determined to sustain morale, assured the citizens that 'everything had gone like clockwork' in the defence of their city. This complacency can hardly have helped press appeals for the evacuation of women and children, for increased vigilance in blackout provision and calls for volunteers to sign up for Civil Defence work, to join anti-aircraft regiments and to fire-watch. But there were those who clearly did heed a lesson from the dockside raid. Moya Woodside noticed that 'the sole topic of conversation is last night's raid' and that though 'down-town everything seemed normal, and no damage visible anywhere' the raid had 'perhaps . . . made people more gas-mask conscious . . . in the space of ½ an hour I saw 2 men and 8 women carrying masks, which is quite unusual.' Her attitude to defence had been vindicated, she felt. 'The raid was actually on a very small scale, and confined in truth to "military objectives". Other damage was apparently incidental. The result goes to prove, in many people's opinion, that the blackout, at any rate on a moon-lit night, is just a waste of time. These last few nights the town must have been spread out to the airman's view as if in a photograph.'

On 15 April 1941 – Easter Tuesday, a traditional Northern Irish bank holiday – the siren sounded at 10.40 p.m. as a convoy of German bombers were flying from their base in Cherbourg to Wales where the formation broke up, some swinging east to attack Tyneside, others heading to Belfast. By 11.45 some 180 aircraft were over the city, dropping flares by parachute that illuminated the night sky. William McCready, a post-office worker from north Belfast, who had gone upstairs to his attic and opened the skylight to look at the sky, thought they were as bright 'as the powerful headlights of a car shining straight down from the sky . . . I had a sinking feeling. I realised that on this occasion the Germans meant business.' The pattern of the raid was as it had been in every major raid since Coventry the previous November: flares followed by incendiaries and high-explosive bombs. In the previous raid on Belfast the docks had been the main target, and the damage to residential areas could be said to have been collateral; now, with the docks screened by dense black smoke   one of the few precautionary measures the government had put in place since the earlier attack – the largely working-class areas to the north and east of the city, back-to-back terraces 'where the poor of Belfast lay unprotected', bore the brunt of the attack.

The raid lasted for five hours, and during that terrible night 674 bombs fell at a rate of approximately two a minute, many specially adapted with their noses covered with steel plates to cause the maximum damage over a wide area since they were less likely to penetrate deep into the ground. Seventy-six parachute bombs landed, as well as 200 tons of high-explosive bombs, though the most terrifying missiles, according to William McCready, were the whistling bombs that had tubes shaped like organ pipes fitted to their tail units. As they fell to earth the wind blowing through the tubes produced an eerie whistling sound. 'Each seemed to be directed at the roof of a house.' Two whole streets were demolished, entire families were killed and, when the residents of one badly bombed street ran out of their ruined homes as the bombs rained down, there was nowhere for them to go. Few shelters had been built in these residential areas since these were far from what were predicted to be the Luftwaffe's targets. People dived into ditches and crouched under bridges – or just carried on running in panic and terror. A parachute mine landed in front of the York Road police barracks, and the vacuum following the explosion sucked out the front of the barracks and nearby shops and houses. The six-storey-high, 60-foot-long rear wall of the massive York Street flax-spinning mill toppled over when it was struck by a parachute mine, pulverising forty-two houses in a nearby street, damaging others and flattening shelters. Frantic residents clawed at the rubble with their bare hands trying to find friends and relatives. Soon the dead and grievously injured were laid out on the pavement: thirty-five were killed in that incident.

Hogarth Street was simultaneously hit by a bomb at both ends, and incendiary bombs 'rained down like confetti' as the residents tore along the street in a desperate search for shelter: forty-five people were killed and seventy houses destroyed. A shelter on the corner of the Antrim Road was flattened by a direct hit: many of the casualties were in party clothes – on their way home from a dance in the Floral Hall their tram had stopped when the alert sounded, and the passengers sought refuge in the nearest shelter. In the narrow streets around the Crumlin Road, terraces concertinaed under the impact of the bombs and seventy were killed. Ewart's weaving mill on the Crumlin Road was so badly damaged by incendiaries that it was still burning fiercely twenty-four hours later. A Hudson Street margarine factory was gutted, its floor awash with grease that would later be used to make candles; Wiltons, Belfast's smartest undertaker, was hit and dozens of the black Belgian horses that, wearing plumes of feathers, were used to pull the hearses, lost their lives. Although both the Falls Road and the Shankill Road largely escaped the devastation, a parachute mine fell within yards of the Percy Street public shelter on the corner of the Shankill Road, and the explosion blew in walls and brought down the heavy concrete roof, killing some and trapping others. A local doctor was obliged to amputate the legs of some victims to release them from their concrete tombs; bits of charred bodies were found in nearby alleyways and backyards. Thirty people died.

At Short and Harland's aircraft factory, four almost complete Stirling aircraft were destroyed in the workshop adjacent to the runway, and fire-watchers were killed; a high-explosive bomb fell on to the roof of Harland and Wolff's boiler house, bringing cranes crashing down and taking the roof off an electrical manufacturing shop. The smokescreen proved ineffective in protecting the docks from damage, and nearly forty fires were reported in the eastern part of the docks, though the port itself was barely touched that night – and a number of those parachute mines that did fall either fell into the water or into mud, and ten failed to explode. The city centre, too, was relatively unscathed, but Trinity Church was hit by a parachute bomb. Some ARP workers returning from a concert in Ulster Hall – where they had obeyed the instructions of the popular singer, Delia Murphy, to sing during the raid – were killed, and no trace was ever found of any of the Hill family who had lived in a house next to the church. Twelve died when an ARP post in Unity Street was hit, and five of the dead were ARP wardens. A large parachute mine that fell on the corner of Oxford Street and East Bridge Street damaged a nearby shelter; fortunately no one was seriously injured, but it put the central telephone exchange out of action, not only isolating Belfast from links with mainland Britain but also cutting a number of local lines, which made the co-ordination of Civil Defence – including anti-aircraft activities – impossible. It also broke the radar plotting lines between Aldergrove airport and the filter station at Preston in Lancashire, which meant that the RAF had no idea how many aircraft were raiding Belfast, nor from which direction they were coming; so at 2 a.m. British fighters withdrew to outside a 5-mile radius of the city and 'the Luftwaffe had the sky to themselves'.

By 3 a.m. Moya Woodside in south Belfast 'could stand it no longer . . . and feeling desperately frightened and somewhat hysterical, put on a dressing-gown and went to join my husband in his vigil under the stairs. I grabbed the whiskey decanter, and with shaking hands drank off about a quarter tumbler neat to try and pull myself together (usually I dislike whiskey and never touch it). We then sat down in the pantry under the stairs, and just waited. After a while I recovered my self control and began to reflect mournfully that this was civilisation in 1941 – sitting shivering, bored and frightened in a cubby hole at 3.30 a.m. I thought too of Madrid and how the Spanish people had neither the defences, nor the sympathy of the outside world. Well now it's our turn!'

Soon fires were threatening to burn out of control, streets were a wall of flame, the sky a vivid red. Rubble blocked many main roads, making it difficult for the emergency services to get through; pumps ran dry as water mains were hit, and by 1.45 a.m. the official verdict was that 'the task was beyond [the] capacity' of the fire services. By 4.30 a.m. there were four conflagrations in Belfast spreading out of control, nineteen 'serious fires' and over a hundred lesser blazes. Crouching under the desk in the study of his home near the Stormont building as bombs fell, fires gripped hold of the city, shrapnel clattered on his roof and an explosion blew out the windows, John MacDermott managed to put in a telephone call to Dublin before the phone lines went down, asking for help. The Taoiseach, Eamon de Valera, 'took what was the possibly the fastest decision of his career' and agreed to send some of neutral Éire's resources over the border. 'They are all our people,' he said, and volunteers came north from Dublin, Dundalk, Drogheda and Dun Laoghaire, driving thirteen fire engines to stricken Belfast. Most did so because, like their Prime Minister, they believed that 'the people of Belfast were Irishmen too', though one, Patrick Finlay from Dublin, was suspicious that Northern firemen 'might only concern themselves with Protestant areas'. The Southern Irish firemen had a hard time of it with little idea of the geography of the city, no waterproof clothing to protect their legs against the freezing water, and sometimes they found that their hose couplings were a different size from the 2½-inch British standard used in Belfast. Moya Woodside believed that 'an action like this does more for Irish Unity than any words of politicians. I hear that the brigades were wildly cheered in towns and villages in Ulster as they passed through . . .' The British government was less generous: the firemen were rewarded by being paid five shillings to cover the cost of their lunch.

An urgent call had also gone out for reinforcements to be sent from mainland Britain. Liverpool, Glasgow and Preston responded, with a total of forty-two pumps and 400 firemen crossing the Irish Sea on a destroyer and several ferries – which 'makes us conscious of a comforting solidarity with Britain', thought Moya Woodside. The fires were not finally brought under control until about two o'clock in the afternoon after the raid – and by this time many had burned themselves out – and the firemen from the south returned home before dusk.

The All Clear had sounded at 4.55 a.m. and policemen toured those areas where the electricity had been cut off, ringing hand bells to tell the people it was safe to come out. As dawn broke, a pall of ochre-coloured smoke hung over the city like a fog, obscuring the daylight – the flares and bombs had illuminated the night. Dust was everywhere, while ambulances and fire engines tore around the streets negotiating craters and fallen masonry, and 'men [were] digging out dead women and children who had been killed in their homes'; glass layered the streets, everywhere 'houses [were] roofless, windowless, burnt out or burning, familiar landscapes gone, and in their places vast craters and mounds of rubble, the desolation indescribable'. People wandered around with 'tear stained, mourning faces', while others looked 'wild-eyed and dazed'. The entire community 'had been dislocated' and the 'citizens wondered how the life of the city could be renewed'. At least two families from the Shankill Road area who had been away for the Easter holiday returned home to find a corpse, or part of a corpse, in their backyard.

South Belfast had largely escaped damage but everyone Moya Woodside met 'has some terrible story of death and damage and disorganisation. Electricity and water still okay but gas off . . . Rang up gas works to order some coke, and the clerk started telling me about his experiences as a warden and about dead bodies . . .'

A day after the raid it was announced that 173 people had been killed; two days later the figure had risen to 363; a week later the Minister for Home Security admitted that 'the dead at present is known to be 500 based on the number of bodies removed to date'. By 1944 the government revised its figures to claim that 745 civilians had been killed and over 430 seriously injured, but the Northern Ireland Fire Authority's figure of 950 dead and 600 seriously injured is probably the closest.

Belfast was not the only victim of the Luftwaffe in Northern Ireland that night: the walled city of Londonderry with its port and shipyards was hit by two parachute mines. One fell on a cluster of ex-servicemen's homes, killing fifteen and injuring the same number, and 150 people were made homeless in the city. A military target, the aerodrome at Newtownards, was also hit; ten guards were killed and three civilians injured; and five civilians were killed and thirty-five injured at Bangor, County Down.

The raid gave Belfast the unwanted distinction of vying with Liverpool as the city that, after London, had lost the most citizens in a single night's raid. Mortuaries were unable to cope with the stream of corpses, 'in the stink of excrement, the acrid smell of disinfectant, these dead were heaped, body on body, flung arm, twisted feet, open mouth, staring eyes, old men on top of young women, a child lying on a policeman's back, a soldier's hand resting on a woman's thigh, a carter still wearing his coal sacks on top of a pile of arms and legs, his own arm outstretched, finger pointing as though he warned of some unseen horror. Forbidding and clumsy, the dead cluttered the morgue room from floor to ceiling,' wrote the novelist Brian Moore, who was then an ARP officer attached to the Mater Hospital.

A bulky, heavy shroud was brought in on a stretcher to the public baths in the Falls Road that was being used as a mortuary: on it was tied a label inscribed 'Believed to be a mother and five children'. The search to give the dead the respect of an identity was particularly painful in Northern Ireland: for the dead, as the living, were segregated. If it was not possible to give a name to a victim, rescuers searched feverishly to find perhaps a rosary or a crucifix, as evidence of the religious denomination of a corpse, so that no Protestant would inadvertently be buried among the Celtic crosses of Milltown cemetery, nor any Roman Catholic interred in the city cemetery at Roselawn to lie for eternity denied the rituals of their own faith, entombed in those of another.

Private funerals took place every day for days; the names of the dead filled three columns of the *Belfast Telegraph* on 19 April 1941, and two days later thousands lined the scarred streets to watch in silence as five army lorries loaded with coffins drove in solemn procession to the public funeral of 150 unclaimed or unidentified bodies that would share a common grave.

Around 20,000 people had been made homeless – with 3,500 houses demolished or irreparably damaged, and a further 10,000 in need of urgent repair; 40,000 dazed and confused people found their way to rest centres and 70,000 were fed in emergency centres, while hundreds left the city as 'ditchers', the Irish equivalent of the 'trekkers', those people who left towns and cities as night fell seeking safety in the countryside away from the city boundaries, sleeping in ditches, under hedges, in woodland or, when the weather was cold, in farm buildings, barns and sheds, and returning in the early hours of the morning when they hoped that danger had passed.

There were also an estimated 100,000 people who fled the city for other parts of the country, chalking 'Gone to Ballymeena' or some similar country address on their doors. 'Such an exodus on foot, in trams, lorries, trailers, cattle floats, bicycles, delivery vans, anything that would move would be utilised. Private cars streamed past laden with women and children, with mattresses tied on top and all sorts of paraphernalia roped on behind. Hundreds were waiting at the main bus-stops. Anxiety on every face ... People are leaving from all parts of town not just from the bombed areas. Where they are going and what they will find even when they get there, nobody knows,' wrote Moya Woodside. 'This business presents a problem of the first priority to Stormont. Belfast is the only large town in Ulster, most of the country towns have also been bombed, and there is absolutely no provision for the reception or feeding of those vast numbers.'

And it was the same at the railway stations: 'thousands of people crowding in, cars, buses, carts and lorries, bathchairs, women pushing prams and go-carts with anything up to 6 or 8 children trailing along, belongings in blankets, pillowcases, baskets and boxes . . . [a] constant stream arriving on foot and on buses, many looking exhausted. It was a heartbreaking sight.' A woman, Dublin-bound for her honeymoon, noticed in horror that of the huge numbers of refugees who crammed on to the train 'some of the women were clutching dead infants in their arms'.

But soon Moya Woodside noted that 'public opinion is now veering round to disapproval of those who bolted from undamaged houses particularly those who did not even have young children' and in an area where 'more than six weeks since the last raid . . . still everywhere one looks are streets of roofless houses, or great piles of bricks and mortar where houses once stood [she] saw the following painted up on the wall in two different places: "Be a man and not a mouse/Come down from the hills and sleep in your house." '

It almost seemed as if the pro-German propagandist Lord Haw Haw had inside information about Belfast when he broadcast a warning to its citizens that Hitler 'will give us time to bury the dead before the next attack. Tuesday was only a sample.' Before it had been possible to clear up the terrible damage the city had suffered, or put new precautions in place – other than hiring an RUC marksman to shoot six wolves, two racoons, a puma, a hyena, five lions, two lionesses, a tiger, a black bear, two brown bears, two polar bears, a lynx, a vulture and a black rat at the

city's Bellevue Zoo in case they escaped in the event of another raid –
Belfast was bombed again.

On 4 May over 200 planes released 235 tons of high explosives and
96,000 incendiaries on the city. This time the targets were specifically
the harbour, shipyards and the aircraft factory, all clustered in north-east
Belfast, and this time it was a clear night and there seemed little to
obstruct the Luftwaffe's vision. The shipbuilding yards of Harland and
Wolff were some of the biggest in the world, with a workforce of 23,000
and contracts to fill for several government departments. Built on the
docks, they were an easily identifiable target, as soon after 1 a.m.
incendiaries, high-explosive bombs and parachute mines fell on the
flimsy, easily flammable factory incinerating nearly completed ships,
igniting piles of timber, and devastating over two-thirds of the company's
entire premises including offices, repair sheds, workshops and drawing
offices, and the electrical manufacturing shop. The fire-fighting
equipment at the works was entirely inadequate and hosepipes proved
too short to reach into the harbour to draw up water as the tide ebbed.
To a German war reporter flying with the Luftwaffe, the fires on the
ground appeared to form one huge conflagration, 'a sea of flame such as
no one had seen before', over the entire harbour and industrial area that
would leave the black skeletons of burnt-out factories and burning silos.

The target may have been the docks but, as in the previous raid,
civilians suffered badly too with bombs falling on commercial and
residential properties particularly in the east of the city. In many streets
around St Patrick's Church of Ireland Church, at least half the houses
were destroyed, and in one, Chater Street, not a house was left standing.
A parachute mine fell within yards of a public shelter, blasting it along
the pavement and killing twenty-five of its occupants; and thirty-five
houses in Witham Street were destroyed when a UXB exploded, killing
nine people. Seven young policemen who had just arrived from training
were killed when Glenraven Street police station received a direct hit,
and many historic Belfast city landmarks were destroyed or damaged,
including the banqueting chamber at City Hall. York Street mill was hit
again and this was time was totally destroyed by fire, the heat so intense
that it could be felt 100 yards away – and venturing on to the pavements
felt like walking on coals. Women in surrounding houses splashed water
on their windows in an attempt to stop them cracking.

Ruptured water mains hampered the work of the fire services – again reinforced by volunteers from south of the border – and when the tide ebbed hoses ran at a trickle. At one point 200 fires were burning, creating 'such an inferno as [those watching from the surrounding hillside] will long remember; below them a great ring of fire as if the whole city was ablaze'. Forty-eight hours after the All Clear – again announced by the ringing of hand bells in some areas since the harbour power station had been damaged – some fires were still burning, and these may have attracted the Germans back again the following night, when east Belfast was attacked, probably by planes making for Clydeside. Fourteen people died, forty were seriously injured and 300 were made homeless when a parachute mine demolished two adjacent public shelters and some nearby houses.

Major roads were blocked by debris, while 150 UXBs throughout the city further dislocated transport and forced people to evacuate their homes and workplaces; numerous gas pipes had been smashed and one area of the city was without gas for a week; the entire city was without electricity for twenty-four hours; the main sewage-pumping station was unable to function; food was almost unobtainable in the shops and thousands of people had only intermittent supplies of water for up to ten days after the raid. However, casualties were markedly lighter in the 'Fire Raid' of early May than in the previous Easter Tuesday attack: by the end of the month it was announced that the death toll for both May raids was 119, though this was to rise later to 191 with 189 seriously injured and three missing. There is no doubt that the toll would have been higher had it not been for the numbers who left the city every night, and perhaps a greater consciousness after the April raids that it was really was sensible to take shelter when the siren went.

Despite the conflagration Harland and Wolff had not been destroyed, though the claim to the British government of almost £3 million for bomb damage to its plants in Belfast and mainland Britain was the highest single amount demanded during the entire war. Work was not able to start again until 8 May and thereafter it slowly increased – hampered by the refusal of workers to do night shifts since their protection against raids was so minimal – until it was back to pre-Blitz levels by November 1941, and much the same was true of the other Belfast war industries.

In total the raids had left more than 1,000 people dead and 650 severely injured, and the damage to property was awesome. Like many of Britain's cities, Belfast had had a housing crisis before the war with overcrowding and sub-standard accommodation; bomb damage added to this substantially – it was estimated that some 56,600 houses were damaged in the raids with 3,200 being completely demolished. In 1944 the Belfast authorities estimated that 23,500 new houses were needed in the city.

Sectarian differences had been overlooked on the night of the 4th in the fear and panic. Protestants from the Shankill Road area had crammed into the Clonard monastery with Catholics from the nearby streets – some 300 women and children taking sanctuary in the crypt. At one moment when it looked as if the chapel would be hit, one of the priests, Father Tom Murphy, donned a tin hat and gave absolution to all present.

But any temporary sectarian reconciliation co-existed with suspicions of Catholics as being 'fifth columnists', as suffering less in the raids (since 'the Pope was in the first airplane') or even as actively encouraging attacks by 'filing up and down the Falls Road' with lights in their hands as the bombers streamed overhead – even of lighting matches in their backyards, presumably as a signal to the planes some 20,000 feet overhead. More Protestant churches than Catholic were hit; however, Catholic schools suffered more damage than those of Protestants. In general Protestant areas suffered proportionately more damage than Catholic. More industrial targets were situated in areas where Protestants lived than in those where Catholics lived.

The Stormont government did little to dampen this sectarianism in time of war: the Home Guard in Northern Ireland continued to be under the control of the almost entirely Protestant RUC despite Opposition objections that this was creating a political and sectarian force; while nationalists were frequently suspected of stirring up industrial disputes, even of passing information directly to Germany. Visiting the Belfast slums in the summer of 1940 for a welfare organisation, Moya Woodside had noticed that 'in the Roman Catholic districts the police barrack windows are almost completely bricked-up; and brick structures, apparently for machine guns, built out over the pavement. It looks as though riots were expected. On walls in these same districts are painted up such slogans as "Join the IRA", "No Conscription Here", "ARP stands for Arrests, Robbery, Police" etc. Some of these have been defaced, but some look quite recent . . . Bigotry is rampant in Ulster,' she declared, 'and the RC manifestations are worse than the Protestant (I speak as one born into the latter persuasion!),' she added.

There also persisted in some minds the conviction that Belfast was an easy target for the Luftwaffe since Dublin acted as a marker for the attack. The German planes were guided by the lights of Southern Ireland, where the blackout was not enforced since it was not at war; whereas for Northern Ireland the Blitz had brought a late and unwanted new affinity with the rest of wartime Britain.

17

'AT THE MOMENT CIVILISATION IS ON THE OPERATING TABLE'

*"Well, **someone's** got to be first off the mark
with a novel about this war."*

*Encased in talent like a uniform
The rank of every poet is well known;
They can amaze us like a thunderstorm,
Or die so young, or live for years alone . . .*
W. H. AUDEN, 'THE NOVELIST'

As the Blitz spread in the autumn of 1940 it became harder to know where the nation's treasures, like the nation's citizens, would be safe. Britain's artistic heritage had to be protected from destruction. In wartime, the arts could be seen as a repository of civilised values against barbarian attack: the symbol of eternal values that were embedded in Britain's artistic patrimony as in its natural landscape.

'Art is an instrument of war; for use as a weapon of defence and attack against the enemy,' Pablo Picasso, the painter of one of the most striking works of twentieth-century warfare, *Guernica*, had written; and during the Second World War painting, music, writing and poetry were all seen as intrinsic to maintaining vital wartime morale, projecting for those at home and abroad an image of a Britain that must be sustained at all costs. Such perceptions were bound to mean that the proper role of the producers of such work in the war effort would come up for lengthy consideration too.

In November 1940 the artist Percy Horton went to a meeting at the National Gallery: 'The damage there is terrific . . .' he noticed. 'There is a huge gap open to the sky & tons of that coloured marble and fragments of pilasters & cornices are heaped at the bottom.' It was the third attack the gallery had suffered. On 30 August a 550lb bomb had destroyed one of the rooms in a raid in which seven people had been killed and over thirty injured. Fortunately the nation's heritage of great art – its Rubens, Rembrandts, Ingres, Botticellis, Van Dycks, Constables and Turners – was not damaged because the paintings had been evacuated. Not that it was only the bombs that the trustees feared: in the event of an invasion, Goering was reputed to have his eye on Poussin's *The Rape of the Sabines* for his own drawing room.

The day before war was declared, the final consignment of paintings from the National Gallery had left London packed on six special freight trains accompanied by guards armed with service revolvers. They had arrived at the small Welsh seaside town of Bangor and been transported in great secrecy to join the other 2,000-odd works of art that had hastily been evacuated to be stored for the duration of the war in various houses and castles in North Wales and Gloucestershire.

A similar exodus of other treasures from the capital had been taking place since late August: Charles Dickens' manuscripts, a first folio edition of Shakespeare, the famed silk carpet from the Mosque of Ardabil in Azerbaijan, illuminated medieval manuscripts, the notebooks of Leonardo da Vinci, 5,000 watercolours, Gobelin tapestries, ivories, fine French and Italian furniture and hundreds of other priceless artefacts had been transported by road from the Victoria and Albert Museum in South Kensington to Montacute House in Somerset, which was owned by the National Trust.

The Duke of Buccleuch, owner of the baroque Boughton House

near Kettering in Northamptonshire, offered sanctuary to objects from the British Museum. Twelve tons of artefacts were sent off in haste, including the coin collection valued at several million pounds, which was unceremoniously dumped on the kitchen floor. Boughton was also to shelter eight sepulchral bronze figures from Westminster Abbey, large numbers of glass cases containing model ships from the Science Museum, and a range of antiquities.

'England is full of large houses,' wrote Sir Kenneth Clark, art critic and Director of the National Gallery, 'and I thought it would be easy to find a proprietor who would have welcomed the quiet occupation of his house by famous pictures rather than rowdy and incontinent evacuees.' 'If there is any threat of evacuees,' the owner of Henley Hall in Shropshire declared, 'I shall spread out the art treasures . . . into more rooms.' But it was not always quite such a pleasure to house the nation's heritage as might have been anticipated. The Buccleuch family soon found that 'in the blackout one stumbled over mummies of incredible rarity'.

Not all the treasures went so far from home. Once the inevitable question of who would pay – the Treasury or the institution concerned – had been resolved, museum basements were strengthened where practical for storage, though unfortunately this did not prevent damage to the National Maritime Museum's collections in Greenwich during a raid in December 1940. There were strongrooms under Bloomsbury that could house some of the British Museum's more robust treasures, and some of the largest and most intractable were simply bricked up – though the Treasury declined to shell out over £2,000 for encasing some statues of Assyrian bulls, enquiring testily, 'Are they worth the expenditure and should they not be left to fend for themselves?' Other treasures including the Elgin Marbles were crated up and stored in the part of the Aldwych branch of the Piccadilly Line that ran under Kingsway. When it was considered that the Aldwych tunnel was no longer suitable, much of the British Museum's collection was relocated to the glass-roofed banqueting hall of Skipton Castle in Yorkshire.

On reflection, Montacute House was considered 'a tinder box' in the event of an air raid with little chance of getting valuables out in time; Boughton was on the bombers' route to the industrial Midlands and North; and Bangor lay on the path the Luftwaffe took to Liverpool. In despair, the National Gallery's trustees suggested sending its pictures to Canada. Sir Kenneth Clark put the idea to Churchill. Back came the curt reply: 'Bury them in the bowels of the earth, but not a picture shall leave this island. WSC.'

So in 1941 as many of the national collections as possible, the National Gallery's included, were moved if not into the very bowels of the earth then as deep underground as possible.

Near Bradford-on-Avon in Wiltshire was a labyrinth of limestone quarries: one had been taken over by the Ministry of Aircraft Production and converted into a massive underground factory extending over 2 million square feet. Another, Westwood quarry – intended for use by the Royal Enfield Company that had turned from making motorcycles to manufacturing bombsights – was under-occupied, and it became home to much of Britain's cultural heritage. Used in peacetime for the cultivation of mushrooms, it was dank and dark, and would cost some £20,000 to convert. As soon as the necessary work was completed in March 1942, artefacts from the British Museum started to arrive (though many books from the British Library remained in Bloomsbury and 250,000 of them had been destroyed by incendiary bombs in the raid of 10 May 1941), as did those from the V&A from their country-house sojourn. These were soon joined by other precious objects, such as the Orville brothers' famous *Kitty Hawk* aeroplane that was on loan from the US to the Science Museum; crates containing thirteenth-century glass from Salisbury Cathedral; 131 boxes of books and manuscripts from the Bodleian Library in Oxford; and pictures from Kenwood House in London's Hampstead Heath. The comprehensive collection of pre-Raphaelite paintings owned by the Walker Art Gallery in Liverpool was eventually transferred to the quarry too. From the National Portrait Gallery came likenesses that had been boarded out at Lord Roseberry's house, Mentmore, in Buckinghamshire – hardly any distance from London but it had nevertheless been 'filled with historic ceilings from Greenwich and Marlborough House and the floor of the Billiards Room covered with recumbent figures of kings and queens from Westminster Abbey . . .' as well as 'tapestries, furniture and Grinling Gibbons wood carvings from Hampton Court', while the eighteenth-century gilded State Coach from Buckingham Palace Mews was stored in Mentmore's stables.

Another major underground storage facility was the honeycomb of disused slate mines, which contained a cave covered by 200 feet of solid rock known as 'The Cathedral', in the Snowdonia mountain range overlooking the town of Blaenau Ffestiniog. This was acquired in September 1940 for the storage of pictures from the National Gallery. Extensive work at the Manod quarries was needed, including building a new approach road and widening the entrance tunnel to transport Van Dyck's 13-foot-high masterpiece *Charles I on Horseback*. Although 'in peace time [the conversion] would have taken seven years, spent in estimates, tenders, scientific tests, disputes about ownership and quarrels with the local authorities, in war time it took a few months'. By September 1941 the transfer of the pictures was able to begin.

Money to convert deep shelters for art was a sensitive issue since the government was initially reluctant to condone such expenditure on sheltering its citizens, and there were complaints that the Aldwych branch tunnel should be used for Londoners taking refuge from the bombs rather than storing Greek friezes. The Cabinet Office somewhat disingenuously deflected the criticism by explaining that no one would actually want to shelter underground in North Wales – which wasn't really the point. As with the Wiltshire quarries, once news of the Welsh facility got out, there were numerous requests for space there from such institutions as the Burrell Collection and the Hunterian Museum in Glasgow, the Fitzwilliam in Cambridge, and the Courtauld Institute and Sir John Soane's Museum in London. Hampton Court Palace stored a few paintings there, Windsor Castle and Buckingham Palace rather more, while the V&A put its Matisse drawings in the Manod quarry for safe keeping, and various individuals stashed their private collections there, including the King, and a young major with a trained connoisseur's eye who would later become Keeper of the Queen's Pictures, Anthony Blunt.

The Wallace Collection was dispersed, part of it going to West Wycombe Park in Buckinghamshire, where Nancy Mitford and James Lees-Milne of the National Trust were also wartime lodgers in the freezing house where snow drifted in through windows that would not shut, and coot, moorhen and swan in aspic were served to eke out wartime rations. The paintings of the First World War that hung in the Imperial War Museum were sent to Bedfordshire and then moved to Surrey; the majority of the documents from the Public Record Office were bundled up for storage in the women's wing of Shepton Mallet prison in Somerset, one of the oldest prisons in the country, which thus became the wartime repository for the Magna Carta, *Domesday Book*, the death warrant for Charles I and, ironically, the scrap of paper that Chamberlain had waved after Munich promising 'peace for our time'.

The Tate Gallery and two major provincial galleries, the Walker in Liverpool and the Manchester Art Gallery, sent some of their pictures on tour to local art galleries and schools, factory canteens, Army camps and work hostels throughout the north of England. This dispersal increased the odds against loss and also brought art to places where it was not usually seen.

The emptied galleries occasioned a sense of loss in some. A letter to *The Times* in January 1942 pointed out wistfully that 'because London's face is scarred and bruised these days, we need more than ever to see beautiful things . . . Would the Trustees of the National Gallery consider whether it were not wise and well . . . to risk one picture for exhibition each week? . . . Music lovers are not denied their Beethoven, but picture lovers are denied their Rembrandts just at a time when such beauty is most potent for good.' In response, one of the National Gallery's paintings was selected as 'Painting of the Month'. Works such as Velázquez's *The Rokeby Venus* (which had survived being slashed by a suffragette in 1912) and Renoir's *Les Parapluies* were carefully wrapped and brought up from Manod quarry by train to be exhibited to the public in a specially reinforced inner room at the gallery, while a train waited on standby in case there was a raid and it suddenly became necessary to rush the picture back to Wales.

The echoing, empty rooms of the National Gallery epitomised the cultural blackout that descended on London in the early days of the war. But Trafalgar Square, its home, was at the heart of the capital, and so when the pianist Myra Hess approached Sir Kenneth Clark with the idea of holding piano recitals in the gallery, he was delighted, and suggested a series of lunchtime concerts in the octagonal room. The first was held on 10 October 1940, admission one shilling. Myra Hess had expected that about forty or fifty of her friends might turn up. In the event it turned out that 'there are thousands of people aching for music at a price they can pay and these concerts have filled a big demand. I love them,' wrote the comedienne Joyce Grenfell, who was performing on the London stage, entertaining the troops, and working as a volunteer in the canteen set up at the gallery to serve cheap and nutritious lunches to the concert goers.

Most people sat on the floor to listen to Hess play. 'The moment she played the opening bars of Beethoven's *Appassionata* will always remain with me as one of the great experiences of my life,' Clark wrote, and when she followed that with her arrangement of Bach's *Jesu, Joy of Man's Desiring* he 'in common with half the audience was in tears. This is what we had all been waiting for – an assertion of eternal values.' The concerts – for piano, chamber groups and small orchestras – were held every weekday throughout the war. Sometimes the audience was as few as 250, on other occasions as many as 1,750 crammed in. 'We made over 1,700 sandwiches,' Joyce Grenfell reported to her mother in April 1940, 'and would have sold more if we'd had the bread . . . by the time the concert started, I was whacked; as were the rest of us. But it was the *Horn Trio* . . . and it did the trick. Heavenly music.'

Should one part of the gallery have to be evacuated, the concerts moved to another part of the building, and on one occasion an unexploded bomb went off while a concert was in progress. No one in the audience moved and the performance of Beethoven's F major 'Rasoumovsky' quartet 'continued . . . without missing a beat'. Myra Hess herself performed 146 times. 'Myra is the whole thing behind these concerts,' Joyce Grenfell considered. 'They were her inspiration and succeed so wonderfully because of her energy and spirit. She plays at least once a week herself on top of all her other work . . . the world's greatest woman pianist.' Myra Hess was made a Dame in 1941.

Musicians were particularly hard hit by the outbreak of war. Artistes had their contracts cancelled, concert halls closed down and composers, unsure of any outlet for their work, stopped composing. Opera, ballet and music would not have survived the war without the help of the Council for the Encouragement of Music and the Arts (CEMA, forerunner of the Arts Council), which took over the funding of a number of principal orchestras including the London Symphony Orchestra, the Hallé, the Liverpool, the Northern and the London Philharmonic, Bournemouth Municipal Orchestra and Scottish Symphony Orchestra. The BBC devoted an increasing amount of airtime to serious music. As Director of Music at the BBC, Arthur Bliss' major contribution was a ballet, *Miracle in the Gorbals*, for Robert Helpmann, and the Corporation continued its policy of commissioning new works from British composers – a policy that was all the more pertinent since most of Wagner's music, quite a lot of Richard Strauss', and even Sibelius' 'Finlandia' (after Finland capitulated) were dropped from the repertoire of BBC orchestras, and records of the music were no longer played. In 1940 the BBC, at the suggestion of the Ministry of Information (MoI), commissioned the composer John Ireland to produce some patriotic music in the vein of Elgar's *Pomp and Circumstance Marches*. Not only was his *Epic March* as thrilling as Elgar's, but Ireland also managed to insert the Morse code V for Victory in its opening bars.

The BBC sponsored Sir Henry Wood's summer Promenade Concerts, which moved to their present-day venue, the Albert Hall, when the Queen's Hall, near the BBC in Langham Place, was bombed in 1941. The Proms drew audiences of up to 5,000 a night, and forty-two works were performed in England for the first time during the 1942–3 seasons. Among them were a number of works by British composers. Ralph Vaughan Williams' *Fifth Symphony* was first heard at a Prom in the summer of 1943 with the composer conducting. Among the younger composers, Benjamin Britten's *Sinfonia da Requiem* (which had been commissioned – and rejected – by the Japanese government to commemorate the 2,600th anniversary of the founding of the Japanese State) was first performed in Britain at the Proms in July 1942; and *Hymn to St Cecilia* (words by W. H. Auden), which Britten had composed during his and Peter Pears' journey home from the US in March 1942, was first heard at the Wigmore Hall that year – appropriately on 22 November, the saint's day.

Britten and Pears, both of whom had been given exemption from military service, gave concerts in prisons during the war, and on one occasion the inmate who turned the pages of the music was Michael Tippett, who, like them, was a Conscientious Objector. Tippett's own oratorio, *A Child of Our Time*, suffused with his pacifist convictions in its telling of the assassination of a German Embassy official by a Polish Jew in Paris, was first performed in 1944.

Four works by Arnold Bax, the Master of the King's Musick, were first heard on the BBC; and Bax also composed *Ode to Russia*. Lennox

Berkeley, who was on the staff of the BBC, wrote chamber music and the score for Jill Craigie's film about the war artists, *Out of Chaos*. Constant Lambert did more conducting than composing during the war, but his *Aubade Héroïque* was inspired by the narrow escape made by the Sadler's Wells Ballet Company (which he was conducting) as the Germans invaded Holland. Other talented younger composers who continued, against the odds, to make music in the war years included Alan Rawsthorne, who was conscripted into the Army and wrote music for a number of films about it, and the Red Army too; Elizabeth Lutyens, whose *Three Pieces for an Orchestra* was in performance the night the Germans launched their air offensive on London on 7 September 1940; and Elizabeth Maconchy, who wrote a ballet, *Puck Fair*, while the Battle of Britain was fought out in the skies above her home, as well as several string quartets.

Vaughan Williams also wrote the music for various films, including *Coastal Command*. Sir William Walton had written the score for *Henry V* and soundtracks for several MoI films including *The First of the Few*, which he developed into a more substantial patriotic offering with *Spitfire Prelude and Fugue*, the first of several in a similar idiom. Towards the end of the war Walton calculated that he had composed the equivalent of eleven symphonies for film and radio – which ensured that his music was heard by a particularly large percentage of the population.

Music may tangibly have filled a space left vacant when paintings were evacuated. But what of the creators, those working as artists when war broke out? Paul Nash, who had been an official war artist in the First World War – his paintings *The Menin Road* and *We Are Making a New World* were among its defining images – was particularly sensitive to the plight of the artist in wartime. How was he or she to earn a living when all the country's energies and resources were to be funnelled to a single goal: winning the war? And how were artists to use their peacetime talents to make a contribution to the war effort? In 1940, as art schools closed down or relocated, and peacetime production and the energies of private patrons were curtailed or redirected, the Central Institute for Art and Design reported that 73 per cent of British artists were out of work. The only profession harder hit was the theatre – in February 1940 the

Spectator reckoned that some 15,000 actors were 'resting' out of the nation's total of 18,000 or so.

Paul Nash, recalling his own struggles as a young artist in 1914, was dogged in his belief that 'unless architects, painters, poets, writers & so on are intelligently used, they will be wanted in ARP & observation posts & and die a lingering death from penury or rheumatism'. From Oxford, where he had moved from London when his wife had a 'sudden hunch' that their Hampstead house would be bombed (it wasn't), Nash had founded the Arts Bureau for War Service, one of a number of organisations concerned with opportunities for artists; these included the Ministry of Labour and National Service's Publicity Artists' Committee, which compiled a register of those who could be employed on propaganda work, designing posters and leaflets, and another of artists who might be particularly suited to camouflage work.

Julian Trevelyan, a surrealist painter, found his own answer. He and another surrealist, Roland Penrose, and others, calling themselves The Industrial Camouflage Unit, rented space from the architect Ernö Goldfinger and set about 'making models and painting them with abstract patterns so as to merge them, so we fondly hoped, into their background. In these early days of the war, Industrial Camouflage was a perfunctory ritual that had very little to do with its proper function which was, presumably, to protect targets from being bombed by enemy aircraft . . . People seemed to feel that the wiggly green stripes somehow brought them immunity from the unknown hazards of war; like the paper strips on the windows it made them feel happy that they had done their little bit . . .' In the summer of 1940 Trevelyan decided to enlist and 'use my little experience in camouflage to step straight into a commission in the Army as a camouflage expert'. He was sent on a six-week training course at Farnham in Kent with a number of others from the creative industries, including the dress designer Victor Stiebel – 'his connections with camouflage being presumably in the design of snipers' suits'. Another trainee was the distinguished Cambridge zoologist, 'Dr Cott, who had written the most authoritative study on the protective coloration of animals, and who now applied the principles he had found in the animal kingdom to the disguise of guns and tanks'. The illusionist and magician Jasper Maskelyne (who would later work wizardry in camouflaging tanks and lorries in what appeared to be the featureless landscape of the

Western Desert – and with a dexterous use of lights even claimed to have made the Suez Canal disappear), was there too, though he couldn't understand for the life of him why he needed to be. At Farnham, Maskelyne 'learned how arctic rabbits suffer a change of colour when snow falls and why tigers hang around tall grass . . . six weeks being told very elementary things, almost drove me out of my mind . . . a lifetime of hiding things on the stage had taught me more about the subject than rabbits and tigers will ever know'.

His training completed, Trevelyan was posted to No 8 Corps at Taunton in Somerset where he replaced the stage designer Oliver Messel as assistant to Geoffrey Baxter, pink-gin-quaffing ex-theatre-producer, who had been responsible for the stage sets at Glyndebourne (and would be shot down over North Africa on an unofficial mission). Baxter held the attention of the troops when he lectured them on camouflage techniques: 'At every dance you have probably noticed that girl with the black velvet dress, with a great hand mark on her bottom where her partner has held her too tight. All he has done is to destroy the contained shadow on the velvet, as you are busy doing when you walk around your gun site.'

Trevelyan himself was to spend eighteen months touring the country 'lecturing ranks of sleepy soldiers in vast Drill Halls on the value of personal concealment, driving home my points with air-views of troops on the move both badly and well concealed' and inserting the odd slide 'of nude girls under a camouflage net to wake up the men when they had dropped off'. He transformed pillboxes all round the coast of Cornwall into cottages complete with lace curtains, into ersatz garages with pumps and a 'closed for the season' notice, public lavatories, cafés, chicken houses and romantic ruins. Asked to give a demonstration, Trevelyan 'would arrive on the barrack square with pots of paint and brushes, and set to work daubing the shield of some anti-tank gun with spots of different greens and browns, touching in the underside of the barrel itself with pure white on the principle of Dr Cott's gazelles'. This principle was the trick of countershading which, from a distance in strong light, flattens out and destroys an animal's form. 'Against the dreary barrack walls it looked an unholy mess, but when it was wheeled out into the country and placed against a hedge, there were cries of astonishment at my magic. This role, half clown, half-magician, was one that I found camouflage officers were more or less expected to fill.'

Apart from the application of art for strictly practical purposes, there were other more subtle ways in which artists could be enlisted to the causes of war. The Pilgrim Trust, which saw its role more widely as keeping Britain's cultural heritage alive in wartime, helped by commissioning a number of artists, as part of its 'Recording Britain' project, to paint or sketch 'any landscape, coast-line, village or city street, or ceremony characteristic of a period and of a district, and in danger of destruction or injury at the present time'. The aim of this Domesday project to compile a register of that which might be lost was also to propagandise 'deep England', emphasising the pastoral values that were conscripted to give the British their reason to fight. The project also contributed to Sir Kenneth Clark's plan for a War Artists Advisory Committee (WAAC) that would 'keep artists in work on any pretext, and, as far as possible, to prevent them from being killed'. In this, sadly, he was not altogether successful, as three artists, Thomas Hennell, Eric Ravilious and Albert Richards – the last the youngest of the war artists and, in the view of Graham Sutherland, 'the one real discovery of the war' – were killed while carrying out commissions.

The work of the WAAC was essentially 'prodding the artist and deciding which artists to prod'. The choice was a sensitive one. The *Tatler* was concerned that it might lean 'towards the abstract school, familiarly called the upside down boys'. Clark accepted this up to a point. 'The War Artists collection cannot be completely representative of modern English art because it cannot include those pure painters who are interested solely in putting down their feelings about shapes and colours, and not . . . drama and human emotions generally.' But there was a larger question than that of form: what could a painting achieve in recording war that a photograph could not? The brief for the artists was to 'report on a landscape' as the poet Henry Reed put it, and the finest would manage to convey something fundamental about the nature of war. ' "What did it look like?" they will ask in 1981, and no amount of description or documentation will answer them . . .'

A number of artists who the committee considered 'can be relied upon to do a workmanlike job under almost any conditions' were offered what amounted to a salaried position; others were commissioned to paint specific subjects, while speculative submissions from artists both professional and amateur, either civilians or serving in the Forces, were encouraged too. The fees were hardly excessive: £300 was the maximum for a large oil painting, though £150–£200 was more usual, and watercolours and drawings could command less than £10.

During the so-called Phoney War, when there wasn't much action to paint, 'recording the war' was amended to 'recording wartime activities'. Artists tended to be commissioned to turn in likenesses of military men, though there were those who were sent to paint ARP preparations, and Ethel Gabain was despatched to make lithographs of East End evacuees as they departed on trains, and when they arrived at their rural billets. She also applied to paint overseas evacuees but this was considered too politically sensitive and permission was refused. Carel Weight took his revenge for spending a winter in deeply uncongenial company digging tanks out of snowdrifts with *Recruit's Progress*, variations on Hogarth's *Rake's Progress*. Other artists were commissioned to fill in time by capturing such bellicose subjects as *Private B. Stockdale, Pastry Section No. 2, Mandora Barracks, Aldershot – Shifting Oven Pans*. 'Somewhat whimsical' was the photographer Cecil Beaton's judgement on much of the artistic output of the Phoney War. The War Office sent four salaried artists to France, including Edward Ardizzone, who was well known to the public through his illustrations for children's books and the *Radio Times*; and Edward Bawden, primarily a calligrapher and book illustrator and stalwart of the Curwen Press. Once there, they tended to mooch around looking at First World War trenches and paint pictures of 'ordinary life' among the soldiers of the BEF, including such works as *Pulling Off the Padre's Boots*. All four were eventually evacuated from Dunkirk.

After the fall of France in June 1940, there were few theatres of war to which artists could be sent: at home their commissions were mainly concerned with training, or, when invasion seemed likely, reassuring views of home defences. On his return, Ardizzone was charged to picture the Home Guard, and made it all look ordinary and reassuring – with more than a touch of the Dad's Army. Abroad the action was mainly in the Middle East. Some artists painted what they were themselves enduring: Keith Vaughan, a homosexual, felt isolated as a Conscientious Objector with the Pioneer Corps, a spectator to the war rather than a participant. He sketched his comrades in the barracks and, later, German POWs. Rodrigo Moynihan had wanted to go into camouflage, but found himself instead coping with 'Morse code and the inside of motorbikes'. He was eventually invalided out of the Army in July 1943 and appointed a civilian war artist, in which capacity he painted numerous portraits of important military figures, scientists and the particularly appealing young *Private Clarke ATS*, who was Moynihan's driver as he searched for subjects. His most telling painting is *The Medical Inspection* (1943), a study in khaki and pallid flesh, which, in its portrayal of resigned and truculent men dropping their trousers for the medical officer, bears eloquent witness to the anonymous indignity of Army life. Miles Chance portrayed the dafter aspects of his training with the Royal Artillery in *Battle Camp: Crawling in Wales* as chickens look on.

Paul Nash, who believed that machines not men were the real protagonists of war, was appointed, on the WAAC's recommendation, to the RAF 'to tackle the sky and aeroplanes'. He painted aerodromes and a number of crashed Nazi planes, paintings that were designed to emphasise the incongruity of the alien machine helpless in the idyllic landscape of the English countryside. When the Battle of Britain started, however, it was considered that crashed planes were not the required motif, and Nash's interest in the planes rather than the men who flew them, coupled with his endless arguments over money with the Air Ministry, led to his contract being terminated. Strongly believing 'in the power of pictorial art as a means of propaganda . . .', he was relieved to be re-employed by the MoI through the good offices of Sir Kenneth Clark, and became one of the foremost aerial artists of the war. His enigmatic masterpiece *Totes Meer* ('Dead Sea') was painted after night visits to the graveyard of crashed planes at Cowley, near Oxford. Nash's *Battle of Britain, August–October, 1940* in 1941, with its scrawling vapour trails – an 'arabesque of white streamers' and a plume of black smoke as a stricken plane plummeted to earth, was 'the epitome of the previous summer's struggle'.

Eric Ravilious had been a student of Paul Nash at the Royal College of Art, but whereas Nash's métier was war in the air, Ravilious – a watercolourist, pottery decorator and wood engraver to compare to Thomas Bewick – was assigned, as a captain, to the Admiralty (his friend and fellow artist Edward Bawden went to the War Office) and painted dockyards, battleships, submarines, coastal defences and naval convoys; he also executed a series of paintings of the Home Security control rooms showing maps of the organisation of Civil Defence on the walls of the underground offices. But as an invasion was considered to be imminent, the censor decided that these could not be shown during the war.

In early 1939 Ravilious had started to paint the huge figures cut out of the landscape of southern England, including the Wilmington Giant and the White Horses at Westbury in Wiltshire and Uffington in Berkshire. He completed the series with the Cerne Abbas Giant, painting it after it had been covered over to prevent it being a navigational aid for the Luftwaffe. The poet Grevel Lindop wrote of memories of a similar exercise at Uffington:

> my father in khaki . . . spreading slabs of turf from the back of a
>   lorry
> to bury the White Horse square by square
> and turf is laid and the blinding chalk goes under
> the rough green skin of the down secure
> from the moon's betrayal, the jealous bomber . . .

In August 1942 Ravilious set off from Iceland on a reconnaissance flight. His plane was never seen again.

The Blitz was to transform the idiom of many of the war artists. 'The background to this war, corresponding to the Western Front in the last war, is the bombed city,' wrote the poet Stephen Spender, and, in compiling its record of the charred and twisted buildings, the WAAC's main concern was to hurry artists to the scene of devastation before the clearance and salvage workers had a chance to spoil the aesthetics. When war broke out, John Piper had volunteered for work with the RAF interpreting aerial reconnaissance photographs. But since he had been painting ruins long before any bombs had fallen, Sir Kenneth Clark stepped in to persuade Piper that, with his intense interest in and knowledge of architecture honed from a childhood fascination with archaeology, he was the perfect artist to chronicle Britain's new 'instant ruins' – blitzed churches in particular. Piper was required to interrupt a brief holiday in November 1940 to hurry to Coventry which had been bombed the previous night, and where the ruins were still smouldering.

Apprehensive at how distressed and angry the local people were as they watched bodies being dug out of the rubble, Piper withdrew to a nearby solicitor's office to make sketches of the devastated cathedral for his paintings. One of the two paintings Piper did of Coventry was used by the MoI as a postcard, and though the detail is not entirely accurate, the picture 'became for Britain what Picasso's *Guernica* had been for Spain . . . a symbol of national resistance to Hitler'. Sixteen years later John Piper was commissioned to design stained glass for one of the huge windows of Basil Spence's new Coventry Cathedral: in it he used the same white light radiating from the altar, suggesting a spiritual presence, that he had used in his wartime painting.

Muirhead Bone (who had been a war artist in the First World War) was summoned from the west coast of Scotland to record his impression of the ruined City of London after the air raids of 29 December 1940; and Graham Sutherland also received a summons from the WAAC 'to stand by and make pictures of debris and damage caused by air raids'. In the City of London he found the skeletal ruins and contorted shapes thrilling. 'A lift shaft, for instance, the only thing left from what had obviously been a very tall building: in the way it had fallen it was like a wounded animal . . . Sometimes the fires were still burning. Everywhere there was a terrible stench – perhaps of burnt dirt: and always the silence . . . Very occasionally there would be the crash of a building collapsing of its own volition.' But when he went east, Sutherland found the atmosphere 'much more tragic . . . In the City one didn't think of the destruction of life. All the destroyed buildings were office buildings and people weren't in them at night. But in the East End one did think of the hurt to people . . . Even a mattress that had been blown out of a house into the middle of the street looked more like a body.' There were 'the shells of long terraces of houses . . . great – surprisingly wide – perspectives of destruction seeming to recede into infinity, the windowless blocks were like sightless eyes.'

Henry Moore was another artist who had fought in the First World War and had come to find 'the sight of a khaki uniform began to mean everything that was wrong and wasteful and anti-life'. In 1940 he admitted, 'I'm still in the process of getting my attitude to the war clear and satisfactory, even to myself.' But on 11 September that year he had an epiphany. Returning home after dinner with friends, Moore and his wife were caught in Belsize Park underground station for an hour because 'of the fierceness of . . . a big anti-aircraft barrage . . . put up all around London', and for the first time encountered those who dwelt underground. There, in front of him, lay row after row of the reclining figures like those he had been drawing and sculpting for years, 'even the holes out of which the trains were coming seemed to me like the holes in my sculpture'. Finally Moore's art could find a wartime translation. The WAAC bought four of the large drawings and gave Moore a commission to continue his work, bringing to the public through the medium of pen and ink, watercolour, chalk and wax crayon 'the group sense of communion in apprehension . . . in a world peopled by figures at once monumental and ghostly'.

These drawings of underground shelterers won acclaim in artistic circles, but less from those members of the public who saw them first at a National Gallery exhibition. Reviewing (anonymously) an exhibition of war artists' work early in 1943, Keith Vaughan regarded it as 'a tragedy, nevertheless understandable, that so many Londoners confronted with these drawings feel baffled and insulted. Here is a whole new underground world from which they feel themselves totally excluded, though the elements were all so familiar.' The shelterers had, in effect, been turned into sculptural forms, unlike Ardizzone's portrayals when 'you are in the midst of a steaming human throng. Here is the familiar moment, the bustling crowds, the burdened mothers with their endlessly tiresome children. The friendly voices, the smells, the chips in newspaper, the easy-going, cheerful society which was certainly part of shelter life . . .' To Moore the underground sleepers – particularly those he drew in the Liverpool Street extension that could hold up to 10,000 people – could seem as objectified as they had been to the government officials who feared the tendency to 'deep shelter' mentality among a part of the population they did not entirely comprehend.

As the poet and editor Alan Ross, who fought in the Second World War, pointed out, the most memorable art of the First was 'painted by artists who were or had been serving soldiers. They not only saw, but they had experienced.' But this was a different war. All artists 'had experienced' war on the civilian front, and many were very directly involved in that experience. John Piper praised *Bombs on Chelsea* on show at a Bond Street gallery. The 'small, rather slight drawings . . .

[which] have a good deal of interest and "actuality" ' were the work of Clifford Hall, who was attached to a Chelsea stretcher party. Leonard Rosoman was a member of the AFS (as were the novelists Henry Green, William Sansom and the poet Stephen Spender) and during the Blitz had helped fight fires all over London, including in the City and docklands, but still somehow managed to find time to paint prodigiously. *A House Collapsing on Two Firemen, Shoe Lane, London EC4* – a painting he came to regard as melodramatic and sentimental – depicts two of his colleagues in the moment before they were killed in an incident from which he only narrowly managed to escape with his life. Rosoman's paintings were regularly hung in exhibitions of work by Firemen Artists (there was a comparable group of Civil Defence Artists) and, after the Blitz subsided, he was invited to provide the illustrations for *The Fire Service Manual*.

Henry Moore grew bored with underground shelters when the occupants, regimented into bunks, ceased to appear as 'a white-grub like race of troglodytes swathed in blankets', so he then went down coalmines, which he found hard to depict in interesting ways. Sutherland was despatched to Cornish tinmines where the 'grand, handsome da Vinci types' hewing the tin attracted his interest. Ceri Richards was employed to depict the next process of turning the tin into tin plate; Michael Ayrton painted a factory engaged in the manufacture of heavy chains; Robert Colquohon was commissioned to paint the weaving of Army cloth (which he found far preferable to his previous occupation of emptying latrines in the RAMC). Mervyn Peake, who was 'quite unsuited to soldiering', had his several applications turned down by the WAAC which stressed that it was 'most important that the Committee should not, in such cases, allow themselves to be influenced by the fact that the artist might wish to get out of the Army'. Peake was finally invalided out of the Forces in May 1943 and six months later was employed by the committee to paint a picture of a glass factory where cathode-ray tubes were made, a process that he saw as a surreal ballet 'of heavy feet and flickering hands'.

Clark was determined that the art of the Second World War should reflect the full participation of the civilian population 'taking it'. In this wider sweep it was essential to depict women 'in spheres formerly considered foreign to their sex . . . that the grim necessities of war' had opened up, in the words of the artist Dame Laura Knight, as well in their more traditional 'womanly' roles as nurses, cooks, and in the voluntary services. Forty-two women artists took part in providing a visual record of the Second World War. Ethel Gabain, who had painted evacuees, executed a series of lithographs of *Children in Wartime* and also painted women building Beaufort planes, operating a weir pump, working on the buses and filling sandbags. Dorothy Coke, who had been a war artist in the First World War, painted women in gas masks making aero-engine parts; and Dame Laura Knight showed them working in aircraft production – *Ruby Loftus Screwing a Breech-ring* became iconic of women's war efforts – and hoisting and repairing barrage balloons. Evelyn Dunbar depicted women in the Land Army practising milking on artificial udders and sorting potatoes in Berwick; and also painted women crawling around making camouflage nets, dutifully listening to a lecture about canning, knitting for the troops and queuing for fish among other wartime activities. Grace Golden captured an emergency food office.

Other paintings by women were not necessarily of women. Anna Zinkeisen, who was a member of the St John's Ambulance Brigade, nursed in the casualty ward of St Mary's Hospital Paddington in the morning and in the afternoon, in a disused operating theatre in the same hospital, reproduced some of what she had seen. Meredith Frampton painted a hyper-realistic portrait of Sir Ernest Gowers, the ARP Controller, plus his team since he insisted that it was absurd to suggest he could run London's Civil Defence on his own; and Lelia Faithfull portrayed American GIs playing baseball in Hyde Park. But it was not only the civilians' war that detained women war artists: Stella Schmolle, a draughtswoman sergeant in the ATS, had been sent to France and Belgium in 1944, but military intransigence had placed so many restrictions on her as a woman at the front that she came back to Britain. However, Dame Laura Knight had her request to go as an official war artist to the Nuremberg war trials in 1946 agreed; and Doris Zinkeisen, the older sister of Anna, was among the first artists to enter Belsen concentration camp in 1945.

Stanley Spencer, the artist of the Resurrection, of sex and divinity, had suggested that he might paint a Crucifixion inspired by the occupation of Poland but, in accord with the policy of getting artists to paint only what they saw, Spencer was sent to paint the shipyards of Port Glasgow on the Clyde where ships were being built at rapid speed to replace those lost in the Battle of the Atlantic. The frail, untidy and eccentric artist found the shipyards very congenial and fortuitously managed to divine religion and sexuality among the furnaces, ropes, great steel sheets and sturdy tarpaulins, and produced a total of fifty-eight feet of powerful large paintings suggesting the hard physical work and team effort that shipbuilding required. At the end of the war Port Glasgow was the location for Spencer's final Resurrection paintings. His inspiration was a cemetery near the gasworks on a hill that did duty for the Hill of Zion on which Christ sat in judgement, the sky filled with angels.

Spencer's younger brother Gilbert was an artist too. Though he was never heavily employed by the War Artists Advisory Committee, his paintings *Grasmere Home Guard* and *Troops in the Countryside* were commissioned by them (though to his chagrin *Grasmere Home Guard* was never hung in the National Gallery because no one could be found to frame the extensive panorama). Spencer had come to choose these subjects because in December 1940 the Royal College of Art, where he taught painting, was evacuated to the Lake District. 'Liverpool was in flames,' he wrote, 'but we were to know Grasmere as Wordsworth had known it, and to hear that strange note ringing round the frozen lake as its waters lowered – rather than the wail of sirens.' 'I thought this war [painting] was a very good one,' wrote Stanley Spencer to Gilbert Spencer about *Troops in the Countryside*. 'I liked the assertion of peace in it: the soldiers being as peaceful as the cows. It was like what a rabbit might have seen and felt, looking from a field opposite, and that would not know the khaki suits, etc. had any other significance than the markings of the cows.'

Most of the college's heavy equipment had to be left in London; the Head of Textiles badgered the Board of Trade for fabrics, and at first the potters had to travel to Lancaster to fire their work until a makeshift kiln was built in the back garden of the Salutation Hotel (where the women students were housed; the men were in Queen's Hotel). 'A throne, a model and a clutter of easels. Paints and canvasses litter the [hotel's] peacetime ballroom. Students design, weave and dye fabrics from experimental formulas in a converted cow shed ... Some have converted old pigeon lofts and garage attics into patched-up whitewashed studios, isolated above rickety ladders. Others may go off into the mountains sketching for several days at a time . . .' The students were either too young or too old to be called up, or they were women or had been invalided out of the Forces – one young man was so traumatised by his experiences that he wore cycle clips day and night to prevent rats climbing up his legs, and others were mutilated and had to learn to paint or sculpt with fingers missing, maybe an arm made useless.

The work of the war artists was regularly exhibited in London when most of the galleries reopened in a limited way from the spring of 1940, bringing life to the denuded walls of the National Gallery, the Royal Academy and the V&A (until it was shut again by a flying bomb in 1944), and selections of artists' work toured the country to hang in provincial museums and galleries (often to coincide with the regular money-raising War Weapons weeks). Meanwhile, under the auspices of the 'Art for the People' programme, paintings were despatched to village halls, munitions factories and Army camps.

Such exhibitions, particularly those 'when . . . artists . . . have turned their subject matter from the Academy rosebud to the Khaki brave', intrigued the public. Galleries all over Britain were gratified to find that such temporary exhibitions drew crowds far in excess of the interest art had excited before the war. Gwladys Cox and her husband tried to see most exhibitions of war art held in London, and in May 1941 they went to the 173rd Summer Exhibition at the Royal Academy. Richard Eurich's *Dunkirk Beaches, 1940* was on show (Mrs Cox much preferred Charles Cundall's version which she saw in July that year at the National Gallery) and 'among other exhibits are skies criss-crossed with search lights and lit with shell bursts, grey battleships on grey seas, a tin-hatted ARP warden rescuing a languishing lady . . . One large canvas in tempera entitled "The Champion" . . . is most comical and should greatly please Lord Woolton . . . some patriotic soul has grown on the *balcony* of his flat, a cauliflower as large as a good-sized dining table . . .'

The BBC complained that no one ever portrayed *its* vital activities and no portrait of Vera Lynn, or Tommy Handley's *ITMA*, was accepted by the WAAC, nor, more surprisingly, any representation of Winston Churchill, until after he had been defeated in the 1945 election. There were, however, plenty of portraits of military men, and of heroes and heroines of the Blitz. Among the portraits of firemen, policemen, ARP workers and nurses, Anthony Devas painted the Matron of Charing Cross Hospital: 'the sort of woman who goes down the ages – one can imagine her being painted by Rembrandt or Hals or Goya'. Rodrigo Moynihan painted Miss Borne, the formidable Matron of Papworth Village Settlement outside Cambridge, which treated cases of tuberculosis, whom he suspected (wrongly) was a spy. A. R. Thomson painted Charity Black, a sixteen-year-old despatch rider from West Bromwich in the Midlands who was the youngest Civil Defence worker to be awarded the George Medal. She 'shone as she sat . . . I would go anywhere to paint another one.' Gilbert Spencer had been commissioned to 'do a number of portrait drawings' of the brave. One was of a young man in the Birmingham Small Arms factory who 'had had his feet shackled, and allowed himself with acetylene welder in one hand, to be lowered, head first, at the end of a hawser, to rescue a mate trapped on the edge of an inferno in a deep gun pit'.

John Piper thought the Official War Art exhibition at the National Gallery in May 1941 'the best yet . . . If anyone still doubts the wisdom of employing artists who can make records of experience during the war he should see these vivid pictures and compare them with what the camera would say about the same subjects; twisted girders pouring over fired rubble-piles; a wall falling like a short man, the broken carcase of a lift shaft; machinery dangling its severed limbs in the bare well of a mantle factory . . .'

As well as exhibitions at home the WAAC mobilised the art it had commissioned in the national interest, mounting exhibitions in Japan in 1940, the Dominions, and, in May 1941, 'Britain at War' opened in New York and later toured the United States. It was a comprehensive exercise in persuasion with over a hundred paintings and some 200 photographs covering all aspects of Britain at war on the Home Front, and the country's plans for post-war reconstruction.

'My little money-sources – (apart from anything else) – are diminishing or dying. Soon there will not be a single paper paying inadequately for serious stories and poems,' bemoaned Dylan Thomas. Artists had the WAAC, while musicians, actors and directors had the support of CEMA. The poet John Betjeman had come up with a scheme for writers who 'are in the unfortunate position of having no single corporate body to

protect their interests – or, in the present case, to direct their activities . . .
In the first instance a register *raisonné* should be made, with the help of
the Authors' Society, indicating different qualifications. Many writers
may not be willing or competent to participate on positive propaganda.
But they could all be used in many ways, drafting, précis-making,
translating, censorship and clerical work.'

But it wasn't that easy. Although Betjeman would for a time be
employed 'at the shameful M of Information, Euston 4321 ext.517',
before being transferred to Éire as Press Attaché to the British
Ambassador, not all who thought they could turn their prose to the
cause of war were wanted. The MoI told Siegfried Sassoon, one of
the foremost poets of the First World War, that 'authors can best serve by
continuing their ordinary work and addressing the public, through
the channels that are open to them'. Sassoon commented ruefully,
'The trouble is, most authors have ceased to earn anything since 1st
September.'

Many writers felt that they had no one to help and the war was closing
in on them. George Orwell saw himself 'sitting on a melting iceberg; he
is an anachronism . . . as surely doomed as a *hippopotamus* . . . from now
onwards the all important fact for the creative writer is going to be that
this is not a writer's world.' The reverse might have been expected. 'The
long dark autumn evenings have merged into the long dark winter
evenings, which in turn will merge into the spring blackout,' wrote
E. M. Delafield, author of the humorous *Diary of a Provincial Lady*, in
December 1939. 'How are you going to spend them? . . . You will . . . be
forced by blackout, rationed petrol and the general state of your finances
to spend the dull dark evenings in your own dull, dark homes; and your
friends and neighbours will remain in theirs . . . whatever your choice,
read *something*. A war spent reading is a *well-spent* war.'

The conditions of war created an unprecedented demand for
something to read, a hunger that did not abate for the duration, and
increased during the Blitz when long hours were spent in shelters. But
the means to satisfy this demand were systematically reduced.

In 1939, 14,904 books had been published; by 1945 this number had
shrunk to just 6,747, and new books were snapped up as soon as they
were published. Although many people had taken their books back to
the public libraries the Monday morning after war was declared on the

Sunday, in a getting-one's-life-in-order sort of way, the same libraries were soon reporting that more people than ever were borrowing from their shelves. Publishers, however, were unable to satisfy this voracious wartime market since their paper stocks had been severely curtailed. The supply of paper was measured against how much each publisher had used between August 1938 and August 1939; each publisher was allowed 60 per cent of that total at first, but this fell to 37.5 per cent by December 1941, and that quota fell disproportionately on small firms.

The publishing and printing industry was hard hit by conscription, too. Skilled men were called up: by the summer of 1940 Penguin Books had many members of staff in the services, and already two of them had been killed in France. Oxford University Press had 'already sent nearly 200 young men to the fighting services'. Twenty out of seventy bookbinding firms had gone out of business and those left were working with only 50 per cent of their staff; and it was impossible to replace machinery for binding and paper-making.

Although the government climbed down over its proposal to impose purchase tax on books, it would not budge on paper allocations, despite the fact that an estimated 20 million books had been lost in the Blitz. When Paternoster Row was destroyed on the night of 29 December 1940, Collins, Ward Lock, Hodder & Stoughton, Eyre & Spottiswoode, Hutchinson and Nelson were among those affected; Longman, which had been trading in the Row since 1724, was demolished, as was its warehouse in Bermondsey, and that night it lost over 3 million books. But the most devastating attack was the destruction of Simpkin Marshall, the largest book distributor in Britain, which lost 6 million books. The firm never recovered and went bankrupt after the war.

The allocation of paper was to affect all publishing decisions from the moment of its imposition on 31 March 1940 until its relaxation in 1948. Publishers tried various solutions: the MoI was sometimes prepared to supply paper from its allocation if it wanted to see a particular book published, though conversely this allowed it a certain censorship of books it did *not* want to see published. George Orwell was convinced that his anti-Stalinist allegory *Animal Farm* had not been able to find a publisher until Secker & Warburg took it up, because the MoI suggested that its publication 'would serve no good purpose'. When the very popular weekly magazine *Picture Post* was critical of the weaponry used in the desert war in North Africa, the MoI temporarily withdrew its subsidy to the wholesalers who were exporting the magazine to the Middle East.

In March 1942 the Ministry of Supply agreed to release an additional 250 tons of paper for books 'of national importance'. There was resistance to what some publishers saw as a state diktat, since it was difficult to agree on which were books of national importance. 'How,' queried the publisher of Left Books, Victor Gollancz, 'was one to decide between a Roman Catholic breviary or a new edition of Karl Marx?'

Frequently, when popular books went out of print, it was not possible to reprint them. Increasingly publishers welcomed shorter books since they used less paper. A. P. Herbert had a remedy.

> The paper situation's worse:
> So I express myself in verse.
> For verse, as everybody knows,
> Is less extravagant than prose . . .

The Book Production War Economy Agreement of January 1942 was a voluntary agreement to standardise production, but those publishers who did not choose to sign found their paper allocation cut to 25 per cent. The quality of the paper, which was made from home-grown straw, declined to that of pre-war toilet paper (while toilet paper 'resembles tin sheet' according to Orwell); but it meant that publishers could probably manage to produce 60 per cent of the books they had produced before the war, despite having only 37.5 per cent of the paper. But by 1943 the paper had been recycled so often and was so thin and yellowing that the Ministry of Supply launched a salvage drive to collect pre-war books. The response was overwhelming – 56 million volumes were collected, the equivalent of more than one from every man, woman and child in the country. Five million of the haul were despatched to the troops, and the remainder pulped to produce more paper – and that included some valuable first editions since it was prohibited to remove any books from the piles for resale.

War reconfigured the literary landscape. Classics that portrayed a calmer, more certain age provided solace and, since fewer new books were being published, V. S. Pritchett turned to reviewing a different classic each week in the *New Statesman*. Anthony Trollope, Charles Dickens, Jane Austen and Henry James were particularly popular wartime reading – or rereading – though D. H. Lawrence no longer seemed to interest anyone. Tolstoy's *War and Peace* became monumentally successful after its serialisation on the BBC, while a more recent blockbuster of war and love, Margaret Mitchell's *Gone with the Wind*, proved as popular a long book as its adaptation did as a long film. But in contrast to such generalisations, James Hadley Chase's 'hard boiled' American-gangster thriller *No Orchids for Miss Blandish* was a best-seller – 'drunk and disorderly reading', as the *Bookseller* described it; 'one of the things that helped to console people for the boredom of being bombed', George Orwell conceded. And the Penguin book that outsold all others was one on aircraft recognition.

In fact Penguin Books were better placed than most to weather the war. The year 1938–9 had been the one in which Penguin Specials had taken off: topical books on important issues of the day, including such titles as *The Air Defence of Britain* and *Europe and the Czechs*; so the baseline from which Penguin's paper allocation was worked out meant the house found itself 'plush beyond the wildest dreams of any aspiring competitor'. Its small, standard format made economical use of paper and was the ideal size to slip into a gas-mask container or the pocket of battledress trousers designed to hold an entrenching tool, and light enough to include in a parcel of cigarettes, socks or a comforter sent out to serving soldiers, sailors and airmen.

The Red Cross, the YMCA and other voluntary organisations organised the bulk despatch of books to the Forces, and in May 1940 the Postmaster General agreed that books left at post offices would be sent on free of charge to those on active service. A note was printed on the half-title page of many new books requesting 'For the Forces, Leave this book at a Post Office when you have read it, so that men and women in the services may enjoy it too.' But this was a haphazard arrangement and fighting men were just as likely to unpack a parcel to find it contained 'unsuitable books from a country parson's own library', a copy of Samuel Smiles' *Self Help* (published in 1859), out-of-date mystery stories, books relating to the last war ('of no interest to the majority of the men') or dated romances such as *East Lynne* or the oeuvre of Elinor Glyn. But among these discards were often a number of dog-eared Penguins, and Allen Lane, Penguin's founder, who had already agreed to produce books for the Canadian government to distribute to its Armed Forces in exchange for shipments of paper, considered the possibility of doing something similar for the British Forces. He consulted one of his editors, W. E. Williams, who was also the Director of the Army Bureau of Current Affairs (ABCA), which had been set up to inform men and women 'most of whom had only the vaguest knowledge of our war aims or of current affairs and no notion of the problems likely to confront this country when the fighting was over'. Weekly ABCA sessions were a compulsory part of a soldier's training. The lectures were given by officers based on material ABCA sent out every week on whatever the topic was – for example, 'What to do with the Germans', 'Women in Industry' and 'Town Planning'. Although these weekly sessions could attempt little more than 'a hedge-hopping of citizenship', they added to the soldier's knowledge and taught him 'the discipline of civilised argument'– a little too effectively, some thought, since the charge of 'socialist propaganda' was frequently levelled at ABCA, which some held responsible for the khaki vote for Labour in the 1945 election.

As someone who also advised on Penguin Specials, Williams could see a fortuitous synergy between the market for these and ABCA's mission, and he was instrumental in brokering an agreement between Allen Lane and the War Office to start a Forces Book Club in Britain, with titles chosen exclusively from the Penguin list and bearing their imprint. Penguin was contracted to produce ten titles a month in runs of an estimated 75,000 subscribers, which added up to 9 million books a year. Units rather than individuals would subscribe, and each month would receive a parcel of that month's titles. Each parcel contained a mixture of popular fiction, crime and world affairs. In November 1942 the contents included Enid Bagnold's *National Velvet*, H. R. Knickerbocker asking *Is Tomorrow Hitler's?*, V. Gordon Childe's *What Happened in History*, and *The Murders in Praed Street* by John Rhodes. The following February the Forces could have enjoyed E. M. Forster's *Howard's End*, *A Short History of the World* by H. G. Wells, *Tarka the Otter* by Henry Williamson, Norman Collins' *Love in Our Time,* two murder mysteries, and a book about steamboatmen. The take-up, however, was never as high as had been hoped, probably due in part to a misreading of what a soldier might like to read in between manoeuvres, and in September 1942 the Forces Book Club was abandoned.

But Penguin was able to rebind much of its Forces Book Club stock and despatch it overseas under the Red Cross scheme to set up libraries in POW camps – by the end of the war the Red Cross estimated that there were a total of 192,335 British POWs in camps in Germany and Japan. The choice of books was censored. The British forbade sending anything that might help the enemy, such as maps and navigational and meteorological charts, while what the Germans permitted varied from camp to camp, but in general all books by Jewish authors, or by H. G. Wells, or George Bernard Shaw, were banned; Baden-Powell's *Scouting for Boys* was not allowed and neither was Palgrave's *Golden Treasury* (because Palgrave was a Jew); Spinoza's *Ethics* was forbidden and so, on moral grounds, was *No Orchids for Miss Blandish*. Less surprisingly, escape stories were not allowed, while books that had titles or chapter headings containing such words as freedom, liberty, democracy, totalitarianism, were likely to be censured.

Many writers were deeply implicated in wartime activities and distilled their experiences in fiction. Henry Green, who served in the AFS, wrote a tribute to his comrades (though not to the regular fire service) in *Caught* (1943). His experiences had taught him that 'the only thing to do was to stick together'. If a fireman didn't act as part of a team, 'you're dead' an old fireman tells Green's character, Richard Roe. 'You're a smell, you're fried.' Graham Greene, who worked in wartime Intelligence, published *The Power and the Glory* in 1940, and *The Ministry of Fear*, his thriller about the Blitz and the Ministry of Information, in 1943, while *The Heart of the Matter* (1948) and *The End of the Affair* (1951) both took the war as settings to explore the complexities of love. Evelyn Waugh, who tried to sign up for war straight away, left *Work Suspended* and, unable to return to it since the world it portrayed had ceased to exist, published just its first two chapters in 1942. His comic novel of the bureaucratic farces and shenanigans of the Home Front – rationing, evacuation and propaganda – *Put Out More Flags*, was also published in 1942. Just as the war ended, *Brideshead Revisited*, which the Army had been very grateful to give Waugh leave to write since he was so unpopular with his men that it was feared that in battle he might be their first casualty, was published. The story of a mansion requisitioned by the

Army, and a world lost, he considered the book to be a souvenir of war, though the story is mainly set in a pre-war arcadia. It was not until 1952 that *Men at Arms*, the first volume of what would become Waugh's masterpiece *Sword of Honour* 'an interminable novel about Army life obsessed by memories of military dialogue' based more directly on his wartime experiences, was published.

For two years Mass-Observation's Tom Harrisson had 'read literally every book which has anything to do with war, fiction or fantasy [and] . . . became totally, immeasurably bogged, engrossed in bad reading'. He read books about politics, peace, 'en route books' like *The Forward March* and *Where Do We Go From Here?* He read of espionage – *The Spy Who Died in Bed*, *The Admiral Was a Spy*, *The Woman in Red* and dozens more. He read about the Army, the Navy and so many books on flying with titles such as *Bomber's Moon*, *Winged Love*, *Air Force Girl* and *Wellington Wendy* that he began to feel that he had never 'owed so little to so many'. He read about evacuation and the Blitz 'but none by working people who have been evacuated or blitzed', and one in which 'the text is liberally bespattered with bomb noises: "Whee-ee-esh . . . bloo-oomp" '. Almost all, Harrisson concluded, were of indifferent quality, the 'chaotic effluvia of a world confused . . .', of the 'uniformed and uninformed' who picked on predictable scapegoats – intellectuals and Jews ('if the villain or shady character or spy was not a painter, he was probably a Jew') – and lauded predictable heroes: cockneys (preferably taxi drivers or charwomen), fighter pilots and those maimed by war 'of pure British (generally aristocratic or near Etonian) extraction'. Harrison was dismissive of 'lady novelists' and did not seem to have read Virginia Woolf's *Between the Acts*, published in 1941, nor to entertain short stories from the pen of such distinguished writers as Elizabeth Bowen or Rosamond Lehmann. But he found some honourable exceptions to the 'overwhelmingly superficial' output. He felt that Rex Warner's allegory *The Aerodrome* had real merit, and in total he 'particularly recommended' seven books including John Strachey's account of his time as an ARP warden during the Blitz, *Post D*, and the account by 'Gun Buster' (John C. Austin) of *Return via Dunkirk*. He concluded, though, that with limited paper supplies publishers stuck to 'their branded lines, the best selling authors of peace'. But while Harrisson believed that publishers could 'sell practically anything' during the war, there is no reason to imagine that most of those people who read more than usual – because they couldn't do much else during air raids, or were endlessly stuck in slow buses and packed trains – were likely to be duped for long by heroic fantasies. The pseudonymous James Hadley Chase was prosecuted for obscenity over his next novel, *Miss Callaghan Comes to Grief*, and spent the rest of the war in the RAF, so Squadron Leader René Raymond (his real name) was in no position to write a sequel to *No Orchids for Miss Blandish* (though his book did not lack pale imitations). But Agatha Christie, who was working as a nurse in a London hospital, continued to write two novels a year (and was considered to be the most-read novelist in air-raid shelters). Patricia Wentworth, whose detective heroine Miss Silver was out of the Miss Marple school, was popular, as was Christiana Brand's fine *Green for Danger* which was set against a background of V-1 raids on southern England; while sales of the former 'true crime' journalist Peter Cheyney's novels such as *Dark Duet* exceeded 2 million between 1944 and 1945.

Books also poured off the presses of the numerous 'mushroom' publishers that had sprung up, managing somehow to get paper from various dubious sources – provincial printers were the most likely, but one consignment consisted of a wholesale grocer's quota for wrapping margarine, and another was made up of the sheets of backing paper from transfers. Two hundred new publishers set up in 1940 alone. While this competition naturally infuriated the established houses who were tied to their paper allocations, the 'mushroomers' were exploiting a different market, publishing mainly westerns and gangster novels – with a liberal lacing of sex thrown in – for a new class of readers who were unlikely to have ever 'picked up a Penguin'. These were mainly young working-class men living away from home in barracks or in hostels, soldiers on leave, and US servicemen stationed in Britain. The paperbacks they bought were often little more than booklets printed on the flimsiest paper, with no margins and type of the size 'required to put the Lord's Prayer on a postage stamp'. Most had alluring covers and some were so salacious that they were passed over the counter of some of the less reputable bookshops in sealed bags at five shillings a copy. They were certainly not cheap – a sixteen-page book that largely consisted of photographs of the film star Rita Hayworth in various poses cost a shilling. Nevertheless, they sold phenomenally well (the Hayworth book sold over 200,000 copies), with print runs inhibited only by lack of paper. So great was the demand for such steamy fiction that the manager of Everybody's Bookshop in the Charing Cross Road, Hector Kelly, a popular fiction publisher, was prepared to buy second-hand books without covers since he knew he'd be able to sell them. He was the brother of Harold Kelly, who himself wrote a series of gangster novels with titles such as *No Mortgage on a Coffin* under the pseudonym Darcy Glinto.

'Mushroom press' authors had little time to consider the role their writing played in wartime: they were production-line workers, paid a fixed fee, and were expected to be able to turn their hand to whatever the public wanted at the time – cowboys, crime, romance. For writers who could stand the pace, it could be well-paid wartime work, and though many mushroom publishers went out of business after the war, those that did manage to survive the austerity years (helped by the fact that the import of US comics and pulp fiction continued to be prohibited) prospered when paper was deregulated.

Elizabeth Bowen was a writer who found herself unable to write a novel during the war, and did not publish her evocation of wartime London with its uncertainties and treacheries, *The Heat of the Day*, until four years later, but instead published collections of short stories. This was a genre that had not been regarded as profitable in the 1930s but the short story, ideally a collection by more than one author, proliferated in wartime. This was partly because short-story reading was rather suited to the interrupted tenor of many wartime lives of minutes snatched, but also because many anthologies were in effect magazines. While it was illegal to start a new magazine during the war, an anthology of verse or prose was permitted. Some were modest affairs, while others, like Cyril Connolly's *Horizon*, or *Penguin New Writing* edited by John Lehmann, were more ambitious. *Penguin New Writing* had a print run of around 75,000 copies and used 5 tons of paper for each issue (equivalent to the entire allocation for the Hogarth Press). With the number of fiction titles falling from 4,222 in 1939 to 1,246 in 1945, such publications were a welcome outlet for writers who felt, like Orwell, that they were sitting on a melting iceberg.

In *Horizon* Cyril Connolly had posed the question: 'Where are the war poets?' The answer was that, like the novelists, they were in a sense everywhere. Some were in uniform: poets writing from a theatre of war that eventually encompassed the deserts of North Africa, the *bocage* of Normandy, the jungles of Borneo, the POW camps of Japan, the Atlantic, the Pacific, the skies over Germany – and from the Nissen huts, barrack rooms and parade grounds that oozed over the English countryside. Keith Douglas, Alun Lewis and Roy Fuller were among the finest. From his Nissen hut, Roy Fuller wanted to pull

> The poets from their safe and paper beds,
> Show them my comrades and the silver pall
> Over the airfield, ask them what they'd sing?

Keith Douglas (who was killed in Normandy three days after the D-Day landings, aged twenty-four) believed that no one who was not in uniform was qualified to write war poetry, but this was a different war. As Robert Graves, who was living through his second world war, wrote, a soldier-poet 'cannot even feel that his rendezvous with death is more certain than that of his Aunt Fanny, the fire-watcher'.

Despite the range of wartime jobs they took – propagandising, recording, morale boosting, fighting and many more – the question of what musicians, artists and writers were *for* in wartime continued to exercise some, though few would have agreed with the literary biographer Lord David Cecil's defence of 'the artist's right to live in his ivory tower . . . [knowing] he may at any moment be bombed out of it . . .' The writer, and editor of *Penguin New Writing*, John Lehmann, put the case for the miscellaneous eddy of writers, poets, painters, musicians and actors who felt deracinated in a world at war, solid in their opposition not to the war itself necessarily, but to the sort of life war demanded. 'We were united in this-has-got-to-seen-through attitude which was taken for granted, and also a determination to guard the free world of ideas from any misguided military encroachment. We *needed* one another, and for purposes larger than our own security or ambition.'

Noel Streatfield, whose *London Under Fire, a Woman's Diary* the publisher William Collins had declined to publish until after the war, when she had lost interest in it, occasionally received 'a telephone call asking me to write a fairy story for children in connection with war weapons week'. She put much of her energy into writing bulletins for the WVS, but when challenged 'about the place of the novelist in the world, I stood up for their value as historians of their age'.

In 1941 Cyril Connolly returned to the itch in a manifesto published in *Horizon* to which Spender, Orwell and Arthur Koestler among others appended their signatures. It demanded that creative writers should be considered as a reserved occupation and 'should be used to interpret the war world so that cultural unity is re-established and war effort emotionally co-ordinated'.

John Betjeman had been mockingly scathing. He wrote to Connolly, 'It was good to see how this spot of bother is affecting you. *Horizon* eh? Some sort of highbrow journal eh? Well, chaps, it's going to give Jerry what for. Teach him to take a slosh at the British Lion by giving him as good as he gives? . . . We must all do our bit . . . But if the best you can find to do is some highbrow paper with a communist-poet fellow, then take my advice and chuck it and get a job in the Sussex Light. *There's a war on, you know . . .*'

18

'GO TO IT! GO TO IT!
THAT'S THE WAY TO DO IT!'

One day when Hitler is no more,
Johnny Brown will come ashore,
Seize again his spade and hoe
And stocks will flourish in a row.
And if I'm not too worn and plain
I'll be a woman once again.

POEMS OF THE LAND ARMY

'IT WAS NOW when you no longer saw, heard, smelled war, that a deadening acclimatisation began to set in,' Elizabeth Bowen wrote, capturing those middle years after the Blitz had abated but before the Allies had been able to count any significant victories against Germany. 'The first generation of ruins, cleaned up, shored up, began to weather – in daylight they took their places as a norm of the scene; the dangerless nights of September two years later blotted them out . . . Reverses, losses, deadlocks, now almost unnoticed bred one another; every day the news hammered one more nail into a consciousness which no longer resounded. Everywhere hung the heaviness of the even worse you could not be told, and could not bear to hear. This was the lightless middle of the tunnel.' For Naomi Mitchison, farming on the Mull of Kintyre, feeling 'ashamed not to be more in it' since she hadn't been in London to share the experience of the Blitz, filling in endless government forms, war had become 'a habit . . . that's the way total war is . . . Dick says it will be over next year; I say it will never be over.'

Food rations were lower in early 1941 than at any time during the war; shipping losses meant that food imports had fallen to two-thirds of their pre-war level, and the government was continually having to revise targets down; and, though farmers were managing to produce ever more home-grown food, this was at the expense of livestock. The meat ration fell from 2s 2d in the autumn of 1940 to 1s 2d in January 1941, the level at which it would remain for most of the war.

What Churchill in June 1940 named the 'Battle of the Atlantic' – which had started with the sinking of the *Athenia* less than twelve hours after the outbreak of war – gained momentum after the fall of France and did not end until 4 May 1945. German U-boats attempted to destroy Allied shipping and blockade British ports so that the country's war industry would grind to a standstill, and its people would starve. In the three months from March to May 1941, 412 British, Allied and neutral ships were lost at sea – the majority to U-boats. In April 1941 Churchill ordered that shipping losses should no longer be reported in the British press: the news could give too much information to the Germans, and it was certain to lower British morale. In November 1942, the worst month of the war at sea, out of a total of 134 ships lost, 117 Merchant Navy vessels – more than 700,000 tons – were sunk, many by 'wolf packs' of U-boats, most of them hunting in the Atlantic. This presented Britain not only with intolerable loss of life, but also a grave import crisis of food and war matériel from the US which, since December 1941, had been a belligerent on the Allied side. In March 1943 half the Allied convoys crossing the Atlantic were attacked and 22 per cent of the ships in those convoys were sunk. At a conference in Casablanca in January, Churchill and Roosevelt had agreed that the Atlantic must be the Allies' first priority. Intelligence intercepts were increasingly able to plot U-boat courses, the Allied air offensive was stepped up, destroyers protecting convoys were increased, the war in the Mediterranean drew off some of the attackers, and by May 1943 the tide had turned decisively in favour of the Allies. The Battle of the Atlantic was, in the words of the official chronicle, 'the hardest-fought victory in history', in which 30,000 men of the Merchant Navy were casualties, plus men of the Royal Naval Reserve and retired naval men who manned naval defences.

As well as those rations denied from the US, other commodities such as rice, sugar and tea that had been imported from the Far East were no longer available after the Japanese advance into Hong Kong, Malaysia and Singapore in the winter of 1941–2, and nor were rubber, tin and other vital raw materials. The standard rate of income tax rose to 50 per cent, and the lowering of personal allowance thresholds meant that 4 million people who had not been eligible to pay income tax were now liable to do so, while a super tax was levied on higher rates of income.

For Julian MacLaren Ross, the novelist and short-story writer, who had been called up for a brief sojourn in the Army, it was the 'Brown Period . . . Browned-off was the phrase one heard most often in X company, the other recruits owing to the difficulty in finding any skirt started jocosely to talk of having Bits of Brown [buggery], the RAF blokes stationed next door called us Brown Jobs, it was autumn and the leaves were brown, and everything was uniquely brown.'

As news of military defeats – Singapore, Hong Kong, Tobruk in North Africa – and rising shipping losses in the Battle of the Atlantic became routine Churchill's popularity fell to a wartime low of 78 per cent in June 1942. The Prime Minister beat off a vote of censure on his direction of the war, but the most serious crisis on the Home Front that the government had to deal with in those 'lightless years' was production of both civilian essentials and war matériel. It was obvious the present system was not working satisfactorily. Although skilled men might have been reserved from the Forces, there was no guarantee that their skills were being deployed in war industries rather than continuing production for civilian consumption, and there were no procedures in place for transferring workers if this was the case. In the early days of war it had been assumed that market forces would sort out the problem: where there was a need for labour, workers would flow in as war industries expanded and peacetime ones contracted, particularly since there were still over a million unemployed eight months after the outbreak of war. But while the munitions and aircraft industries were desperate for labour, far too many workers continued to work in peacetime industries.

The Minister of Labour, Ernest Bevin, insisted that it was not a simple matter of directing men into war-production jobs. What were most needed were skilled workers, and such a pool simply didn't exist: the men needed to be trained. Furthermore, most working people regarded direction into industry as an entirely different matter from conscription into the Armed Forces. Industry was largely in private hands, and memories of the industrial depression of the interwar years, and the bitterness of the General Strike of 1926, ran deep. The successful prosecution of total war had to be built as much as possible on voluntary co-operation, Bevin maintained, if the morale of working people was to be sustained over the duration of what was certain to be a long and arduous war. He was prepared to use compulsion if he had to, but he preferred consultation – 'voluntaryism' as he called it – for as long as it was practicable.

But by 1941, it was already clear that 'voluntaryism' was no longer practicable. There was a serious shortage of skilled workers in war-production industries in the North and Midlands and in the Royal Ordnance factories which, in order to escape raids, were often sited in isolated areas where there was no ready source of labour and little incentive to move there for a job. The turnover of skilled men who were leaving their jobs for increased wages, or to get away from places that were being badly bombed – particularly London and Coventry – was seriously disrupting production, and the allocation of materials and the supply of labour was too frequently out of kilter. At the end of 1940 the Manpower Requirements Committee chaired by Sir William (later Lord) Beveridge had come up with a sobering estimate of what would be required to fight the war. The Army and Navy and Air Force reckoned that between them they needed an additional 1,700,000 men and 84,000 women, and the only way to reach that target would be to withdraw around half a million men from reserved occupations in the munitions industries. But it was no good having fighting forces with insufficient arms to fight with, and in order to ensure the supply of planes and tanks and lorries and weapons, another 1.5 million workers were needed to join the 3.5 million already employed in munitions. The survey showed that at present there simply were not enough people to mobilise to meet the requirements of both the Forces and industry, while maintaining the necessary civilian standards and amenities.

The answers would have to be a 'comb out' of industry to ensure that the maximum use was made of skilled men and that they were not being kept in work that was making no direct contribution to the war effort; an overhaul of the reserved occupations scheme to release more younger men for the Forces; and measures to curtail the high turnover in the industrial workplace. And there was a even more revolutionary solution: the conscription and direction of women for the first time in Britain's history. A total of 1.5 million would have to be drawn into the war effort. Women would have to provide half the number needed in munitions, while another 750,000 would be needed in other industries to replace men who had been called up into the Forces or transferred to munitions, in addition to the women needed for the auxiliary forces.

The Essential Work Order of March 1941 decreed that any privately owned factory could be declared to be doing 'national' work if it was essential to the defence of the country, or the efficient prosecution of the war, or the life of the community. Except in the case of gross misconduct, no worker could either leave or be sacked from such a scheduled establishment without the permission of the local National Service officer, and industrial tribunals were set up to hear appeals from employers and employees.

By the end of 1941, over 4.5 million workers were affected by the provisions of the order, which also regulated collective bargaining for unions to negotiate adequate wages for their workers, and arbitration procedures to settle industrial disputes – while strikes and lockouts had been declared technically illegal in the summer of 1940, in 1941 over a million working days were lost due to strike action and by 1942 the figure had overtaken the pre-war total.

First to come within the scope of the order were the engineering and aircraft industries, and orders were soon extended to building, railways, coalmining and shipbuilding. As a man with a lifetime of experience in the trade-union movement, Bevin was determined to ensure that the increased regulation and regimentation that war demanded would leverage improved working conditions: no enterprise could be scheduled until the Minister had received satisfactory reports about conditions there, including rates of pay and arrangements for welfare and training. While employees could be disciplined for absenteeism or persistent lateness, employers had to guarantee a weekly wage. If a factory was bombed so badly that it could no longer operate, employers were obliged to pay their workers a week's notice and had to make the fullest use of the workforce in getting the factory operational again. The war also gave Bevin, the ex-dockers' leader, an opportunity to improve the persistent problem of casual labour in the docks. Since ports were among the primary targets for air raids in 1941, dockers needed to be available to be diverted to wherever ships could berth, and a system was set up by which registered dockers could enter a labour pool that guaranteed them a weekly wage in return for their agreement to transfer to any port where labour was needed.

Coalmining was another industry with serious labour problems. In 1943 Ernest Bevin reported to the House of Commons that there were only 700,000 men working in the coalmines, and given that the war had offered a new way out of mining for young men – one that some 80,000 of the youngest and strongest had taken – this was an ageing workforce. In order to fuel the nation's war effort, an additional 20,000 men were needed by the end of that year. There had been suggestions that miners who had been called up into the Forces or volunteered should be released, but this had been dismissed as disruptive and impracticable. Appeals for volunteers 'to go down the mines' – since coal production was every bit as essential to Britain's victory as going on to the battlefield – fell largely on deaf ears, as did a similar appeal to ex-miners, only a quarter of whom returned.

In place of voluntaryism in this case came a compulsory no-choice lottery. The 'Bevin Boys' Scheme' applied to all men of twenty-five and under who were not yet enlisted. Ten per cent of them would be selected by ballot to go down the mines. Appeals against being directed down the mines – and there were many, some 40 per cent of all those called objected

– were summarily dealt with. Of the 8,619 appeals the National Service Appeal Boards had dealt with by the end of the war, only 466 had been successful. Five hundred men were prosecuted for refusing to obey the Direction Order and of those 147 were sent to prison.

The scheme was no solution to the industry's long-term structural problems and, having seen for themselves why miners complained about their conditions, almost no ballotees elected to make coalmining a career; but the scheme proved to be a reasonable short-term expedient, with 21,800 young men becoming wartime Bevin Boys, alongside some 16,000 optants – those who had opted for coalmining in preference to the Forces when they were called up.

Frank Collieson, who wanted to be a journalist and had managed to get a job in the London Bureau of the *New York Times*, was dismayed when his promising career was interrupted in January 1944 by a buff envelope containing the news that he had drawn the short straw and was to be a Bevin Boy. When he arrived at his training centre at Cramlington Lamb in Northumberland, 'We stood in the pit yard in a puddle looking at the first pit we had ever seen as the rain poured down. We were herded from one depressing shed to another by Ministry of Labour and colliery officials. Incredibly heavy boots were thrust at us from one side and invariably ill-fitting helmets from another. The importance of coal was stressed over and over again that first day, so much so that the boys were tired of coal before they had ever been near a pit.' The training, which lasted for four weeks, consisted of physical training, training for surface work and coalface work and visits to nearby mines. After this stage, trainees were posted to a working colliery for further training for another couple of weeks before starting work proper, usually at the same colliery. Collieson found at Backworth Colliery where he was sent that 'much of what the Bevin Boys learned at the training pit was . . . useless when we were posted to the collieries, but at least we were taught to look after ourselves, and that alone made the month's training worthwhile . . . a pit man can't be made in a month; both the boys and the Ministry of Labour knew that, but as an emergency measure, it was hoped that by doing an unskilled job, a Bevin Boy would release an old hand to engage in active coal getting.' Older or medically unfit miners were employed as surface workers so almost all Bevin Boys were sent underground, though they were all first given at least two weeks' work on the surface, mostly 'stone shovelling on the top of a slag heap, in fierce winds that lashed coal dust into your eyes, ears, noses and throats. We did this for eight hours, with only 20 minutes off to chew sandwiches with dirt-caked teeth,' recalled Frank Collieson.

Stephen Watson, the youngest of ten children of a country parson and an adventurous mother, had been turned down for the Navy. 'They said I wasn't fit enough, which was ridiculous. I cycled five miles to work every day and five miles back again.' But he was not particularly sorry to be told to report to Cramlington Lamb for training as a Bevin Boy in 1943. 'Some boys minded a lot, and I know of one who took an axe to his foot to get out of it,' but Watson was pleased to get away from the 'Dickensian asbestos and tin roof electrical engineering workshop in Croydon' where he had been working. The training 'didn't really amount to much: we were just told about the dangers of fire damp – methane or marsh gas that is – and warned never to sit on wet stones or we'd get piles'.

After nearly four weeks' training, Watson was sent to Newbiggin colliery where he was billeted in a Nissen hut with some ten other men. 'The place was magical. There was this eerie silence after what had seemed like years and years of bombs and searchlights. I couldn't believe that in the same country there was this oasis, that there could be such a peaceful place in wartime Britain. We'd go for walks along the sands near Morpeth and Alnwick, the country was just so beautiful. And we all used to go into Newcastle for our entertainment. There were sword swallowers and fire eaters and men who would invite you to truss them up with ropes and they would manage to get out just like Houdini. But you couldn't really get away from the war even there. All around Newcastle there were open-cast mines and there'd be men furiously digging out coal, all for the war effort.'

Watson had 'no qualms about working underground. The miners' union had made sure that strict safety precautions were in place before you went down into the mine. The mine I worked in was 11,000 feet deep and the seams stretched two and a half miles out under the North Sea.'

Bevin boys worked alongside experienced miners who hacked and cut coal using a variety of devices, but the 'boys' tended to be engaged in less skilled tasks like salvaging pit props from worked seams, or unloading the coal from the tubs.

'The miners were extraordinary people,' Stephen Watson recalls. 'When you first arrived, it was just like it is in a country pub if you're not a regular. They wouldn't talk to you at all. I worked on a landing at the bottom of a shaft and we sent the tubs up the hill and brought the full ones down. So the old miners had to wait till we gave them the all clear because they were walking. All you could see of them was their lights, six or seven headlights and they'd stand there not speaking a word but spitting. Because you couldn't smoke underground a lot of miners used to chew tobacco, and then they'd spit. Anything that helped to get the saliva going was helpful. It was so dusty down there. Stone dust was actually injected into the air to reduce the explosiveness of the coal dust, so everyone's throat got parched. Anyway they just stood there in silence, in the dark, spitting. It was as if they were ghosts. This went on for at least six or seven weeks. And then like some strange supernatural cult they all agreed that we were OK and they started to talk to us. And then they talked all the time. You never went away empty handed after talking to the miners. You always learned something . . . And because of the ever present danger down a mine there was a great feeling of camaraderie. The roof could fall in, or you could accidentally drill into a pocket of methane gas. On the very few occasions that I felt I was in some danger down the mine, there was always one of them who would know what to do.'

Since more than half the Bevin boys had never wanted to go down the mines in the first place, it was no surprise that absenteeism was high, half as much again as the total figure for other workers. Nor, in a highly unionised industry, were the Bevin boys likely to be interested in joining one of the miners' unions: their interests were focused on obtaining the soonest possible release rather than improving conditions underground or raising wages. J. B. Pick, a Midlands miner, recalled that 'the miners were kindly but non-committal, and watched [the Bevin boys] with a half-humorous, half-bitter smile. Here they were conscripting people for the pits, said the miners, after all these years throwing colliers on the scrap heap and leaving them to rot! . . . It would do the Bevin boys no harm to see what the pits were like, but as for increasing production – a fat lot of difference that would make!'

*

In March 1941 every possible source of man- and womanpower was being squeezed out of the population. The system of block reservation by occupations was abandoned and replaced by one of individual deferment, which would be granted only to men employed in vital war work, and, with a very few exceptions, only to men over twenty-five. Industry apprenticeship schemes were rethought, and deferment suspended for apprentices in industries that did not make a direct contribution to the war. Undergraduates reading science, engineering and medicine continued to be exempt from conscription until they had finished their degrees, as their expertise was a valuable wartime asset, whereas students studying arts subjects had their deferment progressively reduced, and ended altogether in October 1942, unless they were very near to graduation. The age of call-up for men was lowered from nineteen to eighteen and a half, though the government agreed to honour its commitment that no soldier would be sent overseas before he was twenty if at all possible.

The National Service (No 2) Act became law on 18 December 1941. Its terms made Britain the first nation in the world to conscript women. Single women and childless widows between the ages of twenty and thirty were pronounced liable for military service (the age was lowered to nineteen in 1943). Women could in theory elect to join one of the women's auxiliary services – the Auxiliary Territorial Service (ATS), the Women's Royal Naval Service (WRNS) or the Women's Auxiliary Air Force (WAAF) – or be directed into industry or Civil Defence. In practice this usually meant the ATS or the munitions industry, where labour shortages were most acute. By the end of the war 125,000 recruits had been called up into the women's auxiliary services to join a larger number who had volunteered.

The ATS had been created in September 1938: its purpose, like that of the other auxiliary services, was to release men for combatant duty. A wartime publication patronisingly explained: 'The ATS take over the cleaning with the proud name of orderlies . . . Those who have been parlour maids are detailed to wait on officers . . . the ATS look after the stores, fitting men with boots and their equipment as well as women . . . [they] learn . . . that in the army a letter is never addressed "Dear Sir"; it is always in memorandum form . . . Women motor drivers relieve the men of driving the lighter lorries and transport vans, they drive officers and take messages. In their spare time the drivers attend a course of instruction on maintenance and repairs.'

At first, prejudice about the ATS proved hard to overcome. Its khaki uniform hardly had the glamour of the trim navy rig-out of the WRNS, nor the crisp Air Force blue of the WAAFs, and a miasma of immorality garnered by the reputation of the camp follower Women's Auxiliary Army Corps of the First World War ('the ground sheet of the Army') persisted, with some fathers putting their foot down about daughters joining up. Homesickness, the communal life, spartan living and working conditions, rigid discipline and the military-style routine proved dispiriting to a number of volunteers; by December 1940 the discharge rate had soared to 29 per cent and desertion rates had risen too. The only sanction for miscreant behaviour in the ATS in the early days was dismissal – which was hardly a disincentive to a woman who wanted out anyway – but in April 1941 the ATS was incorporated into the Army Act and the service was subject to full military discipline. As a result of the National Service Act of December 1941, and a vigorous campaign by newly appointed ATS directors to improve conditions and smarten up its image, the ATS expanded more than any of the other women's services. By December 1943 it had over 200,000 auxiliaries and 6,000 officers in more than eighty trades, many of them skilled. By 1943 it was reckoned that 80 per cent of the Army's driving was done by women who took the wheel, and maintained and repaired everything from staff cars to three-ton trucks and gun limbers.

Women were seen as the answer to the Anti-Aircraft (Ack-Ack) Command problems too. 'By the end of 1940 . . . we were short of no fewer than 114 officers and 17,965 other ranks,' wrote its commander-in-chief, General Sir Frederick Pile. 'Something drastic had to be done. I suggested . . . that women should be employed in large numbers in an operational role.' The distinguished engineer Caroline Haslett reassured the general that 'women could man searchlights and fire-control instruments and, in fact, do almost everything except fire guns'. Pile could not actually see why women 'should not fire guns too. There is not much essential difference between manning a G.L. set or a predictor and firing a gun: both are means of destroying enemy aircraft.' He was, however, wise enough not to suggest employing women 'on lethal weapons . . . there would be struggle enough to get their employment through in any operational form at all'.

In the end 'pure mathematics' forced the brass hats' hand, and despite problems of mixed accommodation, the attitude of parents – 'always more of a nuisance than the girls themselves ever were [and] . . . disciplinary control [it was] decided to form mixed heavy anti-aircraft batteries'. Churchill suggested the service of his younger daughter, Mary, and on 31 August 1941, after three months' training, the first mixed battery – some 200 men and an equal number of women – was deployed in Richmond Park. In the early days it was 'as good as a visit to the Zoo. Crowds would assemble anywhere where there was a site with ATS on it and stand and gaze in fascination' at the first women to take a combatant role in Britain 'marching, eating and drilling with men'.

At first older men were employed in batteries 'because we felt there would be less trouble'. Nevertheless there were reputed to be some male operators whose files were stamped 'UFM' (Unfit for Mixed – the military equivalent of NST: Not Safe in Taxis) and such lotharios would be sent to a remote, all-male battery somewhere in the middle of the sea. Problems did not disappear overnight but, after six months of operations, a corps commander reported that the employment of ATS members (all volunteers) 'has been an unqualified success . . . [the ATS] learn quickly, and once having mastered the subject very seldom make mistakes . . . Contrary once again to expectations, their voices carry well and can clearly be heard in the din of gunfire.' The commander of the Newcastle battery was surprised to find that 'as an old soldier', if given the choice of an all-male battery and a mixed one, he would opt for one with women as well as men 'without hesitation. They are amazingly keen at going into action, and although they are not supposed to learn how to use the rifle they are as keen as anything to do so.' Pile was impressed too, and though he noticed that the women 'had a tendency to chatter when there was a lull, they behaved like a veteran party, and shot an enemy plane into the sea' during a raid on Newcastle, 'the girls' first taste of blood' on 8 December 1941.

For women to work together in camps was one thing, but how, Pile wondered, would they manage 'in some bleak and desolate spot, five miles or more from the nearest town with night-sentry duties to carry out in a countryside abounding in noise eerie to a townsman, where searchlight batteries sent powerful beams of light into the sky to illuminate and track enemy aircraft or guide Allied aircraft home'. Once again, the 'pure mathematics' of the manpower shortage crisis dictated the solution, and fifty-four ATS between nineteen and thirty-four were trained to operate searchlights, working dutifully at map reading, aircraft recognition, route marches and anti-gas drill for the 'relatively hard open air life'. The 93rd Searchlight Regiment went into action for the first time in the middle of 1942, armed only with pick-axe handles to deal with possible marauders, and dressed in much-coveted 'teddy bear' fur coats with hoods, often in the bitter cold, torrential rain that turned the sites into acres of mud, and intermittent gunfire, bombs and falling shrapnel. Their 'spirits colossal', the women stuck it out. And they even made their bleak, isolated huts like home – especially at Christmas with 'borrowed fairy lights, home made coloured paper chains and tinsel ornaments'. Visiting these scattered, lonely sites, Pile wondered 'why we were ever such fools as to doubt that the thing would work . . . The girls lived like men, fought their lights like men, and, alas, some of them died like men.'

In February 1945 the ATS had a rather grand new recruit. Until then the main contribution to the war effort of the eighteen-year-old heir to the throne, Princess Elizabeth, had been to broadcast to children whose lives had been disrupted by war – and assure them that she understood and was sharing their hardships since her life (and that of her sister Margaret Rose) had been disrupted, living as they did 'somewhere in the country' (usually Windsor Castle) apart from their parents (at least during the day). But in the last months of the war the Princess, apparently largely as a result of her own insistence, was registered as No 230873 Second Subaltern Elizabeth Alexandra Mary Windsor. Her rank was an honorary one, and she slept at home rather than being quartered in barracks or a Nissen hut, but the training in driving and vehicle maintenance that she undertook at Aldershot was real. After six weeks the Princess qualified as a driver, and a few days before VJ day was promoted to the rank of junior commander.

The manpower crisis wrought a change in the Women's Royal Naval Service too. When the women's arm of the Senior Service was re-formed in 1939 it was an exclusive, part-time service to which women applied, references were required, nepotism was rife and going to sea was not what it was about. But in 1941 the service expanded rapidly to meet the needs of war, and during its course more than 100,000 women were in the WRNS (and called Wrens), serving all over the world. The majority worked ashore, initially doing clerical duties, driving and working as cooks, but little by little the Navy cautiously opened its portals a few inches and soon Wrens were acting as coastal mine-spotters – which was hazardous work – training as welders and carpenters to maintain and repair ships in naval bases, and in communications, meteorology and radar; and from 1941 women served as boat crews on small craft such as tug boats and harbour launches, though they were not permitted to go to sea in His Majesty's ships. Their navy-blue uniform was much admired (so much so that after the war the British Overseas Airline Corporation bought up surplus WRNS uniforms, including the tricorn hat, as uniform for its stewardesses).

The Women's Auxiliary Air Force was the descendant of the Women's Royal Air Force, which had been formed on the same day as the RAF in 1918 but had been disbanded exactly two years later and not re-formed until 1939. The Battle of Britain meant that within less than a year of the outbreak of war WAAFs were playing a vital role, and it was clear that 'there is little that the men do that the women cannot – except fly', and even that would change. WAAFs were employed in plotting aircraft and radar signals, interpreting reconnaissance photographs, debriefing RAF crew after raids, packing parachutes and in communications, and by 1944 nearly all the service meteorological officers of the Flying Training Command were women, who also took on the traditional auxiliary roles of drivers and cooks, and administrative and clerical duties.

At first, operational aircraft were definitely off-limits – although those few with a commercial pilot's licence could take up twin-engined planes for reconnaissance flights. But by 1941 women pilots were being sent on a conversion course so they could join the Air Transport Auxiliary (which also numbered the legendary Amy Johnson, who was presumed drowned when her plane came down over the Thames Estuary in 1941, among its members) and deliver fighter planes – and later even four-engined bombers – from the factory to the airfield.

At the start of the war, WAAFs worked on barrage balloons, repairing seams and doping tears in the rubber-proofed fabric. But, again in 1941, the need to release men for combat roles prompted the suggestion that women could take charge of the 500lb hydrogen-filled balloons that were tethered to the ground by heavy steel cables, hoisting the balloons aloft when a raid was threatened, and winching them down again when it was all clear. There were doubts whether women would have the physical strength or the stamina for the task, since the balloons were 66 feet long and 30 feet high when inflated, but in February 1941 a number of WAAF crews volunteered for an intensive ten-week training course. This was so successful that the 'young amazons', as they were dubbed, were running over a thousand barrage-balloon sites throughout the country by 1942 – though *Picture Post* thought it necessary for male morale to point out that: 'The substitution of WAAF for airmen on balloon sites does not imply that the airmen who have operated under all weathers and under aerial bombardment have in any sense been doing a woman's job . . . it requires 16 airwomen to replace 10 airmen . . . and it is only the great progress in and simplification of balloon manipulation . . . that has made the substitution at all possible . . .'

Corporal Irene Storer, who trained as a balloon operator – and was featured training near Coventry in a painting by Dame Laura Knight – found that 'a balloon in a strong and variable wind was like a thing alive. A good winch driver, though, could "feel" the change in tension on the cable, and would haul it in slowly or speed it up . . . like a fisherman playing a large fish on the end of a line. The last 100 ft. or so of hauling in could be precarious as the balloon could sweep right down to the ground – perhaps in the next street. The winch driver needed all her skill and concentration in these circumstances.

'The whole purpose of the balloon was to hold up the cables. It was the cables that were lethal to aircraft. Viewed from the ground, the balloons seemed miles apart but from the air, a balloon barrage was a fearsome sight. Its aims were two-fold: to prevent dive-bombing, and to keep the aircraft high enough up for the ack-ack to reach them . . . Turning a bedded balloon [tethered in a storm by extra sandbags] into the wind was a marathon, especially for two guards on their own in the dark.

'Apart from maintenance, the balloon had to be hauled in in bad weather, and of course if our own aircraft were expected to be in the area. In either case speed was essential. It follows that the winch always had to be in A1 condition . . . however, just in case there was ever a hitch, we had to learn manual handling. About 18 of us, one behind the other, hauled in the balloon, to the rhythm of the counting by a male instructor. For a fraction of a second, the two girls at the front were not quite together with the rest of us and the balloon shot up again causing them to receive severe rope-burns to their hands.'

Hilda Pearce worked on an all-female barrage-balloon site in the centre of London: 'We were based in Grosvenor Gardens and with all the trees around it was quite a hair-raising experience getting the balloon off the ground. The Marines from the American Embassy were very helpful and would come and pull on the ropes if they saw we were having trouble . . . it was tough.'

By 1943 there were nearly half a million women in the ATS, the WRNS and the WAAF. Although their life was regimented and regulated, their work often hard and dangerous – over 600 were killed, 700 seriously wounded and over 100 missing in action or taken prisoner – and their pay derisory (around two-thirds of the low pay of men in the ranks), many civilians were envious of the servicewomen's regular three meals a day when their families were living on ever-reducing rations; the smart uniforms that were provided at a time when rationing made clothes provision a struggle; free medical and dental treatment for numbers of women who had not previously benefited from such care; and three weeks' paid leave a year and free travel warrants.

It didn't always seem so enviable from the inside: girls as young as seventeen who had volunteered, to get away from the confines of home, but had never been away from their families before or even slept in a bed on their own, suffered terrible pangs of homesickness. Middle-class girls who had been through the rigours of a 1930s English boarding-school education found it easier to adjust to the regulated, spartan communal life. Most servicewomen were quartered in corrugated iron Nissen huts with a stove in the middle that was their only hope of getting warm. They slept in iron beds 2 feet 6 inches wide. There were usually twenty-four of these arranged head to toe, with horsehair pillows and 'biscuits' (official-issue mattresses consisting of three unyielding straw-packed cushions). The food, though regular and plentiful, could be appalling – 'lumps of grisly meat and soggy vegetables floating in greasy gravy followed by stodgy spotted dick', tinned pilchards, spam sandwiches with curling edges, rock-hard Eccles cakes – so most WAAFS were 'always clamorously hungry'. The regular routine of button polishing, toothbrush inspection and kit check was onerous when it came after long and tiring working days. 'Everything had to be laid out just right with even the toothbrush facing a certain direction. They would even have got us to polish the coal if they could.'

As a rookie in the ATS, Dorothy Calvert recalled her first taste of 'square bashing'. 'They were yelling orders at us from all directions, and had us moving like "blue-arsed flies"; the worst part of it was not one of us had an inkling of what they were yelling about. Trying to hear each order as it was given, remembering it, and trying to get our feet and arms to work in unison was impossible, and the Instructors saying as if it was something they had rehearsed beforehand, "What a lousy shower you lot are", did not do much to fill us with confidence . . .

'This constant marching and drilling went on and on, until I thought that the idea was for us to march into Germany, fetch old Hitler out, and then have a go at him, and believe me nothing would have given me greater pleasure after all the . . . square bashing we had had to do and the blisters we had got . . . But no such luck. It was just the good old British Bull that we were suffering from, at that time.

'I remember one memorable day . . . lo and behold, we were all marching in step, our arms were swinging at the correct height, the hands making fists with the thumbs on the outside, not tucked in, and each command was carried out perfectly . . . I felt a glow of pride as our feet thudded to a halt, as one foot, like a badly shod caterpillar. We had done it, and what was more, Sgt. was really smiling at us, which must have meant something . . . Now perhaps they would ease up a bit. Did they hell? . . . I began to feel like a mindless, sexless moron. Or a wind up toy.'

'Panda' Carter (her real name was Joan but her friends called her

Panda 'because they said I looked like one') had an elderly widowed mother who wanted to keep her at home and managed to get her a desk job in the Admiralty 'drawing silhouettes of Japanese shipping. I longed for something more adventurous . . .' So when her call-up papers arrived and she had to go into the Forces, she was delighted. She was sent to Telavera racecourse in Northamptonshire for her ATS training. 'I was longing to be issued with a uniform, but at first it was not quite as I expected. I do not know how the sizes were worked out, but they all had to be altered. At first my skirt was nearly down to my ankles and the sleeves of my jacket twice as long as they should have been. My great coat was as heavy as a rock, and so stiff I could not have bent if I wanted to . . .

'Our four weeks training was like a complete new world . . . Each day, rain or shine, or snow, when the camp was shipshape, we spent many hours learning how to march and obey commands. I enjoyed it after a while, and even learned my left from my right. We had learnt discipline. Our uniforms fitted smartly and we were medically A1, having had all the appropriate injections.

'The last part of our training consisted of a variety of tests to decide for what kind of work we were most suited . . . I had just one aim, to become a draughtswoman. When it was my turn to be interviewed by the Commanding Officer, she asked me what I would like to do. When I told her she handed me a huge book about architecture. She asked me if I understood it, and I told a deliberate lie. I said I understood it all. She obviously didn't believe me, and said I was just the right type for a clerk. I tried to protest by telling her I could not spell. Her answer was "None of us can." So that was that . . .'

Stephanie Batstone was doing a clerical job with the Emergency Hospital Service and rather thought she might like to join the Forces. ' "You'll never get in the Wrens," my friends said. "They're awfully choosy. They'll only take girls who've got relations who are naval officers." . . . "You'll be terribly homesick," my family said. "You've never been away from home at all." . . . "But what on earth *for*," they said at work. "You're in a reserved occupation. You can stay here for the rest of the war." That was what I was afraid of.' So towards the end of 1942 Stephanie Batstone said that she was going to the dentist's, left work early and 'went to Westminster, to the WRNS Recruiting Office. There was a poster in the window, of a healthy smiling apple-cheeked girl with dark springing hair, in Wren uniform, with flags in the background. It said "Join the Wrens and Free a Man for the Fleet".

'When I had worked up the queue, across a trestle table I surveyed a woman in a uniform jacket with buttons on the cuffs. She didn't look glowing like the girl on the poster, and neither did I. We both looked pasty. We spent all our evenings down the shelter.

'I said, "I want to be a visual signaller." "Sorry," she said, "I'm afraid that category is closed and there's a waiting list. I doubt if we shall recruit any more. At the moment the only categories open are Writers and Cooks. Can you do shorthand and typing?" "No," I said. "What a pity," she said. "Well, just fill in the form and where it says "category" put "cook". I'm sure you like cooking, don't you?" "No," I said. "I hate it."

'I took the form home and where it said "category" I put "visual signaller" and where it said "second choice" I put "none" and I posted it back.

'Three weeks later a buff card came with an Admiralty stamp requesting my presence for an eye test at the Naval Recruiting Office in the Charing Cross Road.'

When Batstone arrived at her posting, she found what a variety of women had joined up with her. The girl sitting next to her told her she had worked at ' "Woolworfs, Balham High Road . . .' lectrical counter. I'm doing W/T [Wireless Telegraphists]. Me bruvver's a sparks. At Pompey." I didn't know where Pompey was. It sounded foreign.

'The girl on the other side said, "I was a teacher till yesterday." "Where?" I asked. " A village in Anglesey. Miss Williams will have come back today to take over. I wonder how she'll get on. She's nearly seventy." Her voice was soft and lilting. She said, "My fiancé was killed. On the *Hunter* in Narvik. He was a teacher too. I couldn't just do nothing."

'Into the melting pot we all went – conscripts, volunteers, engaged, married, widows, single. Zara from Brazil, Rita from Balham, Cathy from Anglesey, Marianne from Barclay's Bank in Aberdeen, Joy from Sainsbury's cold-meat counter in Birmingham, Clodagh from milking her father's cows near Kinsale in County Cork, Maureen from being a hotel chambermaid in Dublin, with the bright lights and butter and

German Embassy, Joan from helping her mother run a boarding house in Skegness, Judy straight from school, Pauline from an estate agent's in Wood Green, Celia from the Prudential in Exeter, Vivienne, a second-year nurse at Leeds General Infirmary, Patricia from a repertory company in Belfast, Betty who thought life was fun, Irene who wore glasses.

'Four weeks later, out of the melting pot came the coders; sixteen weeks later the VS [Visual Signallers]; and six months later the W/Ts; not yet looking like the girl on the poster, but give or take a few bumps, looking roughly the same size and shape. The prototype Wren, knowing that Pompey was Portsmouth, and gash meant redundant, and slops was snores, and chokker was fed up, and rabbiting was thieving, and a bottle was a row, and a stand-easy bun was elevenses, and a gannet was greedy, and Jimmy the One was the First Lieutenant, and tiddly was for best, and to put the anchor on the bedspread the right way up or the ship would sink. We had entered the only real democracy. We weren't pretending to be equal, we were equal, and might have to go on being equal for years and years. It was a great relief.'

The uniform issued to a Wren consisted of 'two skirts and two jackets, a tiddly [for best] one and an everyday one; two pairs of blackouts [knickers], navy artificial silk and down to the knee; two pairs of black lisle stockings; two pairs of shoes, a raincoat, a greatcoat, a tie. Six collars, two sizes too large because they would shrink in the laundry. Six shirts the right size because they wouldn't. Between the back stud and the front stud there was always a bulge of collar over shirt. The collars did shrink, but before they were down to shirt size they got so worn they rubbed our necks raw even when we put candle grease on. The hat, the crowning glory. A taffeta ribbon with H.M.S. worked in gold on it. And because we would work outdoors, two pairs of thick navy woollen blackouts, two pairs of bellbottoms, a seaman's jersey, and woollen gloves and socks.

'We tottered back clasping our burdens, and about ten of us piled into Betty's cabin. "Look at these woollen knickers!" shrieked Joan. "Just imagine anyone thinking we would be seen dead in them!" We all packed them up and sent them to our elderly aunts who were delighted. By about November, standing about on cliffs in the Hebrides, we would have given anything to have them back.' (Other Wrens sewed along the legs, cut out the gussets, and turned the knickers into warm, if oddly shaped, jumpers.)

The alternative to the auxiliary services, or Civil Defence work such as driving ambulances, the ARP service, the Women's Auxiliary Police Corps or the Women's Auxiliary Fire Service, was to 'come into the factories' as a famous wartime recruiting poster urged, showing a Soviet-style scene of a woman marching to victory in front of a factory from which issued a stream of aircraft. But again simple market mechanisms didn't work effectively.

When war broke out, the closing down of many peacetime workplaces and the changeover of others to war production meant that some 175,000 women found themselves unemployed. Many, including those married to men who had been conscripted and whose families were much worse off as a consequence, sought jobs in munitions factories, on the buses, the trams, railways, the post office – anywhere there were vacancies that men had left when they were called up. But there was considerable resistance from employers, trade unions and other male workers: in 1939 London Transport had opted to cut services rather than employ women, and in the industries where women were most needed – shipbuilding and engineering, for instance – there was often the greatest reluctance to admit them. 'If you ask my candid opinion, girls and women are a very expensive form of labour [since they needed separate lavatories, and increased canteen and restroom provision], and a damned nuisance,' opined one welfare manager (nicknamed 'Illfare' by the staff).

It was becoming clear that, as with men, Bevin's 'voluntaryism' was not working for women: by the summer of 1941 only 87,000 women had been drawn into the auxiliary forces and munitions industry despite continual appeals. Various schemes were tried and government training centres, which had previously dealt only with unemployed men, were opened to women, but there was no rush to enrol. Initiatives such as 'War Work Weeks', recruitment drives held in 1941 and 1942 with parades and processions of women driving round on the tanks and armoured vehicles that they had helped to make, to encourage women into war work, attracted hundreds rather than the thousands of volunteers that were needed.

In a War Work Week parade in Coventry in 1941, girl factory workers carried a poster that read: 'Don't queue with the shirkers, join the women workers' which incensed many onlookers who knew that it wasn't as simple as that. On 13 March 1941 the London *Evening Standard*'s headline read 'Response to Call for Arms Volunteers Disappointing'. The reasons were clear. 'Married women with children were reluctant to volunteer until they'd made arrangements for their care. Ministry of Labour local welfare officers are *recommending* local authorities to establish day nurseries where the children can be accommodated while their mothers are at work in the factory.' Meanwhile the government was calling for half a million more women to register for training in the munitions factories.

Yet any audit recognised that the labour reserve had to be found among married women. In 1931 only 16 per cent of working women were married, and a number of private companies as well as the public sector operated a 'marriage bar'. It was not until two Acts passed in 1944 and 1946 that women were allowed to continue to work as teachers or civil servants after they married. Between 1941 and 1943 the demand for labour tightened the screws of compulsion for some form of war work for an increasingly wide range of women, and by 1943 the number of women in the workforce had risen to 43 per cent.

When her age group became eligible, a woman would be called to her local labour exchange – which may have been hastily set up in a church hall – to be registered for work and questioned about her situation: what family responsibilities did she have? Did she have a soldier or an evacuee billeted with her? Was she already doing voluntary war work with, for example, the WVS (since such women, while required to register, would not be required to move into paid war work)? What work experience did she have? A single woman without dependants would be assessed as 'mobile' and could be directed anywhere in the country where her services were most needed. Just as the country was divided into safe, neutral and reception areas for purposes of evacuation, so it was divided into colour-coded 'supply' and 'demand' areas for production. There was a regional imbalance with 'screaming scarlet' areas where workers were urgently needed in the Midlands, and this is where 'unskilled mobile women' were most likely to be sent, while the south if anything had an oversupply of workers.

Women who were more than three months pregnant, had a child under fourteen living at home, or heavy domestic responsibilities such as an elderly parent – providing it was a father since a household was defined in male terms – would not be directed into war work, though of course they could volunteer. That left married women who were classified as immobile whether they had a husband at home or were servicemen's wives and their husband was away. Such women would not be 'asked to leave home to work', but they could be directed into war work locally at the discretion of the interviewer.

Zelma Katin had been trying on and off for eighteen years to get work and, at the age of forty, had resigned herself 'to the knowledge that in Britain a married woman may not work outside the home except as a charlady'. But soon after her husband had been called up, 'there came a request from the Minister of Labour and National Service that I call at the employment exchange and there be directed to work of national importance . . .

'At the "Labour" they told me I was a year too young to be given clerical work. As you are a non-mobile woman you have two alternatives left: you can go into a factory; or you can go into transport. I thought of the heat, noise, electric light and airlessness of a munitions factory and then I thought of the fresh air that blows from the Yorkshire moors across a tramcar platform in the city. And so I became a tram conductress' – a 'clippie' in her home city of Sheffield.

A couple of days later Mrs Katin found that 'the local Labour Ministry people had been busy with the official comb, and at the Exchange I found women from all walks of life . . . [there] were three housewives, a tailoress, the manageress of a food shop, the manageress of a linoleum store, a typist, an ex-university student, and a music shop assistant . . . I liked the philosophical way we all accepted the situation . . . I stepped back into the main office and asked whether the Minister of Labour could see his way to let me work a short week instead of a full one [since she still had a child at home] . . . it was a young lady of the superior, self confident type to whom I addressed my petition. She spoke with a Girton accent – Girton and Oxford may be tolerable in the South but in a Northern provincial city they stink – and she proceeded to lecture me. The country was at war, she said, it was my duty to accept the job that was offered me, and my boy was old enough to look after himself. As she spoke I reflected that here was an unmarried youngster fit enough to do a full week's work on a tramcar or in a munition works, yet enjoying a soft job which gave her the right to lecture women old enough to have been unlucky enough to bear her. I called her a "whippersnapper" – I am not quite sure what a whippersnapper is but it sounds impressive – and asked her why she didn't give up her job to an older woman if she were so patriotic . . . she didn't reply . . .'

Though popular propaganda at the time spoke of women 'doing a man's job', the job – and the pay – was often not the same at all. Skilled craft jobs were broken down into simpler constituent parts that women could learn in a shorter time, and, in order to assuage men's fears that women would be prepared to work for less and thus price them out of a job, 'dilution agreements' were hammered out between unions and employers in a wide range of industries, whereby women would work on 'women's jobs' for 'women's pay' – around half that of men's. And the commitment was given that any dilution concessions would be for wartime only and that practices would revert to the pre-war norm as soon as hostilities ceased. Sometimes these dilution agreements stuck, but there was often resistance, either active with strikes and walk-outs such as in the Clydeside shipbuilding industry, or passive with male workers making women's lives difficult – failing to tell them all they needed to know to perform a task successfully, loosening the screws on the machine a woman was using, or substituting inferior work for the stuff she had produced. There were contradictory fears that either women would work so slowly that production would fall and so would earnings, or alternatively that they would work so fast that piecework rates would fall.

'Shopping difficulties' were what most women nominated as the main reason not to go out to work. Absenteeism was rife among women workers who were not able to get their shopping done outside working hours, and productivity suffered (absenteeism was not, of course, confined to women, but a Ministry of Labour survey showed it was twice as high). There were numerous attempts by the Minister of Labour to persuade shops to stay open later in the evening, but shortages meant that by then the shops would have little left to sell – certainly not fish or meat or vegetables. As the manager of Slough Co-op reported, 'We did not take enough to pay for the electric light' when he experimented with later opening hours, though Co-operative Society shops were in the vanguard of trying out various schemes to ensure an equitable distribution of food to all women, working or not, and a few employers actually set up 'factory shops' so that women could order their supplies on the premises. There was official encouragement for 'neighbourly' shopping arrangements, and the WVS reluctantly got involved in some schemes, though officially they rejected the idea of voluntary work on behalf of reasonably well-paid factory workers. But for a housewife to get a neighbour to shop for her presumed that the neighbour had the time that she didn't, and this was increasingly not the case. By the end of 1942, 10 million women aged between nineteen and fifty were registered for war work; 7.5 million were in full-time paid work and there were around 380,000 part-timers (though part-time could mean thirty hours a week), plus nearly half a million women in the Forces. In the end the only half-satisfactory solution was either to give women official time off to shop (though most schemes presumed that only married women needed this), or for factory owners to introduce shift working so that women were not always at work when the shops were open.

Increasingly, as the need for labour grew more acute after 1943, pressure grew for mothers to work, but often the necessary child care provision was still not available. Nursery schools in the interwar years had been viewed primarily as welfare provision, a safety net for inadequate parenting, rather than an early educational and socialising opportunity for young children. The provision of nursery places for the children of working mothers threatened the notion of a woman's role in caring for her family; the concept of employer- or State-provided twenty-four-hour nurseries to cater for the needs of women doing shift work was seen as a further wartime erosion of family life. Although much publicity encouraged grandmothers and neighbours to care for the children of younger women so that they could go out to work, the number of government-sponsored nurseries did rise from just fourteen in October 1940 to 1,345 by July 1943.

Two women who had responded to Bevin's call for volunteers rather than waiting to be summoned were Elsie Whiteman and her close friend, Kathleen Church-Bliss, who, aged forty-seven and forty-two respectively, were of an age that employers had previously been wary of taking into the factories. The women started at a Croydon training centre near London in February 1942. After sixteen weeks 'learning about drilling, grinding, boring tapering, cutting screws . . . and cutting pieces of metal to exact sizes', they were offered jobs at Morrison's, a Croydon aircraft-component manufacturer that made parts for Spitfires and Hurricanes. Morrison's had employed around 130 workers before the war, but by June 1942 this had risen to around 500, probably over half of whom were women.

The difficulties encountered by Whiteman and Bliss (Kathleen dropped the Church at work) included not very satisfactory billets, and long hours, sometimes with compulsory overtime – which could mean working an eleven-hour day or more, doing night shifts and sometimes working on a Sunday (though this was discontinued in early 1943 for women at Morrison's). Working conditions were poor, with an overcrowded canteen, entirely inadequate washing facilities often with only cold water to wash the machine oil off the workers' hands, filthy workshops – a nest of baby rats was discovered under a workbench on one occasion – inadequate ventilation, and continuous noise. It took the women months to get the management to supply stools so they could sit at their lathes rather than standing for hours. These complaints were compounded by the frustrations of low basic pay (1s 1d an hour, later raised to 1s 3d, which was less than men doing comparable jobs were paid) supplemented by a bonus system that was frequently in dispute; machines that continually broke down or were set up incorrectly so that much working time (and potential bonus-earning hours) was wasted; and, within a year, exhaustion, recurrent illnesses and 'tear-inducing' boredom. But so conscientious and hard-working were Elsie Whiteman and Kathleen Bliss and some of the other older workers – 'a bunch of nice middle-aged grannies, with kindly worn faces and amiable manners' – that they were soon considered exemplary workers, of much greater value to war production than some of the flighty younger women who spent much time flirting and chatting, and so long making up in the cloakroom that management 'removed the mirror', and who were always being threatened that they would be 'sent to the Midlands' where the need for industrial labour was greatest.

Working in a Royal Ordnance factory – particularly one of the ten filling (cartridges, bullets and bombs) or the eleven explosives factories

– was probably the most dangerous task to which a woman could be directed.

Mabel Dutton worked at an ordnance factory near Warrington in Lancashire. 'I was 19 years old. I was told I had to go to work on Group One. That group was nicknamed the Suicide Group on account of the many workers who had been blown up, killed, or maimed. I didn't know that at the time but I would be working with highly explosive gunpowder for making detonators . . . There were three working shifts – mornings, afternoons and nights . . . I had to wait for a guide to take me to Group One. It was then I noticed that she had only one hand and a finger missing off that. I asked her what had happened and she made up some story or other. I later found out that she had them blown off when she went to work on Group One.

'. . . Outside, we had to leave our coats, shoes, bags, money, hairclips and anything metal in the Contraband Place and change into any old worn shoes, overalls and white turbans . . . On my first afternoon . . . I was put in the Experimental Shop where we had to test the powder by weighing it on brass scales and sealing detonators one at a time. We had to wear goggles and leather gauntlets . . . one day I was given a red box to carry with one person in front and behind carrying red flags walking along the clearways [raised walkways that had to be kept scrupulously clean to avoid the risk of explosion], taking them to magazines to be used later. I didn't know what I was carrying. There was a massive explosion and I dropped the box and was shocked to see a young woman thrown through a window with her stomach hanging out. Luckily the box, which contained detonators, did not explode or we would have had our legs blown off. I was sickened. When I got home I said to my sisters . . . "I'm not going back there again." They laughed at me because they knew that I had to . . .'

As labour shortages worsened, in the middle years of the war more housewives were directed into part-time work – in the face of some opposition from employers who predicted women would have a dilettante attitude, regarding the factory as 'a place where you can drop in for a spot of work just when you feel like it'. By the end of 1943, as a result of government intervention, the number of part-time workers was approaching 900,000, and the pool to draw on grew too when the age limit for women's registration for work was raised to fifty –

'conscripting grandmothers', the press jibed. Even women living in remote rural areas, or housebound for some reason, were brought into the war economy doing outwork tasks such as assembling aircraft components and sorting out the thousands of screws and bolts and rivets dropped daily on factory floors – a scheme that had been suggested by the WVS.

War work was a particular opportunity for women in domestic service who, for want of other work in the interwar years, had been working long hours for low wages – 5s a week was not unusual – and living often very restricted lives in their employer's homes, subject to their employer's rules and fancies. Although interviewers were often accused of being indulgent to middle-class housewives, not calling up servants as soon as they were eligible, many was the middle-class woman who found herself doing her own cooking, cleaning and washing without help for the first time in her life. The scene in Frances Partridge's home in May 1941 was probably replicated in similar form throughout genteel drawing rooms all over England. 'Mrs Partridge', the cook had 'gasped' as she brought in the green tea, 'I want to leave and do war work as Tim's [her husband] being sent abroad . . . she told me that he was going in about three weeks' time and she felt she couldn't bear it unless she was hard at work all day, so she had been to an aeroplane factory in Newbury to see if they would take her on. I didn't know how to show how sorry I was without upsetting her more, her white face and breathless voice were so pitiful . . . Our life gets more domestic and agricultural and when Joan goes it may get more so. If only I could cook!'

In October 1940 yet another appeal for female labour had been broadcast. This time the speaker was the Minister of Agriculture, who explained that 'Total war is a war of endurance and to ensure winning it we must make the most use of all our resources, especially the land . . . without the food you help to produce the bravery of the fighting services would be of no avail and the machinery in our munitions factories would be silent and still. Famine could achieve what no bomb or blitzkrieg or invading force will ever bring about. It is *your* vital task to see that such a thing could in no circumstances arise . . .'

Lady Gertrude Denman, who had been active in promoting the Land

Army in the First World War and had been a pioneer of the Women's Institute for countrywomen, was appointed director of the Second World War version that came into existence on 1 June 1939. By the outbreak of war three months later 17,000 women had volunteered – though there was nowhere to send most of them. The objection to women in agriculture ran along the same lines as that in industry: they would be passengers, unable to do the heavy work required by farm labouring, and they would cut men's already abysmally low wage rates by being prepared to work for less than their male counterparts. The whole idea was 'absurd', decided the farming press.

Dorothy Barton, who had joined the Women's Land Army (WLA) only because she 'couldn't think of anything else to do [and] . . . didn't want to go into the Army and salute everybody' came up against the common 'slip of a girl' prejudice. 'I was sent to a farm quite a long way away . . . I arrived there about teatime one Saturday. I knocked at the door and the farmer answered and took one look at me and said, "Oh no dear, I'm sorry, I wanted a bigger stronger girl than you. It's fairly heavy work round here, I don't think you'll be big enough." ' And of the 6,000 women who had started to work on the land by May 1940, despite the lack of enthusiasm for their services, probably around half were 'paler, streamlined town-bred girls [who] seemed much too fragile for outdoor work'.

The recruiting posters made the Land Army look very appealing, showing healthy-looking young women wearing a workman-like uniform of fawn corduroy breeches (cut like jodhpurs), or khaki-coloured dungarees – when it was still unusual to see a woman in what were then called 'slacks', and all the other women's services wore skirts – with matching Aertex shirts, a green jersey, woollen socks, stout brogues or gumboots and a squashy brown felt trilby 'pork pie' hat. These wholesome lasses were depicted holding a pitchfork, cradling a sheaf of corn, cuddling a lamb in the sunshine, or persuading a motherless calf to suck milk from their fingers. 'Back to the land. We must all lend a hand' trilled the Land Army Song with words and music written by Land Girls – though it was soon adapted to 'backs to the land' in the same 'easy virtue' smear at women in uniform that named ATS girls 'officers' groundsheets' and spoke of being 'up with the lark and to bed with a Wren'.

The writer and gardener Vita Sackville-West wrote an official history of the Land Army that didn't make it sound much fun. 'For the most part its members work isolated and in mouse-like obscurity. Their very uniform seems to suggest a bashful camouflage of green and fawn against the grass or the stubble . . . Instead of silks and georgettes she wears wool and corduroy and clumping boots [though Vita herself was such an aficionado of breeches that she had put them second on her list of what she needed to grab should she need to flee from the invading Germans]; her working-hours seem never definitely to end, for on the land there may always be a sudden urgent call; she lives among strangers, and the jolly atmosphere of homely love or outside fun is replaced often by loneliness and boredom. She gets up when most people are still warmly asleep – and although dawn in spring or summer may be a moment one would be sorry to miss, a dingy wet morning in the winter before the light has even begun to clear the eastern sky is a very different story; she goes to bed with aching muscles after a dull evening, knowing that next morning the horrible alarum will shrill through her sleep calling her back to damp boots, her reeking oil skin, and the mud and numbing cold outside. All this she has done and is doing so that *we* eat.'

Many Land Girls (as members of the WLA were invariably called) were treated well and had comfortable accommodation, plenty of food, friendly hosts and a relaxed atmosphere. But, as most lived with the farmer and his family, this was by no means guaranteed. Given the backward state of agriculture and its low returns, some boarded in very primitive conditions, with no electricity or no heating in the bedrooms, broken windows that let in the wind and rain, and sometimes only a thin blanket to cover the bed, no running water in the house to wash off the caked mud and manure, or clean clothes, the most basic hole-in-the-ground sort of sanitation, and meals that fell far short of the 'manual worker' rations that the women were entitled to. House rules would be made by the farmer's wife and these could be arbitrary or just mean-spirited, with doors locked at 9 p.m. and no baths allowed. Hostel living, it was decided, would be the answer both to improve living standards and to assuage the intense loneliness a girl could feel if she were the only Land Girl staying on a remote farm, where there was almost no communication with the outside world other than the post and maybe a weekly bus into town. Hotels, houses, cottages, barns, stables, hen houses – anything that could be converted to accommodate rows of metal bunks, washing facilities and a dining room – were requisitioned and by 1944 some 22,000 Land Girls were living a regimented life in nearly 700 hostels and getting to work on their farms either by lorry or on a bicycle – their own if they were lucky, or a Land Army issue, black-painted, heavy boneshaker that had been manufactured for export to the Dominions.

At first Land Girls were paid a minimum wage of 28s a week (the average wage for male agricultural workers in 1940 was 38s a week, less than half the national average), and 14s of that was deducted for board and lodging. The basic working week was supposed to be forty-eight hours in winter and fifty in summer; any hours worked over that – and with double summer time that could be until eleven o'clock at night, when the light faded – were paid as overtime. At first there were no guaranteed holidays – paid or unpaid – just a free travel pass after six months' work. By 1943, when the Women's Land Army was at its peak, a 'Land Girl's Charter' stipulated 'a holiday of one week in the working year and an occasional long weekend' off, a minimum wage after board and lodging had been deducted, raised to 22s 6d for those over eighteen and 18s for those under, and 'reasonable working hours with a half day off each week and Sunday work as limited as possible (though on dairy farms the cows still needed milking twice a day every day)'. For her part the Land Girl must be prepared 'to work wherever you are needed' and not leave the Land Army without approval (though this was hard to enforce), and moreover 'while you are in your job you will give the good and cheerful service for which the Land Army has now rightly become famed'.

There were training courses for Land Girls on which they learned how to milk model cows with rubber udders, plough straight furrows and manage stock and poultry, but most girls learned on the job by being pitched straight into shovelling pig manure, clearing land for the plough, milking real cows with swishing tails and hooves that needed watching, delivering calves – whatever the farmer needed help with. 'Reps', voluntary workers who reported to their local county committee, visited the women on their farms once a month to see if conditions were satisfactory, that the girls were not overworked nor too lonely, and that they had the opportunity to meet people through the Women's Institute or the Young Farmers' Club and take correspondence courses and proficiency tests to improve their agriculturalist skills. Lady Dorothy Macmillan, whose husband was the Conservative politician and a post-war prime minister, served as a WLA representative near her home in Sussex walking 'miles through muddy fields' to check up on 'her' girls, and Vita Sackville-West was one of the reps for Kent. Although she did her best in a job that she regarded as 'no sinecure', the Land Girls often struck her as 'unbearably tiresome' and she found it very hard to care whether they were 'served boiled turnips' for supper or not, as she 'painfully and muddily acquired' the information necessary to safeguard the Land Girls' well-being.

By July 1943 there were 87,000 Land Girls; a month later the government, concerned that too many women were plumping for a life on the land over that in the Forces or on the factory floor, banned further recruitment. Much of the initial scepticism had faded: many farmers – some grudgingly – had grown to respect the Land Girls' competence, stamina, conscientiousness and willingness to learn. Productivity had not dropped on farms on which women were employed – in many cases it had increased, and anyway, of necessity Land Girls were now tackling all jobs on the farm. They milked, mucked out, slaughtered, castrated, helped mate, reared, fed, dug, sheared, planted, thinned, picked, harvested, hedged, fenced, ditched, ploughed, drove, excavated, thatched, cleared land, exterminated vermin and – one of the least popular jobs – threshed (picking Brussels sprouts, invariably in drenching rain, was another).

Eileen Jones had learned to milk cows, scythe kale as fodder for the animals, cut wood, saw logs and pull sugar beet on a bleak Yorkshire farm that was her first posting. She then moved to a hostel near Ripon and every day cycled 6 miles to work on a pig farm, boiling swill and mucking out in one of the most malodorous jobs in the Land Army – 'People moved away from us in pubs and in the cinema. No matter how hard you scrubbed you never seemed to be able to get rid of the smell of pig manure.' Towards the end of the war she applied to join the Pest Control Department, travelling to farms to destroy the rats and moles that were eating grain and crops. 'Hitler's helpers' rats were called, since a single rat could eat one hundredweight of food a year, and there were estimated to be over 50 million rats in Britain. Some local authorities, such as Lincolnshire where the problem was particularly acute, offered to pay as much as a shilling for each rat's tail as proof of slaughter. Anti-vermin squads were formed, and in North Wales four Land Girls travelling round on their bicycles managed to kill 35,545 rabbits, 7,689 rats, 1,668 foxes and 1,901 moles in just over a year. Eileen Jones and her fellow workers 'dug for worms from the farmyard, collecting a jarful, cutting them in half and covering them in strychnine poison. We made our way to a field, looking for new mounds of soil where moles were making their new runs and ruining a field. With a walking stick we would probe the field for the run and make a hole and put a worm in it. The hole covered over, we then went round all the mole hills stamping on them to flatten them. Each day we would repeat the operation until no new mole hills appeared.' The women 'also had contracts with the farms to kill rabbits and rats. We poisoned the rats but the rabbits we gassed in their burrows.'

Not all work for Land Girls was on the farm. They could volunteer for the Timber Corps, which was set up in March 1942 to address the shortage of wood. Before the war most telegraph poles and pit props used in coalmines were imported, and the need for home production was urgent, particularly after the fall of France when it was realised that timber would also be needed to construct anti-invasion barricades. Land Girls were sent for a month's training in one of Britain's ancient forests, the New Forest, the Forest of Dean or Savernake Forest, before being posted to scour forests selecting suitable trees for felling.

Doris Benson (later Danher) had volunteered to be a 'Lumber Jill' or 'Pole Cat' 'because the outdoor life appealed to me and after all the bombing [in Liverpool where her father was a publican] . . . I'd always thought that trees were beautiful so I thought the Timber Corps was for me.' Her first posting was to an ex-Army camp near Bury St Edmunds in Suffolk. 'We set off with our mugs and billhooks at about 8 o'clock in the morning. Once we got to the forest . . . we'd light a fire because we had to boil a kettle for the break, and then we'd start felling trees with an axe that weighed about seven and a half pounds. The trees were mainly larch with a diameter of about eight inches. After we'd felled them, we'd cut off the branches and burn all those. Then . . . we'd measure the tree trunks and stack them in lengths for pit props in the coal mines. We used a cross cut to saw them and then stacked them and loaded them onto a lorry for delivery at the station. We cleared all the brushwood and burned it, but we had to make sure at the end of the day that we put out the fire thoroughly because obviously there could be a danger of forest fire. We made lovely toast on those forest fires using a branch as a toasting fork. We all suffered lots of cuts and blisters and bruises and terrible gnat bites, but we took it all in our stride and then we were issued with leather gloves and that made it much better . . .

'I was just given an axe and got on with it. It was as simple as that. But I found it came very naturally to me and I loved the rhythm of it and the sound the axe made. I think most of the girls really loved the life . . . there were about 40 or 50 of us and we all got on extremely well. You'd pick one friend and stay working with her. You had to kneel in front of the tree and put a big cross cut, axing the bottom at an angle and then putting another mark horizontally, and then going to the other side with a cross cut so that when we pushed the tree it would fall in the right direction, and all the time we were doing this we'd be talking about dates and boyfriends and what we going to do and what we were going to wear and stuff like that.

'If you stepped out of line, you were disciplined, but I don't remember many incidents . . . I think we were all too tired after such hard work to get up to much mischief . . . We all got very sunburnt . . . we'd cut the legs off our dungarees and we'd finish up with gorgeous brown legs and as you couldn't get silk stockings in those days, that was really a benefit. When it rained we'd work for as long as we could but when it got too heavy, we'd be sent back to camp – were we glad! There were accidents. I chopped through my thumb with a billhook . . . But I still got paid when I was off sick – not that the pay was very much. After board and lodging you were left with less than £1 a week.'

After a few months, the 'allocation of timber around the area had been used up . . . you can only fell a certain number of trees in an area, so our work was finished', and Doris Benson chose to go to the Lake District. 'We had a lot of freedom there. We were hardly supervised. But we worked hard . . . if there was snow we'd just shovel it out of the way and get on with felling the trees unless it got too deep . . . We left the Lake

District when the quota of trees that needed felling was finished and we had a choice of where to go and my friend Eileen [Coggan], we'd been friends all the way through, decided we'd go to Cardiff, and that was a totally different life altogether. We worked in a sawmill mainly just stacking wood. The men were in charge of the sawing when previously we'd done everything ourselves in the WLA. I can't say I enjoyed that part of my Land Army experience as much as the others and anyway by then I'd met my husband. He was in the RAF and I'd met him when I'd gone home on leave. We married and when I was three or four months pregnant I had to leave the Timber Corps . . . I left with joy at finding a man that I loved and being pregnant and all that to look forward to but I've never really got over leaving the country. As far as I'm concerned the Women's Timber Corps did as good a job as all the other forces but I don't think we got the recognition that the other forces did. For instance you never see us represented at the Cenotaph on Armistice Day and really the work that we did was as vital as all the other services, but it didn't seem to have such status. Perhaps it was because we were in the country we were regarded as not having had such a hard time in the war effort, of being a bit flirty perhaps, a bit flighty. But really we weren't. We were no different at all to other girls of our age.'

On 16 February 1944 Lady Denman resigned as Director of the Land Army when it had become clear that despite the fact that 'the WLA is a uniformed service recruited on a national basis by a Government Department and the work which its members have undertaken . . . is as arduous and exacting as any branch of women's war work and of as great importance to the country', Land Girls were to be excluded from all post-war benefits that might have been regarded as due reward for careers interrupted in the national interest. Unlike women who had served in the Forces, Civil Defence or the Merchant Navy, they would not be eligible for capital grants to restart business enterprises, nor would they be included in any post-war education or training schemes nor in the Reinstatement in Civil Employment Act, which permitted war workers to reclaim their peacetime jobs.

The official argument was that if Land Girls were awarded gratuities and benefits, this would open the door to a torrent of claims from workers in industry. Land Girls were auxiliaries to industry, not the Forces. Nonsense, riposted Lady Denman. Land Girls had always earned less than women in industry, they had never benefited from the wartime perks of the Forces such as free canteens, they *were* an 'army' dressed in government-issue uniform and they had signed a pledge of mobility. The obduracy was particularly galling since the 1943 ban on recruiting had been lifted in early 1945 when it was realised that it would be several months before sufficient men would be demobilised to take over the country's agriculture – and a peacetime population would need feeding as much as a wartime one. Finally the Minister of Agriculture conceded that Land Girls would receive grants to train for work in agriculture or other work at a level commensurate with women in the auxiliary forces or Civil Defence, paid £150,000 into the Land Army Benevolent Fund for cases of hardship, and allowed that on demobilisation Land Girls could keep their heavy greatcoats (provided they dyed them blue), a skirt, their shoes and badge. But no amount of lobbying, meetings, parades, protests and public sympathy improved on what Edith Summerskill – who had taken up the Land Girls' plight in the House of Commons – regarded as a 'mean and niggardly' offer.

By 1939 some 500 miles of canals that had once been the arteries of industrial Britain were no longer navigable, silted up, choked by weeds, their locks rusted, their tunnels collapsed. But 2,000 miles of water were still there and could be used to carry more than 12 million tons of essential goods a year, so the war arrested the decline of the waterways – temporarily.

When Sonia Rolt, an actress who had gone into an engineering factory, and her two flatmates saw an appeal from the Ministry of War Transport in 1944 for volunteers to join a training scheme to work on the barges, it appealed straight away. 'They wanted threesomes. We thought we would all go as a team . . . None of us knew anything about canals. I wasn't even sure that I'd ever seen a canal, but we all fell for the idea.'

The women, all in their early twenties, went for an interview at the Ministry of War Transport in Berkeley Square. 'Lots of girls were very enthusiastic about going on the boats and they had to work out who would stay the course. In fact the more spirited, more bohemian girl seemed to do better. Later, when it became a directed occupation, that was not such a success . . . There were lots of stories of abandoned boats with notes pinned to the cabin doors – "I'd rather face a den of lions than you, Miss March" . . . Then there were these "directed" girls who'd get to a tunnel and couldn't face going through and they'd just all jump off and leg it away . . .'

But Sonia Rolt and her friends took to the life at once. The narrow boats (not strictly speaking barges, which had to have a beam of at least 14 feet while these were only 7 feet wide) were 72 feet long with a small cabin at one end. The rest of the boat was used for carrying goods along the Grand Union canal between London – Limehouse or Brentford most times – and Birmingham. Usually the cargo consisted of 20-foot-long steel rods for aircraft manufacture, or maybe grain going to the Midlands. The boats would then stop off at Longford near Coventry and load up with coal for the return journey to London. Since the boats were capable of a maximum speed of 5 mph empty but only around 3 mph when fully loaded, the round trip would take around a fortnight, and the crew would live entirely on the boats. 'We had to learn to get the boats along the canal, through locks and tunnels. It was dirty and stressful work but extremely invigorating. There was intense physical involvement with your boat, the steering was very heavy, you had to run along narrow planks, coil ropes, clean up your boat and worst of all sheet up your boats when they were fully loaded . . . Boats worked in pairs. There was the oil engine driven boat in front and the butty, or mate boat, which was towed behind. The butty was the woman's boat, where she did the cooking, while the man spent most of his time on the motor boat.'

Naturally there was considerable suspicion of these new, usually rather well-connected female newcomers. The boat people had 'lived through the slump, the depression when times were really hard, and now at last they seemed to be needed, able to do dutiful patriotic things as part of the war effort, and earn a decent wage too. And then along came these women to "free up" the men to go and fight. We knew we could never take the place of the men. We were just extra labour, needed in wartime . . . We had so much to learn. None of us was handy with an engine. If anything went wrong we had to moor up and go along the towpath to find a telephone to ring up the depot and ask an engineer to come out and rescue us . . . locks were a baptism of fire. There were 152 locks between London and Birmingham and you had to tie up the boat and one of us would cycle as fast as she could along the tow path [on a bicycle kept in the hold] to make sure the lock was ready for the boat to pass through and that as little water as possible was wasted.

'We were working *all* the time. We cooked wartime fare – clever sort of risotto things made in a huge frying pan, home made soups, and the boat people caught rabbits and the women on the boats did a lot of baking on their primus stove when the coal was being loaded and sometimes they might give us a pie perhaps. We went to bed as soon as it was dark because of the black out. And we never got away from the war . . . Once we were in Limehouse Basin when a really bad raid was on and all we could do was to lie in the bottom of the boat and watch the raid and hope. No matter how bad the raids were, the canal boats never seemed to get strafed because they lay so low in the water.

'We didn't have a uniform – Meriel wore a leather coat and some ski mittens and I had a roadman's oilskins . . . Baths were a problem. Sometimes we were able to have a bath in a hotel, or maybe in the public baths in Coventry or Northampton or Birmingham. We'd wash ourselves and our hair and our smalls altogether. And we used to go to pubs. There were particularly good pubs in Coventry, right next to the cathedral which was just a blackened shell by then.

'Once they realised that we weren't going to take their men's jobs away, the boat people didn't resent us at all. They got quite fond of us. We made good friends and we were a good subject of yarns for them in the pub – the dire straits we got ourselves into and how they had to rescue us . . .'

Thus in wartime women flooded into jobs where female labour had been unknown, or very rare, in peacetime. On the land, in industry, at sea, in transport and the postal and communication services, in engineering and even shipbuilding, in small numbers. They were applauded from such corners as advertisements for the meat-based drink Bovril, which proclaimed, 'In every sort of wartime task that women can do – and in a great many that women were never expected to do – the women of Britain are scoring triumph after triumph', to the magazine *Woman's Own*, which urged that 'house-pride is no longer the virtue it was. Carry on in comradeship with the women who have put it in their pockets to make munitions, work on the land, hold down a man's job . . . do anything in your capacity to the utmost of your power to hasten victory.' Thousands did. Most found that any simmering male resentment usually evaporated – but that pay differentials with men didn't go away, any more than the often unspoken assumption that such incursions into the labour market were wartime expediencies which, like rationing or the blackout, would be tidied away when peace returned.

19

'OVER HERE'

*It is difficult to go anywhere in London
without having the feeling that Britain is now
occupied territory.*
GEORGE ORWELL, *TRIBUNE*, 3 DECEMBER 1943

THE LAND ARMY was one solution to the wartime demand for
manpower in agriculture as well as in the military and industry. As
early as the summer of 1940 it was estimated that the government's
ambitious programme of agricultural self-sufficiency needed an
additional 82,000 workers. In December that year another solution
suggested itself. Almost 40,000 Italian soldiers had been taken prisoner
at Sidi el Barrani (near the Egyptian border with Libya), and this bounty
was increased after the defeat of the Italians at Bardia and Tobruk. A
message from the Coldstream Guards on 9 December reported that the

officers had had no time yet to count the number of prisoners, but held 'about five acres of officers and two hundred acres of other ranks'. By the beginning of February 1941 some 130,000 soldiers had been captured, including several thousand colonial troops. The Minister of Agriculture asked the War Cabinet to authorise the tapping of this new potential source of labour by arranging for '2,000–3,000 suitable North Italian prisoners to be brought immediately to this country, in order that they may be used for urgent land reclamation work' so the necessary crops could be grown. At first Churchill was 'very doubtful': there was, as he reminded his colleagues, 'still unemployment here'. Furthermore it had only been a year since Britain had hastily rounded up, interned and exported Italians, many of whom had been living in Britain for years. Now the proposal was to import thousands of Italians who had actually been fighting British troops. But by May Churchill had come round to the plan, writing to the Secretary of State for War that 'it might be better to use these docile Italian prisoners of war instead of bringing in disaffected Irish, over whom we have nothing like the same control'.

The rules for POWs as specified by the 1929 Geneva Convention were clear: a prisoner was to be treated no worse than the capturing power's own troops. The International Red Cross was permitted to inspect permanent POW camps. Officers could not be made to work, and NCOs could only be required to act in a supervisory role, but private soldiers could be put to work in any capacity provided that the work was not of military importance. 'Military importance' were weasel words, since in wartime all work in some way contributed to the host nation's war effort. But this was the attraction of the Italian POWs to the British.

The first 2,000-odd Italian POWs arrived at Liverpool in July 1941. The men 'were of good physique . . . well knit, wiry and virile . . . the age range is from 20 to 40 but the majority are under 30 . . . [and] show a keenness to work . . . the selection made by the military authorities in the Middle East seems to be highly satisfactory from the agricultural standpoint'.

The scheme was a success: on the whole the prisoners, who were housed in Nissen-hutted camps and taken out in gangs to work on surrounding farms, found the work was not dissimilar from their working lives in Italy – though any from Naples or Puglia or Calabria found the British winters harsh – and most were disparaging about the food. Farmers were invariably delighted with their new workforce, and one spoke of two prisoners being worth 'ten of the men he could get as casual labourers' and the co-operative behaviour of the Italians led to a relaxation of the rules. In future small parties of two or three men could work for an individual farmer. They would be delivered in the morning and collected at nightfall to spend the night back in their POW camp. Plans to bring an additional 50,000 Italian POWs to Britain in 1942 were curtailed only because there were not sufficient camps to house them.

In January 1942 the Ministry of Agriculture, which had already set up hostels attached to the camps where 'trusty' POWs could live, now announced that as an experiment a number of 'good conduct' Italian POWs would be permitted to 'live in' with the farmers for whom they were working. This would reconfigure the Italian prisoners' relations to their British captors. Fraternisation (which in effect meant consorting with British women) was expressly forbidden by Statutory Rules and Orders published in June 1940, but it was hard to enforce when the prisoners were living in private houses with families, working with Land Girls and cycling along country lanes to work. Jocelyn Greening was a teenager living near a POW camp near Droitwich in Worcestershire, and 'quite prepared to hate the Italian prisoners when we heard that they were going to be housed nearby. . . We were going to be indifferent, ignoring, oblivious and uncaring. After seeing so many newsreels of the smiling happily surrendering little "Eyeties" in the Middle East, we felt utter contempt for them and boo-ed them enthusiastically at the cinema. These feelings, however, were only a temporary state of affairs . . . they were so handsome – black, curly hair, shining eyes, little moustaches, square hands – that we soon found them impossible to ignore.

'In their dark brown uniforms, waving, cheering and blowing kisses, they used to pass our houses every morning and night as the lorries took them to work on the farms. We took great pains to be outside when they passed so that we could glare at them or stick our noses in the air. "Ah! Carrisima [sic]," they yelled, "we love you." In the end we succumbed and laughed with, and at, them.'

But an eighteen-year-old woman was fined £10 at Newbury in Berkshire for fraternising with Italian POWs, though she only admitted to 'having conversed with them in broken English'; in Royston in

Hertfordshire some Land Army girls were accused of consorting with Italian POWs; while in Diss in Norfolk women curbed 'their interest in the prisoners' only when they were warned by the police of the penalty for such an offence.

Italians worked in timber production, limestone quarrying, as labourers in iron-ore mining, brick-making, repairing roads, loading and unloading wagons at railway depots and helping to clear bomb sites. In 1941, the Admiralty requested 2,900 Italian POWs to be sent to Orkney to help build the 'Churchill Barriers' to fence in Scapa Flow, a vast stretch of water that provided 'the true strategic point from which the British Navy can control the exits from the North Sea and enforce blockade'. But the front-line natural harbour was ill-defended, and on the evening of 13 October 1939 a German U-47 had slipped into the Flow and the *Royal Oak*, an elderly iron ship that had seen service in the 1914–18 war, was torpedoed and sank taking 833 of her officers and men down with her. 'Those poor fellows, poor fellows trapped in those black depths . . .' said Churchill, with tears in his eyes, when he was given the news.

Closing the narrow gap through which the German submarine had slipped would require a £2 million building project that would take four years to complete and would change Orkney for ever. In effect four of the islands were to be joined to the mainland by a series of concrete barriers that would give an artificial archipelago to the Orkney mainland, rendering the south-eastern entrance to the Scapa Flow impassable.

Almost from the start there was a shortage of labour. Orkney was not a popular posting: the winters were bitterly cold – the winter of 1939–40 was the coldest for twenty years and the 'peedie' (little) sea at Kirkwall was frozen for weeks with children playing football on it. Gale-force winds whipped up the sea, drifts of snow and sheets of ice covered the landscape, and in winter daylight made a brief appearance – even the summers could be continually overcast and soaked by endless days of near horizontal rain. The population of Orkney in 1939 was just over 22,000: by 1943 it had grown to nearly 60,000 despite the fact that many Orcadians had been called up or sent to work elsewhere. It wasn't just the Navy that came. There was the Army, the Air Force, the ATS, the WRNS, the WAAF – 600 men for every woman, it was claimed – the NAAFI, and a few servicemen's wives braved the elements too.

Thousands of blue and khaki uniforms mingled with those Orcadians still left on the islands, which were the country's first 'Protected Area' – meaning that all civilians, including the Orcadians themselves, had to obtain a permit to enter or leave the islands, and, in addition to the blackout, a nightly curfew was imposed which forbade anyone to be out after 11 p.m. without good reason.

'Orkneyitis' set in. The malady (no stranger to the locals) was a combination of the weather, the landscape, the lack of entertainment, the sparsely populated islands and the feeling of being cut off from the rest of the world at war: 'We'd never seen such isolation,' recalled Edward Partridge, who was stationed on the isle of Hoy.

A local boy watched the arrival of 600 Italian POWs in early January 1942 to augment the local labour force that was building the barriers around Scapa Flow. 'The Italians . . . were dark and suntanned and seemed to be feeling the cold. Many wore cloth capes instead of greatcoats . . . when they marched along the pier road they began to sing army songs, with shouts of "Viva il Duce! Viva il Camerati!" and cheering. We were glad they were well guarded.'

Almost at once the Italians complained that they were being employed 'on works of a warlike nature' in direct contravention of the terms of the Geneva Convention. The War Office agreed to investigate but in the meantime the men must resume work. When the POWs refused they were put on 'punishment diet' – bread and water for three days but normal rations every fourth day. Fortunately the deadlock was broken when a new commander was appointed to Lamb Holm camp. Major T. P. Buckland, a sympathetic officer who spoke fluent Italian, explained to the men that what they were building were not barriers (which they were) but a linking roadway to enable to the people of Orkney to get around the islands more easily. The POWs seem to have accepted that it was likely that a country at war, and still under the possible threat of invasion, would altruistically put in hand a large-scale public works programme on some remote, sparsely populated Scottish islands. They resumed work. Henceforth the barriers were carefully referred to as causeways.

Escape was impossible (which did not stop one prisoner making an elaborate – but fruitless – attempt to do so) and day after day spent in biting wind and cold mixing concrete, digging sodden ground and quarrying stone, sapped energy and – usually – rebellious spirits. The POWs were paid a shilling a day, or 1s 6d (all amounts paid in tokens) for skilled men driving the smaller gauge diesel locomotives that carried rocks from the quarries to be sunk in the sea; some worked as cooks providing pasta (of sorts, given the ingredients supplied), coffee rather than tea and sometimes 'wine' made from potatoes and rice, a diet supplemented by fish the prisoners themselves caught in summer.

The POWs set up a school to teach illiterate prisoners to read, a theatre was constructed fully equipped with scenery, and operas and plays were staged, a recreation hut was equipped with a concrete billiard table and balls, fashioned by the prisoners. But what the Roman Catholic prisoners wanted was a chapel. Two Nissen huts were placed end to end and joined together. Domenico Chiocchetti, an artist from the Dolomites, gathered round him a band of craftsmen and started to transform the corrugated-iron huts: behind the altar he painted a picture of the Madonna and Child based on *Madonna of the Olives* by Nicolo Barabina, a dog-eared reproduction of which, on the insistence of his mother, he had carried in his battledress pocket throughout the war. Tiles retrieved from the lavatory of the sunken block ship *Ilsenstein* surrounded the altar. The corrugated-iron exterior was coated with cement, and an impressive façade was erected to hide the outline of the huts with a campanile, pinnacles, windows and a carving of the head of Christ crowned in thorns surmounting the archway.

The first 1,400-foot causeway was completed by the early autumn of 1943: a straight road between the islands. By that time Italy had surrendered, and the POWs were freer to go around the islands and mingle with the population, offering their services in the evenings as barbers and cooks in the homes of friendly crofter families, and tolerating the children yelling 'Italiano mucho malo' which they imagined meant 'Italians very bad.'

On 4 November 1942 Montgomery's 8th Army had taken 32,000 more Italian prisoners at the battle of El Alamein some 60 miles west of Alexandria. It was an Allied victory at last. In twelve weary days of fighting, British, New Zealand and Australian forces pierced the phalanx of German troops under the command of Rommel 'corseting' Italian soldiers in a line that was strung out across the Western Desert. The Afrika Korps were forced to retreat into Tunisia, and Allied armoured troops pushed on to recapture Tobruk and Benghazi, names that had become part of the grim litany of defeat the previous year. Four days later came more good news when 100,000 British and US troops landed in French North Africa – the first joint military initiative since the US had come into the war after the bombing of Pearl Harbor in December 1941. Within three days the Axis troops had surrendered. The next Sunday, 15 November, church bells pealed out all over Britain for the first time since the dark days of 1940, not to warn of an invasion, but to announce a victory.

The situation for the Italian POWs became even more confused after Italy unconditionally surrendered on 8 September 1943. There were 74,900 Italian POWs in Britain and a further 11,000 were due to arrive from Algiers before the end of 1943. The British government was extremely reluctant to relinquish its Italian labour force. It seemed to want it both ways: retaining the prisoner-of-war status and yet getting round the limitations on the employment of POWs imposed by the Geneva Convention. A scheme was devised whereby Italian prisoners could volunteer to serve in units or formations organised on a military basis, of 'an Italian character . . . under Italian officers and non commissioned officers' but under British command and supervision, and those Italians who volunteered would retain their prisoner-of-war status, but their treatment would be 'ameliorated so far as circumstances permit'.

By the end of 1944 there were already over 155,000 Italian POWs, and thousands of Germans captured in France had begun to arrive, most of them transferred to work in forestry and agriculture, which put pressure on space and supervision in the camps. If only the Italians would co-operate, they could be moved out of the camps and the guards could be used to supervise the Germans. But rather than the 90 per cent of Italians who had been expected to leap at this opportunity, less than 60 per cent did.

The main problem was that there were few incentives. Those who volunteered would still be POWs, but POWs in a 'spruce green' uniform from which the identifying bull's-eye patch would have been removed, the letters POW unpicked and the word Italy substituted. Finally, in the face of Italian recalcitrance and British need, the package was improved:

in August 1944 volunteers – 'co-operators' – were offered a minimum wage for unskilled workers of nine shillings a week; half a POW's pay could be exchanged for sterling and only half would be in tokens (which could be used only in the camps). Prisoners could remit some of their earnings home to their families, and the exchange rate against the lira was increased. In addition volunteers would have more 'privileges' – they could airmail their letters home, and they were allowed to go into shops and cinemas (but not pubs). They were free to talk to British people and accept invitations to their homes.

Still the number of volunteers was slower than had been hoped. Sometimes this was an act of pro-fascist defiance, but more often it was either a wish to stay on the land, or a feeling of camaraderie with fellow Italians from the same village or region and a reluctance for a tight-knit community to be dispersed. Local newspapers carried the usual stories and letters about the alleged 'soft' treatment of the POWs, of their 'idleness', of the 'revulsion' felt by parents who had sons fighting in Italy when they saw the 'cushy' deal the Italians were reputedly getting. Women who fraternised with the Italians were vilified in their pages and it was even suggested that, like women collaborators in occupied France, they should have their heads shaved. But the memoirs of a young man, Ion Megarry, who worked with the YMCA promoting educational and recreational activities for the Italian POWs in Britain, tell a very different story of those who had volunteered to work to help win the war. 'The co-operators . . . experienced disappointment rather than fulfilment; moving among free men, but themselves subject to restrictions . . . they suffered more humiliation than they had ever suffered in their camps; and not only was repatriation as far [away] as ever, but over their heads there always hung the sword: punishment and reversion to the status of non-co-operators . . .'

As wartime Orkney had been transformed by the overwhelming presence of the Italian POWs and the military, so all of Britain had already become a temporary wartime home to a plurality of nations, uniforms and languages. By 1943 there were some 25,000 Polish servicemen in the UK, 3,200 Czechs, around 1,750 Norwegians, approximately 2,000 Belgians and the same number of Dutch, and 35,000 Free French, all 'over here' to join the fight to liberate their homelands.

And to join the fight against Nazi Germany came troops from Australia, New Zealand, South Africa, India and other Dominion countries. Canadians had been among the first.

Canada had abandoned its neutrality within a week of Britain declaring war, and an advance guard of Canadian forces arrived at Greenock on the Clyde on 17 December 1939. By the end of February 1940 there were over 23,000 Canadian troops in the UK, most of them stationed around Aldershot military barracks. For the first few years it was not clear just why the Canadians were in Britain. An expedition planned to defend Norway was cancelled; plans for Canadian divisions to join the BEF in France were confounded; and a contingent that did arrive in Brest in mid June 1940 was almost immediately recalled – leaving one man behind as a prisoner of war.

The Canadians' first winter in Britain was the coldest since 1894, and although many of the soldiers came from parts of Canada where winter temperatures could plunge to minus 11°F and there was deep snow on the ground for months, it could be said to be the wrong sort of cold in Britain. The men were housed in damp and draughty conditions, in a country where most people still regarded central heating as being as unnecessary as air conditioning, and nearly every other soldier seemed to be laid low by flu, bronchitis or a succession of streaming colds. Even though the 'Canucks' were given a more generous coal allowance than the British troops, complaints poured in that no park bench or seat at a bus stop was safe from being carried back to camp and chopped up for firewood.

In the summer of 1941 the entire Canadian Corps moved into position along the Sussex coast to defend the area from possible German attack and invasion. Their commander, General Andrew McNaughton, was determined that the Canadians would fight together – they were not colonials to be thrown in line piecemeal as suited the British military command, and McNaughton refused to let Canadian troops join the Australian and New Zealand forces in what he regarded as a 'side show' in North Africa. In his view the Canadians had come thousands of miles to fight Hitler in Europe. But by the summer of 1942 Canadian troops had been in Britain for well over two years and had got nowhere near any action: they might be intact as a force, but they were inactive. Morale was at rock bottom, the men were 'browned off' – bored, restless and resentful. Their behaviour often reflected this.

There were some positive experiences: the 1st Canadian Division was moved to Northampton and Kettering during the Dunkirk crisis in May and June 1940 as a mobile defence unit in case of invasion. Hundreds of families who could ill afford it refused to take any money for billeting some of the 20,000 Canadians for the short time they spent in the locality – and made them very welcome. But it was an interlude. When the Canadians left, they were back under canvas again with no chance to get to know the locals, no expectation of action, few legitimate diversions and scant attention paid to their plight. The result was more drunken brawls, bothering girls, intimidating road users and vandalising wherever they took their leave.

As the Canadians grew accustomed to life in Britain and more of them were billeted with families rather than living in camp, relations with civilians – which were always much better with the Scots than with the English – did improve, though those French Canadians who spoke little or no English remained lonely and alienated despite some arrangements for them to learn the language. But the monotony of an inactive life in a strange country, with no idea of how long it would last, meant that the Canadian troops' morale remained in a fragile and volatile state throughout 1942–3, and this was a key reason why McNaughton insisted vociferously that his men must see action – any action – in Europe.

Pressure for a 'Second Front Now', to aid a dogged, beleaguered Russia by diverting German troops from the Eastern Front, intensified after February 1942 when US troops started to arrive in the UK. Until then the demand had come largely from the Communist Party, delighted to be able to graft patriotism on to ideology and call for action. But in 1942 the baton was picked up by an unlikely runner, Lord Beaverbrook, who had recently resigned as Minister of Aircraft Production and was convinced that with America at Britain's side an invasion of Europe was feasible. Speaking at a public dinner in New York in late spring, Beaverbrook had been vehement: 'Strike out to help Russia. Strike out violently, strike out even recklessly... Britain should imitate Russia's spirit of attack by establishing somewhere along two thousand miles of occupied coastline a Second Front.'

But when Britain did 'strike out' – recklessly, many would accuse – the result was a terrible disaster that showed how daunting it would be to try to gain a foothold in occupied Europe. It also showed that any assault would be an Allied effort, that Britain did not 'stand alone'.

Operation Rutter was an assault planned to test the German defences of the French port of Dieppe. The Canadian high command insisted that its troops should play a leading role in this more ambitious assault so that at least some could see action at last. Vice Admiral Louis Mountbatten, the ambitious, over-promoted Chief of Combined Operations, took charge and the operation, renamed Jubilee, was mounted from five English ports from Southampton to Newhaven with a force of 4,963 Canadians, 1,075 British personnel and 50 US Rangers on 19 August 1942. It was a tragic fiasco. The troops, landing at dawn at eight points across a 10-mile front, were spotted by a German convoy, so the vital element of surprise was lost. The raid, which Churchill had characterised as a 'butcher and bolt' exercise, turned out to be a slaughter of the Allied troops, and a one-way ticket for thousands. The withdrawal began at 11 a.m. under heavy fire. But 3,367 Canadians were not able to bolt: 907 were killed, others were wounded while 1,946 were taken prisoner, more than in the whole campaign in north-western Europe after D-Day. British casualties were 275.

The official line was that the Dieppe raid taught lessons that would be vital to the planning of D-Day nearly two years later (in which the half a million Canadian troops by then posted to Britain would also play a significant part). But as the military historian John Keegan wrote: 'It is as illuminating to say of Dieppe . . . that it taught important lessons about amphibious exercises as to say . . . of the *Titanic* disaster that it taught important lessons about passenger liner design.' The raid was, 'in ratio to participating forces, the most costly Allied assault of the war'. Rumours persisted that lives had been sacrificed to demonstrate 'the futility of further argument' about invading France in 1942. At all events, calls for a 'Second Front Now' abated, and the next time the Canadians went into action was in July 1943, taking part in the capture of Sicily, and then being consigned to the 'spaghetti league' as part of Montgomery's 8th Army, fighting a slow advance up through Italy.

'If you think we're strange,' Canadian troops had teased British girls, 'you just wait till you see the Yanks.' The largest overseas contingent in

Britain by 1943 – around 770,000 – was that of US troops, who had started to arrive in January 1942. When he had heard the news of the Japanese bombing of the US fleet at Pearl Harbor on 7 December 1941, Churchill 'knew that the United States was in the war, up to the neck and in to the death . . . after seventeen months of lonely fighting . . . We had won the war. England would live; Britain would live; the Commonwealth of Nations and the Empire would live . . . Once again in our long island history we should emerge, however mauled or mutilated, safe and victorious . . .'

Britain, the United States, Canada, governments in exile in London, Latin American countries and others declared war on Japan the following day. Germany and Italy declared war on the United States on 10 December 1941. The circle of war had clamped tight shut. 'We have at least four-fifths of the population of the globe on our side,' Churchill had assured the House of Commons on 7 December, but those who were not wrought terrible defeat within weeks. On 10 December the battleships *Repulse* and the *Prince of Wales*, which had been sent to Singapore in an attempt to deter the Japanese from entering the war, were sunk; on 24 December British forces surrendered Hong Kong to the Japanese; and on 15 February 1942 Singapore fell. But despite the fact that so much 'was molten' in those weeks, Churchill decided his priority must be to zig-zag 'at the best possible speed' across the Atlantic to Washington to speak in person to President Roosevelt and convince him of a 'Europe First' strategy even though it was in the Pacific that the US had been attacked.

The Prime Minister came away with what he wanted: a commitment from the President that his priority was the invasion of occupied Europe, and as evidence 'of the United State's resolve . . . to intervene directly in Europe . . . sixty or seventy thousand US troops' would be sent to Northern Ireland as soon as practicable.

What most ordinary Britons knew about the US had been largely gleaned from the cinema – trigger-happy cowboys up for adventure, or machine-gun-toting Chicago gangsters in slouch hats. Then there were the sophisticated Manhattan apartments where every hour seemed to be cocktail hour, and every man who lit a satin-gowned lady's cigarette or refilled her martini glass looked very like Clark

Gable – who would soon be seen in the flesh with the 351st Bomb Group at Polebrook in Northampton where he was making a training film for aerial gunners (and was reputed to have exchanged the second highest salary in the whole US – $357,000 – for $600 in his new job). Or like James Stewart, who came with the 445th Bomb Group to Tibenham in Suffolk in November 1943 and stayed until VE Day, flying Liberators and then working as a staff officer, and was greatly liked as 'a regular guy'.

Yet a survey taken in October 1940 had revealed that for the British, America was at the bottom of the list of the 'friendly' nations. It was on a par with Italy – which was actually at war with Britain. Even after Pearl Harbor, pro-American sentiment remained muted, with feelings that only now that her own interests were directly threatened would the US be 'kicked into the war'.

The GIs came across the Atlantic – most coming abroad for the first time and with no idea of their destination – in large, purpose-built Liberty ships, or the faster British liners such as the *Queen Mary* or *Queen Elizabeth*, which took only five or six days but were packed to the gunwales, with 15,000 GIs (as compared to the usual 2,000 passengers carried in peacetime) stacked in bunks and hammocks, with endless 'chow lines'. There were fierce Atlantic storms to battle with as the boats clove through the waves to avoid the U-boat menace. The first GIs had landed at Dufferin Quay in Belfast on 26 January 1942. Soon Americans were disembarking at the west coast ports of Clydeside, Liverpool and the Bristol Channel. It made logistical sense to divide the country roughly down the middle, with British troops stationed on the east and US troops on the west, since British and Canadian forces were concentrated in south-east England when the GIs arrived, still on alert for a possible invasion. US ground troops would gradually take over a triangle of Britain stretching from their ports of entry down from Hampshire to Cornwall, and taking in a corridor down the centre for supply.

In addition to the ground troops, a vast US bomber force in Britain was projected to join the RAF in what would become virtually round-the-clock bombing raids of Germany and occupied Europe. It was to prepare the flatlands of East Anglia – the part of Britain nearest to Germany – as a launch pad for the planes of the 8th Air Force that the first GIs came to Britain. Throughout the thousand days that the USAAF operated from Britain, its planes flew a total of 330,523 sorties, including bombing raids, training flights and transport flights to drop supplies over occupied Europe.

'I remember only too well how shocked we were when we disembarked at the sight of all the bomb damage,' wrote Bill Ong, when he arrived, aged eighteen, in April 1942, to help build an airfield in East Anglia. '. . . And if that wasn't enough, I guess it was the whole atmosphere of dirt and dinginess round the docks. Maybe it was the wintry weather, the cold gray days, no leaves on the trees, no sun. I wondered why the Germans wanted England at all! Even so I had to admit that I didn't think that Americans at home could have taken the punishment that the British had. There was precious little food to spare, clothing was rationed and there was no petrol at all except for essential purposes . . . And it wasn't over yet, far from it.'

By the end of 1944 the majority of the 426,000 US airmen in Britain were stationed in Norfolk and Suffolk, which had become a mosaic of airfields – on average one every 8 miles throughout East Anglia. A bomber base might cover as much as 500 acres and be a wartime home for two or three thousand GIs. The effect was devastating to the English countryside. Extensive tracts of high-yield farmland were commandeered for the bases – 100,000 acres in Norfolk alone – and frequently the Air Ministry seemed cavalier in its demands.

The impact of the 'friendly invasion' on most of the rest of the British Isles was profound. By the end of 1942 there were just under a quarter of a million US troops in Britain, the vast majority of whom were service staff and airmen. Ground forces did not start to arrive in large numbers until the autumn of 1943, after which Operation Bolero, the code name given to the build-up of American troops in Britain (after Ravel's composition, to suggest fast music that built to a crescendo with the invasion of Europe), at last seemed appropriate. By May 1944 an invasion force of 1.5 million combat and service troops (including air and ground forces) plus all their equipment was stationed in an already overcrowded island with a population of just over 48 million in an area a third the size of the state of Texas. In some areas the US presence was almost overwhelming by the spring of 1944. There were 71,000 GIs in Suffolk, a county with a population of around 400,000, which meant that every sixth person was a GI, and in Wiltshire the English probably only just outnumbered the GIs by two to one.

'The British will welcome you as friends and allies. But remember that crossing the ocean doesn't automatically make you a hero . . . there are housewives in aprons and youngsters in knee pants who have lived through more high explosives in air raids than many soldiers saw in first-class barrages in the last war,' warned *A Short Guide to Great Britain*, published by the US War and Navy Departments for troops going overseas, 'to start getting you acquainted with the British, their country and their ways'. It explained the peculiarities of the currency with its farthings, halfpenny ('hay-p'ny'), threepence ('thrup'ny bit), and half-crowns. A useful glossary was provided of the English the Brits spoke, with terms such as bloke for guy, cinema for movie house, righto rather than okay, and galoshes meaning rubbers (though rubbers to Americans also signified contraceptives, which caused mirth when English girls used the term when requesting an eraser). They were warned that to say that ' "I look like a bum" is offensive . . . for to the British this means you look like your own backside . . . NEVER criticize the King or Queen [and the Northern Ireland version of the *Guide* warned, 'Don't argue religion. Don't argue politics'] . . . Don't criticize the food, beer or cigarettes to the British. Remember they have been at war since 1939 . . . Don't show off or brag or bluster –"swank" as the British say . . . When you see a girl in khaki or air force blue with a bit of ribbon in her tunic – remember she didn't get that for knitting more socks than anyone else in Ipswich.'

But if the Americans were to be taught to respect the British people and their ways, the British needed some re-education too. They got it in pamphlets issued by the Army Bureau of Current Affairs, which again emphasised, 'Americans are not Englishmen who are different, but foreigners who are rather like us.' Schoolchildren's views were repositioned by the 3,000 or so teachers who attended week-long training courses run by the Board of Education all over the country on American history, politics and society; the Clarendon Press in Oxford commissioned *A Brief History of the United States* with an introduction by the US Ambassador to Britain, John Winant, which was distributed to all secondary schools; and the poet Louis MacNeice was commissioned to write a twenty-four-page illustrated booklet, *Meet the US Army* – 100,000 were printed, explaining that the war was providing 'the opportunity for the ordinary people of the two great English-speaking nations to get to know each other in the mass . . . an opportunity never presented to the tourist traffic in peacetime'. MacNeice stressed the temporary nature of the GI occupation and tried to suggest a common experience shared by 'the average Tommy' and 'the average doughboy', neither of whom came from 'a militaristic nation [that] thinks of war as an end in itself'.

Despite efforts to reassure both sides that the differences between the Americans and the British were fewer than the similarities, the objectives of the two governments were not identical. For the British in need of US manpower and equipment, fearful of any hint of a switch in resources to the Pacific theatre but also with an eye to the post-war economy and balance of power – particularly in relation to Russian ambitions – it wasn't just military co-operation that was the goal but a political 'special relationship' as well. But despite assurance in the *Short Guide* that 'We don't want a mere wartime friendship. We want the real thing – the alliance which survives the peace and becomes a permanent force in the shaping of the new world,' for the US government the Yanks were 'over here' to fight their way back home as soon as possible. The GIs were overwhelmingly a conscript army, from a country whose legislature had only extended the length of the draft by a single vote and many of whose citizens remained extremely reluctant to see their boys involved in another European civil war. As far as possible, American troops would be cocooned in base camps with conditions replicating those at home for the soldiers, many of whom had no particular wish to be either in the Army or in Britain. 'To my mind,' wrote Maurice Gorham, acting Assistant Controller of the BBC, who visited the US several times during the war, 'their troops, especially those who were here for a long time, were too much insulated from the British people. They already had everything laid on in their own camps – their own daily newspaper, their own movies, their own food, and every sort of amenity stocked in the subsidised PX [the equivalent of the British NAAFI] . . . Coming from an environment so scrupulously American, they had nothing in common with the people they met here . . .' US bases were closed environments – islands of little America – off-limits for outsiders except by special invitation.

The GIs were in the streets, loitering 'with discontent', hands stuffed in their pockets, on leave or on a night out and invariably a gaggle of them. 'We never saw an American soldier *doing* anything, or even carrying his own bag,' noted Gorham, but when he was finally sent to a combat zone 'and saw how the Americans could look when they were on a job, I longed to bring a handful of them back to London, and say to the people in Piccadilly, "Look, these are Americans too".'

Clubs run by the American Red Cross (ARC), such as Rainbow Corner in Piccadilly on the corner of Shaftesbury Avenue, where GIs could go for a drink, a meal and a bed for the night, as well as dances, concerts and quizzes, were again off-limits for all but US forces, and so were the smaller venues run by the ARC in towns near US bases. Nothing remotely comparable to these facilities was provided for British troops, even though by 1943 there were some 1.7 million soldiers still stationed in the UK waiting to be sent to battle.

The *Short Guide* had assured the US troops, 'the British are tough. Don't be misled by the British tendency to be soft-spoken and polite. If they need to be, they can be plenty tough. The English language didn't spread across the oceans and over the mountains and jungles and swamps of the world because these people were panty waists.' Nevertheless there was considerable suspicion on both sides about the military capabilities of the other – a vital issue since an Allied offensive depended on both armies fighting together, and that was not something that either side felt sanguine about for some time. GIs taunted that the Union Jack was 'red, white and blue – and yellow'. A Sutton Coldfield office worker recalled that every time 'There'll Always Be an England' was played on the wireless, a GI was bound to wisecrack 'as long as we're here to defend you'. The feeling was mutual. To any jibes the Americans threw at the British about Dunkirk, the British retaliated after the battle of Kasserine Pass in Tunisia in February 1943, by sneering 'how green was my ally . . .' at the Americans. As Laurence Lafore, who had come from Washington to work with the US Information Service in London, discovered, 'The fact of being bombed generates a certain condescension towards people who haven't. To this kind of condescension [the British] could add the pride of having Stood Alone plus their fully justified assurance that they knew a great deal more about fighting a war than we did. We were automatically tenderfeet and due humility was expected of us.'

Unbloodied by conflict, the GIs seemed 'slovenly soldiers ... they were soft ... degenerate ... too damned wealthy ... the hardship of war will do them a lot of good'. Britons were particularly struck by the way the disembarking troops 'marched off in a curious silence on their rubber-soled shoes – it was more like a soft-shoed shuffle than marching'. This was particularly shocking to an older generation: an East Anglian woman's 'father had been a sergeant in the 1914–18 war and he was *very* disparaging when he saw them marching through our village street, their hands in their pockets, chewing gum. "What a shower. They can't march to save their lives! How will they be able to fight?" '

Meet the US Army acknowledged that 'some of the British eyewitnesses ... are somewhat shocked by [the average GI's] informality', but it should be remembered that 'in action the US army is noted for stern discipline ... this army has a victorious history [which] has been unduly ignored in our schools, possibly because many of its victories have been won at our expense ... both the British and American armies are exceedingly tough ... and when you meet a "doughboy" don't be misled ... into thinking that he has any illusion about what he is here for. He regards your island as a halfway house to the front – and he knows what the front will be like.'

The easy-going 'Hiya Sarge' attitude of the GIs was a revelation to the class- and rank-conscious British. 'They were buddies,' recalled a Dorset woman. 'It didn't matter what rank they were, they were always friends. A private would go up to an officer and say "Hi Bud, can I borrow your Cadillac?" and the officer would immediately hand over the keys to his Jeep.' It might be an attractive trait, but it could make a British soldier a bit queasy about going into battle alongside a GI who, he feared, might think it was just fine to put his point of view when given an order, rather than jumping to it straight away.

For their part, the Americans were in despair at the British class system – and what they saw as the British soldier's automatic deference. Robert Raymond, a US pilot who had joined the RAF on the outbreak of war, regarded 'the power of the old school tie in this supposed great stronghold of democracy ... as a dangerous matter'. He sometimes felt 'that England does not deserve to win this war ... it has been well and truly said that General Rommel of the German Army's Afrika Korps would never have risen above the rank of NCO in the British Army'.

'Overfed, overpaid, oversexed and over here' was the enduring British epithet for the GIs – and there were British soldiers who would have tagged 'over medalled' on to the list. The GIs responded that the British troops were 'underfed, underpaid, undersexed and under Eisenhower' – which was at least 75 per cent true. The middle two sneers rankled most – though with food being shipped across the Atlantic, and what was on offer for sale in the PX in the way of tinned ham and fruit, candy and chocolate, there were allegations that an average-sized British family could live for a month on what was scraped into the garbage can after a single meal at a US base.

'American wages and American soldiers' pay are the highest in the world,' the *Short Guide* reminded. The British 'consider you highly paid . . . The British "Tommy" is apt to be specially touchy about the difference between his wages and yours. Keep this in mind . . .' The pay differential was much greater in the lower ranks. A British private was paid 14s a week as compared to his US counterpart's weekly wage of £3 8s 9d, made up of his basic pay and overseas allowance which British did not receive when they went abroad to fight. This meant that a single GI would have a disposable income of around 10s a day, whereas an unmarried British soldier would be left with 3s a day after three months' service. Although Canadian and Australian troops were also 'overpaid' by British standards while they were 'over here', under Army regulations roughly half a Canadian soldier's pay was either deferred (he received it after the war) or assigned (it was sent home to dependants) or both, so a Canadian did not have the same sort of money burning a hole in his pocket as an American did. In grudging recognition that it was perhaps not so much that the GIs were overpaid but that the British were underpaid, in August 1942 a flat-rate pay rise of 20 per cent was awarded to all British troops.

The GIs arrived in Britain at a low point in the war: their arrival signalled new hope that defeats would begin to be reversed, that with US forces and technology the fight back against Hitler in Europe was on its way. But it was a complicated message. Encoded in it was an element of reproach that whatever the rhetoric, Britain might be able to stand alone but she couldn't move forward without US aid. The brash and vulgar incomers with their confidence, their swank, their habit of splashing their big bucks around, sent a shiver down the delicate spine of the 'cultivated' Englishman. The shiver was partly one of fear of the future and Britain's place in it. A post-war world in which the cultural capital of tradition, heritage, manners, deference would be in hock to a new world order of money, technology – and sheer numbers.

For those less concerned with the world order, the reaction was not very different – particularly among men for whom GIs represented unfair competition. A young ATS woman stationed in Wales recounts an evening when an American 'liberty bus' (or 'passion wagon' as they were more appropriately called) arrived at the camp to take the women to a dance at the nearby US base, 'About fifteen girls had primped themselves up – as far as khaki would allow – for the occasion. As we piled into the truck there were, of course, catcalls from a few of our own soldiers who happened to be nearby and shouts of "the Yanks have plenty of dough. No hope for us now!" '

Since Eric Westman was 'a young British serviceman and not an attractive young woman, *my* memories of GIs are pretty sour! The Yanks were the most joyful thing that ever happened to British womanhood. They had *everything* – money in particular, glamour, boldness, cigarettes, chocolate, nylons, Jeeps – and genitalia . . . almost every working-girl aspired to "have a Yank".' A woman from Chippenham, Wiltshire, reflected, 'I cannot recall anyone who had the slightest idea of how tremendous an impact the Americans would have on our lives. The Americans changed England more than the English like to realise and admit.'

For Averil Martin (later Logan), 'the whole world simply changed when the Yanks arrived here in 1943. I thought they were sublime, they were cute . . .'

Quentin Crisp, who was working as an artist's model in London, was mightily taken by the GIs too. 'This brand new army of (no) occupation flowed through the streets of London like cream on strawberries, like melted butter on peas. Labelled "with love from Uncle Sam" and packaged in uniforms so tight that their owners could fight for nothing but their honour, these "bundles for Britain" leaned against the lamp posts of Shaftesbury Avenue or lolled on the steps of thin-lipped statues of English statesmen. As they sat in cafes their bodies bulged through every straining khaki fibre to our feverish hands . . . Above all it was the liberality of their natures that was so marvellous. Never in the history of sex was so much offered to so many by so few.'

It wasn't just the GIs' looks that were so beguiling – and statistically all 1.5 million could not have been second cousin to Adonis. The way many US soldiers and airmen treated the opposite sex was a revelation to a woman who was a teenager in Birmingham during the war. 'We were half starved and drably clothed, but the GIs said we looked good anyway. A lot was said about them being over sexed and things; maybe it applied to a few but it was mainly a myth put about by Lord Haw Haw in his Nazi propaganda broadcasts from Germany to upset British soldiers overseas and try to split up the Allies . . . it was just that British women and the American GIs were in the same place at the same time – it was rather pleasant really.' An aircraft-factory worker in Leicester remarked that 'a British soldier would take a girl for a drink, bore her to death talking about cars or sport etc. Then if he saw any of his mates, he abandoned the girl except to buy her a drink now and then until it was time to go home. With a GI it was very different. He would buy me a drink and entertain me as if I was the only person in the room. I know that when my back was turned he would probably make a date with another girl, but this didn't really seem to matter.'

Many GIs were young, single and thousands of miles away from home for the first time – and, with 'all found', chose to spend their bulging wage packets on drink, fun and girls, buying them presents of candy, gum, chocolates, cigarettes, soap, nylons – 'luxuries we hadn't seen in years. It seemed like Christmas.'

While a degree of indulgence was extended towards 'boys who will be boys', girls were often censured for their behaviour – an attitude that hardened in wartime when so many British men were away fighting, and some British women seemed only too happy to relinquish women's traditional role in wartime of 'keeping the home fires burning' by collaborating with the occupying forces in having a good time. Vivienne Hall thought that it was 'disgusting' the way 'the only ones who show the general mass any friendliness are our most crude specimen of girl and womanhood who flock around the Americans doing anything they want them to do and fleecing them in payment . . . it's they and not the Americans who are bad. Here speaks the crusty old maid I suppose, but

I hate to have the British judged by these little bitches who are showing only our bad side to the Americans.'

A Shropshire man recalled a local square when 'at 7 o'clock on a summer's night and the local girls were all dolled up and scrambling aboard Jeeps after first asking their escorts not to forget to give some gum or candy to their kids left behind in the street . . . some of these local girls, of course, had husbands or fiancés or sweethearts in the British armed forces and they received black looks and jeers from the older women.'

'Maybe they were fresh, but if you are thousands of miles from home and you were lonely and the girls were after you, you would take what you could get, wouldn't you?' reflected a Bristol woman.

Nevertheless the results of sexual laxity in wartime were concerning the authorities. By December 1942, the number of cases of VD among US troops in Britain was 58 cases per thousand men as compared to fewer than 39 per thousand back home. In May 1943 the US forces newspaper, *Stars and Stripes*, published a disturbing cartoon of a GI embracing a girl by a wall on which the 'V' for victory had been crossed out and replaced with 'VD'. Notices started appearing in public lavatories warning of the danger of venereal disease, and a Defence Regulation that came into force in January 1943 required that a suspected carrier named by a VD patient could be compulsorily examined and treated if the testimony was corroborated by two independent witnesses. The regulation applied to both sexes. But this public health exercise did not, in the view of the US authorities, address the urgency of the epidemic. A top level (all male) conference was called in April 1943 with representatives of the US, Canadian (which had its own problems) and British military police and health officials.

Various measures were put in place. Films were shown in army camps and air-bases warning of the dangers, and after some delay VD treatment centres were set up in American Red Cross clubs. At first the US military was reluctant to deal with the problem by providing condoms for fear this would both encourage promiscuity, and be seen to be doing so back home. It was not until early 1943 that US-manufactured condoms were available in PXs, and provision was made for the issue of free contraceptives to the troops. Curfews were imposed if it seemed the situation warranted it, and a police presence was stepped up round sexual hot spots such as London's West End where the 'Piccadilly commandos' shone flashlights on their ankles and murmured 'Hello, Yank!' 'Hallo, soldier!' 'Want to come home with me, dearie?' (though 'home' invariably turned out to be a nearby alley or shop doorway), and Hyde Park where the 'Hyde Park Rangers' were active in the bushes.

The problem of prostitution was not confined to leave-centres like London – though it was certainly more concentrated there. 'Suitcase' girls set up in the New Forest to service GIs on leave from Tidworth, and 'commandos' were found to have been smuggled into bases and camps. Moreover, undesirable sexual liaisons were not confined to professional prostitutes. It was much harder for the police to take action against 'good-time girls' (or 'patriotutes' as such camp followers were called in America) because they did not accost – they simply made it clear that they would welcome advances and this was not a criminal offence. But Lieutenant Colonel Paul Paget, who was in charge of VD control for US troops in Britain, found it necessary to warn that: 'Any woman who has been "picked up" and "made" by an American soldier can be, and certainly has been, "picked up" and "made" by countless others.'

The British authorities feared for the morale of their own troops and the problems of countless illegitimate babies; their American opposite numbers were anxious for the stability of family life back home in the States, and concerned that 'undesirable' girls would latch on to homesick GIs and acquire the right, through marriage, to settle in America. The 'best way of dealing with the problem', as a Ministry of Information regional meeting recognised in late 1943, 'was to find means of introducing troops to a better type of English girl.'

The American Red Cross, as official provider of rest and recreation facilities for the growing number of US troops in Britain, took it upon itself to screen and select 'nice girls' to act as hostesses and partners for GIs at parties and dances. To do this they enlisted the good offices – and local knowledge – of such bodies as the WVS and the Church to supply names of 'suitable girls'. At Rainbow Corner, when a dance was arranged for such an occasion as Hallowe'en or Thanksgiving, a GI was required to submit the name of any partner he wished to bring, forty-eight hours in advance, for approval.

US airbases and army camps also tried to 'vet' the girls who came to dances. Eileen Smithers, living in Norfolk, 'surrounded by US Army Airforce bases', and whose mother's house was on a list for providing beds for US officers when the Red Cross Club was full, 'was also on a list! Most of the bases ran Saturday night dances for which transport was sent to Norwich to collect the local girls. However there were two distinct types of Saturday night dances. Those in the bases that just sent trucks to several pick-up points in the city and collected any waiting girls, and those that were "vetted" by the City Hall. To get such an invitation, a girl was interviewed and if approved her name would go on an official invitation list.'

'British Welcome Clubs' were set up in small towns throughout the country. The WVS, who were often the first British women the GIs saw as they were welcomed to Britain with tea and buns, ran most of these clubs, in church halls, social clubs or even members' own homes. Eventually there were over 200 such clubs – some very small, open only while the GIs were in the area prior to D-Day, others larger, like the one housed in a cinema in Ipswich – but all committed to bridging the divide between US troops and British civilians. They were not an unqualified success and often the pub, the cinema and the street corner proved more of an attraction to the GIs than the tea urn and the wind-up gramophone, however 'nice' the girls who came along.

Some unit commanders made a real effort to get to know the local people and encouraged GIs to participate in local events and find out what the place they'd come to had to offer – other than pubs. But the best way of fostering good Anglo–American wartime relations was to 'get a Yank into a British home' for tea, Sunday lunch or even to stay on leave. Again, the American Red Cross swung into action, and between 1943 and the end of the war managed to arrange over a quarter of a million such visits, and the Anglo–American Hospitality Committee also put willing hosts in touch with potential guests. When one American officer arrived with his company in Wales he found that 'when we first arrived these town people used to gather at the camp gate – sometimes thirty at once – all of them with invitations for the soldiers to come to dinner'.

Sometimes, though, embarrassment about the spread that could be provided was an inhibition. 'After four years of war, the [British] are ashamed of their meagre rations ... and drab, threadbare homes –

particularly when the British think of America as a land of luxury.' Commanding officers began to encourage men to take official 'hospitality rations' when they went visiting, and the men themselves would supplement these with stuff bought from the PX or begged from the cookhouse, turning up with tinned ham, tinned peaches, chocolates, candy, cigarettes – even cigars sometimes, and bourbon.

As many of the GIs were very young and far from home, it was 'Mom' these men missed. Seeing this as an ideal opportunity to establish stable links with the British community, US commanders encouraged schemes whereby a local woman would 'adopt' a lonely GI, inviting him home for tea on a regular basis. Christmas was obviously a time when it was particularly hard to be away from home. As many troops as could be spared were given the day off, and if possible the GIs were entertained in British homes – 'filling the chairs left empty by British fighting men'. The soldiers who accepted such invitations were issued with special rations for each day's stay: 'A typical package will contain fruit or tomato juice, evaporated milk, peas, bacon, sugar, coffee, lard or shortening, butter, rice or available substitutes.' With news of such a cornucopia, so many invitations were extended to the US forces that first Christmas in 1942 that 'the ratio is estimated at fifty invitations for every one soldier available' and a plea went out for GIs to come forward 'and accept some more of those invitations'.

Children, as well as housewives, had reason to be grateful to GIs, many of whom were not long out of childhood themselves, and the uninhibited curiosity children showed made them easier to get to know than more reserved adults. And for family men, time spent with British children was some small compensation for missing their own children who were growing up while they were away at war.

The currency of the relationship was chewing gum – in much the same way as with Canadian troops it was the aircraft 'spotter' cards from Sweet Caporal cigarettes – given, solicited, bartered (coat hangers were always a good bet), used as a bribe. Hard candy (boiled sweets) like Lifesavers, chocolate Hershey Bars, 'Babe Ruths' were much coveted, as among older boys were cigarettes and an introduction to the subculture of the American 'funnies' – comics featuring such characters as Superman, Captain Marvel, Li'l Abner, Bugs Bunny and Loony Toons. Others learned to play baseball, and some villages could even muster a scratch team. And then there were the parties. 'Christmas, New Year, birthdays – any old birthday – Fourth of July, Hallowe'en, Thanksgiving, whatever celebration the GIs cooked up there was *always* – bombs or no bombs – a party for the kids,' particularly at Christmas when an aircraft hangar would be transformed into 'a huge Aladdin's cave . . . with a Christmas tree reaching up to the skies' festooned with 'chaff' – the thin strips of metallic foil thrown out of aircraft to confuse radar – 'and sacks and sacks of sweets'. The highlight would be a red-robed Santa Claus arriving – sometimes by plane, once at Shipham airbase in Norfolk in a Flying Fortress taxiing along the runway – bearing toys that the GIs had made themselves or solicited from home.

When it came to romance with girls, rather than kindness towards their mothers and kid brothers, Anglo–American relations were further strained when it came to the question of GIs marrying, which the US authorities regarded as an impediment to be avoided – particularly marriage to a girl overseas. A single man undistracted by family responsibilities was considered to be superior military material, more likely to make the strong ties with his 'buddies' that generate the selfless and foolhardy courage war demands. The US military authorities shared British concern that it was the 'wrong sort' of woman who might ensnare a GI husband, to share his higher pay and as a ticket to what she imagined would be a chromium-plated life 'over there'. The English girls 'think all Americans are millionaires – and would like to marry one – and go to live in that country where everything is done by Modern Magic', reported Margaret Cotton, who observed the behaviour of her GI countrymen in Devon where she had relocated with her family during the Blitz.

The US authorities were also very concerned about bigamous unions, a concern shared by some British families – the reputation Yanks had among many meant that a father would insist on grilling the prospective suitor about whether he was already married or had a fiancée back Stateside. Even if he could convince them that this wasn't the case, parents frequently opposed such wartime romances, because if their daughter did marry a GI and return with him to the United States after the war, it would in effect be a daughter lost – a one-way air flight across the Atlantic cost around £175 and a sea passage £40 to £60, when the average British weekly wage in 1940 was £4 10s. Some fathers refused to sign the necessary papers, while others did so only with the greatest reluctance: 'I said to my Dad "If you won't sign the papers there won't be a wedding, but there'll be a honeymoon anyway".' Other parents gave their daughters 'a lot of support . . . they felt there was no future for young people in England – and I would have a much better life in the States.'

Then for the US authorities there was public opinion back home to consider. This would hardly be enthusiastic about having the flower of American manhood return from foreign wars accompanied by foreign wives, at the expense of American women seeking husbands. Indeed, so concerned were the US authorities that Margaret Mead, the American anthropologist, whose work on young girls in the Samoan islands had been curtailed by the war, was flown in on a whistle-stop tour to interpret each country's courtship rituals to the other. The problem, she diagnosed, was a mutual misunderstanding of the idea of a date. For the American boy it was 'pre-courtship behaviour', an opportunity 'for flirting and backchat . . . when the boy demands innumerable favours [which the girl] refuses'. Whereas British girls did not seem to understand this at all and 'turn chilly' at the 'speed and assurance of the Americans' approach to them'. Or, worse, 'think he is proposing [which he *isn't*, Mead stressed] . . . and want to take him home to father'.

This disfavour for wartime conjugality with foreigners was not common to all countries. Well over a thousand Poles out of the 30,000 stationed in Britain had taken Scottish brides by the end of 1943, and over 14,000 Canadian servicemen married British women. They were obliged to give notice, but no disciplinary action was taken against a serviceman who married without the requisite permission since 'in general marriage is regarded as a civil right, which should not be interfered with by military regulations'.

In July 1942 Eisenhower ruled that his officers and men could marry only with the permission of their Commanding Officers (COs). Disobeying these regulations would lead to a court martial. Permission would not be granted unless the CO was convinced that such a marriage was 'in the interest of these [European Theatre of Operations (ETO)] forces in particular and military service in general'. Applicants were told that marriage would not entitle them to special treatment in living arrangements, in rental subsidies, travel allowances or medical and PX privileges. A man's wife would not be transported at government expense either within the ETO or to the United States. Furthermore, the marriage would not mean that she would be entitled to automatic US citizenship, rather 'she will be subject to applicable immigration and naturalisation laws'. This startlingly hostile edict, issued when it was clear that US forces would be in Britain for at least two years, was softened somewhat by a revised circular in October, but in effect couples were allowed to marry only when there either was, or soon would be, an illegitimate child to 'bring discredit to the services'. The order was never officially rescinded, and if it was impossible to prove (as it usually must have been) that a marriage would bring 'discredit' to the service, the CO would simply bring out reels of red tape and weave so many complications that all but the brave-hearted wilted.

There was one category of request to marry that was always refused: that between a white British woman and a black GI, since in nineteen out of forty-eight states mixed marriages of colour were illegal. The US Army that came to Britain was a segregated one, a 'Jim Crow' Army, as it had been since the American Civil War. It was not until 1947 that a presidential order ended military apartheid. When black Americans, severely hit by the Depression, began to enlist in the Army in the late 1930s they were assigned almost exclusively to segregated units and trained almost entirely for non-combatant tasks as labourers, transport operators, stevedores, kitchen and domestic staff, and stewards. Blacks could not enlist in the elite Army Air Corps or the Marine Corps, though many were employed on Air Force bases doing a variety of ancillary jobs, some of them hazardous, such as loading bombs.

The British government did not want black GIs to come to Britain. As far as its own black Dominion troops were concerned, the Foreign Office had already made clear that 'the recruitment to the United Kingdom of coloured British subjects, whose remaining in the United Kingdom after the war might create social problems, is not considered desirable'.

In fact around a thousand foresters were brought from British Honduras to fell timber in Scotland, and some 350 engineering and electrical technicians came to work in factories on Merseyside, but this was regarded as a response to a wartime emergency and the workers would not be encouraged to remain to swell the black British community, which, on the outbreak of war, numbered probably no more than 8,000, mainly concentrated in the ports of Cardiff, Liverpool, Newcastle and London. Britain was an overwhelmingly white country, and the British government intended to keep it that way. The Foreign Secretary, Anthony Eden, even suggested to US Ambassador Winant that 'our climate was badly suited to the Negroes'.

But the objections of the British government ran counter to the quota system that President Roosevelt had imposed after his re-election in 1940. The number of blacks in the Army was to be roughly the same as their proportion in the US population – about one in ten – and these men were to serve in all theatres of war.

Initially Eisenhower had hoped to restrict the black GIs to the areas where the black British population was concentrated but, since most were service and supply troops, they were needed initially in East Anglia to build airfields and supply airfields for the USAAF. So to segregate black and white troops when off base, a system of 'rotating passes' was introduced whereby white troops would be allowed to go to the nearest town on one night and black troops on another. Tewkesbury, for example, a market town with a population of under 6,000, was the off-duty town for the GIs stationed some 3 miles away at Ashchurch. By August 1942 there were already 3,000 troops stationed there. White troops were allowed a pass for every Tuesday, Thursday and Saturday, while the black troops' passes were for Mondays, Wednesdays and Fridays: Sundays were alternately black and white. If there were two towns which were feasible options for time off near a camp or base, one might be designated for white troops, the other for black, and when neither of these options was practicable, some pubs (or even separate bars within pubs), cinemas and dance halls would be allocated as whites only, other for blacks only. Thus in Launceston, a small town on the edge of Bodmin Moor in Cornwall – where a gun battle was fought between black and white troops in September 1943 – there was a 'black' fish and chip shop and a 'white' one and there were alternating 'black' and 'white' dances at the town hall.

As the number of black troops increased – there were 130,000 in Britain by D-Day – so did simmering resentment among blacks about this segregation and the over-zealous actions of the military police to enforce it. There had been a clash between black and white US troops in Antrim in Northern Ireland in September 1942: a black GI had been killed and a white GI wounded. A serious near-riot at Bamber Bridge near Preston in Lancashire in June 1943 left one black GI dead and several injured – as were some 'Snowdrops' (US military police, so called for the colour of their helmets rather than the hue of their skin). There were fights and stabbings in Bristol and in December 1944, when some black GIs were driven out of a pub in Newbury, Berkshire, a gunfight developed in which two black GIs and the publican's wife were killed.

Officially the British government distanced itself from what was happening. On 4 September 1942, the Home Office had issued a circular to all chief constables stating: 'It is not the policy of His Majesty's Government that any discrimination as regards the treatment of coloured troops should be made by the British authorities [and] the British police should not make themselves responsible in any way for the enforcement of such an order.' But if there was no official support for US segregationist measures, there were plenty of people in government and local administration who were anxious to strictly limit contact between black GIs and the British population – particularly the female population. Without the co-operation (or at least acquiescence) of the British authorities, it would not have been possible for the US Army to operate a policy of racial segregation.

Although Britain was not innocent of racism towards its own small black population, the attitude of most of the public towards GIs seems to have been 'They're all soldiers. They've come to fight the same war,' and many Britons saw no reason to distinguish between a white American and a black one. They were disturbed by the treatment they saw meted out to the black Americans by their white compatriots, and they responded to what they saw as the black men's humiliation, feeling that such prejudice sat ill in a war being fought to destroy Nazism and its racial attitudes: 'A Jim Crow army cannot fight for a free world.' A Cambridge man 'thought the treatment of the coloured races of the US Army etc. by the white fellows is disgusting . . . After all, both races are doing the same job of work.' And a Birmingham man reported, 'I have personally seen the American troops kick, and I mean kick, coloured soldiers off the pavements, and when asked why, reply "stinking black pigs", or "black trash" or "uppity niggers".'

Publicans, café owners and shopkeepers might not always have been paragons of racial tolerance, but they were often incensed at being dictated to about who they could and could not serve, welcoming 'any soldier of any colour who behaved himself and could pay for his drink'.

But when it came to British women rather than British beer and cigarettes, British attitudes both official and unofficial were less generous, and those of the US authorities intransigent. There was no official encouragement for black GIs to be welcomed into British homes, and no black GI was ever billeted with a British family. The WVS-run 'Welcome Clubs' had a hollow ring to black GIs since the welcome did not extend to them, though just before D-Day a few segregated 'Silver Birch' clubs were established for black GIs.

Miscegenation lay at the heart of the issue. The image of the 'oversexed' Americans and the 'loose' British women calcified around black GIs. Far-fetched tales of black sexual prowess and rapacity spread. A civilian in Leamington Spa found it 'horrible to see white girls running around with the blacks – they do say once a black, never a white, don't they?' A first lieutenant stationed near Wellingborough was outraged. 'I've seen nice-looking English girls out with American soldiers as black as spades. I have not only seen the Negro boys dancing with white girls, but I have actually seen them standing in a doorway *kissing them goodnight.*' A Somerset man, seeing a number of girls peering through the hedge at a black GI, diagnosed that they were 'prick-mazed, that's what they be, prick-mazed'.

Wartime Defence Regulations were used against women found consorting with black GIs on military premises: five women found with black GIs at Melton Mowbray in Lincolnshire in June 1943 were each imprisoned for a month, and the following January two Preston factory workers were given three months' hard labour when they were found sleeping in a hut where black GIs were stationed at Leicester.

On a less serious, but no less mortifying, level women realised that to dance with a black GI was to run the risk of becoming a permanent wallflower at white dances. At a local dance hall near Glasgow, a factory worker reported that 'if you danced with a coloured American, you were blacklisted by the white ones. They kept a list in the camp of these girls and passed it on to the new troops coming in.' And at a dance near Warrington when 'two black Americans came in, the band stopped, and two white Americans walked across the floor and took hold of the blacks by their collar and threw them out of the front door: then the dance went on'.

But Mary Kemp (later Ruau) recalls a dance in her home town of Bridgwater in Somerset, when a contingent of black GIs arrived. 'Nobody talked to them. We thought it was very rude so we decided to ask the band to play a Palais Glide and make it a "ladies' choice", and my sister and I and some friends went over to ask them to dance, which they did. And that broke the ice. But afterwards someone came up to my father and asked him what his daughters were doing dancing with coloured troops. My father replied that he was proud of us. "They're our allies too," he said. "They'll bleed and suffer and die, just like the white men." '

If the 'occupation' of Britain by overseas troops and workers was tolerated by a large percentage of the population – even welcomed by some – it was because it was recognised as a wartime expediency. Relatively few 'occupiers', including some POWs both Italian and German, stayed on to work, to marry British women and settle in British towns, and for most it was an interlude in their lives, as it was for the British. Contact with these wartime visitors from overseas may have expanded the horizons of many, but on the whole neither leaders nor led took this opportunity to learn as much as they might have done about how Britain's place in the world was being reconfigured by the war.

20

PUTTING A FACE
ON THE FUTURE

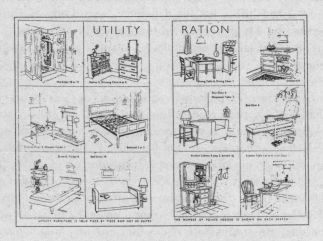

I slept and dreamed that life was Beauty
I woke and found the life was Duty.
ELLEN S. HOOPER

WHAT MIGHT HAVE been a minor irritation in peacetime had come to assume more tragic proportions by 1943 when there were fewer and fewer goods to buy in the shops, so if you smashed a lemon squeezer or cracked a pie dish the chances of replacing it were negligible. 'I'll pamper my equipment,' *Vogue* had resolved as an example to its readers in January. 'I'll pull in my belt, but I'll never pull out an electric light cord roughly again . . . I'll wash up as tenderly as one baths a baby; and dry precious glass and china with hands as safe as a Test Match cricketer's. However few my clothes, I'll have fun with them . . . I vow at least once a week to dress my prettiest; good for boys on leave, and good for me. When my clothes grow old, I'll do much more than "make do". I'll make *new*.'

Clothes rationing had come into effect on 1 June 1941. Churchill had been opposed to the idea, which he believed would be 'unnecessary, unworkable and unpopular', and accused Oliver Lyttelton at the Board of Trade of 'wanting to strip the poor people to the buff'. But Lyttelton managed to convince the Prime Minister that it was essential (or rather slipped it past him while Churchill's attention was focused elsewhere). Supplies of wool and cotton had fallen to 20 per cent of pre-war levels, and there was the fear that at the first hint of a shortage, the better-off would go on a panic-buying spree leaving nothing in the shops for the poorer consumer. It was 'not intended to restrict the quantity of clothes available for the public, that had already been done [by various limitations on production]. The sole object was to provide fair distribution of available supplies' – and also to control consumer spending, release workers in the clothing industry for more important work and free up more factory space. It was to be organised on the basis of quantity, not price. No one was entirely sure what a reasonable allocation was, but it was calculated to be two-thirds of the amount of pre-war clothing bought by an individual.

Just as with food rationing, the purchase of clothes would require coupons as well as money and the number of coupons a piece of clothing 'cost' depended on the amount of cloth and labour used in its manufacture. There was a different tariff for wool and cotton.

Clothes going 'on the ration' had taken most people by surprise that Whit Sunday morning when 'the President of the Board of Trade came on air to announce the imminent rationing of clothes, thereby ruining the Sunday breakfast appetite of millions of women who regretted not having bought that little outfit they dithered about last week'. The market traders of Petticoat Lane in the East End, though, must have 'got wind of something' because they held a free market in clothes on Whit Saturday. But, 'in fact they had only damaged themselves, because they could not replace the stock they had sold on Saturday without coupons'.

At first everyone received sixty-six coupons a year – though the secrecy in which the scheme had been shrouded to avoid pre-emptive buying meant that there weren't any clothing coupons in ration books, and so shops accepted margarine coupons instead. The allocation was slashed to forty in 1943 but rose again slightly to forty-eight in 1944. A man could buy pretty much what he stood up in: a suit took twenty-six coupons, a shirt five, vest and pants eight, socks three, shoes seven and a tie one – leaving sixteen that could be used for handkerchiefs at one coupon each or pyjamas and a dressing gown, each of which took eight. A separate pair of trousers took eight, too (though a Scotsman's kilt took only six). To acquire a woman's suit or outdoor coat would mean the surrender of eighteen coupons; an unlined mackintosh took nine; a dress needed eleven if it was made out of wool, or seven if it was cotton or rayon or some other fabric. Blouses and jumpers were five each, as were shoes (but these soon went up to seven), a pair of stockings two, vests and knickers three each and bras and suspender belts one apiece. Clothes for children under four did not require coupons until August 1941, when they were brought into the scheme. Since clothes for children took less material, they also required fewer coupons, so a child could have more clothes, and from 1942 each child received an additional ten coupons. Pregnant women were given first fifty, then sixty extra coupons to buy maternity clothes and a layette. Wool was also rationed, but it still required fewer coupons to knit garments than to buy them.

At first coalminers had been granted an extra sixty coupons in recognition of the extra wear and tear on their clothes but, after complaints, this was withdrawn and all manual workers were allocated a supplementary ten coupons, while special 'industrial' coupons – 'iron rations' – were shared out by works committees in mines or in factories where the work was particularly heavy, until it was found that the system was being abused. It transpired that those not engaged in heavy industrial work were prepared to dress as if they were if it meant ration-free clothes and the opportunity to save their other garments 'for best'. Thereafter industrial clothing was distributed directly in exchange for a small number of coupons handed in by the worker.

Usually, second-hand clothes did not require coupons, but prices were regulated. Air-raid-damaged stock could be sold at reduced coupon value provided it did not exceed a certain price. At first sheets and furnishing fabric were not rationed but, when it became clear that clever dressmakers were using the supply to add to their wardrobes, these were put on coupons too. Blackout material was coupon-free, and a WVS worker overheard women queuing up to buy tea from the mobile canteen discuss making 'an evening frock from blackout material and trimming it with lace which is unrationed too'.

A thirty-three-year-old woman clerk had 'got a shock' when she first heard the news, but was 'relieved I had got Peter his suits etc. and myself dress length and other things, also stockings last Friday . . . I shall manage on my ration as I always buy good quality . . .' Another woman calculated that she must have used the equivalent of 153 coupons for herself and 45 for her child the previous year, but comforted herself that 'most of that was buying forward and J. has a lot of his cousin's clothes to inherit. Mother and father both ordered two suits apiece when war broke out, having done so last time.' A Mass-Observation survey showed that 70 per cent approved of the policy, and people were 'willing to put up with it as . . . an essential part of the war effort'. Women were more critical than men – and particularly worried about not having enough coupons for the stockings they would need – and those under thirty minded most of all. The consensus among the comfortably off seems to have been that clothes rationing would not be too much of a hardship. Those who had 'had enough money and foresight to lay in a good supply greeted [clothes rationing] with "smug satisfaction" '. 'Most women I know have enough coats, dresses, best dresses, underwear to be smart if the war lasts another ten years!' wrote a northern housewife who considered that 'sixty-six points is quite generous for those who use their hands in wartime'. (The Knightsbridge store, Harrods, agreed, advertising 'A sewing machine can be almost as much a weapon as a spade.') Belfast welfare worker Moya Woodside was characteristically brisk: 'Surely people must have realised that it was inevitable? I think an undue fuss is being made, and probably that in practice it will work out all right. Most of my refugee friends have had no new clothes since they emigrated two or three years ago, and they still manage to look nice and enjoy life (when they can). As long as we have freedom (comparative though it may be), friends, books, music and the countryside, surely these restrictions don't matter.' Chips Channon had all of those things and 'forty [suits] or more' as well. 'If I am not bombed I have enough clothes to last me for years . . .' But even he worried a bit about socks.

Not everyone found it so easy. It was reported that at the end of the first year of clothes rationing the average number of coupons left per person was three, while many had run out altogether. 'People write to the papers endlessly about clothes rationing, struggling to press themselves forward in the guise of exceptions. Surely as expectant mothers they can have extra coupons for maternity gowns? Surely the mothers of sons killed in the war, they can have them for mourning? Or, if not, can they at least have some special armlet to indicate their bereavement?' Those professionals such as doctors, dentists and lawyers who needed special clothes for work thought they should be allocated extra coupons, but the only civilians who were allowed these were those in the Civil Defence services, policemen and fire-fighters – and a few special categories such as newly appointed High Court judges and those high up on the clerical ladder. Civic dignitaries thought they merited special consideration too. In August 1943 the Mayor-elect of Blackpool requested an additional 328 coupons for himself and 178 for his wife, which, considering that the coupon allocation was by then 48 coupons per annum, meant the equivalent of nearly seven years' consumption for him and four for his wife. The official answer was always the same: 'owing to the increasing stringency of supplies . . . The only two classes in the civilian population for whom special provision can be made are the children . . . and the industrial workers . . . In time of war a relaxation of conventional standards of dress is accepted by all . . .' Or, as the rather unloved Chancellor of the Exchequer, Sir Kingsley Wood, prophesied, the day would come when people seeing a man in a shabby suit would say, 'He is a patriotic man carrying out the Chancellor's idea.'

But some were always likely to be shabbier than others: from the outset it was 'obvious that the advantage will tend to lie with those who can afford to buy a garment of good quality which requires the same amount of coupons as a cheap article but which will last twice as long'. And when the President of the Board of Trade, Hugh Dalton (who had replaced Lyttelton in 1942), and the MP Ellen Wilkinson announced that they had not spent any coupons at all, their thrift was greeted with derision: 'Will people in high places ever realise that poor people can't afford clothes that last for years and years?' Or probably could not afford to buy enough clothes in a year to utilise their full coupon allocation. As the war dragged on, everyone got shabbier and made more dispirited by shortages and privations – and unappeased by *Vogue*'s jaunty assertion that *'il faut SKIMP pour être chic'*. Clogs (no coupons) came back into use – if not fashion – in northern towns and cities, though hinged wooden-soled shoes introduced in 1943 to supplement dwindling leather supplies never caught on. The Board of Trade conceded that corsets really were a necessity for the well endowed and those women who had to stand all day at the shop counter or factory bench, and agreed to reserve small amounts of rubber and steel for the manufacture of these wartime stays which almost literally helped give women 'backbone'. Complaints about clothing coupons featured in almost all reports on Home Front morale, and by July 1944 people were finding it 'increasingly difficult to keep themselves even respectable'.

The WVS opened clothing exchanges where clothes of growing children could be swapped for the next size up, and somehow in their busy lives women found the time and energy to be ingenious. What could not be bought could be made or mended. Architects' and engineers' blueprints were soaked so the paper dissolved and the linen could be used for blouses and shirts; butter muslin or curtain nets were stitched into blouses, petticoats and nightdresses – and an advertisement for Lux soap flakes suggested that 'the best parts of worn-out net curtains make lovely brassières – ones that have a pre-war French accent!' Parachute silk was like gold dust, and anyone lucky enough to get any was set up for evening dresses, luxurious underwear – or a wedding dress – while the funereal purple of the lengths of satin that undertakers used to line coffins was salvaged from a bombed-out funeral parlour by one London family, soaked, and the resulting greyish lilac fabric fashioned into party clothes. Almost all garments had an afterlife: shirt tails were cut off and moved up to replace frayed collars; worn sleeves were cut out to leave jerkins; dresses lopped in half to make a skirt or a blouse; adults' clothes were adapted for children; children's clothes cut down for babies. Blankets were turned into coats; candlewick bedspreads into dressing gowns; curtains into dresses and skirts; a woman journalist claimed to have made a whole suit out of the fabric salvaged from old car-seat covers; battered felt hats made clumsy slippers; and the toes cut off too-small children's shoes produced 'sandals'. Petticoats were sewn into camiknickers, knickers regusseted with stockinette or a worn-out tea towel; jumpers were unpicked and the wool knitted into something else; while probably hardly any sheet in the land escaped being turned sides to middle. Women's magazines filled their pages with suggestions, and became fervent advocates of 'jaunty', or 'gay', or 'flattering' hats since these were not on coupons, and gave 'such a lift' to last year's – or the year before that's or the year before that's – outfit. They also became experts in the art of 'primping', adding snippets of lace or feathers, or furnishing trimming or artificial flowers to hats, dresses and suit lapels to individualise and 'refresh' a tired outfit.

The Ministry of Information weighed in too with its 'Make Do and Mend' campaign, producing a booklet and advertisements full of handy hints, often suggested by a wretchedly upbeat 'Mrs Sew and Sew' character. 'Plus fours would make two pairs of shorts for a schoolboy'; 'pyjama legs will make children's vests'; contrasting panels could be let into dresses and skirts – indeed, two frocks could be cannibalised to make one 'coat dress'; replacement sleeves could be knitted to replace those on worn jackets or coats; new stockings should have their heels and toes reinforced *before* wearing; Wellington boots should be kept in the dark for fear of perishing; and men's worn ties shortened for little boys. As Hugh Dalton wrote, 'No doubt there are as many ways of patching and darning as there are of cooking potatoes.'

'We didn't need no one tell us to make and mend,' said Ena Norris, whose family of nine siblings had been bombed out of their home off the Caledonian Road in north London and in 1942 was living in what was effectively a garage in Finsbury while they waited to be rehoused. 'It's what my mum had had to do all her life. Not just in wartime.'

Consumer goods were not rationed but a series of Limitation of Supplies Orders, the first in 1940, had restricted the production of a wide variety of goods, such as pottery, glass, cutlery, games, toys and musical instruments, while the manufacture of other non-essential 'fripperies ranging through jewellery, metal toys, ornamental glassware, bird cages, fancy goods and a miscellany of household gadgets – such as vacuum cleaners, refrigerators, toasters and coffee percolators – was prohibited altogether' in order to divert resources and manpower to wartime production rather than the supply of goods in the shops. By 1942 these restrictions had proved too blunt an instrument, failing to distinguish sufficiently between essential and non-essential items. In these 'lean years' of 1942 onwards, as the war dragged on month after month, 'the search for crockery or something to cook in – both indispensable needs in modern life – consumed more time and temper than the economies in labour or raw materials justified', admit the official historians of the war economy. A Board of Trade survey carried out in 1943 discovered that over a four-week period, half the women trying to buy a saucepan were unsuccessful – and must have bitterly regretted their patriotic impulses back in 1940 when they so willingly gave saucepans for Spitfires. Babies' glass feeding bottles and rubber teats were in desperately short supply, children's toys that contained kapok or plastic or metal were unobtainable – and so the male equivalent of 'make do and mend' was often to repair or make, from bits of salvaged wood, dolls' houses, forts or garages for Christmas and birthday presents. Matches, candles and batteries were sought-after items, and George Beardmore, a London clerk, reckoned that you pretty much had to 'marry a shopkeeper's daughter before one can get hold of a new [razor blade]'.

The Board of Trade walked a knife edge (from which it slipped on occasions) in defining 'essential', in drawing a balance between the need for shipping space, the labour and raw materials required for the production of armaments, and the fact that the war effort might be better served 'by maintaining the supply of tobacco, horse-racing, ice cream, of flowers – things that would strengthen the will to work or brighten dreary lives'.

It seemed as if lives would be made more dreary with the introduction of the Utility scheme – though this was surely an improvement on the 'civilian uniform' that the government had considered introducing. The scheme was the Board of Trade's way of trying to ensure that adequate supplies of good quality clothes were produced, and at a reasonable price – since clothes prices had risen alarmingly since the start of the war: 72 per cent between September 1939 and September 1941 and a further 23 per cent the following year. The Board of Trade asked each member of the Incorporated Society of London Fashion Designers, including Hardy Amies (who was moonlighting from his work as an officer in the Intelligence Corps to design for the House of

Worth), Edward Molyneux (the Irish couturier who had managed to get back to London from Bordeaux on a coal boat after the fall of Paris), Digby Morton, Victor Stiebel (who was given time off from his camouflage duties) and Norman Hartnell (the royal couturier) to submit four outfits – a top coat, suit, afternoon dress and cotton overall dress. When they were given their 'Utility brief', Hardy Amies and Captain Molyneux, whose motto had been 'plainness is all' for years, 'both laughed. "We have been making utility clothes for years," we said.'

The most suitable outfits were selected by the Board to be suggested to manufacturers for mass production. Utility clothes were first shown to the press in September 1942 and the October issue of *Vogue* fell in line at once: 'All women have the equal chance to buy beautifully designed clothes suitable for their lives and income. It is a revolutionary scheme and a heartening thought. It is, in fact, an outstanding example of applied democracy.'

To conform to Board of Trade regulations, the clothes had to be made from specified 'Utility' fabrics and labelled with the 'Utility mark' (two 'cheeses' with a slice cut out disguising the fact that they were two Cs signifying 'civilian clothing' and the number 41 for the year of introduction). The specifications were very strict: the number of buttons on a jacket or coat was prescribed, as was the depth of hems, the length of the skirt (regardless of the height of the wearer); the number of pleats, tucks, pockets and belts was severely restricted; there were to be no superfluous trimmings of velvet, or fur fabric, or decoration such as embroidery, appliqué or lace. Trouser turn-ups were banned for men (which some seem to have minded terribly); the width of the jacket lapel was specified; no double-breasted suits were permitted; and the number of pockets was restricted to three for coats and jackets and two for waistcoats (which didn't go down too well either). With all 'superfluities . . . pared away', cut was all, but for women these simpler, less overtly 'feminine clothes' matched the vernacular of the time since so many women were in uniform or wore dungarees for their war work, their Veronica Lake lookalike peek-a-boo hair tied back in a snood or turban to stop it catching in the machinery.

All clothes manufacture was subject to the same restrictions as to style, including those made by a dressmaker with the customer's own fabric, but with Utility clothes the quality and price were specified, and unlike other garments they did not carry purchase tax. When the clothes first became available in the spring of 1943, many women were impressed. But they were not so impressed by the name 'Utility'. 'I expected them all to be the same,' said a twenty-year-old woman, 'but there's quite a range of styles, and the materials are good.' Ann Seymour, the editor (or editress as the terminology then was) of *Women and Beauty*, ran a feature on Utility clothes in the March 1943 issue: 'The response was immediate and readers are still phoning for details of where the clothes can be obtained.' Miss Seymour thought 'it's an excellent idea. The only thing wrong is the name . . . it's up to the Government to see that the clothes are so good that all women will want to wear them. The word "utility" is awful, but it'll just have to be got over.'

Another product that was designated 'Utility' was furniture – an 'unparalleled example of total state control not only of the supply, but more importantly the design, of an essential commodity'. The manufacture of furniture was a low priority in the early days of the war because it was believed that adequate stocks were already available, and imports of timber had been drastically cut. Home-grown wood was needed for other purposes too, such as in building accommodation for the Forces, making thousands of bunk beds for air-raid shelters, constructing Bailey bridges for the Army and other urgent wartime requirements. Plywood, the staple of inexpensive furniture, was withdrawn in January 1941 since it was extensively used in aircraft production. Furniture manufacture gradually ground to a halt as firms used up their pre-war supplies of timber and were unable to obtain any more. Prices of second-hand furniture soared, since of course those setting up home for the first time (and there were roughly half a million marriages each year of the war) needed to furnish them. The Blitz exacerbated the problem: large numbers of people whose furniture had been destroyed or damaged needed replacements.

Conventional rationing obviously wasn't appropriate – say one bed, two chairs and a table per year – since some (those who had been bombed out, for instance) would need far more, while others would need nothing at all. The solution was allocation: people would be entitled to buy furniture if (and only if) they could prove that they needed it.

As well as timber being scarce, carpenters were in short supply in wartime Britain since only men over forty and women were allowed to work in the furniture industry from 1941: younger men were liable for conscription, or to be drafted into essential war work. Various schemes were considered to deal with the acute furniture shortage, including quota allocations and the imposition of a swingeing rate of purchase tax. There were two considerations: on the one hand, a great deal of materials and effort should not be allowed to go into making elaborate furniture for those who could pay for it. On the other hand, there was the danger that furniture manufacturers would turn out shoddy stuff and sell it at inflated prices to people who simply had to have *some* furniture whatever its cost or quality. Prices were controlled, but quality had to be controlled too.

The answer, as with clothes, was a standard specified design that would be simple, avoid unnecessary use of labour and materials, but be of sufficient quality to ensure that the furniture was useful and long-lasting.

Only twenty items of essential furniture were to be produced and gone were 'such comfortable pieces of furniture as deep-sprung armchairs and the conventional three-piece suite of two armchairs and a settee – a sacrifice made necessary by the shortage of springs and other materials needed for upholstery'. The designs were specified in a booklet produced by the Board of Trade with the help of 'one or two of the best available designers of furniture' including the distinguished Gordon Russell, who considered that 'to raise the whole standard of furniture of the mass of the people was not a bad war job'. The woods specified were oak or mahogany, and the designs were plain and thus simple and quick to make. As Edwin Clinch, one of the designers, wrote, 'All that you see with Utility furniture is pure, it's good . . . the more simple the furniture, the more precise must be the workmanship.' No distracting, labour-absorbing ornamentation was allowed. Utility furniture looks refreshingly minimalist-out-of-the-Arts-and-Crafts-movement to modern eyes, since as Gordon Russell noted, 'austerity and utility have useful astringent qualities'. But to many people in wartime Britain, it looked drab with no barley-sugar turned legs, or Grinling Gibbons-inspired swags. So 'sound, plain and functional' in fact, that some keen do-it-yourselfers would get going with their chisels carving scrolls, rosettes and other decoration in the wood.

A Utility-furniture preview exhibition was held in London in October 1942. It attracted more than 30,000 visitors and subsequently toured the country to show people what they could expect. The *Architects' Journal* sneered that the furniture 'was very ugly to look at' and the furniture trade journal the *Cabinet Maker* reported the comment 'good, solid and sensible . . . that's just what the public doesn't like'. In fact the general public was prepared to concede that the furniture was certainly of good quality (if dull), and it was its availability that interested them more than anything else. Hugh Dalton was very proud of the Utility furniture scheme and was often heard to regret that he was ineligible to procure some for his own home. The Ministry of Information felt satisfied too. 'There is no doubt that the success of the scheme has been remarkable, both in effecting big savings in labour, and in ensuring a distribution which is widely applauded for its fairness. More surprising is the fact that, as with Utility clothing, the need for economy has been turned into a definite and positive advantage by designers and that there has been a real, and no doubt permanent, rise in the standard of public taste.' Or, as Edwin Clinch put it, 'Furniture never went back to how it was before the war — thank God!'

Utility furniture was available only to 'priority classes' who had a permit, and these were issued only to people who had been bombed out, or to newly-weds setting up home for the first time, though there were a few concessions for those who had to move in with parents. Each item of furniture required a certain number of units in addition to the purchase price (which was controlled by the government) – a wardrobe took eight units, for example, a kitchen or dining room chair, one. Bed-settees were available for fifteen units, but only to people living in bed-sitters who had to thus combine their living and sleeping accommodation. No permit was needed for cots, playpens or high chairs and, towards the end of the war, those entitled to furniture were also allowed to obtain curtain material, which, until then, had required the surrender of precious clothes coupons. In the first few months after the scheme came into operation in January 1943, 18,500 'furniture permits' were issued.

Mattresses, quilts and sheets, pillowcases and towels (which to the chagrin of most housewives needed clothing coupons) and pottery all came under the Utility scheme – though pottery was known as 'Victory ware' rather than Utility, which it wasn't strictly anyway, since apart from forbidding decoration (including handles on cups sometimes) and inessential items, the Board of Trade did not provide any specifications to Wedgwood, its manufacturers. Utility pencils (without paint or varnish, though the lead was supposed be 'near pre-war quality') were produced, as were Utility cigarette lighters (since wood for matches was in such short supply).

In such a regulated world, the notion that 'beauty is duty' could sound an injunction too far. Yet the face of the wartime woman was a site of contested signifiers. On the one hand it could seem irremediably frivolous to fuss about lipstick, powder, a shampoo and set and nail polish as bombs rained down and the demands of war production pressed deeper. On the other, a bright slash of lipstick, softly waved hair and a lingering trace of perfume could be seen to represent the persistence of the feminine in a masculinised world of war, a sparky message of defiance, a feisty semaphore of hope, seen at the lathe, in the fish queue, in the air-raid shelter.

When the war news was bad Nella Last cheered herself up by 'slipp[ing] on a gay flowered dress, an old one but I love it for its bright colours. I put rouge and lipstick on – I needed them for I looked a haggard sight . . .' And she reflected that the war had changed her from a 'retiring' woman to one 'who uses too bright lipstick, and on dim days, makes the corners turn up when the lips will not keep smiling'.

By 1942 the supply of cosmetics had fallen to less than a quarter of the immediate pre-war level. The chemicals used in cosmetics were needed to make munitions, and factories that manufactured beauty products in peacetime had increasingly switched to products more directly linked to the needs of war. The Cyclax factory, for example, was concentrating on making creams to protect the skins of the soldiers fighting in North Africa, while at Yardley's more capacity was devoted to making aircraft components and sea-water purifiers than to making lipsticks. In the 1930s the falling prices of mass-produced goods had brought cosmetics within the reach of a large number of women – particularly young women: according to a wartime social survey two-thirds of all women wore make-up, and 90 per cent of those under thirty did. And with clothes rationing, Utility clothes and uniforms, make-up was one wartime 'luxury' that most women were very reluctant to forgo. Cosmetics were never rationed, since the government recognised their morale-boosting properties for a female population who had few other opportunities to express their femininity and individuality – indeed, it granted special rations of good-quality face powder to all women munitions workers in August 1942. But in general production was severely restricted and all legitimately produced cosmetics were in very short supply. A black market flourished from early on in the war, with respectable retailers prepared to stock brands they knew were illegally produced; and many women, who were usually scrupulous about conforming to rationing regulations, were quite prepared to take the opportunity of clinching an 'under the counter deal' when it came to cosmetics and toiletries. Most women became as creative with their ersatz make-up as they were with their make-over clothes: lipstick ends were crumbled into an egg cup standing in a saucepan of hot water to melt, and mixed with cold cream to make rouge. Eyelashes were brushed with castor oil and burnt cork, shoe polish (when that was still available) or even soot when there was no mascara to be had. Used tea leaves in muslin bags were used as a face mask; while 'a teaspoon of Eau-de-Cologne, poured into an almost empty perfume bottle, will give you extra perfume' since scent such as pre-war favourites 'Evening in Paris' and 'California Poppy' had become a luxury only to be dreamed of. 'Powdered camphor blended with cold cream will make a whitening handcream' as would lemon juice, and when cold cream was unobtainable, women would rub a little lard on their skin, or even, in desperation, smooth the greaseproof paper that had wrapped the margarine over their faces – if they hadn't used every last smidgeon for cooking.

Wartime discourse was complicit with the idea that a beautiful face was a brave face. 'No surrender' ran an advertisement for Yardley above a picture of a serious-looking woman in uniform. 'War gives us a chance to show our mettle. We wanted equal rights with men; they took us at our word. We are proud to work for victory beside them. And work is not our only task. We must triumph over routine; keep the spirit of light-heartedness. Our faces must never reflect personal troubles. We must achieve masculine efficiency without hardness. Above all, we must guard against surrender to personal carelessness. Never must we consider careful grooming a quisling gesture. With leisure and beauty-aids so rare, looking our best is specially creditable. Let us face the future bravely and honour the subtle bond between good looks and good morale. Put your best face forward . . .' It was just as well, Quentin Crisp must have reflected, that 'when war was declared' and others were stocking up on sugar and flour and candles and torch batteries, he 'went out and bought two pounds of henna'.

Cyclax named one of its lipstick colours Auxiliary Red – 'the lipstick for service women'. Those who had 'to stay in khaki' shouldn't 'despair – there is a lovely new make-up for you especially created for this rather trying colour. Its name is "Burnt Sugar" . . .' Peggy Sage advertised 'a discreet . . . subtle range of pale [nail] polish shades for those in uniform . . . but when women are in mufti – and what an exciting flavour that dull word has now that women have stolen it from men! – they gaily take their finger-tips out of uniform and turn to Peggy Sage's more burning colours, FEZ, a dark clear red, vibrant and exciting, is an especial favourite . . .' And Tampax, the 'internal sanitary protection', saw the opportunity to promote their product (at a time when many menstruating women still used rags which would have to be soaked in salt water) that was offered by women working 'in a man's job [where] there's no time for "not so good days" . . . war work won't wait . . . a man's job doesn't allow for feminine disability. Tampax . . . has come to the rescue of thousands of women on service. It gives new freedom, complete comfort . . .' And it could be bought from the NAAFI, as could cosmetics when they were available.

Such advertisements, and articles in women's magazines, served several purposes: they were about gratification deferred, keeping brands that were in short supply or unobtainable in women's minds so that they 'would ask for them again when the war's over'. This applied to unobtainable household goods too, and most of the more elegant high fashions pictured in magazines were strictly for export only, and not in the shops. Such copy was also intended to keep up women's morale – and, paradoxically, it was about taking women more seriously, recognising that they were out there in the public sphere, that the home was on the Home Front. That they were part of the wartime agenda. The sales of women's magazines increased (doubled in the case of *Woman's Own*).

The Ministry of Information used several as a vehicle for its Home Front propaganda, and established a committee comprised of the editors of the magazines (and others whom it considered represented the interests of British women) who could be seen as speaking to, and on behalf of, women.

But the 'duty' that conscripted women's 'beauty' to the war effort was a duty to boost not only their morale, but men's too. 'Stay lovely for him' was a common refrain. 'It is axiomatic,' *Vogue* told its readers in 1941, 'that the good spirits of the fighting men depend on the civilians and more particularly the female of the species. And what do hers depend on? Well, largely on clothes . . . this business of looking beautiful is largely a duty.' Women had to make many sacrifices in wartime, but they should not let it look as if they had when their men came home.

In December 1942, amidst all the shortages and making do and daily grind of wartime, the first down payment on a better future seemed to have been made with the publication of what Tommy Handley, in his *ITMA* role as 'His Fatuity the Minister of Social Hilarity', called ' "Gone with the Want" by that stout fellow, Beveridge'. The nation had been reading the report of 'that stout fellow' too. William Beveridge was a civil servant who had 'learned the meaning of poverty and saw the consequences of unemployment' when, as a young man, he had worked as researcher at Toynbee Hall in London's East End.

In June 1941 Beveridge, who between the wars had been Director of the London School of Economics, was appointed Chairman of the Social Insurance Committee. He seized his opportunity and resolved that 'the time has now come to consider social insurance as a whole, as a contribution to a better new world after the war'. The government had hoped that the report would not be published until the war was over, but Beveridge drove his committee hard and produced a blueprint for the future that forced peacetime aims on to the political agenda and brought Beveridge the sobriquet 'father of the welfare state'.

Beveridge's findings were published on 1 December 1942. The night before publication long queues started to form outside His Majesty's Stationery Office's London headquarters in Kingsway, to buy copies of 'this heavy two-shilling slab of involved economics'. It was an instant best-seller: more than 100,000 copies were sold in the first month and the combined sales of the full report and a 3d abridged official summary eventually exceeded 600,000. Not until the Denning Report into the Profumo scandal in 1963 was HMSO to publish another such winner. The day after publication Mass-Observation found that 92 per cent of people in a random sample knew of the report's existence, and this was confirmed by a nationwide survey a fortnight later. Moreover 88 per cent thought the government should implement it.

The BBC broadcast extracts of the report in twenty-two languages, hundreds of copies were shipped to the United States, and Army Bureau of Current Affairs (ABCA) pamphlets containing a summary were prepared for distribution among British troops, but were withdrawn two days later on the orders of the War Office. Newspapers gave saturation coverage. The *Daily Mirror* devoted a page to 'How to be born, bred and buried by Beveridge'. The *Daily Herald* set out the benefits in tabular form and used a fictional working-class family, the Johnsons, to show their 'Life in Beveridge Britain' where they were able to 'manage nicely' thanks to social security. In the weeks after publication, 'the People's William', as Beveridge had become in historian Paul Addison's phrase, toured the country packing town, village and church halls – lobbying for the acceptance of the report.

The genesis of the Beveridge Report lay in pre-war social conditions of poverty and unemployment. The solution he proposed was not revolutionary – or, rather, it was a very British revolution of slow, incremental change, springing out of 'what has already been accomplished in building up security piece by piece'.

The report's proposals basically rationalised and unified the existing complex and unsatisfactory benefits system, and provided a minimum standard of living when a person's ability to earn his or her living was interrupted through illness, old age or unemployment. It was a system essentially based on the principle of insurance: people paid their own way and individual thrift was thus required. The implementation of Beveridge's report would launch an attack on the five 'giants . . . on the road to a just society, those of Want, Disease, Ignorance, Squalor and Idleness'. But rationalising the benefits system was only part of the onslaught on want (Beveridge did not use the word poverty): its co-ordinates – its underpinnings – were in fact much more far-reaching.

There was to be a State allowance for children, a national health service 'available to all members of the community . . . without a charge on treatment at any point' (the most radical feature, and the one that held the greatest appeal for most people), and 'full use of powers of the state to maintain employment and to reduce unemployment' – the spectre that had haunted the 1930s, but had been largely banished by the demands of war production, which had revived many of those industries where it had bitten deepest.

The appeal of Beveridge was clear in its name-shift. What had been a report was, within days, being referred to as a 'plan', something that could be implemented by a State that in wartime had been prepared to seize hold of the economy, take charge of resources, production and people, dictate what could be made and what could be bought. When the report was published Beveridge had insisted that 'the purpose of victory is to live in a better world than the old world', and added that 'each individual citizen is more likely to concentrate upon his war effort if he feels that his Government will be ready with plans for that better world'. With his report coming so soon after victory at El Alamein and the North African landings, it really did seem in the New Year of 1943 that there would be a future to look forward to, but that it could no longer be left to chance: a better peacetime world (whenever that might be) must be planned for in wartime. But could the politicians be trusted to give their approval to a blueprint for a New Jerusalem to be built after the war?

The 'Tory line seems to be to welcome the report in principle,' confided Harold Nicolson, the Bloomsbury-fringe National Labour MP, 'and then to whittle it away by detailed criticism. They will say that it is splendidly Utopian, but we can only begin to know whether we can afford it once we have some idea what our foreign trade will be like after the war.'

Labour politicians hardly seized the ball Beveridge had 'thrown into the scrum' and ran with it either. Bevin reported (erroneously) that his old sparring partner had produced a report that would upset the unions. Attlee was broadly in favour, but limp when it came to pressing for its implementation; only Herbert Morrison raised the flag, arguing in the War Cabinet the moral bankruptcy that the defeat of the report would mean 'to a nation bearing the full burden of total war'. In response to the question 'Can we afford to do this?' Morrison replied, 'Can we afford not to do it?' But the War Cabinet decided they *could* afford not to: for the time being, defence must take absolute priority and no definite commitment to expenditure on the social services could be given.

Since the wartime government was a coalition, Morrison, the plan's most persistent advocate in Cabinet, was obliged to wind up the debate defending the government's refusal to act. When the vote came, 119 voted against: it was the biggest revolt of the war, uniting a number of Liberals (including Lloyd George who was voting for the last time in the Commons in favour of a welfare state he had helped to instigate in 1908), Labour and Independent MPs, one Communist and two Conservatives against the government.

The government's lukewarm attitude to the Beveridge Report convinced a large number of the public that under Conservative steerage the world that emerged from the privations and hardships of war would be no fairer than the one that had gone to war in 1939. In six by-elections in the weeks around the Beveridge debate, the Conservative vote fell significantly, even though under the wartime party truce no official Labour or Liberal Party candidate stood. But left-wing 'Independent Labour' candidates (one was Aneurin Bevan's wife Jennie Lee) and supporters of the new 'Common Wealth Party' challenged the wartime consensus. The Common Wealth Party, the result of a merger between the 1941 Committee, an informal discussion 'ginger' group of the 'progressive establishment', and Sir Richard Acland's Forward Party, was launched in 1942 at a time of great despair about the way the government seemed to be muddling through the war and had no vision for the peace – a perception forged after the loss of Tobruk in the bleak days of November 1941. Acland, an ex-Liberal MP, ran what was in essence a socialist Christian moral crusade and attracted a substantial following among the apolitical middle classes with promises to nationalise industry and banish private property and replace it with classless common ownership. At its peak the Common Wealth Party boasted 300 branches and some 12,000 members, a fifth of whom were in the Forces. During the wartime electoral truce the party won three spectacular by-election victories at the expense of the Conservatives. Although it did not survive into the harsh realities of post-war party politics, the Common Wealth Party's slogan 'Beveridge in Full Now' was another indication of how the plan (or report) crystallised discontent and aspirations in the middle years of the war.

Churchill, who invariably snorted that victory was a sufficient war aim, and had serious concerns about the financial implications of the report's proposals for a country that he knew would come out of the war very deeply in debt to the United States, realised that a political error had been made. In March 1943 the warrior Prime Minister admitted that his was also the duty 'of peering through the mists of future to the end of the war' and promised a plan – including 'national compulsory insurance for all classes and all purposes from the cradle to the grave'. This would be put to the electorate after the war and implemented by the government of the time.

In November 1943 Churchill did what he had refused to do until the Beveridge furore and set up a Ministry of Reconstruction, moving Lord Woolton, with his sure populist touch, across from the Ministry of Food to head it. The following year a series of White Papers were published outlining proposals to slay several of Beveridge's 'five giants'. While those dealing with full employment and health were fudged, since there was insufficient coalition consensus to allow them to be translated into concrete proposals, social security provision stuck closely to Beveridge's recommendations, and the proposals that resulted in the 1944 Education Act were seen (by most people) as an attack on ignorance and a step towards a more equal society – at least for the post-war generation.

Picture Post assumed that people's hopes for the future centred on a post-war world of international peace, social justice, better housing, educational opportunities and enough to eat. They certainly homed in on personal, quotidian things. On not being tired, going back to your old job with your old workmates again or starting a new career, picking up the dropped threads of an education or training, being safe, going home, being together again, being able to buy things on a whim, stopping being anxious, and stopping being bored.

But the point was, as Attlee, the Labour leader, realised, the war had already 'necessitate[d] great readjustments and new departures in the economic and industrial life of the nation'. Wartime expediencies already offered a model for a better post-war world: some of these were supplementary old-age pensions to combat rising prices, and the spread of welfare provision for children in the form of school meals, milk, vitamins and vaccination against infectious diseases. Maybe the 2,000 British Restaurants that had opened between the Blitz and September 1943 offering plain fare for a very reasonable price would be another. Opinions were mixed. Frances Partridge, already rather defeated by the loss of her cook and her husband Ralph's not very helpful assertion that for a woman not to be able to cook was akin to a man being impotent, found the British Restaurant at Swindon prophetic but in an infinitely depressing way. In August 1943 the Partridges followed 'a series of notices . . . to a huge elephant-house, where thousands and thousands of human beings were eating as we did an all-beige meal, starting with beige soup thickened into the consistency of paste, followed by beige mince full of lumps and garnished with beige beans and a few beige potatoes, thin beige apple stew and a sort of skilly. Very satisfying and crushing, and calling up a vision of our future Planned World – all beige also.'

There undoubtedly was a certain beigeness in the air in 1943, a dilute version perhaps of being 'browned off' – a little less active, rather more a sense of flatness for the duration. But there were those who were already able to peer through this wartime gloom. Winifred Williams was one who could see way beyond the soggy cabbage and over-brewed tea. She found in a north country British Restaurant a metaphor for a better world. 'It was quite a pleasant place . . . with yellow walls and small square tables and shiny chairs. I sat between two workmen who swallowed food and news simultaneously (steamed ginger pudding, the *Daily Herald* and the *Daily Express*): a pretty girl in pretty clothes joined us. Black coats and blue overalls seemed to mingle without being aware of their difference in status. This is a very democratic place, I thought, looking to see what my neighbour's paper was saying about Stalingrad . . .

'And as I drank my penny cup of tea I was dreaming – of People's Restaurants of the future, when the war is over and won, of finely decorated buildings with paintings hung on the pale walls, of a gay democracy eating delicious lunches at a price the poorest could afford. The Minister of Food has built something bigger and better than he knows: having once given restaurants to the people will he, when the war is over, snatch them for ever away?

'. . . And having thrown up thousands of fine civic restaurants throughout the land, I started building new schools and new factories, blocks of workers' flats, terraces of shapely houses, fine city streets. And why not? I asked myself, striding to the counter with my tray, looking at the vigorous faces of the workers around me. Why not? They will never again be able to tell us that we haven't any cash. For a country that can finance this sort of war can pay for that sort of peace.'

21

STRIKERS, LOOTERS, TARTS AND SLITHY TOVES

Born with all arms he sought a separate peace.
Responsibilities loomed up like tanks,
And since his manhood marked him of our ranks
He threw if off and scrambled for release . . .
JOHN MANIFOLD, 'THE DESERTER'

IN WARTIME THE British committed more crimes. In 1939 there were 303,771 reported crimes in England and Wales: by 1945 the number had risen by 57 per cent to 478,394. But the difficulty of gathering statistics in wartime means that it is most likely that this number was a gross under-estimate – certainly when it came to such offences as black marketeering.

As the Commissioner of the Metropolitan Police explained in September 1939, crime rose in wartime because there were simply more laws to break. Crimes – acts punishable by law – were added to the wartime statute book by the Emergency Powers (Defence) Bill passed on 24 August 1939, which was renewed on an annual basis throughout the war. In theory all existing laws were set aside. In future ministers and departments would issue new regulations as Orders in Council, which would have the force of law. The government was empowered to enter and search any premises; to prosecute and punish offenders, detaining indefinitely and without trial those whose detention 'appears expedient'; and to suspend or alter any existing laws.

Regulations were abundant and often complicated – the Lighting (Restrictions) Order published in 1942, for example, ran to 'some thirty-three articles and innumerable sub-paragraphs' concerning blackout regulations – but ignorance was no defence. Some crimes were entirely specific to the situation of war: being unable to produce an identity card when required to, entering a restricted zone without a permit, rationing offences, 'defeatist talk', absenteeism at work – and of course contravening blackout regulations. Others were acts that would be crimes in peacetime, but which war made more reprehensible – stealing food and goods from the workplace, sabotaging machinery involved in war production, taking advantage of the blackout to mug pedestrians, stealing from bombed-out properties.

Prosecutions paralleled the course and anxieties of the war. In the first months of the Phoney War, most charges related to contraventions of blackout regulations – in 1940 alone 300,000 people were charged with this – or to 'profiteering' by charging more than the government-regulated price for goods: the fervent capitalist search for profit in the marketplace, which had been so applauded before the war, had become a wartime crime with the punishment a fine of £100, three months in prison or both. When rationing was introduced in December 1940, a whole new range of criminal offences came before the courts. After the fall of France and the evacuation of Dunkirk, 'defeatist' talk was taken very seriously, and spreading 'despondency and alarm' (saying for example 'We can never win the war' in a public place) could result in a fine or prison sentence. And with the threat of invasion, anything that had a whiff of 'fifth column' activity, including inadvertently entering any restricted zones that had been established round the coast, accounted for an increasing number of prosecutions. During the Blitz looting was treated as a particularly heinous crime, and, as the war progressed, productivity became a key issue: the workforce became more tightly regulated; any behaviour that was seen to act against the national interest in the workplace was liable to prosecution. At one end of the spectrum were cases of deliberate sabotage, like that of a young woman working in a Birmingham munitions factory on a secret incendiary bullet who deliberately left out vital screws, which meant that any plane that fired them could have exploded. She was prosecuted under the Treachery Act in 1942. Way further down the scale, but nevertheless potentially injurious to the war effort, were strikes, absenteeism or the refusal to take a job as directed, and these offences would be more likely to result in prosecution as the war dragged on and the controls on labour tightened.

Rationing offences covered the waterfront of criminal activity, from shopkeepers who kept a 'little something under the counter' for favoured customers, or who were prepared to take money over the odds but not demand coupons for goods, to housewives who continued to use the ration book of a deceased relative; from individuals selling coupons (selling clothing coupons, for perhaps the 10s or 12s 6d a book could command, was a real temptation for poor families who could not afford to buy the clothes the coupons entitled them to), to full-scale ration-book heists and forgery. And the small-scale offence could not exist without the larger operation of the black market. A journalist wrote in September 1941 about the 'wholesale evasion' of rationing regulations that he had observed in Romford market in Essex, where no coupons at all seemed to exchange hands between customers and stallholders. The goods that the stallholders were trading on the black market so freely must have been supplied in defiance of the law by a wholesaler who probably obtained them illegally from a manufacturer. If such a web were unpicked, all involved would be prosecuted, including the customer.

The operation of official regulations almost encouraged another scam in the early months of war: retailers handed in envelopes of loose food coupons at the post-office counter in return for vouchers rather than rubber-stamping ration books, but the General Post Office would never have the manpower necessary to check the contents of every envelope. So envelopes containing any scraps of paper other than coupons

In raids on Clydebank in March 1941 only seven of the 12,000 tenements were reported to have completely escaped damage. Victims of the raids survey their salvaged possessions. The Glasgow/Clydeside area suffered a further major attack on 6/7 May.

A policeman stands among the ruins of County Road in Walton, Liverpool after a parachute mine fell during the May Blitz in 1941 'the worst continuous battering any people yet had'.

The burnt-out façade of the International Bar at the corner of York Street and Donegall Street in Belfast after the raid of 4/5 May 1941. Parts of the city were left unrecognisable, 'just smouldering rubble', and it was forty-eight hours before some fires were finally extinguished.

The pianist Myra Hess playing at a lunchtime concert in the National Gallery. The bare-walled gallery was usually packed even at the height of the Blitz. 'The unrolling world of the music overwhelmed them,' wrote John Strachey. 'How could there exist such worlds as this, and that.'

An Entertainments National Service Association (ENSA) party at its Drury Lane Headquarters prepares to go out on tour. At the end of the war *Picture Post* concluded that ENSA had both 'provided a hideout for ham actors' and created a new audience for Shakespeare.

A portrait class where students at the Royal College of Art, which was evacuated to Ambleside on Lake Windemere for the duration, 'paint mostly local characters… in makeshift hotels and barns.'

'The demand now is not for easel pictures, but for murals and decorations for public buildings, – for canteens… children's nurseries, hostels, factories.' The surrealist painter, Julian Trevelyan, at work on a Russian scene for a British Restaurant.

Women of the Auxiliary Territorial Service (ATS) trying to get a six-wheel Army vehicle out of the mud. The largest – though not always the most popular – of the women's services, the ATS peaked at 206,200 in March 1944 when this photograph was taken.

'Come into the Factories.' Sixty-two-year old Edith Leath, one of the many older women who responded to the call for women to help the war effort, working as an acetylene welder in a munitions factory producing shells.

Two Land Girls of the 80,000 members of the Women's Land Army – 'a one-rank force where hard physical labour was the order of the day' – master the art of the straight furrow in October 1942.

The Women's Timber Corps, a section of the Women's Land Army, at Bury St Edmunds, Suffolk. The combination of an open-air life and more regular hours than Land Girls worked on farms proved popular and by the end of 1942 there were nearly 5,000 'pole cats'.

Italian Prisoners of War, wearing a distinctive red circle on the back of their uniform to deter escape, help with the harvest 'somewhere in England' in August 1941. By the end of the war there were 153,779 Italian POWs held in Britain.

A German Prisoner of War hangs out his washing while his compatriots play football at Camp 186 near Colchester in Essex. By May 1945, 381,632 German POWs were held in Britain.

A 'Jim Crow Army' comes to Britain. US policy was not to 'intermingle' black and white enlisted men, and the 100,000 black GIs in Britain were in segregated units, often doing manual work, until high casualty rates by late 1944 meant they too were sent into battle.

Anglo-American co-operation. There were 1.65 million US troops in Britain on the eve of D-Day, 6 June 1944. GIs moving slowly towards the south coast ready to embark while away the time entertaining local children.

An ARP warden surveys the damage caused by a V-1 flying bomb in Aldwych, London at lunchtime on 30 June 1944. A victim lies dead amidst the rubble on the pavement. 5,375 were killed by V-1s, 15,258 were seriously injured and by August 18,000 houses had been totally destroyed.

VE Day, 8 May 1945.
Allied excitement in the streets of London as women workers from the Picture Division at the War Information Office dance with their opposite numbers from the US Army division.

Churchill prepares to speak to the VE Day crowds in London. His Cabinet including Ernest Bevin (*second left*), Herbert Morrison (*far right*) and Lord Woolton (*next to Morrison*) join him on the balcony of the Ministry of Health in Whitehall.

VJ Day. Chinese waiters in London read of the surrender of Japan on 10 August 1945. Their countries had been at war since 1937: in December 1941 the Japanese declared war on the United States. Atomic bombs dropped on Hiroshima and Nagasaki ended the war in the Pacific.

'Face the Future.' Clement Attlee, the Labour party leader, ex-member of the wartime coalition government and future Prime Minister, campaigns in his Limehouse Stepney constituency, east London, on 5 July 1945.

(including torn-up telephone directories in the case of three Stepney youths who were prosecuted for the offence) passed through the system. The vouchers were then sold on to retailers who could claim extra goods on them. Dishonest officials in food offices sold coupons or exchanged them for rationed goods; men and women claimed replacement ration books for those they had lost – some had and some hadn't – but in the first year of clothes rationing 800,000 people claimed to have been careless in this way. A number of ration books were 'lost in the post' when a temporary postman made off with them, while other officials stole coupons due for pulping. If a burglar broke into a house and found ration books lying around, that would be a welcome part of the haul, and on a much larger scale professional thieves raided places where ration books were known to be stored – either food office premises or the printers. In the summer of 1944, 14,000 newly issued ration books, valid for a year, were stolen in a Hertfordshire raid, and were soon changing hands for around £5 in pubs – a £70,000 profit, when in 1939 a three-bedroomed house in a leafy London suburb could be had for well under £1,000. By 1944 there were so many stolen ration books in circulation that the price had fallen to £1.

The demand for clothing coupons made them a more valuable currency than food ration books. Touts disposed of stolen coupons in hotel bars, pubs, nightclubs and restaurants, and made rich pickings. In September 1943 5 million coupons intended for the purchase of civilian clothes for officers and men discharged from the Army – the allowance for some quarter of a million people – were stolen from an Army store near Wandsworth in south-west London. The haul would have flooded the market, so the Board of Trade invalidated the entire issue, and police suspicions that it must have been an inside job – as such thefts often were – proved to be correct.

As well as being stolen, coupons were forged. The owners of printing presses that before the war had produced tote tickets or pornography found it more lucrative to run off clothing and petrol coupons. The official coupons were hurriedly and crudely printed and much easier to counterfeit than banknotes, as well as being less familiar to those handling them. Detection was usually possible because the paper on which the fake coupons were printed was superior to that of the genuine article, or because elementary spelling mistakes – sum for some, for example –

aroused suspicion. Nineteen men – a number of them substantial businessmen – stood trial in Manchester in May 1942 for crimes involving forged clothing coupons. The connection spread from a basement printing press in Salford through wholesalers in the north to London, with the forgers being sufficiently astute to mix genuine coupons in with the forgeries. Counterfeit clothing coupons continued to seep into the market throughout the war – a sheet of forged coupons could be bought for £10 from a pavement tout working Oxford Street – but the swindlers proved hard to track down, and prosecutions were rare.

Petrol was a much coveted wartime commodity for many, since fuel for private motoring was banned from 1942. Periodically the police would swoop on race meetings and interrogate car owners about how they had managed to get the petrol to drive to the course, but in fact counterfeit petrol coupons had a less ready outlet than those for clothing. Since the majority of the population were banned from filling up with petrol, any such transaction was likely to arouse the interest of the police. 'Petrol crimes' were more likely to involve spurious claims for a supplement on the grounds of 'a necessary business allowance' or 'essential war work', and though this did not mean that there was not an active market for forged petrol coupons among the criminal fraternity, fewer filtered down to the general public.

Identities were forged as well as coupons. The National Registration Act which passed into law on 1 September 1939 had made it compulsory for everyone to carry an identity card, green for adults, brown for those under sixteen. That meant 46 million cards, each bearing a combination of letters and numbers that identified where the card was issued and which family or household the bearer belonged to. An ID card had to be produced on request and, without it, it was not possible to obtain ration books, to prove ineligibility or otherwise for military service, or to comply with a morass of other wartime regulations. Forged cards found a ready market among those who wanted to avoid call-up, those who had deserted from the Forces and needed a civilian identity, and those who wished, for whatever nefarious purpose, to assume another persona.

Corrupt medical practitioners could be bribed to produce certificates for exemption or discharge from military service. Dr William St John

Sutton of Stepney was well known for his willingness to produce such certificates without ever seeing the would-be draft dodger, and for this possibly life-saving service he charged only half a crown. In January 1943 Dr Sutton was jailed for nine months. A crook with a crippled leg was reputed to charge a flat fee of £150 to those who wished him to impersonate them at medical boards. Twenty-year-old Jack Brack, of Brick Lane in east London, had a heart condition. For a fee he was prepared to hire out his disability and impersonate another – fit – man at a medical board, and so in demand were his services that his charges soared to £200, which a master tailor thought was a fair price to pay to keep out of the military, even though his weekly wage was probably around £10 a week. Sometimes one man would impersonate another in a misguided act of friendship and no money would change hands, though of course this was still a criminal offence.

Being in a reserved occupation could also keep a man out of the Forces, and those who did not wish to face the loss of earnings or of a business that would have to close, or who were cowardly, or both, might be prepared to pay for documents that falsified their status. A Liverpool city councillor was sent to prison for seven years and fined £2,000 in 1942 for providing such documents for numbers of his business employees. Shady minor officials could sometimes be bribed to alter classifications or, even more simply, 'mislay' papers. A temporary civil servant in Leytonstone in east London managed to 'lose' five sets of papers for £20 a time. A plumber was approached by another temporary civil servant, this time from Islington, who offered to get him 'out of the Home Guard for fifty bob' since this had been included in the National Services Act (1942) which required everyone between the ages of eighteen and sixty to undertake some form of national service. All these crimes could lead to others: whoever supplied these dodgy documents had a hold over the purchaser, who could be blackmailed with the threat that unless further payments were made his papers might be 'found' again, or the 'error' on his form rectified.

Pilfering at work was hardly a unique wartime crime, but the conditions of war – shortages, deprivations, and a ready market for goods in short supply or unobtainable – gave it an unfortunate boost. Kate Phipps, a nurse, reported hearing the case of 'a highly respected lady secretary to a colliery (a leading light in the girl guides) [who] has been helping herself to the company funds over a long period in order to build herself a super air raid shelter with a special place for her parrot'. Such dishonesties could be for the perpetrator's own use, to supplement a family's meagre rations, or to make their wartime lives more comfortable. Often it was opportunistic crime, seizing the moment with the knowledge that good money could be got for the stolen goods.

Sometimes such light-fingeredness was enmeshed in poor pre-war industrial relations, when war increased rather than diminished workers' suspicions that their employer was exploiting them for the company's profit rather than the good of the nation. This was particularly the case in the industrially volatile Merseyside docks, where pilfering was rife at times during the war. Goods for export being loaded at Liverpool docks were regularly depleted by theft, with a variety of easily concealable goods like gin, whisky, cigarettes, tins of food and paint – and peroxide, almost unobtainable for bottle blondes by 1944 – being snitched. It was the same in factories, shops, depots, cinemas, railways, haulage firms, works canteens and other enterprises throughout the country. It appeared that 'virtually everything movable was in danger of being stolen. Shoes, handbags and nylons, (inevitably) but also "grosses of sanitary towels", sacks of sugar; bags of meat; 66,000 knives, forks and spoons from the canteens run by the London Passenger Transport Board (they cost £8,000 to replace); electric fires, dolls; "miscellaneous rubber goods"; radio sets, soap – all of this in the Hackney (east London) and Romford district only.'

Frequently employers were prepared to turn a blind eye to petty pilfering for the sake of good industrial relations and sustained productivity in the face of difficult and sometimes dangerous conditions, and called in the law only when the scale became unacceptable – £500 a week in the case of an Islington radio manufacturer – and clearly systematic in its supply lines to a wartime black market. In the Birkenhead docks a historian of crime, Edward Smithies, has traced a pattern that suggests that prosecutions were orchestrated according to the amount of co-operation needed from the workforce: thus during a campaign to get workers to register under a new scheme in 1941, no prosecutions for theft were reported, but once the campaign was over and only six dockers had failed to register, the prosecutions resumed.

Equally, as the scale of abuse grew, employers were increasingly less tolerant of what at a peacetime level was put down as an unavoidable business cost. They became less prepared to take an offender back, or speak up for him or her in court. Meanwhile magistrates who, in the early years of the war, were often surprisingly lenient, frequently seeming to regard the accused as having a moment of aberration brought on by the strains of war, gradually began to see such crimes as of wider national significance, as sabotaging the war effort rather than just ripping off the employer.

When it came to offences by career criminals, the rate fell by 10 per cent in the early months of the war. In the opinion of the Chief Constable of Essex this was 'probably due to the fact that a large number of youthful offenders, who previously operated from the East End . . . are now serving with HM Forces'. The consequence of this call-up of criminals was to be apparent on the French black market which a few members of the BEF supplied most generously prior to Dunkirk. But the crime rate soon started to rise again. Some previously law-abiding citizens also turned to criminal activities in wartime – sometimes schooled by military training – while others who already had criminal records found that the war offered undreamt-of new opportunities. The value of goods was enhanced by restrictions on production; the population was more transient and peripatetic, which meant homes were left unoccupied and people were harder to trace; while the black market as good as supplied a shopping list to the thief, professional as well as amateur. Rather than the usual lifting of paintings, silver, furs and jewellery from private houses, wartime criminals were more inclined to raid warehouses for large consignments of cigarettes and spirits that were quick to shift on the black market, and it was much harder to trace their provenance.

Then there was the welcome cover of the blackout and the Blitz for illegal activities. Scotland Yard estimated that during the first three months of 1941 gangs of safe-breakers had stolen £20,000 posing as the emergency services using vehicles painted to represent ARP ambulances. A lookout on a moonlit night would hint at a UXB or walls in danger of collapse to any inquisitive passer-by as the gang loaded their spoils.

The crump of bombs, the barrage of ack-ack fire and crash of falling shrapnel added to the blackout blanket to provide ideal cover for any noisy criminal activity. It was impossible to distinguish gelignite explosions from bombs, the noise of shattering glass caused by a brick from that shattered by a bomb. Safes were blown, money, valuables, share certificates – even war bonds – removed and the gang slipped out into the dark streets and the confusion of air-raid-response units.

There was the short-lived notoriety of the 'Blackout Ripper', who murdered four women – including one whose body was found in an air-raid shelter – and almost killed two more, under the cover of near-total darkness. A young RAF cadet, George Cummins, was found guilty of the crimes and hanged – during an air raid. In January 1943 Harry Dobkin was hanged for the murder of his wife, whose mutilated body he had dumped in a badly bomb-damaged Baptist chapel near where he was a fire-watcher, in the hope that she would appear to be another unidentifiable victim of the Blitz.

In the post-Dunkirk 'aliens scare', refugees who had come to expect a knock on the door could open it to find 'policemen' on the step who would drive them somewhere to 'wait' – while the crooks returned to the place where the refugees had been living and stripped it of everything saleable. There were billeting scams when householders claimed for evacuees or billetees long after they had left (or occasionally had never arrived). A cowboy building contractor and the Hammersmith Clerk of Works, who knowingly certified that severely sub-standard public air-raid shelters built in the borough were satisfactory, were charged with manslaughter after one of those 'brick coffins' collapsed when a bomb fell 30 yards away, killing many of its occupants. There were those 'authorised' to inspect locked shelters who, when given access, stripped them of every bunk and cooking facility, and individuals wrenched ladders and ventilation and escape-hatch covers from communal shelters, rendering them death traps in the event of a hit. There were swindlers who tricked money out of urban dwellers in return for a 'guaranteed' place in a deep shelter; those who charged grossly inflated prices to store shelter-bedding during the day; and there were thieves who were the beneficiaries of air-raid anxieties when, at the sound of the alert, citizens packed their life savings and small valuables into a bag to take with them to the shelter, and were relieved of everything as they huddled fearfully listening to the raids overhead. 'Nothing helped the recovery [of air-raid victims] more than the knowledge that their personal treasures were safe,' thought the Rev. John Markham. 'The usual practice of those who took shelter was to put all their cash, Savings Certificates, items of personal jewellery, and personal papers such as birth and marriage certificates in their handbags, which they kept under the chair on which they were sitting, or by their side, if they were in bed. As soon as it was daylight, I used to take two of my wardens, and tunnel through mountains of rubble to find these handbags. We dare not leave them even for a few hours, or they would be gone.'

After raids on Sheffield in December 1940, two full days of the Assize Court sitting had to be devoted to hearing charges of looting. The remarks of the presiding judge unfortunately could have applied equally to London, Manchester, Liverpool, Birmingham, Glasgow... 'When a great city is attacked by bombs on a heavy scale, numbers of houses and their contents are left exposed and deprived of their natural defences. Necessarily these are the homes of comparatively poor people, since they are by far the most numerous ... The task of guarding shattered houses from prowling thieves, especially during the blackout, is obviously beyond the capacity of any police force.' Looting seemed the most despicable crime: an act of meanness that made the perpetrators as odious as the German bombers that had levered open thousands of homes, sometimes killing or injuring the occupants and leaving rich pickings for the deeply unscrupulous. In the first two months of the Blitz, 390 cases of looting were reported (though it was announced in the House of Commons that the final number of looting cases for 1940 was 4,584 in London alone, and there was vague talk of appointing a 'Director of Anti-Looting'). The CID formed a 300-strong anti-looting force and the Lord Mayor of London urged that notices should be posted warning that 'the Legislature has provided that those found guilty of looting from premises damaged or vacated by reasons of attacks by the enemy are, on conviction, liable to suffer death or penal servitude for life. Thus the law puts looters into the category of murderers, and the day may well be approaching when they will be treated as such.' They never were (though in Germany looters were routinely shot), and the maximum penalty available to magistrates was three months' imprisonment, or remitting the case to a higher court where sentences could be exemplary.

Shocked, and perhaps bereaved or injured by an air raid, people would return to their homes in daylight to find not only piles of bricks and rubble, windows shattered and ceilings jagged lumps of plaster, but drawers ransacked, rooms standing empty of all their pictures and ornaments, wardrobes cleared and small items of furniture missing – as had happened to Gwladys and Ralph Cox in London's West Hampstead during the first months of the Blitz. When the couple returned to their mansion block flat the morning after it had been hit in October 1940, 'we wandered from room to room, our feet squelching in the saturated carpets . . . I found that my silver cigarette lighter had disappeared from its drawer. Under my bed, my trinket box was lying open, its contents scattered over the wet carpet. It had been taken out of the dressing table drawer, which had been forced, and everything of the least value removed. Ralph's room had been ransacked and most of his underclothing, as well as a gold watch, taken. All this the work of looters.'

Those who fled from the bombed areas could return to nothing but their blackout curtains flapping, in otherwise undamaged premises. A number of pre-war pickpocket gangs, and those petty criminals who operated at dog tracks and racecourses before the war, were known to take the opportunity of the Blitz – wherever it happened – to 'acquire' the things they knew they could dispose of. Dover, which had been largely evacuated when it was in the front line of German attack in the summer of 1940, suffered from the attention of such London gangs. Residents returning home in 1942 found that whole streets of bombed houses had been systematically stripped of everything: carpets, beds, suites of furniture, cookers – even heavy iron mangles.

On the morning of 17 April 1941, the Rev. John Markham had to 'borrow a ladder belonging to one of my wardens who was a window cleaner' to reach a top flat in a block round the corner from his rectory in Walworth, south London – the block had been bombed and the staircase destroyed. 'We let down on ropes all the furniture and other fittings we could find . . . I can picture to this day a tin bath, which we loaded with a complete dinner service, slowly and jerkily descending three floors on two ropes . . . We stored all we saved from this flat in the ruins of the crypt, from which Mr and Mrs Marsh were able to recover it when they came out of hospital . . . that made a lot of difference. If we had waited another day it would have been looted . . . a few days later a family of another of the blasted flats came to collect their furniture and found that a piano had been taken from an upstairs flat. Two other relatives came to ask me whether they could enter their old mother's flat in Merrow Street, which had been blasted and made unsafe, and I took them there, and found that all her trinkets, including her son's First World War medals, were gone. In fact, the very morning of the raid, the Borough Treasurer's men came to empty the gas and electric meters in the blasted flats, only to find that every one had been broken into and rifled. That was less than six hours after the bomb exploded . . . A rather more macabre side to the looting is illustrated by another precaution that I had to take when I recovered dead bodies. As soon as we found them, I had to put them in an empty room, under the guard of two wardens, until the stretcher party could remove them to the mortuary. Otherwise their clothes would be rifled, there in the midst of the darkness and dust, and falling bombs. It was a good thing I was not armed with a pistol or gun . . .

'A more comic side of looting was shown the same night. I arrived at the scene of the explosion within a couple of minutes of hearing it. I quickly found the body of one of my fire-watchers, lying in the rubble. Then I found his wife shouting and swearing her head off. "Some bleeder," she cried, "has nicked a couple of pounds of bacon I had in my meat safe." It transpired that the said meat safe was sitting on top of the rubble of the block, in which she had occupied the top flat. I do not think she knew then that her husband's dead body lay a few yards away . . . Shock can play funny tricks with people.'

Shops were particularly vulnerable: plate glass shattered by bomb blast opened up treasure troves of easily portable goods – watches, jewellery, silverware – for the opportunistic prowler who had worked out where the bombs were falling that night, and thought it worth risking the danger of the streets rather than taking shelter with his fellow citizens. But on the whole, those who regarded themselves as professional criminals left looting to the little people: they tended to turn to non-bombed areas in the suburbs and further out in the country, where houses were likely to be unoccupied and where a systematically planned, large-scale theft would yield much more than a looter could stuff into his pocket or bags before he bumped into a policeman or ARP warden hurrying to the 'incident'.

Those sent in to deal with bomb incidents were particularly well placed to loot. Sometimes gangs of soldiers detailed to clear bomb sites would appropriate any valuables they found among the debris, as well as loading sheets of lead from the roof – a commodity always easy to sell in the war – on to their lorry. In 1941, thirty-three Royal Engineers, including their NCOs, appeared at the Old Bailey in battledress, accused of stealing over 9 tons of lead from various houses they had been sent to clear or demolish. Four were acquitted. But the rest went to jail, including the sixty-three-year-old scrap-metal dealer who had been the receiver of the booty.

Looting could be a tragically elastic term: unforgivable acts of cruelty were perpetrated on occasions by neighbours, or ARP wardens, who took advantage of a bomb victim's absence in hospital to ensure their homecoming would be even more desolate, with the few precious possessions they had, gone. But some definitions of looting are impossible to condemn given the hellish conditions, gruellingly hard work and acts of courage and heroism of those labouring in the Blitz. An auxiliary fireman, for example, was sent to prison for five years for filling two buckets with food from a bombed-out grocer's shop (though this was quashed on appeal), and there were cases of ARP wardens being prosecuted for pocketing a few lumps of coal, picking up a couple of tins of food that were lying around, taking some sodden cardboard boxes that were no use to anyone. The man in charge of a Heavy Rescue Squad found a quarter-full bottle of gin among the ruins of a London pub which he passed round to revive the spirits of his fellow workers who had been labouring for hours to dig for victims of that particular bomb incident. Leonard Watson was sent to prison for this 'crime'.

Truly noxious wartime crimes – given that there were people in real need and that most authorities were working at full stretch – also included making false claims of having been bombed out to the national assistance office, where the claimants would be given the wherewithal to live, and replacement ration books and ID cards if these were claimed to have been lost. It was simply not possible to check every claim at the height of the bombing, though a Wandsworth man who claimed to have been bombed out nineteen times in five months was finally rumbled and sent to prison for three years in February 1941.

The volume of claims for repairs to property as a result of enemy action (genuine and not), delays in officials assessing the damage and general bureaucratic overload meant that people could wait for months to get any money. Step forward wartime loan sharks, who offered advances on the money in exchange for 'commission' that was invariably exorbitant.

Prosecutions for child cruelty and neglect increased during the war: 751 people were found guilty of these crimes in 1939; by 1944 there were more than twice as many. Though the strains of war may have made such abuse more prevalent, it seems unlikely that there were actually so many more cases. But evacuation schemes opened to the official gaze cases of gross neglect often amounting to deliberate cruelty – children covered in excreta, riddled with sores, scabies, lice, disfigured by cuts and bruises, ill-dressed and cold, starving hungry. And there was a righteous demand that once such atrocities had been brought out into the open, the perpetrators should be prosecuted.

But as well as children being protected, they too were increasingly brought to book in the war years. In 1939, some 52,000 under-seventeen-year-olds had been convicted in magistrates' courts; by 1941 the figure was 72,000, a rise of over 36 per cent. Again, the reasons were complex. Partly it was the dislocation of family life in wartime: there were 34.7 million changes of address during the war among a civilian population of around 45 million; families were split up, fathers away, mothers at work, children evacuated and schools sometimes able to offer only part-time education or closed altogether. At the end of 1940 it was estimated that 80,000 children of school age in London were receiving no education and were left to 'run wild' every day, and in Manchester in April 1941 the tally was 68,000. Magistrates tended to blame lack of parental control (even if that was often almost impossible in some wartime situations) or young people having too much money to spend, since an adolescent could earn as much as £6 a week. Frequently the 'crimes' fell into the category of youthful mischief (as the Commissioner of the Metropolitan Police recognised), such as stealing bikes and petty shoplifting.

Some magistrates were draconian in their treatment of the young offenders who were hauled before them; others recognised how seriously the times were out of joint, how short-changed by society so many children had been, and what temptations war offered the young as well as their elders. The Lord Chief Justice, who 'was no liberal', warned of the dangers of treating young offenders as 'outcasts of society', and the statistics showed how ineffective custodial sentences were in rehabilitating junior criminals in society. On the outbreak of war, in order to clear accommodation, it had been decided that all Borstal boys and girls in approved schools or remand homes who had served at least six months of their sentence would be released. But of the 2,817 boys set free under the scheme, 50 per cent of them were back inside again by 1943 and 56 per cent of the girls by 1946. It confirmed the opinion of some chief constables that Borstal and approved schools offered little more than apprenticeship schemes for crime, and that after-care, poor in the pre-war years, was all but non-existent during the war.

Given the growing demands on police time with the plethora of wartime regulations that could and would be broken every day, many forces instructed their men to try to caution youthful miscreants if their misdemeanours were relatively unimportant. The time-consuming and ultimately not very satisfactory process of prosecution should be reserved for those serious wartime crimes of major theft, damage, assault and gang violence committed by young people.

The imperatives of war brought another potential for criminality into the workplace. Strikes, which might have been considered a usual industrial mechanism in peacetime, were illegal under wartime Defence Regulations in recognition of the nation's need for maximum productivity. But such orders were hard to enforce. By 1942 the number of days lost through industrial action was back to its peacetime high. Employer/employee tensions could be exacerbated rather than assuaged by wartime conditions, and workers were often concerned that concessions they had made in working practices during the war would be fixed into the peace, and were wary about their employment prospects once war production began to wind down. A strike at Betteshanger Colliery in Kent in 1942 pointed up the problems. The dispute was about extracting coal from a newly opened seam that was so difficult to work that it was impossible for the miners to achieve their productivity target of 4 tons a day, no matter how hard they worked.

The arbitration process that had been put in place to settle such disputes in wartime found in favour of the mine owners, and on 12 January all 4,000 miners at the colliery, backed by their union, came out on strike. The strike presented the government with a dilemma. The Minister of Labour, Ernest Bevin, knew how vital the co-operation of the trade unions was to the war effort and his policies had all been designed to avoid confrontation wherever possible. What would be the effect of sending 4,000 miners to prison, even if it was remotely possible to do so? It was decided to prosecute only the 1,000 underground workers, but the threat of legal action, far from intimidating the striking miners, strengthened their resolve and they voted to stay out. The prospect was daunting. If every miner chose to plead not guilty, the cases would take years to get through the courts, and if they were found guilty, as was likely, the jails would be unable to contain 1,000 miscreants and imprisonment might have to operate on a shift system.

The court made it plain that it was not interested in the rights or wrongs of the men's pay claim: by striking in wartime, the miners had broken the law. Coal was a munition of war and the Betteshanger miners had not treated it as such. The three eloquent 'ringleaders' were all sentenced to jail and the rest given the choice of a fine or fourteen days' imprisonment.

Finally the Home Secretary, Herbert Morrison, broke the deadlock by ordering the immediate release of the imprisoned miners' leaders, and when it turned out that only nine of the miners had paid their £1 fine, the government advised the court not to pursue the defaulters with a warrant for their arrest.

After the Betteshanger dispute there were no more prison sentences passed on workers who contravened the anti-strike legislation, though in some cases magistrates imposed swingeing fines on individuals they found guilty. Always prone to see reds under the benches, Bevin was convinced that Trotskyite agitators were inciting industrial disaffection in the coalfields of Yorkshire and South Wales, and in April 1944, on the eve of the invasion of Europe, it was made an indictable offence punishable with draconian penalties to 'instigate or incite other persons . . . to take part in any stoppage . . . in the performance of essential services'. The legislation was never used. In the judicious words of the official historian of manpower in the Second World War, this 'obsession' with political hotheads was misguided. The explanation for strikes and go-slows lay in the legacy of poor pre-war industrial relations, the popular belief that bosses could profit from the war, while all the workers could do was be exploited: feelings intensified by a war weariness that could make bad working conditions seem quite intolerable.

There was one section of wartime society, however, that rarely made an appearance before a British judge or magistrate: the US troops who numbered over 1.5 million in the UK by May 1944. British soldiers who broke the law in war or peace would be tried by civilian courts; courts martial were reserved strictly for military transgressions. It was the same with Canadian and other Dominion or European troops who were in Britain for the duration. The Americans, however, were not prepared to put their troops under the jurisdiction of the British courts. The US State, War and Navy departments demanded exclusive jurisdiction over their Forces in Britain, arguing that theirs was largely a conscript Army that had been sent abroad against its will, and was thus 'on duty' all the time and should therefore be regulated by military law. It was another aspect of the 'cocoon' policy that created little bubbles of America all over Britain.

The US courts were very different from those the British judiciary were used to, with no wigs or gowns, the air thick with cigarette smoke and a feeling of informality. Cases were heard in a courtroom set up near the American Embassy in Grosvenor Square, or in buildings that were considered to impart an air of solemnity and tradition to the proceedings, with the Stars and Stripes nailed on the wall to indicate US home territory.

The proceedings may have seemed casual but the sentences could be punitive. The first trial under the terms of the Visiting Forces Act, which took place four days after it was passed, was of Private Travis Hammond who was accused of a sexual offence against a sixteen-year-old English shop assistant in an air-raid shelter. The facts were not easy to establish, and in the event the death sentence imposed was commuted.

Though a number of thefts by US troops involved their British counterparts in disposing of a haul of cigarettes or whisky or stockings on the black market, a particularly unfortunate example of Anglo–American co-operation was the so-called case of 'Chicago Joe and Blondie'. A twenty-two-year-old American deserter, Private Karl Hulten of the 501st Airborne Division, who was calling himself 'Lieutenant Ricky Allen', embarked on a crime spree with a blonde striptease artiste called 'Georgina Grayson', who was really eighteen-year-old Elizabeth Jones from Neath in South Wales. They attacked and robbed a young woman cyclist, assaulted another young woman with an iron bar, leaving her for dead, and climaxed by killing a taxi driver on the Great West Road, a desolate stretch of highway just outside London. For the first time the US authorities – who could not try Jones, a British citizen – agreed to hand over Hulten to the British courts. Both were found guilty and sentenced to death. Hulten was hanged at Pentonville prison on 8 March 1945: Jones was reprieved.

A disturbing aspect of US law enforcement in Britain was the number of racial crimes between the US troops themselves. It also became clear that more black GIs were prosecuted than white and that, if found guilty, they received longer and harsher sentences. Apart from the ineffectiveness of officers at some bases, morale problems with all-black units, and lax practices over storing arms and ammunition, the thread that ran through all these incidents was resentment at segregation on the part of the black GIs, and objections from white US troops to the blacks consorting with local girls.

Previous convictions had led to disquiet in Parliament about whether rape was a capital offence only when committed by black GIs. The notorious Leroy Henry rape case brought the issue centre stage in 'arguably the most widely publicised and discussed single incident during the whole American presence in Britain'. On 5 May 1944, a thirty-three-year-old woman from Combe Down, a suburb of Bath, claimed that a GI had come to the house asking for directions, while she was in bed with her husband; as she walked along the road allegedly pointing out the way he should take, he had pulled out a knife and threatened to kill her if she didn't have sex with him. The police were called, and some half a mile from where the incident had occurred Leroy Henry, a black truck driver from Missouri, was apprehended – without a knife.

He was handed over to the US authorities and, after having been kept in custody for more than fifteen hours, confessed to the assault.

When Henry stood in the dock, he claimed that his confession had been extracted under duress and that he had in fact met the woman twice before and had had sex with her on both occasions and paid her £1 each time. He claimed that on the night in question, he had gone to her house by arrangement, but this time the women had demanded £2 which Henry had refused to pay. The woman denied his version of events, but even the American officer who was prosecuting counsel found her actions in getting out of bed and walking off with 'a dark stranger rather odd'. Nevertheless the American colonel who was presiding over the trial found Henry guilty, and sentenced him 'by the unanimous vote of every member present to be hanged by the neck till dead'.

There was an immediate public outcry. Led by their Mayor, 33,000 citizens of Bath called for a reprieve since it seemed that a gross miscarriage of justice had occurred. Letters appeared in the press expressing unease about Henry's guilt and concern that his 'crime' was the colour of his skin. Aware of the controversy of the case and petitioned by various organisations, Eisenhower promised to investigate. On 19 June 1944, it was announced that the US commander-in-chief considered the verdict unsafe due to lack of evidence, and Henry was sent back to his unit.

Although US troops were issued with a useful booklet, *How to Stay Out of Trouble*, many chose not to, nor did other lonely servicemen far from home. More prostitutes put in longer hours, especially in the West End of London and other large ports and city centres. Marthe Watts, an enterprising French prostitute who had come to London via a marriage of convenience with an elderly man soon after the outbreak of war, had soon notched up over 400 court appearances through successful participation in the 'vast sellers' market in the commodity we had to offer'. Troops were solicited in the street or themselves sought sex: a simple 'Wanna fuck?' asked of every passing woman in Piccadilly at night was supposed to bring all the gratification a man could handle – or afford. The price for sex, as for almost all wartime commodities for which demand exceeded supply, had spiralled as women passed on to their clients the increased rents of the flats or hotel rooms to which they took them. By 1945 GIs were reputed to be charged £5 'for a short time', a tariff no British soldier could hope to pay. There were also brothels, often attached to hotels or nightclubs, some of which were 'high class', in expensive areas such as Mayfair, catering for officers, while others were tacky and cheap, but both served the same purpose. From 1943 an intensive police campaign was mounted to close down such places and prosecute the women and their pimps.

There was another crime of war that often spiralled down to further illegality. Deserters from the Forces faced severe penalties, though General Auchinleck's call for the return of the death sentence had been rejected. If apprehended by the Redcaps (military police) the miscreant would be returned to his regiment and could in theory face up to ten years in prison, though such sentences were usually reduced to three years, and some deserters were freed after as little as six months – in order to be sent back to the front line.

There were those men who deserted from the field of battle, either because they couldn't take it any more, or because they reckoned they had a good chance of getting away with it, and anyway a spell in prison was better than battle; and there were those who should never have been in the Army anyway. And then there were those who went AWOL in wartime Britain before they had been near any action. Without an ID or a ration book, deserters were seen as fuelling the wartime crime wave. This was probably an exaggeration – though there were a number of cases of deserters driven to burglary, looting, armed hold-ups, even murder. If the deserters were British rather than GIs or other troops from overseas stationed in the UK, they would probably be able to hole up with family or friends, find work on the black market, no questions asked, cash in hand. And it was not so very hard to obtain false papers, particularly if a man had contacts in the criminal fraternity. In 1941, the peak year for desertion, around one in every hundred men in the Forces had deserted and by October 1944 some 80,000 men had gone missing from the Army alone. It was estimated that after the war some 20,000 unpardoned deserters were at large. The deserter became a seedy wartime figure, a precursor of the post-war spiv:

> young man in a purple suit
> doing a little business on the side
> it was not for you that my son died.

Many of those who had deserted went to ground in the anonymity of London and other large cities, where they would also find draft dodgers and those invalided out of the Forces. Between September 1939 and June 1944, 335,000 men and women had been released from the services on medical grounds, 18,000 of them for psychiatric reasons. These could range from psychosis through neurosis and severe learning difficulties, to men who proved so disruptive and unsettling to their fellow soldiers (or airmen or sailors) that they were better out of the services than in. Others were simply society's oddballs, those it was impossible to regulate, unemployable in the usual sense of the word but by no means untalented or unproductive in their fashion. Many found a home in wartime Fitzrovia, the area roughly between Soho and Bloomsbury, which was a location and a magnet, and became a way of life.

Admittedly small and hardly influential, it was nevertheless a dissolute and contemptible canker at the heart of the nation's war effort. Or a besieged bastion of civilised values, toleration, talent and a certain surrealistic sanity, depending on your position and your perception. Here such louche and talented literary figures as Julian Maclaren Ross and Reyner Heppenstall (whose medical report described him as 'a social, disgruntled type, of first-class intelligence and ability' who had 'failed to adjust to the Army') fetched up. They would be surrounded by younger hopefuls, such as the poet Dylan Thomas, who was making films for the Ministry of Information rather than give his 'one and only body' to the war, yet already knew that London was 'his capital punishment' where he drank and grew repetitive and did little work. Young men who had not yet been called up (the 'Slithy Toves' as they were collectively called since they so closely resembled Tenniel's drawings for *Alice in Wonderland*) were regulars, along with the ageing artist Augustus John (whose girlfriend, the beautiful chorus girl and model Caitlin Macnamara, Thomas had stolen, and would marry as soon as he could hang on to sufficient money for the licence). Others frequenting the pubs of Fitzrovia might include George Orwell, Louis MacNeice and Roy Campbell the poet and producer, in his picador's hat, on a break from the BBC just down the road. And these literati and reprobates would be joined by deserters in search of a drink, a bed (or a floor) for the night, for forged ration books or ID cards, pickpockets anxious to unload their takings, Conscientious Objectors who found it hard to find a job and felt adrift in wartime Britain, and petty criminals who wanted to mingle into anonymity. They all washed up in Fitzrovia, to sit out the war in the pubs and coffee bars, and, in the case of many, to fail to make much sense of the peace.

22

'SECOND FRONT NOW'

I said ... I wished something lovely would happen for which I wasn't responsible ... I suppose this is partly this awful ache about the Second Front, the thing one wants and fears so terribly, that it's at the back of one's thoughts all the time, like a wave, a tidal wave coming in from the horizon blotting out everything. In ten years' time nobody will know, one won't know oneself, what the word meant emotionally, to all of us ...
NAOMI MITCHISON, SUNDAY 14 MAY 1944

'WE LIVE FOR D-Day,' wrote Charles Ritchie, a Canadian diplomat who had been posted to London for most of the war, in his diary in early May 1944. There had been many D-Days already during the Second World War as in any war, days targeted for action. D simply stood for day, like H in military speak designated hour, and events were counted back and forward from that point: D+1, D-6 and so on. But the only D-Day that would be remembered by that name is the one that by the spring of 1944 'had become a hallucination – something like the Second Coming, or the End of the World' – when Allied troops would cross the English Channel to invade the fortified beaches of Normandy, and gain a foothold in occupied Europe, from which they would advance in bitter combat towards Germany – and victory.

Churchill had never doubted that the war would have to be won on land; an invasion of 'Fortress Europe' was a prerequisite for Allied victory. But until that moment was ripe, it was the bomber that had been in the front line. Since the dark days of 1940. In early 1942 an Air Ministry directive had instructed Arthur Harris, the newly appointed commander-in-chief of Bomber Command, 'that the primary object of your operations should now be focused on the morale of the enemy civil population, and in particular of the industrial workers' in enemy territory. It was a further step along the road from bombing specific military or industrial targets to an area, or saturation, attack. Civilians would always be the 'incidental' casualties of *any* bombing raid.

The US, however, continued to favour precision bombing with daylight raids on carefully selected military targets, believing that it was preferable to aim to obliterate a few essential industries, rather than causing lesser damage over a wide range. British air strategists considered this to be unrealistic, having by 1942 come to the conclusion that 'precision bombing' was something of a chimera. Daylight raids took a heavy toll on aircraft and crews, and in any case no one knew exactly what to attack and for how long. Where were the bottlenecks, the 'choke' in German war production? What factories or infrastructure were key to the German war effort?

In March and April 1942 Bomber Command mounted intense attacks on the German cities of Lübeck and Rostow. The timbered houses made the narrow, densely packed medieval streets of both towns tinder boxes that immediately burst into flames, laying waste the historic town centres. On the final days of May 1942 came the first '1,000-bomber raid', on Cologne, when 12,840 buildings were destroyed, 600 acres were razed and an estimated 2,500 fires started, followed by similar attacks on Essen and Bremen. In the following months British planes bombed to ruin large parts of Hamburg – the 'city without Nazis' as it was sometimes known as it had such a large Jewish and Left-wing population – killing maybe as many as 50,000 people and injuring 40,000 in the firestorm following a single raid on the night of 27/28 July 1943. From November 1943 to March 1944 Berlin was under continual bombardment. Christina Bielenberg, a British woman, married to a German lawyer who was involved in secret resistance circles and was arrested after the failure of the plot on Hitler's life on 20 July 1944, spent several nights in Berlin during that winter of attrition. 'The bombs fell indiscriminately on Nazis and anti-Nazis, on women and children, on works of art, on dogs and pet canaries,' but 'those wanton, and quite impersonal killings . . . did not so much breed fear and a desire to bow before the storm, but rather a fatalistic cussedness, a dogged determination to survive . . .'

Although the British 'quality' press portrayed the raids as a form of aerial blockade to strangle the German war economy, the popular press was more gung ho, insisting that they were only what the Germans deserved: they were retaliatory raids – at last – for the Blitz. The *Daily Express* blazoned an aerial view of the smouldering ruins of Lübeck on its front page and declared: 'This is what happened to the city of Lübeck, where 150,000 Germans live and work, on the night last night when the RAF decided to render an English translation of the word "blitz". No city in all Britain ever suffered so much in a single attack.' Words like 'Hamburged' (and later 'Dresdened'), reminiscent of the verb to 'Coventrate', were triumphantly coined.

Since they had suffered the Blitz, most of the British public found it hard to condemn intensive bombing. But not all seem to have bought the gloating 'smash 'em' attitude of the popular press. At the beginning of 1944 only six Londoners out of every ten gave 'unqualified approval' to the raids; two had 'qualms' and one in ten felt that they were too terrible to condone. All thought that the raids would shorten the war, but did not like to envisage the human cost, and almost all seemed wilfully unaware that the British were not aiming solely at military targets.

A few Church leaders intervened to express doubts about the morality of area bombardment, but the Bishop of Bristol was slapped down by the mayor of his city, and criticised in the press, for speaking without military knowledge and signing up 'for a war of attrition [that] would last for years longer' if the heavy bombing of Germany were to cease. The Bishop of Chichester, who had argued in 1940 that the bombing of non-combatants was 'a degradation of the spirit for all who take part in it', appealed instead for daylight raids on declared military targets so that the Germans could evacuate the non-combatants.

Although the Blitz had effectively ended in May 1941, Britain had not been free from bombing raids in the next two years. There was a twenty-eight-day embargo on photographs of bomb damage appearing in the press, and captions continued to be imprecise about location and date, but those who suffered 'tip 'n' run raids' – intruder raids, sometimes with a single aircraft mounting lightning attacks from King's Lynn to Middlesbrough, Torquay to East Grinstead – were in no doubt that the threat of death, injury and destruction was still ever present. Nor were the residents of Catford in south-east London, where an elementary school was hit in January 1943 as the children were eating lunch. 'It makes me very bitter. Why young children?' a fire woman who had helped in the rescue asked. Photographs of the bodies of the thirty-eight children (and six teachers) killed were deemed too distressing to be published; over 7,000 attended a funeral service, led by the Bishop of Southwark, for many of the victims who were buried in a mass grave.

In the late spring and early summer of 1942 came 'terror attacks of a retaliatory nature . . . where the greatest possible effect on the civil population was to be expected' in response to the bombing of Rostow and Lübeck. The Deputy Head of the German Information and Press Division announced that in future targets for the Luftwaffe would be chosen from Baedeker's *Great Britain: Handbook for Travellers*. 'We shall go out to bomb every building in Britain marked with three stars in the Guide,' he announced. The cities targeted tended to be those the British had regarded as relatively safe from air raids, where defences were weak and evacuees had relocated. From April to June 1942 the country's most historic cities were pounded. Bath lost its newly renovated Georgian Assembly Rooms, Norwich its sixteenth-century Old Boar's Head, and York its Guildhall, the oldest in Britain since London's had been destroyed; many of Exeter's finest Georgian buildings were lost and the library of the cathedral at Canterbury – which Berlin radio described as 'a main centre of English hypocrisy' – was badly damaged; and as well as buildings lost, so were civilian lives in every attack.

By spring 1943, Londoners still lived with the fear that had been bred into them by the air raids – though ironically on the night of 3 March a tragedy for London's East End arose not through the destructive power of bombs but through fear of them. When the alert sounded at 8.17 p.m., some 1,500 local people hurried to take shelter in Bethnal Green tube station. Work on the Central line had been suspended when war broke out and the underground had been used as a deep shelter. There was a rumour that there would be reprisal raids that night for those the RAF had launched on Berlin and, alarmed by the sound of new anti-aircraft weapons being tested in nearby Victoria Park, people started to surge into the station. Since the tube was still under construction, it had only one main entrance and one narrow staircase with no handrail leading down to the booking hall, which was dimly lit by a single 25-watt bulb. There was pushing and shoving to get down the stairs to safety when a woman, carrying a baby, lost her footing and fell. 'In a matter of seconds there was built an immovable and interlaced mass of bodies five or six or more deep against which the people above and on the stairs continued to be forced by the pressure from behind.' Everything happened at lightning speed: within ninety seconds of the woman stumbling 173 people, 62 of them children, were dead, a third of all the wartime deaths in Bethnal Green. The coroner recorded a verdict of accidental death, adding 'there is nothing to suggest any stampede, any panic, or anything of that kind . . .' The Home Secretary, Herbert Morrison, agreed to an official inquiry, but the report was not released until January 1945, for government fears that it might encourage the enemy to revive air attacks in the hope of causing mass panic. The inquiry found that there had been no one on duty to control the crowds: the police responded that they simply did not have the manpower to guard every potential danger spot.

Rumours that the incident was as a result of a 'Jewish panic' were dismissed as a pernicious 'canard'. Nor, the inquiry chairman concluded, was there any truth to 'the absurdity' that the panic was 'induced by Fascists or criminal persons for nefarious purposes. There were some deaths among men with criminal records. They and their relatives are as much entitled to our sympathy as any of the other victims,' he reproved.

One paragraph of the report was particularly sobering: 'the physical imperfections of this shelter entrance are easily reproduced in scores of other tube entrances in the metropolitan area . . . I confess surprise that the accident has not happened before, and no one . . . can exclude the possibility of it happening elsewhere.'

But despite this salutary warning, in the bitter winter of 1944 the habit of sheltering underground had returned. From January to March the

Luftwaffe came back to bomb London. For Hitler it was Operation Steinbock; for the British the 'little' or a 'baby' blitz compared to the 'big' one, but it was arduous and distressing just the same. 'A city officially enters that class [of a blitz city] when people ring up their friends the day after a noisy night to find out if they're still there,' suggested Mollie Panter-Downes. Though the eight deep shelters, four either side of the Thames to accommodate a total of 64,000 people, agreed as long ago as January 1941, now sported ENTRANCE signs, they were still not open to the public. So when the bombers came back at the end of January 1944 Londoners had had to go back to the shelters they had used in the Blitz. But forty-two tube stations had been closed to shelterers when the raids had abated in 1941, and those shelters that were still open were more crowded than ever. With every bunk taken and people dossing down wherever they could find a space, most of the stations that had been closed had to be reopened, and the dismantled bunks re-erected. In some tube stations there were more shelterers in early 1944 than there had been at the height of the Blitz.

A new type of indoor domestic shelter came into its own during the 'baby blitz'. The 'Morrison' shelter (again named after the Home Secretary in post) was essentially a rectangular steel cage 6 feet 6 inches long, standing 2 feet 9 inches off the ground. Prototypes had provided more headroom – indeed Churchill had been keen on a pointed, neo-Gothic version – but, given the restraints of space in many urban homes, it was decided that a structure that could be used as a table by day was more practical. The base consisted of a steel 'mattress'; the sides were mesh and the top was made of a steel plate ½ inch thick. Tests showed that such shelters could resist the debris produced by the collapse of two floors above. A Morrison shelter could accommodate two adults and two young children (or one older child) lying down, and extended personal shelter facilities to those living in houses without gardens. They could be moved with the family if the house was bombed, though since the steel cage was supposed to be erected on the ground floor, they were of less use to flat dwellers. The first of these shelters were destined for the areas most vulnerable to bombing but, although an order for 400,000 – which would provide shelter for perhaps 1.2 million people – had been placed in January 1941, the distribution was too late for most people to benefit during the Blitz. As with Anderson shelters, the issue of Morrison shelters was dependent on the household income, but now those earning less than £350 a year would get a Morrison shelter free (£250 had been the cut-off point for Anderson shelter eligibility), otherwise it cost £7 12s 6d to buy.

Night after night the bombs came. When it became unbearable, Gwladys Cox and her husband, who had again suffered ceilings down, windows blown out and doors wrenched from their frames on 19 February 1944, the heaviest raid on London since 10 May 1941, would take refuge in a neighbour's ground floor flat in West Hampstead. 'It's a dreadful experience, standing the whole time in an icy, pitch-dark hall.' It was so cold that winter that the Coxes found themselves 'greeting their coalman *affectionately*. We eke out the sitting room fire with chunks of wood from the bombed buildings now. This is thrown on to piles for anyone to help himself who will. At the moment we are burning pieces of Buckingham Mansions [an adjacent bombed-out block of flats], which gives me a sinking feeling, for at this very moment, Buckingham Mansions might quite easily be burning a bit of *us*!' One day Winston Churchill came to see the damage in the area for himself and, with his cigar and fingers held in an almost perpetual 'V sign', 'it was just like 1941 again'.

Gwladys Cox tried to draw comfort listening to 'John Strachey in *War Commentary* tonight assur[ing] us that by our enduring raids on London, the war was being shortened!' The endurance of the 'little blitz' had to last until the final major raid on London on 18/19 April 1944. And by that time everyone's thoughts had turned to the invasion of Europe.

The invasion that would open a Second Front in western Europe, which would take the pressure off the Eastern Front that Russia was holding along its borders, had been top of the agenda at the Anglo–American conference held in Casablanca, North Africa, back in January 1943. Both Allies had had to make concessions. The Americans reluctantly condoned an Allied landing in Sicily, and allowed for the possibility of further operations in Italy, while the British, recognising that a cross-Channel invasion was axiomatic to US policy, and mindful of the need to tie up US forces in Europe rather than see them being sent off to the Pacific, pledged a large-scale assault on France in 1944. Since Churchill's 'interest in terminology even extended to the selection of code names for Operations', he made the choice for this momentous one. 'Facetious names met with vehement disapproval. How would a mother feel if she were to hear that her son had been killed in an enterprise called Bunny Hug?' Operation Overlord, on the other hand, clearly carried the necessary gravitas for the decisive attack of the Second World War.

An operation of the magnitude of Overlord was unprecedented, as *Picture Post* noted: 'Something comparable to the city of Birmingham hasn't merely got to be shifted, it's got to be kept moving when it's on the other side . . . we must take everything with us – and take it in the teeth of the fiercest opposition.' There were precisely seventeen weeks from the acceptance of the final proposals for Overlord and D-Day.

The man appointed to the supreme command of D-Day operations was General Dwight D. Eisenhower, who had risen from the rank of colonel to that of four-star general in just under two years – without ever having been on the battlefield. He seemed to epitomise the American 'armchair soldier' who so unnerved the British, and he was to be in charge of the most crucial military operation of the war. The man who was to have the principal British role in Overlord was 'Monty' – General Sir Bernard Montgomery – the folk hero of both the 8th Army in the Western Desert and the British public. An infantryman, Montgomery was appointed Ground Commander of the Allied Armies (21st Army Corps). The First US Army was placed under the command of Lieutenant General Omar Bradley. D-Day was to be a joint Allied venture, but British, Canadian and US troops were to fight separate battles on allocated code-named beaches, establish a bridgehead and then join up to fight inland.

The obvious place for the landings was the Pas de Calais, which would make the vulnerable sea-crossing short and the turnround of landing craft quick. Landing at Calais also offered the fastest land route to Germany. But since Calais was the obvious place for a landing, the Germans had made the port impregnable and the coastline bristled with pillboxes and gun emplacements. So the Chief of Staff to the Supreme Allied Commander (COSSAC) team plumped for a target further west along the French coast, the stretch of the Normandy beaches around Caen that was much less heavily fortified, and close to the major port of Cherbourg which would allow easy access for US troops to be transported directly across the Atlantic once the port had been secured.

It was essential for the Allies to find out as much as possible about what might await their forces on the coast of France, which had been under scrutiny since 1942. From the Bay of Biscay to the Belgian frontier, British frogmen and swimmers slipped into the sea from small boats and clambered ashore to try to discover the ways in which the Germans were defending the beaches. Members of the British Special Operations Executive (SOE) and MI6 personnel parachuted in to play their part in helping those in the resistance movement in France to paint as full a picture as possible of the disposition and intention of the German forces, and the fortifications the troops would find when they went ashore. The public was enlisted too, with the BBC broadcasting an appeal for snapshots taken on pre-war holidays to France and the Low Countries. The press took up the call and soon over a million pictures had been collected from all over the world, and every out-of-focus Box Brownie snap was scrutinised for the information it might yield to help the troops negotiate the Normandy beaches. Even a picture of a child eating an ice cream in front of a sea wall could indicate the height of the wall.

Deception played a vital role in the success of the D-Day landings. It was a rule that no code-named wartime operation was ever to be instigated without a code name being assigned to a parallel operation to offer German Intelligence a choice of plausible threats if they managed to break the code. A deception plan, Operation Fortitude, would feed the Germans a tissue of lies about Operation Overlord in all theatres of war.

Nothing would persuade the Germans that Allied troops were not going to cross the Channel. What had to be done was try to persuade them that the destination would be the Pas de Calais rather than Normandy. So while every effort was made to keep secret the build-up of men and tanks round the embarkation ports from Sussex through Hampshire and Dorset, elaborate efforts were made for the Germans to 'discover' the concentration of forces in Kent poised to take off from Dover and Folkestone. Operation Fortitude, masterminded by Colonel David Strangeways, was intended to deflect German anticipation of where the Allied landings would take place, and mislead them into thinking that a far greater force was poised to assault the French coast than was the case. Dummy landing craft appeared in the Thames and

Medway estuaries, while the airfields of Kent and Essex filled up with plywood gliders and inflatable rubber tanks that were clearly visible to any German reconnaissance planes that managed to fly over.

Mary Reeves was one of the many people involved in the manufacture of this 'dummy' Army equipment. She worked in a Nottingham factory that had produced silk stockings before the war. It had been in the process of being adapted to turn out nylon stockings instead, and German workers had come over to install the necessary machinery. But when war broke out, the half-ready machinery was abandoned and the factory was equipped to make barrage balloons. In early 1944, 'our . . . gaffer says "we're going into a different product" and we had to sign a form saying that we wouldn't disclose to anyone what we were making in the factory, and we started work on making artificial rubber lorries . . . when they were . . . blown up . . . they looked so real. From a distance you wouldn't have known they weren't the real thing. And in the lunch break we'd be shown films to show us how important the work we were doing was.'

Camouflage presented particular problems for an operation intended to deceive: it must be sufficiently realistic for the Germans to think that Britain had something to hide, but not so effective that the ranks of decoy tanks and guns and lorries would not be spotted. 82nd Group Camouflage Company spent weeks fashioning cover out of brushwood, chicken wire, leaves and netting, and tramping endlessly round in the grass to create the illusion of tyre marks and military manoeuvres when seen from the air. A huge fake oil-storage tank designed by Basil Spence (after the war, the architect of the phoenix Coventry Cathedral) was made at Shepperton film studios and erected in Dover, and the rumour was put about that it fed a huge pipe that ran under the Channel to provide fuel for the armies landing near Calais. To add to its authenticity, the installation was periodically 'inspected' by the King and Queen and by Eisenhower. Dummy 'landing craft' of tubular scaffolding bolted on to oil drums and covered in canvas were 'made at great speed and . . . towed . . . to the sort of place you might expect to find a landing craft to be anchored, and left them there. It was all done at night . . . they looked very real . . . We'd leave the LCs where they were for two or three days and then bring them back inland and dismantle them, so if it looked as if the troops were moving around . . .'

Anyone involved in the preparations for D-Day was soon struck with an ever-growing sense of bewilderment at the sheer size of the enterprise. There were the 'mulberries' constructed in response to the insistence of Captain Hughes-Hallett, Naval Adviser to Combined Operations, that 'if we can't capture a port, we must take one with us'. All around Britain in the spring of 1944, 37,000 workers were making parts – in absolute secrecy – for two prefabricated artificial harbours the size of Dover, with piers for landing ships, which would be towed across the Channel and anchored off the coast of France where they would have to ride tides that could be over 20 feet high and cope with landing 2,500 vehicles and 10,000 tons of stores every day.

Then there was the hardware for the assault: the US DUKW amphibious truck, the DD or 'swimming tank', with its canvas 'skirt' that meant it could be launched at sea and driven, and a selection of Hobart's 'funnies'. These comprised a collection of special-purpose British tanks developed by Major General Sir Percy Hobart, a First World War Distinguished Service Order holder whom Churchill had rescued from being a corporal in the Home Guard to form an armoured division for the invasion. Inventions that the US military persisted in regarding as frankly wacky, the 'funnies' included the 'crab', a mine-clearing flail tank; 'Bobbin' tanks that unspooled canvas and coir matting to lay a path across soft mud, peat or quicksands; a 'fascine' tank that dropped bundles of chestnut palings to fill in anti-tank ditches and bomb craters; the Churchill ARK (Armoured Ramp Carrier) and the AVRE (Armoured Vehicle Royal Engineers) which carried a powerful mortar nicknamed the 'Flying Dustbin' that could blast through concrete pillboxes; and the 'Crocodile' or flame-throwing tank, which could incinerate any obstacle within a 360-foot range. Everything was gradually assembled – lorries, guns, mines for the assault, aircraft for bombing the defences, gliders to convey the parachutists, ambulances, medical supplies . . . All were crucial, but in the end it was the men who were going to have to storm the beaches and fight on inland. Without their courage and fighting skills, the invasion would come to naught. So while the strategists and experts drew up their blueprints and others executed them, the troops slogged it out in training.

Training needs tore into the countryside. Although 165,000 acres of land had already been requisitioned for training purposes, the War Office demanded another 140,000 acres of good agricultural land stretching across Oxfordshire, Hampshire and Wiltshire that was thought to provide the firm subsoil and natural features essential for realistic training – despite warnings from the Minister of Agriculture 'that efforts to maintain and even increase . . . the 1943 level of home food production will be severely affected'.

It was essential to find terrain that was as close as possible to that which the troops would encounter in Normandy. Beaches that had been prohibited areas, mined and ringed with barbed wire when a German invasion threatened, were now cleared to prepare for the invasion of France.

Many schools and organisations that had evacuated to the relative safety of the West Country moved out to make way for the troops. But some stayed on. King's School in Canterbury had been evacuated to Cornwall in 1940. On their walks on the cliffs and scrambling down to the coves and beaches, the boys had a front-row view of Americans training for war. Brian Arnold, then a pupil at the school, recalled 'the American Army were all around in great numbers, preparing for the invasion. Some of the boys . . . were very keen on getting hold of some of their explosives . . . The Americans used to stack all the ammunition up on either side of the road . . . You'd just lean down and pick it up . . . We'd pick up blocks of gelignite which looked like packets of margarine, but luckily without detonators, there were shells of every calibre, anti-aircraft shells, and quite a lot of this stuff found its way into school . . . One day we had a search in the school cupboards and things and amassed quite a considerable pile of weaponry . . . dynamite, shells, mortars, hand-grenades, small arms . . . The area was guarded but there just weren't enough guards. We used to have a whale of a time driving amphibious vehicles out to sea, and really enjoying ourselves knocking bottles off the top of barbed wire entanglements with American carbines. We saw the GIs practising with these DUKWs all the time – they're a cross between a land vehicle and a boat, in fact they are rather better in water. But you have to remember to take the bungs out of the bottom when you got on land to let the water out, and it was rather important to remember to put them back in again before you went back in the sea!'

The villages and hamlets in the hinterland of the 'invasion beaches' were cleared by government order. An area of South Devon known as

South Hams was to be requisitioned under the Defence Regulations and Compensations Act (1939): 30,000 acres comprising parts of six parishes, 3,000 people, 180 farms, village shops and other buildings were to be totally evacuated to make way for the training of US forces. The 750 families affected had just six weeks to find somewhere to live for themselves and any livestock they had. 'As it was winter we had to take all the hay and straw for the cattle – the ricks had to be dismantled – all the farm implements, chickens, dogs, cats, everything had to move out,' remembered Gordon Luscombe, a farmer's son and then sixteen years old. 'There was a war on and we had to go. The old people took it worst. Some of them had never left the village. They never got over it.' The Luscombe family found somewhere to live near Totnes, but they had to sell their dairy herd and sheep – there just wasn't room for the animals in their temporary accommodation.

When the villagers were permitted to return to their homes several months after D-Day, they found every window broken; and Slapton church had received a direct hit – a historic stained-glass window was completely shattered. They also found 'lots of live shells lying around, mortar bombs, everything'. The villagers would ring up the bomb-disposal unit at Plymouth who would come along with lorries and take them away.

A village that 'died for England' was Tyneham in Dorset, surrounded by coastal downland that had been used as a gunnery range in the First World War. The villagers were evacuated at Christmas 1943, and tanks and troops moved in to train for D-Day. 'All day long and every day [the military] dashed past in lorries, in jeeps, in tanks. The clatter of tanks was something awful,' a farm labourer who had watched the despoliation of the countryside recalled. 'They passed in long lines, these chariots of our day, their helmeted riders aloft in their turrets. I sometimes lifted my hand in friendly salute, but there was not much response. The division between us was too great for communication . . . On this side life was everlasting; and over there – History roaring past.' The villagers were never permitted to return to their village, to reclaim their homes as they believed they had been promised they would. In 1948 Attlee's Labour government declared that Tyneham was to be retained permanently as part of the Royal Armoury Corps' tank gunnery range.

*

On 15 May 1944 at St Paul's School in west London, military planners and commanders crowded on to hard wooden benches. The King was there, sitting in an armchair next to Churchill, listening as Montgomery (an ex-pupil) sketched out the plans – and the problems – for D-Day. Then Churchill rose to speak. He admitted that he had had doubts about the wisdom of Overlord and that he was still haunted by the prospect of the English Channel 'running red with the blood of British soldiers, extinguished like the soldiers of the western front, the men of Ypres and Passchendaele' (and no doubt troubled by his own role in the disastrous failed landing at Gallipoli in the Dardanelles in 1917), but that now, a month before the off, he was 'hardening towards this enterprise' and felt resolute in banishing any doubts he might have had.

The military commanders went on the stump like campaigning politicians, travelling round Britain to give their men encouragement. Bradley insisted that his visits must not interfere with the men's training schedules, and once had a battalion commander removed when it was obvious he had rehearsed his men. This was no time to impress the brass hats. Montgomery had a routine on the D-Day trail, always giving the same speech. 'I have come here today so that I can get a look at you and you can get a look at me – not that I'm much to look at . . . we've got to go off and do a job together very soon, you and I . . . and now I have met you, I have complete confidence, absolute confidence . . . And you must have confidence in me.' He once asked a young Welsh Guard, 'What is your most valuable possession?' 'It's my rifle, sir,' the soldier replied dutifully. 'No it's not. It's your life. And I'm going to save it for you . . .' But the soldiers were not impressed: he was booed by the 50th Division, whose 69th Brigade referred to him as 'Flying 'em in Monty' since this would be the second attempt at an amphibious landing.

By late February 150,000 US troops a month were arriving in Britain to join their British, Canadian, French and Polish comrades-in-arms. By May 1944 there were 2,876,600 officers and men organised into thirty-nine divisions, plus air, medical, transport and communication units waiting 'as tense as a coiled spring' for the order to move. To Mollie Panter-Downes, writing to tell the Americans how it was in England in May 1944, it 'uncomfortably resembles living on a vast combination of an aircraft carrier and a warehouse stacked to the ceiling with material labelled "Europe"'. Every week another transatlantic convoy would arrive, and crates of supplies of jeeps, artillery shells, guns, ration packs, blood plasma and much more would be stacked on quaysides. The final plan was that some 150,000 men, 1,500 tanks and 10,000 trucks, jeeps and other vehicles were to be landed in France in the first twenty-four hours, together with the supplies needed to support men and machinery – 1,000 gallons of drinking water, for example. By the end of May Admiral Sir Bertram Ramsay, who had commanded the evacuation from Dunkirk and was appointed Allied naval commander-in-chief for the Normandy landings, had managed to assemble 4,126 ships and landing craft to be used in the initial phase, and the follow-up, in the ports of southern England. It was an awesome sight.

The roads were clogged with endless convoys of tanks, trucks, jeeps and other military vehicles during May as they streamed south towards the marshalling areas. Buildings had to be knocked down, roads widened or newly built, bridges strengthened, and hardstanding and lay-bys constructed to accommodate the huge amphibious trucks and giant transports that poured into the ports. Some unexpected demolition took place when transporters got stuck under road bridges, knocked down parapets and took corners off innumerable buildings.

The convoys would move for five minutes at a time, and then stop for what seemed like hours. 'It was a miracle it all worked,' thought a US infantryman, Bob Sheenan, 'as tens of thousands of men and their vehicles slowly funnelled down to the south coast to pick up the places assigned to them. To do it on time and then do it over again throughout the hours of daylight and darkness marked a major triumph for the bureaucratic mind.' As the convoys stopped along the road, women ran out with cups of tea, sandwiches and cake, anything they could spare for the soldiers, and the US troops would fling out their small change for the children, reckoning they wouldn't be needing British money for much longer.

Tanks, trucks and jeeps camouflaged with netting and foliage were parked along the roadside; piles of ammunition protected by corrugated iron stood in serried ranks in fields, on commons, playing fields, in car parks and hard-standing that was not already occupied by tanks or trucks. In the woods, Red Cross ambulances were parked among the May bluebells, ready to convey the wounded to hospital. 'Troops were everywhere . . . every leaf-roofed lane was parked with vehicles and supply dumps; the air was charged with the vitality and power of all this restrained violence, primed and ready to detonate.'

One of the slogans of the early years of the war had been 'Careless Talk Costs Lives' and now it mattered more than ever. As well as keeping Britain isolated from outside contact, and ensuring that de Gaulle was kept well away in North Africa, the British people had to be kept in the dark in case agents were able to piece together any overheard minutiae and build up an accurate picture of the plans for D-Day. The public must not be allowed to see the build-up of troops and equipment at close quarters, and so from 2 April 1944 those areas dedicated to training and armament storage, from Land's End to the Wash and including a small belt round the Firth of Forth, were designated no-go areas, and civilians were barred from entering. Owners of ships and boats requisitioned for the invasion were not told where their craft were, what they might be used for and when they might get them back. 'Loose Lips Sink Ships' they were reminded.

Once the troops were moved from the concentration areas – most of them south of a line from Milford Haven in Wales to the Wash in East Anglia – to the marshalling areas (sausages as they were called because of their shape) on 26 May, security measures were tightened. 'It's a dump,' thought Gunner Ernest Brewer. 'So far as I can see we are here for security reasons, though I myself can't see what we could give away. We don't know anything.' Barbed-wire barriers were put in place and 'perimeter and interior guards will be established . . . in order to prevent communication between the briefed troops and persons not entitled to operational knowledge', an order from the War Office decreed. No contact with the outside world was allowed to the troops, postboxes were sealed, public phone lines disconnected, and the men entered a strange limbo land of waiting and uncertainty.

Not all the sealed camps were in rural areas. Dennis Bowen, an eighteen-year-old private in the East Yorkshire Regiment, was sent to 'a canvas camp built on a bomb site' in Canning Town in London's East End, from where they would be transported down the Thames for embarkation. 'Then we were paraded . . . and it was said, "You are now all confined to camp, no one will be allowed out." That was the first warning . . . sentries were posted all around, patrolling the perimeter to keep us in . . .

'I got out through a hole in the wire. Lots of other people did too . . . We'd go to the cinema and then crawl back in. In fact the sentries would see us but they'd turn a blind eye. They were soldiers like ourselves . . . I had no secret information or anything. If anybody spoke to me, all I could have said is that we were going abroad . . .'

Meanwhile in the rest of the country life seemed to go on as usual. May 29 was the Whitsun Bank Holiday. The weather was glorious, as it had been for most of the month, and it turned out to be the hottest day of the year with temperatures soaring to 94°F in the sun, 74°F in the shade. Despite government injunctions to 'Holiday at Home' and further travel restrictions announced to come into effect on 1 June, thousands decided to get away, queuing up for hours at Paddington to get to Wales or those parts of the West Country that weren't enclosed in barbed-wire coils.

That Saturday at Lord's Cricket Ground 30,000 spectators watched Australia beat the 'Rest of the World' – in fact a scratch team made up of two New Zealanders, a West Indian and eight Englishmen, including Len Hutton. Others took advantage of a novel spectator sport and went to Notts County football ground to watch a baseball match between two teams from America's 82nd Airborne Division, which was to play such a crucial invasion role only a few days later. It was an unequal contest. The Red Devils thrashed the Panthers 18 to nil.

But, as Mollie Panter-Downes observed, 'until the invasion begins even the most momentous domestic happenings are bound to fall flat. For example, Lord Woolton's first important offering as Minister of Reconstruction, his White Paper dealing with the problem of maintaining full employment after the war, created as little stir as if it had described plans for preventing unemployment among the Hottentots rather than among men who will be coming back from the invasion. In contrast to the Beveridge plan, the lack of excitement . . . was remarkable.'

She had noticed at the end of May it was as though people 'had shouldered the responsibility of being back in the civilian front line again . . . [they] are keyed up to withstand something which they have often imagined but never experienced'. The uncertainty showed in numerous ways: 'Like the phrase "weather permitting" the unspoken phrase "second front permitting" is, more and more, tacked onto all minor plans for the future from a lunch date for next week to a village flower-show announcement that a regimental band will play – if the regiment is still there, that is.

'. . . The big London railway stations, crowded with men in uniform who have rushed up for a few hours' leave, are the only places where the invasion seems real and pressing and dramatic. The women who have come to see their men off nearly always walk to the very end of the platform to wave their elaborately smiling goodbyes as the train pulls out. Sometimes they look . . . as though they're standing on the extreme tip of England itself fluttering their gay, undeceiving handkerchiefs, and possibly they look that way to the boys hanging out of the windows to wave back at them.'

It was double summer time in May so it didn't get dark until well after 10 p.m. There were plenty of activities organised for the soldiers to keep their minds off what was coming: football, volleyball, baseball – and talks. Some wrote letters. Joseph Martin was a sickbay attendant on a landing craft that he knew was going to 'spearhead the invasion, we were to go in even before the minesweepers . . . we were in Southampton Water and I remember the skipper calling everyone together saying, "Right, from such and such a time the ship is sealed off." That meant nobody could go ashore or nobody could come aboard, and then he said, "There's one post going out now, and there'll be one collection of mail." Words to the effect that you'd better write your last letters . . . I remember the difficulty I had in writing those letters because you couldn't write home, "Well I'm going into battle. I'm going into the unknown. I might not come back." You couldn't say any of those things. All you could say was, "Well, we're off on an adventure, and I'm sure we'll be back, and when I get back, we'll look forward to doing this and that. And you know what a wonderful mother and father you've been," and that sort of thing without making it too sloppy or sentimental. At the same time, you could imagine them receiving the letter and reading it. So I didn't want them to say, "My God, you know this is the last letter we're going to receive from our boy," so they were very difficult letters to write, there's no doubt about that.' Martin found it hard to look at his wedding photograph too. 'I kept it on board in my sick bay, but when times were really dodgy I had to put it away. It was a constant reminder that I might not see her again . . . so I used to have to put it out of sight.'

★

D-Day was fixed for Monday 5 June 1944. 'H-hour' was to be soon after dawn. By 3 June 1944 the troops destined for the first assault had hoisted their invasion kit on their backs and set off from their marshalling camp for embarkation 'hards' – hundreds of concrete platforms constructed along beaches, rivers and estuaries to load the vast armada of heavy tanks, guns, trucks and supplies. Dozens of ships had left their harbours and were sailing towards the assembly point in the English Channel south of the Isle of Wight.

A medical officer with the 24th Lancers found he took 'a deeper than normal interest in these last glimpses of England . . . The girls look a lot more attractive when we know we won't see any for a long time to come . . . I occasionally find myself thinking foolish thoughts about not coming back . . .'

The war correspondent Alan Moorhead trundled in a convoy to Southampton. It took for ever. 'Five miles an hour. Down Acacia Avenue. Round the park into High Street; a mile-long column of ducks [DUKWs] and three-ton lorries, of jeeps and tanks and bulldozers. On the pavement, one or two people waved vaguely. An old man stopped and mumbled "Good luck". But for the most part people stared silently and made no sign. They knew we were going. There had been rehearsals before but they were not deceived. There was something in the way the soldiers carried themselves that said all too clearly, "This is it. This is the invasion." '

By 4 June everything was in place. The US Western Task Force was ready to leave from a coastal strip that stretched from Salcombe in Devon to Poole in Dorset, while the British and Canadian forces of the Eastern Task Force were strung along the Solent and Southampton Water. All London railway stations stood empty except for a number of unfortunate would-be travellers, stranded when the trains were peremptorily cancelled. Airfields all over the south and west flew the flag that informed planes 'airfield unserviceable: landing forbidden' above rows of waiting planes.

On Friday the 2nd, Group Captain James Stagg, the chief meteorological officer, had issued Eisenhower with an ominous report: the weather was 'potentially full of menace', and soon after dawn on 4 June Eisenhower ordered a twenty-four-hour postponement. At 11 a.m., true to Stagg's predictions, an angry storm blew up. At 9 p.m. Stagg brought some hope. Conditions were far from ideal, but 'mercifully, miraculously . . . two reports from the Atlantic indicated that there just might be an interlude between two depressions moving towards Ireland . . .' There could be a thirty-six-hour window of opportunity starting on the afternoon of Monday 5 June and lasting until some time late on Tuesday 6 June.

Was it sufficient? Any further delay would mean that Overlord would have to be postponed for a full two weeks. Eisenhower was very well aware of the reasons for going for 6 June, but only if the weather cleared. There could only be one cross-Channel invasion. It had to be right first time, or the war would be prolonged – maybe for years. Montgomery spoke. 'I would say go.' Lieutenant General Walter Bedell Smith, the chief of staff, probably spoke for all those responsible for the invasion when he said, 'It's a helluva gamble, but it's the best possible gamble.' But the decision was Eisenhower's alone. At five o'clock on the morning of the 5th, Stagg was able to report that his forecast stood. Eisenhower confirmed his decision: 'OK – we'll go.'

That day Eisenhower went into Portsmouth to chat to the British troops as they loaded on to the landing craft. 'Good ol' Ike,' they cheered, obligingly. On the spur of the moment he left Portsmouth and, in the company of a posse of reporters and press photographers, drove to Newbury in Berkshire, to watch the US 101st Division preparing to take off in planes and gliders to be parachuted into Normandy. As he left them, Eisenhower had tears in his eyes. His Order of the Day would be distributed to all Allied troops the next morning: 'Soldiers, Sailors, and Airmen of the Allied Expeditionary Forces! You are about to embark upon the Great Crusade, towards which we have striven these many months. The eyes of the world are upon you. The hopes and prayers of liberty-loving people everywhere march with you . . . I have full confidence in your courage, devotion to duty, and skill in battle. We will accept nothing less than full victory! Good luck . . .' But, preparing for bed as the parachutists were setting off for France, Eisenhower carefully folded into his wallet a note he had written at his desk earlier in the day. 'Our landings in the Cherbourg–Le Havre area have failed to gain a satisfactory foothold and I have withdrawn the troops. My decision to attack at this time and place was based on the best information available. The troops, the air and the navy all did the best that bravery and devotion to duty could do. If any blame attaches to the attempt, it is mine alone.'

In London Churchill dined alone with his wife Clementine in the war rooms deep under Whitehall. After dinner he went into the map room to take a final look at the invasion plan and, as she joined him, he turned to her, saying, 'Do you realise that by the time you wake up in the morning, twenty thousand men may have been killed?'

23

'THE WAR WILL NOT BE OVER BY CHRISTMAS'

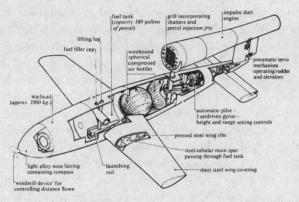

How the flying-bomb worked. The above drawing is based on one issue at the time by the Government, and widely reproduced in the press

The act of destruction and death took a few seconds.
The rescue of the victims took a few days.
The billeting of the homeless took a few weeks.
The healing of the injured will take an indefinite time.
The clearing of the bombed and burned site will take some months.
The rebuilding will take years.
The dead are dead.

MARGARET COTTON, ON THE SMITHFIELD V-2 BOMB INCIDENT, 8 MARCH 1945

As WINSTON CHURCHILL woke on the morning of 6 June 1944, the first reports of the Allied landing were brought in to him. He learned that at 12.16 that morning planes and gliders had started to drop men at both flanks of the 50-mile assault front – 23,400 in total. About half the parachutists made a 'good drop' – that is, landed in the planned zone – others were blown off course, or, weighed down by heavy equipment, men drowned in the sea or ditches the Germans had flooded as a defensive measure; their gliders were hit, they dropped too late and too low, or behind enemy lines. The rest landed over 300 square miles of Normandy. Although some 4,000 US paratroopers failed to join their units after the drop and it was several days before they were able to link up, the essential D-Day tasks were accomplished and the parachutists played a crucial role in holding ground until the seaborne forces landed.

H-Hour – when the first US warship troops would storm ashore – was set for 6.30 a.m, the British and Canadians would follow an hour or so later. An hour earlier the guns ranged along the coast opened up with a salvo of shells, joining the bombs in pounding the gun emplacements in advance of the landing craft bringing the soldiers to the Normandy beaches. During the night minesweepers had succeeded in clearing a wide channel for their manoeuvres.

A WAAF radar operator, whose underground operations block was at the tip of the Isle of Wight, had watched it happen. At 22.40 hours on 5 June the crew of twelve set out for watch duty. Wearing headphones, she observed at the 'tube'. 'At close range it was saturated with "echoes" from hundreds of craft. Slowly they started to move, and we relayed all the information to Filter Room at Stanmore where it was linked to that of other radar stations.

'Gradually the massive area of vessels progressed across our map. At the leading edge towards the Normandy coast, everyone was at fever pitch. Throughout the night we continued to observe. In the morning towards the end of our shift, our plotter called out excitedly, "We're there!" ' The invasion had started. It was D-Day at last.

The planes going over to bomb the beaches in advance of the troops landing had woken a war-production worker in Cheshire. She had to be up by 4.30 a.m. to catch a works bus to the factory. 'The atmosphere on that bus stays with me today. We sang our heads off – mostly the dirtiest ditties we knew – it was our compliment to the boys in the battles to come. When I arrived at work, I didn't feel the least tired and even the most notorious slackers were working like hell that morning . . . I think we all said a prayer as we worked. This was IT and we meant the enemy to know just what we intended to do.'

In East Anglia the sky had been dark with planes as dawn broke and the RAF and USAAF took off from the chequerboard of airfields there. A woman from a village just outside Norwich 'knew "our boys" by the marks on the aircraft tail. We waved, we shouted "Good luck" . . . a neighbour was waving a child's Union Jack . . . We dashed down the garden and frantically waved white tablecloths. Who knows if they were ever seen? By breakfast time it had quietened down. You wouldn't have known anything special was on – although we had lost our voices . . . [someone said], "Let's turn on the radio and see if there's any news." Not that we needed to be told. We KNEW.'

The Sussex woods around Newhaven had been teeming with hundreds of men in tents pitched among the trees for weeks. But on the morning of 6 June they were 'silent and deserted, the tents empty, a line of washing strung between the tents fluttered in the morning breeze, a few personal possessions were scattered on the ground . . . It was so silent, it was as if the whole country had upped and gone across the Channel to settle with Hitler once and for all.'

A VAD billeted in a convent on the outskirts of Plymouth was sent on a special mission to collect pints of Group 'O' blood from surrounding factories and villages. As the blood in unprocessed form would not keep for more than a week, 'we knew that D-Day was imminent'.

The Red Cross was having a flag day on 6 June, and a part-time helper took up her pitch outside Hammersmith underground station at 6.30 a.m. Soon after eight o'clock, Miss Sullivan noticed that instead of just some of those hurrying to work dropping pennies into her tin, nearly everyone was stopping to buy a flag, putting a shilling or two, or even half a crown, into her tin. 'I remember one person remarking, "You'll need all you can get now." My tin was soon full and people were dropping money into my flag tray.'

The first official news had come 'rather calmly as if it were routine night bombing that "Paratroopers had been landed in Northern France" ' on the 8 a.m. BBC bulletin. Gwladys Cox called out 'excitedly' to her husband, *'That's Invasion!'* And at 9.30 that morning, the newsreader John Snagge read 'the First Invasion Report, with a short account of the landing and the vast organisation involved. The weather has not been favourable, cold, cloudy with rough seas.'

Veronica Goddard wrote, 'At 9.45 General Eisenhower issued the official news to the whole world. People were asked to stand to and they would hear something of great interest, and that was it . . . Auntie and Rita at home heard the broadcast and they said it was absolutely thrilling and when they started calling our allies in France, Belgium, Holland and the other European countries with the announcement "Be patient, be patient. We are coming" and issuing them with sabotage instructions, it was just too much.'

Jessie Mosley, who was twenty years old and had been married for only two months to a paratrooper, was doing war work in a local factory when, on 6 June, the wireless programme *Workers' Playtime* was suddenly interrupted soon after ten o'clock with news of the D-Day landings. Everyone cheered – including her. It was only later that she learned that by the time she had heard the announcement her husband was already dead.

Evelyn Waugh had gone away to Devon to get on with writing *Brideshead Revisited*, which was behind schedule. He heard 'that the Second Front had opened . . . I worked through until 4 o'clock and finished the last chapter – dialogue poor – and took it to the post . . . My only fear is lest the invasion upsets my typist at St Leonard's, or the posts to him with my manuscript.' At the other end of the country in Glasgow, the news of the invasion passed quickly along the queue waiting outside a butcher's shop. When the doors opened the butcher announced that in celebration, he would take only coupons for meat that day: no money required.

Tom Hiett, a fourteen-year-old telegram boy, was on his rounds on D-Day. 'Southampton was absolutely deserted, but you could hear the distant rumble of guns and I saw a squadron of B17s fly over, very high up.' Within a few days he had the first death telegram to deliver. 'The lady came to the door and was horrified to see me standing there. I gave her the telegram, muttered, "No answer," and fled. It seemed I could hear crying all down the road and I thought, "Good God, how many more?" '

Just before noon Churchill went to the Commons. 'He looked as white as a sheet . . . we feared he was about to announce some terrible disaster.' Keeping the MPs on tenterhooks as he talked of the success of the battle for Rome the previous day, the Prime Minister finally said, 'I have also to announce to the House that during the night and the early hours of this morning the first of a series of landings in force upon the European continent has taken place . . . So far the commanders who are engaged report that everything is proceeding to plan . . . The battle that has now begun will grow constantly in scale and in intensity for many weeks to come, and I shall not attempt to speculate upon its course . . .'

Esther MacMurray was working in a large aircraft factory, and in the lunch hour all the staff gathered in the canteen, which held 4,000 people, to watch a lunchtime concert. 'Suddenly the Managing Director came on to the stage and everything stopped. "Ladies and gentlemen," he said quietly, "we have landed in France." There was a stunned silence, then a quavering voice started to sing "Land of Hope and Glory." In a moment everybody had joined in a great crescendo of sound . . . some of the women whose sons and husbands were in the forces were singing with the tears running down their faces, while the men were trying to control their emotion. Then we went quietly back to work – for victory.'

Everyone was desperate for news. 'Who would have been a newspaper vendor today?' asked Veronica Goddard. 'They were besieged, literally besieged. I must confess that I had the stupidness (or maybe there's no need to call it that) to queue for a quarter of an hour to get a midday *Evening Standard*. No sooner had I bought it than a woman dashed up and offered me half a crown for it' – which would have been a tidy profit since the paper cost a penny. A Gosport woman was crossing Portsmouth harbour in a ferry later that afternoon when she saw two landing craft being towed into the dockyard. They were full of soldiers, 'bloodstained and bullet-ridden, silent witnesses of the Armageddon they had left behind on the shores of France. We had indeed invaded Hitler's stronghold, but at what a cost!'

At 2 p.m. a sixteen-year-old Red Cross nurse had been alerted that she was needed at Queen Alexandra's Hospital in Portsmouth because 'there were so many wounded coming back from the beaches that they desperately needed help'. When she arrived Naina Beaven found 'lorries were coming up from the dockyards so quickly that there wasn't room for all the wounded . . . Mostly they were conscious but not talking much; they were mostly really, really tired . . . As I worked with these poor exhausted soldiers, I was thinking, "How long will this go on? If I come in tomorrow and the next day, will I still be doing this?"

'While I was washing and cleaning up filthy and dreadful and horrible messes . . . two sisters came round and asked if I would be willing to work in the German prisoners' ward . . . some nurses had refused . . . Win [her friend] looked at me and said, "Oh come on Naina. My Eddie is out there and if somebody said they wouldn't clean him up, Mum would feel terrible." So with that, [I said] I'll do it . . . I couldn't bear the thought of my commander saying to me, "One of my girls wouldn't even give a prisoner a cup of water." . . . One of the rules of the Red Cross is that you are there to help everybody. I'm glad I didn't refuse to help those men.'

Churches opened their doors for impromptu services of prayer and thanksgiving. At St Paul's Cathedral and Westminster Abbey, at churches and chapels all over the country, people slipped in quietly on their way to work or out shopping to kneel briefly in a pew to pray. A Coventry woman heard the news of the invasion while out shopping so she 'went into a local church to pray for victory. The vicar asked why we weren't wearing hats. We put handkerchiefs on our heads. "No woman comes into my church without a hat," he insisted. A woman asked him quietly, "Your church or God's? Have our men over there got hats – or heads?" ' In Manchester, a woman working in a bank opposite St Anne's Church noticed that 'services were being held every half-hour and as midday approached, queues formed outside – the workers of Manchester were waiting to spend their lunch hour today in prayer, myself and colleagues included. Just a simple service, a hymn, a prayer, private meditation and the national Anthem . . .' A Norfolk clergyman 'seized the initiative. He borrowed the police loudspeaker van, the only vehicle then permitted to use a public address system, and toured the streets. Instead of the usual "Police calling!" the surprised townspeople heard "This is the Church calling. I invite you to a special service at eleven o'clock." The response was magnificent. The great church was filled to overflowing and during the moving service tears trickled down many faces.'

By nightfall on D-Day, 75,215 British and Canadian and 57,500 US troops had landed on the beaches of Normandy plus about 20,000 airbourne troops, and were beginning the advance inland. Losses had been lower than expected – but there were still around 4,300 British and Canadian casualties. And the toll of US troops was very high on Omaha beach, the most westerly end of the assault where a crack German unit had, unknown to Allied Intelligence, moved in for training. The worst casualties came within the first two hours, and by the end of the day some 4,500 US troops lay dead or injured on Omaha and Utah beaches, and the soldiers had only just managed to secure the beachhead on Omaha. In total around 10,000 Americans, British and Canadians, from all the services, were killed on D-Day.

Around midnight on D-Day a twenty-three-year-old amphibious platoon commander 'went down to the beach alone . . . It was fairly quiet by then, a few things coming in, but not many. There was still gunfire going on. But it was in the distance.

'It was actually a beautiful night and as I walked along the beach I thought I was stepping on soft seaweed, but when I looked down I saw it was the bodies of our men washed up on the tide. I was actually walking on the bodies of British soldiers. I didn't go any further . . .'

Over the next few weeks thousands more troops and supplies continued to pour into France for the agonisingly slow fight through the *bocage* for, as Roosevelt had warned during his D-Day address: 'The war is by no means over yet . . .' It was 'up to schedule [which strictly speaking it wasn't] but you don't just walk to Berlin. The sooner everyone realises this the better.'

A Corporal Jones and his wife wrote to each other every day during the war. Suddenly the letters stopped coming. 'I knew something desperate was happening and wasn't surprised when the wireless announced landings on the Normandy beaches. It was D-Day. I felt sure my husband was in the terrible affray . . . the BBC announced that we would be soon be receiving a card from the troops who had gone over on D-Day . . . I wrote to him every day for three anxious weeks. Every day I waited for the postman to bring me that longed-for card. The card never came. Instead a letter arrived from the War Office telling me that it was their "painful duty to inform" me that my husband had been killed on D-Day.'

Had they entertained any such illusions, British civilians were very soon to realise how far from over the war was for them, or for the troops fighting in Europe and the Far East.

Exactly one week after the D-Day landings, two part-time members of the Observer Corps were on duty on top of a Martello tower, erected as a coastal defence against invasion during the Napoleonic Wars, at Dymchurch on Romney Marsh in Kent. At eight minutes past four in the morning of Tuesday 13 June, while it was still dark, they noticed a strange black shape the size of a small fighter plane surrounded by a red glare hurtling in their direction and emitting a noise 'like a Model T Ford going uphill'. The first of Hitler's 'secret weapons' had arrived in Britain.

Fears of a German 'secret weapon' stretched back to a speech Hitler had made on 19 September 1939 in Danzig, threatening 'a weapon with which we ourselves could not be attacked'. Although rumours spread of bacterial warfare, death rays and long-range guns, nothing materialised and the whole notion became something of a joke to the public. But not to Whitehall. Dr R. V. Jones, a twenty-eight-year-old physicist who had been a pupil of Churchill's 'Prof', his wartime scientific adviser Frederick Lindemann, was tasked with discovering if this mystery missile existed – and if it did how it could be counteracted. Intelligence reports and reconnaissance photographs were scrutinised, and by February 1943 the War Office had decided that there were 'indications that the Germans may be developing some form of long-range projectors capable of firing on this country from the French coast'. The War Cabinet appointed Churchill's son-in-law Duncan Sandys MP, who was something of an artillery expert, to take charge of the investigation, code-named 'Bodyline' after the style of bowling made notorious by Harold Larwood during the British cricket tour of Australia in 1932, a tactic regarded as distinctly unfair and unEnglish.

For many months Sandys and his team continued to be 'groping in the dark . . . it was as though the parts of two or three jigsaw puzzles had been jumbled together . . .' There were indeed two 'puzzles' in that there were two separate 'secret weapons' being developed simultaneously – a flying bomb and a rocket – each with its own powerful advocate within German military and scientific circles.

It was the first of these pilotless planes (or as the Germans called them V-1s – an abbreviation of *Vergeltungswaffe Eins* or 'Revenge Weapon Number One') to be launched across the Channel that the observers had seen and identified by its code name 'Diver' from their tower on that Tuesday morning. Ten had been launched, of which four had crossed the Channel to fall on English soil; but only one reached its target – London – landing on a railway bridge in Bow, to the east. Railway tracks were torn up, nearby houses and a pub were severely damaged, and the flying bomb claimed its first victims: six dead – including an eight-month-old baby – thirty seriously injured and 200 made homeless. A ten-year-old child staying with her grandmother described for the first time what would become ominously familiar to thousands in London and the south-east in the next few weeks. 'The engine stopped, then there was a sound of whistling . . . and the next thing was a tremendous bang and the front room windows came in . . .'

No reference was made to the attack in the next morning's papers. Since the bomb was reported to have 'dropped like a stone', many presumed that it was a plane that had crashed, and word got around that it was the vanguard of a German counter-invasion, or, remembering Hess's mission in 1942, maybe a peace envoy, and that the pilot had been burned to ashes as the plane crashed. The War Cabinet decided that 'no public statement should be made about the new form of attack until the enemy had made it public or until the weight or extent of attack made a statement desirable'. But that day, as Sir Alan Brooke wrote in his diary, 'Flying bombs have again put us in the front line'.

It was not until the one o'clock bulletin on Friday 16 June that the news broke, putting an end to speculation about planes on fire, pilots baling out or being consumed in the flames. The BBC announced as its third item, after a routine 'No big change in Normandy' story, that 'the enemy has started using pilotless planes against this country'. The report was deliberately cagey. That morning the Chief Censor, Admiral Thomson, had issued strict press guidelines to ensure that the Germans did not know if their weapon was on target. The location of any incidents was to be entirely non-specific; air-raid warnings in the London area were not to be reported, nor was the shooting down or crashing of any plane, with or without a pilot; and obituary notices for people killed by enemy action were limited to a maximum of three people from the same postal district in each issue of a newspaper.

That first weekend of the attack was the worst. Although many bombs crashed on take-off, or failed to make it across the Channel, a steady stream was reaching the capital. St Mary Abbots Hospital in Kensington was so badly damaged that first Saturday, with so many casualties, that it had to be entirely evacuated; bombs fell on shoppers in Battersea, Wandsworth, Streatham and Putney. But the worst incident of that first weekend happened at 11.20 a.m. on Sunday 18 June. The congregation in the Guards Chapel of Wellington Barracks in Birdcage Walk, just around the corner from Buckingham Palace, had just stood to sing the Te Deum 'To Thee all Angels cry aloud, the Heavens and all the Powers therein' when a V-1 hit the building. In all, fifty-eight civilians and sixty-three service personnel were killed, and nearly seventy people seriously injured.

Dr R. V. Jones was working in his office nearby when he heard the explosion. He hurried down to Birdcage Walk. 'I had . . . been used to the flying bomb. I knew its warhead was going to be about a ton. I knew what a ton of high explosive could do . . . [But] it struck me then how very different the academic appreciation of explosions was from the actuality . . . By the time I'd got down to the . . . Chapel they were just carrying out the first dead . . . One lasting impression I had was the whole of Birdcage Walk was a sea of fresh pine tree leaves, the trees had all been stripped and you could hardly see a speck of asphalt for hundreds of yards.'

Within three days of the arrival of the first V-1, 647 bombs had killed 499 people – with the number rising as more bodies were dug out from ruined buildings – and more than 2,000 were seriously injured. The damage to property had been immense, affecting 137,000 buildings, since although the V-1s produced virtually no craters when they fell, their blast power was greater than that of conventional bombs. It was predicted that if attacks continued at the same rate, within two months London would suffer the equivalent destruction as in the whole nine months of the Blitz.

Herbert Morrison recognised that 'after five years of war the civilian population were not as capable of standing the strains of air attacks as they had been during the winter of 1940–41. I will do everything to hold up their courage and spirit – but there is a limit, and the limit will come.' It was Morrison who decided that these new weapons should be called 'flying bombs' rather than the more sinister alternative 'pilotless planes' – though doodlebugs (to be found in Mark Twain's *Tom Sawyer*), buzz bombs, bumble bombs, robot planes – and worse – caught on with the public.

Over the next three months flying bombs were coming over day and night – and alerts became 'like a child pushing a door bell and running away'. An Air Ministry official at work in the Aldwych 'counted over

30 alarms in a single day' and often they came so frequently that people found it difficult to remember whether there was an alert on or not. The noise was very different from that made by bombs dropping from planes – the missiles had a whining, humming note that grew louder as they approached, and when the engine cut out there was an agonising silence before the bomb plunged to earth and exploded. A. P. Herbert recommended that, on such occasions, the 'model citizen' should pray:

> Stop, noise, immediately that I
> And not some other chap may die

but most silently entreated 'Please keep going' as what appeared to be a ball of fire skimmed over the roof tops.

At Morrison's factory in Croydon where Kathleen Bliss and Elsie Whiteman were working, 'the night shift had kept a tally of the number of bombs and red alerts that they had had on the night of 22/23 June – 25 bombs and 18 alerts! Up and down the shelters all day, and meal breaks interrupted too.' The next day George Strauss MP came to the factory, representing Sir Stafford Cripps (Beaverbrook's successor as Minister of Aircraft Production). 'He came to congratulate Morrison's workers on their morale and on their good records for attendance and production during the present blitz . . . He said that we were every bit as much in the front line as the soldiers in Normandy and the civilian casualties to date were much the same as in Monty's army.'

V-1s were simplified, functional weapons, enviably conceived as far as the Allies were concerned. They were cigar-shaped, just over 25 feet long, including the pulse jet engine, and had short, stubby wings with a span of only 17 feet 6 inches. The V-1s weighed 2 tons – nearly half of which consisted of a powerful mixture of TNT and ammonium nitrate. Their course was preset and, if it deviated, devices attached to the fuselage could bring it back on track. The distance was preset too – usually at 140 miles – and when this was reached a circuit closed down and the V-1 plunged down towards the ground. Crossing the English coast at a height of about 2,500 feet and a speed of 340 mph, but getting faster as the fuel burned out, from the ground a V-1 looked like a half-sized Spitfire. Though the crew on some ramps situated in northern

France managed to fire a V-1 every half-hour, the usual rate was around fifteen per site per day, and of those around 10 per cent crashed straight to earth. Since they left a fixed firing ramp aiming for a fixed target – Tower Bridge straddling the Thames at the gateway to the docks – the V-1s flew along a predetermined 'lane' or route, often in rapid succession or in what seemed like convoys fired from a number of sites simultaneously.

The adage that lightning never strikes twice did not hold in the case of the flying bombs, particularly in south London and the area around Croydon. Faulty mechanisms or the action of the defenders, though, caused many to deviate, circling, twisting, diving or even floating eerily when they ran out of fuel miles before they had been programmed to plunge. Although anatomical drawings showing how the V-1 worked appeared in the press, the demystification was not successful. Many people found them a particularly scary form of warfare, an unreckonable mechanical monster impervious to human interference, a science-fiction horror. George Orwell noticed the widespread complaint that the V-1s ' "seem so unnatural" (a bomb dropped by a live airman is quite natural apparently)'. 'After what we have been doing to the Germans over the past two years', he thought it was 'a bit thick' to denounce the flying bombs as 'barbarous, inhumane, and an indiscriminate attack on civilians' – the attacks on Hamburg in July and August 1943 created firestorms in which some 40,000 civilians and 800 servicemen perished, almost five times as many as those killed by the 'revenge weapons' that fell on Britain. But Orwell recognised that it was 'the normal human response to every new weapon. Poison gas, the machine gun, the submarine, gunpowder and even the crossbow were similarly denounced in their day. Every new weapon seems unfair until you have adopted it yourself.'

'People . . . have said to me, "It's a dirty way of waging war." Just as if there was ever such a thing as a "clean war",' was George Britton's riposte. 'War's a dirty business and everybody and everything connected with it gets more or less smudged.'

Vivienne Hall was in no doubt: 'It just seems to be like a colossal and hideous game of spite! Just to send these things over haphazardly to make life a chancy unpleasant thing for we long-suffering Londoners . . . We have had to face up to horrible things for nearly five years, I suppose we shall continue to do so, but, God, how tired we are of it! Just working and living and sleeping through one mad, noisome form of destruction week after week, month after month, without the excitement of battle or the thrill of personal victory, without the knowledge that we count for anything, or that our efforts to keep going are contributing towards the ultimate betterment of conditions in the world.'

Indeed, morale in London and southern England hit rock bottom that cold, wet summer and early autumn when a victory that had seemed graspable after D-Day now started to seem as elusive and high-priced as ever.

Between 100 and 150 V-1s a day were aimed at London. The fear and disruption these weapons – a desperate last-ditch attempt to beat Britain into submission – caused was enormous. Women were reluctant to leave their homes to dash to the shops, they were loath to send their children to school, and those who did go often spent hours in the shelter – everywhere there was a heightened, edgy awareness with everyone's ear permanently cocked for the distinctive sound of a flying bomb.

During the V-1 attacks there was no comforting – albeit deafening – volley of ack-ack fire to reassure Londoners. It had been decided that bringing the flying bombs crashing down in densely populated areas was too dangerous to life and property, and that it was vital to try to fell the weapons before they could reach London. The defence against the V-1s was three-pronged. Ack-ack guns let off salvos around the coast and Thames Estuary; those that managed to get inland were the province of fighter planes; and a vast 260-square-mile shield of barrage balloons covered the area from the South Downs to Essex and Kent. Between mid June and early September this combined defence force managed to bring down a total of 3,463 V-1s – or just over half of all bombs spotted. But that still meant of course that just under half were getting through.

On 30 June, as office workers were taking advantage of some rare summer sunshine in their lunch hour, a V-1 hit the Aldwych in central London. When the choking mist of dust and debris cleared a little it revealed bodies lying across the pavements, the twisted skeleton of a line of burned-out buses that had been parked at the roadside and debris from buildings, including the badly scarred Bush House, home of the BBC overseas service, and Adastral House, the Air Ministry building on the corner of Kingsway – where a 10-foot-high blast wall in front of the windows had been completely demolished. Forty-eight people were dead.

On Thursday 6 July, a month after D-Day, Churchill addressed a sombre House of Commons: 'Up to 6 a.m. today,' he said, '2,752 people have been killed by flying bombs and about 8,000 have been detained in hospital. The firing points in France have been continually attacked for several months . . . the invisible battle has now crashed into the open.'

During the second week of July there was a brief and partial respite for the capital as numbers of V-1s landed in the vicinity of Southampton and around Portsmouth, which suggested that Colonel Max Wachtel, the commander of the V-1 firing units, had in his sights those south coast ports involved in sending troops and supplies across the Channel to reinforce those already in France. It was a highly disruptive but not particularly successful attack since most bombs fell wide of their target, but it did contribute to the ongoing debate about how to deflect the V-1s away from London. By mid July, despite sustained bombing of the launching sites and the triple defence system, twenty-five to thirty V-1s a day were still reaching the capital, though most were falling short of the target. Croydon, 9 miles shy of Tower Bridge, had the most throughout the whole campaign with over 140 V-1s falling in the borough, destroying a thousand houses and severely damaging 57,000. Numbers two and three in this unenviable list were Wandsworth and Lewisham, respectively 5 and 4 miles south-west and south-east of Tower Bridge.

Obviously the Germans wanted to know whether their 'secret weapons' were reaching their targets, and briefed agents in the field to report on when and where the V-1s were landing. What information should those 'turned' agents be fed that would seem plausible to their control, yet deflected as many V-1s as possible from London? 'If we could keep the centre of the pattern [in the south and south-eastern suburbs], or, even better, make them put it back still further, they would in fact do less damage,' Dr R. V. Jones considered. At the end of July a secret report was prepared for the War Cabinet 'to illustrate as accurately as possible the effects of the deception'. It detailed the effect that foreshortening the bombs' mean point of impact at Dulwich would have on various boroughs. Westminster would benefit dramatically, while the situation of such boroughs as Stepney, Islington, Shoreditch and Wandsworth would be much improved, and even Lewisham would have a slightly easier time. But parts of Croydon would be worse off and, in Kent, Bromley, Bexley and particularly Orpington would, if the Germans swallowed the deception, suffer much greater loss of life and property. It was clearly a deeply sensitive and controversial issue, and could only possibly be justified by the argument that the population density was much less in the outer suburbs, and thus each bomb would cause less damage.

The Ministry of Home Security was sceptical whether the plan would save lives and doubted that the Civil Defence services in the outer suburbs would be able to cope with a sudden increase of bombs falling in their area. The Minister, Herbert Morrison, was appalled at the idea, suspecting 'that the attempt to keep the aiming point short was an effort by government officials and others in Westminster, Belgravia and Mayfair, to keep the bombs off themselves at the expense of the proletariat in south London' (including Morrison's own constituency of Lambeth). He was in favour of 'confusing' the enemy with a series of false stories about V-1 attacks but not, in his words, 'playing God' by diverting 'the enemy's attention from certain sections of the population to other sections'. The War Cabinet's decision on the matter – exceptionally – was not minuted in writing, but attempts to deceive the enemy into aiming the V-1s further south, rather than simply to confuse him with contradictory statements, continued.

A month after the Aldwych disaster, on 28 July, there was a second 'Black Friday' for London. Twenty V-1s fell on Kensington and soon after 1 p.m. one of them hit four cafés packed with diners at the junction of Earl's Court Road and Kensington High Street; forty-five people were killed. But earlier that morning south London had had an even more devastating attack when at 9.41 Lewisham street market was hit. Gwyneth Thomas was a sister at Lewisham hospital. Two nights earlier the hospital had received a direct hit 'on the medical block next to our nurses' home where we were sleeping . . . God knows how we got 200 patients out of that furnace; two were trapped, but were rescued just in time . . . one nurse had worked through it all with a severed artery which she had bound up, the others with deep lacerations of the leg, one with a head wound . . . Above all I take my hat off to the firemen.'

On Friday, the Matron ordered an exhausted Nurse Thomas to 'take the day off so I . . . decided if only I could get out of the area for one day, I should feel rested.' Gwyneth Thomas missed the bus she had been aiming for, and that probably saved her life. 'When we reached Lewisham shopping centre, it was to meet with such a sight I shall never forget or wish to see again. Marks & Spencer was ablaze, people trapped, screaming, dead, lying in the roadway, girls with hair and clothes alight, could be seen running wildly in the burning buildings, a girl with half her scalp off, an old lady lying naked in the roadway, people running everywhere, shouting, screaming, dying, burning . . . no battlefield could be worse or more bloody. Suddenly, as if out of the air, ambulances, vans of all descriptions, fire services, rescue squads all working like fury . . . Eventually I reached the station; never have I had a bigger fight to keep from screaming, so at last I reached my friends, and there I broke down. I suppose I knew there was no need to fight any more. I collapsed and screamed and Hilda gave me brandy.'

A former WAAF was with her mother buying mushrooms in the market when 'I suddenly heard a queer sound – a sort of cracking noise . . . I instinctively looked up and there it was, right over the top of us like a huge black whale's head, coming through the cloud almost at roof level, and as I shouted, "Get down, Mum!" and tried to push her to the ground . . . We were thrown into the air and blown about like . . . waste paper and there was dust and screams all round and then awful silence and we were lying on the ground . . . I noticed Mum's white summer coat covered with blood and she was moaning and . . . we could only lie there and wait for help . . . The priest from St Saviour's . . . wandered along and vicars from other churches murmuring prayers over us, then on to the next victim . . .' In September the final casualty figures were released: fifty-one dead (though local ARP workers maintained there were far more), 124 seriously injured and a further 189 treated at first aid posts.

The question of what warning to give preoccupied the government. The approach of a single bomb did not trigger the alert, nor did 'flying bombs passing over', and if there was an alert in the night, the All Clear was not sounded until 6 a.m. the following morning. Some politicians and commentators thought even this was too much, that continual warnings made people nervous and interfered with war work, while others felt uncomfortable at the thought that they might be entirely ignorant of a bomb hastening their way. A woman working in an aircraft factory near Elstree was 'having "Take Cover" warnings as many as 16 times in a nine-hour shift. Production fell well below what we were used to turn out.' The workers were asked 'if they were willing to work through the alerts if there was a look-out on the roof. At the sound of a klaxon everyone would race to the nearest shelter . . . down the middle of the factory and also underground ones; no one was more than a minute from cover. No one HAD to stay working if they were afraid. As the days went on, fewer and fewer people felt they must take cover and production went up to an even higher level than before the bombs.'

Those working in large factories would receive an 'imminent danger' warning which meant that they could ignore any official alert and keep production going until the threat was near, when they could down tools and take shelter. Without this refinement, the endless alerts and daytime all clears meant that either workers took unacceptable risks, or they spent unnecessarily long hours in a shelter. A number of smaller factories had found this so disruptive they had set up their own system by which spotters on the roof would keep an eye on the activities of those large-scale factories that were hooked up to the official 'imminent danger' system and used either bells, or, in the case of particularly noisy establishments, coloured lights, to give their workers a little over a minute to hurry into the shelters. Information about this would be transmitted to the smaller factory's own workers and the shelter routine would start. On 1 August Herbert Morrison announced a similar system of civilian danger warnings. In future a series of klaxon horns linked to the official 'industrial warning system' would emit a signal audible for half a mile when a flying-bomb was within 15 miles 'on the direct line of approach'. The first sounded in mid August from Whitbread's brewery in Chiswell Street in the City, and a week later thirty such devices were set up at the Houses of Parliament, Shell Mex House and various other tall buildings.

Finally the first of the purpose-built 'deep shelters' that had been under construction for so long admitted shelterers at Stockwell in south London on 10 July 1944. The building was 130 feet below ground and had space for 4,000 with reasonably priced canteens, lavatory and washing facilities and even arrangements for laundry. All was very orderly and well run – light years away from the tube-shelter experience of the early days of the Blitz. Unsurprisingly, both this and the two subsequently opened deep shelters were over-subscribed almost at once, and a government spokesman admitted that 'sufficient deep shelters of this new type are not available to meet the demand'. Anderson shelters were cleared out and families once more accustomed themselves to nights spent listening for the whine of the bombs. Once the V-1s arrived, Morrison shelters, metal cages or 'rabbit hutches', started to justify the space they took up in the average semi or terrace house.

Many Londoners, exhausted and afraid and with no reserves of stamina left to counteract this latest offensive after five years of war, simply left the city. By September over a million in the 'priority classes' (mothers with infants under five, school-age children, expectant mothers and the old and infirm) had taken part in the evacuation scheme which the LCC had announced on 1 July, and many more had taken advantage of the 'assisted passage' provision whereby those who had been bombed out received free travel warrants and billeting certificates which entitled them to a weekly allowance, though they had to make their own arrangements.

Churchill was not inclined 'to discourage those . . . who had no essential work to do . . . from leaving London at their own expense if they feel inclined to do so . . . In fact, they assist our affairs by taking such action . . . we do not need more people in London than are required for business purposes of peace and war.' Between July and September 1944 the Post Office registered 1,110,000 changes of address out of London, and that undoubtedly fell well short of the full total of evacuees in all categories. In July Gwladys Cox noted in her diary that she had heard from a friend staying in Southport: her hotel was 'inundated with refugees from London bringing lurid tales of our bombing – evidently an eye opener to those in the north . . . Whereas London is deserted . . . the West End is dead . . . it gives one a queer, lonely feeling.'

All London railway termini were overwhelmed by the numbers of people who wanted to leave the capital, and questions were asked in the House about the 'chaos at Paddington' at the end of July when there were unruly stampedes for every train – and, if they managed to get on a train, pregnant women found that they were having to stand for up to eight hours in the corridor. There were never enough seats on the special trains, suitable billets proved to be as hard to find as ever particularly when it came to placing mothers and babies, and the culture clash between urban and rural Britain continued to jar; but in general the experience of the 1944 evacuation was much more successful than the mass departures of 1939 had been, even though in those areas affected more adults and children were evacuated – officially and unofficially – between June and August 1944, than had been at the start of the war. After five years of war, the quiet of the countryside was a deeply valued antidote to days and nights of bombs, guns, searchlights and danger.

It was almost impossible to find anywhere to live out of London, as Vivienne Hall discovered. Her Putney home had been badly damaged by a V-1 but pronounced 'safe at least until the next bomb', and she went looking for accommodation in Oxted in Surrey. 'The Estate Agents tell me the only way to get a home is to know someone who knows someone who is moving somewhere else!' But for those who were prepared to stay in London, it was a buyers' (or renters') market – every effort was made to patch up and make habitable as many houses as possible. With some 20,000 houses damaged every twenty-four hours, and the backlog increasing by 12,000 a day, London builders could no longer cope, and an appeal was made for tradesmen to be brought in from all over the country to make the houses at least weatherproof. The Empire Pool in Wembley was transformed into a clearing point, sending workers where they were most urgently needed and sorting out accommodation and food for them. On 15 September Lord Woolton, the Minister of Reconstruction, announced that 80,000 men including 5,000 servicemen were at work in a race against the weather to ensure that as many houses as possible were habitable as winter approached.

After a raid the local authority would usually arrange for piles of two-ply wood, roofing felt and clout nails to be delivered to roadside dumps so that householders could help themselves free of charge and undertake some rudimentary DIY first aid to keep their homes and possessions protected from the elements until the workmen arrived. Glass was in desperately short supply and some householders had to go without until after the war had ended. Often all that could be got was opaque, unpolished glass, and this was used in bedrooms and bathrooms to conserve any precious supply of clear glass for downstairs windows.

Most repairs were carried out by private firms under the supervision of the local authority, which could in theory reclaim the cost from the War Damage Commission for all repairs undertaken. Those costing less than £10 could be undertaken without prior permission, and up to £100 it was pretty much a rubber-stamping exercise, but repairs that cost more required a building licence – with many offices and staff bombed out too, and paperwork in chaos, it could take a frustratingly long time to get the required piece of paper. In many of the poorer London boroughs evacuation for non-priority cases was not an option. Families had nowhere else to go, and continued to camp out in what were strictly speaking uninhabitable homes, chalking messages like 'still living here' on the door in case the postman or milkman, noting the tile-less roof and boarded-up windows, presumed otherwise.

In all boroughs Civil Defence services had been cut back in 1943 in response to the constant need for industrial and military manpower, and the depleted services worked at full stretch during the V-bomb campaigns. After the Catford school raid in January 1943, the WVS had been officially asked to set up Incident Inquiry Posts (IIPs) and by the time of the V-1s incident officers in most boroughs were requesting the presence of such a post as routine at each raid. The posts were staffed by specially trained members of the WVS, who requisitioned a suitable space – or just set up shop on the pavement – near an incident. The Blitz had taught that the simple word INFORMATION printed on a tin sign stuck up as near as possible to the site of a bomb incident was the most reassuring sight the bombed could have. Lists of who was expected to be in whatever premises had been bombed were matched with information tactfully gathered about those who had been traced, were at rest centres, in hospital – or in the mortuary. Invariably the lists did not always entirely tally, and people might be missing for days while anxious friends and relations besieged the posts. The WVS workers, who were drawn as much from the local area as possible, became skilled and sympathetic counsellors of the bereaved and the bereft. In Streatham, at one point, there were eight WVS-staffed IIPs operating simultaneously, and at the Lewisham disaster in July 1944 WVS members set up an IIP on a table borrowed from a nearby coffee stall, and tried to answer questions as smoke and debris swirled around. After eleven days there were still unidentified bodies, possibly those of Irish labourers who had been doing road repairs nearby and who were known to the foreman only as Mick or Pat.

By mid September 2,622 bombs had fallen on Kent, 886 on Sussex, 512 on Essex and 295 on Surrey. Now that the southern Home Counties had become hazardous, householders who had previously been ineligible for a Morrison shelter received one; neutral areas such as Bromley, Sidcup, Chislehurst and Orpington were redesignated for evacuation, as were places like Sevenoaks, Tenterden and Tunbridge Wells which had originally been classified as reception areas. Dover and Folkestone, always in the front line of Britain's defences, witnessed numbers of V-1s landing on the beaches and becoming harmlessly embedded in the white chalk cliffs or being brought down by fighter planes and the inshore coastal guns.

The 'alley' that led from the coast to London meant that Kent, Sussex and parts of Hampshire became, in the words of the novelist and journalist. H. E. Bates, a graveyard for intercepted doodlebugs. During the first week of the attack 101 flying bombs were shot down over Kent alone and the unremitting attacks continued day and night. But as Bates wrote in an account that was not published until fifty years after the events of the summer of 1944, 'a shot down bug was not, of course, a dead bug; as it hit the earth whether in cornfield, village street, meadow or churchyard, it exploded just the same, all too often with fatal results'. In his own area of rural Kent, 'more than 3,000 of these intercepted bugs fell in a few weeks, so that a map showing each fallen bug looks like a settlement of dead flies on a dead carcass . . . The people of doodle-bug alley were . . . never free. In eighty days and nights they had every chance to see and hear practically everything that a flying-bomb could do. They saw them fall on their ancient and beloved churches, on schools and hospitals, on some of the loveliest villages in the world. They never knew from one moment to another whether the meal they were eating, the glass of beer they were drinking . . . might not be their last . . . The Battle of Britain which they had been thrilled and proud to see with their own eyes . . . was a memory without fear. The Battle of the Doodlebug . . . was a time entirely without thrill or pride . . .' The chairman of Kent's Civilian Defence Committee queried, 'What is "open country"? Our coastal towns, miles of countryside dotted with villages, cottages, farms and houses. Here and there some big town. A flying-bomb exploding in the air, let alone on the ground, will strip the roof, bring down the ceilings, shatter the windows of all beneath, whether it be a cottage or 500 houses – and whether it be a cottage or a house, it was somebody's home . . . So often [it was] somebody's life taken to save London . . .'

By the end of August V-1 attacks had become sporadic and rumours began to circulate among people desperate for the war to be over that Germany had capitulated and the war was over. Since nearly all areas from which the bombs were launched were already in Allied hands – or soon would be – Duncan Sandys confidently predicted on 7 September 1944 that 'Except for a few shots, the battle for London is over'. It was not. As Sandys spoke, a new phase in the attrition had started. A few V-1s released from aircraft gradually moved up the east coast – and the defences moved to counteract them. Nevertheless, ten days later blackout restrictions were eased. The 'dim out' meant that lights did not have to be blacked out unless the alert was sounded – though George Britton was unable to see the point of having any blackout regulations at all any more since it clearly made no difference to pilotless planes. The result of the relaxation was 'that London is piebald [since] London's regulations are under the control of so many different boroughs, district councils and such like, so consequently each authority has its own system. Some have a master switch whereby all the lights can be put out at once. On the other hand many have not, so perforce they have to remain dark all the time . . . Piccadilly is one of the dark 'uns.'

The day after Sandys' speech, Home Security noted another menace – 'four incidents, all believed to have been caused by long range bombs'. The second of Hitler's 'secret weapons' had arrived in Britain. The V-2 was a rocket, 46 feet long and 5 feet in diameter at the widest part, which carried about a ton of explosives. Since all northern France was in Allied hands and their armies were advancing into Belgium, the only possible site from which to attack was some 200 miles from London on the far side of the Rhine in Holland. The V-2s overcame this. The equipment to launch them was easily transportable and the rockets were moved into position and fired vertically from a small concrete platform that was hard to detect from the air, let alone target. The V-2s had a range of approximately 225 miles and a speed of 3,600 mph – faster than the speed of sound – and as they were launched from Holland, the north-east of London took the worst of the attack. A total news blackout was imposed by the British government, even though the noise of the V-2 was ear-splitting, comparable to a thunderclap followed by a blinding blue flash, and a tremendous roaring sound as the rocket descended to earth – it could be heard for miles. Thirty-six such bombs landed in September 1944, and 131 in October; these 'Big Ben' (as the V-2 was code-named) attacks were referred to as 'air raid incidents' or 'plane crashes' or 'gas main explosions'. They fell on London, the suburbs, Hertfordshire, Kent, Essex, Suffolk and Norfolk with a few penetrating as far as Northampton and Bedford. The death toll was less than that caused by the V-1s: in total 2,754 people were killed by the V-2s (as compared to 6,184 by the V-1s and 51,509 by conventional bombs) and 6,523 were injured. Again the toll on property was heavy: 23,000 homes were destroyed by V-1 and V-2 bombs and nearly a million were damaged – many of which were subsequently found to be unfit for human habitation and had to be demolished.

Even after the *New York Times* reported the scale of the rocket attack on 6 October 1944 the British press was forbidden to reveal that the V-2s were responsible. 'We had to stop the knowledge of their arrival being circulated, first so as not to inform the Germans that they had landed in any particular area, but more important, there was the question of morale of the civilian population, because they were devastating in their effect. One rocket could demolish a whole street in a working-class area. There was no defence against them. And there was no warning that they were on their way and you could not take any shelter of any kind, because you had not even five seconds notice . . .' recalled Dore Silverman, one of the ten censors working at the Ministry of Information combing 'sensitive' copy submitted by newspaper editors for any mention of bomb damage – and removing it.

The incredibly loud double bang that heralded each V-2 could make people up to 10 miles away think it was about to fall on them. Though fewer V-2s fell than V-1s, their terror lay in their unpredictability, and their dreadful impact. A single V-2 could cause a crater as large as 50 feet wide and 10 feet deep. A whole row of perhaps thirty terrace houses in the vicinity of the rocket bomb would be virtually razed, and streets would resemble a battlefield. The effect reverberated up to a quarter of a mile away, causing walls to cave in, skimming tiles off roofs, smashing windows and bringing down clouds of soot. Rockets fell on the usual war-scarred London boroughs – Woolwich, Hackney, Lewisham, West Ham, Lambeth, Wandsworth, as well as Croydon and Beckenham, Bromley, Chislehurst and Orpington in Kent; and there were 3,403 other flying bomb 'incidents' outside the London Civil Defence Region. The worst incident of the offensive came on Saturday 25 November – a month that had a total of 284 incidents – when a V-2 hit a Woolworths store at New Cross in south-east London soon after noon, killing 160 people and seriously injuring 108. June Gaida had been going shopping for her mother, 'and suddenly there was a blinding flash of light, and a roaring, rushing sound and I was lifted off my feet, and all around there was this terrible noise, this din, beating against my eardrums. I fell to the ground [and] curled myself up into a ball to protect myself and I tried to breathe but I couldn't because there was no air. When I picked myself up . . . I was coated in brick dust and splinters of glass, and things were still falling out of the sky, there were bricks and bits of masonry, bits of things and bits of people. I walked towards Woolworths. I remember seeing a horse's head lying in the gutter, and further on there was a pram that stood all twisted and bent and a little baby's hand, still in its woolly sleeve. Outside the pub there was a bus and it had been concertinaed, people were just sitting inside, rows and rows of people covered in dust and they were all dead. When I looked towards where Woolworths had been, it was just a huge empty space. No building, just piles of rubble and bricks and from underneath it all, I could hear people screaming.'

Finally on Armistice Day, 11 November 1944, as Churchill drove up the Champs Elysées in a liberated Paris with General de Gaulle, the British press was at last permitted to tell the people what they already knew. 'The V-2 Rocket Comes to Southern England . . . the most indiscriminate weapon of this or any other war . . . a sinister, eerie form of war. Britain's front line at home is under fire again – from a stratospheric rocket that is dropping on us from 60 to 70 miles up in the air, a rocket that travels faster than sound and flashes across the sky like a "comet trailing fire" . . . There is no siren warning. No time to take shelter.'

The winter of 1944–5 was again bitterly cold, and the lives of those whose homes had been damaged by bombs were made even more insupportable by the freezing weather. In the early hours of what was to be the last Christmas Eve of the war – and the coldest one for more than half a century – the Germans launched a V-1 attack on a part of the country hitherto free of flying bombs. Outflanking the coastal defences, a convoy of planes dropped bombs along the Lincolnshire coast and on the outskirts of Manchester and what was referred to in the press as 'one industrial town', Oldham, where at least ten people were killed, including four members of a wedding party, and fourteen injured.

The bombs dropped on Oldham did not deliver just death and destruction, but propaganda too in the form of an airmail-sized version of *Signal*, the magazine produced for neutral and occupied countries, copies of which had first been found in Kent in August. But this time there was an ingenious new twist – 'POW Post'. Several facsimile letters from prisoners whose homes were in the area were found scattered on the ground. The finder was requested to pass on the letter to the intended recipient as soon as possible and was assured that the original letters were being sent 'through the Red Cross in the usual mail channel'. The idea, presumably, was that the family of the POW would reply to the letter, thus revealing where the V-1 had landed. But the POW Directorate and the Chief Censor decided that though the letters would be sent on, the recipients would be warned not to reply to them.

There were further serious incidents in London in December. Southwark and Duke Street off Oxford Street were hit, and on Boxing Day the Prince of Wales pub in Islington was packed with post-Christmas revellers when a V-2 exploded nearby and demolished the pub, trapping customers under debris in the cellar. Sixty-eight people died and hundreds more were injured.

In January 1945 the London boroughs of West Ham, Hackney, Islington, Tottenham, Southwark, Deptford, Lambeth and Waltham Cross, and Woodford in Essex all experienced the ominous double bang of the V-2 with considerable loss of life – between five and forty deaths per bomb seemed usual – and damage to property. In February the slaughter continued, with attacks falling across the capital, though with most in north-east London and Essex – including Ilford which suffered more than any other borough with thirty-five attacks. The Royal Hospital, home to the Chelsea Pensioners, was badly damaged by enemy action on 3 January. Five were killed, including the hospital doctor.

By the end of January almost half the capital's housing stock had been damaged by the combined flying bomb and rocket attacks, and some areas resembled shanty towns with tarpaulin roofs, boarded-up windows, temporary wood and corrugated-iron huts erected on bomb sites, and a near-Arctic winter to contend with. Strikes were becoming endemic among weary, dispirited workers in the docks, on London Transport, in the factories. George Beardmore was sent to persuade some Heavy Rescue Squad workers in Edgware not to strike over what seemed like a minor matter. 'My country is under attack from a new kind of bombardment . . . My country is short of manpower . . . I have only one question to put to you: "You aren't thinking of going on strike because of a shortage of lockers, are you?" With that I sat down . . .'

'I think that everyone in these dark autumn days is truly unhappy,' Harold Nicolson had written in December 1944. 'Partly war-weariness, partly sadness at things not going right and partly malnutrition.' The advance across Europe had been much slower than expected: Caen – a D-Day objective – had not been fully taken by British and Canadian troops until 18 July; Operation Market Garden – Allied airborne Army landings on 17 September, to aid the advance of Montgomery's 21st Group towards north Germany before the winter set in – was a costly failure and marked the end of any hope that there would be an Allied victory in 1944. On 16 December German panzer and infantry divisions launched what was to be a final counter-offensive across the sparsely defended Ardennes, taking the Allies by surprise. The fighting was bitter and the 'bulge' in the Allied line was not repaired until 16 January 1945 at a cost of some 80,000 Allied casualties. Meanwhile in June Stalin had fulfilled his promise to open an offensive to follow the D-Day landings, and within a month the Russians had advanced into Poland – and by the beginning of February the Red Army was within only 40 miles of Berlin.

The last of the V-1s that Hitler had still imagined could help force Britain to a compromise peace landed at Romford in Essex on Sunday 14 January 1945, but the V-2 attacks continued. In December 1944 there had been 133 incidents; there were 223 in January 1945; 233 in February and 228 in March. 'At present, on average, nineteen people are being killed by V bombs daily, and many more injured with terrible destruction to property all the time. The press, for security reasons, is largely silent,' noted Gwladys Cox in February. Deception exercises similar to those practised to deflect the V-1s south of London moved the impact of the V-2s eastwards by roughly 2 miles a week.

On the night of 13 February 1945 the RAF saturated the city of Dresden with incendiary and high-explosive bombs. The following morning – Ash Wednesday – the USAAF did the same: an Allied total of 4,500 tons of bombs was unleashed on the inadequately defended medieval German city. In the firestorm at least 25,000 died, probably more, maybe as many as 50,000. 'How many died? Who knows the number?' reads the memorial plaque in Dresden cemetery. The dead and wounded included Jews working as slave labourers in the radar and munitions factories, and German refugees fleeing from the advancing Red Army. 'Dresden? There is no such place as Dresden,' Sir Arthur Harris, Chief of Bomber Command, told Jock Colville, Churchill's private secretary.

The *Manchester Guardian* reported tens of thousands of people buried in the Dresden ruins, so badly burned as to make identification impossible. 'What happened on that evening of 13 February?' the newspaper demanded. The question was echoed by Richard Rapier Stokes, Labour MP for Ipswich, who asked in the Commons if the fact that the British people did not know that 'terror bombing' being done in their name was official policy. To a number of cultured Britons, the news of the destruction of 'Florence on the Elbe' came as a shock, while to others it was confirmatory evidence of the 'sickening' nature of war and raised little adverse comment at the time. 'Now they know how we liked the city of London burning,' the journalist Ursula Bloom chided the next month when she heard rumours that 'the Ruhr was on fire'. But with evidence that the end of the war was only a matter of weeks away and thinking as a victor, Churchill, previously a stalwart supporter of area bombing, distanced himself from the campaign. 'It seems to me,' he wrote in late March 1945 in a memo that remained secret for many years, 'that the moment has come when the question of bombing of German cities simply for the sake of increasing the terror, through other pretexts, should be reviewed. Otherwise we shall come into control of an utterly ruined land. We shall not, for example, be able to get housing materials out of Germany for our own needs . . .'

Still the killing went on. On 8 March 1945 at 11.10 a.m. a V-2 hit

Smithfield, the world's largest meat market. It landed in the centre of the complex which was crowded with people, replete with the usual wartime queue stretching along the street. The entire market building collapsed: 110 were killed outright and many more injured. The rockets continued to fall throughout March with mounting death tolls in the same areas that had suffered before – including a lying-in hospital for mothers and babies in Stepney, a Roman Catholic church a little further along the road, Petticoat Lane near Aldgate, a giant crater in some allotments in Canning Town near the Beckton gasworks . . .

On the night of 27 March 1945 a V-2 fell on Stepney in east London in a tragedy comparable to the raid on Woolworths in New Cross: two five-storey blocks of flats were flattened, and a third was badly damaged. By 1 April, after round-the-clock digging – including the use of the RAF-trained sniffer dogs that had been found so useful in locating victims trapped in the debris of a bombed building – it was found that 134 people had been killed, and more died later from their injuries. Just before five o'clock that same day, thirty-four-year-old Ivy Millichamp was in the kitchen of her bungalow in Orpington in Kent while her husband Eric, a shift worker, slept in the front room. When a V-2 landed in a nearby garden Mrs Millichamp was killed instantly by the blast, the last civilian in Britain to die as a result of enemy action.

24

'WE MAY ALLOW OURSELVES A BRIEF PERIOD OF REJOICING'

Oh, won't it be wonderful after the war –
. . . We'll work for the State, and we'll knock off at four
After the war – after the war.
We won't work at all if we find it a bore,
There won't be no rich and there won't be no pore
The beer will be better and quicker and more
But why didn't we have the old wa-er before?
    A. P. HERBERT, 'AFTER THE WAR' IN *PUNCH*, 8 JULY 1942

'THIS MEMORABLE DATE . . . must be in red – Victory red . . . after, it seemed, interminable rumours and false starts it has happened UNCONDITIONAL SURRENDER BY GERMANY TO THE ALLIES something we have longed for for six long years – and once or twice thought it would never happen,' Vivienne Hall wrote in the last entry in her wartime diary on 8 May 1945.

The victory had come haltingly, peace with a whimper. As the Allied armies converged on the River Elbe, German radio announced on 1 May that Hitler had been killed 'in the Battle of Berlin'. In fact he died by his own hand in a bunker deep below Berlin. At 2.41 on the morning of 7 May, in a school building in Rheims in northern France, the unconditional surrender of all German land, sea and air forces was signed by General Jodl. General Bedell Smith signed for the Allied Expeditionary Forces and General Susloparov for the Soviet High Command.

Churchill, Stalin and Harry Truman, the successor as US President to Roosevelt who had died suddenly of a cerebral haemorrhage on 12 April to great shock and sadness in Britain as in the United States, had agreed that the announcement of Germany's surrender should be made simultaneously in all their capital cities. But Stalin insisted that victory in Europe could not be proclaimed until Marshal Zhukov in Berlin had accepted the unconditional surrender of the Germans on the Eastern Front. He proposed the announcement be made at one minute past midnight on 9 May. However, on 7 May the German Foreign Minister broadcast to his countrymen that their troops had surrendered and the war was over. The British press and the BBC picked up the German report. But there was still no official announcement.

'Most people expected peace today . . . flags are being unfurled . . . a press van has a notice "All Over". Waited . . . till 5 o'clock. Still no announcement,' a Mass-Observer noted on 7 May. Unaware of the diplomatic shenanigans, the public felt betrayed. 'They shouldn't keep people hanging about waiting like this. They'll lose all interest. The Govt. needn't be afraid of people going mad, everybody's very sober about it.' 'Churchill had said previously that he wouldn't hold up the news for a minute, and yet here were the papers with definite statements that the war in Europe was over – and no word from him. I know in my own mind that the war in Europe *is* over, for all practical purposes, and I find it very confusing and perplexing.'

Despite the uncertainty, flag-sellers were doing a brisk trade among the crowds. 'Don't forget your victory colours!' shouted some hawkers, while 'two buxom cockney women . . . do twice as much trade as the others . . . mixing among the crowds they shout "'Ere you are luv, 'ere's yer Montgomery's beret. A bob a time. 'Ow much with feathers? Two bob complete, and yer all set ready to 'ave a good time" . . . women and girls of all ages buy their berets allowing the cockney women to put it on for them at the correct sporty angle.'

No coupons were required for flags or bunting. Selfridges department store in Oxford Street, 'the best stocked flag dept. of all the West End stores', reported 'we have been busy for the last 2–3 weeks, People ask for . . . Welcome Home flags . . . in readiness for when their boys come back, perhaps they've been a prisoner of war for years.' A middle-aged woman in Barker's department store in Kensington said cheerfully, 'I've been in so many different queues since the war, it'll be a change to join a flag queue.' But another in Bourne and Hollingsworth in Oxford Street turned away from the silk victory scarves on sale for 24s 6d. 'It's ever so pretty, but after the war you can't wear that. You'll want to get away from the war . . .'

At 7.40 p.m. the BBC interrupted a piano recital to announce that 'Tuesday [8 May 1945] will be treated as Victory in Europe Day, and will be regarded as a holiday.'

'Quietly my father said "It's over" . . . I put the radio on at full blast [for the nine o'clock news] and opened all the windows. Heads came up, spades went down and the whole neighbourhood went indoors. Bedroom windows began to pop open, and within a quarter of an hour some dozens of flags had been put out. On average there is one flag per house in our street. But a few have two or three. I can't say I'm wildly excited . . . just a pleasant feeling of "Well, that's over. What now?" ' For a London window cleaner, 'The holiday is the main issue . . . very few have any definite plans, and these almost exclusively consist of getting drunk . . . for some time now I've been putting a bit by each week so that on V Day I can get really blind drunk, what with getting bombed out in Balham . . . I want to forget it all for a bit.'

When Stuart Hibberd, the BBC announcer, 'said so unemotionally that tomorrow was to be VE Day and Churchill [will] speak at 3 o'clock', Nella Last and a friend 'just *gazed* at each other and Steve said "WHAT a flop. What a FLOP" – we could none of us believe our hearing . . . we felt no pulse quicken, *no* sense of thankfulness, or uplift of any kind . . . I'd heard people say "I'll kneel down and pray if it's in the street when I hear it", "I know I'll cry my eyes out", "I'll rush for the bottle I've kept and open it and get tight for the first time in my life." And so on. I rose placidly and put the kettle on.

'I felt . . . as if I'd sat through a long and tedious play living only for the finale, longing for the time when I could breathe fresh sweet air, go home and do something more interesting and amusing. Instead as each player left the stage they disappeared and the lights gradually dimmed, till the last performer said "That's all, you can go home now!" – and now the audience looked at each other uncertain of the next move – and they too, slowly dispersed.'

While some planned to go to church to give thanks on VE Day and others to get legless, one woman thought that the holiday would be an ideal opportunity 'to get the spring cleaning done', and a Scottish landowner's wife asked one of their tenant farmers 'who was drilling turnips, if he wanted VE Day as a holiday, and should we get the potatoes in? He said VE Day or no VE Day the potatoes are going in tomorrow, which is much what I had felt, so I said I'd help him.' But Lady Gordon nevertheless 'pulled three old flags out of the attic which had been used for the Coronation – old Admiralty stuff I guess – and two enormous blue Ensigns and a huge Union Jack' and set about hanging them up. In Chelsea a woman who didn't want to be the first 'to start putting out my flags . . . and make a fool of myself' saw the block of municipal flats opposite with a flag right across the courtyard, and resolved 'Oooh, I'll go home and get mine up right away'. 'People were putting up decorations in the twilight,' noticed a man cycling home from the pub soon after 10 p.m. in the double summer time of 7 May.

A doctor pronounced that VE Day would *not* be a holiday at Glasgow Royal Infirmary: 'outpatients will still be open . . . babies have to be washed, fed etc'. Kate Hayward, who helped in her brother's grocery shop in Dewsbury, Yorkshire, didn't think she'd be getting much of a victory celebration holiday either. 'The baker told us about their [time] off . . . but when I mentioned ours all customers have a dicky fit – apparently poor grocers are to be still at war. One lady in the shop was lamenting shortage of Spam when old Mrs C rounded on her indignantly. "*Spam!* Don't you know war's over?" '

In Birmingham, the announcement was celebrated at an ARP post by having 'a Post dispersal party – distributed the stores in hand – I got a jar of Bovril', a woman warden reported, 'and we raffled the electric kettle ... proceeds to the Red Cross'. In Trafalgar Square the announcement that 'Mr Churchill is to speak at 3 o'clock tomorrow and that Wednesday is to be VE Day with Thursday VE Day plus 1' also a public holiday was relayed through the public address system. 'Quietly and soberly the crowds dispersed,' reported a Mass-Observer, out on the streets to gauge the public mood. 'We've been waiting long enough,' said a middle-aged man as he made his way home. 'I imagine the enthusiasm will hold good for another day, after six years of waiting.' But some were reluctant to go home, linking arms, singing, blowing hooters, dancing the Lambeth Walk and then the Hokey Cokey, lighting bonfires in Piccadilly and Cambridge Circus until 'amidst shouts and hisses from the crowd fire engines arrived and the AFS turned their hoses on the flames and put them out'.

A London housewife 'cried when I heard the news. I can't grasp the fact that it's all over. We've been bombed out twice, and we've got no roof over our heads, only a tarpaulin. My boy's home on leave after being away for nearly five years, but tomorrow I don't care what happens. I'm going to be really happy. I'm glad of the opportunity to relieve my pent-up feelings.'

VE Day dawned, and for the first time in almost six years the weather forecast could be published in the newspapers. 'Wind freshening; warm and sunny at first but rain can be expected later,' read the *Daily Mirror*. But the forecast was wrong: 'the sudden warm snap' did continue. By the afternoon the temperature in London had risen to 75°F and the celebrating crowds sweltered in the unseasonal heat.

Nothing official had been planned to celebrate Victory in Europe. Resentment still simmered in some quarters. 'A muddle, it was a muddle.' 'Telling us over and over the church bells would be the signal. And then there was *no* signal. Just hanging around.' 'Do 'em no good in the general election. The way they've gone on over this. People won't forget it. An insult that'[s] what it was ... No bells, no All Clears. Nothing to start the people off. That's what they were afraid of ...' A Surrey woman who had been disappointed that 'neither in Reigate nor Dorking have the bells been ringing in the morning ... I thought they would be clanging all day long' was pleased to hear some activity on the wireless. 'I liked most the bells ringing from York Minster, Bath Cathedral and Puddletown village church. They seemed to give the feeling of the whole land rejoicing in the early summer day.'

Some strolled round their neighbourhood looking at the decorations. May Clark found that 'all through the East End the battered little streets are gay with bunting – recent V-2 damage barely tidied up', and her home town of Grays in Essex had its 'shabby paint masked with flags'. Chepstow was 'the gayest place' Mavis Carter, a teacher who lived there, had seen 'with flags out in great numbers obviously saved from the Coronation . . . The main point of interest was the cinema where they were putting up lavish decorations with a centrepiece showing Churchill, Stalin and Roosevelt.' And she noticed in addition to the flags, 'red, white and blue articles of washing hanging on a clothes line'. In Haverfordwest in Pembrokeshire a local authority worker walked round the town 'struck most . . . by the flags. Large flags, small flags, bunting flags, stored since the Coronation, all served to turn the grey stone buildings of the town into a rainbow-like world . . . The Union Jack and the Welsh Dragon flew side-by-side on public buildings and the castle and in the streets were Russian, British, American, Dominion and other Allied flags . . .' In Glasgow 'private houses were snowing flags – Union Jacks were favoured first, and Scottish lions a good second . . . the American Red Cross hostel – the Grand Hotel – flag sat at half mast for Roosevelt and had put up a Union Jack at full mast!' Further north in Argyll, 'there were a few flags up in the village, mostly Scottish lions and a pathetic and obviously home made one on the gate of the poorest family'. But a Suffolk woman was not impressed by her market town's patriotic display. 'When I went to the post I saw that the whole of this silly little town had its flags out. I shall have to keep indoors if I wish to evade the bloody war it seems . . . Aren't people idiots? Don't they read history and learn how other fools hung out flags and then in their turn were trodden underfoot.'

Mavis Carter, walking around Chepstow, 'saw a soldier in a green beret across the road and realised it was Michael Richardson, a Prisoner of War taken at Dieppe, who returned home on Sunday. . . He looked well after nearly three years in prison camp. He went off . . . with his wife – their arms round each other. She looked in her seventh heaven.' Prisoners of war were given priority treatment, shipped back to Britain as soon as possible – including the RAF fighter-pilot hero Douglas Bader who had been in a POW camp in Germany. 'Legless Ace is Back' read the London *Evening News* on VE Day. More than 13,000 former POWs held in the camps of Germany and Italy and the liberated countries arrived in Britain on VE Day, carried by 200 Lancaster bombers, while other Lancasters were dropping food to the starving people of Holland and Belgium. But it would be months before those POWs who survived the war in the Far East would begin their long journey home.

Churchill lunched with the King at Buckingham Palace, where the two men 'congratulated each other on the end of the European War'. Chips Channon's lunch that day was at the Ritz as usual. It 'was beflagged and decorated' and 'everyone kissed me'. The Savoy hotel had rustled up a special VE Day lunch, serving dishes rechristened 'Le Médallion du Soldat', 'La Citronette Joyeuse Déliverances', 'La Coup Glacée des Alliés' costing 5s for the meal plus 3s 6d cover charge.

After lunch the Prime Minister went to the Commons. The questions were sombre: the Secretary of State for War, Sir James Grigg, was non-committal when he was asked whether, since the war against Japan was still being fought, those POWs who had just arrived home at last would be liable to be shipped out to fight after six months. This was one of the many things that would have 'to be reconsidered in light of the events of the last 24 hours', he replied, though he recalled cases of men repatriated from German POW camps on medical grounds who had 'pressed to be allowed to fight against the Japanese'.

At three o'clock Churchill's address was broadcast from Downing Street throughout the world, and relayed by loudspeakers in cities and towns all over Britain. The Prime Minister announced that hostilities with Germany would officially cease at one minute past midnight that night, and that 'our dear Channel Islands are to be freed today'. He went on to recall those who had 'declared war on this foul aggressor', spoke of how 'from this Island and from our united Empire, Britain had maintained the struggle single-handed for a whole year'. He paid tribute to the 'the military might [and prowess in the field] of Soviet Russia and . . . the overwhelming power and resources of the United States of America' before rounding off his brief history of the war: 'finally almost the whole world was combined against the evil-doers who are now prostrate before us.' 'The crowd gasped,' noted Harold Nicolson, who was among their number in Parliament Square. Churchill concluded: 'We may allow ourselves a brief period of rejoicing, but let us not forget for a moment the toil and effort that lie ahead . . . We must now devote all our strength and resources to the completion of our task, both at home and abroad. Advance Britannia! Long live the cause of freedom! God save the King!' On the words 'Advance Britannia!' Churchill's voice broke. At the end of the speech, buglers of the Scots Guards sounded the ceremonial ceasefire and those who were not already standing rose to the strains of the national anthem. Lady Gordon, knitting as she listened to the wireless, 'felt all the time . . . the broadcast was going out what a lovely moment this must be for Churchill. I don't begrudge it him a bit even though my politics are so different – he certainly has the vision and the strategic imagination to get us through to victory as few men could. I felt sorry that poor old Roosevelt had missed this and a little emotional too – the rather obvious emotion we can't help feeling after all these years.'

Churchill drove back to the Commons, standing on the front seat of an open car, giving V-signs for the crowds cheering along the short route as the police cleared a way through. It took the Prime Minister's car half an hour to travel the quarter of a mile. As he entered the Chamber, MPs rose, cheered and waved their order papers in the air. Churchill acknowledged their enthusiasm with an 'odd shy jerk of the head and with a wide grin', and read the House the same speech that had just been broadcast to the nation. He thanked the Commons for 'their noble support during the war years' and moved that 'this House do now attend at the Church of St Margaret's, Westminster, to give humble thanks to Almighty God for our deliverance from the threat of German domination'. The House adjourned, MPs walking across New Palace Yard, for a short service, at the end of which the Speaker read out the names of the twenty-one Members of Parliament who had been killed during the war.

A seething mass gathered beneath the balcony of the Ministry of Health at the corner of Whitehall and Parliament Square where Winston Churchill had been billed to speak at 5 p.m. "E's 'aving a drink, dear,' one onlooker offered in explanation as the Prime Minister failed to respond to the shouts of 'We want Winnie!' 'Five, six, seven, eight. Mr Churchill's always late!' contributed another. At 5.40 p.m. Churchill appeared with members of the Cabinet. Most people picked out Ernest Bevin and Sir John Anderson, but then they were stumped. It was Churchill's victory. His secretary, on an adjoining balcony, thought that the roars and cheers 'exceeded by double anything I can remember at the Coronation'. 'This is your hour,' the Prime Minister told the crowds. 'This is your victory. It is not victory of a party or of any class. It's a victory of the great British nation as a whole.' Ernest Bevin stepped forward: 'Three cheers for victory – 'ip 'ip 'ooray,' urged the Minister of Labour. 'Land of Hope and Glory' floated up: Churchill took his cue and joined in the singing, conducting as he did so. 'For He's a Jolly Good Fellow' the crowds roared.

Reluctantly the Prime Minister went back to his office to deal with the affairs of state of a world half at peace. He noted that 'US troops had advanced 120 miles further than expected' and would have to honour the arrangement made with Russia and pull back. Stalin, he calculated, would have 'eight capitals in his control'.

Outside the crowds partied on: by 8 p.m. the pubs had started to run out of beer, and, arms linked, soldiers, airmen, sailors, women from the ATS, the WAAF, the WRNS and the Land Army, GIs, Canadians, Poles, Free French all eddied along the streets in the balmy May air in search of drink, happenings, ways to celebrate. People waved flags and streamers as they strolled along, sporting rosettes, badges with likenesses of Churchill, paper hats, ribbons. Fireworks were let off, planes overhead periodically released flares. 'A very sprucely dressed young officer of a Scottish regiment is clanging away on two dustbin lids. He heads a procession 100 yards long of young people arms round each other's waists – marching single file. There are scores of such processions.' A 'very pretty girl about 18 . . . in a red frock with white polka dots, a blue neck square and shoeless and stockingless . . . lifting up her skirt, paddles' in the fountain. 'Two officers of the Norfolk Regiment . . . roll up their trousers and follow suit. They climb to the very top of the fountain carrying the girl . . . she kisses them. British Movietone cameramen take photographs . . . "I bet she'll catch it when her mother sees the pictures . . ." ' commented a middle-aged woman in the crowd. 'Two Yanks pass. The face of one is covered in lipstick marks. As he passes an attractive girl, he calls, "Won't you join my collection?" and pushes his face forward.' Anything remotely climbable was climbed – lamp posts, pillar boxes, advertisement hoardings, the plinths of statues, the lions in Trafalgar Square, the boards round the absent statue of Eros in Piccadilly Circus. Searchlights played into the sky, capturing in the V of their probing beams Admiralty Arch, St Martin-in-the-Fields, the National Gallery, Big Ben and, most significantly for Londoners, St Paul's Cathedral. Strangers kissed, couples copulated, condoms were blown up as balloons, bonfires blazed – the one in Green Park fed by park benches dragged on to the flames. The police on duty that night were reputed to have been chosen for their tolerant natures, and most were indulgent of excess and high spirits that night of nights.

The King had broadcast to the nation at 6 p.m., and with the Queen made several appearances on the balcony of Buckingham Palace, he in naval uniform liberally laced with gold braid. With them were Princess Elizabeth in her ATS uniform and Princess Margaret, still a schoolgirl. The crowds below and surging down the Mall went wild, shouting, cheering, waving flags, letting off fireworks. 'It was a spectacular scene,' Julia Strachey told Frances Partridge, '. . . the Palace . . . was brilliantly illuminated with beautiful golden light, and draped with red velvet over the balcony. It was charming, pretty. Everyone was fainting by the roadside, or rather sitting down holding their stockinged feet in their hands and groaning. A few, faint upper-class cries of "Taxi-taxi!" came wailing through the air from voices right down on the pavement; while cockney tones, slightly more robust, could be heard saying, "I'm fucking well all in now." ' The jazz trumpeter Humphrey Lyttelton was there, pushed along in a handcart, and the notes of 'High Society' soared over the crowd's rendition of 'Roll Out the Barrel' and 'Knees Up Mother Brown'.

Every time the royal party turned to go in, the crowd would roar, 'We want the King, we want the King. We want George.' At one point the royal assemblage was joined by Winston Churchill enjoying again – briefly – his finest hour. He had no cigar. He gestured no V sign. He bowed deep to the crowd. Later the princesses slipped out of the palace gates, with a couple of bodyguards following at a distance, to mingle incognito with the celebrating crowds. The heir apparent and her sister had rejoined their parents by 11 p.m. when the King and Queen, picked out by intersecting spotlights, made their sixth and final appearance that day to a still noisy, still good-natured crowd acclaiming victory.

Naomi Mitchison hadn't known it was VE Day until she was told by a porter at Euston station when the family arrived from Scotland. She had set out for Piccadilly Circus, lunched at the Café Royal – which 'wasn't very full or decorated' – and then 'wandered along slowly, looking on. A number of other people were doing the same thing, in fact everyone was tired and wanted to look rather than do . . . most women had lipstick and a kind of put on smile but all but the very young looked very tired when they actually stopped smiling.'

Janetta Woolley 'found the crowds very depressing indeed' – 'I so loathe the look of masses of boiling people with scarlet dripping faces, wearing tiny paper hats with "Ike's babe" or "Victory" written upon them' – yet, like so many, she felt drawn to central London on VE Day. Charles Kohler, a Quaker, also 'stood outside the communal rejoicing. I could not link arms with comrades-in-arms; I had taken no active part in the fight for victory. I had refused military service and registered as a Conscientious Objector . . . I rejoiced in the peace, the end of the war, but I was not among those who had risked their life for victory.' Frances Partridge, remembering how after the First World War 'some pacifists had been turned on by the merry-making crowds . . . wondered if our village neighbours . . . might say to themselves "Well, *they* did nothing to help. *They've* no cause to rejoice." But the warm way Olive and her family welcomed us and exchanged handshakes and kisses did nothing to confirm my fears.'

'I went to bed absolutely happy that night,' wrote Nellie Carver, a supervisor with the Central Telegraph Exchange near Ludgate Circus, who had been allowed to leave an hour and a half early that day (though she had not been given time off to listen to 'this historic moment' of Churchill's broadcast, which she thought was a bit rough 'after all we've been through'). She and her mother wandered round the streets near their home in south London looking at the '*huge* bonfire and people hurrying up with wood and old chairs, tables and lino – in fact everything you can imagine . . . [while] "V" signs and crowns made the night look like day. No street lights on yet, so the illuminations had it all to themselves.'

VE Day turned into something of an *auto-da-fé*. Effigies of Hitler topped many bonfires in the suburbs and provinces. 'Everyone participated in the making of Hitler. One lady gave the jacket, another the trousers and so on . . . A dress maker living in the road gave the dressing up the professional touch. Hitler's clothes fitted to perfection. The Chief Fire Watcher in the road made the face . . . when the gallows were erected and Hitler's body strung up, the foundations of the bonfire was laid. One of the men suggested they burn Goering too, and he volunteered to make him. Goering, complete with medals and two Iron Crosses was seated on a chair at the foot of Hitler. Nearby was a battered doll, face and body daubed with red paint as a reminder of the misery Hitler and Goering had brought to humanity. . . The Chief Fire Watcher was invited to light the bonfire. One of the boys handed him a long pole at the end of which was a rag soaked in paraffin. Immediately the bonfire was lit a great cheer went up. Hitler started to burn too quickly and cries of "Don't let him end up so soon. Let him linger" and the boys promptly doused him with the hose in order to prolong the burning . . .'

In a Coventry suburb 'Hitler was not only burned but first given a ceremonial hanging. This formed the basis of the whole day's celebrations.' But one woman at least felt uneasy. 'Coventry looked almost like a raid night with bonfires in many streets lighting up the sky in all directions.' And in London, Janetta Woolley thought 'some bonfires were wonderful, bringing back the old ecstasies of staring into a fire, but also having that appalling smell of burning debris, too terrifyingly nostalgic of blitzes'.

There were bonfires in Oxford too – 'a huge one in St Giles by the Martyr's Memorial' which people danced round and another one in 'the High between Queen's and University [colleges] and they were bringing furniture out of the university to burn. Goodness knows what they burned, in hindsight I'm thinking about antiques. I think they even brought out a piano.'

Another capital had reason to celebrate: the skies above the crowded streets of Belfast glowed with the light of dozens of bonfires – the city was in a carnival mood and effigies of Hitler were hung from lamp posts. The news of Germany's surrender had been greeted by the ringing of church bells and the celebratory wail of ships' sirens and factory hooters. Long lines of revellers in snake-like procession danced in and out of rows of tramcars immobilised by the crowds. They sang as they danced: 'Tipperary' and 'a completely new number composed for the occasion that began "Hitler thought he had us with a ya, ya, ya" '. On 8 May, Belfast was 'a city without strangers' as Catholics and Protestants celebrated – though not always together – and the biggest crowd since Covenant Day in 1912 gathered outside the City Hall to hear Churchill's broadcast relayed through loudspeakers. Elsewhere in the province there was free beer in the pubs, and some of the effigies of Hitler consumed by flames that night depicted him as the house painter he had once been. At Newtownsbutler 'old political differences were buried for a while with the coming together of Catholic and Protestant bands leading a procession of Orangemen'. At the Giant's Causeway and Lisahally, surrendered German U-boats were tied up in the harbour and proved a tourist attraction on VE Day.

The next day was one for getting up late nursing hangovers, for cringing embarrassment at memories of the excesses of celebration, and for children's parties. In Hackney, east London, Warden Post No 6 organised a party for 1,500 children with a slap-up tea and a Punch and Judy show – and, if there hadn't been enough dismemberment over the last six years, a woman in a box was sawn in half by a magician. In a village near Oxford there was 'a really magnificent tea for the children – jam tarts with a V sign in chocolate being the great delicacies. The children marched along singing and waving flags . . . they looked so pretty. There were 50 of them. Luckily there was enough food. They had 6d stamps for prizes. There was a dance in the village hall at the end of the day. We keep saying to each other that of course it is impossible to believe that peace has really come after all these years of strain and tension, the daily "girding of our loins".'

In Norwood, south London, the people of Rosedale Road 'were busy sweeping up and setting tables for the children's tea to be held there at 3 p.m.', noted Nellie Carver, who had the day off from her supervisor's job at the Central Telegraph Exchange. 'Great excitement . . . The tables looked awfully nice and such a spread. How the mothers must have worked, they only started yesterday. About 150 children arrived looking so clean and bright.' But when Mrs Carver returned to the scene a few hours later 'the children who looked so clean at the party . . . were having the time of their lives – gloriously dirty with soot and smoke, dancing round the fire singing, dogs were barking, and more fireworks going off under one's feet . . . It seemed as tho' the people couldn't get enough light. After six years, it was incredible – the energy, the vitality of everyone after all they had suffered – it was, for this night, as tho' the War had never been. The searchlight display over London was a sight in itself. I stayed until nearly 12 o'clock watching it all, marvelling anew at our people . . .'

The next day was 'a working day again – all shops open . . . and queues of course'. 'Today is a sort of anti-climax. It seems strange that to some extent we could no longer say "there's a war on" . . .' Mrs Carver had to go back to work – 'after 2 days the [telegrams] had piled up terribly . . . to add to the confusion hundreds more P.O.W. wires are coming in and we couldn't let *those* wait'.

There had been a hollow feel to the celebrations for many. 'VE day can't mean much to us as my daughter's husband is a prisoner, and we haven't heard anything since December.' And for those whose loved ones were among the 264,443 British servicemen and 30,248 merchant seamen, or the 63,635 civilians killed, there seemed little cause for rejoicing. 'Mrs Sims says that peace won't bring back her husband killed in the Coventry blitz, nor her house destroyed at the same time.'

Peggie Phillips, whose husband John had been killed in the battle of Monte Cassino, was relieved that the celebrations were over. 'I had lived in dread, like so many other women, for the fortnight of suspense leading up to VE Day,' she wrote to her brother-in-law. 'I was so afraid that I wouldn't be brave. But once the tension had snapped and the day itself had been met, I felt stronger to go on. Johnnie's going must always be an inspiration to me to go forward with greater courage. Heaven knows it's hard enough at times . . .'

Some were cynical about the chances of the peace lasting. 'Niece, 30, very pessimistic, sees no true cessation. Sees her son – now sixteen and a half at war in 20 years time.' 'A solicitor friend of mine has just told me we are going to war again at once – with Russia.'

Others 'felt browned off . . .' by the toll that war had taken. 'I am now years and years older than I was in 1939 – quite 20 years older at least' – and acutely aware of the problems that peace would bring. 'I could see nothing to jubilate about. Bill had been over at the Rose and

Crown. He said it was flat there too. He said the folks were frightened of losing their jobs and didn't feel secure (. . . many folk felt that under our present system having a job, and having a war go together).'

'Personally, although of course I was glad that it was over, I was not particularly excited. For us, the dangerous-to-life part of the war ended just before Easter, when the rockets stopped . . . The Japanese have still to be finished off and materials for civil use are in such short supply, out of which we shall have to do our share in helping the countries of Europe, that I think we shall see very little change for some time to come.'

For Quentin Crisp the transformation was profound. 'The horrors of peace were many. Death-made-easy vanished overnight and soon love-made-easy . . . also disappeared. Even mere friendship grew scarce. Londoners started to regret their indiscriminate expansiveness. People do when some shared moment of danger is past. Emotions that had been displayed now had to be played down; confidences had been uttered that now must be gainsaid. I, who had once been a landmark more cheerful looking and more bomb-proof than St Paul's Cathedral, had ceased to be a talisman. I had become a loathsome reminder of the unfairness of fate. I was still living while so many of the young, the brave and the beautiful were dead.'

And there were those for whom the awesome and enduring suffering of the war – which was still being fought against Japan – drained any pleasure from the celebration of the coming of peace. 'It must be terrible in Europe. How on earth can we get everyone fed? German prisoners abounding . . . I feel sorry for the plight of the German folk and soldiers . . . I am sorry for the people and the soldiers who were compelled.'

'I wondered how people had the heart to rejoice knowing what misery people have had and are still having and with the Japanese war – still likely to have . . . it certainly didn't seem like a day of joy to me . . . I feel we are only touching the fringe of the problem now. Perhaps there is no more fighting . . . but it is as nothing to what is going to happen around the Council Table before very long. What status will Russia have? All these things are going to be hard to solve.'

'There is something about Glasgow that puts a stop on national celebrations . . . because there was still bloodshed in the Far East, the

Council thought it was not quite right to have a celebration at present. As the war is only half won Glasgow's flags will only fly at half mast . . .' wrote a forty-two-year-old woman who worked for the Forth and Clyde Coal Company in the city and whose 'mind is still seething with thoughts of the starvelings of Belsen' as the nation celebrated peace.

The British public had heard about Belsen from a fourteen-minute report broadcast by Richard Dimbleby on 19 April 1945, 'the most horrible day of my life . . . No briefing had prepared me for this . . . I picked my way over corpse after corpse in the gloom . . . Some of the poor starved creatures . . . looked so utterly unreal and inhuman that I could have imagined that they had never lived at all.' Dimbleby's full report was broadcast later, photographs appeared in the press and Pathé newsreels showed film of the atrocities. 'See them – Lest You Forget' a board outside a cinema in Kilburn High Road enjoined passers-by – though the worst of the horrors were deemed unseeable by British audiences and many of those who did watch what was shown stumbled from the cinema in shock.

Evacuees had been coming home since late 1944. Families that had made private arrangements could, of course, bring their children home when they liked, but those who had been evacuated under official schemes were to return in like manner. The first came back from North Wales to Merseyside at the end of November, and those to the Midlands, the coastal areas and Scotland followed. The children were again labelled for despatch and left to clamber on to trains clutching a suitcase which this time might well contain gifts of farm produce – eggs, butter, cheese, even a dead chicken or rabbit – as well as their clothes, toys, ration book and identity card. The V-1 and V-2 attacks made it unsafe to bring evacuees back to London, and Hull and the North East were not yet considered safe, but on 10 April 1945 the Ministry of Health circulated outline plans for the return of some half a million London evacuees – schoolchildren, mothers and babies, the elderly and the disabled. They would be brought back by special trains, or parents could apply for free travel vouchers to collect their children.

On 2 May the London Return Plan was activated. Two weeks later all London schools closed for a week so that teachers could assess the conditions to which the children were returning. 'Home' meant that the evacuees could return, while 'No Home' meant that conditions were not acceptable – dwellings bombed out, perhaps, with the rest of the family living in accommodation that was not fit for a child. Or parents might still be in the Forces or engaged in war work, while one or both parents might have been killed, have disappeared, or be unable or unwilling to care for their children. Such evacuees would have to stay in the reception area until something could be sorted out. The first trainload of schoolchildren accompanied by teachers arrived in early June, and convoys of trains seven days a week for four or five weeks would bring the de-vacuees back to London. By August 1945 around 76,000 children remained in the reception areas – more than had returned under the official scheme – largely because of housing problems in the urban conurbations from which they had been evacuated.

Some children had been living away from home since 1 September 1939, and had grown up strangers to their parents. Some went home very reluctantly. 'It had been pitiful . . . to see so many woebegone faces at the carriage windows. Mrs Fletcher's two were among those who cried bitterly at "going home",' reported Nella Last from Barrow-in-Furness. '[The] boy *begged* to be let stay; he is a big strong lad of 12–13 and said "I know you would get my allowance stopped – but I'd work hard in the garden and help look after the hens and I'd not eat much . . . DO let me stay, let Ethel go back, mother doesn't want me. I was always in the way. *Please* Mr Fletcher write and tell mother you'll let me be your boy and always live with Michael and Mrs Fletcher and you." Mrs Fletcher said that when the mother came she made no secret of the fact that she "disliked boys, they were so rough . . ." but said that he would "soon be earning" and she was going to "have good of him." Mrs Fletcher is very unhappy about it . . . we all liked him, and it is dreadful to think he will not be wanted.'

When the 'official' evacuation scheme ended in March 1946, there were 5,200 unaccompanied children either still billeted with foster-parents or in hostels or residential nurseries in the reception areas. They ceased to be 'evacuees' and became the responsibility of the local authority to which they had originally been sent. Some had been orphaned, while in other cases social problems persisted; in only a very few cases – 29 out of a total of 9,000 in July 1945 – had the children been abandoned by their parents.

*

Just two weeks after VE Day, Labour formally left the coalition. Party politics were *en clair* again. Each party naturally wished to cash in whatever credit it had accumulated during the war. Churchill was believed to be the Conservatives' gilt-edged asset; Labour's appeal was that they were seen to be the party most likely to fulfil the public's demand for post-war social reform that had been whetted by the publication of the Beveridge Report – particularly in the areas of housing and social security – and the fact that they had not been the government in the pre-war decade of appeasement and unemployment. Labour politicians and parliamentary candidates were champing to 'Face the Future', as the Labour manifesto had it, as soon as possible and not wait until the war with Japan was over – which might be months, possibly even years – though Churchill and Attlee would have preferred to prolong the coalition.

It would be the first general election for ten years. Polling day was fixed for 5 July. The result would not be known for a further three weeks since the votes of soldiers still stationed as far away as Burma would take time to come in. In the interim Churchill headed a 'caretaker' government composed of Conservatives and Liberals.

Housing was the key issue in the election. Indeed, it had been evident that it was what most people cared about most, ever since talk about post-war reconstruction had been in the air back in 1942 when it had seemed a brave resolve in the dark days before Britain's first victory at El Alamein. It exemplified the divide between the political philosophies of the two major parties. For Labour, the new homes needed could be achieved only by State planning of resources with municipal-built developments providing community facilities – part of a social services matrix that would also include improved education, and free medical and welfare services. For the Conservatives, it was private enterprise that would produce the homes – and the economic and industrial prosperity needed to rebuild Britain on the ruins of war: over 3.25 million properties had been destroyed by bombing, 92 per cent of which were private dwellings, and half were in London.

Churchill proved weary and erratic on the stump; his oratory seemed to desert him and he was no longer able to 'give the people a tune to hum'. He appeared to be a partisan leader rather than a national hero, and Vita Sackville-West who had an 'admiration . . . amounting to idolatry' for him confessed that if she were a 'wobbler', Churchill's lacklustre party political broadcasts 'would tip me over to the other side'. 'Churchill's all right for the war job, but he's getting too old [he was seventy]. He ought to step down and let a younger man take charge,' suggested a thirty-five-year-old working-class woman. And the Prime Minister incensed more than Labour supporters when he claimed that Labour 'would have to rely on some sort of Gestapo' to implement its policies. He also seemed unable to appreciate the extent of concern over housing among the electorate, 63 per cent of whom plumped for it as the most important issue facing any incoming government. Labour's strategy was to metaphorically link arms with those who had fought the 'people's war' in suggesting commonsense ways in which a fairer people's peace could be achieved: the party played down the ideological aspects of its nationalisation programme, presenting it less as common ownership and more as the efficient use of resources, lessons learned in the wartime version of a command economy.

In the country the prevailing mood seemed to be one of apathy, scepticism and uncertainty. The politician's and planner's vision of the future did not seem to ignite the public's enthusiasm. Naomi Mitchison had spoken of her husband Dick's 'extremely interesting time on [the] Reconstruction [Committee], interviewing municipal authorities in all the bombed London boroughs, saying some of them, especially Poplar, were frightfully keen on re-planning and decent housing (viz the Landsdown estate)', but noted that 'all the inhabitants just want to go back to their own exact houses and neighbourhoods. The poorer the more so. Of course that's logical; they never had the possibility of imagining anything else.'

The outcome was uncertain. 'Of course I shall vote, but I don't know how yet. My mum keeps talking against Morrison; says he was a conchie in the last war and this war he tells women of fifty to "go to it". She says you can't trust a man like that.' In June 1945 Mass-Observation found that 39 per cent of young first-time voters in London were undecided. 'I feel I don't understand politics. I don't want to use my vote. The war's got us down, what with the bombing and the blackout, and the worrying about coupons and queues, women like me haven't the mind to take to politics. We want to be left alone for a bit – not worrying about speeches.'

'I can't make up my mind who to vote for, I'll have to talk it over with my husband and I know what he'll say – he'll say they're all out to suit themselves. I don't think they do care. That's my opinion.'

The Labour landslide, announced in hourly bulletins on the BBC on 26 July, surprised politicians, pundits and public alike: 393 Labour MPs were returned to 213 Conservatives and 12 Liberals – a 146-seat majority. Naomi Mitchison, whose husband successfully challenged the sitting Conservative MP John Profumo at Kettering in Northamptonshire, was so delighted with the news that she plucked a couple of gladioli out of a vase in a pub where she and the Labour Party workers were listening to the results coming in, and stuck them in her hair. The political coloration of the country seemed fundamentally changed: it wasn't just in industrial cities that Labour had cleaned up, it was a number of rural seats too – particularly in Norfolk – and the party had been particularly successful in the middle-class suburbs ringing London.

In fact the British 'first past the post' electoral system meant the result wasn't quite as revolutionary as it at first appeared: although Labour had won 47.8 per cent of the vote, the Conservatives had managed to cling on to 39.8 per cent, and middle-class defections had come mainly from 'clerks, typists, canvassers and agents' while the manual working class remained Labour's bedrock. The 'khaki vote', allegedly radicalised by regular ABCA lectures on citizens' rights and entitlements and just rewards, which was claimed to have made a substantial contribution to the defeat of Churchill, was shown, in fact, to be as apolitical in war as in peace. Again less concerned with a new Jerusalem and more with 'how their own lives will be affected especially in relation to their jobs, their wives and their children', many soldiers had had to be persuaded to enrol on the electoral register. Fewer than half of servicemen voted, and of those some 60 per cent voted Labour.

Harold Nicolson, who had been elected in 1935 for National Labour, fought a less than focused campaign, narrowly persuaded by a local Leicester photographer not to be depicted in a dark-blue shirt that made him look like 'Mosley or Lord Haw Haw' on his election address; he havered about what banner to stand under, refusing to call himself 'Conservative' because he did not feel conservative, but equally would form no part of an alliance ranged against Churchill. Finally he plumped for 'Support Churchill and Vote for Harold Nicolson, the National

Candidate' and lost his seat, as did Harold Macmillan, Churchill's son-in-law Duncan Sandys, Leo Amery and the Ministry of Information's Brendan Bracken – and, oddly, William Beveridge, along with another Liberal, the Air Minister Sir Archibald Sinclair. In Churchill's own constituency, Woodford in Essex, where neither Labour nor Liberal chose to challenge the Great Man, a farmer standing as an Independent did, and walked off with a quarter of the votes. Two Communist Party candidates were elected, but just one Common Wealth Party MP retained his seat, and that only because Labour withdrew from Chelmsford. Birmingham, considered rock solid for working-class Conservatism, went Labour.

A friend accused Nella Last of 'having "more of a tendency to the Left" . . . and I said "maybe, but find me a person who is not in some way, we have grown such arm chair critics in these war years that nothing or no one is safe from our criticism, or feeling "a change could not be worse." [Mary] said "to turn against Churchill so – to throw him out as they did it's one of the 'shames' of England." I looked at her, so plump and prosperous, she has always seemed to get all and everything she needed. Her husband is a shipyard boss, her only daughter married to another, no one in the Services, a grocer who has always sent her order . . . we suspect she has a very well stocked store. I said "They didn't vote against Churchill really, it was against queues and separation and slow demobilisation and all the little irritations of life – and so many had the idea that the Conservatives had let this war drift on till *no* one could stop it." '

In Elizabeth Orchard's opinion, the 'Labour government were not put in by people who wanted socialism. They were put in by people who disliked the last government . . . London has had a dreadful time with the air raids and it affected persons . . . I said discontent in London was obviously a factor in putting in a Labour govt.' A friend 'expressed her surprise at the verdict and said she was sorry about Mr Churchill. That sentiment, I should say, is as near to universal, as any sentiment is likely to be in the political field. At any rate it has been muttered over again and again in my presence, with never a dissident voice. It is clear that the section or sections of the community with which I mix [in Glasgow] was solidly Conservative. However they are reviving. Mrs Stewart [a neighbour] said "it is up to us to give the Labour govt. a fair trial." Miss

Orchard was 'not so sorry as some people are about the Labour victory for I did not want the country to go back to the same stage of capitalism that it was in 1939.'

When Churchill's doctor railed at the ingratitude of the people, the defeated wartime Prime Minister looked up. 'Oh no,' he answered at once. 'I wouldn't call it that. They have had a very hard time.' Later he would be a little less forgiving. 'I won the race – and now they have warned me off the turf.' At 7.30 p.m. on 26 July 1945, Clement Attlee's wife Violet drove the family's modest Standard 10 erratically through the wrought-iron gates of Buckingham Palace for her husband to shake hands with the King and be confirmed in office as Prime Minister. The couple narrowly missed encountering Churchill in his chauffeur-driven Rolls-Royce, sweeping out after surrendering his seals of office.

The wartime leader might have gone: the war in the Far East continued. It was an immensely slow and costly campaign: US troops fought for eighty-two days to wrest the island of Okinawa from the Japanese. 'If and when [the battle for the Japanese homeland] comes it may be a very tough and expensive affair,' warned a *Sunday Times* reporter. On VE Day newspapers reported more men lost in the fighting in Burma. 'How can they celebrate?' a British soldier there wondered when he saw pictures of VE Day. 'For us the real war was still going on and I saw no prospect of its end,' wrote an Australian. 'Only a few days before I had seen another close friend killed in action: none of my real mates survived the war.'

On 21 July the US had appealed to Japan to surrender, threatening that a refusal would result in the virtual destruction of the country and a dictated peace. 'Your opportunity is rapidly passing.' On 27 July the reply came: 'Japan is determined to battle tooth and nail for every inch of her sacred soil.' On 6 August 1945 President Truman, who was crossing the Atlantic on his way home from a visit to Britain, announced that an atomic bomb which was more than 2,000 times more powerful than any bomb dropped before had been unleashed on Japan. It was forty-eight hours before any aerial assessment could be made of Hiroshima, the city against which the world's first nuclear weapon had been used: one aircraft dropping a single bomb. 'Most of Hiroshima no longer exists,' a Japanese broadcast reported. 'The impact of the bomb was so terrific that practically all living things human and animal were literally seared to death . . . Buildings were crushed or wiped out . . . the dead were burned beyond recognition.' The *Manchester Guardian* pointed out that the Allies had already dropped the equivalent of one and a half times the Hiroshima bomb on Cologne. Since it would shorten the war against Japan, its use was 'entirely legitimate'. To the publisher of Left Books, Victor Gollancz, the use of an atomic bomb was not at all 'legitimate': it was a 'further debasement of the human currency'. On 9 August 1945 another atomic bomb was dropped on Japan, this time on Nagasaki.

On 14 August Japan surrendered. 'The last of our enemies is laid low,' wrote Attlee. The news was announced in the midnight bulletin. Nella Last was woken 'at 1 o'clock in the morning . . . slightly alarmed at noise and shouting . . . ships' sirens and church bells and then I realised the longed-for news of peace had come through at last . . . I looked out of my window . . . my neighbour, Mrs Hales, who is very excitable [and had probably kept her promise to drink a tumbler of gin and one of champagne when peace was announced] was half screaming "God Save the King" seemingly knowing all the verses or singing what she did know over and over again . . . I recollected a bit cynically that they had flown out of town when there was raids, had *no one* in the war, never did a damn thing to help, the son-in-law signed on as a baker . . . and snatched at every straw to "keep him out of it" . . .'

Just as for Victory in Europe, Victory in Japan was proclaimed a two-day public holiday – 15–16 August. On the day that the Second World War ended, the King and Queen drove in the golden State Coach in drizzling rain for the opening of Parliament. In the address from the throne George VI announced the nationalisation of the coalmines and of the Bank of England. Outside crowds again filled Piccadilly Circus and Trafalgar Square, and later the royal family again made frequent appearances on the balcony of Buckingham Palace before cheering, singing, dancing crowds. Bonfires were again lit all over the country, fireworks exploded and church bells pealed out. The Dean of St Albans refused to hold a service of thanksgiving in the abbey because the war had been brought to an end by a bomb, and Naomi Mitchison kept 'thinking of this bomb, and what it may make the future look like'. But 'strangely enough,' Joan Wyndham couldn't 'manage to feel much sorrow for the innocent people of Hiroshima and Nagasaki – I think the concentration camps took all my tears and I have none left.'

In war-blitzed Plymouth people made – as always – for the Hoe to dance and to light a huge bonfire that played the historic role of beacon, eliciting answering fires from Devonport and all along the Devon coast. In war-ravaged Liverpool, celebrations lasted for ten days. No one was to be left out of the rejoicings for peace, from the smallest child to the city's 'Aged Poor'. The highlight was when the 'Illuminated Tram' aglow with thousands of coloured lights made its first appearance since the Coronation and toured the streets of the city with a band playing on the open upper deck.

'I really felt *here* we could do nothing to celebrate again, so was delighted when some of the villagers came round to say they were having a bonfire tonight, and would come round this afternoon to collect salvage. Personally I can't of course begin to compare this day with VE Day, the relief then and relaxing of the awful tension from one's own anxiety and anguish is one thing one will never forget,' wrote an Oxfordshire housewife. 'But today there's just the rejoicing of the *whole world* – and the glorious knowledge that the killing is over and the joy of thinking that those who have their dear ones in the Far East . . .'

In Glasgow Elizabeth Orchard thought it was 'like seeing in the New Year for a hundred hogmanies rolled into one'. Yet for her 'there was a world of difference between VE Day and VJ Day . . . I was absolutely stuck to know what to do this holiday. The newspapers did not contain a single suggestion . . . I want to rejoice and there is no way of doing so.'

Nella Last went to look at a bonfire built on some waste ground nearby but found that the people standing about 'looked like a fish queue, so orderly and apathetic! There was no festive air, the north wind was chilling and the grey skies threatened another shower.'

At best victory could only ever be an exhilarating interlude. Peace would mean a return to 'normal' life, but what was that six years on? Expectations were as varied and sometimes confused as people's experience of war had been. Most men who had been away were anxious to get home after six years of an interrupted life. But 'coming out of the Forces into civilian life is rather like a tepid bath', warned a popular guide to demobilisation. 'One finds neither the icy, tingling invigoration of a cold shower enjoyed on first enlisting, nor the steamy, heart-warming glow of a hot bath enjoyed on leave.' From an institutionalised, regulated life of drills and parades and uniform and drill and round-the-clock comradeship, how seamless would the fit back into Civvy Street be?

Eddie Mathieson, who had been a commando fighting in Burma, was 'very, very disturbed' at the prospect. 'You wonder how you're goin' to settle down. I had worries about goin' back to my trade because I hadnae got my apprenticeship completed. I knew there were guys that had worked at their trade all through the war ... But that was a needless ... worry because when I did finally get back into building there wis hundreds o' guys the same as me ... And the guys that hadnae had war service helped you.' Mathieson had collected his demob outfit. 'Everybody had a suit. You had two choices, dark blue or brown, both pin stripe, single breasted or double breasted, wide lapels ... Black shoes or brown ... I think the shirts were all white. And the ties were a nondescript brown or blue. And a soft hat or cap ... I had a hat like Jimmy Cagney! And a raincoat! And it was like another uniform! Everybody walked around with the same. Thousands of men all dressed the same, just the same ... I remember gettin' accosted when I came out of the demob centre in Plymouth. A guy wanted to buy my parcel o' clothes. Ye come out wi' your parcel and touts were waitin' outside tryin' to buy the stuff off ye. Clothes were scarce. You could have got money for that then. But I told the guy to f— off! I wanted tae get into this civvy suit as quick as I could.' But Mathieson found he 'had difficulties fitting into the routine existence of civvy street ... I was quite honestly a wee bit too willing to lift the fists ... I had certain specialist commando trainin' that made it dangerous for anybody to mess wi' me, and I knew that ...'

A committee had been set up as far back as September 1942 to plan for demobilisation in a way that would avoid the injustices and bitterness of the First World War. The simple solution was a reversal of the 1918 diktat 'last in first out' by ensuring that those who had served the longest would be released first. But this did not differentiate between those who had passed their war in Aldershot or fighting in the Far East. Furthermore it was not a scheme that meshed with post-war realities. So although the basis of demobilisation remained the length of service, men who had skills that were urgently needed for post-war reconstruction, house building in particular, were fast-tracked for release – though they were still considered on active service and could be recalled into the military if they left the jobs to which they had been directed. Bevin had presumed that there would be some two years for this ordered return to peacetime employment and accommodation to be realised while the war with Japan continued. In fact there were three months. Release began on 18 June 1945: of the 4 million men and women in the Forces and working in war industries, one-third had been demobbed by Christmas 1945.

The country they returned to was neither the promised land of progressive aspiration, nor was it the country they had left – and grown nostalgic for. Britain was a shabby, drab, battered, ravaged, exhausted, austere victor – and there was worse to come. The country was deeply in debt to the US and to its own dominions. US Lend Lease was abruptly halted on 14 August. By that date Britain had 'borrowed' over £5 billion-worth of goods and had spent some £1.2 billion on 'Reverse Lend-Lease' transactions with the US. Repayment was eventually agreed at £162 million – a net gain of over £3.6 billion for Britain. Almost everything Britain produced in the early post-war years would have be for export only, to close the dollar gap. The government was also £765 million in hock to its citizens through National Savings and post-war credits, and it would not be until the 1970s that these debts could be redeemed. The houses were not built. There would still be 9,000 people on Plymouth's housing waiting list, for example, eight years after the war had ended – production targets set by the government were impossible to fulfil without more skilled men. And rationing continued – indeed gripped ever tighter – well into the 1950s, though it had not been rationed during the war, bread went on coupons in July 1946 and even potatoes were controlled during the winter of 1947–8. Attlee had warned that demobilisation might be slower than hoped since the world remained in such a volatile state. The Prime Minister was thinking of India, Montgomery explained to his men, where the first fatal fissures of Empire had already opened. Others, Churchill in particular, had the Soviet Union in mind. 'You said once,' Peggie Phillips reminded her brother-in-law who was still fighting in the Far East, 'that you were sometimes afraid that perhaps the War might end too soon, before we were equipped for the peace. It does rather look like it . . .'

More than 2 million women had been without their husbands for the duration of the war. Magazines and newspapers were ready with advice on how to cope with the changes that peace would bring to mothers who had learned to be single parents. Thousands of women who had yearned for the return of a husband now began to realise how independent they had had to become, how years of separation could deepen ties – or turn couples into strangers. The number of people getting married rose throughout the war; the birth rate fell until 1941 and then rose steadily until 1947. Divorce rose too, from just under 10,000 in 1938 to 25,000 in 1945, of which 70 per cent were on the grounds of adultery. Children who had dutifully kissed a photograph 'good night' for as long as they could remember now had to adjust to someone who took mummy's attention, shared her bed and maintained that he and the photograph on the mantelpiece were the same man: daddy.

Younger women who had done long hours of menial work in war-production factories, or felt regimented and drilled to death in the Forces, were delighted with the opportunity to resume studies, careers and comfortable home lives, with marriage prospects. Others regretted the loss of freedom, the independence and the camaraderie. Joan Wyndham in the WAAF felt 'the strangest mixture of elation and terror' when she heard that the war was over. 'It was as if five years of my whole world had suddenly come to an end. Five years of security and happy comradeship, the feeling of being needed – and ahead a kind of uncharted wilderness, lonely and frightening . . . It's hard to explain but there has actually been a rather depressed feeling in the Mess . . . not at all like people who have just won a war.'

'Whatever will we do when WVS work is over?' a friend had asked Nella Last. 'I said I felt the same, but surely something would crop up for those of us who were so eager to work for peace as we did for war.' But exhaustion at the 'double shift' involved in running a home and 'going to it' for war work meant that many married women were eager to return to being full-time housewives again. Zelma Katin, who had worked as a 'clippie' on the Sheffield trams, 'was glad I have done this sort of war work . . . like millions of men and women in uniform I cannot pretend I am liking it. Perhaps the sacrifice and hardship are giving us a strength which will enrich us in the future and toughen us for the struggle that lies ahead. I will confess, I am not only thinking of a future for humanity but a future for myself. I want to lie in bed until eight o'clock, to eat a meal slowly, to sweep floors when they are dirty, to sit in front of the fire, to walk on the hills, to go shopping of an afternoon, to gossip at odd minutes.'

For others the chance to work had been a taste of freedom. 'It's such a change after your own house . . . the old home you know too well. It makes you feel younger and it makes you *look* younger, going out to a job each day. I can do my housework and shopping in the morning – and I do let my house go a bit now. My husband comes home at night and I give him a proper dinner. And that's how we live. And now I don't have to scrape every penny together. I wish part time had come to stay,' a forty-five-year-old woman told a Mass-Observation investigator in 1944. And not all married women drawn into the labour force by the exigencies of war were anxious to leave it. By 1947 probably around 22 per cent of all married women were doing paid work; a quarter of working women were doing so part-time and of these most were married women.

The war had made Gwendoline Saunders 'more impatient with some aspects of life, having to do all the things I'd done in the WAAF and all the different people I'd met. I was more confident, I could talk to anyone. When Boots [Circulating Library] offered me my job back, they offered me £1 more than I'd been getting in 1939, but after six years in the WAAF none of us had the attitude to bow to anyone by this time. So the personnel officer had to take it from us all, and when I eventually did go back, I got quite a substantial pay rise.'

But there were still obstacles. For those with children under school age, State-aided nursery provision was dramatically cut almost as soon as the war ended, and there was always the reproach that working women were really only an expediency 'for the duration' and men were entitled to claim their jobs again when peace came.

Margaret Cornish's wartime work had been 'an opportunity to do something I would never have been able to do if it hadn't been for the war'. She would have liked to continue working on the canals but the government had withdrawn its wartime sponsorship and the 'Grand Union Canal Company wasn't keen to employ women. We felt too that we would have to compete with the boat people for cargoes, and fewer and fewer cargoes were coming into Limehouse and Brentford. We thought perhaps it wasn't fair to compete with the men when they came back. It was their living after all – and realistically we wouldn't have been *able* to compete with the men . . .'

Nella Last tried to be optimistic. 'We must hope for the best – it's no use putting patches on old garments, we need new ones even if the coarse sack irks skin used to old comfortable garments which we cling to because of old associations, comfort and inertia . . .'

But even with a husband taking his seat in the reform-minded new Labour House of Commons, and with her own hopes for a revitalised post-war Scotland, Naomi Mitchison still recognised sadly that 'we are going to have hell trying to get people to work the peace, trying to give people a worth-while-ness in their peace time lives comparable with the worth-while-ness of working together during the war. We shall probably fail.'

AFTERWORD

"What was the post-war world like after the last war?"

VERE HODGSON HAD drunk a toast with friends on the day that war ended in Europe. Standing in a garden flat in west London, the assembled company had raised their glasses to '. . . Churchill, Stalin, Auntie Nell, Kit's father in Guernsey . . .' It was a tribute to the figures that had peopled their war, a jumble of the public and the private that in some form exemplified almost everyone's feeling of involvement in Britain's 'finest hour' – which had lasted six long weary years.

The Second World War is now sixty years past: the material evidence of its destruction has been cleared up, built over, tidied away. In city centres the effects of wartime bombs merge indivisibly with the eager intentions of post-war planners. The war's players are growing old: their wartime experiences a lifetime away. Within a decade or so there will be few survivors who were adults on the battlefront or the Home Front. Yet the legacy of the Second World War is still potent. It is ever-present in commemorations that roll round every ten years – Dunkirk, the Blitz, D-Day – in an unceasing output of films and television programmes, books, talks, exhibitions, workshops, school curricula. These serve to remind and reinforce memories, and to acquaint and inform those who came after – long after, now.

But the legacy of the Home Front is more potent even than that. In 2003 Winston Churchill was voted the 'greatest Briton', his life a shorthand for an understanding of the war. Yet as the votes rolled in, shops continued to stock books, and television and radio channels to transmit programmes, that unpacked the 'Forties package' that Churchill represented, and which had been appropriated by politicians of Right and Left to invoke a British spirit of unquestioning unity and dogged resistance that fuelled their particular agendas.

The 'story' of the Second World War in Britain is one of over 48 million people: it is therefore one of courage and cowardice, of selflessness and opportunism, of great vision and intense scepticism, of stoic endurance and deep anger, of 'tiny defeats, tiny victories'. Ultimately it remains a story of a sort of patriotism that was mostly not triumphalist or flag waving, and even managed to ally itself to a dilute form of socialism. As George Orwell famously wrote in 1941: 'Patriotism is usually stronger than class hatred . . . England is the most class-ridden country under the sun. It is a land of snobbery and privilege largely ruled by the old and the silly. But in any calculation one has to take into account its emotional unity, the tendency of nearly all its inhabitants to feel alike and act alike and act together in moments of extreme crisis.'

It is surely how that was, and why that was and the ways in which that was attenuated, that gives the Home Front in the Second World War its continuing interest; and gives the memories, memoirs, diaries and letters of its participants their continuing vitality and importance in understanding something about Britain today.

ACKNOWLEDGEMENTS

T HIS BOOK – AND its author – owes a great number of debts. I would
have not contemplated writing it without prior knowledge of how
helpful a number of people key to the subject would be since this is not
the first time I have relied on their help and expertise. My thanks go to
many of the staff of the Imperial War Museum, primarily to Roderick
Suddaby in the Department of Documents who has been an endless
source of helpful suggestions; he and his entire staff – particularly
Amanda Mason and Katherine Martin – have made working on the
IWM's extensive collection of Second World War letters and diaries a
most rewarding experience. I also again owe a debt to Dr Terry Charman,
historian in the Research and Information Department at the IWM; to
Dr Christopher Dowling, Department of Public Services; to Sue
Breakwell formerly of the Art Department archives; Dr Toby Haggith of
the Film and Archive Department; Penny Ritchie Calder, Head of
Exhibitions; to the staff of the Sound Archives particularly John
Stopford-Pickering; the Photograph Archive; the Department of Printed

Books; to Malcolm Brown and to Clive Richards at IWM Duxford. At the Mass-Observation Archive in Sussex Dorothy Sheridan, Joy Eldridge and their colleagues have once again been extremely helpful, patient and knowledgeable. I am also indebted to the staff of the London Library; the British Library; the London Metropolitan Archives; Heather Creaton at the Centre for Metropolitan History, University of London; Lorraine Chesters at the Museum of Liverpool Life; Tony Lane of the *Liverpool Post and Echo*; Martin Maw, Oxford University Press Archivist; Darleen Maxwell, Archivist to the Royal College of Art; Guy Revel at the RAF Museum, Hendon; Oliver Merrington at the Hall Carpenter Archives; Robert Purves at the British Library Sound Archives; Christopher Whittick at the East Sussex Record Office; Charlotte Derry of Redbridge Museum Services; Alison Fraser at the Orkney Library and Archive, Kirkwall; and to Matt Lyus for his research on my behalf at The National Archive/Public Record Office. When it comes to gathering information today's historian is well-served not only by libraries and archives, but by internet websites: two invaluable ones proved to be the Royal Historical Society Bibliography at www.rhs.ac.uk/bibl and www.abebooks.com, a commercial site that sources – and sells – second-hand books from all over the world, which makes writing a book like this much easier – and much more expensive.

I would particularly like to thank Dr Paul Addison of the Centre for Second World War Studies at the University of Edinburgh who read the manuscript in whole, and Dr J. A. Crang also of the Centre, who read it in part, as did Dr Simon Trew of the Department of War Studies, Royal Military Academy, Sandhurst and Professor Roger Morgan. Professor Peter Hennessey of Queen Mary College, University of London, was most helpful at the beginning of the project, and Jessica Mann and Professor Charles Thomas were extremely hospitable and generous in making material on the WVS and Cornwall's war available to me. Professor Henry Horwitz again proved a tireless and very valued supplier of journal articles and book references, and David Kynaston has been most generous in drawing my attention to useful and sometimes recondite wartime sources that he came across during the research for his own forthcoming book on the post-war period. Dr Robin Woolven kindly lent me his unpublished thesis on *Civil Defence in London, 1935–1945* as did Alice Smith her MA dissertation on evacuation.

Writing this book would have been inconceivable without the

prodigious amount of work by writers and historians on whose books I have drawn in writing my own. My indebtedness to these sources is acknowledged in the bibliography.

I am also most grateful to the following people who have helped me in various ways: Dick and Shirley Annan; Josie Barnard; Professor Brian Barton; Lady Alice Boyd; Dr Angus Calder; Frank Collieson; Charlotte Crow; Vanessa Cunningham; Ann and Mike Dawney; Professor Christopher Elrington and Jean Elrington; Nicholas Faith; Peter Furtado; Geraldine Goller; Sarah Guy; Janie Hampton; Professor Jenny Hartley; Sue Hess; Ruth Ive; Christian, Lady Hesketh; Dave Kendall; Jerry Kuehl; Philippa Lewis; Jill Longmate; Norman Longmate; Professor S. P. MacKenzie; John Manley; Ethel Mattison; John Muir; Vivien Noakes; Edna Norris; Harry and Irene Pepp; David Prest; Hugh Purcell; Phyllis Sellick; Alice Smith; Dr Sally Sokoloff; Dr Jill Stephenson; Victoria Syme Taylor; Antonia Till; Stella Tillyard; Professor Nick Tiratsoo; Stephen Watson; Ian S. Wood; Patrick Wright.

I would like to thank my agent, Deborah Rogers, and my publishers, Headline, where Heather Holden-Brown first suggested the book to me. Martin Neild and Val Hudson took up the idea with enthusiasm, and Emma Tait my editor has worked without ceasing to make this a very much better (and shorter) book than it would otherwise have been, as has my copy editor Christine King, and Emma's assistant, Eleanor Maxfield. I am also most grateful to the sales, marketing and publicity teams at Headline for their support: Kerr MacRae, James Horobin, Paul Erdpresser, Sabine Edwards and Caitlin Raynor.

My family have, as always, been encouraging, enthusiastic, supportive and challenging. My thanks to Alexander, Sophie and Sebastian.

It can be no other way, but despite all this help, any errors or omissions that persist are my responsibility alone.

ENDNOTES

viii: *Every true story* . . . Hustvedt p. 367

xiv: *I don't know* . . . Orwell (1968 Vol. II) p. 590

xv: *Peace was dying* . . . Cowles p. 139

1: *Today was a* . . . 'Autumn Journal' MacNeice pp. 101–53

1: *The sun is* . . . 3 Sep 1939 M-OA Diarist 5383

2: Reach of the wireless, O'Sullivan in Kirkham & Thoms p. 175

2: *Literally everyone in* . . . Orwell (1937) p. 83

2: *the accumulator man* . . . Roose IWM Dept of Documents 89/14/1 p. 11

2: Listening figures for BBC news, Curran & Seaton p. 148

2: *the most delightfully* . . . Miles 3 Sep 1939 IWM Dept of Documents 99/74/1

3: *could eat no* . . . Quoted in Mass-Observation (1940) p. 39

3: *held her chin* . . . M-OA Diarist 5282

3: *safe and temporary* . . . Author interview with Angela Culme-Seymour 15 Oct 2002

3: *L[eonard] and I* . . . V. Woolf pp. 233–4

4: *sound[ed] like a* . . . 3 Sep 1939 Mitchison p. 35

4: *even when someone* . . . Nicolson (1967) p. 30

4: *If only we* . . . Channon p. 215

5: *I saw from* . . . 3 Sep 1939 M-OA Diarist 5269 5

5: *voice sounded very* . . . Brittain (1989) p. 28

5: *a feeling of* . . . 3 Sep 1939 M-OA Diarist 5324 3

6: *This is the . . .* Laurence Olivier quoted in Sinclair (1989) p. 27

6: *If I am . . .* 5 Sep 1939 M-OA Diarist 5269 5

7: *had been convinced . . .* Masel 3 Sep 1939 M-OA Diarist 5370

8: *As we went . . .* Anonymous M-OA Diarist

8: *to see what . . .* Churchill (1948) pp. 361–2

9: *police on bicycles . . .* Mass-Observation (1940) pp. 45–6

9: *Of course we . . .* Author interview with Shirley Annand 11 Sep 2002

9: *it would be . . .* Beardmore p. 34

9: *They ought not . . .* Leo Amery quoted in Nicolson (1967) p. 421

9: *Hardly had he . . .* Nicolson (1967) p. 421

10: *hardly digested the . . .* 3 Sep 1939 M-OA Diarist 5342 3

10: *unspeakable astonishment . . .* Cox 3 Sep 1939 IWM Dept of Documents 86/46/1 (P)

11: *to advise me . . .* 3 Sep 1939 M-OA Diarist 5276 3

12: *prepared a short . . .* Churchill (1959) p. 361

12: *barks of a . . . New York Times* 4 Sep 1939

12: *Too much like . . .* Nicolson (1967) p. 422

13: *sorting out all . . .* 3 Sep 1939 M-OA Diarist 5269 5

13: Plan to circulate King's message, Wheeler-Bennett (1958) p. 406

14: *this dimmed lighting . . .* 3 Sep 1939 M-OA Diarist 5336

15: *All the time . . .* Jim Bartley quoted in Parsons p. 9

16: *We are dropping . . .* Phipps 19 Sep 1939 IWM Dept of Documents P178

16: *the people of . . .* Kee p. 336

16: *Great Britain is . . . Observer* 8 Oct 1939

17: *Committee of Evacuation . . . Evacuation: The True Story* BBC Radio 4, Aug 1999

17: *Exodus of the . . . Dorset Daily Echo* 1 Sep 1939 quoted in Parsons p. 17

18: *The scheme is . . .* MoI Public Information Leaflet No 3

18: *It does not . . . Liverpolitan* quoted in Wallis p. 5

19: Evacuation of public schools, Robinson p. 47

19: Highgate school evacuation, Mallinson IWM Sound Archives 220703

20: *The headmistress sent . . .* Margaret Cronin quoted in Brown (2000) p. 10

20: *card games, gym . . .* Quoted in M. Brown (2000) p. 5

20: *realise what war . . .* Quoted in M. Graham p. 28

20: *Each morning my . . .* Mel Calman quoted in Johnson p. 35

21: Percentages of evacuees who left, Titmuss p. 103

21: Reasons for regional variations, Titmuss p. 103

22: *it would not . . .* MoI Public Information Leaflet No 3

22: *The Government was . . .* Titmuss p. 105

22: Children missing out on education, Titmuss p. 133

23: Percentages of evacuees who left, Titmuss p. 105

23: *There are still . . .* MoI Public Information Leaflet No 3

23: *most vividly . . .* Sylvia Woodeson quoted in Inglis pp. 13–4

23: *I want to . . .* Kops pp. 51–2

24: *Come the Friday . . .* Edna Griffiths (née Kirby) quoted in Wallis p. 27

24: *the idea began . . .* Marjorie Lamb quoted in Wallis p. 25

24: *a bit of . . .* Baker IWM Sound Archives 006498

25: *It is now . . .* Eileen Donald quoted in Johnson p. 69

25: *We were put . . .* Betty Jones quoted in M. Brown (2000) p. 17

26: *the most depressing . . .* Quoted in Boyd p. 57

26: Lack of lavatories on trains, Titmuss p. 108

26: *Once on the* . . . Eileen Donald quoted in Johnson p. 69

26: *was carried out* . . . Hylton p. 35

27: *It was not* . . . Titmuss p. 111

27: Appointment of billeting officers, Crosby p. 31

28: *No one knows* . . . Renée Humphries quoted in M-OA, F/R 11

28: Misdirection of evacuees in Oxfordshire, M. Graham pp. 31–2

28: Misdirection of evacuees in Wales, Wallis pp. 37–9

29: *The scene that* . . . Quoted in Mass-Observation (1940) p. 299

29: *all the girls* . . . Bill Wilkinson quoted in Wallis p. 45

29: *herded like cattle* . . . Quoted in Ferguson p. 9

30: *a burly man* . . . Ron Freedland quoted in Wallace p. 5

30: *because I didn't* . . . Charles Crebbin quoted in Wallis pp. 42–3

30: *When we had* . . . Joyce Light quoted in Wallis p. 42

30: *Stick together* . . . Dorothy Wharton quoted in Wallis p. 43

30: *nearly thirteen years* . . . Kops p. 53

31: *it's not our* . . . Kops p. 55

31: Attitudes towards Jewish evacuees, Crosby p. 5

31: *seemed to have* . . . Ruth Fainlight quoted in Johnson p. 90

31: Problems Jewish evacuees experienced, Crosby pp. 40–1

31: *I certainly wasn't* . . . Mitchell IWM Sound Archives 20371

32: *on Sundays we* . . . Hugh Jones quoted in Wallis p. 144

32: *the physical danger* . . . Quoted in Padley & Cole pp. 236–7

32: Mary Datchelor's School, Crosby p. 67

33: *They got all* . . . Crompton pp. 1, 5

33: Finding space for schools, Parsons p. 76

34: Unemployment and poor relief figures, Branson & Heinemann p. 341

34: *Those children may* . . . Patrick Dollan in *Glasgow Herald* 14 Sep 1939 quoted in Rose p. 59

34: *one of* . . . Quoted in Mass-Observation (1940) p. 327

34: O's research into evacuation problems, Mass-Observation (1940) p. 305

35: *The rumours of* . . . Quoted in Mass-Observation (1940) p. 305

35: *who have gone* . . . Margaret Cassidy quoted in Wallace p. 37

35: *a great deal* . . . Quoted in Mass-Observation (1940) p. 311

35: *half-fed, half-clothed* . . . Quoted in Macnicol in H. L. Smith (1986)

35: *quite unknown to* . . . Women's Group on Public Welfare p. xiv

35: *children in rags* . . . Women's Group on Public Welfare

35: *many Manchester and* . . . Ministry of Health report quoted in Titmuss p. 117

36: *he never had* . . . Baker IWM Sound Archives 006498

36: Lice infestation in Bridgenorth, Crosby p. 33

36: Percentage of evacuees with vermin, Women's Institute survey quoted in Crosby p. 33

38: Punishment of evacuees, Parsons & Starns p. 116

38: Invention of bedwetting cases, Macnicol in H. L. Smith (1986) pp. 17–18

38: *a visit to* . . . Quoted in Welshman in *Twentieth Century British History* p. 21

39: Dealing with problem evacuees, Macnicol in H. L. Smith (1986) p. 17

39: Evacuation surveys, Titmuss pp. 179–80

39: *These children* . . . Jesse & Harwood p. 29

39: *low slum type* . . . Quoted in Lily Bos 'Preliminary Report on Evacuation' in Hinton (2002) p. 150

39: *If the mothers* . . . M-OA TC Box
     5 Folder I/1

40: *there is evidently* . . . *Farmers' Weekly*
     27 Oct 1939 quoted in Rose
     pp. 207–8

40: *Rural life has* . . . Women's Group
     on Public Welfare p. 6

40: *Growth rates in children,* Welshman
     in *Twentieth Century British History*
     p. 45

41: *the servant problem* . . . Letter to
     Ministry of Health 14 Mar 1940
     quoted in Crosby p. 50

41: *disgruntled butlers* . . . Mass-
     Observation (1940) p. 329

41: *over and over* . . . Quoted in
     Crosby p. 47

41: *It's always the* . . . M-OA TC Box
     5 Folder 2/L

41: *whose one sitting* . . . 31 Aug 1939
     Miles IWM Dept of Documents
     99/74/1

41: *quite happy* . . . M-OA TC Box 5
     Folder 2/A

42: *brings in no* . . . *Home and Country*
     Jun 1942 quoted in M. Andrews
     pp. 115–16

42: *the appalling conditions* . . .
     Parliamentary Secretary to the
     Ministry of Health quoted in
     Titmuss p. 177

42: Collecting payment for evacuees'
     billets, Titmuss p. 160

43: *the children were* . . . Letter from
     Dorothy Mainwaring to Helena
     Britton Sep 1939 IWM Dept of
     Documents Con. Shelf

43: Evacuation to non-English-
     speaking countries, Jackson
     p. 72

43: Percentages of Welsh-only
     speakers, Wallis p. xviii

44: *went to the* . . . Elsa Chatterton
     quoted in Wallis p. 155

44: *the indiscriminate transfer* . . . D. H.
     Davies p. 232

45: Billeting tribunals, Crosby p. 32

45: *I gather these* . . . *St Ives Times*
     quoted in *The Evacuee* 1997 p. 9

45: Miss Hoyles' experiences, Hoyles

46: Catholic families from Clydeside,
     Boyd p. 29

46: *found it hard* . . . Women's
     Institute survey quoted in Matless
     p. 183

47: Figures for expectant mothers,
     Titmuss p. 113

47: *Who pays for* . . . Dorset County
     Council minutes Sep 1939
     quoted in Parsons p. 150

47: Payment for expectant mothers,
     Parsons p. 110

48: *not so much* . . . Baker IWM Sound
     Archives 006498

48: Abuse of evacuees, *Evacuation:
     The True Story* BBC Radio 4, Aug
     1999

49: *They reason* . . . Burlingham and
     Freud p. 26

49: *very few parents* . . . Quoted in
     Wallis p. 68

49: Contact with home, Barnett
     House Study Group pp. 41, 101

49: *a feeling of* . . . Isaacs p. 140

50: Ronald Hodgson's father visiting,
     Letter from Ronald Hodgson to
     author 2003

50: *After a bit* . . . Baker IWM Sound
     Archives 006498

50: Preference for camps, Isaacs
     p. 140

51: *had had a* . . . Quoted in Parsons
     p. 118

51: *the Dead End* . . . Ritchie Calder
     in *Daily Herald* 26 Oct 1939

51: Percentages of children in full-
     time education, Titmuss p. 58

53: *It oughtn't to* . . . Struther p. 129

53: Blackout as the most hated thing,
     Mass-Observation (1940) p. 185

53: *Daily Mail* survey, Conrad Russell
     quoted in Cooper p. 506

54: Blackout regulations, O'Brien
     p. 137

55: *with curtains drawn* . . . Cotton
     IWM Dept of Documents 93/3/1
     p. 48

55: Lord Alfred Douglas, Thomas
     p. 38

55: *one of the . . .* Quoted in Livesey p. 18

55: *kitchen window cost . . .* Cotton IWM Dept of Documents 93/3/1 p. 47

56: *afford a pot . . .* Haldane p. 84–5

57: Man fined £2, Smithies (1982) p. 84

57: Man who lit bonfire, Smithies (1982) p. 84

57: *to protest most . . .* Letter to *The Times* 16 Sep 1939

57: *the merest glimmer . . .* Nellie Turner quoted in Longmate (1971) p. 30

58: *For weeks it . . .* Cotton IWM Dept of Documents 93/3/1 p. 53

58: *so stygian . . .* Burgon Bickerstein quoted in Smart in Gledhill & Swanson p. 84

58: *a tag I've . . .* 5 Sep 1939 Last p. 129

58: *My dear boy . . .* Dorothy L. Sayers in *Spectator* 17 Nov 1939

58: *I yield to . . .* 'Y. Y.' in *New Statesman and Nation* 16 Dec 1930 p. 890

59: *suffering from sexual . . .* Crisp pp. 154–5

60: *if the London . . .* Dorothy L. Sayers in *Spectator* 17 Nov 1939

61: Figures for blackout fatalities, A. Calder (1969)

61: *the means of . . .* Sir John Anderson quoted in O'Brien p. 322

62: *A friend of . . .* 'Y. Y.' in *New Statesman and Nation* 16 Dec 1930 p. 890

62: *wanted to see . . .* Cox 18 Nov 1939 IWM Dept of Documents 86/46/1 (P)

64: Man with light in fish tank, E. S. Turner p. 62

64: Dixon's Blazes, E. S. Turner p. 64

65: *every British adult . . .* O'Brien p. 330

65: *to the Army . . .* Haldane p. 203

66: Lectures on gas, Allingham p. 35

67: *swank . . .* J. P. McHutchison IWM Dept of Documents P151 p. 66

67: *with a scandalised . . .* F. Tennyson Jesse quoted in Colenbrander

67: *My God . . .* Mike Bree quoted in M. Brown (1999) p. 3

68: *army of volunteers . . .* M-O Archive F/R A24

68: *found themselves confronted . . .* Quoted in O'Brien p. 341

69: Home Secretary defends the ARP, O'Brien p. 344

69: Reasons for joining Fulham ARP, M-OA F/R A24

70: *bring home to . . .* Graves (1948) p. 2

71: *Woman of various . . .* 'Lady Reading: Unforgettable Founder of the WVS' in *Reader's Digest* Oct 1972

71: *Willingness versus . . .* WVS Bulletin No. 22, Aug 1941

72: *we have learned . . .* Lady Reading quoted in Beauman

72: What the WVS did, WVS Bulletin No. 15, Jan 1941; No. 39, Jan 1943; No. 23, Sep 1941

73: *the dust and . . .* Westwood in *History Today*

73: *a million magnificent . . .* Herbert Morrison quoted in Westwood in *History Today*

73: *a many faceted . . .* M. Andrews p. 101

74: WI jam making, M. Andrews p. 107

74: *Life in the . . .* Quoted in M. Andrews p. 104

74: *is no doubt . . .* Home and Country Jan 1941 quoted in M. Andrews p. 104

75: *Now the war . . .* Rosamond Lehmann quoted in Struther p. 140, 143

76: *He had got . . .* Bowen (1948) p. 51

76: Recruitment in the First World War, Gilbert (1994) pp. 37–8

77: *not prepared . . .* C. W. G. Eady (Deputy Sec of State, Home Office) 26 Oct 1938 quoted in Dennis p. 229

78: *The support of . . .* Sir Henry

Pownall quoted in Bond p. 286

78: *Opinion poll on conscription,* Gallup poll quoted in French p. 49

79: *The 'Terries'* . . . Eddie Mathieson quoted in MacDougall p. 216

78: Preference for the RAF and Navy, Crang pp. 6–7

79: *There is the* . . . Captain 'X' p. 78

79: *looked at my* . . . 6 Sep 1939 Last pp. 13–15

80: *as a Civil Servant* . . . Mattison IWM Dept of Documents Con. Shelf

80: *Uniform does something* . . . Letter from John Phillips to Peggie Phillips 12 Nov 1940 IWM Dept of Documents 61/47/2

80: *for the first* . . . Sir D. Fraser p. 98

80: *sloppy civilians into* . . . Waller IWM Dept of Documents 87/42/1

80: *soldiers used to* . . . Captain 'X' p. 93

81: *Really when one* . . . Earl of Derby (TNA/PRO WO) quoted in Dennis p. 236

82: Growth in size of Army, War Office report on manpower problems (TNA/PRO W. 277/12) July 1944 quoted in Crang p. 144

82: *battle-hardened troops* . . . Crang in Addison & Calder p. 60

82: Army still based in Britain, Crang in Addison & Calder p. 60

82: *daring deeds at* . . . Crang in Addison & Calder p. 60

83: *My soldier has* . . . 1 Oct 1941, 2 Oct 1941, 7 Oct 1941 M-OA Diarist 4523 quoted in Sheridan p.144–7

83: *cogs in [a]* . . . French p. 230

83: Problems of Army on Home Front, Sokoloff (1999) p. 41

84: *Getting involved in* . . . Letter from John Phillips to Peggie Phillips 12 Nov 1940 IWM Dept of Documents 61/47/2

84: *bored and browned* . . . Army morale report May–Jul 1942 (TNA/PRO WO 163/161) quoted in Crang in Addison & Calder p. 63

84: *Pay and allowances* . . . Captain 'X' p. 32–3

84: *It is generally* . . . Army morale report May–Jul 1942 (TNA/PRO WO 163/161) quoted in Englander & Mason p. 12

85: Deductions to wives' grants, Captain 'X' p. 73

85: Problems with renting rooms, Dewey pp. 300–1

85: Cost of living increases, Hancock & Gowing p. 166

85: Prof. John Hilton's advice bureau, War office report on morale in the army Nov 1942–Jan1943 (TNA/PRO WO 163/161) quoted in Englander & Mason p. 13

86: RAF airman's colleagues' marriages, M-OA F/R 64

86: *I had been* . . . Bowmer 12 Jul 1940 IWM Dept of Documents 61/47/2

86: *delay, irregularities or* . . . Quoted in Minns p. 175

87: *I haven't used* . . . Letter from John Phillips to Peggie Phillips 11 Aug 1942 IWM Dept of Documents 61/47/2

87: *Well my darling* . . . Letter from John Phillips to Peggie Phillips (posted) Mar 1942 IWM Dept of Documents 61/47/2

87: *Thank you very* . . . Bowmer 12 Jul 1940, 9 Nov 1941 IWM Dept of Documents Con. Shelf

88: *We went to* . . . Letter from Peggie Phillips to John Phillips IWM Dept of Documents 61/47/2

88: *It was fine* . . . Mattison IWM Dept of Documents Con. Shelf p. 30

89: *I can't get* . . . Hill p. 45

89: *About leaves* . . . Hill p. 43

90: *My long weekend* . . . 24 Oct 1941, 26 Oct 1941 M-OA Diarist 5284 quoted in Sheridan p. 140

90: LAWOs, Crang p. 91

90: Soldiers finding out about Blitz, Crang p. 101

91: Compassionate leave requests, Sokoloff (1999) p. 36

91: *It was touch* . . . Quoted in Sokoloff in *Women's History Review* pp. 59–67

91: *This depends on* . . . Hillary p. 48

92: *war is a mass* . . . Slater & Woodside p. 215

92: *mentioned the sex* . . . Slater & Woodside p. 219

93: *that the fidelity* . . . Slater & Woodside p. 222

93: *some men admitted* . . . Slater & Woodside p. 219

93: *Listen, darling* . . . 'Sarah Russell' (Marghanita Laski) p. 73

93: *took place under* . . . Slater & Woodside p. 219

93: *Every married man* . . . Letter from John Phillips to Peggie Phillips 1 Nov 1943 IWM Dept of Documents 61/47/2

94: *kept on about* . . . Quoted in Slater & Woodside p. 220

94: *Affairs in wartime* . . . Author interview with Ethel Mattison

94: *said to me* . . . Cartland pp. 221–2

95: Figures for illegitimate births, Ferguson & Fitzgerald p. 91

95: Illegitimate births in Birmingham, Ferguson & Fitzgerald p. 98

95: Husbands' responses to illegitimate babies, Ferguson & Fitzgerald p. 99

95: *A friend of* . . . Mattison (née Britton) 22 Jul 1941 IWM Dept of Documents Con. Shelf

96: *Figures for abortion,* Ferguson & Fitzgerald pp. 77–8

96: *much as we* . . . Letter from John Phillips to Peggie Phillips Jun 1941 IWM Dept of Documents 61/47/2

96: *didn't quite trust* . . . Letter from Peggie Phillips to John Phillips (prior to) 3 Jul 1941 IWM Dept of Documents 61/47/2

96: *The woman* . . . Letter from John Phillips to Peggie Phillips Oct 1941 IWM Dept of Documents 61/47/2

96: *Jack is now* . . . Mattison 1 Jan 1940, 22 Aug 1943 IWM Dept of Documents Con. Shelf

97: *one of the* . . . Quoted in Haste p. 110

98: Figures for divorce, Annual Abstract of Statistics 1947 quoted in Ferguson & Fitzgerald p. 20

98: *not one that* . . . Quoted in Sokoloff in *Women's History Review* p. 39

98: Printed appeal to women, Crang in Addison & Calder p. 71

98: *telling him to* . . . Mattison IWM Dept of Documents Con. Shelf

99: *Jack was only* . . . Author interview with Ethel Mattison

99: *was not quite* . . . Mary Cole quoted in Humphries & Gordon pp. 245–6

99: *This is the* . . . Miles 28 Nov 1939 IWM Dept of Documents 99/74/1

100: Navy losses in 1939, *Lloyd's War Losses*

100: *The Royal Navy's* . . . Panter-Downes (1972) p. 32

100: *the Nazi air force* . . . Walmsley p. 46

100: *There was no* . . . Walmsley p. 47

102: *Your conscience thinks* . . . A.A. Milne quoted in Hayes p. 65

102: *I admit that* . . . Fenner Brockway quoted in Hayes p. 61

103: *the meaning of* . . . Barker p. 16

103: *It is immaterial* . . . Judge Burgis quoted in Barker p. 17

104: *The tribunals could* . . . Barker pp. 17–26

104: *R's beliefs are* . . . Partridge p. 155

104: *Someone who has* . . . Quoted in Turner p. 170

105: *I have the greatest* . . . Judge Richardson quoted in Turner p.177

105: *these miserable creatures* . . . Sir Edmund Phipps (London Chairman) quoted in Hayes p. 40

106: *to waste my* . . . Dylan Thomas quoted in Fitzgibbon p. 246

106: *The editor of* . . . D. H. Davies p. 228

106: *have occupations where* . . . M-OA TC6

107: *Quite frankly Jags* . . . Letter from a girl to a pacifist July 1940 M-OA TC6

108: *our discussion of* . . . Letter from Arnold Monk-Jones to Eileen Bellermy 23 Apr 1939 IWM Dept of Documents 01/50/1

108: *I am very* . . . Letter from Eileen Bellermy to Arnold Monk-Jones 25 Apr 1939 IWM Dept of Documents 01/50/1

108: *Re pacificism you* . . . Letter from Arnold Monk-Jones to Eileen Bellermy 30 Apr 1939 IWM Dept of Documents 01/50/1

109: *There is no* . . . Letter from Eileen Bellermy to Arnold Monk-Jones 7 May 1939 IWM Dept of Documents 01/50/1

109: *wobbling like a* . . . Letter from Arnold Monk-Jones to Eileen Bellermy 19 May 1939 IWM Dept of Documents 01/50/1

109: *insists that once* . . . Letter from Arnold Monk-Jones to Eileen Bellermy 19 May 1939 IWM Dept of Documents 01/50/1

109: *That is a* . . . Letter from Eileen Bellermy to Arnold Monk-Jones 31 May 1939 IWM Dept of Documents 01/50/1

109: *I think it* . . . Letter from Eileen Bellermy to Arnold Monk-Jones 4 Jun 1939 IWM Dept of Documents 01/50/1

109: *Arnold dear* . . . Letter from Eileen Bellermy to Arnold Monk-Jones Jun 1939 IWM Dept of Documents 01/50/1

109: *I am only* . . . Letter from Arnold Monk-Jones to Eileen Bellermy 26 Jun 1939 IWM Dept of Documents 01/50/1

109: *all this ugliness* . . . Letter from Arnold Monk-Jones to Eileen Bellermy 14 Sep 1939 IWM Dept of Documents 01/50/1

110: *You won't be* . . . Quoted in J. Lewis p. 26

110: *I could hardly* . . . Letter from Arnold Monk-Jones to Eileen Bellermy 2 Sep 1939 IWM Dept of Documents 01/50/1

110: *He felt that* . . . Blishen p. 13

110: *I was brought* . . . Bottini IWM Sound Archives 00461/04

111: *Hardly dared glance* . . . Len Richardson, www.peacenow.org.uk

112: *Among its members* . . . Ceadel p. 295

112: *An organisation of* . . . Fenner Brockway quoted in Hayes p. vii

112: *Not all pacifists* . . . M-OA F/R 312 p. 6

113: *Conchies learn the* . . . *Daily Express* 14 Apr 1940

113: Questions asked of COs, MacDougall p. 265

114: *I shall never* . . . Bottini IWM Sound Archives 00461/04

115: *forbids [us] to* . . . Benjamin Britten quoted in Carpenter pp. 134–5

115: *The whole of* . . . Britten p. 1046

115: *going for a* . . . Ethel Bridge quoted in Britten p. 1049

115: *a wise and* . . . Quoted in Carpenter p. 177

115: *I was given* . . . Tippett pp. 120–1

116: *could respect and* . . . Barker p. 18

116: *In all, 18,495 men* . . . Barker p. 26

117: *of the 5852* . . . Hayes p. 207

117: *of the 16,000* . . . Barker p. 121

117: *for committing a* . . . Leonard Bird, www.ppu.org.uk/learn/infodocs/cos

117: *some people may* . . . *Aberdeen Evening Express* 4 Sep 1941 quoted in Barker p. 97

118: *Nancy-Elsie to* . . . Stanford p. 54

118: *felt it was* . . . Quoted in MacDougall p.285

119: *Eventually almost 2,400* . . . Hayes p. 387

119: *overcome by pictures* . . . Christopher Wren quoted in Jappy p. 92

119: *some members of . . .* Christopher Wren quoted in Jappy p. 97

120: *who showed his . . .* Eric Gill quoted in MacCarthy p. 289

120: *a nice funkhole . . . Sunday Pictorial* 6 Sep 1942 quoted in Rose p. 173

120: *made compulsory for . . .* Lieutenant-Colonel Ackland-Troyte (MP) quoted in Barker p. 47

121: *so you would . . .* Archibald Black quoted in MacDougall p. 278

121: *wrote to the . . .* Bottini IWM Sound Archives 00461/04

121: *Eventually Bottini was . . .* Bottini IWM Sound Archives 00461/04

121: *never had any . . .* Bottini IWM Sound Archives 00461/04

121: *who wanted to . . .* Bill Prentice quoted in MacDougall p. 271

122: *national pansies...with . . .* Bernard Gray in *Sunday Pictorial* 9 Jun 1940 quoted in Rose pp. 175–6

122: *A Yorkshire Vicar,* Hayes pp. 203–4

122: *She didn't want . . .* Walter Wright, www.ppu.org.uk/learn/infodocs/cos

122: *could find no . . .* D. S. Savage 'Treatment of a Conscientious Objector' in Simmons pp. 106–7

122: *Cut out his . . .* www.ppu.org.uk/learn/infodocs/cos

122: *Conscientious Objectors were . . .* K. O. Morgan p. 296

122: *There were reports . . . New Statesman and Nation* 2 Mar 1940 p. 268

122: *on several . . .* Barker p. 59

123: *They should be . . .* CBCO LAD Portsmouth 12 Jun 1940 quoted in Barker pp. 61–2

123: *They are like . . .* CBCO LAD Merton, Surrey quoted in Barker p. 59

123: *Men who register . . .* CBCO LAD Essex 21 Nov 1940 quoted in Barker p. 59

123: *In the end . . .* Barker p. 69

123: *What would be . . .* Quoted in Rose p. 177

123: *As a serving . . .* Hemel Hempstead

Gazette quoted in Barker p. 70

123: *And Leeds Education . . . News Chronicle* quoted in Rose p. 177

123: *no reason to . . . Hansard* 10 Apr 1940 quoted in Barker p. 70

124: *We were against . . .* Trory IWM Sound Archives 004693

125: *Under the provisions . . .* H. M. D. Parker p. 113

126: *That might be . . .* Hayes p. 49

126: *The first woman . . .* Hayes pp. 266–7

126: *My father wouldn't . . .* Hayes p. 89

130: *I do think . . .* Wigham IWM Sound Archives 004761

131: *A long face . . . Picture Post* 10 Dec 1939

132: *A total of . . .* Nicholas p. 27

132: *the unaffectionate . . .* Hickman p. 16

132: *For amusement only . . .* Nicholas pp. 27–8

132: *the first and . . . Listener* 7 Sep 1939 p. 464

133: *in maintaining national . . .* Nicholas p. 92

133: *The BBC monotonously . . . New Statesman and Nation* 9 Sep 1939

133: *By the beginning . . .* Curran & Seaton p. 139

133: *These 'black propaganda' . . .* M. Doherty p. 19–29

134: *The gent . . .* Jonah Barrington in *Daily Express* 14 Sep 1939

134: *His broadcasts were . . .* 'The Effect of the Hamburg Propaganda in Great Britain' Jan 1940 quoted in Briggs (1970) p. 135

134: *the best entertainment . . .* Briggs (1970) p. 128

134: *I learn some . . .* 'Hamburg Broadcast Propaganda' 8 Mar 1940 quoted in M. Doherty p. 97

134: *At first the . . .* M. Doherty p. 103

135: *The almost war-long . . .* Hickman p. 47

135: *one of the . . .* 1 Feb 1940 M-OA TC 'Radio' Box 3B

136: *is that five . . .* Quoted in Curran & Seaton p. 137

136: *which was as . . .* Briggs (1970) p. 291

136: *There were inevitable . . .* Briggs (1970) pp. 509–10

137: Establishment of Forces Programme, Nicholas p. 71

137: *if we give . . .* A. P. Ryan (soon to become Controller of Home Service) quoted in Nicholas p. 51

137: Restriction of football crowds, Lanfranchi & Taylor in Kirkham & Thoms p. 189

138: Matt Busby during war, Lanfranchi & Taylor in Kirkham & Thoms p. 191

138: Stanley Matthews during war, Lanfranchi & Taylor in Kirkham & Thoms p. 192

138: Aldershot football team, Lanfranchi & Taylor in Kirkham & Thoms p. 193

138: Norwich City football team, Longmate (1971) p. 463

138: Football pools, McCarthy p. 46

139: *large underground offices . . .* Stanford p. 245

139: *I had the . . .* Sir P. Warner p. 245

139: *business as usual . . .* Sir Stafford Cripps quoted in Baker in Hayes & Hill p. 131

140: Red Cross and greyhound racing, Baker in Hayes & Hill p. 133

140: *evening dress . . .* Quoted in Noble p. 14

140: West End shows, Noble p. 13

140: Vic Oliver, Turner p.101

141: *require morale boosters . . .* Dean p. 280

142: *they listened with . . .* Haskell et al p. 108

142: *What madness is . . . Daily Express* quoted in Hewison p. 23

142: *music-making and . . .* Leventhal in *Twentieth Century British History* p. 297

142: *culturally deprived . . .* Leventhal in *Twentieth Century British History* p. 291

143: concert at Vauxhall works, Leventhal in *Twentieth Century British History* pp. 299–301

143: CEMA concerts in 1944, Hewison p. 157

143: *is not a . . .* Clark

143: CEMA re-forms companies, Leventhal in *Twentieth Century British History* p. 313

143: *to refuse people . . .* Sybil Eaton quoted in Leventhal in *Twentieth Century British History* p. 310

143: *orchestra of four . . .* Hewison p. 154

144: *the distinctive cultural . . .* C. E. M. Joad in *New Statesman and Nation* 11 Oct 1941

144: Dance halls, McKibbin p. 393

145: Sales of 'There'll Always Be An England', Steinberg et al p. 29

145: Success of 'I Don't Want to Set the World on Fire', Steinberg et al p. 61

146: Popular songs at the end of the war, G. Morgan pp. 26–7

146: *A masterstroke of . . .* Letter to *The Times* 5 Sep 1939

146: Sales of cinema tickets, McKibbin p. 419

146: Bolton Odeon, McKibbin p. 423

146: Re-opening of cinemas, Aldgate & Richards p. 2

147: *it took a . . .* Dilys Powell in Haskell et al p. 83

147: *bowler-hatted . . .* Lejeune p. 55

148: *a year of . . .* Lejeune p. 71

148: *almost as well . . .* Sinclair p. 38

148: MoI production figures, Thorpe et al p. ix

149: *they could not . . .* Dilys Powell in Haskell et al p. 66

149: 86 MoI films, Swann p. 167

149: *dearth of information . . .* Swann p. 170

149: Jennings' films, Swann p. 159

150: *decisively shaped and . . .* Aldgate & Richards p. 220

150: *the woolliest concept . . .* Addison (1994) p. 121

150: *What is 'morale'...* Last p. 135

150: *ultimately measured not . . .* Stephen Taylor quoted in MacKay (2002) p. 2

150: *panic, hysteria, grumbling*... MacKay p. 3

151: *this precise peer*... Mass-Observation (1940) p. 416

151: *became efficient and*... Lord Hood quoted in McLaine p. 7

151: Founders of M-O, Jeffery p. 2

151: *an anthropology of*... Letter to *New Statesman and Nation* 2 Jan 1937

152: *Madge's lab boys*... Quoted in Cunningham p. 336

152: Survey sources for M-O, McLaine p. 52

153: Postal and Telegraph Censorship reports, McLaine p. 53

153: Mary Adams, MacKay p. 10

153: *they're a bit*... Thomson p. 3

154: *a dumping ground*... Riley p. 17

154: *socially favoured amateurs*... *New Statesman and Nation* 11 May 1940

154: *The people must*... J. T. MacCurdy 13 Sep 1939 quoted in McLaine p. 280

155: Changes to content of newspapers, McCarthy p. 47

156: *Midnight Mass at*... Wyndham (1985) p. 33

156: *feeling quite sick*... M-OA Diarist 4342

157: *a fine holly*... Cox IWM Dept of Documents 86/46/1 (P)

157: *The toy display*... Panter-Downes (1972) p. 29

157: *Father Christmas tradition*... M-OA TC 282 Folder 1/E

157: *This Christmas saw*... Miles 27 Dec 1939 IWM Dept of Documents 99/74/1

158: *shortly before Christmas*... Milburn pp. 18–19

158: Figures for Armed Forces, *Fighting with Figures* p. 393

158: The BEF, Bond p. 41

159: New Year pantomime, Turner p. 99

159: *got rather tiddly*... Wyndham (1985) p. 34

160: *Julia...noticed*... Taylor pp. 40–1

160: Winter 1939–1940, Cox 3 Jan 1940 IWM Dept of Documents 84/46/1 (P)

162: *Pigs now wander*... Quoted in Ward p. 13

163: Increase in land under cultivation, R. J. Hammond p. 392

163: Figures for days Britain could feed itself, Wilt p. 68–9, 225

164: *to keep hens*... 4 Sep 1939 Last p. 11

164: Setting up of horticultural committees, J. Davies p. 30

164: *people soon found*... Fred Daw (Parks Superintendent for Oldbury) quoted in J. Davies p. 30

164: The King's contribution to food production, Bishop p. 47

164: *for every five*... Frederick A. Talbot 'Those Amazing Allotments' in *World's Work* Jan 1919 quoted in Crouch & Ward p. 71

164: *the pass with*... F. E. Green 'The Allotment Movement' in *Contemporary Review* Jul 1918 quoted in Crouch & Ward p. 72

165: Allotment service, J. Davies p. 106

165: Allotments on Hackney football pitches, Golden p. 92

165: Figures for allotments in cities, J. Davies p. 106

165: LMS railway allotments, J. Davies p. 108

165: Planting at British Museum, Ziegler (1995) p. 257

166: *went to a*... Letter from George Britton to Elizabeth (Florence) Elkus 27 Feb 1940 IWM Dept of Documents Con. Shelf

166: *vegetables are very*... Letter from Helena Britton to Elizabeth (Florence) Elkus 1 Mar 1940 IWM Dept of Documents Con. Shelf

166: Figures for allotment holders, Crouch & Ward pp. 75–6

166: Pig club at Ladies' Carlton Club, Ziegler (1995) p. 258

166: Pig club at Hyde Park police station, Ziegler (1995) p. 258

166: Figures for imports, Felton p. 92

166: Figures for water brought in with imports, *The Times* 29 Aug 1942

167: *the shortages are* . . . M-OA TC 'Rationing'

167: *the public should* . . . *Daily Express* 21 Nov 1939

167: *a general campaign* . . . *New Statesman and Nation* 13 Jan 1940

168: Rations for institutions, Impresario p. 9

169: summer concession, Impresario p. 54

169: Variation of allowances, Impresario p. 54

169: Meat for male workers, Smithies (1984) p. 76

169: *During most of* . . . Impresario p. 26

170: Tobacco rationing, Alford pp. 399–401

170: Rises in beer consumption, Hancock & Gowing pp. 493, 485

171: *Fish was* . . . *unrationed* . . . FitzGibbon pp. 67–8

172: *little Willie would* . . . Impresario p. 33

172: Availability of sweets, Longmate (1971) p. 181

173: *fresh butter had* . . . Letter from Ethel Mattison to Elizabeth Elkus 17 Oct 1939 IWM Dept of Documents Con. Shelf

173: *the 4 ounces* . . . Letter from Helena Britton to Elizabeth Elkus 30 Jan 1940 IWM Dept of Documents Con. Shelf

173: *poorer section of* . . . Cambridge Regional Information Office report quoted in Zweiniger-Bargielowska p. 71

174: Employment figures, *Ministry of Labour Gazette* quoted in Andrew Thorpe 'Britain' in Noakes p. 27

174: Wage rises, *Fighting with Figures* p. 236

174: Subsidies, Felton p. 26

174: *the Food office* . . . Letters from Ethel Mattison to Elizabeth Elkus 12 Jun, 18 Jul 1940 IWM Dept of Documents Con. Shelf

175: Kosher food, Kushner pp. 135–6

175: *the pinched* . . . Cotton 30 Apr 1945 IWM Dept of Documents 93/3/1 p. 329

176: *All the extras* . . . TNA/PRO MAF 75/68 quoted in Zweiniger-Bargielowska p. 130

176: *in spite of* . . . Kushner p. 137

177: *London lives well* . . . Channon p. 272

177: Complaints about rationing, Gallup poll 1 Feb 1941

178: Price of a meal at a British Restaurant, Felton pp. 23–4

178: Description of a meal at a British Restaurant, Longmate (1971) p. 151

178: Location of British Restaurants in London, Mack & Humphries p. 86

178: Figures for spread of British Restaurants, Felton p. 24

178: *one potato* . . . Regan IWM Dept of Documents Con. Shelf

178: *one needs to* . . . Sir William Darling quoted in Ziegler (1995) p. 251

178: Percentages of people who ate in a British Restaurant, 'Wartime Social Surveys, Food: I: Food Schemes: A Collection of Short Reports on Inquiries Made by the Regional Organisation of the Wartime Social Survey May 1942– Jan 1943' quoted in Zweiniger-Bargielowska pp. 74, 114

179: Advice for using all of the animal, *Farmer and Stockbreeder* quoted in Ward p. 63

179: *We grew up* . . . Ward p. 69

179: *Home to a* . . . Partridge p. 93

180: *what were once* . . . Henry pp. 15–16

181: Swapping rations, Zweiniger-Bargielowska pp. 175–6

181: *The public would* . . . Lord Woolton quoted in Ward pp. 174–5

181: *Many vital decisions* . . . MoI British Women at War 1944 TNA/PRO

182: *Yours is a* . . . *Good Housekeeping* Aug 1941

182: Figures for female employment, Ministry of Labour and National Service report for the years 1939–1946 pp. 2–3

182: *home life will* . . . Quoted in C. Harris (2000) p. 7

183: *No errand boys* . . . Cox 19 Sep, 8 Oct, 27 Nov 1941 IWM Dept of Documents 84/46/1 (P)

183: Queuing times, Zweiniger-Bargielowska p. 118

185: 'Food Facts Quiz' *Food Facts* 31 Dec 1943

185: *working-class housewives* . . . Home Intelligence Special Report No.44: Housewives Attitudes towards Official Campaigns and Instructions quoted in Zweiniger-Bargielowska pp. 111–12

186: Recipe suggestions, Patten pp. 16, 52, 61, 74, 75, 85 and Corbishley pp. 19, 23

187: Figures for listeners to *Gert and Daisy*, Nicholas p. 82

188: Percentages of mothers giving supplements, Hammond p. 371

188: *a really nice* . . . Goddard 24 Mar 1940 IWM Dept of Documents Con. Shelf

188: *had never seen* . . . Miles 23 Mar 1940 IWM Dept of Documents 99/74/1

188: *Much screaming and* . . . Hall 4 Apr 1940 IWM Dept of Documents DS/Misc/88

190: *When no allies* . . . Dorothy L. Sayers 'The English War' in *Times Literary Supplement* 7 Sep 1940

190: James Isbister, *Orkney Herald* 20 Mar 1940

191: *Poor James perished* . . . Miles 18 March 1940 IWM Dept of Documents 99/74/1

191: *Hold on tight* . . . Neville Chamberlain quoted in Blake & Louis p. 243

191: *a speech of* . . . Churchill (1959) p. 203

192: *she phoned me* . . . Beardmore p. 49

192: *aircraft, anti-aircraft* . . . Churchill (1959) p. 211

192: *tocsin sounded* . . . Churchill (1959) p. 213

192: *made a very* . . . Nicolson (1967) p. 76

192: *Members in front* . . . 'Sagittarius' (Olga Katyin) in *New Statesman and Nation* 11 May 1940 p. 612

193: *full of young* . . . Dalton (1957) p. 306

193: *I thought Winston* . . . Cadogan p. 281

193: *Winston licked his* . . . Colville p. 121

193: *Just as it* . . . Wyndham (1985) pp. 65–6

194: *It's like trying* . . . Brendan Bracken quoted in Lysaght p. 173

194: *H[alifax] was not* . . . George VI quoted in Wheeler-Bennett pp. 443–4

194: *prompted by the* . . . Wheeler-Bennett (1958) p. 446

194: *by the staff* . . . Wheeler-Bennett (1958) pp. 48–9

194: *don't trust Winston* . . . Lord Davidson quoted in Cadogan p. 272

194: Newspaper headlines, Channon p. 250

195: *So at last* . . . C. King p. 39

195: *I have always* . . . Beardmore p. 52

195: *had to spend* . . . Last p. 55

195: *Isn't he a* . . . Phipps 11 May 1940 IWM Dept of Documents P178

195: *to pass a* . . . Churchill (1959) p. 228

195: *as patriotic gadflies* . . . Dalton p. 297

196: *with a profound* . . . Churchill (1959) p. 220

196: *His interests were* . . . Colville p. 127

196: *Winston has slipped* . . . Miles 11 May 1940 IWM Dept of Documents 99/74/1

196: *who seem to* . . . Priestley (1940) p. 5

196: *strong German forces* . . . General Ironside quoted in Gilbert (1983) pp. 333–4

196: *I have nothing...* Winston Churchill quoted in Gilbert (1983) p. 333

197: *Everyone is asking...* Beardmore p. 52

197: Bombing of Rotterdam, Gilbert (1983) p. 339

197: *We are beaten...* Paul Reynaud quoted in Gilbert (1983) p. 349

198: *I don't know...* Nicolson (1967) p. 88

198: *Mortimer has promised...* Channon p. 254

198: *more a symbol...* Harman p. 69

198: *I saw my...* Sir Hugh Dowding quoted in Overy (2000) p. 9

199: *nothing but a...* Alanbrooke p. 67

199: *All day and...* BBC News 31 May 1940 quoted in Harman p. 237

200: *were halted by...* Cotton 26 May 1940 IWM Dept of Documents 93/3/1

200: *All our boats...* Walmsley pp. 209–16

201: Details of the Little Ships, Atkin p. 198

202: *to be depended...* George Mallory (master of the ferry *Malines*) quoted in Atkin p. 203

202: *to lie helpless...* Hadley

203: *they were probably...* Harman p. 184

203: Lieutenant C.W. Read, Atkin p. 202

203: Figures for the BEF, Gilbert (1983) p. 465

203: *saw my first...* V. Woolf p. 289

203: *the longest day...* Milburn pp. 40, 41, 43, 48

204: *There is no...* Lady Reading quoted in Graves (1948) p. 57

204: *as the troops...* Quoted in Graves (1948) pp. 65–6

204: *a never-ending stream...* Graves (1948) p. 66

205: *The amazing welcome...* Hadley p. 143

205: *Typical of the...* Tom Harrisson M-OA F/R 182

205: *across some fields...* Darwin pp. 28–9

205: Reception at Penge, Darwin p. 30

205: Decorations on houses, Tom Harrisson M-OA F/R 182

206: *passed through London...* Hadley pp. 143–4

206: *The men were...* Phillips IWM Dept of Documents 80/6/1 pp. 1–10

206: *were told to...* Phipps Aug 1940 IWM Dept of Documents P178

207: Condition of returning forces, Shephard pp. 169–71

209: *Auntie Olive...* Roose IWM Dept of Documents 89/14/1 pp. 8–9

210: *total and abject...* Sargant pp. 86–7

210: *a case of...* Phipps 13 Jun 1940 IWM Dept of Documents P178

210: Fazakerly Hospital, Shephard pp. 171–2

211: *as much part...* Harman p. 164

211: *72,000 soldiers left...* Harman p. 184

211: *no retreat can...* Partridge p. 44

211: *typically English...* Priestley pp. 1–4

212: *A miracle is...* 5 Jun 1940 'Cato' pp. 11–12

212: *the accounts of...* Last p. 63

212: *they could no...* Dean p. 123

213: *Harry came back...* V. Woolf pp. 297–8

213: *the Dunkirk episode...* C. King p. 85

214: *We must be...* Winston Churchill 4 Jun 1940 quoted in Gilbert (1983) pp. 463–8

214: *a motorised column...* C. King pp. 53–4

214: *quite extraordinary capacity...* Lord Woolton quoted in MacKenzie (1995) p. 47

214: *We shall not...* Winston Churchill 4 Jun 1940 quoted in Gilbert (1983) pp. 463–8

216: *Last night a...* Day-Lewis p. 28

216: *having groped our...* Cooper pp. 39, 40

217: *When the news* . . . Churchill (1953) pp. 564–5

217: *whatever happened in* . . . Winston Churchill quoted in Cannadine p. 168

217: *I expect that* . . . Winston Churchill quoted in Cannadine pp. 177–8

218: *reassuring about defence* . . . V. Woolf p. 297

218: *it was only* . . . Churchill quoted in Gilbert (1983) p. 571

218: *another magnificent achievement* . . . Bishop of Durham 19 Jun 1940 quoted in Henson p. 116

218: aircraft losses, Gilbert (1983) p. 609

219: *in most people's* . . . 24 May 1940 Panter-Downes (1972) p. 60

219: *For the first* . . . Cowles pp. 216–17

219: *personally I feel* . . . King George VI quoted in Wheeler-Bennett (1958) p. 460

219: *Well! Now it* . . . Air Marshal Dowding quoted in Gilbert (1983) p. 564

219: *without reason the* . . . Cooper p. 41

219: *white as a* . . . Wyndham (1985) pp. 81–2

220: *only one or* . . . Hall 22 Jun 1940 IWM Dept of Documents DS/MISC/88

220: *possibility of our* . . . M-OA F/R 4/6/40

220: *people...walked among* . . . Rebecca West quoted in Ziegler (1995) p. 82

220: *the country is* . . . C. King p. 54

220: polling results, Ziegler (1985) p. 84

220: *It would be* . . . 22 Jun 1940 Panter-Downes (1972) pp. 70–1

221: *They bombed the* . . . 4 Jul 1940 V. Woolf pp. 299–300

221: *The older men* . . . Banger p. 18

221: Daylight raids, Collier (1957) pp. 163–4

221: *disguised as nuns* . . . Quoted in Glover p. 29

221: Stories in the press, Glover p. 30

222: *enemy parachutists* . . . *The Times* 11 May 1940

222: *We talked endlessly* . . . Cooper p. 41

222: *and announced that* . . . Phipps 22 May 1940 IWM Dept of Documents P178

222: *everyone makes jokes* . . . Partridge p. 39

223: *defend our island* . . . Winston Churchill 4 Jun 1940 quoted in Gilbert (1983) p. 468

223: *with a couple* . . . Lady Helena Gleichen quoted in Graves (1943) p. 15

223: *running an anti-invasion* . . . Phipps 16 Jun 1940 IWM Dept of Documents P178

223: *about 100 strong* . . . Bishop of Romford quoted in Glover p. 27

223: *oiling up their* . . . Quoted in Mackenzie (1995) p. 27

223: *We should use* . . . Josiah Wedgwood quoted in Glover p. 11

223: *gave the impression* . . . Nicolson (1967) p. 76

224: *the bulk of* . . . Collier (1957) pp. 123–4

224: *should the Germans* . . . the chiefs of staff quoted in Collier (1957) p. 125

224: *countless ordinary citizens,* Glover p. 27, Mackenzie (1995) pp. 33–4

225: *starting a war* . . . Miles 15 May 1940 IWM Dept of Documents 99/74/1

225: *was at our* . . . E. Raymond p. 70

226: *carpenters, masons, farm* . . . M. Graham p. 80

226: *to have poaching* . . . Graves (1943) p. 39

226: *all that happened* . . . E. Raymond p. 71

226: Committee of American Aid weapons, Mackenzie (1995) p. 66

226: *The whole thing* . . . Alanbrooke p. 98

227: LDV previous service experience, Mackenzie (1995) p. 37

227: Eightieth birthday, Longmate (1971) p. 20

227: *at the usual* . . . Miles 18 May 1940 IWM Dept of Documents 99/74/1

227: Knox reprimanding Eden, Mackenzie (1995) p. 39

227: Wintringham as Left's theorist, David Fernbach 'Tom Wintringham and the Socialist Defence Strategy' pp. 63–91

228: *Superficially alike in* . . . *Picture Post* 21 Sep 1940

229: *a Buffalo Bill* . . . Mackenzie (1995) p. 73

229: *a crumpled uniform* . . . Warburg p. 36

229: *as much as* . . . Warburg p. 37

229: Number of attendees, *Picture Post* 21 Sep 1940

230: *In the absence* . . . E. Raymond p. 71

230: *petrol or paraffin* . . . Graves (1943) p. 53

230: *two thirds petrol* . . . Lieutentant-Colonel Treve Holman 'Looking Back' in Choughs Annual Register No. 2

231: *the Local Defence* . . . Josiah Wedgwood quoted in Mackenzie (1995) pp. 43–4

231: *It was young* . . . Eddie Mathieson quoted in MacDougall p. 218

231: *He was very* . . . I. Thomas pp. 30–1

231: *the long summer* . . . Raymond pp. 71–2

232: *sticky mixture* . . . Knight p. 168

232: *men of valour* . . . E. Raymond p. 70

233: *Static defence in* . . . Quoted in Ironside p. 343

233: *Orders and suggestions* . . . Cooper pp. 41–2

234: *the one normally* . . . *Field* 29 Jun 1940

234: Queen being instructed, Nicolson (1967) p. 100

235: *it is absurd* . . . Nicolson (1967) pp. 95–6

235: *We are continually* . . . MoI Directive Letter to Clergy and Others 5 Jul 1940 quoted in McLaine p. 72

235: *the Bosches [sic] have* . . . General Sir Edmund Ironside quoted in Glover p. 49

236: *suggestions as to* . . . War Directive No. 16 quoted in Glover p. 112

238: Melting down railings, Glover p. 105

238: Melting down cannons, Gill

238: *remember it's guts* . . . M-OA F/R 298

238: Members of the public, McLaine p. 83

239: *alarm and despondency* . . . MoI quoted in McLaine p. 81

239: *There is no* . . . Harold Nicolson quoted in McLaine pp. 83–5

239: Leaky cistern, Morgan p. 27

239: *Wall chalkings and* . . . M-OA TC 44 Folder 1/A

240: *hardly realised what* . . . M-OA F/R 167 quoted in Lafitte p. 116

240: *we do not* . . . General Sir Edmund Ironside quoted in Mackenzie (1995) p. 57

241: Overzealous Home Guard, Scott (1959) p. 134

242: *as with a* . . . M. Graham p. 81

242: *Crossbow men of* . . . *Daily Mail* 6 Feb 1942

244: *Tom fall in* . . . Tom Basford quoted in J. R. Lewis p. 34–6

244: *are those least* . . . Lt-General (ret'd) Sir Douglas Brownrigg quoted in Mackenzie p. 79

245: Oxford ranks, *Oxford Mail* 27 Nov 1944 quoted in M. Graham p. 79

245: *even women, must* . . . Churchill, 12 July 1940, quoted in Colville p. 193

245: *women cannot be* . . . War Office quoted in Mackenzie (1995) p. 83

246: *a few million* . . . Murrow p. 108

246: *Why should women* . . . Quoted in Summerfield & Peniston-Bird in *Women's History Review* p. 236

246: *fifty indignant female* . . . Lampe p. 7

246: *a woman's duty* . . . Quoted in Lampe p. 238

247: *The Germans are* . . . Nicolson (1967) p. 99

247: *It so happens* . . . Quoted in Agar p. 79

248: *not suggesting that* . . . *Tribune* 20 Dec 1940

249: *Orwell helped the* . . . Crick p. 399

249: *nostalgic veterans clustered* . . . David Fernbach 'Tom Wintringham and the Socialist Defence Strategy' p. 74

250: *What is the* . . . 'Birthday Behind Barbed Wire' in Laurent

250: *to keep contact* . . . Bing 25 Jun 1940 IWM Dept of Documents

251: Government attitude to Jewish immigration, London p. 169

251: Figures for refugees in Britain, Stent p. 21

252: Focus for the Defence of Freedom and Peace movement, Spier

252: Prominent Germans who were arrested, Gillman & Gillman p. 33

253: Figures and grades for tribunals, Stent p. 37

254: Regional variations of tribunals, Gillman & Gillman p. 44

254: Evolving rules of tribunals, Thurlow p. 160

255: The Kuczynski family, *New Statesman and Nation* 9 Mar 1940

255: *spoke very little* . . . *Spectator* 17 Nov 1939

256: *I think it* . . . Sir John Anderson quoted in Stammers p. 37

256: *I cannot bring* . . . Norman Birkett quoted in Hyde p. 470

256: Attitude of the *Daily Mail*, Stent p. 470

257: Citizens' Advice Bureaux report, Stent p. 51

257: *there should be* . . . Winston Churchill quoted in *News Chronicle* 29 Jul 1940

257: Home Office Directives of 27 May 1940, Stammers p. 39

257: WVS assistance with arrests, Gillman & Gillman p. 33

259: *the most ruthless* . . . War Cabinet recommendation quoted in Stent p. 70

259: *the most dangerous* . . . War Cabinet recommendation quoted in Gillman & Gillman p. 164

259: *Like everyone else* . . . Joseph Pia quoted in MacDougall p. 308

259: *to see whether* . . . Orwell (1968) p. 347

259: Violent attacks against Italians in England and Wales, Sponza pp. 76–7

259: Violent attacks against Italians in Scotland, *The Scotsman* 11 Jun 1940 quoted in Sponza p. 78

259: *Restaurants, ice-cream shops* . . . *Edinburgh Evening Dispatch* 11 Jun 1940

260: Mobs in Glasgow, Colpi in Cesarani & Kushner pp. 172–3

260: *three Italian shops* . . . 11 Jun 1940 Mitchison p. 65

260: Opportunity to vent xenophobia, Sponza p. 86

260: *these fellows who* . . . Joseph Pia quoted in MacDougall p. 308

261: *I said* . . . Joseph Pia quoted in MacDougall p. 309

261: *the majority* . . . Orwell Vol. 1 (1968) p. 347

261: *Virgie Cresci* . . . *South Wales Evening Post* 11 Jun 1940 quoted in Sponza p. 81

262: *as, say, a* . . . Professor Bruno Foa quoted in Sponza p. 115

262: *90 per cent* . . . Joseph Pia quoted in MacDougall p. 309

262: Variation in belief of Italians in Britain, Sponza p. 141

263: Warth Mills, Lafitte pp. 101–2

263: Hierarchy in Isle of Man camps, Colpi in Cesarani & Kushner pp. 182–3

263: Variety of detainees sent to Canada, Stent p. 97

264: *to pack for* . . . *Islington Gazette* 7 Jun 1940

264: *Of course the* . . . Dominic Crolla

quoted in MacDougall pp. 291–2

265: *a transport with* . . . Bing IWM Dept of Documents

265: The *Dunera*, Quoted in Stent p. 122

268: *Prisoners of War* . . . Dominic Crolla quoted in MacDougall p. 291

268: *It was very* . . . Hallgarten IWM Sound Archive 004494

268: *because in the* . . . Hallgarten IWM Sound Archive 004494

270: *mini civil service* . . . Gilman p. 162

270: Artists scratching designs, Klaus E. Hinrichsen 'Visual Art Behind the Wire' in Cesarani & Kushner p. 191

271: *unforgettable depressing picture* . . . Stent p. 184

271: *Women's activities in camps,* Cere in Kirkham & Thoms pp. 225–6

272: *not met a* . . . Letter to Francis C. Scott 23 Jul 1940 Keynes pp. 190–1

272: *there are German* . . . *Evening Standard* Jun 1940

273: *wasn't anxious about* . . . Hallgarten IWM Sound Archive 004494

273: Bishop Bell's visit, Stent p. 241

274: *There is nothing* . . . Bing 8 Oct 1940 IWM Dept of Documents

275: *I still cannot* . . . Bing 26 Sep 1940 IWM Dept of Documents

275: *wanted to put* . . . Hallgarten IWM Sound Archive 004494

276: *an ARP warden* . . . Hallgarten IWM Sound Archive 004494

277: *Love your enemies* . . . 'Notes for an Unwritten Autobiography' *Modern Reading* No. 13, 1945

278: *He was completely* . . . D. Mosley p. 95

278: *a long line* . . . D. Mosley p. 158

278: *none of the* . . . D. Mosley p. 98

278: Hitler wedding guest, Dalley pp. 213–14

279: *a well organised* . . . *Daily Mail* 14 Jan 1934

279: Thugs' party, Thurlow p. 71

280: *big Jews* . . . Thurlow p. 75

280: BU member numbers, Robert Skidelsky quoted in S. J. Woolf p. 275

281: *Why don't the* . . . Lady Redesdale to Lord Cranborne 13 Oct 1940 quoted in Gottlieb p. 239

281: *As a matter* . . . Note on the Question: Why Prisoners Detained Under Defence Reg 18B have not been brought to trial TNA/PRO HO45 24893/23

281: Numbers of citizens detained, Simpson p. 78

282: BU security risk, Simpson p. 168

282: *have or have* . . . Skidelsky p. 448

283: *he found a* . . . Skidelsky p. 405

283: *perceived behind the* . . . Maule Ramsay quoted in Griffiths p. 354

283: Leese internment, Cross p. 196

284: *a little larger* . . . Domvile (1947) p. 99

285: *you can drive* . . . Domvile (1936) pp. 235, 236–7

285: *Judmas (my copyright* . . . Domvile (1947) p. 98

285: *clubs should not* . . . Luttman-Johnson IWM Dept of Documents 72/32/1

285: *had asked Watts* . . . Gottlieb p. 230

286: *you don't see* . . . Gottlieb p. 236

286: Tea dance, Gottlieb p. 245

286: *what shred of* . . . Oswald Mosley quoted in Simpson p. 275

287: *when Hitler appeared* . . . D. Mosley (1977) p. 108

287: *saw* . . . *this extraordinary* . . . D. Mosley (1977) pp. 123, 156

288: *extremely dangerous and* . . . Guinness pp. 492–4

288: *thankful Sir Oswald* . . . Mitford pp. 97–8

288: *silly questions* . . . Mitford p. 253

288: *Sir Oswald Mosley's* . . . Simpson p. 249

289: *unembittered* . . . Robert Swann quoted in D. Mosley (1985) p. 183

290: Communist Party membership, Branson p. 271

290: Sales of *Daily Worker,* M-OA F/R 552

290: Sales of *Action,* Simpson p. 130

290: Sales of *Peace News,* Hinsley & Simkins p. 20

291: *one of those . . .* Beckett p. 92

291: *Thereby it forged . . .* Quoted in Branson p. 369

291: *It was a . . .* Author interview with Ethel Mattison March 2003

292: Home Office would have argued, Branson (1985) p. 296

292: *insulting words and . . . Labour Research* Sept 1940 quoted in Branson (1985) p. 297

293: List of customers, TNA/PRO HO45 25581

293: *The emptying of . . .* Quoted in Branson p. 298

293: *A most admirable . . .* Quoted in Hinsley & Simkins p. 58

294: *the Communist Party . . .* Quoted in Hinton in *History Workshop Journal* p. 93

294: *a handful . . .* Branson (1985) p. 299

295: Mason's internment, Hinsley & Simkins p. 320; Branson (1985) p. 299.

295: *duty . . . Tribune* 8 Sep 1940 quoted in Calder (1991) p. 79

295: Editor removed, Calder (1991) p. 79

296: Political truce, Labour Party Annual Report 1940 quoted in Branson p. 276

296: Complaining about Army pay, Branson p. 276

297: Chairman of committee, Pritt (1965) Part 1, p. 252

298: Proletarian overthrow, Pritt (1941) p. 252

298: *2,234 delegates directly . . .* Pritt (1941) p. 260

298: *Left-wing psychopaths . . .* Home Office report quoted in McLaine p. 8

298: *democratic imperialism . . . People's Convention: Official Report,* 1941 pp. 40, 50–1, 58–9

299: *overwhelming feeling . . .* Quoted in Calder & Sheridan pp. 199–202

299: *honest-to-God British . . . Daily Mirror* 13 Jan 1941 quoted in Branson p. 310

299: *that a 'people's . . .* MacEwen pp. 73–4

299: *in a style . . .* Herbert Morrison quoted in Branson pp. 310–11

301: *No one has . . . The Times* 23 Jun 1941

301: *I've been teaching . . .* Quoted in MacEwen p. 82

302: *It must be . . .* Sheean p. 165

303: *see no reason . . .* Adolf Hitler quoted in Shirer p. 754

303: *Hitler may plant . . .* Lord Halifax quoted in Roberts p. 249

303: *overpower the English . . .* Quoted in Overy (2000) p. 31

304. Operational aircraft, Overy (2000) p. 34

304: Aircraft replacements, Overy (2000) p. 37

304: *the muddle and . . .* Churchill (1949) p. 561

304: *the solemn duty . . .* Lee p. 129

304: *I asked very . . .* Quoted in A. J. P. Taylor p. 549

305: *after Dunkirk they . . .* Nancy Deacon quoted in Bruley p. 41

305: *wanted the factories . . .* Quoted in A. J. P. Taylor p. 551

305: *This was just . . .* Lee pp. 130–1

307: *the flash of . . .* Sheean p. 157

307: *The Minister of . . .* Lady Reading quoted in Graves (1948) p. 58

307: Tons of aluminium collected by WVS, Graves (1948) pp. 58–9

308: Money to pay for planes, Addison & Crang p. 256; Beckles p. 58

308: *as you put . . .* Beckles p. 248

309: Donations in Hackney, Golden p. 96

309: *the designer of . . .* Knowles pp. 144–6

309: Choices of names, www.spitfiresociety.demon.co.uk/present

311: *for the purchase . . .* Quoted in Fisk pp. 152–3

311: *the fund was . . .* A. J. P. Taylor p. 550

311: Beaverbrook's quarry schemes, McCamley (1998) pp. 146–81

311: Castle Bromwich as shadow factory, Sebastian Cox 'The RAF's Response' in Addison & Crang pp. 61–2

312: Component manufacture, Wood & Dempster p. 209

312: *filing parties* . . . Wood & Dempster p. 101

312: *We knew it* . . . Sheean p. 153

312: *The fate of* . . . Cowles pp. 424–6

313: *The war will* . . . Wood & Dempster p. 174

314: Communications hub, Wood & Dempster p. 175

315: Pip Squeak device, Wood & Dempster p. 198

315: *long, harrowing weeks* . . . Wyndham (1986) p. 1

316: *Would you like* . . . Quoted in Hough & Richards p. 329

316: *I would often* . . . Aileen Morris quoted in Clayton & Craig p. 39

316: *a flurry of* . . . Overy (2000) p. 41

317: *suddenly heard terrific* . . . Partridge p. 54

318: Grave for shelter, M. Parker pp. 248–52

318: *If any aerodrome* . . . Quoted in Wellum p. 130

319: *appalled at the* . . . Quoted in Kaplan & Collier p. 83

319: Fate of Manston, Kaplan & Collier p. 83

320: Pilot training cut, Kaplan & Collier p. 154

320: *You are not* . . . Wellum p. 95

321 *war as it* . . . Hillary p. 17

321: Sand in coffin, Faulkes pp. 195–6

321: *a speck of* . . . Robinson

322: Pilots killed, missing or imprisoned, Kaplan & Collier p. 222

322: Strain on pilots, Kaplan & Collier p. 463

323: Aircraft over southern England, Kaplan & Collier p. 173

323: *the Battle of* . . . Howard p. 88

323: *a Heinkel III* . . . Gale p. 66

324: *We're Cinque Port* . . . Quoted in Robertson p. 49

324: *a narrow dark* . . . Sevareid p. 167

324: *a superb place* . . . Robertson p. 82

325: *a sort of* . . . Quoted in Robertson p. 87

325: *The daily spectacle* . . . Sheean p. 161

325: *like a tortured* . . . Clayton & Craig p. 41

325: *It was at* . . . Sheean p. 157

326: *If we can* . . . Winston Churchill 18 Jun 1940 quoted in Gilbert (1983) p. 570–1

326: Churchill's arguments to bring in the US, Cull pp. 72–3

326: *Propaganda is all* . . . Winston Churchill quoted in Colville p. 175

326: *British planes getting* . . . Quoted in Cull p. 88

327: Nationality of pilots killed in Battle of Britain, Deighton p. 298

327: *homeless men. Motivated* . . . Deighton p. 298

329: *I think we* . . . Nicolson (1967) p. 126

330 *Autumn seems a* . . . Bowen (1950)

331: *every detail on* . . . Stahl p. 76

331: Bill for war damage to the docks, Pudney p. 152

332: Thames threatened to silt up, Byrant p. 57

332: *When they declare* . . . Shirer pp. 778–80

332: *Most people believe* . . . Murrow

333: Raiders aimed straight for London, Knight p. 128

333: Planes all making for the East End, *Front Line* pp. 10–11

333: *the East End* . . . Nixon pp. 12–13

334: *ordered out, our* . . . George Woodhouse quoted in Waller & Vaughan-Rees (1991) pp. 18–19

335: Army of rats in factory in Silvertown, Ramsey Vol. II p. 57

335: Tower Bridge ablaze, Wallington p. 79

335: *with the object* . . . Ray p. 18

336: *a raging inferno* . . . *Front Line* p. 26

336: Woolwich Arsenal fireman fought the flames, *Front Line* p. 25

337: Calls for additional fire engines, Firebrace p. 16

338: Churchill meeting East Enders, Ismay pp. 183–4

338: *between 2.0 & 3.0 . . .* Brittain (1989) p. 53

339: Local population alerted by Home Guard, Mackenzie (1995) p. 63

340: Single-seater fighters ineffective for night flying, Collier (1957) pp. 238–9

340: Defence resting on 264 anti-aircraft guns, Collier (1957) p. 238

340: *We had depended on . . .* Regan IWM Dept of Documents Con Shelf

341: *it bucked people . . .* Pile pp. 130–4

342: *could comfortably accommodate . . .* Plaistow pp. 23–5

343: Incendiaries heavier, Ray pp. 84–5; Plaistow p. 28

343: *It was as . . .* Allan 20 Sep 1940 IWM Dept of Documents 95/8/7 and Con. 344 Shelf

344: *Every night, one's . . .* Hodgson p. 44

344: *There is much . . .* Nicolson (1967) pp. 114–15

345: Desert tummy, Brendon & Whitehead p. 114

345: 350 tons of bombs dropped on Britain, O'Brien p. 390

345: *like a charred . . .* Quoted in Ramsey Vol. II p. 109

345: *Bombs were dropped . . .* Nixon p. 103

346: *The dining room . . .* Cox 2 Oct 1940 IWM Dept of Documents 86/46/1 (P)

347: *For days on . . .* Nixon p. 45

348: *People were lying . . .* Mack & Humphries pp. 71–2

348: *One of the . . .* Markham 28 Oct 1940 IWM Dept of Documents 91/5/1

349: *It's an awfully . . .* Letters of George and Helena Britton 11 Oct–19 Nov 1940 IWM Department of Documents Con. Shelf

350: *We are speechless . . .* Hodgson p. 67

350: Luftwaffe attack, *Aeroplane* 21 Feb 1941 quoted in Ray p. 263

350: Mid November attack, T. Lewis p. 54

351: *My father turned . . .* Mrs A. Zebrzuski quoted in Waller & (1990) Vaughan-Rees pp. 102–3

351: *it was impossible . . .* BBC quoted in T. Lewis p. 129

352: Figures for dead and injured, Longmate (1976) p. 190

352: *The centre of . . .* T. Lewis p. 158

353: *We had as . . .* Longmate (1976) p. 223

353: *back over the . . .* Rev. Leslie E. Cooke quoted in Burrow

354: Factory damage . . . Ray p. 61

356: *The trauma of . . .* Joe Lucas quoted in Maritime Museum, Liverpool: Spirit of the Blitz Exhibition Jul 2003–Aug 2004

356: *Almost everyone in . . .* Marion Browne quoted in Maritime Museum, Liverpool: Spirit of the Blitz Exhibition Jul 2003–Aug 2004

356: Bristol Fire Brigade, Belsey & Reid p. 46

357: Bristol damage, Reid p. 10

357: Bombing 12 December, Abrahams p. 15

357: *got a direct . . .* Quoted in Waller & Vaughan-Rees (1990) p. 128

358: Civilian deaths and injuries, Abrahams p. 21

358: *we realised how . . .* Geoffrey Hill quoted in Waller & Vaughan-Rees (1990) pp. 166–7

358: Diners joined in with hotel orchestra, Whittington-Egan p. 40

359: *stood like the . . .* Front Line p. 84

359: *There was no . . .* Front Line p. 84

359: *It was possible . . .* Front Line p. 84

360: *madrigal in stone . . .* Quoted in Trench p. 51

362: *was easily put* . . . Matthews p. 46

362: *without a bucket* . . . Trench p. 122

362: *This must never* . . . Donoghue & Jones p. 293

363: Fire-watching percentages, Hayes pp. 297–8

363: Conscientious Objectors as fire-watchers, Hayes p. 302

364: *looked at Wren's* . . . Schweeitzer p. 20

364: *a group of* . . . Schweeitzer p. 20

365: *We were looking* . . . Schweeitzer pp. 20–1

365: *went to St* . . . Beaton p. 59

365: *all we could* . . . Harrisson

366: *the least effect* . . . Trevor-Roper pp. 102–4

367: *The bodies had* . . . John Strachan 'Digging for Mrs Miller' in *New Statesman and ion* 9 Nov 1940

367: *Am sitting in* . . . Allan 20 Oct 1940 IWM Dept of Documents 95/8/7 and Con. Shelf p. 205

368: *When Dad was* . . . Stewart IWM Sound Archives 005334

369: *There'll be more* . . . M-OA F/R 436 p. 8

369: Anderson shelter survey, M-OA F/R 431 p. 50

370: Domestic shelter use, Titmuss p. 343

370: *the Banshee Howl* . . . Cotton 9 Aug 1939 IWM Dept of Documents 93/3/1

371: *The public showed* . . . Government report 23 Jan 1941 quoted in O'Brien p. 507

371: *THIS IS NOT* . . . Wilson pp. 14–15

372: *They are no* . . . M-OA F/R A14 p. 8

372: *definitely unsafe* . . . R. Calder *Carry on London* p. 39

372: *Over everything is* . . . M-OA F/R 431 pp. 46–7

373: *everyone there was* . . . M-OA F/R 431 pp. 47–8

373: *People should not* . . . Masel Oct 1940 M-OA Diarist 5370

373: *the resulting stampede* . . . M-OA F/R 431 p. 50

373: *men, women and children* . . . John H. Smith quoted in Waller & Vaughan-Rees (1990) p. 257

374: *I had to* . . . Markham IWM Dept of Documents 91/5/1

375: *as there was* . . . Helen Sandys quoted in Waller & Vaughan-Rees (1990) p. 259

375: Anderson shelter cost, Woolven (unpublished) p. 213

375: Proposal turned down, Woolven (unpublished) pp. 123–4

376: *orderly and obedient* . . . Gregg p. 5

376: *the shelter policy* . . . *Daily Worker* 7 Sep 1940

376: *quite secure* . . . Ziegler (1991) p. 202

376: *It's certainly more* . . . Cooper p. 60

377: *It's a great victory* . . . Kops pp. 67–8

377: *insofar as it* . . . Gregg pp. 22–3

378: *I am just* . . . M-OA F/R 425 p. 1

378: *From the platforms* . . . *South London Press* 1 Oct 1940 quoted in Gregg p. 24

378: *We were underground* . . . Kops pp. 68–9

379: Adaptation of tube stations, Gregg p. 28

379: Activities in shelters, Gregg p. 28

380: Glenn Miller concert, Gregg p. 63

380: *too much publicity* . . . Woolven (unpublished) p. 176

380: *undesirable to give* . . . 19 Dec 1940 quoted in Woolven (unpublished) p. 176

380: *had a frightful* . . . Goddard 21 Oct 1940 IWM Dept of Documents Con. Self

381: *underneath a glass* . . . M-OA F/R 436

381: Gestetnered newsletters, Quoted in Gregg p. 67

382: *could not burn* . . . Quoted in Longmate (1971) p. 216

382: Evacuation of pets, Longmate (1971) p. 216

384: ARP wardens' frozen jobs, O'Brien p. 375

385: Post warden had been an electrician, Nixon pp. 82–3

385: *had been to...* Nixon p. 85

385: *multitudinous things . . .* Nixon p. 10

385: *to the shelters . . .* Faviell p. 115

388: Ambulances in the war, M. Brown (1999) p. 58

388: *been picked for . . .* Keith Barber quoted in M. Brown (1999) p. 64

388: Bread vans as ambulances, Tim Clarke quoted in M. Brown (1999) p. 65

389: *the stench was . . .* Faviell p. 115

390: *I looked at . . .* Reagan IWM Dept of Documents 88/10/1 pp. 29–30

391: *when the storm . . .* Titmuss p. 255

392: *Dim figures in . . .* Titmuss p. 261

392: *battered away at . . .* M-OA F/R 431 p. 79

392: *machinery of government . . .* M-OA F/R 431 p. iv

393: Notices not in Yiddish, M-OA F/R 431 pp. 41–2

394: Ministry of Information leaflets, 9 Jan 1941 quoted in McLaine

397: *East London comes . . .* Allan IWM Dept of Documents 95/8/7 and Con. Shelf

398: *few windows left . . .* Last pp. 138–9

399: Debris used for building of airfields, Woolven (unpublished) p. 276

399: Figures for children evacuated, Titmuss p. 285

400: Nearest to making evacuation of children compulsory, Titmus p. 358

400: 'Hostels for problem children' on notepaper, Titmuss p. 380

401: Improvement in welfare for children, Titmuss p. 380–7

401: The Oxford Health Settlement in Bethnal Green, Titmuss pp. 377–8

402: *new territories unhampered . . .* Brittain (1941) p. 55

402: *America must say . . .* Quoted in Parsons p. 159

402: *A queue of . . .* Brittain (1941) p. 56

404: *one or more . . .* Parsons p. 163

404: *Boys from a . . .* Hylton p. 47

404: *not to get . . .* Cooper p. 44

404: *sitting on your . . .* Ziegler (1991) p. 200

405: *I am very . . .* Marjorie Maxse quoted in Fethney p. 133

405: *the little ones . . .* Marjorie Day quoted in Fethney p. 138

406: *People will say . . .* Shakespeare p. 257

407: Exceptions made to damage, McLaine pp. 64–5

408: War Cabinet restricts casualty information, McLaine pp. 65

409: *The street was . . .* M-OA F/R 844

410: *the most important . . .* Directive No. 23 'Directions for operations against the English war economy' 6 Feb 1941 quoted in Trevor-Roper pp. 102–4

410: *vital harbour installations . . .* Directive No. 9 'Instructions for warfare against the economy of the enemy' 29 Nov 1939 quoted in Trevor-Roper pp. 56–9

410: *they kept singing . . . Front Line* p. 11

411: *a scene of . . . The Times* 3 Jan 1941 quoted in K. O. Morgan p. 51

411: *like a wedding . . .* K. O. Morgan p. 54

411: Figures for homes destroyed and damaged, Ramsey Vol. II p. 384

411: *two houses might . . .* MacInnes p. 100

411: 'Satan' bomb, MacInnes p. 80

412: *It is said . . .* Hodgson p. 114

413: Forty acres razed to the ground, Alban pp. 16–17

413: Swansea damage, Alban p. 114

413: Canon J. J. Tallon killed, Whittington-Egan p. 43

414: Girl's parents killed, Perret p. 10

414: *without the slightest . . .* Perret p. 97

414: *the tally of . . .* Whittington-Egan p. 13

414: Inland Revenue Building, Whittington-Egan p. 14

414: *I shudder to . . .* Quoted in Perret p. 113

415: WVS workers killed, Whittington-Egan p. 16

415: *the longest unbroken . . .* O'Brien p. 418

415: *simple murder . . .* Colonel J. T. C. Moore-Brabazon quoted in Ramsey Vol. II p. 560

416: *Glasgow houses are . . .* Webb & Duncan p. 110

417: *indecorous . . .* Ramsey Vol. II p. 481

417: Clydebank damage, McKendrick p. 12

417: *a bad knock . . .* McHutchison IWM Dept of Documents P151

419: Bristol tram service, Dike p. 71

419: *battered ruins . . .* Colville p. 373

420: *There was devastation . . .* Colville p. 373

420: *kept on arriving . . .* Mary Soames quoted in Gilbert (1983) p. 1059

420: *They have such . . .* Harriman & Able pp. 29–30

420: Plymouth on day of bombing, O'Brien p. 414

420: UXB exploded, Twyford p. 148

421: *When I arrived . . .* Doreen Jessop (née Herd) quoted in Waller & Vaughan-Rees (1990) pp. 146–7

421: City 'eradicated', Ray p. 219

421: *nothing but twisted . . .* Anne-Lee Mitchell quoted in Webb & Duncan p. 154

421: *Nothing I had . . .* Q. Reynolds

421: *The civic and . . .* M-OA F/R 626

421: *practically wiped out . . .* Anne-Lee Mitchell quoted in Webb & Duncan pp. 146–7

421: *stand in the . . .* Hammond p. 342

421: I *saw a . . .* Colville p. 381

422: *where bombs had . . .* Colville p. 381

422: Editorial and printing staff to Exeter, Twyford p. 157

423: *children were being . . . Daily Herald* 16 Nov 1940

424: Centres crowded with homeless people, Titmuss p. 307

424: Queue had formed, Titmuss p. 308

424: *have a depressed . . .* PRO Home Intelligence Report on Merseyside TNA PRO/INF1/292

425: Population of Bootle come back to work, Titmuss p. 311

425: 'Yellow convoy', Reid pp. 37–8

425: *It seems that . . .* Titmuss p. 307

425: Robert Garton PC, Geraghty p. 13

426: Hull left without gas, Geraghty p. 19

426: Deputy Chief Constable killed, Geraghty p. 20

426: *where passenger coaches . . .* Ray p. 224

427: *There was nothing . . .* Fred Kummer and Rev Frederick Ralph quoted in Ramsey 248. II p. 603

428: *young men in . . .* Roose IWM Dept of Documents 89/41/1 p. 23

428: *It was a . . .* Nixon p. 103

430: *We called and . . .* Markham IWM Dept of Documents 91/5/1 pp. 29–30

431: Royal Hospital in Chelsea, Ziegler (1995) p. 152

431: *rents had dropped . . .* FitzGibbon p. 66

432: *Young and old . . .* FitzGibbon pp. 88–91

432: *dressed in borrowed . . .* FitzGibbon p. 93

432: 6,065 civilians killed, Gilbert (1983) p. 1062

432: *at London's landmarks . . .* Colville p. 376

433: *into a great . . . Front Line* p. 33

433: *Towards morning the . . .* C. King pp. 124–8

434: *bits of paper . . .* Channon p. 304

434: Hospital paperwork, Titmuss pp. 335, 557–61

434: *not until over . . .* Titmuss p. 336

435: Total risen to 535, Henderson IWM Dept of Documents p. 3

436: *On the Shankill . . .* Quoted in Fisk p. 497

436: *Would be to* . . . Carroll p. 12

437: US entering war, Roberts p. 165

437: Close watch kept on German agents, O'Halpin p. 30

437: *is not a* . . . Gilbert (1983) pp. 67–8

439: Peter Barnes and Frank Richards condemned for murder, Kee (1984) p. 300–1

439: IRA was main target, O'Halpin p. 34

439: Germany planned attack on Ireland, Foster p. 560

440: *nobody knew how* . . . *Irish Times* Aug 1947 quoted in Coogan pp. 214–5

440: *was staggered* . . . Fisk p. 504

441: German Federal Government to pay settlement, Barton (1989) p. 249

441: Explanation for bombs, Barton (1989) pp. 249–52

441: Allied ships in convoy, Fisk p. 252

441: 98,296 Irishmen in the war, R. Doherty pp. 22, 25

441: Southern Irishmen decorations, Carroll p. 163

441: *have been given* . . . Girvin & Roberts p. 107

441: *believed that that* . . . Kavanagh p. 85

442: *blossoms of blood* . . . Girvin & Roberts p. 87

442: *no slacking in* . . . Barton (1995) p. 476

442: *hundreds of men* . . . Barton (1995) p. 7

443: *Well-off women from* . . . Woodside 9 Oct 1940 M-OA Diarist 5462

443: *fit young men* . . . *Sunday Pictorial* 4 Apr 1943 quoted in Barton (1995) p. 15

444: *it will come* . . . Fisk p. 87

444: BBC ignore Northern Ireland in its morale-boosting, Nicholas p. 232

444: *letters addressed to* . . . Woodside 13 Oct 1940 M-OA Diarist 5462

445: Carringtons, Barton (1989) p. 33

445: *is the most* . . . Fisk p. 477

446: *The inadequacy of* . . . Foster p. 561

446: *don't press for* . . . Lady Craigavon quoted in Barton (1995) p. 17

447: 26,000 volunteers coming forward, Blake p. 180

447: Sir John Anderson concludes status quo should pertain, Mackenzie pp. 84–5

448: Evacuation unsuccessful, Fisk p. 479

448: *we are another* . . . Woodside 25 Aug 1940 M-OA Diarist 5462

448: *in this professional* . . . Woodside 25 Aug 1940 M-OA Diarist 5462

448: *wondered if Belfast's* . . ., Emma Duffin quoted in Barton (1989) p. 77

449: *less well-defended than* . . . Barton (1989) p. 72

449: *in one of* . . . Woodside 23 Aug 1940 M-OA Diarist 5462

449: Figures for shelter provision, Blake p. 218

449: Belfast defence, Blake p. 208

450: Workers killed in explosion, Barton (1989) pp. 86–7

450: *the sole topic* . . . Woodside 8 Apr 1941 M-OA Diarist 5462

450: *The raid was* . . . Woodside 9 Apr 1941 M-OA Diarist 5462

451: *as the powerful* . . . Barton (1989) p. 106

451: *where the poor* . . . Barton (1989) p. 108

451: *Each seemed to* . . . Barton (1989) p. 108

452: Thirty-five killed in incident, Barton (1989) p. 112

452: Passengers seek refuge in nearest shelter, Barton (1989) p. 114

452: Streets around the Crumlin road, Barton (1989) p. 115

452: Mine near Percy Street, Barton (1989) p. 118

452: Bomb on Harland and Wolff's boiler house, Fisk p. 487

453: *the Luftwaffe had* . . . Fisk pp. 489–90

453: *could stand it* . . . Woodside 16 Apr 1941 M-OA Diarist 5462

454: *took what was* . . . Longford p. 383

454: *might only concern* . . . Barton (1989) p. 137

454: Couplings different size, Fisk p. 491

454: *an action like* . . . Woodside 17 Apr 1941 M-OA Diarist 5462

454: Firemen rewarded with lunch money, Patrick Finlay quoted in Fisk p. 498

454: *makes us conscious* . . . Woodside 17 Apr 1941 M-OA Diarist 5462

455: *men digging out* . . . William McCready quoted in Barton (1989) p. 135

455: *houses roofless, windowless* . . . Woodside 16 Apr 1941 M-OA Diarist 5462

455: *tear stained, mourning* . . . Belfast *Telegraph* quoted in Barton (1989) p. 133

455: *had been dislocated* . . . William McCready quoted in Barton (1989) p. 139

455: *citizens wondered how* . . . Blake p. 232

455: Part of corpse in backyard, Fisk p. 493

455: *has some terrible* . . . Woodside 17 Apr 1941 M-OA Diarist 5462

455: Fire Authority's figure, Barton (1989) p. 150

455: Aerodrome at Newtownards hit, Blake p. 230

455: Belfast as city with third highest loss of life, Blake p. 233

455: *in the stink* . . . Moore p. 231

456: *Believed to be* . . . Joseph McCann quoted in Fisk p. 493

456: Public funeral, *The Times* 7 Oct 1974

456: 'Ditchers' leave city, Fisk p. 497

457: *Such an exodus* . . . Woodside 16 Apr 1941 M-OA Diarist 5462

457: *This business presents* . . . Woodside 17 Apr 1941 M-OA Diarist 5462

457: *thousands of people* . . . Woodside 16 Apr 1941 M-OA Diarist 5462

457: *some of the* . . . Mrs E. M. Sweeney quoted in Barton (1989) p. 161

457: *public opinion* . . . Woodside 17 Apr 1941 M-OA Diarist 5462

457: *will give us* . . . Woodside 17 Apr 1941 M-OA Diarist 5462

458: Belfast bombed again, Fisk p. 499

458: *a sea of* . . . Ernst von Kuhren quoted in Barton (1989) p. 184

458: Water on windows to stop them cracking, Barton (1989) p. 200

459: *such an inferno* . . . Blake p. 237

459: Harland and Wolff's claim for bomb damage, Barton (1989) pp. 214–5

460: Figures for new houses needed, Barton (1989) p. 256

460: Accusations against nationalists, Barton (1989) pp. 268–9

460: *in the Roman* . . . Woodside 15 Aug 1940 M-OA Diarist 5462

461: *and the RC* . . . Woodside 30 Mar 1940 M-OA Diarist 5462

462: *Encased in talent* . . . Auden p. 124

463: *There is a* . . . Letter from Ronald Horton to Percy Horton 10 Nov 1940 quoted in *Artist as Evacuee* p. 39

463: Goering reputed to have his eye on Poussin, Secrest p. 148

463: Art evacuated to North Wales and Gloucestershire, McCamley (2003) p. 1

463: Boughton House to shelter art, Seebohm p. 149

464: *England is full* . . . Clark p. 1

464: *I shall spread* . . . J. Robinson p. 86

464: *in the blackout* . . . Seebohm p. 147

464: *Are they worth* . . . McCamley (2003) p. 30

465: *Bury them in* . . . Clark p. 5

465: *tapestries, furniture and* . . . Seebohm p. 146

466: *in peace time* . . . Clark p. 5

466: Private collections stashed in Manod, McCamley (2003) p. 113

466: West Wycombe Park, Lees-Milne (1975) p. 93

467: *peace for our* . . . McCamley (2003) pp. 133–4

467: *because London's face* . . . *The Times* 3 Jan 1942

467: *I love them* . . . Grenfell p. 156

468: Joyce Grenfell entertaining troops, Hampton p. 104

468: *We made over* . . . Grenfell pp. 188–9

468: *continued* . . . *without missing* . . . Haskell et al p. 116

468: *They were her* . . . Grenfell p. 162

469: Music dropped by BBC, Mackay p. 145

469: John Ireland's *Epic March*, Mackay p. 167

469: *Hymn to St Cecilia* first heard at Wigmore Hall, Stansky & Abrahams pp. 156–7, 163

470: Theatre profession hit hard, David p. 183

471: *unless architects, painters* . . . Letter from Paul Nash to Robert Byron Sep 1940 473ted in J. King p. 198

471: *making models and* . . . Trevelyan pp. 112–13

471: *Dr Cott, who* . . . Trevelyan pp. 117–18

472: *learned how arctic* . . . Maskelyne p. 17

472: *At every dance* . . . Trevelyan p. 123

472: *Against the dreary* . . . Trevelyan p. 130

473: *any landscape, coast-line* . . . CEMA Bulletin 28 Aug 1942

473: *the one real* . . . Clark p. 22

473: *prodding the artist* . . . Newton p. 7

473: *towards the abstract* . . . Harries & Harries pp. 160–1

473: *The War Artists* . . . Sir Kenneth Clark quoted in Harries & Harries p. 161

473: *What did it* . . . *War Pictures in the National Gallery by British Artists*

474: *Somewhat whimsical* . . . Beaton p. 5

474: salaried artists in France, Harries & Harries p. 168

475: *to tackle the* . . . Ross p. 26

475: *in the power* . . . Paul Nash quoted in Ross p. 76

475: *arabesque of white* . . . *War Pictures in the National Gallery by British Artists* p. 103

476: *my father in* . . . Lindop p. 28

476: *The background to* . . . Spender p. 6

477: Piper withdrew to solicitor's office, Jenkins p. 33

477: *became for Britain* . . . Jenkins p. 33

477: *to stand by* . . . Harries & Harries p. 187

477: *A lift shaft* . . . Ross pp. 43–4

477: *much more tragic* . . . Harries & Harries pp. 188–9

477: *the sight of* . . . J. Andrews p. 16

477: *I'm still in* . . . J. Andrews p. 198

478: *the group sense* . . . Rothestein

478: *a tragedy, nevertheless* . . . Keith Vaughan quoted in Lewis in Kirkham & Thoms p. 18

478: *you are in* . . . Keith Vaughan quoted in Lewis in Kirkham & Thoms p. 198

478: *painted by artists* . . . Ross p. 13

479: Leonard Rosoman, Ross pp. 167–8

479: *a white-grub like* . . . Eric Newton in *The Sunday Times* 18 May 1941 quoted in Lewis in Kirkham & Thoms p. 120

479: *of heavy feet* . . . Peake pp. 19–20

479: *In this wider* . . . Knight p. 5

480: Stella Schmolle, Harries & Harries p. 338

480: Stanley Spencer suggested Crucifixion painting, Ross p. 54

481: *Liverpool was in* . . . Gilbert Spencer quoted in *Artist as Evacuee* p. 135

481: *I liked the* . . . Gilbert Spencer quoted in *Artist as Evacuee* p. 138

481: Women students housed in Salutation Hotel, *Artist as Evacuee* p. 9

481: *A throne, a* . . . *Picture Post* 3 Jul 1943

482: Students traumatised and mutilated, Edward Berry 'A Three and Seven Penny Half Penny Man' quoted in *Artist as Evacuee* p. 73

482: *when* . . . *artists* . . . *have* . . . Wyndham Lewis quoted in Harries & Harries

482: *among other exhibits* . . . Cox 6 May 1941 IWM Dept of Documents 86/46/1 (P)

483: *the sort of* . . . Miss M. S. Cochrane quoted in Harries & Harries p. 185

483: Rodrigo Moynihan painted Miss Borne, Shone pp. 18–19

483: *shone as she* . . . Harries & Harries p. 181

483: *had had his* . . . Gilbert Spencer quoted in *Artist as Evacuee* p. 138

483: *the best yet* . . . *Spectator* 23 May 1941

483: *My little money-sources* . . . Letter from Dylan Thomas to John Davenport 14 Sep 1940 quoted in Thomas p. 410

483: *are in the* . . . Letter from John Betjeman to Oliver Stoner 14 Sep 1939 Betjeman pp. 237–8

484: *at the shameful* . . . Letter from John Betjeman to William Plomer 17 Mar 1940 Betjeman p. 257

484: *authors can best* . . . Letter from John Betjeman to Siegfried Sassoon 15 Sep 1939 Betjeman p. 231

484: *sitting on a* . . . Orwell Vol. I. (1968) p. 576

484: *How are you* . . . E. M. Delafield 'The War and the Author or The Author and War' in *Punch* 20 Dec 1939

484: Number of books published, Brophy p. 51

484: Appetite for new books, Hewison p. 76

485: Penguin staff killed in France, Morpurgo p. 155

485: *already sent nearly* . . . Letter from John Johnson (printer to the university) 27 Aug 1940 in Oxford University Press Archives

485: Impossible to replace machinery, Hewison p. 77

486: MoI withdrawal of its subsidy, Hopkinson pp. 203–4

486: *was one to* . . . Warburg p. 27

487: *drunk and disorderly* . . . *Bookseller* 7 Mar 1940 quoted in McAleer p. 77

487: *one of the* . . . Orwell (1944)

487: *plush beyond the* . . . Morpurgo p. 157

488: *a hedge-hopping of* . . . Pearson pp. 21–3

489: British POWs in camps, Pearson pp. 38–41

489: *No Orchids for Miss Blandish,* National Book League *A Time to Read*

489: Censorship of books for POWs, Pearson pp. 42–3

489: *you're dead* . . . Green p. 20

490: *an interminable novel* . . . Evelyn Waugh quoted in Hastings p. 546

490: *read literally every* . . . Harrisson p. 417

490: *owed so little* . . . Harrisson p. 417

490: *but none by* . . . Harrisson p. 432

490: Harrisson dismissive of 'lady novelists', Harrisson p. 435

490: *sell practically everything* . . . Harrisson p. 435

491: Paper from dubious sources, Holland p. 14

491: *required to put* . . . Chibnell in Kirkham & Thoms p. 144

491: Sales of Rita Hayworth book, Holland p. 13

493: *cannot even feel* . . . Robert Graves quoted in Sinclair (1989) pp. 566–7

493: *the artist's right* . . . *Times Literary Supplement* 11 Jan 1941

493: *We were united* . . . John Lehman 'Why Not War Writers' in *Horizon* Vol. IV No. 22, 22 Oct 1941 p. 165

493: *a telephone call* . . . Bull p. 180

494: *should be used* . . . Horizon Vol. IV No. 22, 22 Oct 1941 pp. 236–9

494: *It was good* . . . Letter from John Betjeman to Cyril Connolly 19 Oct 1940 Betjeman pp. 243–4

495: *One day when* . . . *Poems of the Land Army*

495: *It was now* . . . Bowen (1948) pp. 92–3

496: *a habit . . . that's . . .* 29 May 1942
Mitchinson p. 198

497: *the hardest-fought victory . . . Battle of
the Atlantic* pp. 5, 104

497: *Brown Period . . . Browned-off . . .*
MacLaren-Ross p. 85

499: 1.5 million workers needed to
join munitions, H. M. D. Parker
p. 102

499: Survey results, H. M. D. Parker
p. 176

501: National Service Appeal Boards
appeals, H. M. D. Parker p. 255

501: Men sent to prison for refusing
to obey the Direction Order, W.
Taylor p. 24

501: *We stood in . . .* Author interview
with Frank Collieson 2003

503: *the miners were . . .* Pick p. 100

504: Women's auxiliary services, H. M.
D. Parker pp. 286–7

504: *The ATS take . . .* Hammerton &
Gwynn pp. 416–7

505: Discharge rate, C. Harris (2003)
p. 29

505: Percentage of driving done by
women, Lynn p. 65

505: *By the end . . .* Pile p. 164

505: *should not fire . . .* Pile p. 164

506: *always more of . . .* Pile p. 168

506: *marching, eating and . . .* Pile
pp. 169, 171

506: *as an old . . . Roof Over Britain*
pp. 60–1

506: *the girls' first . . .* Pile p. 170

506: *in some bleak . . .* Pile p. 199

507: *relatively hard open . . . Roof Over
Britain* p. 61

507: *why we were . . .* Pile p. 200

508: Admiration of uniform, C. Harris
(2003) p. 91

508: *there is little . . .* Hammerton &
Gwynn p. 418

508: WAAFs employment, C. Harris
(2003) p. 63

508: Women pilots sent on conversion
courses, Adie p. 142

509: *young amazons . . .* Escott p. 16

509: *The substitution of . . . Picture Post*
1942

509: *a balloon in . . .* Lynn p. 76

510: *We were based . . .* Hilda Pearce
quoted in C. Harris (2003)
p. 75

511: *Everything had to . . .* Minns p. 46

511: *They were yelling . . .* Calvert
pp. 12–13

512: *I was longing . . .* Zeepvat IWM
Dept of Documents 82/33/1

512: *The last part . . .* Zeepvat IWM
Dept of Documents 82/33/1

512: *You'll never get . . .* Batstone IWM
Dept of Documents 82/61/1
pp. 3, 5

514: *Four weeks later . . .* Batstone IWM
Dept of Documents 82/61/1
pp. 10–11

514: *We tottered back . . .* Lynn pp. 71–2

515: *If you ask . . .* Ellis p. 34

516: *Don't queue with . . .* 18 Nov 1941
M-OA Town Box 'Coventry' File
3708

516: Acts passed to allow women to
continue to work after they
married, Summerfield in *Labour
History Review* p. 89

516: Percentage of women in the
workforce, Summerfield in
Labour History Review p. 68

517: *to the knowledge . . .* Katin pp. 5–6

517: *the local Labour . . .* Katin pp. 6–7

519: Figures for part-time workers,
Ministry of Labour report quoted
in Smith in H. L. Smith (1986)
p. 216

519: Government sponsored
nurseries, Summerfield in *Labour
History Review* p. 94

520: Young workers threatened they
would be 'sent to the Midlands',
25 Jul 1942 Bruley p. 56

521: *I was 19 . . .* Quoted in Harris
(2000) pp. 77–9

522 *I want to . . .* Partridge pp. 91–2

523: Objections to women in
agriculture, Tyrer pp. 17–18

523: *couldn't think of . . .* Hyndman
p. 81

524: *For the most . . .* Sackville-West
pp. 7–8

524: Vita Sackville-West aficionado of breeches, Glendenning p. 305

525: *while you are* . . . Tyrer pp. 65–6

527: Anti-vermin squads, Tyrer p. 128

527: *also had contracts* . . . Verrill-Rhys & Beddoe pp. 114–15

528: *allocation of timber* . . . Danher IWM Sound Archives 9/526/3/1

530: Peacetime population would need feeding, Tyrer pp. 214–22

530: *mean and niggardly* . . . Quoted in Ward p. 45

530: Crew on the boats, Wollfitt pp. 11–12

531: *We had to* . . . Rolt IWM Sound Archives 22902/8

532: *house-pride is no* . . . *Woman's Own* 20 Mar 1942

534: *It is difficult* . . . George Orwell in *Tribune* 3 Dec 1943

535: *about five acres* . . . Quoted in M. R. D. Foot 'Prisoners-of-War' in Dear & Foot p. 914

535: 130,000 soldiers captured, Sponza p. 186

535: *2,000–3,000 suitable North* . . . Sponza p. 186

535: *it might be* . . . Letter from David Margesson to the Ministry of Agriculture 29 May 1941 quoted in Sponza p. 187

535: *were of good* . . . Labour Advisory for the Midlands report quoted in Sponza p. 197

536: *In their dark* . . . Greening p. 161

537: *their interest in* . . . Sponza pp. 214–15

537: *the true strategic* . . . Churchill (1959) p. 171

537: *Those poor fellows* . . . Gilbert (1983) p. 63

537: Orkneys population, Tinch p. xiii

538: *We'd never seen* . . . Quoted in Brown & Meehan p. 194

538: *The Italians* . . . *were* . . . *Churchill's Prisoners* p. 7

539: POWs offering services, Author interview with John Muir 2003

539: *Italians very bad* . . . Tinch p. 32

540: POWs uniform, Albert Bertin quoted in Sponza p. 255

541: Women who fraternised with the Italians, Sponza p. 280

541: *The co-operators* . . . Ion Megarry quoted in Sponza pp. 45–6

542: Canadians in Britain, Stacey & Wilson pp. 3–5

543: *Strike out help* . . . Lord Beaverbrook quoted in P. M. H. Bell p. 78

544: *It is as* . . . Keegan (1989) p. 124

544: *in ratio to* . . . Hamilton (1983) p. 518

544: *the futility of* . . . Eisenhower p. 96

545: *knew that the* . . . Churchill (1950) pp. 538–40

546: America at bottom of list of 'friendly' nations, M-OA F/R 523B

547: *I remember only* . . . Bill Ong quoted in Hale & Turner pp. 78–9

547: 1.5 million combat and service troops, Ruppenthal pp. 100, 129, 133

547: 71,000 GIs in Suffolk, Quoted in D. Reynolds p. 112

548: *The British will* . . . *A Short Guide to Great Britain* issued by US War Department 1942 pp. 2, 3, 24, 18–19, 30–2, 38

548: *Americans are not* . . . Current Affairs No. 26 19 Sep 1942

549: *we don't want* . . . *A Short Guide to Great Britain* issued by US War Department 1942 p. 37

549: *their troops, especially* . . . Gorham p. xiii

550: *We never saw* . . . Gorham p. xiii

550: *the British are* . . . *A Short Guide to Great Britain* issued by US War Department 1942 p. 51

550: *There'll Always Be* . . . Gardiner (1992) p. 56

551: *some of the* . . . *Meet the Army*

551: *that England does* . . . R. S. Raymond p. x

552: *American wages and* . . . *A Short Guide to Great Britain* issued by US War Department 1942 pp. 3–4

552: British and American wages, Longmate (1975) pp. 377–9

552: Disposable incomes of soldiers, D. Reynolds p. 152

553: *About fifteen girls . . .* Quoted in Hale & Turner p. 108

553: *a young British . . .* Author interview with Eric Westman 1991

553: *I cannot recall . . .* Author interview with Avice Wilson 1991

553: *This brand new . . .* Crisp pp. 156–7

554: *luxuries we hadn't . . .* Brenda Devereux quoted in Gardiner (1992) p. 114

554: *the only ones . . .* Hall 3 Mar 1944 IWM Dept of Documents DS/MISC/88

555: *at 7 o'clock . . .* Gardiner (1992) p. 119

556: *was to find . . .* PRO/NA FO, 371/3

559: *think all Americans . . .* Cotton 17 Jul 1942 IWM Dept of Documents 93/3/1/ (P) pp. 230–1

560: *in general marriage . . .* Stacey & Wilson p. 138

561: *she will be . . .* ETO Circular 20, 28 Jul 1942

562: *our climate was . . .* D. Reynolds p. 217

564: Women with black GIs imprisoned, quoted in Reynolds p. 229

565: *Nobody talked to them . . .* Author interview with Mary Ruau (née Kemp) 1991

566: *I slept and . . .* Ellen S. Hooper quoted in Collier & Kaplam p. 56

566: *I'll pamper my . . .* Vogue Jan 1943

567: *unnecessary, unworkable . . .* Winston Churchill quoted in Zweinger-Bargielowska p. 48

567: Lyttleton convinces Churchill about clothes rationing, Chandos p. 205

567: *not intended to . . .* Hargreaves & Gowing pp. 312–13

567: *the President of . . .* Panter-Downes (1972) p. 152

567: *got wind of . . .* Chandos p. 206

568: Industrial clothing, Gardiner (2000) pp. 191–2

569: *an evening frock . . .* M-OA F/R 791

569: Public response to clothes rationing, M-OA F/R 830 p. 68–9

569: *had enough money . . .* M-OA F/R 756

569: *Surely people must . . .* Moya Woodside quoted in M-OA F/R 791

569: *forty [suits] or . . .* Channon p. 307

570: *People write to . . .* Partridge p. 95

570: Responses to requests for more coupons, Applications for Supplementary Clothing from Public Dignitaries quoted in Zweinger-Bargielowska p. 89

570: *He is a . . .* Sir Kingsley Wood quoted in E.S. Turner 'Flashes of 15 Denier' in London Review of Books 20 Mar 1997

570: *Will people in . . .* Ellen Wilkinson quoted in Zweinger-Bargielowska p. 88

571: *il faut SKIMP . . .* Vogue 1941 quoted in Sladen p. 13

571: *increasingly difficult to . . .* TNA/PRO INF 1/292 18–20 Jul 1944

572: *No doubt there . . .* Hugh Dalton in Make Do and Mend

572: *We didn't need . . .* Author interview with Ena Norris 22 Aug 2002

573: *the search for . . .* Hancock & Gowing p. 491

573: *marry a shopkeeper's . . .* Beardmore p. 114

573: *by maintaining the . . .* Hancock & Gowing p. 494

573: Request to Hardy Amies, Sladen p. 39

574: *both laughed . . .* Hardy Amies and Captain Molyneux quoted in McDowell p. 114

574: *All women have . . .* Vogue Oct 1942 quoted in CC41 p. 33

575: *The response was . . .* Women and

Beauty 9 Mar 1943 quoted in M-OA F/R 1143

575: *unparalleled example of . . . CC41* p. 7

576: Considerations for the furniture industry, *CC41* p. 5

576: *All that you . . .* Edwin Clinch quoted in *CC41* p. 13

576: *austerity and utility . . .* Gordon Russell in a letter to *Cabinet Maker* quoted in Dover p. 19

577: *was very ugly . . . Architects' Journal* quoted in Gillian Naylor 'The Attitude of the Furniture Trade' in *CC41* p. 28

577: *Furniture never went . . .* Edwin Clinch quoted in *CC41* p. 13

577: Other items in the Utility scheme, Felton p. 45

578: *slipp[ing] on a . . .* Last p. 64

578: Cosmetics factories put to industrial use, McDowell p. 70

578: Percentages of women wearing make-up, Zweinger-Bargielowska p. 91

579: Face powder for munitions workers, Kirkham in Kirkham & Thoms p. 152

579: *No surrender . . .* Quoted in Waller & Vaughan-Rees (1987) p. 104

580: *when war was . . .* Crisp p. 105

580: Advertisements for make-up, Waller & Vaughan-Rees (1987) p. 101

580: *internal sanitary protection . . .* Quoted in Waller & Vaughan-Rees (1987) p. 105

580: Use of women's magazines for propaganda, Winship in Gledhill & Swanson p. 127

581: *It is axiomatic . . . Vogue* 1941

581: Tommy Handley's description of Beveridge, Kavanagh p. 164

581: *learned the meaning . . .* Quoted in Timmins p. 127

581: *this heavy two-shilling . . .* Panter-Downes (1972) p. 253

581: Sales of the Beveridge and Denning reports, Timmins p. 23

582: Percentage of people aware of the Beveridge report, M-OA F/R 1538

582: Newspapers' response to the Beveridge report, *Daily Mirror* 2 Dec 1942, *Daily Herald* 3 Dec 1942 quoted in Bromley in Hayes & Hill pp. 110–14

582: *the People's William . . .* Addison (1992) pp. 211–28

582: *what has already . . .* Beveridge p. 14

583: *available to all . . .* Beveridge p. 14

583: *full use of . . .* D. Fraser p. 265

583: *the purpose of . . .* Beveridge p. 171

583: *Tory line seems . . .* Nicolson (1967) p. 264

583: *to a nation . . .* Donoghue & Jones pp. 314–15

584: *Can we afford . . .* Herbert Morrison quoted in Donoghue & Jones p. 229

584: War Cabinet decision not to pursue Beveridge's recommendations, Addison (1994) p. 223

585: Steps taken by the Cabinet, Mackay pp. 221–47

585: *necessitate[d] great readjustments . . .* Clement Attlee quoted in Addison (1994) p. 223

586: *a series of . . .* Partridge p. 169

586: *It was quite . . .* Williams p. 836

588: *Born with all . . .* Manifold

588: Crime rose because more laws, Scott (1957) p. 68

590: The Treachery Act, D. Thomas p. 336

591: Inside jobs, D. Thomas p. 164

591: Fake coupons detection, D. Thomas p. 172

593: Dr Sutton jailed for nine months, D. Thomas p. 49

593: Impersonation at medical boards, Smithies (1982) p. 49

593: Weekly wage £10 a week, D. Thomas p. 47

593: Liverpool city councillor, D. Thomas p. 49

593: *out of the . . .* Smithies (1982) p. 50

593: *a highly respected . . .* Phipps 30 Apr 1944 IWM Dept of Documents P178

594: *virtually everything movable . . .* Smithies (1982) p. 34

594: Birkenhead docks, Smithies (1982) p. 30

595: Prosecutions resumed, Smithies (1982) p. 37

595: *probably due to . . .* Smithies (1982) pp. 47–8

597: *The usual practice . . .* Markham IWM Dept of Documents 91/5/1 p. 29

597: *When a great . . .* Quoted in D. Thomas p. 76

597: Talk of appointing a 'Director of Anti-Looting', D. Thomas pp. 84–5

597: *the Legislature has . . .* Quoted in D. Thomas p. 77

598: *we wandered from . . .* Cox 2 Oct 1940 IWM Dept of Documents 86/46/1 (P)

598: *borrow a ladder . . .* Markham IWM Dept of Documents 91/5/1 p. 30

600: Leonard Watson sent to prison, D. Thomas p. 83

601: Prosecutions for child cruelty and neglect, Smithies (1982) p. 165

601: Dislocation of family life in wartime, Titmuss p. 413

602: Borstal boys and girls set free, Smithies (1982) pp. 178–9

603: Miners dispute in Kent, Burton in *BBC History* pp. 12–15

603: Imprisonment on a shift system, Burton in *BBC History* p. 13

603: Coal munition of war, Lord Hawarden quoted in Burton in *BBC History* p. 14

604: *obsession with political . . .* H. M. D. Parker p. 471

604: Stars and Stripes to indicate US home territory, D. Thomas p. 229

604: *arguably the most . . .* G. Smith p. 185

606: *vast sellers' market . . .* Watts p. 234

607: Deserters freed after six months, French p. 141

608: *young man in . . .* V. Graham p. 97

610: *I said . . .* Mitchison p. 284

610: *We live for . . .* Ritchie p. 165

610: *had become a . . .* Ritchie p. 166

611: *that the primary . . .* Air Ministry Directive quoted in Connelly p. 63

611: Infrastructure key to German war effort, Connelly p. 68

612: *The bombs fell . . .* Bielenberg p. 125

612: *This is what . . .* Quoted in Connelly in *Contemporary British History* p. 49

612: British not solely aiming at military targets, M-OA F/R 2000

613: Victims buried in a mass grave, Ramsey Vol. II pp. 209–11

614: *In a matter . . .* 'Tragedy at Bethnal Green' inquiry report 1945 p. 10

614: Lack of police manpower, 'Tragedy at Bethnal Green' inquiry report 1945 p. 22

614: *the physical imperfections . . .* 'Tragedy at Bethnal Green' inquiry report 1945 p. 35

615: *A city officially . . .* Panter-Downes (1972) p. 27, 312

615: Stations reopened and bunks re-erected, Gregg p. 83

615: Morrison shelter price, O'Brien pp. 527–9

616: *it was just . . .* Cox 15 Apr 1944 IWM Dept of Documents 84/46/1 (P)

616: *John Stachey in . . .* Cox 19 Feb–15 Apr 1944 IWM Dept of Documents 84/46/1 (P)

617: *Facetious names met . . .* Ismay p. 187

617: *Something comparable to . . .* Picture Post 6 May 1944

619: *our . . . gaffer says . . .* Gardiner (1994) p. 74

619: *made at great . . .* Lieutenant-Colonel White quoted in Gardiner (1994) p. 75–6

621: *the American Army . . .* Brian Arnold quoted in Gardiner (1992) p. 97

622: *All day long . . .* John Stewart Collis quoted in Wright (2002) p. 234

623: *uncomfortable resembles living* . . . Panter-Downes (1972) p. 322

624: *Troops were everywhere* . . . Cawthon p. 38

625: *So far as* . . . Letter from Ernest Brewer 28 May 1944 quoted in D-Day Museum, Portsmouth

626: *until the invasion* . . . Panter-Downes (1972) p. 325

626: *had shouldered the* . . . Panter-Downes (1972) p. 322

627: *The big London* . . . Panter-Downes (1972) p. 324

627: *spearhead the invasion* . . . Gardiner (1994) pp. 120–1

628: *a deeper than* . . . Willis p. 131

628: *Five miles an* . . . Moorehead

631: *The act of* . . . Cotton 8 Mar 1945 IWM Dept of Documents 93/3/1 p. 39

632: *At close range* . . . Quoted in Gardiner (1994) p. 169

632: *The atmosphere on* . . . Quoted in Gardiner (1994) p. 170

633: *rather calmly as* . . . Cox 6 Jun 1944 IWM Dept of Documents 84/46/1 (P)

633: *At 9.45 General* . . . Goddard 6 Jun 1944 IWM Dept of Documents Con. Shelf

634: *Southampton was absolutely* . . . Tom Hiett quoted in D-Day Museum, Portsmouth

634: *He looked as* . . . Nicolson (1967) p. 375

635: *Who would have* . . . Goddard 6 Jun 1944 IWM Dept of Documents Con. Shelf

635: *there were so* . . . R. Miller (1993) pp. 443–5

637: *went down to* . . . Lieutenant Donald Holman quoted in R. Miller (1993) p. 473

638: *groping in the* . . . Babington Smith pp. 200–9

639: *The engine stopped* . . . Quoted in Longmate (1981) p. 95

639: *Flying bombs have* . . . Alanbrooke p. 560

640: Congregation deaths and injuries, *ARP and NFS News Review* Jun 1945 quoted in Ramsey Vol. III p. 393

640: *I had been* . . . Longmate (1981) p. 122

640: Predictions about rate of attack, Longmate (1981) p. 127

640: *after five years* . . . Herbert Morrison quoted in Mack & Humphries p. 140

642: *the normal human* . . . George Orwell in *Tribune* 30 Jun 1944

642: *People…have said* . . . Letter from Helena Britton to Elizabeth (Florence) Elkus 21 Jun 1944 IWM Dept of Documents Con. Shelf

642: *It just seems* . . . Hall 10–16 Jun 1944 IWM Dept of Documents DS/MISC/88

643: Air Ministry building wall demolished, Ramsey Vol. III p. 403

644: *If we could* . . . Jones pp. 422–3

646: *When we reached* . . . Thomas 28 Jul 1944 IWM Dept of Documents 90/30/1 pp. 49–50

646: *I suddenly heard* . . . Longmate (1981) pp. 185–6

648: *inundated with refugees* . . . Cox 6 Jun 1944 IWM Dept of Documents 86/46/1 (P)

649: *safe at least* . . . Hall IWM Dept of Documents DS/MISC/88

651: *a shot down* . . . Bates pp. 22–4, 43

651: *What is 'open* . . . *Kent Messenger* 15 Sep 1944 quoted in Longmate (1981) p. 384

652: *that London is* . . . Letter from George Britton to Elizabeth (Florence) Elkus 14 Nov 1944 IWM Dept of Documents Con. Shelf

653: Death toll caused by V-2s, O'Brien p. 678

653: Property having to be demolished, Collier (1964) p. 528

653: *We had to* . . . Quoted in Mack & Humphries p. 143 h

654: V-2 attack on Woolworths store, Ramsey Vol. III p. 490

654: *and suddenly there*... June Gaida quoted in Mack & Humphries p. 328

654: *The V-2 Rocket*... *Daily Herald* 11 Nov 1944

655: Recipients warned not to reply, Longmate (1981) pp. 460–1

656: *My country is*... Beardmore p. 171

656: *I think that*... Nicolson (1967) p. 420

656: *At present, on*... Cox 12 Feb 1945 IWM Dept of Documents 86/46/1 (P)

657: *Dresden? There is*... Colville p. 562

657: *Now they know*... Bloom p. 209

659: *Oh, won't it*... A. P. Herbert in *Punch* 8 Jul 1942

659: *This memorable date*... Hall 11 May 1945 IWM Dept of Documents DS/MISC/88

660: *Most people expected*... Quoted in M-OA F/R 2263 p. 18

660: *Churchill had said*... Quoted in M-OA F/R 2263 p. 17

660: *Don't forget your*... Quoted in M-OA F/R 2263 p. 24

661: *It's ever so*... Quoted in M-OA F/R 2263 pp. 13–14

661: *Quietly my father*... Quoted in M-OA F/R 2263 p. 11

662: *I felt*... 7 May 1945 M-O Diarist 5353

662: *who was drilling*... 17 May 1945 M-OA Diarist 5314

662: *to start putting*... M-OA F/R 2263 p. 15

662: *outpatients will be*... 7 May 1945 M-OA Diarist 5390

662: *The baker told*... 7 May 1945 M-OA Diarist 5331

662: *a Post dispersal*... 7 May 1945 M-OA Diarist 5307

663: *quietly and soberly*... Quoted in M-OA F/R 2263 p. 24

663: *We've been waiting*... Quoted in M-OA F/R 2263 p. 29

663: *cried when I*... Quoted in M-OA F/R 2263 p. 32

663: *A muddle*... Quoted in M-OA F/R 2263 p. 35

663: *neither in Reigate*... 7 May 1945 Anonymous M-OA Diarist

664: *all through the*... 7 May 1945 M-OA Diarist 5358

664: *the gayest place*... 7 May 1945 M-OA Diarist 5282

664: *struck most*... Directive Reply from government official in Haverfordwest quoted in M-OA F/R 3657

664: *private houses were*... 8 May 1945 M-OA Diarist 5390

664: *there were a*... 7 May 1945 M-OA Diarist 5314

664: *When I went*... 7 May 1945 M-OA Diarist 1896

664: *saw a soldier*... 8 May 1945 M-OA Diarist 5282

665: Return of POWs, Rolf p. 186

665: *was beflagged and*... Channon p. 405

665: Savoy's VE Day lunch, Pocock p. 101

665: *to be reconsidered*... Sir James Grigg quoted in Gilbert (1995) p. 156

665: *The crowd gasped*... 8 May 1945 Nicolson (1967) p. 456

666: *We may allow*... Marian Holmes (one of Churchill's secretaries) quoted in Gilbert (1995) p. 174

666: *Felt all the*... 8 May 1945 M-OA Diarist 5314

666: Chants outside Ministry of Health, M-OA F/R 2263

667: *exceeded by double*... Elizabeth Layton (one of Churchill's secretaries) quoted in Gilbert (1995) p. 209

667: *A very sprucely*... M-OA F/R 2263 p. 45

667: *very pretty girl*... M-OA F/R 2263 p. 43

668: *the Palace*... Julia Strachey 10 May 1945 quoted in Partridge pp. 214–15

669: *wasn't very full* . . . Mitchison M-OA Diarist 5378

669: *found the crowds* . . . Janetta Woolley quoted in Partridge p. 215

669: *stood outside the* . . . Charles Kohler quoted in Miller pp. 171, 174

669: *some pacifists had* . . . Partridge p. 215

669: *I went to* . . . Carver 8 May 1945 IWM Dept of Documents 90/16/1

670: *Everyone participated in* . . . M-OA F/R 2263 p. 50

670: *Hitler was not* . . . M-OA F/R 2263 p. 50

670: *Coventry looked almost* . . . 8 May 1945 M-OA Diarist 5318

670: *some bonfires were* . . . Janetta Woolley quoted in Partridge p. 214

670: *in the High* . . . Mary Grice quoted in R. Miller (1995) p. 195

670: Singing in the streets of Belfast, Barton (1995) p. 135

671: Celebrations in Belfast, Barton (1995) p. 137

671: *old political differences* . . . Barton (1995) p. 138

671: Party arranged by Warden Post No 6, Golden pp. 109–10

671: *a really magnificent* . . . 9 May 1945 M-OA Diarist 5337

671: *were busy sweeping* . . . Carver 9 May 1945 IWM Dept of Documents 90/16/1

672: *a working day* . . . Carver 9 May 1945 IWM Dept of Documents 90/16/1

672: *Today is a* . . . M-OA F/R 2263 p. 59

672: *after 2 days* . . . Carver 10 May 1945 IWM Dept of Documents 90/16/1

672: *Mrs Sims says* . . . Quoted in M-OA F/R 2263 p. 11

672: *I had lived* . . . Letter from Peggie Philips to Luigi 'Laddie' Day 3 Jun 1945 IWM Dept of Documents 61/47/2

672: *Niece, 30, very* . . . 8 May 1945 M-OA Diarist 5318

672: *A solicitor friend* . . . M-OA F/R 2263 p. 10

672: *felt browned off* . . . 8 May 1945 M-OA Diarist 5271

672: *I could see* . . . M-OA F/R 2263 p. 28

673: *Personally, although of* . . . M-OA F/R 2263 p. 56

673: *The horrors of* . . . Crisp p. 173

673: *It must be* . . . 8 May 1945 M-OA Diarist 5296

673: *I wondered how* . . . M-OA F/R 2263 p. 56

673: *There is something* . . . 8 May 1945 M-OA Diarist 5390

674: Return of evacuees, Wallis p. 248

675: *It had been* . . . Last 10 Jul 1945 M-OA Diarist 5353

675: Unaccompanied evacuees, Titmuss pp. 431–41

676: Figures for destroyed buildings, R. Miller (1995) p. 246

676: *give the people* . . . Enoch Powell quoted in Hennessy p. 83

677: *admiration* . . . *amounting to* . . . Vita Sackville-West quoted in Nicolson (1967) p. 472

677: *would have to* . . . Kenneth Lindsay in *Spectator* 3 Aug 1945

677: *extremely interesting time* . . . 17 May 1941 Mitchison M-OA Diarist 5378

678: *I can't make* . . . Quoted in M-OA F/R 2257

678: Figures for servicemen voting, Fielding et al pp. 64–5

679: *having 'more of* . . . Last 13 Aug 1945 M-OA Diarist 5353

679: *Labour government were* . . . 1 Aug 1945 M-OA Diarist 5390

680: *Oh no he* . . . Winston Churchill quoted in Moran p. 352

680: *I won the* . . . Winston Churchill quoted in Nicolson (1967) p. 479

680: *For us the* . . . John Laffin quoted in Gilbert (1995) p. 317

681: *at 1 o'clock* . . . Last 15 Aug 1945 M-OA Diarist 5353

681: *thinking of this* . . . 10 Aug 1945 Mitchison MO-A Diarist 5378

681: *strangely enough* . . . Wyndham (1986) p. 190

682: Celebrations in Plymouth, Twyford p. 183–4

682: Celebrations in Liverpool, Perrett p. 164–5

682: *I really felt* . . . 15 Aug 1945 M-OA Diarist 5337

682: *like seeing in* . . . 15 Aug 1945 M-OA Diarist 5390

682: *coming out of* . . . Rooke & D'Egville p. 12

683: *very, very disturbed* . . . Eddie Mathieson quoted in MacDougall pp. 255–7

684: Figures for Reverse Lend-Lease, Dimbleby & Reynolds p. 164–5

684: Figures for governments debt to people and lack of housing, Tiratsoo in *Contemporary British History* p. 30

684: *You said once* . . . Letter from Peggie Philips to Luidi 'Laddie' Day 3 Jun 1945 IWM Dept of Documents 61/47/2

685: Marriage figures, Ferguson & Fitzgerald p. 19

685: Birth rate figures, Ferguson & Fitzgerald p. 19

685: *the strangest mixture* . . . Wyndham (1986) pp. 189–90

685: *Whatever will we* . . . Last 13 Jul 1945 M-OA Diarist 5353

685: *was glad I* . . . Katin

686: *It's such a* . . . Quoted in Mass-Observation (1944)

686: Percentages of married women working, Summerfield in Brivati & Jones pp. 73, 76

686: *more impatient with* . . . Saunders IWM Sound Archive 09106

686: *an opportunity to* . . . Cornish Ridout IWM Sound Archive 23089

687: *we are going* . . . 12 Aug 1945 Mitchison p. 338

688: *a garden flat* . . . Hodgson p. 589

689: *tiny defeats* . . . Orwell (1941) p. 40

689: *Patriotism is usually* . . . Orwell (1941) pp. 10, 13

BIBLIOGRAPHY

Books

Abrahams, James S., *Sheffield Blitz* (Sheffield: Pawson & Brailsford, 1941)

Addison, Paul, *The Road to 1945: British Politics and the Second World War* (London: Pimlico, 1994)

Addison, Paul, *Churchill on the Home Front, 1900–1955* (London: Jonathan Cape, 1992)

Addison, Paul, and Angus Calder (eds), *Time To Kill: The Soldier's Experience of War in the West* (London: Pimlico, 1997)

Addison, Paul, and Jeremy A. Crang (eds), *The Burning Blue: A History of the Battle of Britain* (London: Pimlico, 2000)

Adie, Kate, *Corsets to Camouflage: Women and War* (London: Hodder & Stoughton, 2003)

Agar, Herbert, *Britain Alone: June 1940–June 1941* (London: Bodley Head, 1972)

Alanbrooke, Field Marshal Lord, *War Diaries, 1939–1945*, ed. Alex Danchev and Daniel Todman (London: Weidenfeld & Nicolson, 2001)

Alban, J. R., *The 'Three Nights' Blitz': Select Contemporary Reports relating to Swansea's Air Raids of February, 1941* (Swansea: City of Swansea, 1994)

Aldgate, Anthony and Jeffrey Richards, *Britain Can Take It: The British Cinema in the Second World War*, (Edinburgh: Edinburgh University Press, 2nd edn, 1994)

Alford, B. W. E., *W. D. & H. O. Wills and the Development of the UK Tobacco Industry, 1786–1965* (London: Methuen, 1973)

Allingham, Margery, *The Oaken Heart* (London: Michael Joseph, 1941)

Anderson, Verily, *Spam Tomorrow* (London: Rupert Hart-Davis, 1956)

Andrews, Julian, *London War: The Shelter Drawings of Henry Moore* (Aldershot: Lund Humphries, 2002)

Andrews, Maggie, *The Acceptable Face of Feminism: The Women's Institute as a Social Movement* (London: Lawrence & Wishart, 1997)

The Artist as Evacuee: The Royal College of Art in the Lake District 1940–1945 (Grasmere: Wordsworth Trust, 1987)

Atkin, Ronald, *Pillar of Fire: Dunkirk, 1940* (London: Sidgwick & Jackson, 1990)

Attfield, Judy (ed.), *Utility Reassessed: The Role of Ethics in the Practice of Design* (Manchester: Manchester University Press, 1999)

Auden, W. H., *Collected Shorter Poems, 1927–1957* (London: Faber & Faber, 1966)

Babington Smith, Constance, *Evidence in Camera: The Story of Photographic Intelligence in World War II* (London: Chatto & Windus, 1958)

Balchin, Nigel, *The Small Back Room* (1943; London: Cassell, 2000)

Banger, Joan, *Norwich at War* (Norwich: Wensum Books, 1974)

Barker, Rachel, *Conscience, Government and War: Conscientious Objectors in Britain, 1939–1945* (London: Routledge, 1982)

Baring, Norah, *A Friendly Hearth* (London: Jonathan Cape, 1946)

Barnett House Study Group, *London Children in Wartime Oxford: A Survey of Social and Educational Results of Evacuation* (Oxford: Oxford University Press, 1947)

Barton, Brian, *The Blitz: Belfast in the War Years* (Belfast: The Blackstaff Press, 1989)

Barton, Brian, *Northern Ireland in the Second World War* (Belfast: Ulster Historical Foundation, 1995)

The Battle of the Atlantic (London: HMSO, 1946)

Bates, H. E., *Flying-Bombs over England* (Westerham, Kent: Froglets Publications Ltd, 1994)

Beardmore, George, *Civilian at War: Journals, 1938–1946* (London: John Murray, 1964)

Beaton, Cecil, *The Years Between: Diaries 1939–44* (London: Weidenfeld & Nicolson, 1965)

Beauman, Katherine Bentley, *Green Sleeves: The Story of WVS/WRVS* (London: Seeley Service, 1977)

Beckett, Francis, *Enemy Within: The Rise and Fall of the British Communist Party* (London: Merlin Press, 1995)

Beckles, Gordon, *Birth of a Spitfire: The Story of Beaverbrook's Ministry* (London: Collins, 1941)

Bell, George, *The Church and Humanity, 1939–1946* (London: Longman, 1946)

Bell, P. M. H., *John Bull and the Bear: British Public Opinion, Foreign Policy and the Soviet Union, 1941–1945* (London: Edward Arnold, 1990)

Bell, Reginald, *Bull's Eye* (London: Cassell, 1943)

Belsey, James, and Helen Reid, *West at War* (Bristol: Redcliffe Press, 1990)

Betjeman, John, *Letters Volume I: 1926 to 1951*, ed. Candida Lycett-Green (London: Methuen, 1994)

Beveridge, William, *Social Insurance and Allied Services: Report by Sir William Beveridge*, Cmnd 6404 (London: HMSO, 1942)

The Bickersteth Family World War II Diary: Dear Grandmother: Volume I, 1939–1942, (ed.) Nick Smart (Lampeter: The Edwin Mellen Press, 1999)

Bielenberg, Christina, *The Past is Myself* (London: Chatto & Windus, 1985)

Bishop, James, *Illustrated London News History of the First World War* (London: Angus & Robertson, 1982)

Blake, John W., *Northern Ireland in the Second World War* (London: HMSO, 1956)

Blake, Robert, and William Roger Louis (eds), *Churchill* (Oxford: Oxford University Press, 1993)

Blishen, Edward, *A Cack–Handed War* (London: Thames & Hudson, 1972)

Bloom, Ursula, *War Isn't Wonderful* (London: Hutchinson, 1961)

Bond, Brian, *British Military Policy between the Two World Wars* (Oxford: Clarendon Press, 1980)

Boston, Anne (ed.), *Wave Me Goodbye: Stories of the Second World War* (London: Virago, 1988)

Bousquet, Ben and Colin Douglas, *West Indian Women at War: British Racism in World War II* (London: Lawrence & Wishart, 1991)

Bowen, Elizabeth, *The Heat of the Day* (1948; London: Vintage, 1998)

Bowen, Elizabeth, *Collected Impressions* (London: Longman, 1950)

Bowker, Gordon, *George Orwell* (London: Little Brown, 2003)

Boyd, William (ed.), *Evacuation in Scotland: A Record of Events and Experiments* (Bickley, Kent: University of London Press, 1944)

Bradford, Sarah, *George VI* (London: Weidenfeld & Nicolson, 1989)

Bradley, General Omar N., *A General's Life* (London: Sidgwick & Jackson, 1982)

Brand, Chistianna, *Green for Danger*, (1944; San Diego: University of California, 1978)

Branson, Noreen, *History of the Communist Party of Great Britain 1941–1951* (London: Gollancz, 1957)

Branson, Noreen, *History of the Communist Party of Great Britain 1941–1951* (London: Lawrence & Wishart, 1997)

Branson, Noreen, and Margot Heinemann, *Britain in the Nineteen Thirties* (London: Weidenfeld & Nicolson, 1971)

Branson, Noreen, *History of the Communist Party of Great Britain, 1927–1941* (London: Lawrence & Wishart, 1985)

Braybon, Gail, and Penny Summerfield, *Out of the Cage: Women's Experience in Two World Wars* (London: Pandora, 1987)

Brendon, Piers and Philip Whitehead, *The Windsors: A Dynasty Revealed* (London: Hodder & Stoughton, 1994)

Briggs, Asa, *The History of Broadcasting in the UK, Volume III: The War of Words* (Oxford: Oxford University Press, 1970)

Briggs, Asa, *Go To It! Working for Victory on the Home Front 1939–1945* (London: Mitchell Beazley, 2000)

Briggs, Susan, *Keep Smiling Through: The Home Front 1949–1945* (London: Weidenfeld & Nicolson, 1975)

Brittain, Vera, *England's Hour* (London: Macmillan, 1941)

Brittain, Vera, *Testament of Experience: An Autobiographical Story of the Years 1925–1950* (London: Gollancz, 1957)

Brittain, Vera, *Wartime Chronicle: Vera Brittain's Diary, 1939–1945*, ed. Alan Bishop and Y. Aleksandra Bennett (London: Gollancz, 1989)

Britten, Benjamin, *Letters from a Life: Selected Letters and Diaries of Benjamin Britten, Volume II, 1939–1945*, eds Donald Mitchell and Philip Reed (London: Faber & Faber, 1991)

Brivati, Brian, and Harriet Jones (eds), *What Difference Did the War Make?* (Leicester: Leicester University Press, 1993)

Brophy, John, *Britain Needs Books* (London: National Book Council, 1942)

Brown, Lieutenant John Mason, *Many a Watchful Night* (New York: Whittlesey House, 1944)

Brown, Malcolm, and Patricia Meehan, *Scapa Flow: the Story of Britain's Greatest Naval Anchorage in Two World Wars* (1968; London: Pan Books, 2002)

Brown, Mike, *Put That Light Out! Britain's Civil Defence Services at War 1939–1945* (Stroud: Sutton Publishing, 1999)

Brown, Mike, *Evacuees: Evacuation in Wartime Britain, 1939–1945* (Stroud: Sutton Publishing, 2000)

Bruley, Sue (ed.), *Working for Victory: A Diary of Life in a Second World War Factory* (Stroud: Sutton Publishing, 2001)

Bryant, Arthur, *Liquid History: To Commemorate Fifty Years of the Port of London Authority* (London: Port of London Authority, 1960)

Bryher, Winifred, *The Days of Mars: A Memoir 1940–1946* (London: Calder and Boyars, 1972)

Bull, Angela, *Noel Streatfield: A Biography* (London: Collins, 1984)

Bullock, Alan, *Ernest Bevin: A Biography*, (1960–83; abridged London: Politico's Publishing, 2002)

Burlingham, Dorothy, and Anna Freud, *Young Children in Wartime: A Year's Work in a Residential War Nursery* (London: George Allen & Unwin, 1942)

Cadogan, Sir Alexander, *The Diaries of Sir Alexander Cadogan OM, 1938–1945*, ed. David Dilks (London: Cassell, 1971)

Calder, Angus, *The People's War* (London: Jonathan Cape, 1969)

Calder, Angus, *The Myth of the Blitz* (London: Jonathan Cape, 1991)

Calder, Angus, and Dorothy Sheridan (eds), *Speak for Yourself: A Mass-Observation Anthology, 1937–49* (London: Jonathan Cape, 1984)

Calder, Ritchie, *Carry On London* (London: The English Universities Press, 1941)

Calder, Ritchie, *The Lessons of London* (London: Secker & Warburg, 1941)

Calvert, Dorothy, *Bull, Battledress, Lanyard and Lipstick* (London, New Horizon, 1978)

Cannadine, David (ed.), *Blood, Toil, Tears and Sweat: The Speeches of Winston Churchill* (London: Cassell, 1989)

Capa, Robert, *Images of War* (London: Paul Hamlyn, 1964)

Captain 'X', *A Soldier Looks Ahead* (London, George Routledge & Sons, 1944)

Carpenter, Humphrey, *Benjamin Britten: A Biography* (London: Faber & Faber, 1992)

Carroll, Joseph T., *Ireland in the War Years: 1939–1945* (Newton Abbot: David & Charles, 1975)

Cartland, Barbara, *The Years of Opportunity 1939–1945* (London: Hutchinson, 1948)

'Cato', *Guilty Men* (London: Gollancz, 1940)

Cawthon, Charles R., *Other Clay: A Remembrance of the the World War II Infantry* (Colorado: University of Colorado Press, 1990)

CC41: Utility Fashion and Furniture, 1941–1951 (London: Geffrye Museum Trust, 1995)

Ceadel, Martin, *Pacifism in Britain, 1914–1945: The Defining of a Faith* (Oxford: Clarendon Press, 1980)

Cesarani, David, and Tony Kushner (eds), *The Internment of Aliens in Twentieth-Century Britain* (London: Frank Cass, 1993)

Chandos, Viscount (Oliver Lyttelton), *The Memoirs of Lord Chandos* (London: Bodley Head, 1962)

Channon, Sir Henry, *Chips: The Diaries of Sir Henry Channon*, ed. Robert Rhodes James (London: Weidenfeld & Nicolson, 1967)

Churchill, Winston S., *The Second World War*
    Volume I: The Gathering Storm (London: Cassell, 1948)
    Volume II: Their Finest Hour (London: Cassell, 1949)
    Volume III: The Grand Alliance (London: Cassell, 1950)
    Volume IV: The Hinge of Fate (London: Cassell, 1951)
    Volume V: Closing the Ring (London: Cassell, 1952)
    Volume VI: Triumph and Tragedy (London: Cassell, 1954)

Churchill, Winston S., *The Second World War* (London: Cassell, 1959),

Churchill's Prisoners: The Italians in Orkney, 1942–1944 (Kirkwall, Orkney: Wireless Museum, 1987)

Clark, Kenneth, *The Other Half: A Self Portrait* (London: John Murray, 1977)

Clarke, Peter, *Hope and Glory: Britain 1900–1990* (London: Allen Lane, 1996)

Clarke, Peter, *The Cripps Version: The Life of Sir Stafford Cripps, 1889–1952* (London: Allen Lane, 2002)

Clayton, Tim, and Phil Craig, *Finest Hour* (London: Hodder & Stoughton, 1999)

Cockburn, Claud, *Crossing the Line* (London: MacGibbon & Kee, 1959)

Cole, J. A., *Lord Haw Haw and William Joyce: The Full Story* (London: Faber & Faber, 1964)

Colenbrander, Joanna, *A Portrait of Fryn: A Biography of F. Tennyson Jesse* (London, André Deutsch, 1984)

Collier, Basil, *The Defence of the United Kingdom* (London: HMSO, 1957)

Collier, Basil, *The Battle of the V-Weapons, 1944–1945* (London: Hodder & Stoughton, 1964)

Colpi, Terry, *The Italian Factor: The Italian Community in Great Britain* (Edinburgh: Mainstream Publishing, 1991)

Colville, John, *The Fringes of Power: 10 Downing Street Diaries, 1939–1955* (London: Hodder & Stoughton, 1985)

Connelly, Mark, *Reach for the Stars: A New History of Bomber Command in World War II* (London: I. B. Tauris, 2001)

Coogan, Tim Pat, *The IRA* (1995; London: HarperCollins, 2000)

Cooper, Diana, *Trumpets from the Steep* (London: Rupert Hart Davis, 1960)

Corbishley, Gill, *Ration Book Recipes: Some Food Facts, 1939–1954* (London: English Heritage, 1990)

Cowles, Virginia, *Looking for Trouble: An account of the author's experiences as a journalist in various countries, 1937–1940* (London: Hamish Hamilton, 1941)

Crang, Jeremy A., *The British Army and the People's War* (Manchester: Manchester University Press, 2000)

Crick, Bernard, *George Orwell: A Life* (London: Secker & Warburg, 1980)

Crisp, Quentin, *The Naked Civil Servant* (London: Jonathan Cape, 1968)

Crompton, Richmal, *William and the Evacuees* (London: George Newnes, 1940)

Crosby, Travis L., *The Impact of Civilian Evacuation in the Second World War* (Beckenham, Kent: Croom Helm, 1986)

Cross, Colin, *The Fascists in Britain* (London: Barrie & Rockwell, 1961)

Crouch, David, and Colin Ward, *The Allotment: its Landscape and Culture* (London: Faber & Faber, 1988)

Crowther, J. G. and R. Whiddington, *Science at War* (London: HMSO, 1947)

Cull, Nicholas, *Selling War: The British Propaganda Campaign Against American 'Neutrality' in World War II* (Oxford: Oxford University Press, 1995)

Culme-Seymour, Angela, *Bolter's Grand-daughter* (Oxford: Bird Island Press, 2001)

Cunningham, Valentine, *British Writers of the Thirties* (Oxford: Oxford University Press, 1998)

Curran, James, and Jean Seaton, *Power Without Responsibility: The Press and Broadcasting in Britain* (London: Routledge, 4th edn 1991)

Dalley, Jan, *Diana Mosley: A Life* (London: Faber & Faber, 1999)

Dalton, Hugh, *The Fateful Years: Memoirs 1931–1945* (London: F. Muller, 1957)

Dalton, Hugh, *The Political Diary of Hugh Dalton: 1918–40, 1945–60*, ed. Ben Pimlott (London: Jonathan Cape, 1986)

Darwin, Bernard, *War on the Line* (1946; Midhurst, West Sussex: Middleton Press, 1984)

David, Hugh, *The Fitzrovians: A Portrait of Bohemian Society, 1900–1955* (London: Michael Joseph, 1988)

Davies, D. Hwyel, *The Welsh Nationalist Party 1925–1945: A Call to Nationhood* (Cardiff: University of Wales Press, 1983)

Davies, Jennifer, *The Wartime Kitchen Garden: The Home Front 1939–45* (London: BBC Books, 1993)

Davin, Dan, *Night Attack: Short Stories from the Second World War* (Oxford: Oxford University Press, 1982)

Day, David, *The Bevin Boy* (Kineton, Warwickshire: The Roundwood Press, 1975)

Day-Lewis, Cecil, *World All Over* (London: Jonathan Cape, 1943)

Dean, Basil, *Mind's Eye: An Autobiography, 1927–1972* (London: Hutchinson, 1973)

Dear, I. C. B. and M. R. D. Foot (eds), *The Oxford Companion to the Second World War* (Oxford: Oxford University Press, 1995)

Deighton, Len, *Fighter: The True Story of the Battle of Britain* (London: Macmillan, 1940)

Delafield, E. M., *The Provincial Lady in Wartime* (London: Jonathan Cape, 1977)

Dennis, Peter, *The Territorial Army, 1907–1940* (London: The Royal Historical Society, 1987)

D'Este, Carlo, *Eisenhower: A Soldier's Life* (New York: Henry Holt, 2002)

Dewey, Peter, *War and Progress: Britain 1914–1945* (Harlow: Longman, 1997)

Dike, John, *Bristol Blitz Diary* (Bristol: Redcliffe Press, 1982)

Dimbleby, David, and David Reynolds, *An Ocean Apart: The Relationship Between Britain and America in the Twentieth Century* (London: BBC Books and Hodder & Stoughton, 1988)

Doherty, Martin, *Nazi Wireless Propaganda: Lord Haw Haw and British Public Opinion in the Second World War* (Edinburgh: Edinburgh University Press, 2000)

Doherty, Richard, *Irish Men and Women in the Second World War* (Dublin: Four Courts Press, 1999)

Domvile, Admiral Sir Barry, *By and Large* (London: Hutchinson, 1936)

Domvile, Admiral Sir Barry, *From Cabin Boy to Admiral* (London: Boswell Publishing, 1947)

Donnelly, Mark, *Britain in the Second World War* (London: Routledge, 1999)

Donnison, David, *The Government of Housing* (Harmondsworth: Penguin, 1967)

Donoghue, Bernard, and G. W. Jones, *Herbert Morrison: Portrait of a Politician* (London: Weidenfeld & Nicolson, 1973)

Dover, Harriet, *Home Front Furniture: British Utility Design 1941–1951* (Aldershot: Scolar Press, 1991)

Einzig, Paul, *In the Centre of Things: The Autobiography of Paul Einzig* (London: Hutchinson, 1960)

Eisenhower, David, *Eisenhower at War, 1943–1945* (London: Collins, 1986)

Ellis, A. William, *Women in War Factories* (London: Gollancz, 1943)

Englander, David, and Tony Mason, *The British Soldier in World War II* (Coventry: Warwick Papers in Social History, 1984)

Escott, Squadron Leader Beryl, *The WAAF: A History of the Women's Auxiliary Air Force in the Second World War* (Princes Risborough, Buckinghamshire: Shire Publications, 2003)

Faulkes, Sebastian, *The Fatal Englishmen: Three Short Lives* (London: Hutchinson, 1996)

Faviell, Frances, *Chelsea Concerto* (London: Cassell, 1959)

Felton, Monica, *Civilian Supplies in Wartime Britain* (1945; London: Imperial War Museum, 1997)

Ferguson, Margaret, *Our Evacuee* (Oswestry, Shropshire: Oswestry Heritage Centre, 1995)

Ferguson, Sheila, and Hilde Fitzgerald, *Studies in the Social Services* (London: HMSO, 1954)

Fethney, Michael, *The Absurd and the Brave* (Lewes: The Book Guild, 1990)

Fighting with Figures: A Statistical Digest of the Second World War (London: Central Statistics Office, 1995)

Fielding, Steven, Peter Thompson and Nick Tiratsoo, *'England Arise!': The Labour Party and Popular Politics in 1940's Britain* (Manchester: Manchester University Press, 1995)

Firebrace, Commander Sir Aylmer, *Fire Service Memories* (London: Andrew Melrose, 1949)

Fisk, Robert, *In Time of War: Ireland, Ulster and the Price of Neutrality, 1939–45* (London: André Deutsch, 1983)

Fitzgibbon, Constantine, *The Life of Dylan Thomas* (London: Dent, 1965)

FitzGibbon, Theodora, *With Love: An Autobiography, 1938–46* (London: Century Publishing, 1982)

Foster, R. F., *Modern Ireland, 1600–1972* (London: Allen Lane, 1988)

'Fougasse' (Cyril Kenneth Bird), *The Changing Face of Britain* (London: Methuen, 1940)

Frankland, Noble, *History at War: The Campaigns of a Historian* (London: Giles de la Mare, 1988)

Fraser, Sir David, *And We Shall Shock Them: The British Army and the Second World War* (London: Hodder & Stoughton, 1983)

Fraser, Derek, *The Evolution of the British Welfare State: A History of Social Policy since the Industrial Revolution* (Basingstoke: Macmillan, 3rd edn 2003)

Freedman, Jean R., *Whistling in the Dark: Memory and Culture in Wartime London* (Lexington, Kentucky: Kentucky University Press, 1999)

Freeman, Roger, *Airfields of the Eighth: Then and Now* (London: After the Battle, 6th edn 1992)

French, David, *Raising Churchill's Army: The British Army and the War Against Germany, 1919–1945* (Oxford: Oxford University Press, 2000)

Front Line, 1940–41: The Official Story of the Civil Defence of Britain (London: Ministry of Information, 1942)

Fussell, Paul, *Wartime: Understanding and Behaviour in the Second World War* (Oxford: Oxford University Press, 1989)

Gale, John, *Clean Young Englishman* (London: Hodder & Stoughton, 1965)

Gardiner, Juliet, *Over Here: The GIs in Wartime Britain* (London: Collins & Brown, 1992)

Gardiner, Juliet, *Picture Post Women* (London: Collins & Brown, 1993)

Gardiner, Juliet, *D–Day: Those Who Were There* (London: Collins & Brown, 1994)

Gardiner, Juliet, *The 1940s House* (London: Channel 4 Books, 2000)

Gardner, Brian (arr.), *The Terrible Rain: The War Poets, 1939–1945: An Anthology* (London: Methuen, 1966)

Gayford, Eily, *The Amateur Boatwoman: Canal Boating, 1941–1945* (Newton Abbot: David & Charles, 1973)

Geraghty, T., *A North East Coast Town: Ordeal and Triumph: The Story of Kingston Upon Hull in the 1939–1945 Great War* (1951; Hull: Hull Academic Press, 2002)

Gilbert, Martin, *Finest Hour: Winston S. Churchill, 1939–1941* (London: Heinemann, 1983)

Gilbert, Martin, *Road to Victory: Winston S. Churchill, 1941–1945* (London: Heinemann, 1986)

Gilbert, Martin, *Never Despair: Winston S. Churchill, 1945–1965* (London: Heinemann, 1988)

Gilbert, Martin, *Second World War* (London: Weidenfeld & Nicolson, 1989)

Gilbert, Martin, *The First World War: A Complete History* (London: Weidenfeld & Nicolson, 1994)

Gilbert, Martin, *The Day the War Ended: May 8, 1945 Victory in Europe* (London: HarperCollins, 1995)

Gill, Peter, *Cheltenham at War* (Stroud: Alan Sutton, 1994)

Gillman, Peter, and Leni Gillman, *Collar the Lot: How Britain Interned and Expelled its Wartime Refugees* (London: Quartet Books, 1980)

Girvin, Brian, and Geoffrey Roberts (eds), *Ireland and the Second World War: Politics, Society and Remembrance* (Dublin: Four Courts Press, 2000)

Glass, Fiona, and Philip Marsden-Smedley (eds), *Articles of War: The Spectator Book of World War II* (London: Grafton Books, 1989)

Gledhill, Christine, and Gillian Swanson (eds), *Nationalising Femininity: Culture, Sexuality and British cinema in the Second World War* (Manchester: Manchester University Press, 1996)

Glendenning, Victoria, *Elizabeth Bowen: Portrait of a Writer* (London: Weidenfeld & Nicolson, 1977)

Glover, Michael, *Invasion Scare, 1940* (London: Leo Cooper, 1990)

Golden, Jennifer, *Hackney at War* (Stroud: Alan Sutton Publishing, 1995)

Gordon, Jane, *Married to Charles* (London: Heinemann, 1950)

Gorham, Maurice, *Sound and Fury: Twenty-One Years at the BBC* (London: Percival Marshall, 1948)

Gottlieb, Julie V., *Feminine Fascism: Women in Britain's Fascist Movement* (London: I. B. Tauris, 2003)

Grafton, Pete, *You, You and You: The People Out of Step with World War II* (London: Pluto Press, 1981)

Graham, Malcolm, *Oxfordshire at War* (Stroud: Alan Sutton Publishing, 1994)

Graham, Virginia, *Consider the Years, 1938–1946* (1946; London: Persephone Books, 2000)

Graham, Ysenda Maxtone, *The Real Mrs Miniver: Jan Struther's Story* (London: John Murray, 2001)

Graves, Charles, *The Home Guard of Britain: A Comprehensive History of the Home Guard Movement, 1940–1943* (London: Hutchinson, 1943)

Graves, Charles, *Women in Green: The Story of the WVS in Wartime* (London: Heinemann, 1948)

Green, Henry, *Caught* (1943; London: The Harvill Press, 2001)

Greene, Graham *The Ministry of Fear: An Entertainment* (London: Heinemann, 1943)

Greening, Jocelyn, *The Way We Were* (Upton-upon-Severn, Worcestershire: The Self-Publishing Association, 1991)

Gregg, John, *The Shelter of the Tubes: Tube Sheltering in Wartime London* (Harrow: Capital Transport Publishing, 2001)

Grenfell, Joyce, *Darling Ma: Letters to Her Mother, 1932–1944*, ed. James Roose-Evans (London: Hodder & Stoughton, 1988)

Griffiths, Richard, *Fellow Travellers of the Right: British Enthusiasts for Nazi Germany* (London: Constable, 1980)

Guinness, Jonathan with Catherine Guinness, *The House of Mitford* (London: Hutchinson, 1984)

Hadley, Peter, *Third Class to Dunkirk* (London: Hollis and Carter, 1944)

Haldane, J. B. S., *A.R.P.* (London: Gollancz, 1938)

Hale, Edwin R.W., and John Frayn Turner (eds), *The Yanks Are Coming* (Tunbridge Wells, Kent: Midas Books, 1983)

Hambley, John A. S., *London Transport Buses and Coaches, 1939–1945* (London: Images in conjunction with J. A. S. Hambley, 1995)

Hamilton, Nigel, *Montgomery*
    Volume I: The Making of a General 1887–1942 (London: Hamish Hamilton, 1981)
    Volume II: Master of the Battlefield 1942–1944 (London: Hamish Hamilton, 1983)
    Volume III: The Field Marshall 1944–1976 (London: Hamish Hamilton, 1986)

Hamilton, Nigel, *The Full Monty: Montgomery of Alamein, 1887–1942* (London: Allen Lane, 2001)

Hammerton, Sir John, and Major-General Sir Charles Gwynn (eds), *The Second Great War: A Standard History* (London: The Amalgamated Press, 1939–46)

Hammond, R. J., *Food* (London: HMSO, 1951–1962)

Hampton, Janie, *Joyce Grenfell* (London: John Murray, 2002)

Hancock, W. K., and M. M. Gowing, *British War Economy* (London: HMSO, 1951)

Hargreaves, E. L., and Margaret Gowing, *Civil Industry and Trade* (London: HMSO, 1952)

Harman, Nicholas, *Dunkirk: The Necessary Myth* (London: Hodder & Stoughton, 1980)

Harries, Meirion, and Susie Harries, *The War Artists: British Official War Art of the Twentieth Century* (London: Michael Joseph, 1988)

Harriman, J. Averell, and Elie Able, *Special Envoy to Churchill and Stalin, 1941–1946* (London: Hutchinson, 1976)

Harris, Arthur, *Bomber Offensive* (London: Collins, 1947)

Harris, Carol, *Women at War, 1939–1945: The Home Front* (Stroud: Sutton Publishing, 2000)

Harris, Carol, *Women at War in Uniform* (Stroud: Sutton Publishing, 2003)

Harrisson, Tom, *Living through the Blitz,* (London: Collins, 1976)

Harrisson, Tom and Charles Madge (arr.), *Britain by Mass-Observation* (1939; London. The Cresset Library, 1986)

Haskell, Arnold L. and Dilys Powell, Rollo Myers and Robin Ironside, *Since 1939 (1): Ballet, Films, Music, Painting* (London: Phoenix House by arrangement with the British Council, 1948)

Hartley, Jenny, *Millions Like Us: Women's Fiction of the Second World War* (London: Virago, 1984)

Hartley, Jenny (ed.), *Hearts Undefeated: Women's Writing of the Second World War* (London: Virago, 1994)

Haste, Cate, *Rules of Desire: Sex in Britain, World War One to the Present* (London: Pimlico, 1992)

Hastings, Selina, *Evelyn Waugh: A Biography* (London: Sinclair-Stevenson, 1994)

Haugland, Vern, *The Eagle Squadrons: Yanks in the RAF* (New York: Ziff Davis, 1979)

Hayes, Denis, *Challenge of Conscience* (London: Allen & Unwin, 1949)

Hayes, Nick, and Jeff Hill (eds), *Millions Like Us: British Culture in the Second World War* (Liverpool: Liverpool University Press, 1999)

Heimann, Judith, *The Most Offending Soul Alive: Tom Harrisson and his Remarkable Life* (London: Aurum Press, 2002)

Hennessy, Peter, *Never Again: Britain 1945–1951* (London: Jonathan Cape, 1992)

Henry, Stuart (ed.), *Can I Have it in Cash? A Study of Informal Institutions and Unorthodox Ways of Doing Things* (London: Astragal, 1981)

Henson, Herbert Hensley, *Retrospective on an Unimportant Life* (Oxford: Oxford University Press, 1950)

Heppenstall, Rayner, *The Lesser Infortune* (London: Jonathan Cape, 1953)

Hewison, Robert, *Under Siege: Literary Life in London, 1939–45* (Oxford: Oxford University Press, 1977)

Hickman, Tom, *What Did You Do In The War, Auntie?* (London: BBC Books, 1995)

Hill, Heywood and Anne Hill, *A Bookseller's War*, ed. Jonathan Gathorne-Hardy (Norwich: Michael Russell, 1997)

Hillary, Richard, *The Last Enemy* (London: Macmillan, 1942)

Hillier, Bevis, *John Betjeman: New Fame, New Love* (London: John Murray, 2002)

Hinsley, F. H., and C. A. G. Simkins, *British Intelligence in the Second World War, Volume IV: Security and Counter Intelligence* (London: HMSO, 1990)

Hinton, James, *Shop Floor Citizens: Engineering Democracy in 1940s Britain* (Cheltenham: Edward Elgar, 1994)

Hinton, James, *Women, Social Leadership and the Second World War: Continuities of Class* (Oxford: Oxford University Press, 2002)

Hodgson, Vere, *Few Eggs and No Oranges: The Diaries of Vere Hodgson, 1940–45* (1971; London: Persephone Books, 1999)

Holland, Steve, *The Mushroom Jungle* (Westbury, Wiltshire: Zeon Books, 1993)

Hopkinson, Tom, *Of This Our Time: A Journalist's Story, 1905–50* (London: Hutchinson, 1982)

Hough, Richard, and Denis Richards, *The Battle of Britain* (London: Penguin, 2001)

Howard, Elizabeth Jane, *Slipstream: A Memoir* (London: Macmillan, 2002)

Huggett, Frank E., *Goodnight Sweetheart: Songs and Memories of the Second World War* (London: W. H. Allen, 1979)

Humphries, Steve, and Pamela Gordon, *A Labour of Love: The Experiences of Parenthood in Britain, 1900–1950* (London: Sidgwick & Jackson, 1993)

Hustvedt, Siri, *What I Loved* (London: Sceptre, 2003)

Hyde, Montgomery H., *Norman Birkett: The Life of Lord Birkett of Ulverston* (London: Hamish Hamilton, 1964)

Hylton, Stuart, *The Darkest Hour: The Hidden History of the Home Front, 1939–1945* (Stroud: Sutton Publishing, 2001)

Hyndman, Oonagh (comp.), *Wartime Kent: A Selection of Memories from the BBC Kent Series* (Rainham, Kent: Meresborough Books, 1990)

'Impresario', *The Market Square: the Story of the Food Ration Book, 1940–1944* (1944; London: Imperial War Museum, 1997)

Inglis, Ruth, *The Children's War: Evacuation 1939–1945* (London: Collins, 1989)

Inman, P., *Labour in the Munitions Industries* (London: HMSO, 1957)

Ironside, General Sir Edmund, *The Ironside Diaries, 1937–1940*, ed. R. Macleod and D. Kelly (London: Constable, 1962)

Isaacs, Susan (ed.), *The Cambridge Evacuation Surveys: A Wartime Study in Social Welfare and Education* (London: Methuen, 1941)

Ismay, Lord, *The Memoirs of General the Lord Ismay* (London: Heinemann, 1960)

Jackson, Carlton, *Who Will Take Our Children?* (London: Methuen, 1985)

Jappy, M. J., *Danger UXB: The Remarkable Story of the Disposal of Unexploded Bombs During the Second World War* (London: Channel 4 Books, 2001)

Jasper, Ronald, *George Bell, Bishop of Chichester* (Oxford: Oxford University Press, 1967)

Jeffery, Tom, *Mass-Observation: A short history*, Occasional Paper No 10 (Falmer, Sussex: University of Sussex Library, 1999)

Jeffrey, Andrew, *Present Emergency: Edinburgh, the River Forth and South-East Scotland and the Second World War* (Edinburgh: Mainstream Publishing, 1992)

Jenkins, David Fraser, *John Piper: The Forties* (London: Philip Wilson/Imperial War Museum, 2000)

Jesse, F. Tennyson and H. M. Harwood etc., *London Front: Letters Written to America, August 1939–July 1940* (London: Constable, 1940)

Johnson, B. S., *The Evacuees* (London: Gollancz, 1968)

Jones, R. V., *Most Secret War: British Scientific Intelligence, 1939–45* (London: Hamish Hamilton, 1978)

Jordan, Heather Bryant, *How Will the Heart Endure: Elizabeth Bowen and the Landscape of War* (Ann Arbor: University of Michigan Press, 1992)

Kaplan, Philip and Richard Collier, *The Few: Summer 1940, The Battle of Britain* (London: Blandford, 1989)

Katin, Zelma, *'Clippie': The Autobiography of a Wartime Conductress* (London: John Gifford, 1944)

Kavanagh, Ted, *Tommy Handley* (London: Hodder & Stoughton, 1949)

Kee, Robert, *The World We Left Behind: A Chronicle of the Year 1939* (London: Weidenfeld & Nicolson, 1984)

Kee, Robert, *The World We Fought For* (London: Hamish Hamilton, 1985)

Keegan, John, *Six Armies in Normandy: From D-Day to the Liberation of Paris* (Harmondsworth: Penguin, 1983)

Keegan, John, *The Second World War* (London: Hutchinson, 1989)

Kenny, Mary, *Germany Calling: A Personal Biography of William Joyce, 'Lord Haw Haw'* (Dublin: New Island, 2003)

Kershaw, Ian, *Hitler 1936–1945: Nemesis* (London: Allen Lane, 2000)

Keynes, John Maynard, *The Collected Writings of John Maynard Keynes, Volume XXII Activities 1939–45: Internal War Finance*, ed. Donald Moggeridge (Cambridge: Cambridge University Press, 1978)

King, Cecil, *With Malice Towards None: A War Diary*, ed. William Armstrong (London: Sidgwick & Jackson, 1970)

King, James, *Interior Landscapes: A Life of Paul Nash* (London: Weidenfeld & Nicolson, 1987)

Kirkham, Pat, and David Thoms (eds), *War Culture: Social Change and Changing Experience in World War Two* (London: Lawrence & Wishart, 1995)

Kirkup, James, *I, of All People: An Autobiography of Youth* (London: Weidenfeld & Nicolson, 1988)

Knight, Dennis, *Harvest of Messerschmitts: The Chronicle of a Village at War, 1940* (London: Frederick Warne, 1981)

Knowles, Bernard, *Southampton: The English Gateway* (London: Hutchinson, 1951)

Kohan, C. M., *Works and Buildings* (London: HMSO, 1952)

Kops, Bernard, *The World is a Wedding* (London: MacGibbon and Kee, 1963)

Kushner, Tony, *The Persistence of Prejudice: Anti-Semitism in British Society During the Second World War* (Manchester: Manchester University Press, 1989)

Kynaston, David, *The City of London, Volume III: Illusions of Gold 1914–1945* (London: Chatto & Windus, 1999)

Lafitte, François, *The Internment of Aliens* (Harmondsworth: Penguin, 1940)

Laity, Paul (ed.), *Left Book Club Anthology* (London: Gollancz, 2001)

Lampe, David, *The Last Ditch: The Secrets of the Nationwide British Resistance Organisation and the Nazi Plans for the Invasion of Britain, 1940–1944* (London: Cassell, 1968)

Last, Nella, *Nella Last's War: A Mother's Diary 1939–45*, ed. Richard Fleming and Suzie Broad (Bristol: Falling Wall Press, 1981)

Laurent, Livia, *A Tale of Internment* (London: George Allen & Unwin, 1942)

Lawlor, Sheila, *Churchill and the Politics of War, 1940–1941* (Cambridge: Cambridge University Press, 1994)

Lee, Jennie, *My Life with Nye* (London: Jonathan Cape, 1980)

Lees-Milne, James, *Ancestral Voices* (London: Chatto & Windus, 1975)

Lees-Milne, James, *Prophesying Peace* (London: Chatto & Windus, 1977)

Lehman, John, *I Am My Brother: Autobiography II* (London: Longman, 1960)

Lejeune, C. A., *Chestnuts in her Lap, 1936–1946* (London: Phoenix House, 1947)

Lewis Cohen Urban Studies Centre, *Brighton Behind the Front: Photographs and Memories of the Second World War* (Brighton: QueenSpark Books, 1990)

Lewis, June R., *The Cotswolds at War* (Stroud: Alan Sutton Publishing, 1992)

Lewis, Peter, *A People's War* (London: Methuen, 1986)

Lewis, Tim, (arr.) *Moonlight Sonata* (Coventry: Tim Lewis and Coventry City Council, 1990)

Lilly, Robert, *La Face Cachée des GIs: les viols commis par des soldats Americains en France, en Angleterre et en Allemagne pendant la Seconde Guerre Mondiale* (Paris: Payot, 2003)

Lindop, Grevel, *Selected Poems* (Manchester: Carcanet, 2000)

Livesey, Anthony, *Are We at War? Letters to the Times, 1939–1945* (London: Times Books, 1989)

Lloyd's War Losses: The Second World War 3 September–14 August 1945 Volume I: British, Allied and Neutral Merchant Vessels Sunk or Destroyed by War Causes (London: Lloyd's of London Press, 1989)

London, Louise, *Whitehall and the Jews, 1933–1948: British Policy and the Holocaust* (Cambridge: Cambridge University Press, 2000)

Longford, Lord (with Thomas P. O'Neil), *Eamon de Valera* (London: Arrow Books, 1974)

Longmate, Norman, *How We Lived Then: A History of Everyday Life during the Second World War* (London: Hutchinson, 1971)

Longmate, Norman, *The Real Dad's Army: The Story of the Home Guard* (London: Arrow Books, 1974)

Longmate, Norman, *The GIs: The Americans in Britain, 1942–1945* (London: Hutchinson, 1975)

Longmate, Norman, *Air Raid: The Bombing of Coventry, 1940* (London: Hutchinson, 1976)

Longmate, Norman, *The Doodlebugs: The Story of the Flying Bombs* (London: Hutchinson, 1981)

Longmate, Norman (ed.), *The Home Front: An Anthology, 1939–1945* (London: Chatto & Windus, 1981)

Lukacs, John, *Five Days in London, May 1940* (New Haven, Connecticut and London: Yale University Press, 1999)

Lynn, Vera, with Robin Cross and Jenny de Gex, *Unsung Heroines: The Women Who Won the War* (London: Sidgwick & Jackson, 1990)

Lysaght, C. E., *Brendan Bracken* (London: Allen Lane, 1979)

MacCarthy, Fiona, *Eric Gill* (London: Faber & Faber, 1989)

MacDougall, Ian (ed.), *Voices from War: Personal recollections of war in our century by Scottish men and women* (Edinburgh: The Mercat Press, 1995)

MacEwen, Malcolm, *The Greening of a Red* (London: Pluto Press, 1991)

MacInnes, C. M., *Bristol at War* (London: Museum Press, 1962)

Mack, Joanna, and Steve Humphries, *The Making of Modern London, 1939–1945: London at War* (London: Sidgwick & Jackson, 1985)

MacKay, Robert, *The Test of War: Inside Britain 1939–45* (London: UCL Press, 1999)

MacKay, Robert, *Half the Battle: Civilian Morale in Britain during the Second World War* (Manchester: Manchester University Press, 2002)

Mackenzie, S. P., *The Home Guard: The Real Story of 'Dad's Army'* (Oxford: Oxford University Press, 1995)

Mackenzie, S. P., *British War Films 1939–1945: The Cinema and the Services* (London: Hambledon, 2001)

MacLaren-Ross, Julian, *Memoirs of the Forties* (London: Alan Ross, 1965)

MacLeish, Archibald, *In Honour of a Man and an Ideal: Three Talks on Freedom* (New York: CBS, 1942)

Macleod, Joseph, *A Job at the BBC: Some Personal Reminiscences* (Glasgow: William McLellan, 1947)

MacNeice, Louis, *Collected Poems of Louis MacNeice* (London: Faber & Faber, 1979)

Manifold, John, *More Poems from the Forces*, ed. K. Rhys (London: Routledge, 1943)

Martland, Peter, *Lord Haw Haw: The English Voice of Nazi Germany* (Richmond, Surrey: The National Archive, 2003)

Marwick, Arthur, *The Home Front: The British and the Second World War* (London: Thames & Hudson, 1976)

Maskelyne, Jasper, *Magic – Top Secret* (London: Stanley Paul, 1949)

Mass-Observation, *War Begins at Home* (London: Chatto & Windus, 1940)

Mass-Observation, *People in Production* (Harmondsworth: Penguin Specials, 1942)

Mass-Observation, *War Factory: A Report by Mass-Observation* (London: Gollancz, 1943)

Mass-Observation, *The Journey Home* (London: John Murray, 1944)

Matless, David, *Landscape and Englishness* (London: Reaktion Books, 1998)

Matthews, The Very Rev. W. R., *St Paul's Cathedral in Wartime, 1939–1945* (London: Hutchinson, 1946)

Mayhew, Patricia (ed.), *One Family's War* (London: Hutchinson, 1985)

McAleer, Joseph, *Popular Reading and Publishing in Britain, 1914–50* (Oxford: Clarendon Press, 1992)

McCamley, N. J., *Secret Underground Cities* (London: Leo Cooper, 1998)

McCamley, N. J., *Saving Britain's Art Treasures* (London: Leo Cooper/Pen and Sword Books, 2003)

McCarthy, Tony, *War Games: The Story of Sport in World War Two* (London: Queen Anne Press, 1989)

McDowell, Colin, *Forties Fashion and the New Look* (London: Bloomsbury, 1997)

McKendrick, Tom, *Clydebank Blitz* (Glasgow: McNaugton and Sinclair, 1986)

McKibbin, Ross, *Classes and Cultures: England 1918–1951* (Oxford: Oxford University Press, 1998)

McLaine, Ian, *Ministry of Morale: Home Front Morale and the Ministry of Information in World War II* (London: George Allen & Unwin, 1979)

Megarry, Ion, *The YMCA and the Italian Prisoners of War* (Luton: Dragon Press for the World's Alliance of Young Men's Christian Associations, War Prisoners' Aid, Geneva, Switzerland, c. 1946/7)

Milburn, Mrs, *Mrs Milburn's Diaries: An Englishwoman's Day-to-Day Reflections, 1939–45*, ed. Peter Donnelly (London: Harrap, 1979)

Miller, Betty, *On the Side of the Angels* (1945; London: Virago, 1985)

Miller, Betty, *Farewell Leicester Square* (1941; London: Persephone Books, 2000)

Miller, James, *Scapa: Britain's Famous Wartime Naval Base* (Edinburgh: Birlinn, 2000)

Miller, Russell, *Nothing Less Than Victory: The Oral History of D-Day* (London: Michael Joseph, 1993)

Miller, Russell with Renate Miller, *Ten Days in May: The People's Story of VE Day* (London: Michael Joseph, 1995)

Ministry of Labour and National Service, *Report for the Years 1939–1946* (London: HMSO, 1947)

Minns, Rayner, *Bombers and Mash: The Domestic Front 1939–1945* (London: Virago, 1980)

Mitchison, Naomi, *Among You Taking Notes: The Wartime Diaries of Naomi Mitchison, 1939–1945*, ed. Dorothy Sheridan (Oxford: Oxford University Press, 1986)

Mitford, Nancy, *The Letters of Nancy Mitford*, ed. Charlotte Mosley (London: Hodder & Stoughton, 1993)

Montgomery Hyde, H., *Norman Birkett: The Life of Lord Birkett of Ulverston* (London: Hamish Hamilton, 1964)

Moore, Bob and Kent Fedorowich, *Prisoners of War and Their Captors in World War II* (Oxford: Berg, 1996)

Moore, Brian, *The Emperor of Ice Cream* (London: André Deutsch, 1966)

Moorehead, Alan, *Eclipse* (London: Hamish Hamilton, 1946)

Moran, Lord, *Churchill at War 1940–1945* (1966; London: Constable & Robinson, 2002)

Morgan, Dennis, *Cardiff, a City at War* (Cardiff: Dennis Morgan, 1998)

Morgan, Guy, *Red Roses Every Night: An Account of London Cinemas Under Fire* (London: Quality Press, 1948)

Morgan, Kenneth O., *Rebirth of a Nation: Wales, 1880–1980* (Oxford: Oxford University Press, 1981)

Morpurgo, J. E., *Allen Lane: King Penguin* (London: Hutchinson, 1979)

Morrison, Herbert (Lord Morrison of Lambeth), *Herbert Morrison: An Autobiography* (London: Odhams Press, 1960)

Mosley, Diana, *A Life of Contrasts: The Autobiography of Diana Mosley* (London: Hamish Hamilton, 1977)

Mosley, Diana, *Loved Ones: Pen Portraits* (London: Sidgwick & Jackson, 1985)

Mosley, Nicholas, *Beyond the Pale: Sir Oswald Mosley 1933–1980* (London: Secker & Warburg, 1983)

Mosley, Sir Oswald, *My Life* (London: Nelson, 1988)

Mountevans, Admiral Lord, *Adventurous Life* (London: Hutchinson, 1946)

Moynihan, Michael (ed.), *People at War 1939–1945* (Newton Abbot: David & Charles, 1974)

Murray, Keith A.H., *Agriculture* (London: HMSO, 1955)

Murrow, Ed, *This is London* (London: Cassell, 1941)

Nel, Elizabeth, *Mr Churchill's Secretary* (London: Hodder & Stoughton, 1958)

Newton, Eric (ed.), *War Through Artists' Eyes: Paintings and Drawings by British War Artists* (London: John Murray, 1945)

Nicholas, Siân, *The Echo of War: Home Front propaganda and the wartime BBC, 1939–45* (Manchester: Manchester University Press, 1996)

Nicolson, Harold, *Why Britain is at War* (Harmondsworth: Penguin Specials, 1939)

Nicolson, Harold, *The Diaries and Letters of Harold Nicolson, Volume II, The War Years, 1939–45*, ed. Nigel Nicolson (London: Collins, 1967)

Nixon, Barbara, *Raiders Overhead: A Diary of the London Blitz* (London: Scolar Press, 1980)

Noakes, Jeremy (ed.), *The Civilian in War: The Home Front in Europe, Japan and the USA in World War Two* (Exeter: University of Exeter Press, 1992)

Noble, Peter, *British Theatre* (London: British Yearbooks, 1947)

O'Brien, Terence H., *Civil Defence* (London: HMSO, 1955)

O'Halpin, Eunan (ed.), *MI5 and Northern Ireland, 1939–1945: The Official History* (Dublin: Irish Academic Press, 2003)

Once, Catherine (ed.), *Life in Cornwall, 1939–42: Extracts from the 'West Briton' newspaper* (Truro: Truran, 2001)

Orwell, George, *The Road to Wigan Pier* (London: Gollancz, 1937)

Orwell, George, *The Lion and the Unicorn: Socialism and the English Genius* (London: Secker & Warburg, 1941)

Orwell, George, *The Collected Essays, Journalism and Letters of George Orwell*, eds Sonia Orwell and Ian Angus (London: Secker & Warburg, 1968)
> *Volume I: An Age Like This, 1920–1940*
> *Volume II: My Country Right or Left, 1940–1943*
> *Volume III, As I Please, 1943–1945*

Overy, R. J. (Richard), *The Air War, 1939–1945* (London: Europa, 1980)

Overy, Richard, *Why the Allies Won* (London: Jonathan Cape, 1995)

Overy, Richard, *The Battle* (London: Penguin Books, 2000)

Overy, Richard and Andrew Wheatcroft, *The Road to War* (London: Penguin, rev. edn 1999)

Padley, Richard and Margaret Cole (eds), *Evacuation Survey: A Report to the Fabian Society* (London: Routledge, 1940)

Panter-Downes, Mollie, *London War Notes, 1939–1945*, ed. William Shawn (London: Longman, 1972)

Panter-Downes, Mollie, *Good Evening Mrs Craven: The Wartime Stories of Mollie Panter-Downes* (London: Persephone Books, 2002)

Parker, H. M. D., *Manpower: A Study of War-time Policy and Administration* (London: HMSO, 1957)

Parker, Matthew, *The Battle of Britain: July–October 1940* (London: Headline, 2000)

Parker, R. A. C., *Chamberlain and Appeasement: British Policy and the Coming of the Second World War* (Basingstoke: Macmillan, 1993)

Parker, R. A. C., *Churchill and Appeasement* (Basingstoke: Macmillan, 2000)

Parsons, Martin, *I'll Take That One: Dispelling the Myths of Civilian Evacuation, 1939–45* (Peterborough: Beckett and Carlson, 1998)

Parsons, Martin, and Penny Starns, *The Evacuation: The True Story* (London: DSM, 1999)

Partridge, Frances, *A Pacifist's War: Diaries 1939–1945* (London: The Hogarth Press, 1978)

Patten, Marguerite, *We'll Eat Again: A Collection of Recipes from the War Years* (London: Hamlyn, 1985)

Peake, Mervyn, *The Glass Blower* (London: Eyre & Spottiswood, 1950)

Pearson, Joe, *Penguins March On: Books for the Forces during World War II*, Miscellany 11 (London: Penguin Collectors Society, 1996)

Pentelow, Mike, and Marsha Rowe, *Characters of Fitzrovia* (London: Chatto & Windus, 2001)

Perrett, Bryan, *Liverpool: A City at War* (London: Robert Hale, 1990)

Pick, J. B., *Under the Crust* (London: John Lane, 1946)

Pile, General Sir Frederick, *Ack-Ack: Britain's Defence Against Air Attack in the Second World War* (London: Harrap, 1949)

Plaistow, Norman, *Safe as Houses: Wimbledon at War, 1939–1945* (London: The Wimbledon Society, 1972)

Playfair, Jocelyn, *A House in the Country* (1944; London: Persephone Books, 2002)

Pocock, Tom, *1945: The Dawn Came Up Like Thunder* (London: Collins, 1983)

Poems of the Land Army: An Anthology of Verse by Members of the Women's Land Army (London: Imperial War Museum, 1997)

Pollit, Harry, *How to Win the War* (London: Communist Party, 1939)

Powell, Anne (ed.), *Shadows of War: British Women's Poetry of the Second World War* (Stroud: Sutton Publishing, 1999)

Powell, Anthony, *Books Do Furnish a Room* (London: Heinemann, 1971)

Priestley, J. B., *Postscripts* (London: Heinemann, 1940)

Priestley, J. B., *Black-Out in Gretley: A Story of – and for – Wartime* (London: Heinemann, 1942)

Priestley, J. B., *British Women Go to War* (London: Collins, n. d.)

Pritt, D. N., *Choose Your Future* (London: Lawrence & Wishart, 1941)

Pritt, D. N., *The Autobiography of D. N. Pritt, Part I: From Right to Left* (London: Lawrence & Wishart, 1965)

Pudney, John, *London Docks* (London: Thames & Hudson, 1975)

Ramsey, Winston G. (ed.), *The Blitz: Then and Now*
> Volume I: September 1939–September 1940 (London: Battle of Britain Prints International, 1987)
> Volume II: September 1940–May 1941 (London: Battle of Britain Prints International, 1988)
> Volume III: May 1941–May 1945 (London: Battle of Britain Prints International, 1990)

Ravilious, Eric, *Ravilious at War: The Complete Works of Eric Ravilious, September 1939–September 1942*, ed. Anne Ullmann (Huddersfield: Fleece, 2002)

Ray, John, *The Night Blitz* (London: Arms and Armour Press, 1996)

Raymond, Ernest, *Please You Draw Near: Autobiography 1922–1968* (London: Cassell, 1969)

Raymond, Robert S., *A Yank in Bomber Command*, ed. Michael Moynihan (Newton Abbot: David & Charles, 1977)

Reid, Helen, *Bristol Blitz: The Untold Story* (Bristol: Redcliffe Press, 1988)

Reilley, Catherine (ed.), *Chaos of the Night: Women's Poetry and Verse of the Second World War* (London: Virago, 1984)

Reynolds, David, *Rich Relations: The American Occupation of Britain, 1942–1945* (London: HarperCollins, 1995)

Reynolds, Quentin, *Only the Stars are Neutral* (Bath: Chivers, 1977)

Riley, Norman, *999 and All That* (London: Gollancz, 1940)

Ritchie, Charles, *The Siren Years: A Canadian Diplomat Abroad, 1937–1945* (Toronto: Macmillan, 1974)

Roberts, Andrew, *The Holy Fox: The Life of Lord Halifax* (London: Weidenfeld & Nicolson, 1997)

Robertson, Ben, *I Saw England* (London: Jarrolds, 1941)

Robinson, Derek, *A Piece of Cake* (London: Hamish Hamilton, 1983)

Robinson, John, *The Country House at War* (London: Bodley Head, 1989)

Rolf, David, *Prisoners of the Reich: Germany's Captives, 1939–1945* (London: Leo Cooper, 1988)

Roof over Britain: The Official Story of Britain's Anti-Aircraft Defences, 1939–1942 (London: Ministry of Information, 1943)

Rooke, Dennis, and Alan D'Egville, *Call Me Mister! A Guide to Civilian Life for the Newly Mobilised* (London: Heinemann, 1946)

Rose, Sonya O., *Which People's War? National Identity and Citizenship in Wartime Britain, 1939–1945* (Oxford: Oxford University Press, 2003)

Ross, Alan, *Colours of War* (London: Jonathan Cape, 1983)

Rothestein, John, *Modern English Painters, Vol. II* (London: Macdonald, 1984)

Rothnie, Niall, *The Baedeker Blitz: Hitler's Attack on Britain's Historic Cities* (Shepperton, Surrey: Ian Allan Ltd, 1992)

Ruppenthal, Roland G., *Logistical Support of the Armies, Volume I* (Washington DC: Department of the Army, 1953)

'Russell, Sarah', *To Bed With Grand Music* (London: The Pilot Press, 1946)

Sackville-West, Vita, *The Women's Land Army* (London: Michael Joseph, 1944)

Sargant, William, *The Unquiet Mind: The Autobiography of a Physician in Psychological Medicine* (London: Heinemann, 1967)

Schweeitzer, Pam (ed.), *Londoners Remember Living Through the Blitz* (London: Age Concern Publications, n.d.)

Scott, Sir Harold, *Scotland Yard* (Harmondsworth: Penguin Books, 1957)

Scott, Sir Harold, *Your Obedient Servant* (London: André Deutsch, 1959)

Secrest, Meryle, *Kenneth Clark: A Biography* (London: Weidenfeld & Nicolson, 1984)

Seebohm,Caroline, *The Country House: A Wartime History, 1939–1945* (London: Weidenfeld & Nicolson, 1989)

Sevareid, Eric, *Not So Wild a Dream* (New York: Alfred Knopf, 1946)

Shakespeare, Geoffrey, *Let Candles Be Brought In* (London: John Murray, 1949)

Sheean, Vincent, *Between the Thunder and the Sun* (London: Macmillan, 1943)

Shelden, Michael, *Cyril Connolly and the World of Horizon* (London: Hamish Hamilton, 1989)

Shelden, Michael, *Orwell: The Official Biography* (London: Heinemann, 1991)

Shephard, Ben, *A War of Nerves: Soldiers and Psychiatrists, 1914–94* (London: Jonathan Cape, 2000)

Sheridan, Dorothy (ed.), *Wartime Women* (London: Heinemann, 1990)

Shirer, William, *The Rise and Fall of the Third Reich* (New York: Simon & Schuster, 1960)

Shone, Richard, *Rodrigo Moynihan: The End of the Picnic: Paintings and Drawings, 1939–47* (London: Imperial War Museum, 1998)

Simmons, Clifford (ed.), *The Objectors* (Isle of Man: Times Press and Anthony Gibbs and Philips, n.d.)

Simpson, A. W. Brian, *In the Highest Degree Odious: Detention without trial in Wartime Britain* (Oxford: Clarendon Press, 1992)

Sinclair, Andrew, *War Like a Wasp: The Lost Decade of the Forties* (London: Hamish Hamilton, 1989)

Skidelsky, Robert, *Oswald Mosley* (Basingstoke: Macmillan, 1975)

Sladen, Christopher, *The Conscription of Fashion: Utility Cloth, Clothing and Footwear, 1941–1951* (Aldershot: Scolar Press, 1995)

Slater, Eliot, and Moya Woodside, *Patterns of Marriage: A Study of Marriage Relationships in the Urban Working Classes* (London: Cassell, 1951)

Smith, Emma, *Maiden's Trip* (1948; Cleobury Mortimer, Shropshire: M & M Baldwin, 1987)

Smith, Graham, *When Jim Crow Met John Bull: Black American Soldiers in World War II Britain* (London: I. B. Tauris, 1987)

Smith, Harold L. (ed.), *War and Social Change in British Society in the Second World War* (Manchester: Manchester University Press, 1986)

Smith, Harold L. (ed.), *Britain in the Second World War: A Social History* (Manchester: Manchester University Press, 1996)

Smith, Malcolm, *Britain and 1940: History, Myth and Popular Memory* (London: Routledge, 2000)

Smithies, Edward, *Crime in Wartime: A Social History of Crime in World War II* (London: George Allen & Unwin, 1982)

Smithies, Edward, *The Black Economy in England since 1914* (Dublin: Gill & Macmillan, 1984)

Soames, Mary, *Clementine Churchill* (London: Cassell, 1979)

Speaight, Robert and Henry Reed, Stephen Spender and John Hayward, *Since 1939 (2): Drama, the Novel, Poetry, Prose Literature* (London: Phoenix House by arrangement with the British Council, 1949)

Spender, Stephen, 'Introduction' to *War Pictures by British Artists: Second Series no. 4. Air Raids* (Oxford: Oxford University Press, 1943)

Spier, Eugen, *Focus: A Footnote to the History of the Thirties* (London: Oswald Wolff, 1963)

Sponza, Lucio, *Divided Loyalties: Italians in Britain during the Second World War* (Bern, Switzerland: Peter Lang, 2000)

Stacey, C. P., and Barbara M. Wilson, *The Half Million: The Canadians in Britain, 1939–1946* (Toronto: University of Toronto Press, 1987)

Stafford, David, *Ten Days to D-Day: Countdown to the Liberation of Europe* (London: Little, Brown, 2003)

Stagg, James, *Forecast for Overlord* (London: Ian Allen, 1971)

Stahl, P., *The Diving Eagle: A Ju.88 Pilot's Diary*, trans. Alex Vangas-Baginskis (London: Kimber, 1984)

Stammers, Neil, *Civil Liberties in Britain During the Second World War* (Beckenham, Kent: Croom Helm, 1983)

Stanford, Derek, *Inside the Forties: Literary Memoirs, 1937–1957* (London: Sidgwick & Jackson, 1977)

Stansky, Peter and William Abrahams, *London's Burning: Life, Death and Art in the Second World War* (London: Constable, 1994)

Starns, Penny, *Nurses at War: Women on the Frontline, 1939–45* (Stroud: Sutton Publishing, 2000)

Steinberg, Steven, Maurice Sellar and Lou Jones, *You Must Remember This . . . Songs at the Heart of War* (London: Boxtree, 1995)

Stent, Ronald, *A Bespattered Page: The Internment of His Majesty's 'Most Loyal Enemy Aliens'* (London: Andre Deutsch, 1980)

Strachey, John, *Post D* (London: Gollancz, 1941)

Streatfeild, Noel, *Saplings* (1945; London: Persephone Books, 2000)

Struther, Jan, *Mrs Miniver* (1939; London: Virago, 1989)

Summerfield, Penny, *Women Workers in the Second World War* (Beckenham, Kent: Croom Helm, 1984)

Summerfield, Penny, *Reconstructing Women's Wartime Lives: Discourse and Subjectivity in Oral Histories of the Second World War* (Manchester: Manchester University Press, 1998)

Swann, Paul, *The British Documentary Film Movement, 1926–1946* (Cambridge: Cambridge University Press, 1989)

Taylor, A. J. P., *Beaverbrook* (London: Hamish Hamilton, 1972)

Taylor, Elizabeth, *At Mrs Lippincote's* (1945; London: Virago, 1988)

Taylor, Frederick, *Dresden, Tuesday 13 February 1944* (London: Bloomsbury, 2004)

Taylor, Philip M., *Britain and the Cinema in the Second World War* (Basingstoke: Macmillan, 1988)

Taylor, D. J., *Orwell* (London: Chatto & Windus, 2003)

Taylor, Warwick, *The Forgotten Conscript: A History of the Bevin Boy* (Durham: The Pentland Press, 1995)

Thomas, Donald, *An Underworld at War: Spivs, Deserters, Racketeers and Civilians in the Second World War* (London: John Murray, 2003)

Thomas, Dylan, *The Collected Letters of Dylan Thomas*, ed. Paul Ferris (London: Dent, 1985)

Thomas, Irene, *The Bandsman's Daughter: An Autobiography* (Basingstoke: Macmillan, 1979)

Thomson, Rear-Admiral George P., *Blue Pencil Admiral: The Inside Story of Press Censorship* (London: Sampson, Law, Marston & Co., 1947)

Thorpe, Andrew, *The British Communist Party and Moscow, 1920–43* (Manchester: Manchester University Press, 2000)

Thorpe, Frances, and Nicholas Pronay with Clive Coultass, *British Official Films in the Second World War: A Descriptive Catalogue* (Oxford: Oxford University Press, 1980)

Thurlow, Richard, *Fascism in Britain: From Oswald Mosley's Blackshirts to the National Front* (London: I. B. Tauris, 1998)

Timmins, Nicholas, *The Five Giants: A Biography of the Welfare State* (London: HarperCollins, 1995)

Tinch, Dave, *The Shore: Growing up in Wartime Kirkwall* (Kirkwall: Orcadian, 2003

Tippett, Michael, *Those Twentieth Century Blues: An Autobiography* (London: Hutchinson, 1991)

Tiquet, Stanley (comp.), *It Happened Here: The Story of Civil Defence in Wanstead and Woodford, 1939–1945* (Ilford, Essex: Redbridge Libraries, 1994)

Tiratsoo, Nick (ed.), *From Blitz to Blair: A New History of Britain since 1939* (London: Weidenfeld & Nicolson, 1997)

Titmuss, Richard M., *History of the Second World War: Problems of Social Policy* (London: HMSO, 1950)

Treglown, Jeremy, and Bridget Bennett (eds), *Grub Street and the Ivory Tower: Literary Journalism and Literary Scholarship from Fielding to the Internet* (Oxford: Clarendon Press, 1998)

Trench, Richard, *London Before the Blitz* (London: Weidenfeld & Nicolson, 1989)

Trevelyan, Julian, *Indigo Days* (London: MacGibbon & Kee, 1957)

Trevor-Roper, Hugh (ed.), *Hitler's War Directives, 1939–45* (London: Sidgwick & Jackson, 1964)

Turner, Barry, and Tony Rennell, *When Daddy Came Home: How Family Life Changed Forever in 1945* (London: Hutchinson, 1995)

Turner, E. S., *The Phoney War on the Home Front* (London: Michael Joseph, 1961)

Twyford, H. P., *It Came to Our Door: The Story of Plymouth Throughout the Second World War* (Plymouth: Underhill, 1945)

Tyrer, Nicola, *They Fought in the Fields: The Women's Land Army: The Story of a Forgotten Victory* (London: Sinclair Stevens, 1996)

Verrill-Rhys, Leigh, and Deidre Beddoe (eds), *Parachutes and Petticoats: Welsh Women Writing on the Second World War* (Dinas Powis: Honno, 1992)

Wallace, Lorne A. (ed.), *'Here Come the Keelies': Vivid Recollections of World War II Evacuees and a Wee Scottish Village* (Dunning Parish Historical Society, 1999)

Waller, Jane and Michael Vaughan-Rees, *Woman in Wartime: The Role of Women's Magazines 1939–1945* (London: Macdonald Optima, 1987)

Waller, Jane, and Michael Vaughan-Rees, *Blitz: The Civilian War, 1940–45* (London: Macdonald Optima, 1990)

Waller, Maureen, *London 1945: Life in the Debris of War* (London: John Murray, 2004)

Wallington, Neil, *Fireman at War: The Work of the London Fire-fighters in the Second World War* (Newton Abbot: David & Charles, 1981)

Wallis, Jill, *A Welcome in the Hillside? The Merseyside and North Wales Experience of Evacuation, 1939–1945* (Bebbington, Wirral: Avid Publications, 2000)

Walmsley, Leo, *Fishermen at War* (London: Collins, 1941)

War Pictures in the National Gallery by British Artists (London: 1942)

Warburg, Frederic, *All Authors are Equal* (London: Hutchinson, 1976)

Ward, Sadie, *War in the Countryside, 1939–1945* (Newton Abbot: David & Charles, 1988)

Warner, Sir Pelham, *Lord's, 1787–1945* (London: Harrap, 1946)

Warner, Rex, *The Aerodrome* (1941; Oxford: Oxford University Press, 1982)

Watts, Marthe, *The Men in My Life* (London: Christopher Johnson, 1960)

Waugh, Evelyn, *Put Out More Flags* (London: Chapman Hall, 1948)

Waugh, Evelyn, *Sword of Honour* (London: Chapman Hall, 1965)

Weale, Adrian, *Renegades: Hitler's Englishmen* (1994; London: Pimlico, 2002)

Webb, Edwin, and John Duncan, *Blitz Over Britain* (Tunbridge Wells, Kent: Spellmount, 1990)

Webb, Kaye (ed.), *Lilliput Goes to War* (London: Hutchinson, 1985)

Weight, Richard, *Patriots: National Identity in Britain, 1940–2000* (London: Macmillan, 2002)

Wellum, Geoffrey, *First Light* (London: Viking, 2002)

Wheal, Elizabeth-Anne and Stephen Pope (eds), *The Macmillan Dictionary of the Second World War* (London: Macmillan, 1995)

Wheeler-Bennett, John W., *King George VI: His Life and Reign* (London: Macmillan, 1958)

Wheeler-Bennett, John W. (ed.), *Action This Day* (London: Macmillan, 1968)

White, Jerry, *London in the Twentieth Century* (London: Viking, 2001)

Whittington-Egan, Richard, *The Great Liverpool Blitz* (Liverpool: Gallery Press, 1987)

Willetts, Paul, *Fear and Loathing in Fitzrovia: The Bizarre Life of the Writer, Actor, Soho Dandy Julian Maclaren-Ross* (Stockport: Dewi Lewis Publishing, 2003)

Williams, Raymond, *George Orwell* (London: Fontana, 1971)

Willis, Leonard, *None Had Lances: the Story of the 24th Lancers* (Old Coulsdon, Surrey: 24th Lancers Association, 1985)

Wilson, H. A., *Death Over Haggerston* (London and Oxford: A. W. Mowbray, 1941)

Wilt, Alan F., *Food for War: Agriculture and Rearmament in Britain before the Second World War* (Oxford: Oxford University Press, 2001)

Wintringham, Tom, *New Ways of War* (London: Penguin Specials, 1940)

Wollfitt, Susan, *Idle Women* (London: Ernest Benn, 1947)

Women's Group on Public Welfare, *Our Towns: A Close Up* (Oxford: Oxford University Press, 1943)

Wood, Derek, and Derek Dempster, *The Narrow Margin: The Battle of Britain and the Rise of Air Power, 1930–1940* (London: Hutchinson, 1961)

Wood, Ian S., *Ireland During the Second World War* (London: Caxton Editions, 2000)

Woolf, Leonard, *The Journey Not the Arrival Matters: An Autobiography of the*

Years 1939–1969 (London: The Hogarth Press, 1969)

Woolf, S. J. (ed.), *Fascism in Europe* (London: Methuen, 1981)

Woolf, Virginia, *The Diary of Virginia Woolf: Volume 5: 1936–41* (London: Chatto & Windus/The Hogarth Press, 1984)

Worsley, Francis, *ITMA, 1939–1948* (London: Vox Mundi, 1948)

Wright, Patrick, *Tank: The Progress of a Monstrous Machine* (London: Faber & Faber 2000)

Wright, Patrick, *The Village That Died for England: The Strange Story of Tyneham* (1995; London: Faber & Faber 2002)

Wyndham, Joan, *Love Lessons: A Wartime Diary* (London: Heinemann, 1985)

Wyndham, Joan, *Love is Blue* (London: Heinemann, 1986)

Ziegler, Philip, *Crown and People* (London: Collins, 1978)

Ziegler, Philip, *Diana Cooper: A Biography* (London: Hamish Hamilton, 1991)

Ziegler, Philip, *London at War, 1939–1945* (London: Sinclair-Stevenson, 1995)

Zweiger-Bargielowska, Ina, *Austerity in Britain: Rationing, Controls, and Consumption, 1939–1955* (Oxford: Oxford University Press, 2000)

Articles and Essays

Addison, Paul and J. A. Crang, 'A Battle of Many Nations' in Addison and Crang, *The Burning Blue*, pp. 243–63

Alberti, Johanna, 'A Time for Hard Writers: The Impact of War on Women Writers' in Hayes and Hill, *Millions Like Us?*, pp. 156–78

Baker, Norman, 'A More Even Playing Field? Sport During and after the War' in Hayes and Hill, *Millions Like Us?*, pp. 125–55

Baxendale, Michael, 'You and I – All of Us Ordinary People: Renegotiating Britishness in Wartime' in Hayes and Hill, *Millions Like Us?*, pp. 295–322

Bromley, Michael, 'Was it the *Mirror* Wot Won It? The Development of a Tabloid Press During the Second World War' in Hayes and Hill, *Millions Like Us?*, pp. 93–124

Bruley, Sue, 'A New Perspective on Women Workers in the Second World War: The Industrial Diary of Kathleen Church-Bliss and Elsie Whiteman' in *Labour History Review* (August 2003) 68:2

Brunt, Rosalind, 'The Family Firm Restored: Newsreel Coverage of the British Monarchy, 1936–45' in Gledhill and Swanson, *Nationalising Femininity*, pp. 140–51

Burton, Sarah, 'Workers Walk Out in Wartime' in *BBC History* (January 2002) pp. 12–15

Calder, Angus, 'The Battle of Britain and Pilots' Memoirs' in Addison and Crang, *The Burning Blue*, pp. 191–206

Cere, Rina, 'Women Internment and World War Two' in Kirkham and Thoms, *War Culture*, pp. 219–28

Chapman, James, 'British Cinema and "The People's War" ' in Hayes and Hill, *Millions Like Us?*, pp. 33–61

Charman, Terry, '"The number one radio personality of the war": Lord Haw Haw and his British Audience during the Phoney War' in *Imperial War Museum Review* (1992) 9

Chibnell, Steve, 'Pulp versus Penguins: Paperbacks go to War' in Kirkham and Thoms, *War Culture*, pp. 131–50

Colpi, Terri, 'The Impact of the Second World War on the British Italian Community' in Cesarani & Kushner, *The Internment of Aliens*

Connelly, Mark, 'The British People, the Press and the Strategic Air Campaign Against Germany, 1939–45 in *Contemporary British History* (Summer 2002) 16:2 pp. 39–58

Crang, J. A. 'The British Soldier on the Home Front: Army Morale Reports, 1940–45' in Addison and Calder, *Time to Kill*, pp. 60–74

Edwards, Owen Dudley, 'The Battle of Britain and Children's Literature' in Addison and Crang, *The Burning Blue*, pp. 163–90

Featherstone, Simon, 'The Nation as Pastoral in British Literature of the Second World War' in *European Studies*, (1986) xvi pp. 155–68

Fernbach, Davis, 'Tom Wintringham and the Socialist Defence Strategy' in *History Workshop Journal* (1982) 14 pp. 63–91

Gregory, Adrian, 'The Commemoration of the Battle of Britain' in Addison and Crang, *The Burning Blue*, pp. 217–28

Haggith, Toby, 'Post-war Reconstruction as depicted in Official British Films of the Second World War' in *IWM Review*, (1992–3) 7–8 pp. 34–45

Harper, Sue, 'The Years of Total War: Propaganda and Entertainment' in Gledhill and Swanson, *Nationalising Femininity*, pp. 193–212

Harris, José, 'Political Ideas and the Debate on State Welfare' in Smith, *War and Social Change*, pp. 133–63

Harris, José, 'War and Social History: Britain and the Home Front during the Second World War' in *Journal of Contemporary History* (1992) 1 pp. 17–35

Hayes, Nick, 'More Than "Music-While-You-Eat"? Factory and Hostel Concerts, "Good Culture" and the Workers' in Hayes and Hill, *Millions Like Us?*, pp. 209–35

Hill, Jeff, '"When Work is Over": Labour, Leisure and Culture in Wartime Britain' in Hayes and Hill, *Millions Like Us?*, pp. 236–60

Hinton, James, 'Coventry Communism: A Study of Factory Politics in the Second World War' in *History Workshop Journal* (1980) 10 pp. 90–118

Howkins, Alan, 'A Country at War: Mass-Observation and Rural England, 1939–45' in *Rural History* (1998) 9 pp. 75–97

Kirkham, Pat, 'Beauty and Duty: Keeping Up the (Home) Front' in Kirkham and Thoms, *War Culture*, pp. 13–28

Kirkham, Pat, 'Fashioning the Feminine: Dress, Appearance and Femininity in Wartime Britain' in Gledhill and Swanson, *Nationalising Femininity*, pp. 152–74

Lanfranchi, Pierre and Taylor, Matthew, 'Professional Football in World War Two Britain' in Kirkham and Thoms, *War Culture*, pp. 187–97

Leventhal, F. M., ' "The Best for the Most": CEMA and State Sponsorship of the Arts in Wartime, 1939–1945' in *Twentieth Century British History* (1990) 1

Lewis, Adrian, 'Henry Moore's "Shelter Drawings": Memory and Myth' in Kirkham and Thoms, *War Culture*, pp. 87–98

Mackay, Robert, 'Safe and Sound: New Music in Wartime Britain' in Hayes and Hill, *Millions Like Us?*, pp. 179–208

Mackay, Robert 'Being Beastly to the Germans: Music Censorship and the BBC in World War II' in *Historical Journal of Film, Radio and Television* (2000) 20:4 pp. 513–25

Mackay, Robert, 'Leaving out the Black Notes: The BBC and "enemy music" in the Second World War" in *Media History* (2000) 6:1 pp. 75–80

MacKenzie, S.P. 'The Real Dad's Army: the British Home Guard. 1940–44 in Addison and Calder, *Time to Kill*, pp. 50–9

Macnicol, John, 'The Effect of the Evacuation of Schoolchildren on Official Attitudes to State Intervention' in Smith, *War and Social Change*, pp. 3–31

Newsinger, John, 'My Country, Right or Left: Patriotism, Socialism and George Orwell, 1939–41' in Kirkham and Thoms, *War Culture*, pp. 29–37

Nicholas, Siân, 'The People's Radio: The BBC and its Audience, 1939–1945' in Hayes and Hill, *Millions Like Us?*, pp. 62–92

Oram, Alison, '"Bombs Don't Discriminate!" Women's Political Activities in the Second World War', in Gledhill and Swanson, *Nationalising Femininity*, pp. 53–69

O'Sullivan, Tim, 'Listening Through: The Wireless and World War Two' in Kirkham and Thoms, *War Culture*, pp. 173–86

Overy, Richard, 'How Significant *was* the Battle?' in Addison and Crang, *The Burning Blue*, pp. 267–80

Panayi, Panikos, 'Immigrants, Refugees, and the British State and Public Opinion During World War Two' in Kirkham and Thoms, *War Culture*, pp. 201–8

Peniston-Bird, Corinna, M., and Penny Summerfield, ' "Hey, you're dead!" The Multiple Uses of Humour in Representations of British National Defence in the Second World War' in *Journal of European Studies* (2001) 31:3:4 pp. 413–55

Richardson, Robert, 'Closings and Openings: Leading Public Art Galleries During the Second World War' in Kirkham and Thoms, *War Culture*, pp. 87–98

Rose, Nigel. 'Dear Mum and Dad: An RAF Pilot's Letters to His Parents, June–December, 1940' in Addison and Crang, *The Burning Blue*, pp. 138–60

Sheridan, Dorothy, 'Ambivalent Memories: Women and the 1939–45 War in Britain' in *Oral History* (Spring 1990)

Smart, Carol, 'Good Wives and Moral Lives: marriage and divorce 1937-51' in Gledhill and Swanson, *Nationalising Femininity*, pp. 91–105

Smith, Harold L., 'The Effect of War on the Status of Women' in Smith, *War and Social Change*, pp. 208–29

Smith, Malcolm, 'The RAF' in Addison and Crang, *The Burning Blue*, pp. 22–36

Sokoloff, Sally, 'Soldiers or Civilians? The Impact of Army Service in World War Two on Birmingham men' in *Oral History* (1997) 25:2 pp. 59–66

Sokoloff, Sally, '"How Are They at Home?" Community, State and Servicemen's Wives in England, 1939–45', *Women's History Review* (1999) 8:1 pp. 27–52

Sokoloff, Sally. 'The Home Front in the Second World War and Local History' *Local Historian* (2002) 32:1 pp. 22–40

Summerfield, Penny, 'The "levelling of class"' in Smith, *War and Social Change*, pp. 179–207

Summerfield, Penny, 'Approaches to Women and Social Change in the Second World War' in Brivati and Jones, *What Difference Did the War Make?* pp. 63–79

Summerfield, Penny, ' "They didn't want women back in that job": The Second World War and the Construction of Gendered Work Histories' in *Labour History Review* (1998) 63:1 pp. 83–104

Summerfield, Penny, ' "The girl that makes the thing that drills the hole that holds the spring . . .": Discourses of Women and Work in the Second World War' in Gledhill and Swanson, *Nationalising Femininity*, pp. 35–52

Summerfield, Penny, and Peniston-Bird, Corinna, M., 'Women in the Firing Line: the Home Guard and the Defence of Gender Boundaries in Britain in the Second World War' in *Women's History Review* (2000) 9:2 pp. 231–5

Swanson, Gillian, '"So much money and so little to spend it on": morale, consumption and sexuality" in Gledhill and Swanson, *Nationalising Femininity*, pp. 70–90

Thoms, David, 'The Blitz, Civilian Morale and Regionalism, 1940–1942' in Kirkham and Thoms, *War Culture*, pp. 3–10

Tiratsoo, Nick, 'The Reconstruction of Blitzed British Cities, 1945–55:

Myths and Realities' in *Contemporary British History* (Spring 2000) 14:1

Weight, Richard, 'State, Intelligentsia and the Promotion of National Culture in Britain, 1939-45', *Historical Research* (1996) 69 pp. 83–101

Welshman, John, 'Evacuation and Social Policy During the Second World War: Myth and Reality' in *Twentieth Century British History* (1998) 9:1

Welshman, John, 'Evacuation, Hygiene and Social Policy: The *Our Towns* Report of 1943' in *Historical Journal* (1999) 42:3

Westwood, Louise, 'WVS: More than Tea and Sympathy' in *History Today* (June 1998) 48:6

Winship, Janice, 'Women's Magazines: Times of War and Management of the Self in *Woman's* Own' in Gledhill and Swanson, *Nationalising Femininity*, pp. 127–39

Wood, Ian S., '"Twas England Bade Our Wild Geese Go": Soldiers of Ireland in the Second World War' in Addison and Calder, *Time to Kill*, pp. 77–92

Unpublished Sources

War Diaries of Henrietta Munro: D1/297 Highland Regional Archives, Inverness, deposited in Orkney Islands, Kirkwall, Orkney, August 1940

Woolven, Robin, *Civil Defence in London, 1939–1945: The Formation and Implementation of the Policy for, and the Performance of, the Air Raid Precautions (later Civil Defence) Services in the London Region* (unpublished PhD thesis, Department of War Studies, King's College, University of London, 2001)

Mass-Observation

I would like to thank the Trustees of the Mass-Observation Archive, University of Sussex, for permission to quote from diaries, file reports and topic collections held in the M-O Archive.

M-O Diarists

Under the terms of deposition of diaries kept for Mass-Observation, the diarists are anonymous. However, interested readers can check those numbers against a list held by the M-O Archive to discover the name, location and brief biographical details of each diarist. Occasionally, a diary has been published using the correct name of the diarist, where that is the case these names are included in this list. In cases of numbers only, the name in the text, if there is one, is pseudonymous.

1896
2263

5269
5271
5276
5282
5296
5307
5314
5318
5324 3
5331
5336
5337
5342 3
5353 Nella Last
5358
5370 Nina Masel (later Hibbin)
5378 Naomi Mitchison
5383
5390
5462 Moya Woodside

M-O File Reports

Part of the 3,000 typed original reports summarising Mass-Observation's methods and conclusions carried out between 1937 and 1955.

26: 1 June 1939: *They Speak for Themselves* BBC Programme on Mass-Observation.
182: 10 June 1940: Dover: Return of the BEF troops from Dunkirk.
298: 26 July 1940: Rout the Rumour Rally, Hendon.
312: June 1940: Conscientious Objectors.
425: 28 September 1940: Young Men in Tubes.
431: September 1940: Survey of Volunteers and Official Bodies during Bombing in the East End.
436: October 1940: Shelters in London. How People Behave in Shelters.
495: November 1940: Coventry: the Effects of Bombing.
532: December 1940: Result of December Directive: Cheerfulness, Depression: analysis of panel's response.
756: June 1941: Clothes Rationing. First Reactions.
759: June 1941.
780: 18 November 1941: War Work, Coventry, 1941.
791: 17 July 1942: Clothes Rationing.

844: 23 August 1941: Hull: Effect of War on Industries, Evacuation, Blitz and Food Situation.

1143: 9 March 1943: Report on Utility Clothing Scheme.

1501: November 1942: What the British think of the Americans.

1569: January 1943: Feelings about America and the Americans.

1923: October 1943: Public Opinion and the Americans.

2000: 14 January 1944: Vengeance. Public Opinion about Air Raids on Germany.

2121: July 1944: A Survey of Pilotless Planes.

2201: January 1945: Wartime Shortages of Consumer Goods.

2205/6: February 1945: Sex, Morality and the Birth Rate.

2249: May 1945: Post VE Day Celebrations.

2263: June 1945: Victory in Europe.

2257: June 1945: Youth and the Election.

2283: September 1945: Forces' Views on Demob.

14 March 1939: Air Raids Shelters by Celia Fremlin.

Report on attitudes to USA

M-O Archive Topic Collections

Raw material generated by Mass-Observation studies, including observations, questionnaires, interviews, descriptions and printed ephemera.

TC 2 (1, 2 & 3): Reconstruction, 1941–43.

TC 5 (1 & 2): Evacuation, 1939–44.

TC 6 (2): Conscientious Objectors.

TC 15 (1) Demolition in London, 1941

TC 18 (4 & 5): Personal Appearance and Clothes.

TC 19 (1): Day Nurseries.

TC 23 (2 & 4): Air Raids.

TC 29 (1, 2 & 4): Public Morale During Raids.

TC 32 (1, 2 & 3): Women in Wartime.

TC 40 (1 & 2): Post-War Hopes.

TC41: Wall Chalkings, 1939–43.

TC 42: Poster Surveys.

TC 43 (1, 3, 4 & 5): Propaganda and Morale, 1939–44.

TC44 (1): Public Administration and Social Services in Wartime, 1941–2.

TC 47 (1 & 2): Shopping, 1939–63.

TC 49 (1&2): Victory Celebrations, 1945–46.

TC 62: Attitude to Jews.

TC 74 (3B): Radio Listening, 1939–44.

Imperial War Museum

I am grateful both to the Trustees of the Imperial War Museum and to the individual copyright holders for allowing me access to the collections of papers and recordings held by the IWM; and for permission to publish extracts from them.

IWM Sound Archives

Reginald Baker 006498
Reginald Norman Bottini, CBE 00461/04
Doris Danher (née Benson) 9/526/3/1
Kathleen Derbyshire (née Wigham) 004761
Friedel Hallgarten (née Liebmann) 004494
Theodore Mallinson 220703
Lily Mitchell 20371
Margaret Cornish Ridout 23089
Sonia Rolt 22902/8
Mrs Gwendoline Saunders 09106
Gwendoline Olive Stewart (neé Watts) 005334
Ernest Walter Trory 004693

IWM Department of Documents

The Papers of Miss M. E. Allan (Diaries) 95/8/7 and Conservation Shelf
The Papers of Stephanie Batstone ('Worm's Eye View') 86/61/1
The Papers of Heinz Bing (Internment diary) No Reference
The Papers of Muriel Bowmer Conservation Shelf
The Papers of George and Helena Britton (Letters, including those from Ethel Mattison) Conservation Shelf
The Papers of Mrs N. V. Carver 90/16/1
The Papers of Mrs E. H. Cotton 93/3/1
The Papers of Gwaldys Cox ('The War Diary of Gwaldys Cox') 86/46/1 (P)
The Papers of Veronica Goddard ('My Scrapbook Part I (1939–1943)', 1946) Conservation Shelf
The Papers of Vivienne Hall ('The Second World War Diary of Vivienne Hall') DS/MISC/88
The Papers of Major D.V. Henderson GM, (Ret'd) ('Dragoons Undefeated: The Complete History of the George Medal' 1993) No Reference
The Papers of Miss D. M. Hoyles 77/50/1
The Papers of Captain H. W. Luttman-Johnson 72/32/1
The Papers of Reverend J. G. Markham 91/5/1

The Papers of J. P. McHutchison (Diary) P151

The Papers of Ethel Mattison *see* Britton

The Papers of Constance Miles ('Mrs Miles War Journal') 99/74/1

The Papers of Mr and Mrs A Monk-Jones 01/50/1 and Conservation Shelf

The Papers of Mrs I Phillips 80/6/1

The Papers of John and Peggie Phillips (Letters) 61/47/2

The Papers of Miss K. M. Phipps (later Harding) ('The Second World War Diary of Kate Phipps') P178

The Papers of Violet I Regan ('The German Blitzkreig') Conservation Shelf

The Papers of W. B. Regan 88/10/1

The Papers of Barbara Roose ('Got Any Gum Chum?') 89/14/1

The Papers of Miss G. Thomas 90/30/1

The Papers of Joan Zeepvat (née Carter) ('A Time to Tell. My Life in the ATS') 82/33/1

The Papers of Len Waller 87/42/1

INDEX